AIR FRYER COOKBOOK

1000 DELICIOUS, EASY AND QUICK "15 MINUTES" RECIPESTHAT YOU CAN DO WITH YOUR AIRFYER.

Contents

3

4

INTRODUCTION

Hello and welcome to my book about air fryers! Did you know that you can get healthy, lose weight, save dollars and still enjoy delicious, indulgent, utterly yummy foods? Does it sounds like something you would hear in an infomercial? No, it's not. It's 100% true. You just need to join the art of air frying!

You'll love this book if you're new to air fryer cooking and also if you're an experienced air fryer user. It contains fantastic recipes for great meals that everyone will enjoy.

The air fryer is a brilliant kitchen appliance - it lets you cook delicious food without using lots of fat and oil. You'll be able to create yummy dishes that are healthy too! You'll find the recipes in this book can be used with any brand and model of an air fryer.

And go ahead and modify any of the recipes for the air fryer you have, such as the temperature and time. Or adjust the number of ingredients if you want to make more or less than the recipe calls for. No matter what type of recipe you searching for, I've got one for you.

Breakfast, snacks, appetizers, meat, seafood, and desserts. There are also vegan and vegetarian options that are sure to delight.

When it comes to breakfast and dessert, I've got some healthy choices for you with decadent and delicious recipes, using ingredients that are sure to make your mouth water in anticipation. Be warned – the recipes in this book aren't for those who are watching their weight and stick to their diet all day, every day.

These are recipes that are to be savored and enjoyed. But even if you're watching what you eat, it all comes down to balancing your diet.

Use this cookbook to create delightful meals when you're having a cheat day and want to treat yourself to something tasty. Let's jump into what an air fryer is and how it works, and then you can start cooking!

Every recipe here is healthy for you.

1. Panko-Crusted Avocado and Slaw Tacos

Preparation Time: 15 minutes
Cooking Time: 6 minutes
Servings: 4

Ingredients
- ¼ cup all-purpose flour
- ¼ teaspoon salt, plus more as needed
- ¼ teaspoon ground black pepper
- 2 large egg whites
- 1¼ cups panko bread crumbs
- 2 tablespoons olive oil
- 2 avocados, peeled and halved, cut into 1/2-inch-thick slices
- 1/2 small red cabbage, thinly sliced
- 1 deseeded jalapeño, thinly sliced
- 2 green onions, thinly sliced
- 1/2 cup cilantro leaves
- ¼ cup mayonnaise
- Juice and zest of 1 lime
- 4 corn tortillas, warmed
- 1/2 cup sour cream
- Cooking spray

Directions:
1. 1.Spritz the air fry basket with cooking spray.
2. Pour the flour in a large bowl and sprinkle with salt and black pepper, then stir to mix well.
3. Whisk the egg whites in a separate bowl. Combine the panko with olive
4. oil on a shallow dish.
5. Dredge the avocado slices in the bowl of flour, then into the egg to coat. Shake the excess off, then roll the slices over the panko.
6. Arrange the avocado slices in a single layer in the basket and spritz the
7. cooking spray.
8. 6. Place the basket on the air fry position.
9. 7. Select Air Fry, set temperature to 400°F (205ºC) and set time to 6minutes. Flip the slices halfway through with tongs.
10. 8. When cooking is complete, the avocado slices should be tender and lightly browned.
11. 9. Combine the cabbage, onions, jalapeño, cilantro leaves, lime juice, mayo, and zest, and a touch of salt in a separate large bowl. Toss to mix well.
12. 10. Unfold the tortillas on a clean work surface, then spread with cabbage slaw and air fried avocados. Top with sour cream and serve.

2. Bacon-Wrapped Herb Rainbow Trout

Preparation Time: 15 minutes
Cooking Time: 15 minutes
Servings: 4

Ingredients:
- 4 (8- to 10-ounce / 227- to 283-g) rainbow trout, butterflied and boned
- 2 teaspoons kosher salt, divided
- 1 tablespoon extra-virgin olive oil, divided
- 1 tablespoon freshly squeezed lemon juice, divided
- 2 tablespoons chopped fresh parsley, divided
- 2 tablespoons chopped fresh chives, divided
- 8 thin bacon slices
- Lemon wedges, for serving

Directions:
1. Lightly oil a sheet pan.
2. Sprinkle the inside and outside of each trout with the salt.Brush the inside with the oil and drizzle with the lemon juice. Scatter the parsley and chives on one side of each butterflied trout. Fold the trout closed and wrap each one with two slices of bacon. Transfer to the sheet pan.
3. Select Bake. Set temperature to 400°F (205ºC) and set time to20 minutes. Select Start to begin preheating.
4. Once preheated, slide the pan into the oven. Flip the trout halfway through the cooking time.
5. When done, the bacon will be crisp.
6. Serve with lemon wedges.

3. Crab Cheese Enchiladas

Preparation Time: 15 minutes
Cooking Time: 15 minutes
Servings: 4

Ingredients:
- 8 (6-inch) corn tortillas
- Nonstick cooking spray or vegetable oil, for brushing
- 2 cups mild tomatillo salsa or green enchilada sauce
- ½ cup heavy (whipping) cream
- 8 ounces (227 g) lump crab meat, picked through to remove any shells
- 3 or 4 scallions, chopped
- 8 ounces (227 g) Monterey Jack cheese, shredded

Directions:
1. 1Spray the tortillas on both sides with cooking spray or brush lightly with oil. Arrange on a sheet pan, overlapping as little as possible.
2. Select Bake. Set temperature to 350ºF

14

(180°C) and set time to5 minutes. Select Start to begin preheating.
3. Once preheated, slide the pan into the oven.
4. When done, the tortillas will be warm and flexible.
5. Meanwhile, stir together the salsa and cream in a shallow, microwave-safe bowl and heat in the microwave until very warm, about 45 seconds.
6. Pour a quarter of the salsa mixture into a baking pan. Place a tortilla in the sauce, turning it over to coat thoroughly. Spoon a heaping tablespoon of crab down the middle of the tortilla, then top with a teaspoon of scallions and a heaping tablespoon of cheese. Roll up the tortilla and place it seam- side down at one end of the pan. Repeat with the remaining tortillas, forming a row of enchiladas in the pan. Spoon most or all of the remaining sauce over the enchiladas so they are nicely coated but not drowning. Sprinkle the remaining cheese over the top.
7. Bake for 15 to 20 minutes, until the cheese is melted and the sauce is bubbling.

4. Salmon Fillet with Spinach, and Beans

Preparation Time: 10minutes
Cooking Time: 15 minutes
Servings: 4
Ingredients:
- 2 tablespoons olive oil, divided
- 1 garlic clove, thinly sliced
- 1 (9- to 10-ounce / 255- to 283-g) bag baby spinach
- 1 (15-ounce / 425-g) can cannellini or navy beans, rinsed and drained
- 1½ teaspoons kosher salt, divided
- ½ teaspoon ground cumin
- ½ teaspoon ground coriander
- ¼ teaspoon red pepper flakes
- 4 (6-ounce / 170-g) skinless salmon fillets

Directions:
1. 1Heat 1 tablespoon of oil in a large, oven-safe skillet over medium-high heat. Add the garlic and cook, stirring, until fragrant, about 30 seconds. Add the spinach a handful at a time and cook, tossing, until slightly wilted, adding more as you have room. Stir in the beans, ¾ teaspoon of salt, cumin, coriander, and red pepper flakes.
2. Season the salmon with the remaining ¾ teaspoon of salt. Place the fillets in a single layer on top of the spinach mixture and drizzle with the remaining 1 tablespoon of oil.
3. Select Bake. Set temperature to 300°F (150°C) and set time to35 minutes. Select Start to begin preheating.
4. Once preheated, put the skillet in the oven.
5. When done, the salmon will be opaque in the center.

5. Sherry Tilapia and Mushroom Rice

Preparation Time: 15minutes
Cooking Time: 15 minutes
Servings: 4

Ingredients:
- 4 tablespoons unsalted butter
- 12 ounces (340 g) cremini or white button mushrooms, trimmed and sliced
- 4 to 6 scallions, chopped
- 1 teaspoon kosher salt, divided
- 2 tablespoons all-purpose flour
- ¾ cup dry sherry or dry white wine
- ¾ cup low-sodium vegetable or fish broth
- 3 tablespoons heavy (whipping) cream
- 1 tablespoon chopped fresh parsley, divided
- 2 cups cooked white or brown rice
- 4 (6-ounce / 170-g) tilapia fillets
- ⅛ teaspoon freshly ground black pepper

Directions:
1. In a large cast-iron or other oven-safe skillet, melt the butter over medium heat until foaming. Sauté the mushrooms and scallions until the mushrooms are soft. Stir in ½ teaspoon of salt and the flour. Cook for 1 minute, stirring constantly. Gradually stir in the sherry. Let the sauce simmer for 3 to 5 minutes, until some of the alcohol evaporates. Add the broth, cream, and 1½ teaspoons of parsley and bring back to a simmer.
2. Stir the rice into the sauce. Place the fish fillets in a single layer on top of the rice and sauce. Sprinkle the fish with the remaining ½ teaspoon of salt and the pepper, then spoon a little of the sauce over the fillets.
3. Select Bake. Set temperature to 325°F (163°C) and set time to 15 minutes. Select Start to begin preheating.
4. Once preheated, put the skillet in the oven.

5. When done, the fish will flake with a fork.
6. To serve, spoon some rice onto each plate and top with a fillet. Sprinkle with the remaining 1½ teaspoons of parsley.

6. Marinated Catfish Fillet

Preparation Time: 10minutes
Cooking Time: 15 minutes
Servings: 4

Ingredients:
- 4 (6-ounce / 170-g) catfish fillets
- Marinade Ingredients:
- 1 tablespoon olive oil
- 1 tablespoon lemon juice
- ¼ dry white wine
- 1 tablespoon garlic powder
- 1 tablespoon soy sauce

Directions:
1. Combine the marinade ingredients in an ovenproof baking dish. Add the fillets and let stand for 10 minutes, spooning the marinade over the fillets every 2 minutes.
2. Select Broil. Set temperature to 400°F (205°C) and set time to 15 minutes. Select Start to begin preheating.
3. Once preheated, place the baking dish in the oven.
4. When done, the fish will flake easily with a fork.

7. Mackerel with Mango and Chili Salad

Preparation Time: 15minutes
Cooking Time: 15 minutes
Servings: 4

Ingredients:
For the Fish:
- 2 garlic cloves, finely grated
- 1½in fresh ginger, peeled and finely grated
- ¾ teaspoon ground turmeric
- 1½ teaspoons ground cumin
- ½ teaspoon ground fenugreek
- 2½ tablespoons tamarind paste
- ¼ cup lime juice, plus more to serve, plus lime wedges to serve
- 1 tablespoon light brown sugar
- 2 tablespoons peanut oil
- Sea salt flakes and freshly ground black pepper, to taste
- 4 whole Boston mackerel, gutted and washed
- Rice, or warmed naan bread and plain yogurt, to serve
For the Salad:
- 2 just-ripe or slightly under-ripe mangoes
- Juice of 2 limes
- 1 red Fresno chili and 1 green chili, halved, seeded, and very finely shredded
- ½ cup cilantro leaves and stalks (make sure the stalks aren't toolong or thick)

Directions:
1. Mix together the garlic, ginger, and all the spices for the mackerel, adding the lime juice, sugar, oil, and seasoning. Spread this all over each fish, inside and out. Cover and put in the refrigerator for about 15 minutes.
2. Now make the salad. Peel the mangoes and cut off the 'cheeks' (the fleshy bits that lie alongside the stone). Cut the cheeks into neat slices.
3. Put the mango slices in a serving bowl and add the lime juice, chilies, some salt, and the cilantro, and toss.
4. Line a baking pan with foil or parchment paper and put the mackerel in it.
5. Select Bake. Set temperature to 400°F (205°C) and set time to 20 minutes. Select Start to begin preheating.
6. Once preheated, slide the pan into the oven.
7. When done, squeeze some lime juice over the fish and serve with rice, or warmed naan bread and yogurt, lime wedges, and the mango and chili salad.

8. Lemony Shrimp with Arugula

Preparation Time: 10minutes
Cooking Time: 10 minutes
Servings: 4

Ingredients:
- 4 tablespoons unsalted butter, melted
- 2 tablespoons extra-virgin olive oil
- 1 teaspoon kosher salt
- 6 garlic cloves, minced
- ¼ cup chopped fresh parsley, divided
- 2 pounds (907 g) large shrimp, peeled and deveined
- 2 tablespoons freshly squeezed lemon juice
- 1 (9- to 10-ounce / 255- to 283-g) bag arugula

Directions:
1. In a baking pan, add the butter, oil, salt, garlic, and half the parsley. Stir well. Add the shrimp and toss to coat, then arrange the shrimp in a single layer.
2. Select Bake. Set temperature to 375°F (190°C) and set time to 5 minutes. Select Start to begin preheating.

3. Once preheated, slide the pan into the oven.
4. When done, the shrimp will be opaque and pink.
5. Remove the pan from the oven. Add the lemon juice, arugula, and remaining parsley. Toss well to wilt the arugula. Serve immediately.

9. Broiled Lemony Salmon Steak

Preparation Time: 10minutes
Cooking Time: 15 minutes
Servings: 2

Ingredients:
- 2 (6-ounce / 170-g) salmon steaks
- Brushing Mixture:
- 2 tablespoons lemon juice
- 2 tablespoons olive oil
- 1 tablespoon soy sauce
- 1 teaspoon dried dill or dill weed
- ½ teaspoon garlic powder
- 1 teaspoon soy sauce

Directions:
1. Combine the brushing mixture ingredients in a small bowl and brush the salmon steak tops, skin side down, liberally, reserving the remaining mixture. Let the steaks sit at room temperature for 10 minutes, then place on a broiling rack with a pan underneath.
2. Select Broil. Set temperature to 400°F (205°C) and set time to 20 minutes. Select Start to begin preheating.
3. Once preheated, slide the pan into the oven.
4. After 15 minutes, remove from the oven, and brush the steaks with the remaining mixture. Broil again for 5 minutes, or until the meat flakes easily with a fork.

10. Crispy Fish Fillet

Preparation Time: 10minutes
Cooking Time: 14 minutes
Servings: 4

Ingredients:
- 4 (6-ounce / 170-g) fish fillets, approximately ¼- to ½-inch thick
- 2 tablespoons vegetable oil
Coating Ingredients:
- 1 cup cornmeal
- 1 teaspoon garlic powder
- 1 teaspoon ground cumin
- 1 teaspoon paprika
- Salt, to taste

Directions:
1. Combine the coating ingredients in a small bowl, blending well. Transfer to a large plate, spreading evenly over the surface. Brush the fillets with vegetable oil and press both sides of each fillet into the coating.
2. Place the fillets in an oiled or nonstick square baking (cake) pan, laying them flat.
3. Select Broil. Set temperature to 400°F (205°C) and set time to 14 minutes. Select Start to begin preheating.
4. Once preheated, slide the pan into the oven.
5. Broil for 7 minutes, then remove the pan from the oven and carefully turn the fillets with a spatula. Broil for another 7 minutes, or until the fish flakes easily with a fork and the coating is crisped to your preference. Serve immediately.

11. Swordfish Steaks with Lemon

Preparation Time: 5minutes
Cooking Time: 10 minutes
Servings: 4

Ingredients:
- 1 pound (454 g) swordfish steaks
- 2 tablespoons olive oil
- 2 tablespoons chopped fresh mint leaves
- 3 tablespoons fresh lemon juice
- 1 teaspoon garlic powder
- ½ teaspoon shallot powder
- Sea salt and freshly ground black pepper, to taste

Directions:
1. Start by preheating the air fryer to 400°F (205°C).
2. Toss the swordfish steaks with the remaining ingredients and place them in a lightly oiled crisper tray.
3. Place the crisper tray in the corresponding position in the air fryer. Select Air Fry and cook the swordfish steaks for about 10 minutes, turning them over halfway through the cooking time.
4. Bon appétit!

12. Mackerel Patties Muffins

Preparation Time: 5minutes
Cooking Time: 10 minutes
Servings: 4

Ingredients:
- 1 pound (454 g) mackerel fillet, boneless and chopped
- 1 tablespoon olive oil
- ½ onion, chopped
- 2 garlic cloves, crushed
- 1 teaspoon hot paprika
- 1 tablespoon chopped fresh cilantro
- 2 tablespoons chopped fresh parsley
- Sea salt and ground black pepper, to taste
- 4 English muffins, toasted

Directions:
1. Start by preheating the air fryer to 400ºF (205ºC).
2. Mix all ingredients , except for the English muffins, in a bowl. Shape the mixture into four patties and place them in a lightly oiled crisper tray.
3. Place the crisper tray in the corresponding position in the air fryer. Select Air Fry and cook the fish patties for about 14 minutes, turning them over halfway through the cooking time.
4. Serve on English muffins and enjoy!

13. Calamari with Lemon

Preparation Time: 15minutes
Cooking Time: 5 minutes
Servings: 4

Ingredients:
- 1 pound (454 g) calamari, sliced into rings
- 2 garlic cloves, minced
- 1 teaspoon red pepper flakes
- 2 tablespoons dry white wine
- 2 tablespoons olive oil
- 2 tablespoons fresh lemon juice
- 1 teaspoon chopped basil
- 1 teaspoon chopped dill
- 1 teaspoon chopped parsley
- Coarse sea salt and freshly cracked black pepper, to taste

Directions:
1. Start by preheating the air fryer to 400ºF (205ºC).
2. Toss all ingredients in a lightly greased crisper tray.
3. Place the crisper tray in the corresponding position in the air fryer. Select Air Fry and cook the calamari for 5 minutes, tossing crisper tray halfway through the cooking time.
4. Bon appétit!

14. Pollock Fishcakes

Preparation Time: 15minutes
Cooking Time: 5 minutes
Servings: 4

Ingredients:
- 1 pound (454 g) pollock, chopped
- 1 teaspoon chili sauce
- Sea salt and ground black pepper, to taste
- 4 tablespoons all-purpose flour
- 1 teaspoon smoked paprika
- 2 tablespoons olive oil
- 4 ciabatta buns

Directions:
1. Start by preheating the air fryer to 400ºF (205ºC).
2. Mix all ingredients , except for the ciabatta buns, in a bowl.Shape the mixture into four patties and place them in a lightly oiled crisper tray.
3. Place the crisper tray in the corresponding position in the air fryer. Select Air Fry and cook the fish patties for about 14 minutes, turning them over halfway through the cooking time.
4. Serve on hamburger buns and enjoy!

15. Squid Tubes with Cheese

Preparation Time: 6minutes
Cooking Time: 5 minutes
Servings: 4

Ingredients:
- 1½ pounds (680 g) small squid tubes
- 2 tablespoons butter, melted
- 1 chili pepper, chopped
- 2 garlic cloves, minced
- 1 teaspoon red pepper flakes
- Sea salt and ground black pepper, to taste
- ¼ cup dry white wine
- 2 tablespoons fresh lemon juice
- 1 teaspoon Mediterranean herb mix
- 2 tablespoons grated Parmigiano-Reggiano cheese

Directions:
1. Start by preheating the air fryer to 400°F (205°C).
2. Toss all ingredients , except for the Parmigiano-Reggiano cheese, in a lightly greased crisper tray.
3. Place the crisper tray in the corresponding position in the air fryer. Select Air Fry and cook the squid for 5 minutes, tossing crisper tray halfway through the cooking time.
4. Top the warm squid with the cheese. Bon appétit!

16. Turkey Burrito

Preparation Time: 10minutes
Cooking Time: 10 minutes
Servings: 2

Ingredients:
- 4 slices of turkey breast that have already been cooked.
- 1/2 sliced red bell peppers 2 eggs
- peeled and pitted. 1 small avocado (cut into slices). Salsa (about 2 teaspoons)
- Season with salt and black pepper to taste. 1/8 cup mozzarella cheese, with shredded tortillas on the side

Directions:
1. In a large mixing bowl, whisk together the eggs and season with salt and pepper to taste. Pour the mixture into a pan and place it in the air fryer basket.
2. Cook for 5 minutes at 400°F before removing the pan from the fryer and transferring the eggs to a serving plate.
3. Arrange the tortillas on a work surface and divide the eggs among them, as well as the turkey meat, bell pepper, cheese, salsa, and avocado among them.
4. After you've prepared your air fryer with tin foil, roll your burritos and place them in the air fryer to cook.
5. Bake the burritos for 3 minutes at 300°F, then divide them among plates and serve.
6. Enjoy!

17. Tofu Scramble

Preparation Time: 5minutes
Cooking Time: 15 minutes
Servings: 2

Ingredients:
- Ingredients: 1 brick of tofu, cubed
- 1 teaspoon turmeric, freshly ground
- Another 2 tblsp. of extra virgin olive oil 4 cups of broccoli florets (optional)
- 1/2 tsp onions powder
- 1/2 tsp. garlic powder
- 2 and a 1/2-cup red potato, cut into cubes.
- 1/2 cup chopped yellow onion, salt and black pepper to taste

Directions:
1. In a large mixing bowl, combine the tofu, 1 tablespoon oil, salt, pepper, soy sauce, garlic powder, onion powder, turmeric, and onion. Set aside after thoroughly mixing.
2. Combine the potatoes with the remaining oil and seasonings (salt and pepper to taste) in a separate bowl and toss well to coat.
3. Preheat your air fryer to 350°F and bake the potatoes for 15 minutes, shaking halfway through.
4. Bake the tofu in the air fryer for 15 minutes at 350 °F with the marinade.
5. Add the broccoli to the fryer and cook for another 5 minutes, or until the broccoli is tender.
6. Put the dish on the table as soon as possible. Enjoy!

18. Oatmeal Casserole

Preparation Time: 10minutes
Cooking Time: 15 minutes
Servings: 8

Ingredients:
- 2 cups of rolled oats (or equivalent)
- 1 tsp baking powder (optional) third cup of brown sugar
- Optional: 1 tsp cinnamon powder
- 1 pound chocolate chipsA third cup of blueberries
- 1 banana that has been peeled and mashed. 2 quarts of milk.
- 1 egg
- 2 teaspoons of melted butter.
- 1 tsp vanilla extractCooking spray 1 tablespoon

of olive oil

Directions:
1. In a large mixing basin, combine the sugar, baking powder, cinnamon, chocolate chips, blueberries, and banana, stirring constantly.
2. In a separate bowl, whisk together the eggs, vanilla extract, and butter until well combined.
3. Preheat your air fryer to 320°F and spray the inside with cooking spray before adding the oats to the bottom.
4. Stir in the cinnamon-egg mixture and bake for 15 minutes.
5. Stir it one more time, divide it into bowls, and serve it for breakfast the next morning. Enjoy!

19. Ham Breakfast

Preparation Time: 10minutes
Cooking Time: 15 minutes
Servings: 6

Ingredients:
- 6 cups of French bread, cubed
- 4 ounces chopped green chilies 10 ounces cubed ham 4 ounces shredded cheddar cheese 2 cups milk
- 5 eggs
- 1 tablespoon of Dijon mustard.
- Season with salt and black pepper to taste. Using cooking spray

Directions:
1. Before using your air fryer, preheat it to 350 degrees
2. Fahrenheit and coat it with cooking spray.
3. In a large mixing bowl, whisk together the eggs, milk, cheese, mustard, salt, and pepper.
4. Toss bread cubes with chilies and ham in the air fryer until well combined.
5. Pour in the egg mixture, smooth it out, and bake it for 15 minutes.
6. Distribute the mixture among the plates and serve.
7. Enjoy!

20. Tomato and Bacon Breakfast

Preparation Time: 10minutes
Cooking Time: 15 minutes
Servings: 6

Ingredients:
- 1 pound cubed white bread
- 1 pound cooked and chopped smoked bacon
- 1 tablespoon extra virgin olive oil
- 1 finely sliced small yellow onion
- 28 ounces of canned tomatoes, finely minced
- 1 and 12 teaspoons of crushed red pepper flakes.
- 1/2 pound cheddar cheese, shredded
- 2 teaspoons chives, finely chopped
- 1/2 pound of shredded Monterey Jack cheese with 2 teaspoons of chicken broth.
- Season with salt and black pepper to taste. 8 eggs, lightly whisked

Directions:
1. Prepare your air fryer by filling it halfway with oil and heating it to 350 degrees F.
2. In a large mixing bowl, combine the bread, bacon, onion, tomatoes, red pepper, and stock.
3. Add the eggs, cheddar, and Monterey jack cheeses and continue to cook for another 15 minutes.
4. Divide the mixture among the plates and garnish them with chives before serving. Enjoy!

21. Tasty Hash

Preparation Time: 10minutes
Cooking Time: 15 minutes
Servings: 6

Ingredients:
- Hash browns (16 oz.)
- 1 tablespoon extra virgin olive oil
- paprika, 1/2 teaspoon
- 1/2 tsp. garlic powder
- Salt and black pepper to taste. 1 whisked egg
- 2 tablespoons chopped chives 1 cup shredded

cheddar

Directions:
5. Heat the oil in your air fryer to 350 degrees F, then add the hash.
6. Toss in the paprika, garlic powder, salt, pepper, and egg, and cook for 15 minutes.
7. Toss in the cheddar and chives, divide among plates, and serve!

22. Lunch Egg Rolls

Preparation Time: 10minutes
Cooking Time: 15 minutes
Servings: 4

Ingredients:
- 1/2 cup mushrooms, chopped1/2 cup grated carrots2 tbsp. grated zucchini green onions, chopped 2 tbsp of soy sauce8 egg roll wrappers (for 8 egg rolls) 1/2 cups of mushrooms, chopped 12 cups of carrots, grated
- 1 lightly whisked egg
- 1 tbsp cornstarch (optional).

Directions:
1. In a large mixing basin, combine the carrots, mushrooms, zucchini, green onions, and soy sauce, stirring well.
2. Lay out the egg roll wrappers on a work surface, divide the veggie mixture among them, and roll them tightly.
3. In a separate dish, whisk together the cornstarch and the egg until well combined. Brush the egg rolls with this mixture.
4. Seal the edges of the rolls and place them in a preheated air fryer for 15 minutes at 370 degrees F.
5. Prepare them on a platter and offer them as a side dish with your lunch. Enjoy!

23. Veggie Toast

Preparation Time: 10minutes
Cooking Time: 15 minutes
Servings: 4

Ingredients:
- 1 red bell pepper, peeled and thinly sliced1 cup sliced cremini mushrooms 1 cup sliced cremini mushrooms
- 1 chopped yellow squash 2 thinly sliced green onions 1 chopped yellow squash
- 1 tbsp olive oil (extra virgin)4 slices of sourdough bread
- 2 tablespoons of melted butter (softened)
- 1/2 cup goat cheese, crumbled

Directions:
1. Toss together the red bell pepper, mushrooms, squash, green onions, and oil in a large mixing bowl. Transfer the vegetables to an air fryer and cook at 350 degrees F for 10 minutes, shaking the fryer once, until the vegetables are tender.
2. Cook the bread slices at 350 degrees F for 5 minutes after spreading butter on them in an air fryer.
3. To serve, divide the veggie mixture among the bread slices and top with cheese crumbles.
4. Enjoy!

24. Stuffed Mushrooms

Preparation Time: 10minutes
Cooking Time: 15 minutes
Servings: 4

Ingredients:
- 4 large Portobello mushroom tops (optional). 14 cups of ricotta cheese 1 tbsp olive oil (extra virgin)
- 5 tbsp parmesan cheese, grated1 cup spinach, shredded
- A third of a cup of bread crumbs
- 14 teaspoon finely chopped rosemary

Directions:
1. Toss the mushroom caps with the oil, then put them into your air fryer's basket and cook them for 2 minutes at 350 degrees F.
2. In the meantime, in a large mixing bowl, combine half of the parmesan with the

ricotta, spinach, rosemary, and bread crumbs, stirring thoroughly.
3. Place the mushrooms in the air fryer basket once again and cook at 350 degrees Fahrenheit for 10 minutes. 3. Stuff the mushrooms with the mixture and sprinkle the remaining parmesan on top.
4. To serve them for lunch, divide them among plates and accompany them with a side salad. Enjoy!

25. Quick Lunch Pizzas

Preparation Time: 10minutes

Cooking Time: 7 minutes

Servings: 4

Ingredients:
- pitas (four pitas)
- 1 tbsp olive oil (extra virgin)
- one-quarter cup pizza sauce
- 2 cups chopped canned mushrooms, 4 ounces sliced canned mushrooms
- 1/2 teaspoons of basil (dried), 2 green onions (chopped), 2 cups of mozzarella (grated), 12

teaspoons of basil
- 1 cup (optional) sliced grape tomatoes

Directions:
1. Using your fingers, spread pizza sauce over each pita bread, then top with green onions and basil, then divide the mushrooms and cheese.
2. Arrange the pita pizzas in your air fryer and cook them for 7 minutes at 400°F.
3. Before serving, place tomato slices on top of each pizza and divide them among plates. Enjoy!

26. Scallops and Dill

Preparation Time: 10minutes

Cooking Time: 5 minutes

Servings: 4

Ingredients:
- Two cups of debearded sea scallops 1 teaspoon lemon juice one pound sea scallops
- 2 teaspoons extra-virgin olive oil, 1 teaspoon finely chopped dill
- Season with salt and black pepper to taste.

Directions:
1. In your air fryer, combine the scallops with the dill, oil, salt, pepper, and lemon juice, cover, and cook at 360 degrees F for 5 minutes until done.
2. Discard those that have not been opened, and divide the scallops and dill sauce among the dishes for lunch.
3. Enjoy!

27. Hot Bacon Sandwiches

Preparation Time: 10minutes
Cooking Time: 7 minutes
Servings: 4

Ingredients:
- A third cup of barbecue sauce
- Honey (about 2 tablespoons)
- Bacon (boiled and chopped into thirds): 8 slices bacon1 peeled and sliced red bell pepper
- One small yellow bell pepper, thinly sliced, divided into three pita pockets, each half
- 15-cup butter lettuce leaves, divided into quarters; 2 tomatoes, thinly sliced

Directions:
4. In a large mixing bowl, whisk together the barbecue sauce and honey until thoroughly combined.
1. Brush the bacon and all of the bell peppers with some of this mixture, then place them in your air fryer and cook for 4 minutes at 350 degrees Fahrenheit.
2. Shake the fryer and cook them for a further 2 minutes.
3. Stuff pita pockets with the bacon mixture, as well as tomatoes and lettuce, and then put the remaining barbecue sauce on top and serve for lunch.
4. Enjoy!

28. Fish And Chips

Preparation Time: 10minutes
Cooking Time: 7 minutes
Servings: 4

Ingredients:
- 2 medium cod fillets, skinless and boneless, cooked in a skillet with salt and black pepper to taste.
- 1/4 cup buttermilk
- 3 cups drained and cooled kettle chips

Directions:

1. Combine the fish, salt, pepper, and buttermilk in a large mixing bowl; toss well and set aside for 5 minutes.
2. Place the chips in a food processor and pulse until they are crushed. Spread the chips on a platter.
3. Place the fish on top and press down firmly on all sides.
4. Place the fish in the basket of your air fryer and cook at
400°F for 12 minutes.
5. Prepare a hot meal for your guests. Enjoy!

29. Hash Brown Toasts

Preparation Time: 10minutes
Cooking Time: 7 minutes
Servings: 4

Ingredients:
- 4 hash brown patties, defrosted from the freezer. 1 tbsp olive oil (extra virgin)
- 1/4 cup chopped cherry tomatoes
- grated 2 tbsp. shredded parmesan cheese3 tablespoons shredded mozzarella
- 1 tbsp. balsamic vinegar, 1 tbsp. minced basil, 1 tbsp. olive oil

Directions:
1. Place the hash brown patties in the air fryer, drizzle with oil, and cook for 7 minutes at 400 degrees F, or until crispy.
2. In a large mixing bowl, combine the tomatoes, mozzarella, parmesan, vinegar, and basil. Stir thoroughly.
3. Assemble the hash brown patties on plates and top each with a tomato mixture before serving them for lunch.
4. Enjoy!

30. Delicious Beef Cubes

Preparation Time: 10minutes
Cooking Time: 12 minutes
Servings: 4

Ingredients:
- 1 pound sirloin steak, cubed
- Jarred spaghetti sauce (about 16 ounces) Bread crumbs (about
- 1/2 cup) 2 tbsp olive oil (extra-virgin)
- 1/2 teaspoons of ground marjoram, preferably dried.
- ready-to-serve white rice that has already been cooked.

Directions:
1. In a large mixing bowl, combine the meat cubes with the pasta sauce and toss thoroughly.
2. In a separate bowl, combine the bread crumbs, marjoram, and oil, stirring thoroughly.
3. Coat the beef cubes with this mixture and place them in your air fryer at 360 degrees F for 12 minutes.
4. Arrange the mixture on individual plates and serve with white rice on the side. Enjoy!

31. Beignets

Preparation Time: 10minutes
Cooking Time: 5 minutes
Servings: 24

Ingredients:
- ¾ cup water, lukewarm
- 1 tbsp. yeast, active-dry
- 1/4 cup of sugar
- 4 cups all-purpose flour
- 2 tbsp. butter, unsalted, and cut into small pieces
- 1/2 cup evaporated milk
- 1 lightly beaten egg
- 1/4 cup butter, melted
- 1 cup sugar, confectioners

Directions:
1. Mix the water, yeast, plus a pinch of sugar in a medium bowl, then let the mixture proof for about 5 minutes until frothing a little. If it does not froth, start again using new yeast.

2. Combine flour, unsalted butter, salt, and remaining sugar in a large bowl. Add milk, egg, and yeast mixture, then mix with a spatula until dough forms.

3. Transfer the dough into a bowl, oiled, then cover with a kitchen towel. Let it rest for about 2 hours in a warm place and let it rise. You can refrigerate the dough overnight.

4. Now roll the dough into ½ -inch thick, then cut the dough into diamond-shaped or rectangular-shaped pieces.

5. Preheat your air fryer to 350F/180C. Brush both sides of the beignets with melted butter. Air fry for about 5 minutes turning over halfway through.

6. Transfer the cooked beignets onto a plate, then dust with confectioners sugar and serve with raspberry sauce or chocolate.

32. Blueberry Muffins

Preparation Time: 10minutes
Cooking Time: 15 minutes
Servings: 12
Ingredients:
- 1-1/2 cups all-purpose flour
- 3/4 cup oats, old fashioned
- 1/2 tbsp. cinnamon
- 1/2 tbsp. salt
- 1/2 cup light brown sugar
- 1 tbsp. baking powder
- 1 cup milk
- 2 tbsp. vanilla
- 2 eggs
- 1/4 cup melted butter, unsalted
- 1 cup blueberries

Directions:
1. Combine flour, oats, cinnamon, salt, sugar, and baking powder in a mixing bowl. Mix well. Combine milk, vanilla, eggs, and butter in another mixing bowl. Stir to combine.

2. Add wet batter to the dry batter and stir. Stir in blueberries.

Now divide the batter into 12 silicone muffin cups.

3. Place the cups in an air fryer. Air fry for about 11-15 minutes at 350F/180C until a toothpick comes out clean when inserted in the middle. Serve and enjoy.

33. Quiche Lorraine

Preparation Time: 10minutes
Cooking Time: 12 minutes
Servings: 1
Ingredients:
- 1/2 pie crust, refrigerated
- 1 cooked bacon slice, diced
- 2 tbsp. scallions, minced
- 1/4 cup Swiss cheese, shredded
- 1 egg, large
- 1/4 cup milk
- 1/2 tbsp. salt
- 1/2 tbsp. pepper

Directions:
1. Cut your pie crust to fit into the pan, then place bacon at the bottom of the dough spread scallions and cheese on top of your bacon.

2. Meanwhile, crack the egg into a bowl, small, then add milk.

Add salt and pepper, then beat well.

3. Pour the mixture over ingredients in the pan, then place in an air fryer basket. Air fry for about 12 minutes at 350F/180C.

4. Let cool before removing it from the basket. Serve and enjoy.

34. Pumpkin French Toast

Preparation Time: 10minutes
Cooking Time: 15 minutes
Servings: 2

Ingredients:
- 4 oz. pumpkin
- A pinch of nutmeg
- 2 tbsp. honey
- 1 egg, small
- 3 tbsp. whole milk
- 1 ½ oz. pumpkin pie filling
- 4 slices whole meal bread

Directions:
1. Chop your pumpkin into cubes, small, and place them in a bowl, mixing. Add nutmeg and honey, then mix until pumpkin cubes are coated well.

2. Place the cubes in your air fryer and air fry for about 8 minutes at 360F/182C.

3. Meanwhile, place egg and milk in the mixing bowl and mix well with a fork until the egg is beaten well. Add pumpkin pie filling and mix again well.

4. Now remove the pumpkin from your air fryer and set it aside.

Soak bread slices in French toast batter, drowning them and removing excess moisture, if any.

5. Place them on a grill pan then in the air fryer. Air fry for about 4 minutes at 400F/205C. Use tongs to turn them over.

6. Add the set-aside pumpkin and air fry for another 4 minutes at 400F/205C. Sprinkle with a little honey and extra pumpkin juices. Serve.

35. Chicken Cheese Quesadilla

Preparation Time: 10minutes
Cooking Time: 6 minutes
Servings: 4

Ingredients:
- 2 flour tortillas
- 1 cup chicken, precooked and diced
- 1 cup cheese, shredded

Directions:
1. Place one tortilla in your air fryer, then top and evenly spread chicken and cheese.

2. Top a second tortilla and place a metal rack over the second tortilla. This is to prevent the tortillas from moving.

3. Air fry for about 6 minutes at 370F/188C, flipping halfway through. Slice, serve and enjoy.

36. Asparagus Frittata

Preparation Time: 5minutes
Cooking Time: 8 minutes
Servings: 1

Ingredients:
- 2 eggs, large
- 2 tbsp. milk
- 1 tbsp. fresh parmesan cheese, grated
- Pepper, to taste
- Salt, to taste
- Non-stick cooking spray
- 5 asparagus tips, steamed

Directions:
1. Whisk together eggs, milk, cheese, pepper, and salt in a medium bowl. Spray the air fryer-safe dish with cooking spray, then place it in your air fryer basket.

2. Pour the mixture into the dish, then top with asparagus. Air fry for about 8 minutes at 400F/205 C until a toothpick comes out clean when inserted in the center. Serve and enjoy.

37. Lemon Muffins

Preparation Time: 10minutes
Cooking Time: 15 minutes
Servings: 4

Ingredients:
- 1/2 cup cream cheese softened
- 2/3 cup butter softened
- 1/2 cup caster sugar
- 2 eggs
- A pinch of salt
- 1/2 tbsp. baking powder
- 2/3 cup self-rising flour
- 2 tbsp. lemon juice

Directions:
1. Preheat your air fryer to 370F (188 C). Beat cheese plus butter in a bowl until consistency is light and creamy. Add sugar, beating for about 5 minutes until light and fluffy mixture.

2. Add eggs each time, then fold in salt, baking, and flour. Add lemon juice mixing well. Now spoon the mixture into silicone cups.

3. Place the cups in an air fryer basket in your air fryer. Air fry for about 15 minutes at 370F/188 C until a toothpick comes out clean once inserted. Enjoy!

38. Cornmeal Pancake

Preparation Time: 10minutes
Cooking Time: 12 minutes
Servings: 4

Ingredients:
- 1½ cups yellow cornmeal
- ½ cup all-purpose flour
- 2 tablespoons sugar
- 1 teaspoon salt
- 1 teaspoon baking powder
- 1 cup whole or 2% milk
- 1 large egg, lightly beaten
- 1 tablespoon butter, melted

- Cooking spray

Directions:
1. Line the air fryer basket using parchment paper. Mix the cornmeal, flour, sugar, salt, plus baking powder in your large bowl. Mix the milk, egg, and melted butter, then whisk to combine.

2. Drop tablespoonfuls of the batter onto your parchment paper for each pancake.

3. Spray the pancakes with cooking spray, then bake at

350F/180C for 3 minutes. Flip the pancakes, spray with cooking spray again, and bake for an additional 2 to 3 minutes.

4. Remove from the basket to a plate and repeat with the remaining batter. Cool for 5 minutes and serve immediately.

39. Air Fried Omelet

Preparation Time: 5minutes
Cooking Time: 10 minutes
Servings: 2

Ingredients:
- 4 eggs
- ½ cup milk
- Salt, to taste
- Diced fresh meat and veggies – ½ cup (mushrooms, ham, green onions, red bell pepper, etc.)
- 1 teaspoon breakfast seasoning

- ½ cup shredded cheese (mozzarella or cheddar)
- Green onions, for garnish

Directions:
1. Mix the milk and eggs in a bowl until well combined.

Season with salt. Add the meat and vegetables to the egg mixture.

2. Pour the mixture into a greased pan. Place the pan into the air fryer basket.

3. Cook 10 minutes at 350F/177C. Around the 5-minute mark, sprinkle the mixture with seasoning and cheese. Finish cooking.

4. Remove from the basket, garnish with green onions, and serve.

40. Olives Bake

Preparation Time: 10minutes
Cooking Time: 15 minutes
Servings: 4

Ingredients:
- ½ cup cheddar; shredded
- 4 eggs; whisked
- 2 cups black olives pitted and chopped.
- 1 tbsp. Cilantro; chopped.

- ¼ tsp. Sweet paprika
- A pinch of salt and black pepper
- Cooking spray

Directions:
1. Take a bowl and mix the eggs with the olives and all the ingredients except the cooking spray and stir well.

2. Heat your air fryer at 350F/177C, grease it with cooking spray, pour the olives and eggs mixture, spread and cook for

20 minutes. Divide between plates and serve.

41. Mustard Greens Salad

Preparation Time: 5minutes Cooking Time: 15 minutes Servings: 4

Ingredients:
- ½ lb. Cherry tomatoes; cubed
- 2 cups mustard greens
- 2 tbsp. Chives; chopped.
- 1 tsp. Olive oil
- A pinch of salt and black pepper

Direction:
1. Heat your air fryer with the oil at 360F/182C, add

all the ingredients, toss, cook for 15 minutes shaking halfway, divide into bowls and serve for breakfast.

42. Spinach and Shrimp

Preparation Time: 10minutes
Cooking Time: 0 minutes
Servings: 4

Ingredients:
- 15 oz. shrimp; peeled and deveined
- ¼ cup veggie stock
- 2 tomatoes; cubed
- 4 spring onions; chopped

- 2 cups baby spinach
- 1 tbsp. garlic; minced
- 2 tbsp. cilantro; chopped
- 1 tbsp. lemon juice
- ½ tsp. cumin, ground
- Salt and black pepper to taste

Directions:
1. In a pan that fits your air fryer, mix all the ingredients except the cilantro, toss, introduce in the air fryer and cook at
360F/182C for 15 minutes.
2. Add the cilantro, stir, divide into bowls. Serve.

43. Mustard Chicken Thighs

Preparation Time: 10minutes
Cooking Time: 15 minutes
Servings: 4

Ingredients:
- 1 ½ lb. chicken thighs, bone-in
- 2 tbsp. Dijon mustard
- Cooking spray
- A pinch of salt and black pepper

Directions:
1. Take a bowl and mix the chicken thighs with all the other ingredients and toss.
2. Put the chicken in your Air Fryer's basket and cook at
370F/188C for at least 15 minutes shaking halfway. Serve.

44. Broccoli Stew

Preparation Time: 50minutes
Cooking Time: 15 minutes
Servings: 4

Ingredients:
- 1 ½ lb. chicken thighs, bone-in
- 2 tbsp. Dijon mustard
- Cooking spray
- A pinch of salt and black pepper

Directions:
1. Take a bowl and mix the chicken thighs with all the other ingredients and toss.
2. Put the chicken in your Air Fryer's basket and cook at
370F/188C for 30 minutes shaking halfway. Serve.

45. Tomato Stew

Preparation Time: 10minutes
Cooking Time: 15 minutes
Servings: 4

Ingredients:
- 25 oz. canned tomatoes; cubed
- 4 spring onions; chopped.
- 2 red bell peppers; cubed
- 1 tbsp. cilantro; chopped.
- 1 tsp. sweet paprika
- Salt and black pepper to taste.

Directions:
1. In a pan that fits your air fryer, mix all the ingredients, toss, introduce the pan in the fryer and cook at 360F/182C for 15 minutes
2. Divide into bowls and serve.

46. Mushroom and Spinach Cups

Preparation Time: 5minutes
Cooking Time: 15 minutes
Servings: 6

Ingredients:
- Olive oil cooking spray
- 6 large eggs
- 1 garlic clove, minced
- ½ teaspoon salt
- ½ teaspoon black pepper
- Pinch red pepper flakes
- 8 ounces (227 g) baby bella mushrooms, sliced
- 1 cup fresh baby spinach

- 2 scallions, white parts and green parts, diced

Directions:
1. Preheat the air fryer to 320°F (160°C). Lightly coat the inside of six silicone muffin cups or a six-cup muffin tin with olive oil cooking spray.
2. In a large bowl, beat the eggs, garlic, salt, pepper, and red pepper flakes for 1 to 2 minutes, or until well combined.
3. Fold in the mushrooms, spinach, and scallions.
4. Divide the mixture evenly among the muffin cups.
5. Place into the air fryer and bake for 12 to 15 minutes, or until the eggs are set.
6. Remove and allow to cool for 5 minutes before serving.

47. Spinach and Mushroom Frittata

Preparation Time: 10 minutes
Cooking Time: 15 minutes
Servings: 4

Ingredients:
- Olive oil cooking spray
- 8 large eggs
- ½ teaspoon salt
- ½ teaspoon black pepper
- 1 garlic clove, minced
- 2 cups fresh baby spinach
- 4 ounces (113 g) baby bella mushrooms, sliced
- 1 shallot, diced
- ½ cup shredded Swiss cheese, divided

- Hot sauce, for serving (optional)

Directions:
1. Preheat the air fryer to 360°F (182°C). Lightly coat the inside of a 6-inch round cake pan with olive oil cooking spray.
2. In a large bowl, beat the eggs, salt, pepper, and garlic for
1 to 2 minutes, or until well combined.
3. Fold in the spinach, mushrooms, shallot, and ¼ cup of the Swiss cheese.
4. Pour the egg mixture into the prepared cake pan, and sprinkle the remaining ¼ cup of Swiss over the top.
5. Place into the air fryer and bake for 15 minutes, or until the eggs are set in the center.
6. Remove from the air fryer and allow to cool for 5 minutes. Drizzle with hot sauce (if using) before serving.

48. Parmesan Egg Pita

Preparation Time: 5 minutes
Cooking Time: 6 minutes
Servings: 2

Ingredients:
- 1 whole wheat pita
- 2 teaspoons olive oil
- ½ shallot, diced
- ¼ teaspoon garlic, minced
- 1 large egg
- ¼ teaspoon dried oregano
- ¼ teaspoon dried thyme
- ⅛ teaspoon salt
- 2 tablespoons shredded Parmesan cheese

Directions:
1. Preheat the air fryer to 380°F (193°C).
2. Brush the top of the pita with olive oil, then spread the diced shallot and minced garlic over the pita.
3. Crack the egg into a small bowl or ramekin, and season it with oregano, thyme, and salt.
4. Place the pita into the air fryer basket, and gently pour the egg onto the top of the pita. Sprinkle with cheese over the top.

5. Bake for 6 minutes.
6. Allow to cool for 5 minutes before cutting into pieces for serving

49. Sweet Potato Hash with Mushrooms

Preparation Time: 5 minutes
Cooking Time: 6 minutes
Servings: 2

Ingredients:
- 2 medium sweet potatoes, peeled and cut into 1-inch cubes
- ½ green bell pepper, diced
- ½ red onion, diced
- 4 ounces (113 g) baby bella mushrooms, diced
- 2 tablespoons olive oil
- 1 garlic clove, minced
- ½ teaspoon salt
- ½ teaspoon black pepper
- ½ tablespoon chopped fresh rosemary

Directions:
1. Preheat the air fryer to 380°F (193°C).

2. In a large bowl, toss all ingredients together until the vegetables are well coated and seasonings distributed.

3. Pour the vegetables into the air fryer basket, making sure they are in a single even layer. (If using a smaller air fryer, you may need to do this in two batches.)

4. Cook for 9 minutes, then toss or flip the vegetables. Cook for 9 minutes more.

5. Transfer to a serving bowl or individual plates and enjoy.

50. Peach Oatmeal

Preparation Time: 5 minutes
Cooking Time: 30 minutes
Servings: 6

Ingredients:
- Olive oil cooking spray
- 2 cups certified gluten-free rolled oats
- 2 cups unsweetened almond milk
- ¼ cup honey, plus more for drizzling (optional)
- ½ cup plain Greek yogurt
- 1 teaspoon vanilla extract
- ½ teaspoon ground cinnamon
- ¼ teaspoon salt
- 1½ cups diced peaches, divided, plus more for serving (optional)

Directions:
1. Preheat the air fryer to 380°F (193°C). Lightly coat the inside of a 6-inch cake pan with olive oil cooking spray.

2. In a large bowl, mix together the oats, almond milk, honey, yogurt, vanilla, cinnamon, and salt until well combined.

3. Fold in ¾ cup of the peaches and then pour the mixture into the prepared cake pan.

4. Sprinkle the remaining peaches across the top of the oatmeal mixture. Bake in the air fryer for 30 minutes.

5. Allow to set and cool for 5 minutes before serving with additional fresh fruit and honey for drizzling, if desired.

51. Apples Stuffed with Granola

Preparation Time: 10 minutes
Cooking Time: 15 minutes
Servings: 4

Ingredients:
- 4 Granny Smith or other firm apples
- 1 cup granola
- 2 tablespoons coconut sugar
- ¾ teaspoon cinnamon
- 2 tablespoons cashew butter
- 1 cup water or apple juice

Directions:
1. Working one apple at a time, cut a circle around the apple stem and scoop out the core, taking care not to cut all the way through to the bottom. (This should leave an empty cavity in the middle of the apple for the granola.) Repeat with the remaining apples.

2. In a small bowl, combine the granola, coconut sugar, and cinnamon. Pour the butter over the ingredients and stir with a fork. Divide the granola mixture among the

apples, packing it tightly into the empty cavity.

3. Place the apples in the cake pan insert for the air fryer.

Pour the water or juice around the apples. Bake at 350°F (177°C) for 20 minutes until the apples are

soft all the way through.

4. Serve warm with a dollop of crème fraîche or yogurt, if desired.

52. Red Potatoes with Red Bell Pepper

Preparation Time: 10 minutes
Cooking Time: 15 minutes
Servings: 4

Ingredients:
- 2 cups diced waxy red potatoes
- 2 teaspoons olive oil, divided
- Kosher salt, to taste
- ½ cup chopped yellow onion
- 1 cup chopped red bell pepper
- 1¾ cups ketchup
- 2 chipotle peppers in adobo plus 1 tablespoon adobo sauce
- ½ teaspoon smoked paprika

Directions:
1. In a medium bowl, toss the potatoes with 1 teaspoon of oil and season with a pinch of salt. Place them in the air fryer basket and cook at 400°F (204°C) for 10 minutes. In the meantime, in a small bowl toss the onion and pepper with the remaining teaspoon of oil and season with salt.

2. After 10 minutes, add the onion and pepper to the air fryer basket and toss to combine. Cook for an additional

10 to 12 minutes until the peppers are softened and charred at the edges and the potatoes are crispy outside and cooked through.

3. While the vegetables are cooking, prepare the chipotle ketchup. Combine the ketchup, 2 chipotle peppers, and

1 tablespoon of the adobo sauce in a blender and purée until smooth. Pour the chipotle ketchup into a serving bowl.

4. When the vegetables are cooked, remove them from the air fryer and toss them with the smoked paprika. Serve immediately with chipotle ketchup on the side.

53. Whole Wheat Biscuits

Preparation Time: 10 minutes

Cooking Time: 10 minutes

Servings: 6

Ingredients:
- 4 cups whole wheat flour
- 1 tablespoon baking powder
- 1 teaspoon salt
- 6 tablespoons cashew butter, plus more for brushing on the biscuits (optional)
- ¾ cup unsweetened coconut milk
- 1 to 2 tablespoons oil

Directions:
1. In a large bowl, whisk the flour, baking powder, and salt until blended.

2. Add the cashew butter. Using a pastry cutter or 2 forks, work the dough until pea-size balls of the butter-flour mixture appear. Stir in the coconut milk until the mixture is sticky.

3. Preheat the air fryer to 330°F (166°C). Line the air fryer tray with parchment paper and spritz it with oil.

4. Drop the dough by the tablespoonful onto the prepared tray, leaving 1 inch between each, to form 10 biscuits.

5. Bake for 5 minutes. Flip the biscuits and cook for 4 minutes more for a light brown top, or 5 minutes more for a darker biscuit. Brush the tops with the butter, if desired.

54. Cinnamon Muffins with Pecans

Preparation Time: 15 minutes Cooking Time: 13 minutes Servings: 12

Ingredients:
- 4 cups whole wheat flour
- 1 tablespoon ground cinnamon
- 2 teaspoons baking soda
- 2 teaspoons allspice
- 1 teaspoon ground cloves
- 1 teaspoon salt
- 1 cup cashew butter
- 2 cups honey
- 2 large eggs, lightly beaten
- 2 cups unsweetened applesauce
- ¼ cup chopped pecans
- 1 to 2 tablespoons oil

Directions:
1. In a large bowl, whisk the flour, cinnamon, baking soda, allspice, cloves, and salt until blended.

2. In another large bowl, combine the butter and honey.

Using an electric mixer, beat the mixture for 2 to 3 minutes until light and fluffy. Add the beaten eggs and stir until blended.

3. Add the flour mixture and applesauce, alternating between the two and blending after each addition. Stir in the pecans.

4. Preheat the air fryer to 325°F (163°C). Spritz 12 silicone muffin cups with oil.

5. Pour the batter into the prepared muffin cups, filling each halfway. Place the muffins on the air fryer tray.

6. Air fry for 6 minutes. Shake the basket and air fry for 7 minutes more. The muffins are done when a toothpick inserted into the middle comes out clean.

55. Rosemary Potato Fries with Garlic

Preparation Time: 5 minutes

Cooking Time: 15 minutes

Servings: 4

Ingredients:
- 2 cups cubed potato (small cubes from 2 medium potatoes)
- 1½ teaspoons olive oil
- 3 medium cloves garlic, minced or pressed
- ¼ teaspoon sea salt
- ¼ teaspoon onion granules
- ⅛ teaspoon freshly ground black pepper
- Cooking oil spray
- ½ tablespoon dried rosemary or fresh rosemary, minced

Directions:
1. In a medium bowl, toss the potatoes with the oil, garlic, salt, onion granules, and black pepper. Stir to evenly coat the potatoes with the seasonings. Place the potato mixture in the air fryer basket and roast at 390°F (199°C) for 8 minutes. Set the bowl aside.

2. Remove, shake the basket or stir the contents and cook for another 7 minutes, or until the potatoes are tender and nicely browned. Add the potatoes back to the bowl and spray with oil. Add the rosemary, toss, and serve immediately.

56. Shrimp with Garlic Olive Oil

Preparation Time: 15 minutes
Cooking Time: 6 minutes
Servings: 4

Ingredients:
- 1 pound (454 g) medium shrimp, cleaned and deveined
- ¼ cup plus 2 tablespoons olive oil, divided
- Juice of ½ lemon
- 3 garlic cloves, minced and divided
- ½ teaspoon salt
- ¼ teaspoon red pepper flakes
- Lemon wedges, for serving (optional)
- Marinara sauce, for dipping (optional)

Directions:
1. Preheat the air fryer to 380°F (193°C).

2. In a large bowl, combine the shrimp with 2 tablespoons of the olive oil, as well as the lemon juice, ⅓ of the minced garlic, salt, and red pepper flakes. Toss to coat the shrimp well.

3. In a small ramekin, combine the remaining ¼ cup of olive oil and the remaining minced garlic.

4. Tear off a 12-by-12-inch sheet of aluminum foil. Pour the shrimp into the center of the foil, then fold the sides up and crimp the edges so that it forms an aluminum foil bowl that is open on top. Place this packet into the air fryer basket.

5. Roast the shrimp for 4 minutes, then open the air fryer and place the ramekin with oil and garlic in the basket beside the shrimp packet. Cook for 2 more minutes.

6. Transfer the shrimp on a serving plate or platter with the ramekin of garlic olive oil on the side for dipping. You may also serve with lemon wedges and marinara sauce, if desired.

57. Basil Crostini with Goat Cheese

Preparation Time: 5 minutes
Cooking Time: 5 minutes
Servings: 4

Ingredients:
- 1 whole wheat baguette
- ¼ cup olive oil
- 2 garlic cloves, minced
- 4 ounces (113 g) goat cheese
- 2 tablespoons fresh basil, minced

Directions:
1. Preheat the air fryer to 380°F (193°C).

2. Cut the baguette into ½-inch-thick slices.

3. In a small bowl, mix together the olive oil and garlic, then brush it over one side of each slice of bread.

4. Place the olive-oil-coated bread in a single layer in the air fryer basket and bake for 5 minutes.

5. Meanwhile, in a small bowl, mix together the goat cheese and basil.

6. Remove the toast from the air fryer, then spread a thin layer of the goat cheese mixture over the top of each piece and serve.

58. Artichoke Pita Flatbread with Olives

Preparation Time: 5 minutes
Cooking Time: 10 minutes
Servings: 4

Ingredients:
- 2 whole wheat pitas
- 2 tablespoons olive oil, divided
- 2 garlic cloves, minced
- ¼ teaspoon salt
- ½ cup canned artichoke hearts, sliced
- ¼ cup Kalamata olives
- ¼ cup shredded Parmesan
- ¼ cup crumbled feta
- Chopped fresh parsley, for garnish (optional)

Directions:
1. Preheat the air fryer to 380°F (193°C).

2. Brush each pita with 1 tablespoon olive oil, then sprinkle the minced garlic and salt over the top.

3. Distribute the artichoke hearts, olives, and cheeses evenly between the two pitas, and place both into the air fryer to bake for 10 minutes.

4. Remove the pitas and cut them into 4 pieces each before serving. Sprinkle parsley over the top, if desired.

59. Crab Cakes with Red Bell Pepper

Preparation Time: 10 minutes
Cooking Time: 10 minutes
Servings: 6

Ingredients:
- 8 ounces (227 g) lump crab meat
- 2 tablespoons diced red bell pepper
- 1 scallion, white parts and green parts, diced
- 1 garlic clove, minced
- 1 tablespoon capers, minced
- 1 tablespoon plain Greek yogurt
- 1 egg, beaten
- ¼ cup whole wheat bread crumbs
- ¼ teaspoon salt
- 1 tablespoon olive oil
- 1 lemon, cut into wedges

Directions:
1. Preheat the air fryer to 360°F (182°C).
2. In a medium bowl, mix the crab, bell pepper, scallion, garlic, and capers until combined.
3. Add the yogurt and egg. Stir until incorporated. Mix in the bread crumbs and salt.
4. Divide this mixture into 6 equal portions and pat out into patties. Place the crab cakes into the air fryer basket in a single layer, making sure that they don't touch each other. Brush the tops of each patty with a bit of olive oil.
5. Bake for 10 minutes.
6. Remove the crab cakes from the air fryer and serve with lemon wedges on the side.

60. Chicken Wings with Honey Mustard

Preparation Time: 10 minutes
Cooking Time: 20 minutes
Servings: 2

Ingredients:
- 2 pounds (907 g) chicken wings
- Salt and freshly ground black pepper
- 2 tablespoons cashew butter
- ¼ cup honey
- ¼ cup spicy brown mustard
- Pinch ground cayenne pepper
- 2 teaspoons Worcestershire sauce

Directions:
1. Prepare the chicken wings by cutting off the wing tips and discarding (or freezing for chicken stock). Divide the drumettes from the wingettes by cutting through the joint. Place the chicken wing pieces in a large bowl.
2. Preheat the air fryer to 400°F (204°C).
3. Season the wings with salt and freshly ground black pepper and air fry the wings in two batches for 10 minutes per batch, shaking the basket half way through the cooking process.
4. While the wings are air frying, combine the remaining ingredients in a small saucepan over low heat.
5. When both batches are done, toss all the wings with the honey-mustard sauce and toss them all back into the basket for another 4 minutes to heat through and finish cooking. Give the basket a good shake part way through the cooking process to redistribute the wings. Remove the wings from the air fryer and serve.

61. Avocado Eggs

Preparation Time: 10 minutes
Cooking Time: 15 minutes
Servings: 4

Ingredients:
- 2 large avocados, sliced
- 1 cup breadcrumbs
- ½ cup flour 2 eggs, beaten
- ¼ tsp. paprika
- Salt and pepper to taste

Directions:
1. Pre-heat your Air Fryer at 400°F for 5 minutes.
2. Sprinkle some salt and pepper on the slices of avocado.
Optionally, you can enhance the flavor with a half-tsp. of dried oregano.
3. Lightly coat the avocados with flour. Dredge them in the eggs, before covering with breadcrumbs. Transfer to the fryer and cook for 6 minutes.

62. English Muffin Sandwiches

Preparation Time: 10 minutes
Cooking Time: 15 minutes
Servings: 4

Ingredients:
- 4 English muffins
- 8 pepperoni slices
- 4 cheddar cheese slices
- 1 tomato, sliced

Directions:
1. Preheat air fryer to 370°F. Split open the English muffins along the crease. On the

bottom half of the muffin, layer
2 slices of pepperoni and one slice of the cheese and tomato. Place the top half of the English muffin to finish the sandwich. Lightly spray with cooking oil. Place the muffin sandwiches in the air fryer. Bake for 8 minutes, flipping once. Let cool slightly before serving.

63. Medium Rare Simple Salt And Pepper Steak

Preparation Time: 10 minutes
Cooking Time: 15 minutes
Servings: 3

Ingredients:
- 1 ½ pounds skirt steak
- Salt and pepper to taste

Directions:
1. Preheat the air fryer at 390°F.
2. Place the grill pan accessory in the air fryer.
3. Season the skirt steak with salt and pepper.
4. Place on the grill pan and cook for 15 minutes per batch.
5. Flip the meat halfway through the cooking time.

64. Bagels

Preparation Time: 5 minutes
Cooking Time: 10 minutes
Servings: 4

Ingredients:
- 1 cup self-rising flour
- 1 cup plain full-fat Greek yogurt
- 2 tablespoons granulated sugar
- 1 large egg, whisked

Directions:
1. Preheat the air fryer to 320°F.
2. In a large bowl, mix flour, yogurt, and sugar together until a ball of dough forms.
3. Turn dough out onto a lightly floured surface. Knead dough for 3 minutes, then form into a smooth ball. Cut dough into four sections. Roll each piece into an 8" rope,
then shape into a circular bagel shape. Brush top and bottom of each bagel with egg.
4. Place in the air fryer basket and cook 10 minutes, turning halfway through cooking time to ensure even browning. Let cool 5 minutes before serving.

65. The Simplest Grilled Cheese

Preparation Time: 5 minutes
Cooking Time: 10 minutes
Servings: 1

Ingredients:
- 2 slices bread
- 3 slices American cheese

Directions:
Preheat the air fryer to 370°F. Spread one tsp of butter on the outside of each of the bread slices. Place the cheese on the inside of one bread slice. Top with the other slice. Cook in the air fryer for 4 minutes. Flip the sandwich over and cook for an additional 4 minutes. Serve cut diagonally

66. Pigs In A Blanket

Preparation Time: 10 minutes
Cooking Time: 8 minutes
Servings: 10
Ingredients:
- 1 cup all-purpose flour, plus more for rolling
- 1 teaspoon baking powder
- ¼ cup salted butter, cut into small pieces
- ½ cup buttermilk
- 10 fully cooked breakfast sausage links

Directions:
1. In a large mixing bowl, whisk together the flour and baking powder. Using your fingers or a pastry blender, cut in the butter until you have small pea-size crumbles.
2. Using a rubber spatula, make a well in the center of the flour mixture. Pour the buttermilk into the well, and fold the mixture together until you form a dough ball.
3. Place the sticky dough onto a floured surface and, using a floured rolling pin, roll out until ½-inch thick. Using a round biscuit cutter, cut out 10 rounds, reshaping the dough and rolling out, as needed.
4. Place 1 fully cooked breakfast sausage link on the left edge of each biscuit and roll up, leaving the ends slightly exposed.
5. Using a pastry brush, brush the biscuits with the whisked eggs, and spray them with cooking spray.
6. Place the pigs in a blanket into the air fryer basket with at least 1 inch between each biscuit. Set the air fryer to 340°F and cook for 8 minutes.

67. Cheesy Sausage Sticks

Preparation Time: 10 minutes
Cooking Time: 8 minutes
Servings: 3

Ingredients:
- 6 small pork sausages
- ½ cup almond flour
- ½ cup Mozzarella cheese, shredded
- 2 eggs, beaten
- 1 tablespoon mascarpone
- Cooking spray

Directions:
1. Pierce the hot dogs with wooden coffee sticks to get the sausages on the sticks". Then in the bowl mix up almond flour, Mozzarella cheese, and mascarpone. Microwave the mixture for 15 seconds or until you get a melted mixture. Then stir the egg in the cheese mixture and whisk it until smooth. Coat every sausage stick in the cheese mixture. Then preheat the air fryer to 375°F. Spray the air fryer basket with cooking spray. Place the sausage stock in the air fryer and cook them for 4 minutes from each side or until they are light brown.

68. Bacon Eggs

Preparation Time: 10 minutes
Cooking Time: 5 minutes
Servings: 2

Ingredients:
- 2 eggs, hard-boiled, peeled
- 4 bacon slices
- ½ teaspoon avocado oil
- 1 teaspoon mustard

Directions:
1. Preheat the air fryer to 400°F. Then sprinkle the air fryer basket with avocado oil and place the bacon slices inside. Flatten them in one layer and cook for 2 minutes from each side. After this, cool the bacon to the room temperature. Wrap every egg into 2 bacon slices. Secure the eggs with toothpicks and place them in the air fryer. Cook the wrapped eggs for 1 minute at 400°F.

69. Easy Egg Bites

Preparation Time: 10 minutes
Cooking Time: 9 minutes
Servings: 2

Ingredients:
- 2 large eggs
- ¼ cup full-fat cottage cheese
- ¼ cup shredded sharp Cheddar cheese
- ¼ teaspoon salt
- ⅛ teaspoon ground black pepper
- 6 tablespoons diced cooked ham

Directions:
1. Preheat the air fryer to 300°F. Spray six silicone muffin cups with cooking spray.

2. In a blender, place eggs, cottage cheese, Cheddar, salt, and pepper. Pulse five times until smooth and frothy.

3. Place 1 tablespoon ham in the bottom of each prepared baking cup, then divide egg mixture among cups.

4. Place in the air fryer basket and cook 9 minutes until egg bites are firm in the center. Carefully remove cups from air fryer basket and cool 3 minutes before serving. Serve warm.

70. Cheese Pie

Preparation Time: 10 minutes
Cooking Time: 15 minutes
Servings: 4

Ingredients:
- 8 eggs
- 1 1/2 cups heavy whipping cream
- 1 lb cheddar cheese, grated
- Pepper
- Salt

Directions:
1. Preheat the air fryer to 325°F.

2. In a bowl, whisk together cheese, eggs, whipping cream, pepper, and salt.

3. Spray air fryer baking dish with cooking spray.

4. Pour egg mixture into the prepared dish and place in the air fryer basket.

5. Cook for 15 minutes or until the egg is set.

6. Serve and enjoy.

71. Spinach Spread

Preparation Time: 5 minutes
Cooking Time: 10 minutes
Servings: 4

Ingredients:
- 2 tablespoons coconut cream
- 3 cups spinach leaves
- 2 tablespoons cilantro
- 2 tablespoons bacon, cooked and crumbled
- Salt and black pepper to the taste

Directions:
1. In a pan that fits the air fryer, combine all the ingredients except the bacon, put the pan in the machine and cook at
360°F for 10 minutes. Transfer to a blender, pulse well, divide into bowls and serve with bacon sprinkled on top.

72. Egg Muffins

Preparation Time: 5 minutes
Cooking Time: 11 minutes
Servings: 4

Ingredients:
- 4 eggs
- salt and pepper
- olive oil
- 4 English muffins, split
- 1 cup shredded Colby Jack cheese
- 4 slices ham or Canadian bacon.

Directions:
1. Preheat air fryer to 390°F.

2. Beat together eggs and add salt and pepper to taste. Spray air fryer baking pan lightly with oil and add eggs. Cook for
2minutes, stir, and continue cooking for 4minutes, stirring every minute, until eggs are scrambled to your preference. Remove pan from air fryer.
3. Place bottom halves of English muffins in air fryer basket.
Take half of the shredded cheese and divide it among the muffins. Top each with a slice of ham and one-quarter of the eggs. Sprinkle remaining cheese on top of the eggs. Use a fork to press the cheese into the egg a little so it doesn't slip off before it melts.
4. Cook at 360°F for 1 minute. Add English muffin tops and cook for 4minutes to heat through and toast the muffins.

73. Fried Eggs

Preparation Time: 5 minutes
Cooking Time: 7 minutes
Servings: 2

Ingredients:
- 2 eggs
- 3 slices bacon

Directions:

1. Heat some oil in a deep fryer at 375°F.
2. Fry the bacon.
3. In a small bowl, add the 2 eggs.
4. Quickly add the eggs into the center of the fryer.
5. Using two spatulas, form the egg into a ball while frying.
6. Fry for 2-3 minutes, until it stops bubbling.
7. Place on a paper towel and allow to drain.
8. Enjoy!

74. Strawberry Pastry

Preparation Time: 10 minutes
Cooking Time: 15 minutes
Servings: 8

Ingredients:
- 1 package refrigerated piecrust
- 1 cup strawberry jam
- 1 large egg, whisked
- ½ cup confectioners' sugar
- 2 tablespoons whole milk
- ½ teaspoon vanilla extract

Directions:
1. Preheat the air fryer to 320°F. Cut parchment paper to fit the air fryer basket.
2. On a lightly floured surface, lay piecrusts out flat. Cut each piecrust round into six 4" × 3" rectangles, reserving excess dough.
3. Form remaining dough into a ball, then roll out and cut four additional 4" × 3" rectangles, bringing the total to sixteen.
4. For each pastry, spread 2 tablespoons jam on a pastry rectangle, leaving a 1" border around the edges. Top with a second pastry rectangle and use a fork to gently press all four edges together. Repeat with remaining jam and pastry.
5. Brush tops of each pastry with egg and cut an X in the center of each to prevent excess

steam from building up.

6. Place pastries on parchment in the air fryer basket, working in batches as necessary. Cook 12 minutes, then carefully flip and cook an additional 3 minutes until each side is golden brown. Let cool 10 minutes.

7. In a small bowl, whisk confectioners' sugar, milk, and vanilla. Brush each pastry with glaze, then place in the refrigerator 5 minutes to set before serving.

75. Almond Oatmeal

Preparation Time: 5 minutes
Cooking Time: 15 minutes
Servings: 4

Ingredients:
- 2 cups almond milk
- 1 cup coconut, shredded
- 2 teaspoons stevia
- 2 teaspoons vanilla extract

Directions:
1. In a pan that fits your air fryer, mix all the ingredients, stir well, introduce the pan in the machine and cook at
360°F for 15 minutes. Divide into bowls and serve for breakfast.

76. Air Fryer Sweet Potato Wedges

Preparation Time: 10 minutes
Cooking Time: 15 minutes
Servings: 2

Ingredients
- 2 Sweet Potatoes, skin on, washed & cut into wedges
- 2 tablespoons Olive Oil
- 1 tablespoon Corn Flour / Corn Starch
- 1 tablespoon Paprika
- Salt, to taste

Directions:
1.Combine sweet potato wedges, corn flour/starch, paprika, and olive oil in a large mixing bowl. To blend, whisk everything together thoroughly.

2. Place wedges in an air fryer basket or rack in a single layer, ensuring they don't touch. Cook for 15 minutes at
200°C/390°F, rotating the wedges halfway through.

When the wedges are golden and crisp, they're done.

3. Transfer to a platter and season liberally with salt. Serve right away.

77. Crispy Chicken Wings

Preparation Time: 15 minutes Cooking Time: 15 minutes Servings: 4

Ingredients
- 500g / 1 lbs. Chicken Wings
- 3 tablespoons butter
- ¼ cup Frank's Hot Sauce (or more, to taste)
- 1 tablespoon Brown Sugar
- 1 tablespoon Baking Powder
- 1 teaspoon Paprika
- 1 teaspoon Garlic Powder
- Salt and Pepper, to taste
- 1 teaspoon Worcestershire Sauce
- ½ teaspoon Garlic Powder

Directions:
1. Dry the wings as much as possible; the less moisture remaining on them, the crispier the skin! Toss the chicken wings with the baking powder, paprika, garlic powder, salt, and pepper in a mixing basin using your hands to ensure they are uniformly covered.

2. In the air fryer basket, arrange the wings in a single layer with a little space between each wing.

3. Cook at 150°C/300°F for fifteen minutes, then at
200°C/400°F for 10-15 minutes, or until thoroughly cooked. You may confirm this by checking the interior temperature of the wings using a meat thermometer. You can top it with your favorite sauce right away if you're serving it plain.

4. In a small saucepan over medium heat, combine the ingredients. Cook stirring periodically until the sauce has slightly thickened and decreased.

5. Toss your wings in the buffalo sauce and toss to coat them.

Return the wings to the air fryer for another 2 minutes at
200°C to crisp up the sauce. Serve right away.

78. Quesadillas

Preparation Time: 10 minutes
Cooking Time: 10 minutes
Servings: 2

Ingredients
- Two flour tortillas
- 4 tablespoon Refried Beans, or more if needed
- Quarter cup Cheese, or more if needed

Directions:
1. Place the tortilla on a flat surface. Next, spread refried beans on the tortilla's (half).

Fold the tortilla in half and sprinkle cheese on top of the beans. Using the remaining tortilla, repeat the process.

2. Place the tortillas in the air fryer basket and cook for 8 minutes, flipping halfway, or till the quesadillas are crisp & golden and the cheese is melted. Check on your quesadillas in the very first few minutes of cooking and check whether the tortilla has lifted slightly away from the fillings, push it back down with a spatula.

3. If desired, serve with guacamole & sour cream or Greek yogurt right away.

79. Mozzarella Sticks

Preparation Time: 15 minutes
Cooking Time: 2 minutes
Servings: 6

Ingredients
- 16 oz. mozzarella block cheese
- 1/4 cup all-purpose flour
- 2 large eggs
- 3 tbsp. nonfat milk
- 1 cup plain breadcrumbs

Directions:
1. Create 3 by 1/2-inch cheese sticks.

2. In a mixing bowl, add the bread crumbs. In a mixing bowl, insert flour. In a mixing bowl, combine the egg and milk.

3. Flour, egg, and bread crumbs are used to coat cheese sticks.

4. Place the breaded sticks on a cookie sheet and spread them out flat.

5. Freeze for 2 hours or till completely solid.

6. Preheat the air fryer to 390° F for around 5 minutes. Using nonstick cooking spray, coat the basket. Remove the basket from the air fryer before spraying.

7. Fill the fryer basket with small batches of breaded sticks. Do not overcrowd the area.

8. Cook for 2 minutes at 390°F. Cook for another two minutes after flipping the mozzarella sticks.

80. Vanilla Bean Air Fryer Doughnuts

Preparation Time: 12 minutes
Cooking Time: 15 minutes
Servings: 3

Ingredients:
- Twelve ounces' fresh sea scallops, defrosted
- 2 tbsp. olive oil
- Half tsp. sea salt
- 1/2 tsp. ground black pepper
- Half tsp. garlic powder
- 1/2 tsp. onion powder
- Quarter cup traditional bread crumbs
- One tsp. Old Bay seasoning

Directions:
1. In a large mixing bowl or resealable bag, pour the olive oil. Add the scallops and coat them completely.

2. Mix the salt, pepper, garlic, and onion powder in a second bowl or bag. Toss the scallops in the seasonings after removing them from the olive oil.

3. In a third bowl or bag, mix bread crumbs & Old Bay seasoning. Toss the scallops with the bread crumb mixture to coat them.

4. Remove the air fryer basket and coat it lightly with nonstick cooking spray. In the basket, arrange the scallops in a beautiful pattern. Scallops may need to be cooked in two batches to avoid overcrowding.

5. Preheat oven to 400°F and bake for 12 minutes. If the scallops are larger, cook for up to 15 minutes or until they reach an internal temperature of 145°F.

81. Air Fryer Baked Apples

Ingredients
- 2 medium apples
- 2 tablespoons (25 grams) brown sugar or coconut sugar
- 2 tablespoons (28 grams) unsalted butter or coconut oil, melted and cooled (coconut oil for vegan)
- 2 tablespoons (15 grams) pecans optional
- 1/2 cup (46 grams) rolled oats (if gluten-free, use GF oats)
- 2 tablespoons (15 grams) all-purpose flour, white whole wheat flour or for GF, use 2

tablespoons (18 grams) Bob's Red Mill
- 1-to-1 Gluten-free Baking Mix
- 3/4 teaspoon ground cinnamon
- pinch of salt

Directions:
1. If the air fryer is large enough to accommodate whole apples, you can cut and fill them the same way you would in the oven. If your air fryer can't fit a whole apple, cut it in half, as well as remove the core and stem. Make sure they're the right size for your air fryer and, if necessary, cut more away.
2. Some toppings will splatter, so prepare your air fryer accordingly.
3. Preheat the air fryer to 325 degrees Fahrenheit (162 degrees Celsius).
4. Combine everything except the apples and raisins in a small mixing bowl.
5. In the center of each apple, place ½ tablespoon of raisins. To prevent the raisins from burning, place them between the crumble and the apples.
6. To keep the crumble from blowing around in the air fryer, divide it among the 4 apple halves and press it down over the raisins to compact it.
7. With crumble topping side on the upper side place them in the air fryer very gently.
8. Then cook for about 15-18 minutes, or until the vegetables are softened. The apples should have softened slightly but not become mushy, and the crumble mixture should have begun to brown. As they sit, they'll soften a little more.

82. Cinnamon and Sugar Doughnuts

Preparation Time: 12 minutes
Cooking Time: 14 minutes
Servings: 9

Ingredients:
- ½ cup white sugar
- 1 teaspoon salt
- ½ cup sour cream
- ⅓ cup white sugar
- 2 ½ tablespoons butter, at room temperature
- 2 large egg yolks
- 2 ¼ cups all-purpose flour
- 1 ½ teaspoons baking powder
- 1 teaspoon cinnamon
- Two tbsp. butter, melted, or as needed

Directions:

1. In a mixing bowl, combine ½ cup white butter and sugar until crumbly. Stir in the egg yolks until completely mixed.
2. Sift together the flour, baking powder, and salt in a separate basin. One-third of the flour mixture and half of the sour cream should be added to the sugar and egg mixture. Combine the remaining flour & sour cream in a mixing bowl. Keep the dough refrigerated till ready to use.
3. In a bowl, combine 1/3 cup sugar & cinnamon.
4. Roll out the dough to a thickness of 1/2 inch on a lightly floured work surface. To make doughnut shapes, cut nine large circles in the dough and a little circle out of the middle of each large round.
5. Preheat your air fryer to 350°F (175 degrees C).
6. Brush both sides of the doughnuts with 1/2 of the melted butter.
Place half doughnuts in the air fryer basket and cook for 8 minutes. Cooked donuts are brushed with melted butter and then dipped in the cinnamon-sugar mixture. Carry on with the rest of the doughnuts in the same manner

83. Air Fryer Breakfast Cookies

Preparation Time: 15 minutes
Cooking Time: 10 minutes
Servings: 12

Ingredients
- One cup mashed ripe bananas (about 2 medium)
- A half-cup chunky peanut butter
- A half-cup honey
- One teaspoon vanilla extract
- One cup old-fashioned oats
- A half-cup whole wheat flour
- A quarter cup nonfat dry milk powder
- two teaspoons ground cinnamon
- A half teaspoon of salt

- 1/4 teaspoon baking soda
- One cup dried cranberries or raisins

Directions:
1. Preheat air fryer to 300° F. Beat banana, peanut butter, honey and vanilla until blended. In another bowl, add flour, oats, milk powder, salt cinnamon, and baking soda; gradually beat into the banana mixture. Add in dried cranberries.
2. In batches, drop dough by 1/4 cupful's.
3. Cook until lightly browned, 6-8 minutes. Cool in the basket for 1 minute. Remove to wire racks.
4. Serve warm or at room temperature.
5. Freeze cookies in freezer containers, separating layers with waxed paper. To use, thaw before serving or, if desired, reheat in a preheated 300° air fryer until warmed, about 1 minute.

84. Breakfast Burritos

Preparation Time: 10 minutes
Cooking Time: 5 minutes
Servings: 6

Ingredients
- 6 medium flour tortillas
- 6 scrambled eggs
- 1/2 lb. ground sausage – browned
- 1/2 bell pepper – minced
- One third cup bacon bits
- 6 medium flour tortillas
- 6 scrambled eggs
- A half-cup shredded cheese
- oil for spraying

Directions:
1. Combine scrambled eggs, bell pepper, cooked sausage, bacon bits & cheese in a big bowl. Stir to blend.
2. A half-cup of the mixture is spooned into the middle of a flour tortilla.
3. Fold the sides and then roll.
4. For the remaining ingredients, you have to repeat the same process.
5. Put filled burritos in the air fryer's basket & liberally spray with oil.
6. Cook for 5 minutes at 330 degrees F.

85. Beef Empanadas

Preparation Time: 15 minutes
Cooking Time: 10 minutes
Servings: 12

Ingredients
- 12 Goya Empanadas wrappers thawed
- 1/2 teaspoon onion powder
- 1/2 teaspoon garlic powder
- 1/2 teaspoon paprika
- 1 egg
- 2 teaspoons water
- 1/2 tablespoon chili powder
- 1/2 teaspoon cumin
- 1/2-pound ground beef
- 1/2 cup chopped onion
- 2 garlic cloves minced
- 1 cup shredded Mexican Blend cheese shredded
- salt and pepper to taste

Directions:
1. Spritz your air fryer basket with oil or use parchment paper to line it.
2. In the air fryer basket, place the empanadas.
3. Air fry for 8-10 minutes at 350°F or until crisp.

86. Kale Chips

Preparation Time: 15 minutes
Cooking Time: 7 minutes
Servings: 12

Ingredients:
- 10 oz. fresh kale ribs removed and chopped into large pieces
- One tablespoon olive oil
- salt and pepper to taste
- Quarter cup grated parmesan cheese

Directions:
1. Combine the kale and olive oil in a large bowl and sprinkle the salt and pepper to taste throughout.
2. Place the kale in the air fryer basket.
3. Air-fry the kale at 270 degrees for 5 minutes.
4. Open the air fryer and shake the basket. Cook for an additional 2 minutes.
5. Open the air fryer and sprinkle the parmesan cheese throughout. Cook for an additional 2 minutes.

87. Zucchini Chips

Preparation Time: 15 minutes
Cooking Time: 15 minutes
Servings: 5

Ingredients
- 1 large zucchini
- 1/4 cup of shredded parmesan cheese
- Pepper and salt to taste
- 2 beaten eggs
- 1/2 cup of all-purpose flour
- 1 teaspoon of Italian Seasoning
- 1 teaspoon of Smoked Paprika
- 1 1/2-2 cups of breadcrumbs

Directions:
1. Spray your air fryer basket with some cooking oil.
2. Add flour, eggs, and breadcrumbs to separate bowls.
3. Thinly slice the zucchini into 1/4-inch thick pieces. A mandolin may also be used for fine slicing. To ensure that the zucchini chips fry at the same temperature, make sure they are all

approximately the same size.

4. Season the flour with salt, pepper, and paprika to taste, then top with grated parmesan.

5. Toss the zucchini in flour, egg, and breadcrumbs before placing in the air fryer. To ensure that the breadcrumbs stay, completely cover the chip in the eggs.

6. Keep a moist towel nearby because your hands will get sticky.

7. Spray the zucchini chips with the cooking oil spray.

8. Air Fry for about 5 minutes at 400 degrees.

9. Flip the chips. Spray with additional oil and cook for 4-7 minutes at 400 degrees. The zucchini chips will brown by

8 minutes; cook them a little longer if you like them crispy.

88. Tortilla Chips

Preparation Time: 15 minutes
Cooking Time: 10 minutes
Servings: 48

Ingredients
- Six corn tortillas
- Kosher salt to taste
- cooking oil spray

Directions:
1. Spray both sides of each tortilla with cooking oil, then rotate the stack and cut again to make 4 pieces.

2. Lay the tortillas in 1 stack. Use a knife or pizza cutter and cut the stack in half.

3. Then you will cut down the middle again, both horizontally and vertically, to form 8 total chips per layer.

4. Sprinkle salt throughout the chips. You can add any additional seasonings if you wish.

5. Load the chips into the air fryer. Do not overcrowd the basket. Cook in batches if needed. Overcrowding will lead to some chips that taste stale.

6. Air-fry the chips for 6 minutes at 370 degrees.

89. Avocado Fries

Preparation Time: 15 minutes
Cooking Time: 10 minutes
Servings: 4

Ingredients
- Half cup of panko breadcrumbs
- Half teaspoon salt
- One Haas avocado - peeled, pitted, and sliced
- aquafaba from one 15 ounces can of white beans or garbanzo beans

Directions:
1. Toss the panko and salt together in a shallow bowl. Into another shallow bowl, put the aquafaba.

2. In the aquafaba and then in the panko, dredge the avocado slices and obtain a clean, even coating.

3. Arrange the slices in your air fryer basket in a single layer. The single layer is important. Air fry at 390F for 10 minutes (do not preheat), shaking well 5 minutes later.

4. Serve with your favorite dipping sauce instantly.

90. Chicken Tenders

Preparation Time: 10 minutes
Cooking Time: 15 minutes
Servings: 2

Ingredients
- Twelve ounces of Chicken Breasts
- 1 Egg White
- 1/8 Cup Flour
- Thirty-five grams Panko Bread Crumbs
- Salt and Pepper

Directions:
1. Trim the chicken breast and slice into tenders.

2. With salt and pepper, season each side.

3. Dip chicken tenders into egg whites. Then panko bread crumbs and then into flour.

4. Load and spray with olive spray into the air fryer basket.

5. It has to be cooked for about ten minutes or until fully cooked at 350 degrees F.

91. Cheesy Chicken Omelet

Preparation Time: 5 minutes
Cooking Time: 10 minutes
Servings: 2

Ingredients
- Black pepper, to taste
- 4 eggs
- Chicken breast: half cup, cooked & diced
- Cheese: 2 tbsp., shredded
- Salt, to taste
- 1/4 tsp. of onion powder
- 1/4 tsp. of granulated garlic

Directions:
1. Take 2 ramekins and spray them with oil.
2. Add two eggs to each ramekin.
3. Add seasonings and cheese in each ramekin, mix well.
4. Add in ¼ cup of diced chicken to every ramekin.
5. Let the air fryer oven preheat to 330 F.
6. Air fry for 14-18 minutes at 330 F.
7. Serve right away.

92. Air-Fried English Breakfast

Preparation Time: 5 minutes
Cooking Time: 15 minutes
Servings: 4

Ingredients
- 8 sausages
- 8 bacon slices
- 4 eggs
- 1 (16-ounce) can of baked beans
- 8 slices of toast

Directions
1. Add the sausages and bacon slices to your air fryer and cook them for 10 minutes at a 320°F.
2. Using a ramekin or heat-safe bowl, add the baked beans, then place another ramekin and add the eggs and whisk.
3. Change the temperature to 290°F.
4. Place it inside your air fryer and cook it for an additional 5 minutes or until everything is done.
5. Serve and enjoy!

93. Bacon BBQ Burgers

Preparation Time: 15 minutes Cooking Time: 8 minutes Servings: 3

Ingredients
- 6 slices of bacon
- Minced onion: 2 tbsp.
- Bbq sauce: 1 tbsp.
- Seasoned salt: half tsp.
- Ground beef: 1 pound
- 3 slices of cheese
- Pepper: half tsp.
- 3 buns

Sauce
- mayonnaise: 2 tbsp.
- BBQ sauce: 2 tbsp.

Directions:
1. Let the air fryer oven preheat to 400 F.
2. Air fry the bacon for 8-10 minutes, flipping halfway through.
3. In a bowl, add the rest of the ingredients except for buns and cheese. Mix and make into 3 patties.
4. Air fry for five minutes at 360 F, flip and cook for 3 to 4 minutes.
5. Add cheese slices on each patty, air fry for 1 to 2 minutes.
6. In a bowl, mix the sauce's ingredients and spread on one half
of the bun.
7. Add patty and desired toppings and serve.

94. Stuffed Mushrooms

Preparation Time: 15 minutes
Cooking Time: 15 minutes
Servings: 16

Ingredients:
- 1/4 cup breadcrumbs
- Shredded mozzarella: 2 tbsp.
- 36 white button mushrooms, without stem
- Chopped fresh parsley: 1 tbsp.
- Grated pecorino-romano: ¼ cup
- Olive oil: 4 tbsp.
- Chopped fresh mint: 1 tsp.
- 1 minced garlic clove

Directions:
1. In a bowl, add cheeses, mint, breadcrumbs, parsley, garlic, olive oil (2 tbsp.), salt and pepper. Toss to combine.
2. Coat the mushrooms in the rest of the olive oil and place on the tray, cavity facing up.
3. Add the crumbs mixture to the cavity.

4. Let the air fryer oven preheat to 360 F.

5. Air fry for ten minutes until bubbling.

6. Serve right away.

95. Yummy Breakfast Italian Frittata

Preparation Time: 5 minutes
Cooking Time: 15 minutes
Servings: 6
Ingredients
- 6 eggs
- 1/3 cup of milk
- 4-ounces of chopped Italian sausage
- 3 cups of stemmed and roughly chopped kale
- 1 red deseeded and chopped bell pepper
- ½ cup of a grated feta cheese
- 1 chopped zucchini
- 1 tablespoon of freshly chopped basil
- 1 teaspoon of garlic powder
- 1 teaspoon of onion powder
- 1 teaspoon of salt

- 1 teaspoon of black pepper

Directions:
1. Turn on your air fryer oven to 360°F.
2. Grease the air fryer pan with a nonstick cooking spray.
3. Add the Italian sausage to the pan and cook it inside your air fryer for 5 minutes
4. While doing that, add and stir in the remaining ingredients until it mixes properly.
5. Add the egg mixture to the pan and allow it to cook inside your air fryer for 5 minutes
6. Thereafter carefully remove the pan and allow it to cool off until it gets chill enough to serve.
7. Serve and enjoy!

96. Breakfast Grilled Ham and Cheese

Preparation Time: 5 minutes
Cooking Time: 10 minutes
Servings: 2

Ingredients:
- 1 teaspoon butter
- 4 slices bread
- 4 slices smoked country ham
- 4 slices Cheddar cheese
- 4 thick slices tomato

Directions:
1. Spread ½ teaspoon of butter onto one side of 2 slices of bread. Each sandwich will have 1 slice of bread with butter and 1 slice without.

2. Assemble each sandwich by layering 2 slices of ham, 2 slices of cheese, and 2 slices of tomato on the unbuttered pieces of bread. Top with the other bread slices, buttered side up.

3. Place the sandwiches in the air fryer buttered-side down.

Cook for 4 minutes

97. Omelet Frittata

Preparation Time: 10 minutes
Cooking Time: 6 minutes
Servings: 2

Ingredients
- 3 eggs, lightly beaten
- 2 tbsp cheddar cheese, shredded
- 2 tbsp heavy cream
- 2 mushrooms, sliced
- 1/4 small onion, chopped
- 1/4 bell pepper, diced
- Pepper
- Salt

Directions:
1. In a bowl, whisk eggs with cream, vegetables, pepper, and salt.

2. Preheat the air fryer oven to 400°F.
3. Pour egg mixture into the air fryer oven pan. Place pan in air fryer and cook for 5 minutes
4. Add shredded cheese on top of the frittata and cook for 1 minute more.
5. Serve and enjoy.

98. Cheesy Spinach Omelet

Preparation Time: 10 minutes
Cooking Time: 6 minutes
Servings: 2

Ingredients
- Melted unsalted butter, 3 tbsps.
- Powdered sugar, ¼ cup
- Refrigerated biscuits, 8.
- Semisweet chocolate chips, 48

Directions
1. Cut the biscuits into thirds then flatten them and place 2 chocolate chips at the center.
2. Wrap the chocolate with dough to seal the edges.
3. Rub each dough hole with some butter.
4. Set the dough into your air fryer oven to cook for 12 minutes at 340°F.
5. Set aside to add powdered sugar.
6. Serve and enjoy.

99. Apple Chips

Preparation Time: 5 minutes
Cooking Time: 10 minutes
Servings: 2

Ingredients
- Granulated sugar: 2 tsp.
- Cinnamon: half tsp.
- 2 apples, sliced thin

Directions:
1. In a bowl, toss apples with sugar and cinnamon.
2. Place the apples on the tray of the air fryer.
3. Let the air fryer oven preheat to 350 F on bake.
4. Bake for 12 minutes, flip every 4 minutes.

100. Stuffed Jalapeno

Preparation Time: 5 minutes
Cooking Time: 10 minutes
Servings: 2

Ingredients
- 1 lb. ground pork sausage
- 1 (8 oz.) package cream cheese, softened
- 1 cup shredded Parmesan cheese
- 1 lb. large fresh jalapeno peppers halved lengthwise and seeded
- 1 (8 oz.) bottle Ranch dressing

Directions:
1. in Mix pork sausage ground with ranch dressing and cream cheese in a bowl. But the jalapeno in half and remove their seeds. Divide the cream cheese mixture into the jalapeno halves.
2. Place the jalapeno pepper in a baking tray. Set the Baking tray inside the Air Fryer toaster oven and close the lid. Select the Bake mode at 350°F for 10 minutes. Serve warm.

101. Zucchini Fries

Preparation Time: 15 minutes
Cooking Time: 12 minutes
Servings: 4

Ingredients:

Garlic Aioli
- Olive oil: 2 tbsp.
- Salt & pepper, to taste
- Mayonnaise: half cup
- Roasted garlic: 1 tsp.
- Half lemon's juice

Zucchini Fries:
- 1 large zucchini, sliced into half-inch sticks
- Flour: half cup
- seasoned breadcrumbs: 1 cup
- 2 eggs, whisked

- salt & pepper

Directions:
1. In a bowl, add all ingredients of aioli and mix. Adjust seasoning.
2. In a bowl, add flour and season with salt and pepper.
3. In another bowl, add whisked eggs.
4. In the third bowl, add seasoned breadcrumbs.
5. Coat the zucchini fries in flour, then in eggs and lastly in breadcrumbs.
6. Place them on the air fryer tray. Let them rest for ten minutes.
7. Let the air fryer oven preheat to 400 F.
8. Oil spray the zucchini fries and air fry for 12 minutes, flipping halfway through.
9. Serve with aioli.

102. Deep Dish Pizza

Preparation Time: 15 minutes
Cooking Time: 22 minutes
Servings: 2

Ingredients
- Button mushrooms: 3 oz., sliced
- Pizza dough: 12 oz.
- Spinach: half cup
- Olive oil: 1 tbsp.
- Prosciutto: 3 oz., sliced
- Italian seasoning: ¼ tsp.
- Pizza sauce: 1/3 cup
- Grated mozzarella cheese: 1½ cups

Directions:
1. Coat the mushrooms with olive oil, Italian seasonings. Let it rest for 15 minutes.
2. Let the air fryer oven preheat to 370 F.
3. Oil spray a 7" baking pan and roll the dough, and place in the pan.
4. Pierce with a fork, air fry for five minutes.
5. Take out and flip the crust, air fry for five minutes.
6. Add sauce and cheese on top.
7. On half of the pizza, add spinach and add mushrooms to the other half.
8. Add prosciutto on top.
9. Air fry for 10-12 minutes.
10. Slice and serve.

103. Avocado Fries with Lime Dipping Sauce

Preparation Time: 10 minutes
Cooking Time: 10 minutes
Servings: 4-5

Ingredients
- Panko breadcrumbs: 3/4 cup
- 2 small avocados, sliced into 16 wedges
- seasoning salt (lime chili): 1 1/4 tsp.
- 1 egg, whisked

Lime dipping sauce
- Mayonnaise: 3 tbsp.
- kosher salt: 1/8 tsp.
- Greek Yogurt: 1/4 cup
- lime juice: 2 tsp.

- seasoning salt (lime chili): half tsp.

Directions:
1. Let the air fryer oven preheat to 390 F.
2. In a bowl, whisk egg.
3. In another bowl, add panko with seasoned salt.
4. Season the avocado with seasoned salt, coat in egg and then in crumbs.
5. Spray with oil and air fry for 7-8 minutes, flip halfway through.
6. Serve with dipping sauce.
7. In a bowl, add all ingredients of dipping sauce and mix.

104. Mini Calzones

Preparation Time: 15 minutes
Cooking Time: 10-15 minutes
Servings: 16

Ingredients
- Pizza dough: 1 pound
- Mini pepperoni: 6 oz., chopped
- Pizza sauce: 1 cup
- Mozzarella cheese: 8 oz., shredded

Directions:
1. Roll the dough into 1/4" thick.
2. Slice into 8-10 circles. Make a total of 16 circles.
3. Add pizza sauce, pepperoni and cheese to each circle.
4. Fold the circle in half and seal the edges.
5. Let the air fryer oven preheat to 374 F.
6. Air fry the calzones for 8 minutes. Serve right away.

105. German Currywurst Recipe

Preparation Time: 10 minutes
Cooking Time: 12 minutes
Servings: 4

Ingredients
- Canned tomato sauce 1 cup
- Cayenne pepper ¼ teaspoon
- Diced onion ½ cup.
- Bratwurst 1 lb.
- Vinegar 2 tablespoons.
- Curry powder 2 teaspoons
- Sweet paprika 2 teaspoons
- Truvia 1/2 teaspoon, or sugar 1 teaspoons

Directions:
1. Whisk together the tomato sauce, curry powder, paprika, vinegar, sugar, & cayenne pepper in a heatproof container 6 x

44

3. Stir the onions in.
2. Slice the bratwurst into 1" thick chunks on the diagonal. To the sauce, apply bratwurst and mix well.
3. The pan is placed in the air fryer.
4. Till the sausage is cooked & the sauce is bubbling, to 400F, set the air fryer for 12 minutes.

106. Hot Pockets

Preparation Time: 5 minutes
Cooking Time: 14 minutes
Servings: 8

Ingredients:
- 1 bag gluten-free crescent rolls
- 8 slices prosciutto
- 8 slices Edam cheese
- 2 tbsp melted butter
- 2 tsp sea salt
- 2 tbsp mayonnaise, optional

Directions:
1. Lay the crescent rolls on a floured work surface and pinch together two triangles to create rectangles for the hot pocket.
2. Then, seal the perforated edges with your fingers. Lay a slice of ham and Edam on one side of the dough. Add a dab of mayonnaise on top of the slices.
3. Cover the slices with the other side of the dough and seal edges with a fork. Brush each hot pocket with melted butter and sprinkle with sea salt.
4. Cook hot pockets in the air fryer at 300 °F for 14 minutes.

107. Egg Cups

Preparation Time: 10 minutes
Cooking Time: 15 minutes
Servings: 4

Ingredients:
- 4 large eggs
- 4 slices whole-wheat bread
- 2 tbsp butter
- ¼ cup chopped bacon or 2 slices
- 2 tbsp chopped parsley
- Salt and pepper to taste

Directions:
1. Cook bacon in the air fryer at 350 °F for 7-10 minutes and chop into bite-sized pieces. Cut the crusts off the whole wheat bread and spread a layer of butter on each side.
2. Lightly coat silicone egg molds or ramekins with non-stick spray and add the buttered bread.
3. Crack each egg into the bread cups, sprinkle bacon on each, and place in the air fryer at 400 °F for 14 minutes. Top with parsley, salt, and pepper to taste.

108. French Toast Sticks

Preparation Time: 5 minutes
Cooking Time: 10 minutes
Servings: 6

Ingredients:
- 6 slices brioche bread
- 2 large eggs
- ⅓ cup heavy cream (of any milk)
- 1 tbsp melted butter
- 2 tbsp granulated sugar
- 1 tsp cinnamon
- ½ tsp vanilla extract
- ½ tsp salt
- ¼ cup maple syrup

Directions:
1. Slice brioche into strips. In a shallow bowl, whisk together eggs, heavy cream, butter, and vanilla extract. Separately, mix the dry ingredients: sugar, cinnamon, and salt.
2. Dunk each brioche stick into the wet mixture and then sprinkle the dry mixture onto each side. Set the air fryer to 350 °F and cook the strips for 8-10 minutes or until crisp. Pour the maple syrup into a small bowl for dipping.

109. Scotch Eggs

Preparation Time: 10 minutes
Cooking Time: 15 minutes
Servings: 6

Ingredients:
- 6 large eggs, soft-boiled and peeled
- 1 lb breakfast sausage
- 1 tsp onion powder
- 1 tsp garlic powder

- ¼ cup grated parmesan
- 1 tbsp chopped chives
- 1 tbsp sriracha
- ½ cup mayonnaise
- 2 tsp lemon juice

Directions:
1. In a bowl, combine onion powder, garlic powder, parmesan, and chives. Once combined, separate and grind the breakfast sausages by hand and add to the dry ingredients.

2. Make 3-inch patties with the sausage mixture. Pat dry the soft- boiled eggs, lightly coat with flour, and surround the eggs with the breakfast sausage mix.

3. In a 350 °F air fryer, cook the scotch eggs for 15 minutes or until the outside is crispy. In a small bowl, mix the sriracha, mayonnaise, and lemon juice.

110. Breakfast Frittata

Preparation Time: 5 minutes
Cooking Time: 15 minutes
Servings: 2

Ingredients:
- 4 eggs
- ½ lb breakfast sausage
- ½ cup milk
- ½ cup red bell pepper
- ½ cup shredded cheese
- ½ diced red onion
- 1 diced green onion
- 1 pinch cayenne pepper
- Salt, pepper, and paprika to taste

Directions:
1. In a mixing bowl, combine eggs, crumbled breakfast sausage, cheese, milk, bell pepper, red onion, cayenne pepper, salt, pepper, and paprika. In a 360 °F air fryer, spray a cake pan with non-stick spray and pour in the frittata mixture.

2. Cook in the air fryer for 15-20 minutes. Check with a toothpick that the eggs are cooked through. Remove the frittata from the air fryer, top with green onion.

111. Glazed Apple Fritters

Preparation Time: 5 minutes
Cooking Time: 10 minutes
Servings: 10

Ingredients:
- 2 Honeycrisp apples
- ¼ cup sugar
- 1 ½ tsp cinnamon
- ¼ cup milk, plus 1 tbsp
- 2 large eggs
- ¼ cup butter
- 2 tsp baking powder
- 1 ½ cups flour
- 1 cup powdered sugar

Directions:
1. In a mixing bowl, combine sugar, flour, baking powder, and 1 tsp cinnamon. In a separate bowl, combine milk, butter, and eggs. Add to dry ingredients and stir in the apples. Place parchment paper in a 350 °F air fryer.

2. Scoop 2 tablespoon balls of the apple mixture into the air fryer and fry for 10 minutes. For the glaze, mix the powdered sugar,

1 tbsp of milk, and ½ tsp of cinnamon in a bowl. After the fritters cool, coat in the glaze.

112. Churros

Preparation Time: 5 minutes
Cooking Time: 20 minutes
Servings: 4

Ingredients:
- ¼ cup butter
- 2 large eggs
- ½ cup milk
- ½ cup flour
- ¼ cup white sugar
- ½ tsp cinnamon
- 1 tsp salt

Directions:
1. In a saucepan over medium heat, boil the milk with a pinch of salt.

Add the flour and stir until a wet dough forms. Allow the dough to cool for 5 minutes. Combine the eggs into the dough and place into a plastic bag.

2. Cut off the tip of the plastic bag, and in a parchment-lined air fryer, pipe the churro dough into the air fryer. Cook each batch for 10 minutes at 375 °F or until golden. Coat each churro with cinnamon and sugar.

113. Chicken Taquitos

Preparation Time: 10 minutes
Cooking Time: 15 minutes
Servings: 4

Ingredients:
- 1 shredded rotisserie chicken
- 4 flour tortillas (8-inch)
- ½ cup shredded Mexican blend cheese
- ¼ cup sour cream
- 3 tbsp Mexican-style salsa
- 1 clove minced garlic
- 2 tbsp diced onion
- Salt and pepper to taste

Directions:
1. In a skillet, cook onions until translucent. Add the garlic, salsa, cheese, chicken, salt, and pepper to the skillet. sauté the ingredients until the cheese is melted.

2. Spoon about 3 tablespoons of the taquito mix onto the center of the tortillas and roll. Place a half-inch apart in the air fryer at 400

°F and lightly spray with cooking oil. Fry the taquitos for 10 to 15 minutes, flipping halfway.

114. Asiatic Orange Chicken

Preparation Time: 10 minutes
Cooking Time: 15 minutes
Servings: 2

Ingredients:
- 1 lb cubed chicken breast
- 3 tbsp cornstarch
- ½ cup orange juice
- 2 tbsp brown sugar
- 1 tbsp rice wine vinegar
- 1 tsp minced garlic
- 1 tsp minced ginger
- 2 tbsp soy sauce
- 2 tsp sesame seeds

Directions:
1. Cube the chicken and lightly coat in the cornstarch. Fry in the air fryer at 400 °F for 10 minutes, shaking the basket halfway to flip the chicken.

2. Meanwhile, in a skillet, combine the orange juice, rice wine vinegar, brown sugar, garlic, ginger, and soy sauce. Simmer for 5 minutes. Add a dash of water and cornstarch to the orange mixture and simmer for another minute.

3. Coat chicken with sauce and sprinkle with sesame seeds.

115. Southern Country Sandwich

Preparation Time: 10 minutes
Cooking Time: 15 minutes
Servings: 4

Ingredients:
- 1 lb chicken breast
- 4 burger buns or biscuits
- 1 cup flour
- ½ cup cornstarch
- 1 tbsp garlic powder
- 2 cups buttermilk
- 2 tsp each of salt, pepper, and paprika
- Pickles and mayonnaise for topping

Directions:
1. Use two shallow bowls to create the coating for the chicken. In the first bowl, combine the flour, cornstarch, and garlic powder.

2. In the second bowl, combine the buttermilk, salt, pepper, and paprika. Dunk the chicken in the flour mixture, then the buttermilk mixture, then back in the flour.

3. Spray chicken with cooking oil and place in the air fryer at 400 °F for 20 minutes. Flip the chicken halfway and spray again. Assemble on a bun with pickles and mayonnaise.

116. Chicken Nuggets

Preparation Time: 5 minutes
Cooking Time: 15 minutes
Servings: 5

Ingredients:
- ½ lb chicken breast
- 2 large eggs
- ¼ cup lemon juice
- ¼ cup panko breadcrumbs
- ¼ cup grated parmesan cheese
- 1 tsp onion powder
- 1 tsp garlic powder
- 1 tsp each of salt, pepper, and paprika

Directions:
1. Cube the chicken breasts into bite-size pieces. In a bowl, whisk together the eggs, lemon juice, garlic powder, onion powder, salt, pepper, and paprika. In a separate bowl, combine the panko and parmesan cheese.

2. Dunk the chicken bites into the egg mixture and then thoroughly coat in the panko. Place in the air fryer at 400 °F for 12-15 minutes and lightly spray with cooking oil.

117. Italian Chicken Piccata

Preparation Time: 10 minutes
Cooking Time: 15 minutes
Servings: 4

Ingredients:
- 1 lb boneless chicken breast
- 2 large eggs
- 2 tbsp lemon juice
- 1 cup breadcrumbs
- ¼ cup grated parmesan cheese
- ½ cup butter
- 1 cup chicken broth
- ¼ cup capers
- 1 tsp each of salt, pepper, and garlic powder

Directions:
1. Using a mallet, flatten the chicken breasts until ¼-inch thick. In a shallow bowl, mix the eggs, 1 tbsp of lemon juice, and garlic powder. In another bowl, combine the breadcrumbs and parmesan. Dip chicken breasts into the egg mixture and then the breadcrumb mixture.
2. Spray the air fryer with cooking oil and cook at 350 °F for 15 minutes. Meanwhile, on a medium-heat skillet, whisk together the chicken broth, lemon juice, butter, capers, salt, and pepper. Simmer until the sauce is reduced. Pour over the chicken.

118. Buffalo Wings

Preparation Time: 10 minutes
Cooking Time: 15 minutes
Servings: 4

Ingredients:
- 2 lbs chicken wings
- 1 tbsp olive oil
- ¼ cup hot sauce of choice
- ¼ cup butter
- 1 tsp garlic powder
- 1 tsp onion powder
- 1 tsp Worcestershire sauce
- 1 tsp salt and pepper

Directions:
1. Pat the chicken wings dry and separate into drums and flats. In a large bowl, coat chicken in olive oil, onion powder, salt, and pepper. Place in the air fryer at 400 °F for up to 20 minutes, checking every 5 minutes for desired crispiness.
2. Meanwhile, in a smaller bowl, combine the hot sauce, butter, garlic powder, and Worcestershire sauce. Remove chicken from the air fryer and generously coat in the buffalo sauce.

119. Turkey Meatballs

Preparation Time: 5 minutes
Cooking Time: 8 minutes
Servings: 6

Ingredients:
- 1 lb ground turkey
- 1 large egg
- 1 tbsp dijon mustard
- ⅓ cup breadcrumbs
- ¼ cup parmesan cheese
- 1 tbsp olive oil
- 1 tsp garlic powder
- 1 tsp dried parsley
- Salt and pepper to taste

Directions:
1. In a large mixing bowl, combine the ground turkey, egg, dijon mustard, breadcrumbs, parmesan, olive oil, garlic powder, parsley, salt, and pepper.
2. Roll each meatball into 2-inch balls. Place a piece of parchment in your air fryer and spray the meatballs with cooking oil. Do not overlap meatballs. Fry at 400 °F for 8 minutes.

120. Stuffed Peppers

Preparation Time: 15 minutes
Cooking Time: 15 minutes
Servings: 4

Ingredients:
- 4 bell peppers
- 1 lb lean ground beef
- 1 can diced tomatoes
- 1 can corn
- 1 can of black beans
- 2 cups cooked rice
- 1 cup shredded cheese
- 1 tbsp olive oil
- 1 tsp each of salt, pepper, garlic powder, and parsley

Directions:
1. In a medium-heat skillet, sauté the ground beef. Add the olive oil, tomatoes, corn, black beans, and rice. Season with salt, pepper, garlic powder, and parsley.
2. sauté for 5-7 minutes. Meanwhile, cut the tops off the bell peppers and clean out any seeds. Pour filling into the bell peppers and place in the air fryer at 360 °F for 10 minutes.
3. Add the cheese to the tops of the peppers and fry for another 2-4 minutes.

121. Banana Bread

Preparation Time: 10 minutes Cooking Time: 15 minutes Serve: 6

Ingredients:
- 1 egg
- ¼ cup butter, melted
- 1/3 cup walnuts, chopped
- 1 cup sugar
- 3 bananas, overripe & mashed
- 1 tsp baking soda
- 1 ½ cups all-purpose flour

- ½ tsp salt

Directions:
1. In a mixing bowl, mix together flour, baking soda, sugar, walnuts, and salt.
2. Add melted butter, egg, and mashed bananas and mix until well combined.
3. Pour batter into the greased loaf pan.
4. Place loaf pan into the air fryer basket and cook at 350 F for
12-15 minutes.
5. Slice and serve.

122. Roasted Asparagus

Preparation Time: 10 minutes
Cooking Time: 15 minutes
Serve: 1

Ingredients:
- 1 bunch fresh asparagus, trimmed
- avocado oil cooking spray
- ½ teaspoon garlic powder
- ½ teaspoon Himalayan pink salt
- ¼ teaspoon ground multi-colored peppercorns

- ¼ teaspoon red pepper flakes
- ¼ cup freshly grated Parmesan cheese

Directions:
1. Preheat the air fryer carefully to 375°F (190 degrees C). Using parchment paper, line the basket.
2. Mist the asparagus stalks with avocado oil and place them in the air fryer basket. Garlic powder, pink Himalayan salt, pepper, and red pepper flakes are optional. Garnish with Parmesan cheese.
3. 7 to 9 minutes in the air fryer until asparagus spears brown

123. Mixed Veggies

Preparation Time: 10 minutes
Cooking Time: 10 minutes
Serve: 4

Ingredients:
- 1 small zucchini, cut into ½-inch sliced
- 1 cup mushrooms, sliced
- 1 bell pepper, chopped
- 1 tbsp parmesan cheese, grated
- ½ tsp Italian seasoning
- 1 tbsp olive oil
- 1 tsp garlic, minced
- Pepper
- Salt

Directions:
1. Preheat the air fryer to 390 F.
2. In a mixing bowl, toss together zucchini, mushrooms, bell pepper, Italian seasoning, oil, garlic, pepper, and salt.
3. Pour veggie mixture into the air fryer basket and cook for 6 minutes.
4. Sprinkle parmesan cheese on top of veggie and cook for 4 minutes more.

124. Balsamic Tomatoes

Serve and enjoy.
Preparation Time: 10 minutes
Cooking Time: 8 minutes
Serve: 4

Ingredients:
- 2 large tomatoes, cut into 4 slices
- 1/4 cup balsamic vinegar
- 1 tsp red pepper flakes, crushed
- 1 tbsp oregano, dried
- 1/4 tsp black pepper
- 1/2 tsp sea salt

Directions:
1. Preheat the air fryer to 360 F.
2. In a bowl, mix together vinegar, red pepper flakes, oregano, pepper, and salt.
3. Dip each tomato slice into the vinegar mixture and place into the air fryer basket and cook for 5-8 minutes.
4. Serve and enjoy.

125. Herb Mushrooms

Preparation Time: 10 minutes
Cooking Time: 14 minutes
Serve: 4

Ingredients:
- 1 lb. mushrooms
- 1 tsp thyme, chopped
- 2 garlic cloves, minced
- 1 tbsp basil, minced
- 1 tsp rosemary, chopped
- 1/2 tbsp vinegar
- Pepper
- Salt

Directions:
1. Preheat the air fryer to 350 F.
2. Add mushrooms and remaining ingredients into the large bowl and toss well.
3. Spread mushrooms into the air fryer basket and cook for 14 minutes.
4. Serve and enjoy.

126. Green Beans

Preparation Time: 10 minutes
Cooking Time: 10 minutes
Serve: 2

Ingredients:
- 2 cups green beans, cut in half
- 2 tbsp canola oil
- 1 tbsp shawarma spice
- 1/2 tsp salt

Directions:
1. Preheat the air fryer to 370 F.
2. In a bowl, toss green beans with shawarma spice, oil, and salt.
3. Add beans into the air fryer basket and cook for 10 minutes. Turn halfway through.
4. Serve and enjoy.

127. Curried Cauliflower

Preparation Time: 10 minutes
Cooking Time: 10 minutes
Serve: 4

Ingredients:
- 1 medium cauliflower, cut into florets
- ¼ tsp paprika
- 1 tbsp canola oil
- 1 tsp curry powder
- 1/4 tsp pepper
- 1/4 tsp salt

Directions:
1. Preheat the air fryer to 390 F.
2. Add cauliflower florets and remaining ingredients into the mixing bowl and toss well.
3. Place cauliflower florets into the air fryer basket and cook for 10 minutes. Stir halfway through.
4. Serve and enjoy.

128. Lemon Garlic Broccoli

Preparation Time: 10 minutes
Cooking Time: 8 minutes
Serve: 4

Ingredients:
- 3 cups broccoli florets
- 1 tbsp canola oil
- 3 garlic cloves, chopped
- 2 tbsp fresh lemon juice
- Pepper
- Salt

Directions:
1. Preheat the air fryer to 375 F.
2. In a bowl, toss broccoli florets with olive oil.
3. Add broccoli florets into the air fryer basket and cook for 8 minutes.
4. Transfer cooked broccoli into the bowl. Add lemon juice, garlic, pepper, and salt and toss well.
5. Serve and enjoy.

129. Herb Carrots Slices

Preparation Time: 10 minutes
Cooking Time: 14 minutes
Serve: 4

Ingredients:
- 6 carrots peel and slice into thick chips
- 1 tbsp oregano
- 2 tbsp canola oil
- 1 tbsp fresh parsley, chopped
- Pepper
- Salt

Directions:
1. Preheat the air fryer to 360 F.
2. In a bowl, toss carrots with oil.
3. Add carrots slices into the air fryer basket and cook for 12 minutes.
4. Add pepper, oregano, and salt and stir well and cook for 2 minutes more.
5. Garnish with parsley and serve.

130. Apple Oats

Preparation Time: 10 minutes
Cooking Time: 15 minutes
Serve: 1

Ingredients:
- ½ cup gluten-free oats
- 1 tbsp Greek yogurt
- ½ cup unsweetened almond milk
- 2 tbsp date spread
- ½ tsp cream of tartar
- ½ tsp baking powder
- 1 tbsp protein powder
- ¼ cup apple, chopped

Directions:
1. In a mixing bowl, mix together oats, baking powder, and protein powder.
2. Add yogurt, milk, date spread, and cream of tartar and mix until well combined.
3. Add apple and fold well.
4. Pour oat mixture into the greased air fryer baking dish.
5. Place baking dish into the air fryer basket and cook at 330 F
for 15 minutes.
6. Serve and enjoy.

131. Roasted Cauliflower Florets

Preparation Time: 10 minutes
Cooking Time: 12 minutes
Servings: 4

Ingredients:
- 1 ½ lb. Cauliflower florets
- ½ tsp. Black pepper
- ¼ tsp. salt
- 1 tbsp. cooking oil

Directions:
1. In a bowl, add cauliflower with cooking oil, salt, and pepper, toss well to combine.
2. Preheat your Air fryer to a temperature of 400°F.
3. Place cauliflower florets into the fryer basket and set time to
12 minutes.
4. After halftime, turn cauliflower florets so that they can cook evenly from both sides.
5. Serve!

132. Air Fried Breaded Mushrooms

Preparation Time: 9 minutes
Cooking Time: 7 minutes
Servings: 5

Ingredients:
- ½ lb. button mushrooms
- 1 large Egg
- 3 oz. Grated cheese
- Breadcrumbs – as required to coat
- Flour – as necessary to coat
- ¼ tsp. Ground pepper
- ⅛ Tsp. Salt

Directions:
1. In a bowl, mix well the bread crumbs with grated cheese then keep it aside.
2. Beat the egg in another bowl and keep it aside.
3. Wash the mushrooms and dry pat.
4. Put the flour on a flat surface then roll the mushroom in the flour.
5. Dip the flour rolled mushroom in the beaten egg.
6. Now dip the mushroom again in the cheese & bread crumb mixture.
7. Place the coated mushroom in the Air fryer

cooking basket.
8. Set the temperature of your Air fryer at 356°F and time for 7 minutes.
9. Shake the basket intermittently so that it can have an even frying.

133. Carrot Sticks

Preparation Time: 6 minutes
Cooking Time: 12 minutes
Servings: 2

Ingredients:
- 1 large carrot, peeled and cut into sticks
- 1 tbsp. fresh rosemary, finely chopped
- 1 tbsp. olive oil
- 2 tsp. Sugar
- ¼ tsp. cayenne pepper
- Salt and black pepper to taste

Directions:
1. Set the temperature of your Air fryer to 390 °F and time to 12 minutes.
2. In a bowl, add all the listed ingredients tossing to coat thoroughly.
3. Place the carrot sticks in a Air fryer basket in a single layer.
4. Serve when ready.

134. Crispy Eggplant Slices

Preparation Time: 7 minutes
Cooking Time: 15 minutes
Servings: 4

Ingredients:
- 1 medium eggplant, peeled and cut into ½-inch round slices
- Salt, as required
- ½ cup all-purpose flour
- 2 eggs, beaten
- 1 cup Italian-style breadcrumbs
- ¼ cup olive oil

Directions:
1. In a colander, add the eggplant slices and sprinkle with salt.
2. Set aside for about 30 minutes and pat dry the eggplant slices.
3. Add the flour in a shallow dish.
4. Crack the eggs in a second dish and beat well.
5. In a third dish, mix the oil, and breadcrumbs.
6. Coat each eggplant slice with flour, then dip into beaten eggs, and finally, evenly coat with the breadcrumbs mixture.
7. Set the temperature of your Air fryer at 390 °F and time to 8 minutes.
8. Arrange the eggplant slices in Air fryer basket in a single layer in 2 batches.
9. Serve.

135. Banana-Choco Brownies

Preparation Time: 7 minutes
Cooking Time: 15 minutes
Servings: 4

Ingredients:
- 2 cups almond flour
- 3 tsp. Baking powder
- ½ tsp. salt
- 1 over-ripe banana
- 3 large eggs
- ½ tsp. stevia powder
- ¼ cup coconut oil
- 1 tbsp. vinegar
- 1/3 cup almond flour
- 1/3 cup cocoa powder

Directions:
1. Preheat the Air fryer for 5 minutes.
2. Pulse all the listed ingredients in a food processor until well-combined.
3. Pour the batter into a baking tin will fit in the Air fryer.
4. Place in the Air fryer basket and set the temperature to
350°F, and time to 30 minutes.
If a toothpick inserted in the middle, it should come out clean.

136. Cherry-Choco Bars

Preparation Time: 8 minutes
Cooking Time: 15 minutes
Servings: 10

Ingredients:
- ¼ tsp. salt
- ½ cup almonds, sliced
- ½ cup chia seeds
- ½ cup dark chocolate, chopped
- ½ cup dried cherries, chopped
- ½ cup prunes, pureed
- ½ cup quinoa, cooked
- ¾ cup almond butter
- 1/3 cup honey

- 2 cups old-fashioned oats
- 2 tbsp. coconut oil

Directions:
1. Preheat the Chefman Air fryer to 375°F for 5 minutes.
2. In a bowl, combine the oats, quinoa, chia seeds, almond, cherries, and chocolate.
3. In a saucepan, heat the almond butter, honey, and coconut oil.
4. Pour the butter mixture over the oat mix. Add salt and prunes.
5. Mix until well combined.
6. Pour over a baking dish that can fit inside the Chefman Air fryer.
7. Cook for 15 minutes.

137. Cod with Basil Vinaigrette

Preparation Time: 8 minutes
Cooking Time: 15 minutes
Servings: 10

Ingredients:
- ¼ cup olive oil
- 4 cod fillets
- A bunch of basil, torn
- Juice from 1 lemon, freshly squeezed
- Salt and pepper to taste

Directions:
1. Preheat the Air fryer at 350°F for 5 minutes.
2. Season the fillets accordingly with salt and pepper.
3. Place in the Air fryer and Set the temperature to 350°F
4. , and set time to 15 minutes.
5. Mix the other ingredients in a bowl and toss to combine.
6. Serve the air fried cod with the basil vinaigrette.

138. Cod Fillet

Preparation Time: 8 minutes
Cooking Time: 15 minutes
Servings: 4

Ingredients:
- ¼ cup coconut milk, freshly squeezed
- 1 tbsp. lime juice, freshly squeezed
- 1 lb. cod fillet, cut into bite-sized pieces
- Salt and pepper to taste

Directions:
1. Preheat the Air fryer at 325°F for 3 minutes.
2. Place all ingredients in a baking dish that will fit in the Air fryer.
3. Place in the Air fryer.
4. Cook for 20 minutes at 325°F

139. Zesty Chili Clams

Preparation Time: 6 minutes Cooking Time: 15 minutes Servings: 3

Ingredients:
- ½ cup basil leaves
- ½ cup tomatoes, chopped
- 1 tbsp. fresh lime juice
- 25 clams
- 4 cloves of garlic, minced

- 6 tbsp. unsalted butter
- Salt and pepper to taste

Directions:
1. Preheat the Air fryer to 390°F for 5 minutes.
2. Place the grill pan accessory in the Air fryer.
3. On a large foil, place all ingredients. Fold over the foil and close by crimping the edges.
4. Set the time to 15 minutes.
5. Serve with bread when ready.

140. Beer Battered Cod Filet

Preparation Time: 6 minutes
Cooking Time: 15 minutes
Servings: 3

Ingredients:
- ½ cup all-purpose flour
- ¾ tsp. baking powder
- 1 ¼ cup lager beer
- 2 cod fillets
- 2 eggs, beaten
- Salt and pepper to taste

Directions:
1. Preheat the Air fryer to 390°F for 3 minutes.
2. Pat the fish fillets dry then set aside.
3. In a bowl, combine the rest of the ingredients to create a batter.
4. Dip the fillets on the batter and place it on the double layer rack.
5. Set the time to 15 minutes.

141. Bacon-Wrapped Shrimps

Preparation Time: 6 minutes
Cooking Time: 15 minutes
Servings: 3

Ingredients:
- 1lb. Shrimp
- ½ lb. Bacon strips
- ¼ tsp. salt

Directions:
1. Preheat your Air fryer to a temperature of 370°F for 3 minutes.
2. Wrap each bacon strip around the shrimps and sprinkle salt.
3. Place them into a fryer basket and set time to 8 minutes.
4. Serve!

142. Crispy Fried Fish

Preparation Time: 8 minutes
Cooking Time: 12 minutes
Servings: 2

Ingredients:
- 2 fish fillets
- 1 tsp. salt
- 3 tbsp. gram flour
- 2 tbsp. Apple Cider vinegar
- 1 tbsp. Lime juice
- ½ tsp. chili powder
- 1 tsp. Garlic paste
- ¼ tsp. turmeric powder

Directions:
1. In a bowl, add garlic, lime juice, vinegar, salt, chili powder, flour, and turmeric powder, mix, and rub on fish fillets.
2. Preheat your Chefman Air fryer to a temperature of 400°F for 4 minutes.
3. Place fish fillets into the Chefman Air fryer and set time to 12 minutes.
4. Serve!

143. Sea Scallop Bake

Preparation Time: 8 minutes
Cooking Time: 10 minutes
Servings: 4

Ingredients:
- 16 sea scallops, rinsed and drained
- 5 tbsp. butter, melted
- 5 cloves garlic, minced
- 2 shallots, chopped
- 3 pinches nutmeg
- Salt and pepper to taste
- 1 cup bread crumbs

- 4 tbsp. olive oil
- 1/ 4 cup chopped parsley

Directions:
1. Lightly grease baking pan of the Air fryer with cooking spray.
2. Mix in shallots, garlic, melted butter, and scallops — season with pepper, salt, and nutmeg.
3. In a small bowl, whisk well the olive oil and bread crumbs.
Sprinkle over scallops.
4. Set temperature to 390°F, and set time to 10 minutes.
5. Cook until tops become brown
6. Serve and garnish with parsley.

144. Grilled Spicy Halibut

Preparation Time: 10 minutes
Cooking Time: 13 minutes
Servings: 6

Ingredients:
- 3 lbs. halibut fillet, skin removed
- Salt and pepper to taste
- 4 tbsp. dry white wine
- 4 tbsp. olive oil
- 2 cloves of garlic, minced
- 1 tbsp. chili powder

Directions:
1. Place all ingredients in a Ziploc bag.
2. Allow marinating for two hours in the refrigerator.
3. Preheat the Air fryer at 390°F for 5 minutes
4. Place the grill pan accessory in the Air fryer.
5. Set the time to 13 minutes, making sure to flip every 5 minutes.

145. Fried Sesame Squid

Preparation Time: 4 minutes
Cooking Time: 10 minutes
Servings: 3

Ingredients:
- 1 ½ lb. squid, cleaned
- 2 tbsp. toasted sesame oil
- Salt and pepper to taste

Directions:
1. Preheat the Air fryer at 390°F for 5 minutes.
2. Place the grill pan accessory in the Air fryer.
3. Season the squid with sesame oil, salt, and pepper.
4. Set the time to 10 minutes and cook tossing halfway through.

146. Air Fried Thai Salad

Preparation time: 10 minutes
Cooking time: 5 minutes
Servings: 4

Ingredients:
- 1 cup carrots, grated
- 1 cup red cabbage, shredded
- A pinch of salt and black pepper
- A handful cilantro, chopped
- 1 small cucumber, chopped
- Juice from 1 lime
- 2 teaspoons red curry paste
- 12 big shrimp, cooked, peeled and deveined

Directions:
1. In a pan that fits your air fryer, combine the cabbage with the carrots, cucumber, and shrimp, stir, and cook for 5 minutes at 360°F.
2. Stir in the remaining ingredients (cilantro, lime juice, red curry paste, salt and pepper) and serve immediately.
3. Enjoy!

147. Coconut and Chicken Casserole

Preparation time: 10 minutes
Cooking time: 25 minutes
Servings: 4

Ingredients:
- 4 lime leaves, torn
- 1 cup veggie stock
- 1 lemongrass stalk, chopped
- 1 inch piece, grated
- 1 pound chicken breast, skinless, boneless and cut into thin strips
- 8 ounces mushrooms, chopped
- 4 Thai chilies, chopped
- 4 tablespoons fish sauce
- 6 ounces coconut milk

- ¼ cup lime juice
- ¼ cup cilantro, chopped
- Salt and black pepper to the taste

Directions:
1. Place the stock in a skillet that is large enough to hold your air fryer and put to a simmer over medium heat. Add the lemongrass, ginger, and lime leaves and cook for 10 minutes, stirring occasionally.
2. Cook at 360 degrees F for 15 minutes in your air fryer after straining the soup. 2. Return the soup to the pan and toss in the chicken and mushrooms. Add the chilies, fish sauce, lime juice, cilantro, salt and
pepper to taste.
3. Divide the mixture into dishes and serve.
4. Enjoy!

148. Turkey Burgers

Preparation time: 10 minutes
Cooking time: 8 minutes
Servings: 4

Ingredients:
- 1 pound turkey meat, ground
- 1 shallot, minced
- A drizzle of olive oil
- 1 small jalapeno pepper, minced
- 2 teaspoons lime juice
- Zest from 1 lime, grated
- Salt and black pepper to the taste
- 1 teaspoon cumin, ground
- 1 teaspoon sweet paprika

- Guacamole for serving

Directions:
1. In a large mixing bowl, combine the turkey meat with the salt, pepper, cumin, paprika, shallot, jalapeño, lime juice, and zest. Stir well. Form burgers from the turkey meat mixture, sprinkle the oil over them, and cook them at 370 degrees F for 8 minutes on each side.
2. Divide the mixture among the dishes and serve with guacamole on the side.
3. Enjoy!

149. Roly Poly Air Fried White Fish

Preparation Time: 10 minutes
Servings: 4

Ingredients:
- 4 lbs. of white fish fillets
- 2 ½ teaspoons of sea salt
- 4 mushrooms, sliced
- 1 teaspoon liquid stevia
- 2 tablespoons of Chinese winter pickle
- 2 tablespoons of vinegar
- 2 teaspoons chili powder
- 2 onions, thinly sliced
- 1 cup vegetable stock
- 2 tablespoons soy sauce

Directions:
1. Stuff the mushroom and pickle mixture into the fish fillets. Cut the onions into thin slices and set them aside. The onions should be spread over the fish fillets. Combine the chicken stock, soy sauce, vinegar, sea salt, and stevia in a large mixing bowl. Toss the mixture over the fish fillets and set aside. Place the fish fillets in your air fryer and cook at 350 degrees Fahrenheit for 10 minutes until they are cooked through. Warm the dish before serving.

150. Dragon Shrimp

Preparation Time: 15 minutes
Servings: 2

Ingredients:
- ½ lb. shrimp
- ¼ cup almond flour
- Pinch of ginger
- 1 cup chopped green onions
- 2 tablespoons olive oil
- 2 eggs, beaten
- ½ cup soy sauce

Directions:
1. Boil the shrimps for 5 minutes in salted water. Make a paste out of ginger and onion and set it aside. Now, whisk together the eggs with the ginger paste, soy sauce, and almond flour until thoroughly combined and fluffy. Place the shrimps in a baking dish and spray with oil once they have

been added to the mixture. Cook the shrimps for 10 minutes at 390 degrees Fahrenheit.

151. Simple Tomato Cheese Sandwich

Preparation time: 8-10 minutes
Cook Time: 6 minutes
Servings: 2

Ingredients:
- 8 tomato slices
- 4 bread slices
- 2 Swiss cheese slices
- Black pepper and salt as needed
- 4 teaspoons margarine

Directions:
1. On a flat kitchen surface, plug your air fryer and turn it on.

2. Preheat your air fryer for about 4-5 minutes to 355 degrees F.

3. Gently coat an air frying basket with cooking oil or spray.

4. In the basket, place one cheese slice over one bread slice.

5. Then add 2 tomato slices on top. Sprinkle with salt and pepper.

Top with another bread slice.

6. Insert the basket inside the air fryer. Let it cook for about 5 minutes.

7. Remove the basket; spread 2 teaspoons of margarine on both sides of each sandwich. Cook for about one more minute.

8. Serve warm!

152. Coconut Veggie and Eggs Bake

Preparation time: 5 minutes
Cook Time: 30 minutes
Servings: 6

Ingredients:
- Cooking spray
- 2 cups green and red bell pepper, chopped
- 2 spring onions, chopped
- 1 teaspoon thyme, chopped
- Salt and black pepper to the taste
- 1 cup coconut cream
- 4 eggs, whisked
- 1 cup cheddar cheese, grated

Directions:
1. Place all the ingredients except the cooking spray and cheese in a mixing bowl and mix up to combine.

2. Using the cooking spray to grease a suitable pan.

3. Pour the eggs mixture and bell peppers evenly

on your pan.

4. Sprinkle the top with the cheese.

5. Transfer the pan inside your air fryer and close the air fryer.

6. Cook at 350 degrees F for 30 minutes.

7. When cooked, transfer onto plates and serve for breakfast.

153. Classical Eggs Ramekins

Preparation time: 5 minutes
Cook Time: 6 minutes
Servings: 5

Ingredients:
- 5 eggs
- 1 teaspoon coconut oil, melted
- ¼ teaspoon ground black pepper

Directions:
1. Using coconut oil, grease the ramekins and whisk in eggs.
2. Sprinkle on the top with ground black pepper.
3. Then place in your air fryer and cook at 355 degrees F for 6 minutes.

154. Cinnamon French Toast

Preparation time: 12 minutes
Cook Time: 9 minutes
Servings: 2

Ingredients:
- ⅓ cup almond flour
- 1 egg, beaten
- ¼ teaspoon baking powder
- 2 teaspoons Erythritol
- ¼ teaspoon vanilla extract
- 1 teaspoon cream cheese
- ¼ teaspoon ground cinnamon
- 1 teaspoon ghee, melted

Directions:
1. Mix up baking powder, ground cinnamon, and almond flour in a mixing bowl.

2. Add in vanilla extract, cream cheese, egg, and ghee and stir together with a fork until smooth.

3. Place baking paper on the bottom of the mugs.

4. Add in almond flour mixture and use a fork to flatten well.

5. Before cooking, heat your air fryer to 255 degrees F.

6. Transfer the mugs with toasts inside your air fryer basket.

7. Cook in your air fryer for 9 minutes.

8. When cooked, cool for a while. To serve, sprinkle Erythritol on the toasts.

155. Breakfast Cobbler with Blueberries

Preparation time: 15 minutes
Cook Time: 15 minutes
Servings: 4

Ingredients:
- ⅓ cup whole-wheat pastry flour
- ¾ teaspoon baking powder
- Dash salt
- ½ cup 2% milk
- 2 tablespoons pure maple syrup
- ½ teaspoon vanilla extract
- Cooking oil spray
- ½ cup fresh blueberries
- ¼ cup Granola, or plain store-bought granola

Direction
1. In a suitable bowl, whisk the flour, baking powder, and salt.

2. Add maple syrup, the milk, and vanilla and gently whisk.

3. Spray a suitable 6-by-2-inch round baking pan

with cooking oil and pour the prepared batter into the pan.

4. Top evenly with the blueberries and granola.

5. At 350 degrees F, preheat your air fryer and cook for almost 15 minutes.

6. Garnish and serve.

156. Egg Peppers Cups

Preparation time: 10 minutes
Cook Time: 12 minutes
Servings: 12

Ingredients:
- 6 green bell peppers
- 12 egg
- ½ teaspoon ground black pepper
- ½ teaspoon chili flakes

Directions:
1. Before cooking, heat your air fryer to 395 degrees F.

2. While preheating, cut the green bell peppers

into halves and remove the seeds.

3. In the bell pepper halves, whisk the eggs.

4. Sprinkle the top with chili flakes and ground black pepper.

5. Arrange evenly the bell pepper halves onto a suitable baking pan.

6. Cook in the preheated air fryer for 4 minutes. (2 to 3 halves per batch)

157. Spinach Bacon Spread

Preparation time: 5 minutes

Cook Time: 10 minutes

Servings: 4

Ingredients:
- 2 tablespoons coconut cream
- 3 cups spinach leaves
- 2 tablespoons cilantro
- 2 tablespoons bacon, cooked and crumbled
- Salt and black pepper to the taste

Directions:

1. Combine coconut cream, spinach leaves, salt, and black pepper in a suitable baking pan.

2. Transfer the baking pan into your air fryer and cook at 360 degrees F for 10 minutes.

3. When cooked, transfer to a blender and pulse well.

4. To serve, sprinkle the bacon on the top of the mixture.

158. Mozzarella Rolls

Preparation time: 15 minutes   Cook Time: 6 minutes Servings: 6

Ingredients:
- 6 wonton wrappers
- 1 tablespoon keto tomato sauce
- ½ cup Mozzarella, shredded
- 1 ounce pepperoni, chopped
- 1 egg, beaten
- Cooking spray

Directions:

1. Before cooking, heat your air fryer to 400 degrees F.

2. Grease the air fryer basket with cooking spray.

3. Mix the pepperoni, shredded Mozzarella cheese, and tomato sauce in a big bowl until homogenous.

4. Separate the mixture onto wonton wraps.

5. Roll the wraps into sticks.

6. Use the beaten eggs to brush the sticks.

7. Arrange evenly on the air fryer basket and cook in your air fryer for 6 minutes and flip the sticks halfway through cooking.

159. Parmesan Spinach Pancake

Preparation time: 5 minutes

Cook Time: 15 minutes

Servings: 4

Ingredients:
- 2 eggs, whisked
- Cooking spray
- 1 and ½ cups coconut milk
- 1 tablespoon baking powder
- 4 ounces baby spinach, chopped
- 2 ounces parmesan cheese, grated
- 3 ounces almond flour

Directions:

1. Grease the muffin molds with cooking spray.

2. Mix the whisked eggs, coconut milk, baking powder, baby spinach, parmesan cheese, and almond flour together in a mixing bowl.

3. Transfer onto the greased molds.

4. Cook in your air fryer at 380 degrees F for 15

minutes.

5. When the cooking time is up, serve on plates.

6. Enjoy your breakfast.

160. Bacon Muffins

Preparation time: 15 minutes

Cook Time: 15 minutes

Servings: 8

Ingredients
- 6 large eggs
- 3 slices of cooked and chopped bacon
- ½ cup of chopped green and red bell pepper
- ½ cup of shredded cheddar cheese
- ¼ cup of shredded mozzarella cheese
- ¼ cup of chopped fresh spinach
- ¼ cup of chopped onions
- 2 tablespoons of any milk
- Black pepper and salt, to taste

Instructions:

1. Put eggs, milk, black pepper, and salt into a suitable mixing bowl.
2. Whisk it until well combined.
3. Add in chopped bell peppers, spinach, black peppers, onions, ½
of shredded cheeses, and crumbled bacon. Mix it well.
4. First, place the silicone cups in the air fryer, then pour the egg mixture into them and add the remaining cheeses.
5. At 300 degrees F, preheat your Air fryer.
6. Cook the prepared egg muffins for almost 12–15 minutes.
7. Serve warm and enjoy your Egg Muffins with Bacon!

161. Hard-Boiled Eggs

Preparation time: 8 minutes
Cook Time: 16 minutes
Servings: 2

Ingredients:
- 4 eggs
- ¼ teaspoon salt

Directions:
1. Cook the eggs in your air fryer at 250 degrees F for 16 minutes.
2. When the cooking time is up, cool the eggs in ice water.
3. Then peel the eggs and cut them into halve.
4. Season the egg halves with salt and serve.

162. Creamy Eggs and Leeks

Preparation time: 5 minutes
Cook Time: 7 minutes
Servings: 2

Ingredients:
- 2 leeks, chopped
- 4 eggs, whisked
- ¼ cup Cheddar cheese, shredded
- ½ cup Mozzarella cheese, shredded
- 1 teaspoon avocado oil

Directions:
1. Before cooking, heat your air fryer to 400 degrees F.
2. Using avocado oil, grease your air fryer basket.

3. Combine the whisked eggs with the remaining ingredients.
4. Cook in your air fryer for 7 minutes.
5. When the cooking time is up, remove from the air fryer and serve warm.

163. Cauliflower Tots

Preparation time: 15 minutes
Cook Time: 8 minutes
Servings: 4

Ingredients:
- 1 teaspoon cream cheese
- 5 ounces Monterey Jack cheese, shredded
- 1 cup cauliflower, chopped, boiled
- ¼ teaspoon garlic powder
- 1 teaspoon sunflower oil

Directions:
1. In a blender, add the boiled cauliflower, garlic powder, shredded
Monterey Jack cheese, and cream cheese and mix until smooth.
2. Then make the cauliflower tots and cool them in the refrigerator for 10 minutes.
3. Before cooking, heat your air fryer to 365 degrees F.
4. Transfer the broccoli tots inside the air fryer basket.

5. Sprinkle sunflower oil on the top and cook in your air fryer for 8 minutes. Flip to the other side halfway through cooking.

164. Spicy Bean Meal

Preparation time: 8-10 minutes
Cook Time: 8 minutes
Servings: 4

Ingredients:
- ½ teaspoon black pepper
- 1 teaspoon sea salt flakes
- ½ cup all-purpose flour
- 1 teaspoon smoky chipotle powder
- 2 eggs, beaten
- 10 ounces wax beans
- ½ cup saltines, crushed

Directions:
1. Mix the black pepper, salt, flour, and chipotle powder in a medium sized bowl. Then whisk in eggs.
2. In another bowl, add the crushed saltines.

3. Coat the beans with the flour mixture, then dip in the whisked eggs. Coat the beans with the crushed saltines.
4. Spray the beans with non-stick cooking spray.
5. On a flat kitchen surface, plug your air fryer and turn it on.
6. Before cooking, heat your air fryer to 360 degrees F for 4 to 5 minutes.
7. Place the mixture into the air fryer basket.
8. Cook in your air fryer for 4 minutes.
9. Then shake for a while and continue cooking for 3 minutes or more.
10. Serve warm.

165. Creamy Cauliflower Puree

Preparation time: 10 minutes
Cook Time: 8 minutes
Servings: 2

Ingredients:
- 1 ½ cup cauliflower, chopped
- 1 tablespoon butter, melted
- ½ teaspoon salt
- 1 tablespoon fresh parsley, chopped
- ¼ cup heavy cream
- Cooking spray

Directions:
1. Spray the air fryer basket with cooking spray.
2. Place the cauliflower in the air fryer basket.
3. Cook in your air fryer at 400 degrees F for 8 minutes. Stir the cauliflower every 4 minutes.
4. Heat the heavy cream until it is hot. Then pour in a blender, add parsley, butter, salt, and cauliflower.
5. Blend until it is smooth.

166. Italian Seasoned Chicken Tenders

Preparation Time: 10 minutes
Cooking Time: 10 minutes
Servings: 2

Ingredients:
- 2 eggs, lightly beaten
- 1 1/2 lbs. chicken tenders
- 1/2 tsp onion powder
- 1/2 tsp garlic powder
- 1 tsp paprika
- 1 tsp Italian seasoning
- 2 tbsp. ground flax seed
- 1 cup almond flour
- 1/2 tsp pepper
- 1 tsp sea salt

Directions:
1. Preheat the air fryer to 400 F.
2. Season chicken with pepper and salt.
3. In a medium bowl, whisk eggs to combine.
4. In a shallow dish, mix together almond flour, all seasonings, and flaxseed.
5. Dip chicken into the egg then coats with almond flour mixture and place on a plate.
6. Spray air fryer basket with cooking spray.
7. Place half chicken tenders in air fryer basket and cook for 10 minutes. Turn halfway through.
8. Cook remaining chicken tenders using same steps.
9. Serve and enjoy.

167. Vegetable Egg Pancake

Preparation Time: 10 minutes
Cooking Time: 15 minutes
Servings: 2
- Ingredients:
- 1 cup almond flour
- ½ cup milk
- 1 tbsp. parmesan cheese, grated
- 3 eggs
- 1 potato, grated
- 1 beet, peeled and grated
- 1 carrot, grated
- 1 zucchini, grated
- 1 tbsp. olive oil
- ¼ tsp. nutmeg
- 1 tsp. onion powder
- 1 tsp. garlic powder
- ½ tsp. black pepper

Directions:
1. Preheat your air fryer to 390°F.
2. Mix the zucchini, potato, beet, carrot, eggs, milk, almond flour, and parmesan in a bowl.
3. Place olive oil into an oven-safe dish.
4. Form patties with the vegetable mix and flatten them to form patties.
5. Place patties into an oven-safe dish and cook in the air fryer for 15 minutes.
6. Serve with sliced tomatoes, sour cream, and toast.

168. Monkey Bread

Preparation Time: 2 minutes
Cooking Time: 10 minutes
Servings: 8

Ingredients:
- 1 cup non-fat Greek yogurt
- 1 cup self-rising flour
- 1 tsp. sugar
- ½ tsp. cinnamon

Directions:
1. Combine in a medium bowl the self-rising flour and yogurt; mix well to form into dough.

2. Custom the dough into a large ball and cut into fourths.

3. Remove each dough wedge to shape into a flattened circular disc, and then cut into eight pieces, similar to a pizza. Remove each wedge from the disc and roll it to form into balls.

4. Combine cinnamon and sugar in a Ziploc or resealable plastic bag. Add the dough balls and seal the bag; shake to coat the balls well.

5. Prepare a mini loaf pan by lightly misting it with non-stick spray.

6. Arrange the dough balls in the pan and sprinkle lightly with the sugar-cinnamon mix.

7. Put the loaf pan inside the air fryer. Bake the bread for 7 minutes, at 375°F. Let cool.

8. Enjoy!

169. Meatballs in Tomato Sauce

Preparation Time: 10 minutes
Cooking Time: 10 minutes
Servings: 3–4

Ingredients:
- 1 egg
- ¾ lb. lean ground beef
- 1 onion, chopped
- 3 tbsp. breadcrumbs
- ½ tbsp. fresh thyme leaves, chopped
- ½ cup tomato sauce
- 1 tbsp. parsley, chopped
- Pinch salt
- Pinch pepper, to taste

Directions:
1. Preheat the Air Fryer to 390°F
2. Place all ingredients in a bowl. Mix until well-combined.
Divide mixture into 12 balls. Place them in the cooking basket.
3. Cook meatballs for 8 minutes.
4. Put the cooked meatballs in an oven dish. Pour the tomato sauce on top. Put the oven dish inside the cooking basket of the Air Fryer.
5. Cook for 5 minutes at 330°F.

170. Scallion Sandwich

Preparation Time: 10 minutes
Cooking Time: 10 minutes
Servings: 1

Ingredients:
- 2 slices wheat bread
- 2 tsp. butter, low fat
- 2 scallions, sliced thinly
- 1 tbsp. parmesan cheese, grated
- ¾ cup cheddar cheese, reduced-fat, grated

Directions:
1. Preheat the Air fryer to 356°F.
2. Spread butter on a slice of bread. Place inside the cooking basket with the butter side facing down.
3. Place cheese and scallions on top. Spread the rest of the butter on the other slice of bread, put it on top of the sandwich, and sprinkle with parmesan cheese.
4. Cook for 10 minutes.

171. Rosemary Beef Tips

Preparation Time: 10 minutes
Cooking Time: 12 minutes
Servings: 4

Ingredients:
- 1 lb. steak, cut into 1-inch cubes
- 1 tsp. paprika
- 2 tsp. onion powder
- 1 tsp. garlic powder
- 2 tbsp. coconut aminos
- 2 tsp. rosemary, crushed
- Pepper
- Salt

Directions:
1. Add meat and remaining ingredients into the mixing bowl and mix well and let it sit for 5 minutes.
2. Select Air Fry mode.
3. Set time to 12 minutes and temperature 380°F then press
START.
4. The air fryer display will prompt you to ADD FOOD once the temperature is reached then place steak cubes in the air fryer basket. Stir halfway through.
5. Serve and enjoy.

172. Mushroom Cheese Salad

Preparation Time: 10 minutes
Cooking Time: 15 minutes
Servings: 2

Ingredients:
- 10 mushrooms, halved
- 1 tbsp. fresh parsley, chopped
- 1 tbsp. olive oil
- 1 tbsp. mozzarella cheese, grated
- 1 tbsp. cheddar cheese, grated
- 1 tbsp. dried mix herbs
- Pepper

Directions:
1. Add all ingredients into the bowl and toss well.
2. Transfer bowl mixture into the air fryer baking dish.
3. Place in the air fryer and cook at 380°F for 15 minutes.
4. Serve and enjoy.

173. Lettuce Salad with Beef Strips

Preparation Time: 10 minutes
Cooking Time: 12 minutes Servings: 5

Ingredients:
- 2 cup lettuce
- 10 oz. beef brisket
- 2 tbsp. sesame oil
- 1 tbsp. sunflower seeds
- 1 cucumber
- 1 tsp. ground black pepper
- 1 tsp. paprika
- 1 tsp. Italian spices
- 2 tsp. butter
- 1 tsp. dried dill
- 2 tbsp. coconut milk

Directions:
1. Cut the beef brisket into strips.
2. Sprinkle the beef strips with the ground black pepper, paprika, and dried dill.
3. Preheat the air fryer to 365 F.
4. Put the butter in the air fryer basket tray and melt it.
5. Then add the beef strips and cook them for 6 minutes on each side.
6. Meanwhile, tear the lettuce and toss it in a big salad bowl.
7. Crush the sunflower seeds and sprinkle over the lettuce.
8. Chop the cucumber into the small cubes and add to the salad bowl.
9. Then combine the sesame oil and Italian spices together. Stir the oil.
10. Combine the lettuce mixture with the coconut milk and stir it using 2 wooden spatulas.
11. When the meat is cooked – let it chill to room temperature.
12. Add the beef strips to the salad bowl.
13. Stir it gently and sprinkle the salad with the sesame oil dressing.

174. Cayenne Rib Eye Steak

Preparation Time: 10 minutes
Cooking Time: 13 minutes
Servings: 2

Ingredients:
- 1-lb. rib eye steak
- 1 tsp. salt
- 1 tsp. cayenne pepper
- ½ tsp. chili flakes
- 3 tbsp. cream
- 1 tsp. olive oil
- 1 tsp. lemongrass
- 1 tbsp. butter
- 1 tsp. garlic powder

Directions:
1. Preheat the air fryer to 360°F.
2. Take a shallow bowl and combine the cayenne pepper, salt, chili flakes, lemongrass, and garlic powder together.
3. Mix the spices gently.
4. Sprinkle the rib eye steak with the spice mixture.
5. Melt the butter and combine it with cream and olive oil.
6. Churn the mixture.
7. Pour the churned mixture into the air fryer basket tray.
8. Add the rib eye steak.
9. Cook the steak for 13 minutes. Do not stir the steak during the cooking.
10. When the steak is cooked transfer it to a paper towel to soak all the excess fat.
11. Serve the steak. You can slice the steak if desired.

175. Juicy Pork Chops

Preparation Time: 10 minutes
Cooking Time: 11 minutes
Servings: 3

Ingredients:
- 1 tsp. peppercorns
- 1 tsp. kosher salt
- 1 tsp. minced garlic
- ½ tsp. dried rosemary
- 1 tbsp. butter
- 13 oz. pork chops

Directions:
1. Rub the pork chops with dried rosemary, minced garlic, and kosher salt.
2. Preheat the air fryer to 365°F.
3. Put the butter and peppercorns in the air fryer basket tray.
Melt the butter.

4. Place the pork chops in the melted butter.
5. Cook the pork chops for 6 minutes.
6. Turn the pork chops over.
7. Cook the pork chops for 5 minutes more.
8. When the meat is cooked dry gently with a paper towel.
9. Serve the juicy pork chops immediately.

176. Garlic Salmon Balls

Preparation Time: 6–7 minutes
Cooking Time: 10 minutes
Servings: 2

Ingredients:
- 6 oz. tinned salmon
- 1 large egg
- 3 tbsp. olive oil
- 5 tbsp. wheat germ
- ½ tsp. garlic powder
- 1 tbsp. dill, fresh, chopped
- 4 tbsp. spring onion, diced
- 4 tbsp. celery, diced

Directions:
1. Preheat your air fryer to 370°F. In a large bowl, mix the salmon, egg, celery, onion, dill, and garlic.
2. Shape the mixture into golf ball size balls and roll them in the wheat germ. In a minor pan, warm olive oil over medium-low heat. Add the salmon balls and slowly flatten them. Handover them to your air fryer and cook for 10 minutes.

177. Onion Rings

Preparation Time: 7 minutes
Cooking Time: 10 minutes
Servings: 3

Ingredients:
- 1 onion, cut into slices, then separate into rings
- 1 ½ cup almond flour
- ¾ cup pork rinds
- 1 cup milk
- 1 egg
- 1 tbsp. baking powder
- ½ tsp. salt

Directions:
1. Preheat your air fryer for 10 minutes. Cut onion into slices, then separate into rings. In a container, supplement the flour, baking powder, and salt.
2. Whisk the eggs and the milk, then combines with flour.
Gently dip the floured onion rings into the batter to coat them.
3. Spread the pork rinds on a plate and dredge the rings in the crumbs. Abode the onion rings in your air fryer and cook for 10 minutes at 360°F.

178. Garlic Tomatoes

Preparation Time: 7 minutes
Cooking Time: 15 minutes
Servings: 4

Ingredients:
- 3 tbsp. vinegar
- ½ tsp. thyme, dried
- 4 tomatoes
- 1 tbsp. olive oil
- Salt and black pepper to taste
- 1 garlic clove, minced

Directions:
1. Preheat your air fryer to 390°F. Scratch the tomatoes into halves and remove the seeds. Please place them in a big bowl and toss them with oil, salt, pepper, garlic, and thyme.
2. Place them into the air fryer and cook for 15 minutes. Drizzle with vinegar and serve.

179. Cheese & Onion Nuggets

Preparation Time: 7 minutes
Cooking Time: 12 minutes
Servings: 4

Ingredients:
- 7 oz. Edam cheese, grated
- 2 spring onions, diced
- 1 egg, beaten
- 1 tbsp. coconut oil
- 1 tbsp. thyme, dried
- Salt and pepper to taste

Directions:
1. Mix the onion, cheese, coconut oil, salt, pepper, thyme in a bowl. Make 8 small balls and place the cheese in the center.
2. Place in the fridge for about an hour. With a pastry brush, carefully brush the beaten egg over the nuggets. Cook for 12 minutes in the air fryer at 350°F.

180. Beef and Mango Skewers

Preparation Time: 10 minutes
Cooking Time: 4–7 minutes
Servings: 4

Ingredients:
- ¾ lb. (340-g.) of beef sirloin tip, cut into 1-inch cubes
- 2 tbsp. balsamic vinegar
- 1 tbsp. olive oil
- 1 tbsp. honey
- ½ tsp. dried marjoram

63

- Pinch salt
- Freshly ground black pepper to taste
- 1 mango

Directions:
1. Put the beef cubes in a medium bowl and add the balsamic vinegar, olive oil, honey, marjoram, salt, and pepper. Mix well, then rub the marinade into the beef with your hands. Set aside.

2. To prepare the mango, stand it on end and cut the skin off using a sharp knife. Then carefully cut around the oval pit to remove the flesh. Cut the mango into 1-inch cubes.

3. Thread metal skewers alternating with 3 beef cubes and 2 mango cubes. Place the skewers in the air fryer basket.

4. Air fry at 390ºF (199ºC) for 4 to 7 minutes or until the beef is browned and at least 145ºF (63ºC).

181. Asian Sirloin Steaks

Preparation time: 10 minutes
Cook Time: 15 minutes
Servings: 2

Ingredients:
- Twelve ounces of sirloin steaks
- One tablespoon of minced garlic
- One tablespoon of grated ginger
- Half tablespoon of Worcestershire sauce
- One and a half tablespoons of soy sauce
- Two tablespoons of Erythritol
- Pepper
- Salt

Directions:
1. Add steaks in a large zip-lock bag along with the remaining ingredients. Shake well and place in the refrigerator overnight.
2. Spray air fryer basket with cooking spray.
3. Place marinated steaks in an air fryer basket and cook at 400 F for 10 minutes.
4. Turn steaks to another side and cook for 10-15 minutes more.
5. Serve and enjoy.

182.. Bacon Pudding

Preparation time: 10 minutes
Cook Time: 15 minutes
Servings: 2

Ingredients:
- Two cooked and chopped bacon strips
- One tablespoon of softened butter
- One cup of corn
- One chopped yellow onion
- A quarter cup of chopped celery
- Half cup of chopped red bell pepper

- One teaspoon of chopped thyme
- Two teaspoons of minced garlic
- Salt and black pepper to the taste
- Half cup of heavy cream
- One and a half cups of milk
- Two whisked eggs
- Two cups of cubed bread
- Two tablespoons of grated parmesan
- Cooking spray

Directions:
1. Grease your air fryer's pan with cooking spray.

2. In a bowl, mix bacon with butter, corn, onion, bell pepper, celery, thyme, garlic, salt, pepper, milk, heavy cream, eggs and bread cubes, toss, pour into greased pan and sprinkle cheese all over

3. Add this to your preheated air fryer at 320 degrees and cook for 15 minutes.

4. Divide among plates and serve warm for a quick lunch.

5. Enjoy!

183. Basil Parmesan Shrimp

Preparation time: 10 minutes
Cook Time: 10 minutes
Servings: 2

Ingredients:
- One lb. of peeled and deveined shrimp
- One teaspoon of basil
- Half teaspoon of oregano
- One teaspoon of pepper
- 2/3 cup of grated parmesan cheese
- Two minced garlic cloves
- Two tablespoons of olive oil
- One teaspoon of onion powder

Directions:
1. Add all ingredients into the bowl and toss well.
2. Spray air fryer basket with cooking spray.
3. Transfer shrimp into the air fryer basket and cook at 350 F
for 10 minutes.
4. Serve and enjoy.

184. Broccoli Beef

Preparation time: 10 minutes
Cook Time: 12 minutes
Servings: 2

Ingredients
- Half lb. of round steak, cut into strips
- Half lb. of broccoli florets
- Two drops of liquid stevia
- One teaspoon of soy sauce
- 1/3 cup of sherry
- Two teaspoons of sesame oil
- 1/3 cup of oyster sauce

- One minced garlic clove
- One tablespoon of sliced ginger
- One teaspoon of arrowroot powder
- One tablespoon of olive oil

Directions:
1. In a small bowl, merge together oyster sauce, stevia, soy sauce, sherry, arrowroot, and sesame oil.
2. Add broccoli and meat to a large bowl.
3. Pour oyster sauce mixture over meat and broccoli and toss well. Place in the fridge for 60 minutes.
4. Add marinated meat broccoli to the air fryer basket. Drizzle with olive oil and sprinkle with ginger and garlic.
5. Cook at 360 F for 12 minutes.
6. Serve and enjoy

185 Cajun Cheese Shrimp

Preparation time: 10 minutes
Cook Time: 5 minutes
Servings: 2

Ingredients:
- One lb. of shrimp
- Half cup of almond flour
- One teaspoon of olive oil
- One tablespoon of Cajun seasoning
- Two tablespoons of parmesan cheese
- Two minced garlic cloves

Directions:
1. Add all ingredients into the bowl and toss well.
2. Spray air fryer basket with cooking spray.
3. Transfer shrimp mixture into the air fryer basket and cook at
390 F for 5 minutes. Shake halfway through.
4. Serve and enjoy.

186. Chicken Pie

Preparation time: 10 minutes
Cook Time: 5 minutes
Servings: 2

Ingredients:
- Two boneless, skinless and cubed chicken thighs
- One chopped carrot
- One chopped yellow onion
- One chopped potato
- Two chopped mushrooms
- One teaspoon of soy sauce
- Salt and black pepper to the taste
- One teaspoon of Italian seasoning
- Half teaspoon of garlic powder
- One teaspoon of Worcestershire sauce
- One tablespoon of flour
- One tablespoon of milk

- Two puff pastry sheets
- One tablespoon of melted butter

Directions:
1. Heat up a pan over medium-high heat, add potatoes, carrots and onion, stir and cook for 2 minutes.
2. Add chicken and mushrooms, salt, soy sauce, pepper, Italian seasoning, garlic powder, Worcestershire sauce, flour and milk, stir really well and take off the heat.
3. Place one puff pastry sheet on the bottom of your air fryer's
pan and trim edge excess.
4. Add chicken mix, top with the other puff pastry sheet, trim excess as well and brush pie with butter.
5. Place in your air fryer and cook at 360 degrees F for 6 minutes.
6. Leave the pie to cool down, slice and serve for breakfast.
7. Enjoy!

187. Chili Garlic Shrimp

Preparation time: 10 minutes
Cook Time: 8 minutes
Servings: 2

Ingredients
- One lb. of peeled and deveined shrimp
- One tablespoon of olive oil
- One sliced lemon
- One sliced red chili pepper
- Half teaspoon of garlic powder
- Pepper
- Salt

Directions:
1. Preheat the air fryer to 400 F.
2. Spray air fryer basket with cooking spray.
3. Add all ingredients into the bowl and toss well.
4. Add shrimp into the air fryer basket and cook for 5 minutes.
Shake basket twice.
5. Serve and enjoy.

188. Brussels Sprout Chips

Preparation time: 10 minutes
Cook Time: 15 minutes
Servings: 2

Ingredients:
- Two cups of thinly sliced Brussels sprouts
- One tablespoon of olive oil
- One teaspoon of garlic powder
- Salt and pepper to taste

- Two tablespoons of grated Parmesan cheese

Directions:
1. Toss the Brussels sprouts in oil.
2. Sprinkle with garlic powder, salt, pepper and Parmesan cheese.
3. Choose bake function.
4. Add the Brussels sprouts to the air fryer.
5. Cook at 350 degrees F for 8 minutes.
6. Flip and cook for seven more minutes.

189. Crunchy Fried Cabbage

Preparation time: 10 minutes
Cook Time: 10 minutes
Servings: 2

Ingredients:
- Half cabbage head, sliced into 2-inch slices
- One tablespoon of olive oil
- Pepper
- Salt

Directions:
1. Drizzle cabbage with olive oil and season with pepper and salt.
2. Add cabbage slices into the air fryer basket and cook at 375 F
for 5 minutes.
3. Toss cabbage well and cook for 5 minutes more.
4. Serve and enjoy.

190. Pork Sliders

Preparation time: 10 minutes
Cook Time: 15 minutes
Servings: 2

Ingredients
- Half pound of ground pork
- One tablespoon of Thai curry paste
- One tablespoon of fish sauce
- A quarter cup of thinly sliced scallions
- Two tablespoons of minced peeled fresh ginger
- One tablespoon of light brown sugar
- One teaspoon of ground black pepper
- Two to four slider buns split open lengthwise, warmed
- Cooking spray

Directions:
1. Set the air fryer basket with cooking spray.
2. Combine all the ingredients, except for the buns, in a large bowl. Stir to mix well.
3. Divide and shape the mixture into six balls, then bash the balls into six 3-inch-diameter patties.
4. Arrange the patties in the basket and spritz with cooking spray.
5. Slide the basket into the air fryer. Cook at the corresponding preset mode or Air Fry at 375F (190C) for 14 minutes.
6. Set the patties halfway through the cooking time.
7. When cooked, the patties should be well browned.
8. Assemble the buns with patties to make the sliders and serve immediately.

191. Pork Wontons

Preparation time: 10 minutes
Cook Time: 15 minutes
Servings: 2

Ingredients
For dough
- One and a half cups of all-purpose flour
- Two teaspoons of salt
- Five tablespoons of water
For filling
- Two cups of minced pork
- Two tablespoons of oil
- Two teaspoons of ginger-garlic paste
- Two teaspoons of soya sauce
- Two teaspoons of vinegar

Directions:
1. Knead the dough and cover it with plastic wrap, and set it aside. Next, cook the ingredients for the filling and try to ensure that the pork is covered well with the sauce.
2. Roll the dough and place the filling in the center. Now, wrap the dough to cover the filling and pinch the edges together.
3. Preheat the Air fryer at 200° F for 5 minutes. Place the wontons in the fry basket and close it. Let them cook at the same temperature for another 15 minutes.
4. Recommended sides are chili sauce or ketchup.

192. Sweet and Spicy Peanuts

Preparation time: 5 minutes
Cook Time: 5 minutes
Servings: 2

Ingredients:
- Two cups of shelled raw peanuts
- One tablespoon of hot red pepper sauce
- Two tablespoons of granulated white sugar

Directions:
1. Put the peanuts in a large bowl, then drizzle with hot red pepper sauce and sprinkle with sugar. Toss to coat well.
2. Pour the peanuts into the air fry basket.
3. Place the basket on the air fry position.
4. Select Air Fry, set the temperature to 400F (205C) and set time to 5 minutes. Set the peanuts halfway through the cooking time.
5. When cooking is complete, the peanuts will be crispy and browned. Remove from the air fryer grill.
6. Serve immediately.

193. Sweet Baby Carrots

Preparation time: 15 minutes
Cook Time: 10 minutes
Servings: 2

Ingredients:
- One tablespoon of brown sugar
- Two cups of baby carrots
- Two tablespoons of melted butter
- Black pepper and salt

Directions:
1. Mix butter, sugar, pepper, carrot, and salt in a bowl.
2. Transfer the mix to the Air Fryer Grill pan.
3. Set the Air Fryer Grill to the air fry function.
4. Cook for 10 minutes at 350 degrees F.
5. Serve immediately.
6. If desired, serve with maple syrup.

194. Sweet Popcorn

Preparation time: 10 minutes
Cook Time: 10 minutes
Servings: 2

Ingredients
- Two tablespoons of corn kernels
- Two tablespoons of butter
- Two ounces of brown sugar

Directions:
1. Put corn kernels in your air fryer's pan, cook at 400 degrees F for 6 minutes, transfer them to a tray, spread and leave aside for now.
2. Heat up a pan over low heat, add butter, melt it, add sugar and stir until it dissolves.
3. Add popcorn, toss to coat, take off the heat and spread on the tray again.
4. Cool down, divide into bowls and serve as a snack.
5. Enjoy.

195. Tuna Cakes

Preparation time: 10 minutes
Cook Time: 10 minutes
Servings: 2

Ingredients:
- Six ounces of drained and flaked canned tuna
- Two eggs
- Half teaspoon of dried dill
- One teaspoon of dried parsley
- A quarter cup of chopped red onion
- One teaspoon of garlic powder
- Salt and black pepper to the taste
- Cooking spray

Directions:
1. In a bowl, mix tuna with salt, pepper, dill, parsley, onion, garlic powder and eggs, stir well and shape medium cakes out of this mix.
2. Place tuna cakes in your air fryer's basket, spray them with cooking oil and cook at 350 degrees F for 10 minutes, flipping them halfway.
3. Arrange them on a platter and serve as an appetizer.
4. Enjoy!

196. Broccoli Salad

Preparation time: 15 minutes
Cook Time: 10 minutes
Servings: 2

Ingredients
- Six cloves of garlic
- One head of broccoli
- Black pepper and salt
- One tablespoon of Chinese rice wine vinegar
- One tablespoon of peanut oil

Directions:
1. Mix oil, salt, broccoli, and pepper.
2. Place the mixture on the Air Fryer Grill pan.
3. Set the Air Fryer Grill to the air fry function.
4. Cook for 9 minutes at 350 degrees F.
5. Place the broccoli in the salad bowl and add peanuts oil, rice vinegar, and garlic.
6. Serve immediately.

197. Creamy Endives

Preparation time: 10 minutes
Cook Time: 10 minutes
Servings: 2

Ingredients:
- Six trimmed and halved endives
- One teaspoon of garlic powder
- Half cup of Greek yogurt
- Half teaspoon of curry powder
- Salt and black pepper to the taste
- Three tablespoons of lemon juice

Directions:
1. In a bowl, mix endives with garlic powder, yogurt, curry powder, salt, pepper and lemon juice, toss, leave aside for 10 minutes and transfer to your preheated air fryer at 350 degrees F.
2. Cook endives for 10 minutes, divide them among plates and serve as a side dish.
3. Enjoy!

198. Shrimp Sandwiches

Preparation time: 10 minutes
Cook Time: 5 minutes
Servings: 2

Ingredients:
- 1+1/4 Cups cheddar, shredded
- 6 Oz. canned tiny shrimp, drained
- 3 Tbsp mayonnaise
- 2 Tbsp green onions, chopped
- 4 Whole wheat bread slices
- 2 Tbsp butter, soft

Directions:
1. In a bowl, mix shrimp with cheese, green onion, mayo, and stir well.
2. Spread this on half of the bread slices, top with the other bread slices, cut into halves diagonally, and spread butter on top. Place sandwiches in your air fryer and cook at 350°F for

5 minutes.
3. Divide shrimp sandwiches between plates and serve them for breakfast. Enjoy!

199. Crispy Eggplant

Preparation time: 5 minutes
Cook Time: 15 minutes
Servings: 2

Ingredients:
- 1 Eggplant, cut in half.
- 1/2 Tsp Italian seasoning
- 1 Tsp paprika
- 1/2 Tsp red pepper
- 1 Tsp garlic powder
- 2 Tbsp olive oil

Directions:
1. In a mixing basin, add all ingredients and mix well.
2. Then transfer the combination of eggplant into the air fryer basket.
3. Cook at 375°F for 15 minutes. Halfway through the shake basket. Serve and enjoy!

200. Roasted Macadamia

Preparation time: 5 minutes
Cook Time: 10 minutes
Servings: 2

Ingredients:
- 1 Lb. Macadamia nuts
- Salt to taste

Directions:
1. Spread the macadamia nuts in the air fryer basket.
2. Cook at 250°F for 10 minutes, shaking the basket halfway through.
3. Sprinkle with salt.
4. As a serving suggestion, sprinkle with herbs or grated Parmesan cheese.
5. Store in an airtight container for up to 3 days.

201. Walnut and Cheese Filled Mushrooms

Preparation time: 5 minutes
Cook Time: 10 minutes
Servings: 2

Ingredients:
- 4 Large Portobello mushroom caps
- 1/3 Cup walnuts, minced
- 1 Tbsp canola oil
- 1/2 Cup mozzarella cheese, shredded
- 2 Tbsp fresh parsley, chopped

Directions:
1. Preheat your air fryer to 350°F, and spray the air fryer basket with cooking oil.
2. Rub the mushrooms with canola oil, fill them with mozzarella cheese.
3. Sprinkle with minced walnuts and place in the bottom of a greased air fryer basket.
4. Bake for 10 minutes or until golden on top. Remove, let cool for a few minutes and sprinkle with freshly chopped parsley to serve. Enjoy!

202. Crispy Zucchini Fries

Preparation time: 10 minutes
Cook Time: 10 minutes
Servings: 4

Ingredients:
- 2 Medium zucchinis, cut into fries shape
- 1/2 Tsp garlic powder
- 1 Tsp Italian seasoning
- 1/2 Cup parmesan cheese, grated
- 1/2 Cup almond flour
- 1 Egg, lightly beaten
- Pepper
- Salt

Directions:
1. In a bowl, add egg and stir thoroughly.
2. Mix almond flour, spices, parmesan cheese, and salt together in a small dish.
3. Spray the spray cooking spray air fryer basket.
4. Dip zucchini fries in egg, coat with almond flour mixture, and place in the air fryer basket.

203. Bok Choy Stir Fry

Preparation time: 10 minutes
Cook Time: 10 minutes
Servings: 2

Ingredients:
- 1 Lb. Bok Choy rinsed and drained
- 1 Tbsp oyster sauce
- 3 Tbsp chicken broth
- 2 Tbsp peanut oil
- 2 Cloves garlic, minced
- Salt to taste

Directions:
1. Mix all the ingredients in a bowl.
2. Add the bok Choy into your air fryer.
3. Air fry at 350°F for 10 minutes, stirring twice.
4. Serving Suggestions: Garnish with crispy garlic slices.
5. Preparation Tips: Use low sodium oyster sauce.

204. Brussels Sprouts and Pomegranate

Preparation time: 5 minutes
Cook Time: 10 minutes
Servings: 2

Ingredients:
- 1 Pound Brussels sprouts, trimmed and halved
- Salt and black pepper to the taste
- 1 Cup pomegranate seeds
- 1/4 Cup pine nuts, toasted
- 1 Tbsp olive oil
- 2 Tbsp veggie stock

Directions:
1. In a heat-proof dish that fits your air fryer, mix Brussels sprouts with salt, pepper, pomegranate seeds, pine nuts, oil, and stock. Stir, place in your air fryer's basket and cook at
390°F for 10 minutes.
2. Divide among plates and serve as a side dish. Enjoy!

205. Collard Greens Mix

Preparation time: 10 minutes
Cook Time: 10 minutes
Servings: 2

Ingredients:
- 1/2 Bunch collard greens, trimmed
- 1 Tbsp olive oil
- 1 Tbsp tomato paste
- 1/2 Yellow onion, chopped
- 2 Cloves garlic, minced
- Salt and black pepper to taste
- 1/2 Tbsp balsamic vinegar
- 1/2 Tsp sugar

Directions:
1. In a bowl, mix tomato puree, onion, vinegar, garlic, and oil. Whisk.
2. Add sugar, salt, pepper, and collard greens. Mix.
3. Place the bowl in the air fryer and cook at 320°F for 10 minutes and serve. Enjoy!

206. Oriental Roasted Eggplant

Preparation time: 10 minutes
Cook Time: 15 minutes
Servings: 2

Ingredients:
- 1+1/2 Pounds eggplant, cubed
- 1 Tbsp olive oil
- 1 Tsp garlic powder
- 1 Tsp onion powder
- 1 Tsp sumac
- 2 Tsp za'atar
- Juice from 1/2 lemon
- 2 Bay leaves

Directions:
1. Mix eggplant cubes with oil, garlic powder, onion powder, sumac, za'atar, lemon juice, and bay leaves in your air fryer. Toss and cook at 370°F for 15 minutes.
2. Divide among plates and serve as a side dish. Enjoy!

207. Jicama Fries

Preparation time: 10 minutes
Cook Time: 15 minutes
Servings: 2

Ingredients:
- 1 Tbsp dried thyme
- 3/4 Cup arrowroot flour
- 1/2 Large Jicama
- 2 Eggs

Directions:
1. Slice the jicama into fries.
2. Whisk the eggs together and pour over fries. Toss to coat.
3. Mix a Pinch of salt, thyme, and arrowroot flour. Toss the egg- coated jicama into the dry mixture, coat well.
4. Spray the air fryer basket with olive oil and add fries. Cook for 15 minutes on the "chips" setting. Toss halfway into the cooking process. Serve and enjoy!

208. Asparagus Fries

Preparation time: 15 minutes Cook Time: 6 minutes Servings: 2

Ingredients:
- 1 Large egg, beaten
- 1 Tsp honey
- 1/2 Cup Parmesan cheese, grated
- 1 Cup panko bread crumbs
- 12 Asparagus spears, trimmed
- 1 Pinch cayenne pepper, optional
- 1/4 Cup Greek yogurt
- 1/4 Cup stone-ground mustard

Directions:
1. Preheat your air fryer to 400°F.
2. Get a long, narrow dish, and in it combine egg and honey.
Beat together and set aside.
3. On a separate plate, combine the Parmesan cheese and panko.
4. After coating each asparagus stalk in the egg mixture, roll it also in the panko mix and allow thorough coating.
5. Arrange six spears in the air fryer and allow cooking to the desired brownness; this takes 4 to 6 minutes. Do the same for the other spears.
6. Get a small bowl, and mix the cayenne pepper, yogurt, and mustard in it. Serve the asparagus spears with the dipping sauce. Enjoy!

209. Batter-Fried Scallions

Preparation time: 5 minutes
Cook Time: 5 minutes
Servings: 2

Ingredients:
- 2 Trimmed scallion bunches
- 1 Cup white wine
- 1 Tsp salt
- 1 Cup flour
- 1 Tsp black pepper

Directions:
1. Preheat your air fryer to 390°F. Using a bowl, add and mix the white wine, flour and stir until it gets smooth. Add salt, black pepper, and mix again. Dip each scallion into the flour mixture until it is adequately covered and remove any excess batter. Grease your air fryer basket with nonstick cooking spray and add the scallions. At this point, you may need to work in batches.
2. Leave the scallions to cook for 5 minutes or until it has a golden-brown color and crispy texture, while still shaking it after every 2 minutes. Carefully remove it from your air fryer. Allow it to cool before serving. Serve and enjoy!

210. Delicious Wrapped Shrimp

Preparation time: 15 minutes
Cook Time: 11 minutes
Servings: 2

Ingredients:
- 10 Oz. already cooked shrimp, peeled and deveined
- 2 Tbsp olive oil
- 1/3 Cup blackberries, ground
- 11 Prosciutto sliced
- 1/3 Cup red wine
- 1 Tbsp mint, chopped

Directions:
1. Wrap each shrimp in a prosciutto slice, drizzle the oil over them, rub well, place in your preheated air fryer at 390°F and fry them for 8 minutes.
2. Meanwhile, heat a pan with ground blackberries over medium heat, add mint and wine; stir, cook for 3 minutes, and take off the heat. Arrange shrimp on a platter, drizzle blackberries sauce over them, and serve as an appetizer. Enjoy!

211. Pumpkin Pancakes

Preparation time: 15 minutes
Cook Time: 12 minutes
Servings: 2

Ingredients:
- 1 Square puff pastry
- 3 Tbsp pumpkin filling
- 1 Small egg, beaten

Directions:
1. Preheat your air fryer to 355°F.
2. Roll out a puff pastry square and layer it with pumpkin pie filling, leaving about 1/4-inch space around the edges. Cut it up into eight equal-sized square pieces and coat the edges with beaten egg.
3. Arrange the squares into a greased "Sheet Pan" and insert
them in the oven. Cook for 12 minutes. Serve warm. Enjoy!

212. Lemony Raspberries Bowls

Preparation time: 5 minutes
Cook Time: 12 minutes
Servings: 2

Ingredients:
- 1 Cup raspberries
- 2 Tbsp butter
- 2 Tbsp lemon juice
- 1 Tsp cinnamon powder

Directions:
1. In your air fryer, mix all the ingredients, toss, cover, cook at
350°F for 12 minutes, divide into bowls and serve for breakfast. Enjoy!

213. Pita-Style Chips

Preparation time: 5 minutes
Cook Time: 15 minutes
Servings: 4

Ingredients:
- 1 large egg
- ¼ c blanched finely ground almond flour
- ½ oz. pork rinds, finely ground
- 1 c shredded Mozzarella cheese

Directions:
1. Put Mozzarella in a wide oven-safe dish and microwave for about 30 seconds or until melted Add the rest of the ingredients and mix until largely smooth dough shapes into a ball quickly; if your dough is too hard, microwave for an additional 15 seconds
2. Roll the dough into a wide rectangle among 2 parchment paper sheets and then use a sharp knife to make the triangle- shaped chips Put the prepared chips in the bucket of your Air Fryer
3. Set the temperature and adjust the clock to about 350°F for around 5 minutes

214. Flatbread

Preparation time: 5 minutes
Cook Time: 20 minutes
Servings: 4

Ingredients:
- 1 oz. full-fat cream cheese softened
- ¼ c blanched finely ground almond flour
- 1 c shredded Mozzarella cheese

Directions:
1. Melt some Mozzarella in your microwave for about 30 seconds in a wide oven-safe container Mix in some almond flour to make it smooth, and add some cream cheese to the mix Proceed to blend until dough shapes, slowly kneading using wet hands if needed

2. Split the dough into 2 parts and roll between 2 pieces of parchment paper to a thickness of about ¼-inch Cut an extra piece of parchment paper to fit in the container of your Air Fryer

3. Put a small piece of flatbread; try working in 2 batches if necessary, on your parchment paper and into the Air Fryer

4. Set the temperature and adjust the clock to about 320°F for around 7 minutes

5. Rotate the flatbread midway through the cooking process

Serve it hot

215. Radish Chips

Preparation time: 10 minutes
Cook Time: 15 minutes
Servings: 4

Ingredients:
- 2 tbsps. coconut oil, melted
- ½ tsp garlic powder
- ¼ tsp paprika
- ¼ tsp onion powder
- 1 lb. radishes
- 2 c water

Directions:
1. Put the water in a medium-sized saucepan and bring the water to a boil

2. Cut the upper part and bottom of each radish, then cut each radish thinly and evenly using a mandolin At this stage, you can use the cutting blade in your food processor

3. For about 5 minutes or until transparent, put the radish pieces in hot water To trap extra humidity, extract them from the boiling water and put them on a dry paper towel

4. In a wide pot, combine the radish pieces and the rest of the ingredients until thoroughly covered in oil and seasoned Put the radish chips in the basket of an Air Fryer

5. Set the temperature and adjust the clock to about 320°F for around 5 minutes

6. During the cooking process, rotate the basket at least 2–3 times Serve it hot

216. Dinner Rolls

Preparation time: 10 minutes
Cook Time: 15 minutes
Servings: 6

Ingredients:
- 1 large egg
- ½ tsp baking powder
- ¼ c ground flaxseed
- 1 c blanched finely ground almond flour
- 1 oz. full-fat cream cheese
- 1 c shredded Mozzarella cheese

Directions:
1. In a big oven-safe dish, put the cream cheese, Mozzarella, and almond flour Microwave for about 1 minute Blend until smooth

2. When thoroughly mixed and soft, add baking powder, flaxseed, and egg Suppose the dough is too hard, microwave for an extra 15 seconds

3. Split your dough into 6 portions and shape it into small balls

Put the balls into the bucket of your Air Fryer

4. Set the temperature and adjust the clock to about 320°F for around a 12 minutes timer

5. Let the rolls cool fully before serving

217. Buffalo Cauliflower

Preparation time: 10 minutes
Cook Time: 10 minutes
Servings: 4

Ingredients:
- ¼ c buffalo sauce
- ½ (1 oz.) dry ranch seasoning packet
- 2 tbsps. salted butter, melted
- 4 c cauliflower florets

Directions:
1. Toss the cauliflower with the butter and dry ranch in a wide pot Place it in the bucket of your Air Fryer
2. Set the temperature and adjust the clock to about 400°F for around 5 minutes
3. During frying, rotate the basket at least 2–3 times Take out the cauliflower from the fryer basket when soft, and then toss in the buffalo sauce Serve it hot

218. Garlic Herb Butter Roasted Radishes

Preparation time: 10 minutes
Cook Time: 15 minutes
Servings: 4

Ingredients:
- ¼ tsp ground black pepper
- ¼ tsp dried oregano
- ½ tsp dried parsley
- ½ tsp garlic powder
- 2 tbsps. unsalted butter, melted
- 1 lb. radishes

Directions:
1. Remove the radish roots and split them into quarters
2. Put seasonings and butter in a shallow dish In the herb butter, turn the radishes and put them in your Air Fryer basket
3. Set the temperature and adjust the clock to about 350°F for around 10 minutes
4. Simply throw the radishes in the Air Fryer basket midway through the cooking time Keep cooking until the edges start to turn dark brown
5. Serve it hot

219. Roasted Peppers

Preparation time: 8 minutes
Cook Time: 15 minutes
Servings: 4

Ingredients:
- 2 yellow onions, chopped
- 6 yellow bell peppers, cut into medium strips
- 6 green bell peppers, cut into medium strips
- 6 red bell peppers, cut into medium strips
- 2 tbsps. olive oil
- 2 tbsps. sweet paprika
- Salt and black pepper according to your taste

Directions:
1. Mix the red bell peppers with the green and yellow ones in your Air Fryer
2. Add some oil, paprika, salt, onion, and black pepper, mix, and bake for about 15 minutes at around 350°F
3. Split as a side dish between plates and eat Enjoy!

220. Cheddar Biscuits

Preparation time: 15 minutes
Cook Time: 15 minutes
Servings: 10

Ingredients:
- 2 c flour
- 2 ⅓ c buttermilk
- 1 c Cheddar cheese, grated
- 3 tbsps. sugar
- 1 c butter + 1 tbsp. melted
- 3 ⅓ c self-rising flour

Directions:
1. Mix 1 c butter, Cheddar cheese, sugar, and buttermilk in a bowl of self-rising flour and mix until you have a dough
2. On a working surface, place 1 c flour, shape the dough, flatten it, slice 10 circles with a cookie cutter and cover them with flour
3. Cover the basket of your Air Fryer with aluminum foil, add the cookies, spray them with some melted butter and fry them for about 15 minutes at around 380°F
4. Split between plates and serve them as a side dish Enjoy!

221. Fried Tomatoes

Preparation time: 5 minutes
Cook Time: 15 minutes
Servings: 5

Ingredients:
- Cooking spray
- 1 tbsp. Creole seasoning
- 2 c panko breadcrumbs
- 2 c buttermilk
- 1 c flour
- Salt and black pepper according to your taste
- 3 green tomatoes, sliced

Directions:
1. With some salt and black pepper, spice the tomato slices

2. Put some flour in a bowl, buttermilk in a different bowl, and panko crumbs Add Creole seasoning in the final bowl

3. Dig the tomato slices in flour then placed them in your buttermilk and the panko breadcrumbs Put them in the oiled Air Fryer basket with some cooking spray, and fry them for about 5 minutes at around 400°F

4. Split as a side dish between dishes and eat Enjoy!

222. Mushrooms and Sour Cream

Preparation time: 10 minutes

Cook Time: 15 minutes

Servings: 8

Ingredients:
- Salt and black pepper according to your taste
- 1 ½ c Cheddar cheese, grated
- 1 ½ c sour cream
- 2 carrot, grated
- 28 mushrooms, stems removed
- 2 green bell pepper, chopped
- 2 yellow onion, chopped
- 4 bacon strips, chopped

Directions:
1. Heat a skillet over medium-high heat; add onion, bacon, carrot, and bell pepper Mix and cook for about 1 minute

2. Add some salt, black pepper, and some sour cream, cook for an extra minute Remove from flame and cool off

3. Stuff the mushrooms with this combination; sprinkle the cheese on top, and simmer for about 8 minutes at around

360°F

4. Split as a side dish between plates and serve Enjoy!

223. Eggplant Side Dish

Preparation time: 10 minutes

Cook Time: 13 minutes

Servings: 5

Ingredients:
- 2 tomato chopped
- 2 yellow onion, chopped
- 2 tbsps. olive oil
- 1 tsp garlic powder
- 2 bunch cilantros, chopped
- 2 tbsps. tomato paste
- 2 green bell pepper, chopped
- 1 pinch of oregano, dried
- Salt and black pepper according to your taste
- 10 baby eggplants, scooped in the center and pulp reserved

Directions:
1. Over medium-high heat, warm a pan with some oil, add the onion, mix and cook for about 1 minute

2. Add some salt, the pulp of eggplant, black pepper, green bell pepper, oregano, tomato paste, cilantro, powdered garlic, and tomato, mix, cook for about 1–2 more minutes, take off the flame and cool down

3. Pack the eggplants with this blend, put them in the basket of your Air Fryer, and cook for about 8 minutes at around 360°F

4. On bowls, split the eggplants and offer them as a side dish with your choice of food Enjoy!

224. Garlic Potatoes

Preparation time: 15 minutes

Cook Time: 15 minutes

Servings: 8

Ingredients:
- ⅔ c Parmesan, grated
- 3 tbsps. butter
- Salt and black pepper according to your taste
- 3 tbsps. olive oil
- 2 tsps. thyme, dried
- 5 lbs. red potatoes, halved
- 1 tsp oregano, dried
- 1 tsp basil, dried
- 6 garlic cloves, minced
- 3 tbsps. parsley, chopped

Directions:
1. Mix the potato halves with garlic, parsley, oregano, basil, thyme, pepper, salt, oil, and butter in a bowl, mix very well and move to the basket of your Air Fryer

2. Cover and cook for about 15 minutes at around 400°F, switching them over once

3. Toss on top some Parmesan, split the potatoes on the dishes, and serve them as a side dish Enjoy!

225. Roasted Pumpkin

Preparation time: 15 minutes

Cook Time: 12 minutes

Servings: 5

Ingredients:
- 1 pinch of cinnamon powder
- 1 pinch of nutmeg, ground
- 1 pinch of brown sugar
- 1 pinch of sea salt
- 2 tbsps. olive oil
- 4 garlic cloves, minced
- 2 ½ lb. pumpkin, deseeded, sliced, and

roughly chopped

Directions:
1. Combine the pumpkin with oil, garlic, brown sugar, salt, nutmeg, and cinnamon in the Air Fryer's basket, mix good, cover and cook for about 12 minutes at around 370°F
2. Split as a side dish between dishes and serve Enjoy!

226. Corn With Lime and Cheese

Preparation time: 15 minutes
Cook Time: 15 minutes
Servings: 4

Ingredients:
- Juice from 3 limes
- 4 tsps. sweet paprika
- 1 c Feta cheese, grated
- 1 drizzle of olive oil
- 4 corns on the cob, husks removed

Directions:
1. Rub the corn with the oil and some paprika, bring it in your Air Fryer, and steam for about 15 minutes at around 400°F, turning once

2. Split the corn into bowls, cover with the cheese, drizzle with the lime juice and serve as a side dish with your choice of food Enjoy!

227. Chili and Parsley Soufflé

Preparation time: 5 minutes
Cooking time: 9 minutes
Servings: 3

Ingredients:
- 3 eggs
- 2 tablespoons heavy cream
- 1 red chili pepper, chopped
- 2 tablespoons parsley, finely chopped
- Salt and white pepper to taste

Directions:
1. In a large mixing basin, whisk together all of the ingredients before pouring them into three ramekins.
2. Preheat your air fryer at 400 degrees F and cook for 9 minutes with the ramekins in the basket.
3. Remove the soufflés from the oven and serve immediately.

228. Parmesan Breakfast Muffins

Preparation time: 5 minutes
Cooking time: 15 minutes
Servings: 4

Ingredients:
- 2 eggs
- 2 tablespoons olive oil
- 3 ounces almond milk
- 1 tablespoon baking powder
- 4 ounces white flour
- A splash of Worcestershire sauce
- 2 ounces parmesan cheese, grated

Directions:
1. In a large mixing bowl, whisk together the eggs, 1 tablespoon of the oil, the milk, the baking powder, the flour, the Worcestershire sauce, and the parmesan; set aside.
2. Pour 1 tablespoon of oil into a muffin pan that will fit in your air fryer, divide the cheesy mixture equally among the cups, and set the pan in the air fryer to bake for 15 minutes.
3.320 degrees Fahrenheit for 15 minutes is the recommended temperature.
4..Enjoy.

229. Long Beans Omelet

Preparation time: 10 minutes
Cooking time: 10 minutes
Servings: 3

Ingredients:
- ½ teaspoon soy sauce
- 1 tablespoon olive oil
- 3 eggs, whisked
- A pinch of salt and black pepper
- 4 garlic cloves, minced
- 4 long beans, trimmed and sliced

Directions:
1. In a large mixing bowl, whisk together the eggs, a bit of salt, black pepper, and soy sauce until thoroughly combined.
2. Preheat your air fryer to 320 degrees Fahrenheit, add the oil and garlic, swirl, and cook for 1 minute until the garlic is golden brown.
3. Spread the long beans and egg mixture on a baking sheet and bake for
10 minutes.
4. Divide the omelet among the dishes and serve it for brunch.
5. Enjoy!

230. French Beans and Egg Breakfast Mix

Preparation time: 10 minutes
Cooking time: 10 minutes
Servings: 3

Ingredients:
- 2 eggs, whisked
- ½ teaspoon soy sauce
- 1 tablespoon olive oil
- 4 garlic cloves, minced
- 3 ounces French beans, trimmed and sliced diagonally
- Salt and white pepper to the taste

Directions:
1. In a large mixing bowl, whisk together the eggs, a bit of salt, black pepper, and soy sauce until thoroughly combined.
2. Preheat your air fryer to 320 degrees Fahrenheit, add the oil and garlic, swirl, and cook for 1 minute until the garlic is golden brown.
3. Spread the long beans and egg mixture on a baking sheet and bake for
10 minutes.
4. Divide the omelet among the dishes and serve it for brunch.
5. Enjoy!

231. Creamy Breakfast Tofu

Preparation time: 15 minutes
Cooking time: 15 minutes
Servings: 4

Ingredients:
- 1 block firm tofu, pressed and cubed
- 1 teaspoon rice vinegar
- 2 tablespoons soy sauce
- 2 teaspoons sesame oil
- 1 tablespoon potato starch
- 1 cup Greek yogurt

Directions:
1. In a large mixing basin, combine tofu cubes, vinegar, soy sauce, and oil;
stir well and set aside for 15 minutes.
Cook for 15 minutes, shaking halfway through, after dipping tofu cubes in potato starch. 2. Place tofu cubes in air fryer and heat at 370 degrees F for
15 minutes.
3. Dish out the mixture into bowls and serve it for breakfast with a dollop of plain Greek yogurt.
4. Enjoy!

232. Veggie Burritos

Preparation time: 10 minutes
Cooking time: 10 minutes
Servings: 4

Ingredients:
- 2 tablespoons cashew butter
- 2 tablespoons tamari
- 2 tablespoons water
- 2 tablespoons liquid smoke
- 4 rice papers
- ½ cup sweet potatoes, steamed and cubed
- ½ small broccoli head, florets separated and steamed
- 7 asparagus stalks
- 8 roasted red peppers, chopped
- A handful kale, chopped

Directions:
1. In a large mixing basin, whisk together the cashew butter, water, tamari, and liquid smoke until thoroughly combined.
2. Wet the rice sheets and lay them on a work area to be used later.
Divide the ingredients into four equal portions and wrap them in burritos, dipping each one in the cashew mixture.
4. Arrange the burritos in your air fryer and cook them for 10 minutes at
350 degrees Fahrenheit.
5. Arrange the vegetarian burritos on plates and serve immediately.

233. Breakfast Fish Tacos

Preparation time: 10 minutes
Cooking time: 13 minutes
Servings: 4

Ingredients:
- 4 big tortillas
- 1 red bell pepper, chopped
- 1 yellow onion, chopped
- 1 cup corn
- 4 white fish fillets, skinless and boneless
- ½ cup salsa
- A handful mixed romaine lettuce, spinach and radicchio
- 4 tablespoon parmesan, grated

Directions:
1. Place the fish fillets in the air fryer and cook for 6 minutes at 350 degrees F.
2. In the meantime, heat a pan over medium high heat and add the bell pepper, onion, and corn, stirring constantly, for 1-2 minutes until the vegetables are tender.
3. Arrange tortillas on a work surface, divide fish

fillets, pour salsa over them, divide mixed vegetables and mixed greens, and sprinkle parmesan cheese over each at the conclusion of the process.

4. Roll your tacos and throw them in an air fryer that has been preheated to 350 degrees F for 6 minutes.

5. Divide the fish tacos among the dishes and serve them like a breakfast dish.

6. Enjoy!

234. Spinach Breakfast Parcels

Preparation time: 10 minutes
Cooking time: 4 minutes
Servings: 2

Ingredients:
- 4 sheets filo pastry
- 1 pound baby spinach leaves, roughly chopped
- ½ pound ricotta cheese
- 2 tablespoons pine nuts
- 1 eggs, whisked
- Zest from 1 lemon, grated
- Greek yogurt for serving
- Salt and black pepper to the taste

Directions:
1. In a large mixing bowl, combine spinach, cheese, egg, lemon zest, salt, pepper, and pine nuts, stirring constantly.

2. Prepare filo sheets on a work area, divide spinach mixture, fold diagonally to make your packages, and put them in your preheated air fryer set to 400 degrees F. 3.

3. Cook the parcels in the oven for 4 minutes, then divide them onto plates and serve them with Greek yogurt on the side as a condiment.

4. Enjoy

235. Ham Rolls

Preparation time: 10 minutes
Cooking time: 10 minutes
Servings: 4

Ingredients:
- 1 sheet puff pastry
- 4 handful gruyere cheese, grated
- 4 teaspoons mustard
- 8 ham slices, chopped

Directions:
1. On a work surface, stretch out puff pastry and divide the cheese, ham, and mustard evenly. Roll up tightly and cut into medium circles.

2. Place all of the rolls in an air fryer and cook for 10 minutes at 370 degrees Fahrenheit until golden brown.

3. Arrange the buns on plates and serve them as breakfast.

236. Shrimp Frittata

Preparation time: 10 minutes
Cooking time: 15 minutes
Servings: 4

Ingredients:
- 4 eggs
- ½ teaspoon basil, dried
- Cooking spray
- Salt and black pepper to the taste
- ½ cup rice, cooked
- ½ cup shrimp, cooked, peeled, deveined and chopped
- ½ cup baby spinach, chopped
- ½ cup Monterey jack cheese, grated

Directions:
1. In a large mixing bowl, whisk together the eggs, salt, pepper, and basil. Rice, shrimp, and spinach are added to the pan of your air fryer after it has been sprayed with cooking spray.

3. Pour in the egg mixture and top with cheese, then cook for 10 minutes at 350 degrees F in your air fryer.

4. Distribute the mixture among the dishes and serve for breakfast.

5. Enjoy!

237. Buttery Shrimp Skewers

Preparation Time: 15 Minutes
Cooking time: 15 minutes
Servings: 2

Ingredients:
- 8 shrimps; peeled and deveined
- 8 green bell pepper slices
- 1 tbsp. rosemary; chopped.
- 1 tbsp. butter; melted
- 4 garlic cloves; minced
- Salt and black pepper to the taste

Directions:
1. Put shrimp in a large mixing basin and toss to cover with the garlic and butter. Season with salt and pepper and add the rosemary and bell pepper slices. Set aside for 10 minutes.

2. Thread 2 shrimp and 2 bell pepper slices onto a skewer, then repeat with the remaining shrimp and bell pepper pieces. 3. Serve immediately.

3. Place all of the ingredients in the air fryer's basket and cook for 6 minutes at 360 degrees Fahrenheit. Divide the mixture among the dishes and serve immediately.

238. Crusted Salmon Recipe

Preparation Time: 15 Minutes
Cooking time: 10 minutes
Servings: 4

Ingredients:
- 1 cup pistachios; chopped.
- 4 salmon fillets
- 1/4 cup lemon juice
- 2 tbsp. honey
- 1 tbsp. mustard
- 1 tsp. dill; chopped
- Salt and black pepper to the taste

Directions:
1. In a large mixing bowl, whisk together the pistachios, mustard, honey, lemon juice, salt, black pepper, and dill; distribute over the salmon.
2. Place the ingredients in your air fryer and cook for 10 minutes at 350 degrees Fahrenheit. Toss the mixture among the dishes and serve with a side salad

239. Tasty Grilled Red Mullet

Preparation Time: 15 minutes
Cooking time: 15 minutes
Servings: 8

Ingredients:
- 8 whole red mullets, gutted and scales removed
- Salt and pepper to taste
- Juice from 1 lemon
- 1 tablespoon olive oil

Directions:
1. Preheat the air fryer to 3900 degrees Fahrenheit.
2. Secondly, insert the grill pan attachment into the air fryer.
3. Salinity, pepper, and lemon juice should be used to season the red mullet.
4. Apply a light coat of olive oil.
5. Grill for 15 minutes on each side.

240. Spiced Salmon Kebabs

Preparation Time: 15 minutes
Cooking time: 15 minutes
Servings: 3

Ingredients:
- 2 tablespoons chopped fresh oregano
- 2 teaspoons sesame seeds
- 1 teaspoon ground cumin
- Salt and pepper to taste
- 1 ½ pounds salmon fillets
- 2 tablespoons olive oil
- 2 lemons, sliced into rounds

Directions:
1. Preheat the air fryer to 390 degrees Fahrenheit. Secondly, insert the grill pan attachment into the air fryer.
Make the dry rub by combining oregano, sesame seeds, cumin, salt and
pepper in a small mixing bowl.
4. Rub the salmon fillets with the dry rub and then brush them with oil to finish them off.
5. Grill the salmon for 15 minutes on a hot grill.
6. Once the dish is finished, garnish with lemon slices.

241. Garlicky-Grilled Turbot

Preparation Time: 15 minutes
Cooking time: 15 minutes
Servings: 2

Ingredients:
- 2 whole turbot, scaled and head removed
- Salt and pepper to taste
- 1 clove of garlic, minced
- ½ cup chopped celery leaves
- 2 tablespoons olive oil

Directions:
1. Preheat the air fryer to 390 degrees Fahrenheit.
2. Add the grill pan attachment to the air fryer and turn it on.
3. Season the turbot with salt, pepper, garlic, and celery leaves before grilling or baking.
4. Brush with a little oil.
5. Place the fish on a grill pan and cook for 15 minutes, or until it is flaky and cooked through.

242. German Pancakes

Preparation Time: 15 minutes
Cooking Time: 12-16 minutes
Servings: 4

Ingredients:
- 3 eggs, beaten
- 2 tbsp butter, melted
- 1 cup flour
- 2 tbsp sugar, powdered
- ½ cup milk
- 1 cup fresh strawberries, sliced

Directions:
1. Preheat air fryer to 330 F. In a bowl, mix flour, milk, and eggs until fully incorporated. Grease a baking pan that fits in your air fryer with the butter and pour in the mixture.
2. Place the pan in the air fryer's basket and Air Fry for 12-16 minutes until the pancake is fluffy and golden brown. Drizzle powdered sugar and arrange sliced strawberries on top to serve.

243. Kale and Cottage Cheese Omelet

Preparation Time: 10 minutes Cooking Time: 10 minutes Servings: 3

Ingredients:
- 5 eggs
- 3 tbsp cottage cheese
- 1 cup kale, chopped
- ½ tbsp basil, chopped
- ½ tbsp fresh parsley, chopped
- Salt and black pepper to taste

Directions:
1. Beat the eggs, salt, and pepper in a bowl. Stir in the rest of the ingredients. Pour the mixture into a greased baking pan and fit in the air fryer. Bake for 10 minutes at 330 F until slightly golden and set.

244 Fennel Frittata

Preparation Time: 15 minutes
Cooking Time: 10-15 minutes
Servings: 6

Ingredients:
- 1 fennel bulb; shredded
- 6 eggs; whisked
- 2 tsp. cilantro; chopped.
- 1 tsp. sweet paprika
- Cooking spray
- A pinch of salt and black pepper

Directions:
1. Take a bowl and mix all the ingredients except the cooking spray and stir well.
2. Grease a baking pan with the cooking spray, pour the frittata mix and spread well
3. Put the pan in the Air Fryer and cook at 370°F for 15 minutes.
4. Divide between plates and serve them for breakfast.

245. Tofu Omelet

Preparation Time: 10 minutes
Cooking Time: 10 minutes
Servings: 2

Ingredients:
- 3 eggs, lightly beaten
- ¼ cup onion, chopped
- 2 tbsp green onion, chopped
- 2 tbsp soy sauce
- 1 tsp cumin
- 1 tsp coriander
- 1 /4 cup tofu, cubed
- Pepper
- Salt

Directions:
1. Add all ingredients into the large bowl and stir until well combined.
2. Spray air fryer baking pan with cooking spray.
3. Pour bowl mixture into the prepared baking pan and place into the air fryer.
4. Cook at 400 F for 10 minutes.
5. Serve and enjoy.

246. Coconut Cream Cheese Pancakes

Preparation Time: 10 minutes
Cooking Time: 5-10 minutes
Servings: 1

Ingredients:
- 2 oz cream cheese
- 2 eggs
- ½ tsp cinnamon
- 1 tbsp coconut flour
- ½ to 1 packet of Sugar

Directions:
1. Mix together all the ingredients until smooth.
2. Heat up a non-stick pan or skillet with butter or coconut oil on medium-high.
3. Make them as you would normally make pancakes.
4. Cook it on one side and then flip to cook the other side!
5. Top with some butter and/or sugar.

247. Florentine Eggs

Preparation Time: 15 minutes
Cooking Time: 10 minutes
Servings: 2

Ingredients:
- 1 cup washed, fresh spinach leaves
- 2 tbsp freshly grated parmesan cheese
- Sea salt and pepper
- 1 tbsp white vinegar
- 2 eggs

Directions:
1. Cook the spinach the microwave or steam until wilted.
2. Sprinkle with parmesan cheese and seasoning.
3. Slice into bite-size pieces and place on a plate.
4. Simmer a pan of water and add the vinegar. Stir quickly with a spoon.
5. Break an egg into the center. Turn off the heat and cover until set.
6. Repeat with the second egg.
7. Place the eggs on top of the spinach and serve.

248. Smoked Salmon Omelet

Preparation Time: 10 minutes
Cooking Time: 10 minutes
Servings: 2

Ingredients:
- 3 eggs
- 1 smoked salmon
- 3 links pork sausage
- ¼ cup onions
- ¼ cup provolone cheese

Directions:
1. Whisk the eggs and pour them into a skillet.
2. Follow the standard method for making an omelet.
3. Add the onions, salmon and cheese before turning the omelet over.
4. Sprinkle the omelet with cheese and serve with the sausages on the side.
5. Serve!

249. Peanut Oats and Chia Porridge

Preparation Time: 10 minutes
Cooking Time: 5 minutes
Servings: 4

Ingredients:
- 4 cups milk
- 2 tbsp. peanut butter
- 2 cups oats
- 1 cup chia seeds
- 4 tbsp. honey
- 1 tbsp. butter, melted

Directions:
1. Pre-heat the Air Fryer to 390°F.
2. Put the peanut butter, honey, butter, and milk in a bowl and mix together using a whisk. Add in the oats and chia seeds and stir.
3. Transfer the mixture to a fryer-proof bowl that is small enough to fit inside the fryer and cook for 5 minutes. Give another stir before serving.

250. Nutmeg Cranberry Scones

Preparation Time: 5 minutes
Cooking Time: 10 minutes
Servings: 4

Ingredients:
- 1 cup of fresh cranberries
- ⅓ cup of sugar
- One tablespoon of orange zest
- ¾ cup of half and half cream
- 2 cups of flour
- ¼ teaspoon of ground nutmeg
- ¼ teaspoon of salt
- ¼ cup of butter, chilled and diced
- ¼ cup of brown sugar
- One tablespoon of baking powder
- One egg

Directions:
1. Set an Air fryer to 365 degrees F for 10 minutes. Strain nutmeg, flour, baking powder, salt, and sugar in a bowl. Blend in the cream and egg. Fold in the orange zest and cranberries to form a smooth dough.
2. Roll the dough and cut into scones. Place the scones on the cooking tray. Insert the cooking tray in the Air fryer when it displays "Add Food." Flip the sides when it shows "Turn Food." Remove from the oven when cooking time is complete. Serve warm.

251. Pizza Omelet

Preparation Time: 15 minutes
Cooking Time: 12 minutes
Servings: 2

Ingredients:
- 4 eggs
- 2 tablespoons milk
- Pinch of salt
- Ground black pepper, as required
- 8-10 turkey pepperoni slices

Directions:
1. In a bowl, crack the eggs and beat well.
2. Add the remaining ingredients and gently, stir to combine.
3. Place the mixture into a baking pan.
4. Press "Power Button" of Air Fry and turn the dial to select the
"Air Fry" mode.
5. Press the Time button and again turn the dial to set the cooking time to 12 minutes.
6. Now push the Temp button and rotate the dial to set the temperature at 355 degrees F.
7. Press "Start/Pause" button to start.
8. When the unit beeps to show that it is preheated, open the lid.
9. Arrange pan over the "Wire Rack" and insert in the oven.
10. Cut into equal-sized wedges and serve hot.

252. Streusel Donuts

Preparation Time: 15 minutes
Cooking Time: 15 minutes
Servings: 6

Ingredients:
- 1 cup plus 2 tablespoons all-purpose flour, divided, plus additional to dust the work surface
- 5 tablespoons dark brown sugar, divided
- 1 teaspoon baking powder
- Pinch sea salt
- ¼ cup whole milk
- 1 large egg, yolk and white separated
- 3 tablespoons granulated sugar
- ½ teaspoon ground cinnamon
- ¼ cup butter, melted
- Cooking oil spray

Directions:
1. In a medium bowl, combine 1 cup of flour, 2 tablespoons of brown sugar, the baking powder, and salt and mix well.
2. In a small bowl, whisk together the milk and egg yolk. Add this to the flour mixture and mix just until a dough forms.
3. In another small bowl, combine the remaining 3 tablespoons of brown sugar, granulated sugar, cinnamon, remaining 2 tablespoons of flour, and butter and mix until a crumbly streusel forms Set aside.
4. Dust the work surface with some flour. Turn the dough out onto the surface and pat it to ⅓-inch thickness. Using a 3-inch cookie cutter, cut out 6 rounds. We'll skip the donut holes so we can have more streusel on top.
5. Beat the egg white until frothy in a small bowl, then brush the tops of the rounds with some of the egg white.
6. Sprinkle each dough round with some of the streusel topping, patting the topping onto the dough so it sticks.
7. Cut two pieces of parchment paper to fit in your air fryer basket.
8. Place a parchment paper round into the air fryer basket and add the donuts, three at a time, depending on the size of your air fryer. Spray the tops with cooking oil.
9. Set or preheat the air fryer to 350°F. Fry the donuts for 4 to 6 minutes or until they are light golden brown. Remove and cool on a wire rack. Remove and discard the parchment paper and replace with a fresh round. Air fry the remaining donuts.

253. Pesto Omelet

Preparation Time: 15 minutes
Cooking Time: 15 minutes
Servings: 3

Ingredients:
- 1 tablespoon olive oil
- 1 shallot, minced
- 1 garlic clove, minced
- ½ cup diced red bell pepper
- ¼ cup chopped fresh tomato
- 4 large eggs
- 2 tablespoons light cream
- ¼ teaspoon sea salt
- ½ cup shredded mozzarella cheese
- 3 tablespoons basil pesto

Directions:
1. In a 6-inch round pan, place the olive oil. Add the shallot, garlic, bell pepper, and tomato and toss to coat in the oil.
2. Set or preheat the air fryer to 350°F. Put the pan with the vegetables in the basket and the basket in the air fryer. Cook for 3 to 5 minutes, stirring once halfway through cooking time, until the veggies are tender.
3. Meanwhile, whisk together the eggs, cream, and salt until smooth.
4. When the vegetables are done, remove the basket. Pour the egg mixture into the pan. Return the basket to the air fryer and cook for 8 minutes.
5. Sprinkle with the cheese and cook another 2 minutes or until the cheese is melted and the eggs are set. Top with the pesto and serve immediately.

254. Berry and Nuts Granola

Preparation Time: 15 minutes
Cooking Time: 12 minutes
Servings: 6

Ingredients:
- 1½ cups rolled oats (not quick-cooking oats)
- 1 cup chopped pecans or walnuts, or a combination
- 3 tablespoons flaxseed
- ½ teaspoon cinnamon
- ⅛ teaspoon nutmeg
- ¼ cup maple syrup
- 3 tablespoons vegetable oil
- 1 teaspoon vanilla
- ¼ teaspoon sea salt
- ½ cup dried blueberries
- ½ cup dried cherries

Directions:
1. In a large bowl, combine the oats, nuts, flaxseed, cinnamon, and nutmeg and mix well.
2. In a 2-cup glass measuring cup, combine the maple syrup, oil, vanilla, and salt and mix well. Pour this over the oat mixture and stir to combine.
3. Spread the mixture in a 7-inch round pan.
4. Set or preheat the air fryer to 350°F. Place the pan in the air fryer basket and the basket in the air fryer. Bake for 12 minutes, stirring halfway through cooking time, until the granola is golden brown and fragrant.
5. Transfer the granola to a serving bowl and let cool for 3 minutes.

Stir in the dried blueberries and cherries. Let stand until cool, then

serve, or store in an airtight container at room temperature for up to 4 days.

255. Kale Muffins

Preparation Time: 10 minutes
Cooking Time: 12-15 minutes
Servings: 8

Ingredients:
- 6 large eggs
- 1/2 cup almond milk
- 1 cup kale, chopped
- 1/4 cup chives, chopped
- Pepper
- Salt

Directions:
1. Add all ingredients into the bowl and whisk well.
2. Pour egg mixture into the 8 silicone muffin molds.
3. Place the dehydrating tray in a multi-level air fryer basket and place basket in the air fryer.
4. Place 6 muffin molds on dehydrating tray.
5. Seal pot with air fryer lid and select bake mode then set the temperature to 350 F and timer for 30 minutes.
6. Bake remaining muffins using the same method.
7. Serve and enjoy.

256. Creamy Mac and Cheese

Preparation Time: 10 minutes
Cooking Time: 15 minutes
Servings: 4

Ingredients:
- 2 1/2 cups macaroni
- 1/4 tsp garlic powder
- 2 cups crackers, crushed
- 1/3 cup parmesan cheese, shredded
- 2 2/3 cups cheddar cheese, shredded
- 8 tbsp butter
- 1 1/4 cup heavy cream
- 2 cups vegetable stock
- Pepper
- Salt

Directions:
1. Add heavy cream, 4 tbsp butter, and stock into the air fryer and stir well.
2. Add macaroni and stir well.
3. Seal the pot with pressure cooking lid and cook on high pressure for 4 minutes.
4. Once done, release pressure using quick release. Remove lid.
5. Add 2 cups of cheese and stir until cheese is melted.
6. Mix together remaining butter and crushed crackers.
7. Spread remaining cheddar cheese, parmesan cheese, and crushed crackers.
8. Seal pot with air fryer lid and select air fry mode then set the temperature to 400 F and timer for 5 minutes.
9. Serve and enjoy.

257. Cauliflower Florets

Preparation Time: 10 minutes
Cooking Time: 10 minutes
Servings: 4

Ingredients:
- 1/4 cup sultanas or golden raisins
- ¼ teaspoon salt
- 1 tablespoon curry powder
- 1 head cauliflower, broken into small florets
- ¼ cup pine nuts

Directions:
1. In a cup of boiling water, soak your sultanas to rehydrate. Preheat your air fryer to 350˚ Fahrenheit. Add oil and pine nuts to air fryer and toast for a minute or so.
2. In a bowl toss the cauliflower and curry powder as well as salt, then add the mix to air fryer mixing well. Cook for 10-minutes. Drain the sultanas, toss with cauliflower, and serve.

258. Apple Steel Cut Oats

Preparation Time: 10 minutes
Cooking Time: 15 minutes
Servings: 6

Ingredients:
- 1 ½ cups water
- 1 ½ cups coconut milk
- 2 apples, cored, peeled, and chopped
- 1 cup steel-cut oats
- ½ tsp. cinnamon powder
- ¼ tsp. ground nutmeg
- ¼ tsp. ground allspice
- ¼ tsp. ginger powder
- ¼ tsp. ground cardamom
- 1 tbsp. ground flaxseed
- 2 tsp. vanilla extract
- 2 tsp. stevia
- A drop oil, for greasing

Directions:
1. Grease the air fryer with a drop of oil, add apples, milk, water, cinnamon, oats, allspice, nutmeg, cardamom, ginger, vanilla, flaxseeds, and stevia. Stir, cover, and cook at 360°F for 15 minutes.
2. Divide into bowls and serve.

259. Carrot Mix

Preparation Time: 10 minutes
Cooking Time: 15 minutes
Servings: 4

Ingredients:
- 2 cups coconut milk
- ½ cup steel cut oats
- 1 cup shredded carrots
- 1 tsp. ground cardamom
- ½ tsp. agave nectar
- A pinch saffron
- A drop oil, for greasing

Directions:
1. Grease the air fryer with a drop of oil, then add the milk, oats, carrots, cardamom, and agave nectar. Stir, cover, and cook at
2. 365°F for 15 minutes.
3. Divide into bowls, sprinkle saffron on the top, and serve.

260. Blueberries Vanilla Oats

Preparation Time: 10 minutes
Cooking Time: 10 minutes
Servings: 4

Ingredients:
- 1 cup blueberries
- 1 cup steel cut oats
- 1 cup coconut milk
- 2 tbsp. agave nectar
- ½ tsp. vanilla extract
- A drop oil, for greasing

Directions:
1. Grease the air fryer with a drop of oil, then add the oats, milk, agave nectar, vanilla, and blueberries. Toss, cover, and cook at
365°F for 10 minutes.
2. Divide into bowls and serve.

261. Chickpeas and Lentils Mix

Preparation Time: 10 minutes
Cooking Time: 15 minutes
Servings: 6

Ingredients:
- 1 yellow onion, chopped
- 1 tbsp. olive oil
- 1 tbsp. minced garlic
- 1 tsp. sweet paprika
- 1 tsp. smoked paprika
- Salt and black pepper, to taste
- 1 cup red lentils, boiled
- 15 oz. canned chickpeas, drained
- 29 oz. canned tomatoes and juice

Directions:
1. In the air fryer, mix the onion with the oil, garlic, sweet and smoked paprika, salt, pepper, lentils, chickpeas, and tomatoes. Then stir, cover, and cook at 360°F for 15 minutes.
2. Ladle it into bowls and serve hot.

262. Roasted Chickpeas

Preparation Time: 2 minutes
Cooking Time: 8 minutes
Servings: 4

Ingredients:
- ¼ tsp. dried mango powder
- ½ tsp. cinnamon powder
- ¼ tsp. cumin powder
- 3 cups boiled chickpeas
- 1 tsp. salt
- ¼ tsp. dried coriander powder
- ½ tsp. chili powder
- 1 tsp. olive oil
- ¼ tsp. rosemary

Directions:
1. Preheat and set the air fryer's temperature to 370°F.
2. Transfer the chickpeas with olive oil into the air fryer basket.
3. Cook for 8 minutes.
4. Shake after every 2 minutes.
5. Take a bowl, add the chickpeas with all the spices, and toss to combine.
6. Serve and enjoy!

263. Tomatoes and Bell Peppers Mix

Preparation Time: 10 minutes
Cooking Time: 15 minutes
Servings: 4

Ingredients:
- 2 red bell peppers, chopped
- 2 garlic cloves, minced
- 1 lb. cherry tomatoes, halved
- 1 tsp. dried rosemary
- 3 bay leaves
- 2 tbsp. olive oil
- 1 tbsp. balsamic vinegar
- Salt and black pepper, to taste

Directions:
1. Mix the tomatoes with black pepper, salt, garlic, rosemary, half of the oil, bay leaves, and half of the vinegar in a bowl. Toss to coat, introduce them in the air fryer, and roast them at 320°F for 15 minutes.

2. In a food processor, mix the bell peppers with salt, black pepper, the rest of the oil, and the rest of the vinegar. Blend very well.
3. Divide the roasted tomatoes between plates, drizzle the bell peppers sauce over them, and serve.

oil over medium-high heat. Then add eggplant slices and cook for 2 minutes.
2. Add the chili pepper, garlic, green onions, ginger, coconut aminos, and vinegar. Then put it in your air fryer and cook at
320°F for 7 minutes.
3. Divide between plates and serve.

264. Spiced Peppers with Jalapeños

Preparation Time: 10 minutes
Cooking Time: 16 minutes
Servings: 4

Ingredients:
- 4 bell peppers, cut into medium chunks
- ½ cup tomato juice
- 2 tbsp. chopped jarred jalapenos
- 1 cup chopped tomatoes
- ¼ cup chopped yellow onion
- ¼ cup chopped green peppers
- 2 cups tomato sauce
- Salt and black pepper, to taste
- 2 tsp. onion powder
- ½ tsp. crushed red pepper
- 1 tsp. chili powder
- ½ tsp. garlic powder
- 1 tsp. ground cumin
- Oregano

Directions:
1. Mix the tomato juice, jalapeños, tomato sauce, tomatoes, onion, green peppers, salt, pepper, onion powder, red pepper, chili powder, cumin garlic powder, and oregano in a pan that fits the air fryer. Stir well, introduce the pan in the air fryer, and cook at 350°F for 6 minutes.
2. Add the bell peppers and cook at 320°F for 10 minutes more.
3. Divide the peppers mixture between plates and serve.

265. Garlic Eggplants

Preparation Time: 10 minutes
Cooking Time: 9 minutes
Servings: 4

Ingredients:
- 2 tbsp. olive oil
- 2 garlic cloves, minced
- 3 eggplants, halved and sliced
- 1 red chili pepper, chopped
- 1 green onion stalk, chopped
- 1 tbsp. grated ginger
- 1 tbsp. coconut aminos
- 1 tbsp. balsamic vinegar

Directions:
1. Heat up a pan that fits the air fryer with the olive

266. Banana Chips

Preparation Time: 10 minutes
Cooking Time: 10 minutes
Servings: 4

Ingredients:
- 4 bananas, peeled and sliced into thin pieces
- A drizzle olive oil
- A pinch black pepper

Directions:
1. Put the banana slices into the air fryer, drizzle the oil, season with pepper, toss to coat gently, and cook at 360°F for 10 minutes.
2. Serve as a snack.
3. Enjoy!

267. Polenta Biscuits

Preparation Time: 10 minutes
Cooking Time: 25 minutes
Servings: 4

Ingredients:
- 18 oz. cooked polenta roll, cold
- 1 tbsp. olive oil

Directions:
1. Cut the polenta into medium slices and brush them with the olive oil.
2. Place the polenta biscuits into the air fryer and cook at 400°F for 25 minutes, flipping them after 10 minutes.
3. Serve the biscuits as a snack.

268. Sweet Potato and Beans Dip

Preparation Time: 10 minutes
Cooking Time: 10 minutes
Servings: 10

Ingredients:
- 19 oz. canned garbanzo beans, drained
- 1 cup sweet potatoes, peeled and chopped
- ¼ cup sesame paste
- 2 tbsp. lemon juice
- 1 tbsp. olive oil
- 5 garlic cloves, minced

- ½ tsp. ground cumin
- 2 tbsp. water
- Salt and white pepper, to taste

Directions:
1. Put the potatoes in the air fryer's basket, cook them at 360°F for 10 minutes, cool them down, peel them, put them in a food processor, and pulse well.
2. Add the sesame paste, garlic, beans, lemon juice, cumin, water, oil, salt, and pepper. Then pulse again, divide the mixture into bowls, and serve cold.

269. Rice Balls

Preparation Time: 10 minutes
Cooking Time: 35 minutes
Servings: 6

Ingredients:
- 1 small yellow onion, chopped
- 1 cup Arborio rice
- 1 tbsp. olive oil
- 1 cup veggie stock
- Salt and black pepper to the taste
- 2 oz. tofu, cubed
- ¼ cup sun-dried tomatoes, chopped
- 1 ½ cups vegan breadcrumbs
- A drizzle olive oil

Directions:
1. Heat up a pan with 1 tablespoon of oil over medium heat, add onion, stir, and cook for 5 minutes.
2. Add the rice, stock, salt, and pepper. Stir, cook over low heat for 20 minutes, spread the rice on a baking sheet, and leave aside to cool down.
3. Transfer the rice to a bowl, add the tomatoes and half of the breadcrumbs, and stir well.
4. Shape 12 balls, press a hole in each ball, stuff them with the tofu cubes, and mold balls again.
5. Dredge them in the rest of the breadcrumbs, arrange all the balls into the air fryer, drizzle the oil over them, and cook at 380°F for 10 minutes.
6. Flip them and cook for 5 minutes more.
7. Arrange them on a platter and serve them as a snack.

270. Avocado Chips

Preparation Time: 10 minutes
Cooking Time: 10 minutes
Servings: 3

Ingredients:
- 1 avocado, pitted, peeled, and sliced
- Salt and black pepper, to taste
- ½ cup vegan breadcrumbs
- A drizzle olive oil

Directions:
1. In a bowl, mix the breadcrumbs with salt and pepper and stir.

2. Brush the avocado slices with the oil, coat them in the breadcrumbs, place them in the air fryer's basket, and cook at
390°F for 10 minutes, shaking halfway through the cooking.
3. Divide the mixture into bowls and serve them as a snack

271. Basil Crackers

Preparation Time: 10 minutes
Cooking Time: 17 minutes
Servings: 6

Ingredients:
- ½ tsp. baking powder
- Salt and black pepper, to taste
- 1 ¼ cups whole wheat flour
- ¼ tsp. dried basil
- 1 garlic clove, minced
- 2 tbsp. vegan basil pesto
- 2 tbsp. olive oil
- 1 tsp. cayenne

Directions:
1. In a bowl, mix the flour with salt, pepper, baking powder, garlic, cayenne, basil, pesto, and oil. Stir until you obtain a dough and spread it onto a lined baking sheet that fits the air fryer. Introduce the sheet in the fryer at 325°F and bake for
17 minutes.
2. Leave aside to cool down, cut the crackers, and serve them as a snack.

272. Potato Patties with Parsley

Preparation Time: 10 minutes
Cooking Time: 12 minutes
Servings: 4

Ingredients:
- 3 big potatoes, boiled, drained, and mashed
- 2 tbsp. chopped parsley
- 2 tbsp. chopped dill
- Salt and black pepper, to taste
- 1 tbsp. flax meal combined with 1 tbsp. water
- 2 tbsp. vegan breadcrumbs
- A drop oil, for greasing

Directions:
1. In a bowl, mix the potatoes, salt, pepper, dill, parsley, flax meal, and breadcrumbs. Stir well and shape 8 patties out of this mixture.

2. Grease the air fryer with a drop of oil, place patties into the air fryer's basket, and cook them at 360°F for 12 minutes, flipping them halfway through the cooking. Then transfer them to a platter and serve.

273. Swordfish Skewers with Cherry Tomato

Preparation Time: 10 minutes
Cooking Time: 8 minutes
Servings: 4

Ingredients:
- 1 pound (454 g) filleted swordfish
- ¼ cup avocado oil
- 2 tablespoons freshly squeezed lemon juice
- 1 tablespoon minced fresh parsley
- 2 teaspoons Dijon mustard
- Sea salt, black pepper, to taste
- 3 ounces (85 g) cherry tomatoes

Directions:
1. Cut the fish into 1½-inch chunks, picking out any remaining bones.
2. In a large bowl, whisk together the oil, lemon juice, parsley, and Dijon mustard. Season to taste with salt and pepper. Add the fish and toss to coat the pieces. Cover and marinate the fish chunks in the refrigerator for 30 minutes.
3. Remove the fish from the marinade. Thread the fish and cherry tomatoes on 4 skewers, alternating as you go.
4. Set the air fryer to 400°F (205°C). Place the skewers in the air fryer basket and cook for 3 minutes. Flip the skewers and cook for 3 to 5 minutes longer, until the fish is cooked through and an instant-read thermometer reads 140°F (60°C).

274. Cod with Tomatillos

Preparation Time: 10 minutes
Cooking Time: 15 minutes
Servings: 4

Ingredients:
- 2 oz tomatillos, chopped
- 1-pound (454-g) cod fillet, roughly chopped
- 1 tablespoon avocado oil
- 1 tablespoon lemon juice
- 1 teaspoon keto tomato paste

Directions:
1. Mix avocado oil with lemon juice and tomato paste.
2. Then mix cod fillet with tomato mixture and put in the air fryer.
3. Add lemon juice and tomatillos.
4. Cook the cod at 370F (188°C) for 15 minutes.

275. Tuna Steak

Preparation Time: 10 minutes
Cooking Time: 12 minutes
Servings: 4

Ingredients:
- 1-pound (454-g) tuna steaks, boneless and cubed
- 1 tablespoon mustard
- 1 tablespoon avocado oil
- 1 tablespoon apple cider vinegar

Directions:
1. Mix avocado oil with mustard and apple cider vinegar.
2. Then brush tuna steaks with mustard mixture and put in the air fryer basket.
3. Cook the fish at 360F (182°C) for 6 minutes per side.

276. Air Fried Tofu

Preparation Time: 10 minutes
Cooking Time: 15 minutes
Servings: 4

Ingredients:
- 1 (16-ounce / 454-g) block extra-firm tofu
- 2 tablespoons coconut amino
- 1 tablespoon toasted sesame oil
- 1 tablespoon olive oil
- 1 tablespoon chili-garlic sauce
- 1½ teaspoons black sesame seeds
- 1 scallion, thinly sliced

Directions:
1. Press the tofu for at least 15 minutes by wrapping it in paper towels and setting a heavy pan on top so that the moisture drains.
2. Slice the tofu into bite-size cubes and transfer to a bowl.
Drizzle with the coconut amino, sesame oil, olive oil, and chili-garlic sauce. Cover and refrigerate for 1 hour or up to overnight.
3. Preheat the air fryer to 400°F (205°C).
4. Arrange the tofu in a single layer in the air fryer basket.
Pausing to shake the pan halfway through the cooking time, air fry for 15 minutes until crisp. Serve with any juices that accumulate in the bottom of the air fryer, sprinkled with the sesame seeds and sliced scallion.

277. Air Fried Zucchini Salad

Preparation Time: 5 minutes
Cooking Time: 7 minutes
Servings: 4

Ingredients:
- 2 medium zucchini, thinly sliced
- 5 tablespoons olive oil, divided
- ¼ cup chopped fresh parsley
- 2 tablespoons chopped fresh mint
- Zest and juice of ½ lemon
- 1 clove garlic, minced
- ¼ cup crumbled feta cheese
- Freshly ground black pepper

Directions:
1. Preheat the air fryer to 400°F (205ºC).
2. In a large bowl, toss the zucchini slices with 1 tablespoon of the olive oil.
3. Working in batches if necessary, arrange the zucchini slices in an even layer in the air fryer basket. Pausing halfway through the cooking time to shake the basket, air fry for 5 to 7 minutes until soft and lightly browned on each side.
4. Meanwhile, in a small bowl, combine the remaining 4 tablespoons olive oil, parsley, mint, lemon zest, lemon juice, and garlic.
5. Arrange the zucchini on a plate and drizzle with the dressing.
6. Sprinkle the feta and black pepper on top. Serve warm or at room temperature.

278. Zucchini and Tomato Boats

Preparation Time: 5 minutes
Cooking Time: 10 minutes
Servings: 4

Ingredients:
- 1 large zucchini, ends removed, halved lengthwise
- 6 grape tomatoes, quartered
- ¼ teaspoon salt
- ¼ cup feta cheese
- 1 tablespoon balsamic vinegar
- 1 tablespoon olive oil

Directions:
1. Use a spoon to scoop out 2 tablespoons from center of each zucchini half, making just enough space to fill with tomatoes and feta.
2. Place tomatoes evenly in centers of zucchini halves and sprinkle with salt. Place into ungreased air fryer basket. Adjust the temperature to 350°F (180°C) and set the timer for 10 minutes. When done, zucchini will be tender.
3. Transfer boats to a serving tray and sprinkle with feta, then drizzle with vinegar and olive oil. Serve warm.

279. Roast Chicken Leg

Preparation Time: 15 minutes
Cooking Time: 15 minutes
Servings: 6

Ingredients:
- 2 leeks, sliced
- 2 large-sized tomatoes, chopped
- 3 cloves garlic, minced
- ½ teaspoon dried oregano
- 6 chicken legs, boneless and skinless
- ½ teaspoon smoked cayenne pepper
- 2 tablespoons olive oil
- A freshly ground nutmeg

Directions:
1. In a mixing dish, thoroughly combine all ingredients, minus the leeks. Place in the refrigerator and let it marinate overnight.
2. Lay the leeks onto the bottom of an Air Fryer cooking basket.
Top with the chicken legs.
3. Roast chicken legs at 375°F (190°C) for 15 minutes, turning halfway through. Serve with hoisin sauce.

280. Chicken with Bacon and Tomato

Preparation Time: 15 minutes
Cooking Time: 10 minutes
Servings: 4

Ingredients:
- 4 medium-sized skin-on chicken drumsticks
- 1½ teaspoons herbs de Provence
- Salt and pepper, to taste
- 1 tablespoon rice vinegar
- 2 tablespoons olive oil
- 2 garlic cloves, crushed
- 12 ounces (340 g) crushed canned tomatoes
- 1 small-size leek, thinly sliced
- 2 slices smoked bacon, chopped

Directions:
1. Sprinkle the chicken drumsticks with herbs de Provence, salt and pepper; then, drizzle them with rice vinegar and olive oil.
2. Cook in the baking pan at 360°F (182ºC) for 8 to 10 minutes.
Pause the Air Fryer; stir in the remaining ingredients and continue to cook for 15 minutes longer; make sure to check them periodically. Bon appétit!

281. Air Fried Flank Steak

Preparation Time: 5 minutes
Cooking Time: 10 minutes
Servings: 6

Ingredients:
- ½ cup avocado oil
- ¼ cup coconut amino
- 1 shallot, minced
- 1 tablespoon minced garlic
- 2 tablespoons chopped fresh oregano, or 2 teaspoons dried
- 1½ teaspoons sea salt
- 1 teaspoon freshly ground black pepper
- ¼ teaspoon red pepper flakes
- 2 pounds (907 g) flank steak

Directions:
1. In a blender, combine the avocado oil, coconut amino, shallot, garlic, oregano, salt, black pepper, and red pepper flakes. Process until smooth.

2. Place the steak in a zip-top plastic bag or shallow dish with the marinade. Seal the bag or cover the dish and marinate in the refrigerator for at least 2 hours or overnight.

3. Remove the steak from the bag and discard the marinade.

4. Set the air fryer to 400°F (205°C). Place the steak in the air fryer basket (if needed, cut into sections and work in batches). Cook for 4 to 6 minutes, flip the steak, and cook for another

4 minutes or until the internal temperature reaches 120°F (49°C) in the thickest part for medium-rare (or as desired).

282. Cheesy Filet Mignon

Preparation Time: 15 minutes
Cooking Time: 13 minutes
Servings: 4

Ingredients:
- 1 pound (454 g) filet mignon
- Sea salt and ground black pepper, to taste
- ½ teaspoon cayenne pepper
- 1 teaspoon dried basil
- 1 teaspoon dried rosemary
- 1 teaspoon dried thyme
- 1 tablespoon sesame oil
- 1 small-sized egg, well-whisked
- ½ cup Parmesan cheese, grated

Directions:
1. Season the filet mignon with salt, black pepper, cayenne pepper, basil, rosemary, and thyme. Brush with sesame oil.

2. Put the egg in a shallow plate. Now, place the Parmesan cheese in another plate.

3. Coat the filet mignon with the egg; then, lay it into the Parmesan cheese. Set your Air Fryer to cook at 360°F (182°C).

4. Cook for 10 to 13 minutes or until golden. Serve with mixed salad leaves and enjoy!

283. Cheesy Chicken

Preparation Time: 10 minutes
Cooking Time: 14 minutes
Servings: 4

Ingredients:
- 2 pounds (907 g) boneless, skinless chicken breasts or thighs
- Sea salt
- Freshly ground black pepper
- 8 ounces (227 g) cream cheese, at room temperature
- 4 ounces (113 g) Cheddar cheese, shredded
- 2 jalapeños, seeded and diced
- 1 teaspoon minced garlic
- Avocado oil spray

Directions:
1. Place the chicken in a large zip-top bag or between two pieces of plastic wrap. Using a meat mallet or heavy skillet, pound the chicken until it is about ¼-inch thick. Season both sides of the chicken with salt and pepper.

2. In a medium bowl, combine the cream cheese, Cheddar cheese, jalapeños, and garlic. Divide the mixture among the chicken pieces. Roll up each piece from the long side, tucking in the ends as you go. Secure with toothpicks.

3. Set the air fryer to 350°F (180°C). Spray the outside of the chicken with oil. Place the chicken in a single layer in the air fryer basket, working in batches if necessary, and cook for 7 minutes. Flip the chicken and cook for another 7 minutes, until an instant-read thermometer reads 160°F (71°C).

284. Kohlrabi Fries

Preparation Time: 10 minutes
Cooking Time: 15 minutes
Servings: 4

Ingredients:
- 2 pounds (907 g) kohlrabi, peeled and cut into ¼–½-inch fries
- 2 tablespoons olive oil
- Salt and freshly ground black pepper

Directions:
1. Preheat the air fryer to 400°F (205°C).

2. In a large bowl, combine the kohlrabi and olive oil. Season to taste with salt and black pepper. Toss gently until thoroughly coated.

3. Working in batches if necessary, spread the kohlrabi in a single layer in the air fryer basket. Pausing halfway through the cooking time to shake the basket, air fry for 15 minutes until the fries are lightly browned and crunchy.

285. Steak with Butter

Preparation Time: 5 minutes Cooking Time: 10 minutes Servings: 6

Ingredients:
- ½ cup olive oil
- 2 tablespoons minced garlic
- Sea salt, black pepper to taste
- 1½ pounds (680g) New York strip or top sirloin steak
- Unsalted butter, for serving (optional)

Directions:
1. In a bowl or blender, combine the olive oil, garlic, and salt and pepper to taste.
2. Place the steak in a shallow bowl or zip-top bag. Pour the marinade over the meat, seal, and marinate in the refrigerator for at least 1 hour and up to 24 hours.
3. Place a grill pan or basket in the air fryer, set it to 400°F (205°C), and let preheat for 5 minutes.
4. Place the steak on the grill pan in a single layer, working in batches if necessary, and cook for 5 minutes. Flip the steak and cook for another 5 minutes, until an instant-read thermometer reads 120°F (49°C) for medium-rare (or cook to your desired doneness).
5. Transfer the steak to a plate, and let rest for 10 minutes before serving. If desired, top the steaks with a pat of butter while they rest.

286. Olive Muffuletta

Preparation Time: 10 minutes
Cooking Time: 6 minutes
Servings: 8

Ingredients:
- ¼ pound (113 g) thinly sliced deli ham
- ¼ pound (113 g) thinly sliced pastrami
- 4 ounces (113 g) low-fat Mozzarella cheese, grated
- 8 slider buns, split in half
- Cooking spray
- 1 tablespoon sesame seeds

Olive Mix:
- ½ cup sliced green olives with pimentos
- ¼ cup sliced black olives
- ¼ cup chopped kalamata olives
- 1 teaspoon red wine vinegar
- ¼ teaspoon basil
- ⅛ teaspoon garlic powder

Directions:
1. Combine all the ingredients for the olive mix in a small bowl and stir well.
2. Stir together the ham, pastrami, and cheese in a medium bowl and divide the mixture into 8 equal portions.
3. Assemble the sliders: Top each bottom bun with 1 portion of meat and cheese, 2 tablespoons of olive mix, finished by the remaining buns. Lightly spritz the tops with cooking spray. Scatter the sesame seeds on top.
4. Arrange the sliders on the air flow racks.
5. Slide the racks into the air fryer oven. Press the Power Button and cook at 360°F (182°C) for 6 minutes.
6. When cooking is complete, the cheese should be melted.
Remove the racks from the air fryer oven and serve.

287. Pepperoni Pizza Bites

Preparation Time: 5 minutes
Cooking Time: 12 minutes
Servings: 8

Ingredients:
- 1 cup finely shredded Mozzarella cheese
- ½ cup chopped pepperoni
- ¼ cup Marinara sauce
- 1 (8-ounce / 227-g) can crescent roll dough
- All-purpose flour, for dusting

Directions:
1. In a small bowl, stir together the cheese, pepperoni and
Marinara sauce.
2. Lay the dough on a lightly floured work surface. Separate it into 4 rectangles. Firmly pinch the perforations together and pat the dough pieces flat.
3. Divide the cheese mixture evenly between the rectangles and spread it out over the dough, leaving a ¼-inch border. Roll a rectangle up tightly, starting with the short end. Pinch the edge down to seal the roll. Repeat with the remaining rolls.
4. Slice the rolls into 4 or 5 even slices. Put the slices on a sheet pan, leaving a few inches between each slice.
5. Slide the pan into the air fryer oven. Press the Power Button and cook at 350°F (180°C) for 12 minutes.
6. After 6 minutes, rotate the pan and continue cooking.
7. When cooking is complete, the rolls will be golden brown with crisp edges. Remove from the air fryer oven. Serve hot.

288. Roasted Yogurt Grapes

Preparation Time: 5 minutes
Cooking Time: 10 minutes
Servings: 6

Ingredients:
- 2 cups seedless red grapes, rinsed and patted dry
- 1 tablespoon apple cider vinegar
- 1 tablespoon honey
- 1 cup low-fat Greek yogurt
- 2 tablespoons 2 percent milk
- 2 tablespoons minced fresh basil

Directions:
1. Spread the red grapes on the air flow racks and drizzle with the cider vinegar and honey. Lightly toss to coat.

2. Slide the racks into the air fryer oven. Press the Power Button and cook at 380°F (193°C) for 10 minutes.

3. When cooking is complete, the grapes will be wilted but still soft. Remove from the air fryer oven.

4. In a medium bowl, whisk together the yogurt and milk.

Gently fold in the grapes and basil.

5. Serve immediately.

289. Sausage and Cheese Balls

Preparation Time: 10 minutes
Cooking Time: 10 minutes
Servings: 8

Ingredients:
- 12 ounces (340 g) mild ground sausage
- 1½ cups baking mix
- 1 cup shredded mild Cheddar cheese
- 3 ounces (85 g) cream cheese, at room temperature
- 1 to 2 tablespoons olive oil

Directions:
1. Line the air flow racks with parchment paper. Set aside.

2. Mix the ground sausage, baking mix, Cheddar cheese, and cream cheese in a large bowl and stir to incorporate.

3. Divide the sausage mixture into 16 equal portions and roll them into 1-inch balls with your hands. Arrange the sausage balls on the parchment, leaving space between each ball. Brush the sausage balls with the olive oil.

4. Slide the racks into the air fryer oven. Press the Power Button and cook at 325°F (163°C) for 10 minutes.

5. Flip the balls halfway through the cooking time.

6. When cooking is complete, the balls should be firm and lightly browned on both sides. Remove from the air fryer oven to a plate and serve warm.

290. Lemon-Honey Pears

Preparation Time: 10 minutes
Cooking Time: 10 minutes
Servings: 8

Ingredients:
- 2 large Bartlett pears, peeled, cut in half, cored
- 3 tablespoons melted butter
- ½ teaspoon ground ginger
- ¼ teaspoon ground cardamom
- 3 tablespoons brown sugar
- ½ cup whole-milk ricotta cheese
- 1 teaspoon pure lemon extract
- 1 teaspoon pure almond extract
- 1 tablespoon honey, plus additional for drizzling

Directions:
1. Toss the pears with butter, ginger, cardamom, and sugar in a large bowl. Toss to coat well. Arrange the pears in a baking pan, cut side down.

2. Slide the pan into the air fryer oven. Press the Power Button and cook at 375°F (190°C) for 8 minutes.

3. After 5 minutes, remove the pan and flip the pears. Return to the air fryer oven and continue cooking.

4. When cooking is complete, the pears should be soft and browned. Remove from the air fryer oven.

5. In the meantime, combine the remaining ingredients in a separate bowl. Whip for 1 minute with a hand mixer until the mixture is puffed.

6. Divide the mixture into four bowls, then put the pears over the mixture and drizzle with more honey to serve.

291. Corn on the Cob

Preparation Time: 10 minutes
Cooking Time: 10 minutes
Servings: 8

Ingredients:
- 2 tablespoons mayonnaise
- 2 teaspoons minced garlic
- ½ teaspoon sea salt
- 1 cup panko bread crumbs
- 4 (4-inch length) ears corn on the cob, husk and silk removed
- Cooking spray

Directions:
1. Spritz the air flow racks with cooking spray.

2. Combine the mayonnaise, garlic, and salt in a bowl. Stir to mix well. Pour the panko on a plate.

3. Brush the corn on the cob with mayonnaise mixture, then roll the cob in the bread crumbs and press to coat well.

4. Transfer the corn on the cob on the air flow racks and spritz with cooking spray.

5. Slide the racks into the air fryer oven. Press the Power Button and cook at 400°F (205°C) for 10 minutes.

6. Flip the corn on the cob at least three times during the cooking.

7. When cooked, the corn kernels on the cob should be almost browned. Remove from the air fryer oven.

8. Serve immediately.

292. Fried Edamame

Preparation Time: 5 minutes
Cooking Time: 7 minutes
Servings: 6

Ingredients:
- 1½ pounds (680 g) unshelled edamame
- 2 tablespoons olive oil
- 1 teaspoon sea salt

Directions:
1. Put the edamame in a large bowl, then drizzle with olive oil.

Toss to coat well. Transfer the edamame to the air flow racks.

2. Slide the racks into the air fryer oven. Press the Power Button and cook at 400°F (205°C) for 7 minutes.

3. Stir the edamame at least three times during cooking.

4. When done, the edamame will be tender and warmed through.

5. Transfer the cooked edamame onto a plate and sprinkle with salt. Toss to combine well and set aside for 3 minutes to infuse before serving.

293. Chili Okra

Preparation Time: 5 minutes
Cooking Time: 7 minutes
Servings: 6

Ingredients:
- 3 tablespoons sour cream
- 2 tablespoons flour
- 2 tablespoons semolina
- ½ teaspoon red chili powder
- Salt and black pepper, to taste
- 1 pound (454 g) okra, halved
- Cooking spray

Directions:
1. Spray the air flow racks with cooking spray. Set aside.

2. In a shallow bowl, place the sour cream. In another shallow bowl, thoroughly combine the flour, semolina, red chili powder, salt, and pepper.

3. Dredge the okra in the sour cream, then roll in the flour mixture until evenly coated. Transfer the okra

to the air flow racks.

4. Slide the racks into the air fryer oven. Press the Power Button and cook at 400°F (205°C) for 10 minutes.

5. Flip the okra halfway through the cooking time.

6. When cooking is complete, the okra should be golden brown and crispy. Remove from the air fryer oven. Cool for 5 minutes before serving.

294. Crunchy Eggplant Slices

Preparation Time: 5 minutes
Cooking Time: 7 minutes
Servings: 6

Ingredients:
- 1 cup all-purpose flour
- 4 eggs
- Salt, to taste
- 2 cups bread crumbs
- 1 teaspoon Italian seasoning
- 2 medium eggplants, sliced
- 2 garlic cloves, sliced
- 2 tablespoons chopped parsley
- Cooking spray

Directions:
1. Spritz the air flow racks with cooking spray. Set aside.

2. On a plate, place the flour. In a shallow bowl, whisk the eggs with salt. In another shallow bowl, combine the bread crumbs and Italian seasoning.

3. Dredge the eggplant slices, one at a time, in the flour, then in the whisked eggs, finally in the bread crumb mixture to coat well.

4. Lay the coated eggplant slices on the air flow racks.

5. Slide the racks into the air fryer oven. Press the Power Button and cook at 390°F (199°C) for 12 minutes.

6. Flip the eggplant slices halfway through the cooking time.

7. When cooking is complete, the eggplant slices should be golden brown and crispy. Transfer the eggplant slices to a

plate and sprinkle the garlic and parsley on top before serving.

295. Parmesan Salmon Patties

Preparation Time: 10 minutes
Cooking Time: 13 minutes
Servings: 4

Ingredients:
- 1 pound (454 g) salmon, chopped into ½-inch pieces
- 2 tablespoons coconut flour
- 2 tablespoons grated Parmesan cheese

- 1½ tablespoons milk
- ½ white onion, peeled and finely chopped
- ½ teaspoon butter, at room temperature
- ½ teaspoon chipotle powder
- ½ teaspoon dried parsley flakes
- ⅓ teaspoon ground black pepper
- ⅓ teaspoon smoked cayenne pepper
- 1 teaspoon fine sea salt

Directions:
1. Put all the ingredients for the salmon patties in a bowl and stir to combine well.
2. Scoop out 2 tablespoons of the salmon mixture and shape into a patty with your palm, about ½ inch thick. Repeat until all the mixture is used. Transfer to the refrigerator for about 2 hours until firm.
3. When ready, arrange the salmon patties on the air flow racks.
4. Slide the racks into the air fryer oven. Press the Power Button and cook at 395ºF (202ºC) for 13 minutes.
5. Flip the patties halfway through the cooking time.
6. When cooking is complete, the patties should be golden brown. Remove from the air fryer oven and cool for 5 minutes before serving.

297. Crisp Pork Chops

Preparation Time: 10 minutes
Cooking Time: 12 minutes
Servings: 2

Ingredients:
- Half lbs. pork chops, boneless
- One teaspoon of paprika
- One teaspoon of creole seasoning
- One teaspoon of garlic powder
- A quarter cup of grated parmesan cheese
- 1/3 cup of almond flour

Directors:
1. Preheat the air fryer to 360 F.
2. Add all ingredients except pork chops in a zip-lock bag.
3. Add pork chops to the bag. Seal bag and shake well to coat pork chops.
4. Remove pork chops from the zip-lock bag and place them in the air fryer basket.
5. Cook pork chops for 10-12 minutes.
6. Serve and enjoy.

296. Sheet Pan Shakshuka

Preparation Time: 10 minutes
Cooking Time: 13 minutes
Servings: 4

Ingredients
- Two large eggs
- One chopped Anaheim chili
- One tablespoon of vegetable oil
- Half cup of chopped onion
- One teaspoon of ground cumin
- Two minced garlic cloves
- Half cup of feta cheese
- Half teaspoon of paprika
- Half of the tomatoes
- Salt and pepper

Directions:
1. Sauté the chili and onions in oil until tender.
2. Pour in the remaining ingredients apart from eggs and cook until thick.
3. Make two pockets to pour in the eggs.
4. Bake for 10 minutes at 191C or 375F in the Air Fryer Grill.
5. Top it off with feta.

298. Crispy Chicken Breast

Preparation Time: 10 minutes
Cooking Time: 30 minutes
Servings: 2

Ingredients:
- Two chicken breasts, skinless and boneless
- Four eggs
- Two cups of buttermilk
- Two cups of all-purpose flour
- Two cups of yellow cornmeal
- One ounce of applewood smoked salt
- One ounce of. old bay seasoning
- One tablespoon of ground black pepper
- Cooking spray

Director:
1. Merge the wet ingredients in a mixing bowl, and then combine the dry ingredients in a separate bowl.
2. Place the pizza rack on position 2 in your Air Fryer.
3. Dip each chicken breast in the wet mixture, then in the dry mixture. Spray the chicken with cooking spray and place them on the crisper tray.
4. Place the crisper tray on a level higher than the pizza rack.
Select the bake setting. Set the temperature at 425F for 30 minutes. Press the start button.
5. Check the meat when cooking is complete. The meat should at least have an internal temperature of 165F.
6. Serve and enjoy.

299. Crispy Fish Sticks

Preparation Time: 10 minutes
Cooking Time: 10 minutes
Servings: 2

Ingredients:
- Half lb. of white fish, cut into pieces
- 3/4 teaspoon of Cajun seasoning
- Half cup of crushed pork rind
- Two tablespoons of water
- Two tablespoons of Dijon mustard
- A quarter cup of mayonnaise
- Pepper
- Salt

Directions:
1. Spray air fryer basket with cooking spray.
2. In a small bowl, merge together mayonnaise, water, and mustard.
3. In a shallow bowl, merge together pork rind, pepper, Cajun seasoning, and salt.
4. Dip fish pieces in mayo mixture and coat with pork rind mixture, and place in the air fryer basket.
5. Cook at 400 F for 5 minutes. Turn fish sticks to another side and cook for 5 minutes more.
6. Serve and enjoy.

300. Meatloaf Sliders

Preparation Time: 10 minutes
Cooking Time: 15 minutes
Servings: 2

Ingredients:
- Half lb. of ground beef
- Half teaspoon of dried tarragon
- One teaspoon of Italian seasoning
- One tablespoon of Worcestershire sauce
- A quarter cup of ketchup
- A quarter cup of coconut flour
- Half cup of almond flour
- One minced clove of garlic
- A quarter cup of chopped onion
- Two lightly beaten eggs
- A quarter teaspoon of pepper
- Half teaspoon of sea salt

Directions:
1. Set all ingredients into the mixing bowl and mix until well combined.
2. Make the equal shape of patties from the mixture and place them on a plate. Place in refrigerator for 10 minutes.
3. Spray air fryer basket with cooking spray.
4. Preheat the air fryer to 360 F.
5. Place prepared patties in an air fryer basket and cook for 10 minutes.
6. Serve and enjoy.

301. Pesto Fish

Preparation Time: 10 minutes
Cooking Time: 15 minutes
Servings: 2

Ingredients:
- One tablespoon of olive oil
- Two fish fillets
- Salt and pepper to taste
- One cup of olive oil
- Two cloves of garlic
- Half cup of fresh basil leaves
- Two tablespoons of grated Parmesan cheese
- Two tablespoons of pine nuts

Directions:
1. Set olive oil over fish fillets and season with salt and pepper.
2. Add remaining ingredients to a food processor.
3. Pulse until smooth.
4. Bring pesto to a bowl and set it aside.
5. Add fish to the air fryer.
6. Select grill setting.
7. Cook at 320 degrees F for 5 minutes per side.
8. Spread pesto on top of the fish before serving.

302. Pork with Mushrooms

Preparation Time: 10 minutes
Cooking Time: 15 minutes
Servings: 2

Ingredients:
- Half lb. of rinsed and pat dry pork chops
- Half teaspoon of garlic powder
- One teaspoon of soy sauce
- Two tablespoons of melted butter
- Four ounces of halved mushrooms
- Pepper
- Salt

Directions:
1. Preheat the air fryer to 400 F.
2. Cut pork chops into the 3/4-inch cubes and place them in a large mixing bowl.
3. Add remaining ingredients into the bowl and toss well.
4. Transfer pork and mushroom mixture into the air fryer basket and cook for 15 minutes. Shake basket halfway through.
5. Serve and enjoy.

92

303. Spicy Shrimp

Preparation Time: 10 minutes
Cooking Time: 15 minutes
Servings: 2

Ingredients:
- Half lb. of peeled and deveined shrimp
- Half teaspoon of old bay seasoning
- One teaspoon of cayenne pepper
- One tablespoon of olive oil
- A quarter teaspoon of paprika
- 1/8 teaspoon of salt

Directions:
1. Preheat the air fryer to 390 F.
2. Add all ingredients into the bowl and toss well.
3. Transfer shrimp into the air fryer basket and cook for 6 minutes.
4. Serve and enjoy.

304. Squash Fritters

Preparation Time: 10 minutes Cooking Time: 8 minutes Servings: 2

Ingredients:
- One and a half ounces of cream cheese
- One whisked egg
- Half teaspoon of dried oregano
- A pinch of salt and black pepper
- One grated yellow summer squash
- 1/3 cup of grated carrot
- 2/3 cup of bread crumbs
- Two tablespoons of olive oil

Directions:
1. In a bowl, mix cream cheese with salt, pepper, oregano, egg, breadcrumbs, carrot and squash and stir well.
2. Shape medium patties out of this mix and brush them with the oil.
3. Place squash patties in your air fryer and cook them at 400 degrees F for 7 minutes.
4. Serve them for lunch.
5. Enjoy!

305. Turkish Koftas

Preparation Time: 10 minutes
Cooking Time: 15 minutes
Servings: 2

Ingredients:
- One chopped leek
- Two tablespoons of crumbled feta cheese
- Half pound lean minced beef
- One tablespoon of ground cumin
- One tablespoon of chopped mint
- One tablespoon of chopped parsley
- One teaspoon of minced garlic
- Salt and black pepper to the taste

Directions:
1. In a bowl, mix beef with
2. leek, cheese, cumin, mint, parsley, garlic, salt and pepper, stir well, shape your koftas and place them on sticks.
3. Add koftas to your preheated air fryer at 360 degrees F and cook them for 15 minutes.
4. Serve them with a side salad for lunch.
5. Enjoy.

306. Yummy Kabab

Preparation Time: 10 minutes
Cooking Time: 15 minutes
Servings: 2

Ingredients:
- One lb. of ground beef
- A quarter cup of chopped fresh parsley
- One tablespoon of olive oil
- Two tablespoons of kabab spice mix
- One tablespoon of minced garlic
- One teaspoon of salt

Directions:
1. Set all ingredients into the bowl and merge until combined. Place in the fridge for 60 minutes.
2. Divide the meat mixture into four sections and wrap around four soaked wooden skewers.
3. Spray air fryer basket with cooking spray.
4. Place kabab into the air fryer and cook at 370 F for 10 minutes.
5. Serve and enjoy.

307. Quick Paella

Preparation Time: 10 minutes
Cooking Time: 18 minutes
Servings: 2

Ingredients:
- One (Ten-ounce) package of thawed frozen cooked rice
- One (Six-ounce) jar of drained and chopped artichoke hearts
- A quarter cup of vegetable broth
- Half teaspoon of turmeric
- Half teaspoon of dried thyme
- One cup of frozen cooked small shrimp
- Half cup of frozen baby peas
- One diced tomato

Directions:
1. In a 6-by-6-by-2-inch pan, combine the rice, artichoke hearts, vegetable broth, turmeric, and

thyme, and stir gently.

2. Set in the air fryer and bake for 8 to 9 minutes or until the rice is hot.

3. Remove from the air fryer and gently stir in the shrimp, peas, and tomato. Cook for 5 to 8 minutes or until the shrimp and peas are hot and the paella is bubbling.

4. Substitution tip: If you like intensely flavored food, try using marinated artichoke hearts in this recipe. Be sure you taste the marinade first! For even more flavor, use the liquid in the jar of artichokes in place of the vegetable broth.

308. Salmon and Avocado Salsa

Preparation Time: 10 minutes
Cooking Time: 18 minutes
Servings: 2

Ingredients:
• Two to four salmon fillets
• One tablespoon of olive oil
• Salt and black pepper to the taste
• One teaspoon of ground cumin
• One teaspoon of sweet paprika
• Half teaspoon of chili powder
• One teaspoon of garlic powder

For the salsa:
• One chopped small red onion
• One pitted, peeled and chopped avocado
• Two tablespoons of chopped cilantro
• Juice from two limes
• Salt and black pepper to the taste

Directions:
1. In a bowl, mix salt, pepper, chili powder, onion powder, paprika and cumin, stir, rub salmon with this mix, drizzle the oil, rub again, transfer to your air fryer and cook at 350 degrees F for 5 minutes on each side.

2. Meanwhile, in a bowl, mix avocado with red onion, salt, pepper, cilantro and lime juice and stir.

3. Divide fillets on plates, top with avocado salsa and serve.

309. Seafood Tacos

Preparation Time: 15 minutes
Cooking Time: 12 minutes
Servings: 2

Ingredients:
• One pound of white fish fillets, such as snapper
• One tablespoon of olive oil
• Three tablespoons of lemon juice, divided
• One and a half cups of chopped red cabbage
• Half cup of salsa

• 1/3 cup of sour cream
• Four to six soft flour tortillas
• Two peeled and chopped avocados

Directions:
1. Brush the fish with olive oil and sprinkle with One tablespoon of lemon juice. Place in the air fryer basket and air-fry for 9 to 12 minutes or until the fish just flakes when tested with a fork.

2. Meanwhile, combine the remaining two tablespoons of lemon juice, cabbage, salsa, and sour cream in a medium bowl.

3. When the fish is cooked, remove it from the air fryer basket and break it into large pieces.

4. Let everyone assemble their own taco combining the fish, tortillas, cabbage mixture, and avocados.

310. Tabasco Shrimp

Preparation Time: 10 minutes
Cooking Time: 10 minutes
Servings: 2

Ingredients:
• One pound of peeled and deveined shrimp
• One teaspoon of red pepper flakes
• Two tablespoons of olive oil
• One teaspoon of Tabasco sauce
• Two tablespoons of water
• One teaspoon of dried oregano
• Salt and black pepper to the taste
• Half teaspoon of dried parsley
• Half teaspoon of smoked paprika

Directions:
1. In a bowl, mix oil with water, Tabasco sauce, pepper flakes, oregano, parsley, salt, pepper, paprika and shrimp and toss well to coat.

2. Transfer shrimp to your preheated air fryer at 370 degrees F and cook for 10 minutes, shaking the fryer once.

3. Divide shrimp on plates and serve with a side salad.

311. Thai Shrimp

Preparation Time: 10 minutes
Cooking Time: 10 minutes
Servings: 2

Ingredients:
• One lb. of peeled and deveined shrimp
• One teaspoon of toasted sesame seeds
• Two minced cloves of garlic
• Two tablespoons of soy sauce
• Two tablespoons of Thai chili sauce

- One tablespoon of arrowroot powder
- One tablespoon of sliced green onion
- 1/8 teaspoon of minced ginger

Directions:
1. Spray air fryer basket with cooking spray.
2. Toss shrimp with arrowroot powder and place them into the air fryer basket.
3. Cook shrimp at 350 degrees F for 5 minutes. Shake basket well and cook for 5 minutes more.
4. Meanwhile, in a bowl, mix together soy sauce, ginger, garlic, and chili sauce.
5. Add shrimp to the bowl and toss well.
6. Garnish with green onions and sesame seeds.
7. Serve and enjoy.

312: Sweet & Spicy Mussels

Preparation Time: 10 minutes
Cooking Time: 7 minutes
Servings: 2

Ingredients:
- 2 pounds Blue Mussels
- 2 teaspoons Granulated Sugar
- 1/4 cup Mayonnaise
- 2 tablespoons chopped Fresh Scallion
- 1 Persian Lime juice
- 2 tablespoons Sweet Chili Sauce

Directions:
1. Wash the mussels in cold water.
2. Combine all the ingredients in a medium mixing bowl.
3. Then add half of the sauce over the mussels.
4. Place the mussels in the air fryer basket.
5. Cook the mussels for 5–7 minutes at 390°Fahrenheit.
6. Cook until mussels are opened.
7. Remove the mussels from the shells.
8. Serve the mussels with sauce and enjoy.

313. Clams In The Air Fryer

Preparation Time: 10 minutes
Cooking Time: 10 minutes
Servings: 2

Ingredients:
- 1 cup bread crumb
- salt and black pepper, to taste
- ½ cup mozzarella
- cup parsley
- ½ teaspoon of lemon zest
- 6 tablespoons of butter
- 2 garlic cloves
- 1 dozen clams
- 1 lemon, wedges

Directions:
2. Take a mixing bowl and add cheese, breadcrumbs, lemon zest, garlic, parsley, and melted butter.
3. Mix the ingredients well and put the mixture on the clams in a large bowl.
4. Add salt and black pepper to taste
5. Cook the clams in the air fryer basket for 5 minutes at 400 degrees Fahrenheit.
6. Once the clams are cooked, serve with lemon slices.

314. Coconut Cod Fillets

Preparation Time: 10 minutes
Cooking Time: 12 minutes
Servings: 2

Ingredients:
- 1 pound of codfish fillet
- 1 cup of coconut milk
- ¼ teaspoon of smoked paprika
- Salt and black pepper

Directions:
1. Preheat the Air Fryer Air fryer for 5 minutes to 375 degrees Fahrenheit.
2. Prepare the mixture by combining salt, black pepper, coconut milk, and paprika.
3. Marinate the fish for 2-3 hours.
4. Then bake the fish for 12 minutes at 375 degrees F, in an air fryer.
5. Serve hot coconut codfish and enjoy.

315. Prawns Snack

Preparation Time: 15 minutes
Cooking Time: 6 minutes
Servings: 2

Ingredients:
- 12 Fresh king prawns
- 1 tablespoon wine vinegar
- 4 tablespoons mayonnaise
- 1 teaspoon ketchup
- 1 teaspoon chili flakes
- Salt and black pepper, to taste
- ½ teaspoon chili powder

Direction:
1. Preheat the Air Fryer air fryer for 2-3 minutes to 320 degrees Fahrenheit.
2. Combine all the spices and add prawns to the mixing bowl.
3. Place the prawns into the basket of Air Fryer.
4. Cook the prawns for 6 minutes.
5. Serve and enjoy.

316. Masala Fish

Preparation Time: 15 minutes
Cooking Time: 6 minutes
Servings: 2

Ingredients:
- 2 pounds white fish fillets
- 4 tablespoons extra virgin olive oil
- 3/4 teaspoon turmeric
- 1 teaspoon cayenne pepper
- 1 teaspoon salt
- 1 tablespoon Fenugreek leaves
- 1 and 1/2 teaspoon freshly ground cumin
- 2 teaspoons amchoor powder
- 2 tablespoons ground almonds

To garnish
- Extra lemon juice
- Chopped coriander leaves
- Sliced almonds

Directions:
1. Take a mixing bowl and add oil, turmeric, cayenne, salt, fenugreek leaves, cumin, and amchoor powder.
2. Combine the grounded almonds in a separate bowl.
3. Put the fish in the spicy Masala, then keep aside for 15 to 20 minutes.
4. Then dip the fish in the almond flour.
5. Arrange the fish in the air fryer basket.
6. Cook the fish for 12 minutes at 450 degrees.
7. Serve the fish with lemon juice, chopped cilantro, and sliced almonds on top.
8. Spicy fish is now ready to serve.

317. SWAI Fish

Preparation Time: 15 minutes
Cooking Time: 15 minutes
Servings: 2

Ingredients:
- 24 ounces SWAI fillets
- 1 teaspoon olive oil
- Blackened seasoning to taste

Directions:
1. Preheat the Air Fryer to 390°Fahrenheit.
2. Coat the air fryer basket by using olive oil spray/ nonstick cooking spray/ parchment paper.
3. Brush both sides of the fish fillets with olive oil.
4. Season the fish with the blackened seasoning on both sides.
5. Cook for 10 minutes in the air fryer basket by then flipping back and forth.
6. Serve the fish with a side dish of your choice.

318. Divine Salmon

Preparation Time: 15 minutes
Cooking Time: 15 minutes
Servings: 2

Ingredients:
- 20 ounces of salmon fillets, 2 pieces
- 4 cloves of garlic, minced
- ½ tablespoon ginger, grated
- ½ tablespoon brown sugar
- 4 teaspoons sesame seeds
- 1/3 cup tamari
- 1/3 cup water
- 1/3 cup dry sherry
- 4 tablespoons sesame oil

Directions:
1. Take a bowl and mix the tamari sauce, garlic, water, sesame oil, dry sherry, sesame seeds, ginger, and brown sugar.
2. Mix until the ingredients get dissolved in the bowl.
3. Marinate the fish in this mixture for 30 minutes.
4. Using aluminum foil, cover the baking tray.
5. Place the fish fillet in the baking tray.
6. Cover the fish with aluminum foil.
7. In the air fryer, cook the fish at 390 degrees for 5 minutes by selecting air fry mode.
8. Flip the fish halfway through to ensure even cooking.
9. Remove the aluminum foil and bake it for 4 more minutes.
10. Salmon is ready to serve and enjoy.

319. Seafood, Shrimp Omelet

Preparation Time: 15 minutes
Cooking Time: 15 minutes
Servings: 1

Ingredients:
- 6 large shrimp
- 6 eggs
- ½ tablespoon melted butter
- 2 tablespoon sliced green onions
- 1/3 cup of mushrooms, chopped
- 1 pinch paprika
- Salt and black pepper
- Oil spray for greasing

Directions:
1. Take a large bowl, add eggs, chopped shrimp, butter, green onions, mushrooms, paprika, salt, black pepper, and mix.
2. Spray oil on the Grease the cake pan using oil spray.
3. Keep the cake pan in the air fryer basket and pour the egg mixture into it.
4. Bake the shrimp for 15 minutes at 320 degrees

Fahrenheit in the air fryer.

5. Repeat the same process for the remaining shrimp.

6. Once the cooking is done, serve the shrimp and enjoy.

320. Swordfish With Herb Vinaigrette

Preparation Time: 15 minutes
Cooking Time: 15 minutes
Servings: 2

Ingredients:
- ½ cup parsley leaves
- 1 cup basil leaves
- ½ cup mint leaves
- 2 tablespoons thyme leaves
- 1/4 teaspoon red pepper flakes
- 2 cloves of garlic
- 4 tablespoons of red wine vinegar
- ¼ cup of olive oil
- Required salt
- 1.5 pounds codfish fillets
- 2 tablespoons olive oil
- Salt and black pepper
- 1 teaspoon of paprika
- 1 teasbpoon of Italian seasoning

Directions:
1. Add all the dressing ingredients to the food processor and pulse until a creamy consistency is formed. And transfer it to a bowl.

2. Season the swordfish fillet with salt, oil, paprika, Italian spice, pepper, and baste it with mixed sauce.

3. Place the fillets on a foiled-lined basket of the air fryer.

4. Set the timer to 15 minutes at 390 degrees Fahrenheit, by pressing the fish button.

5. Once cooked, serve with the remaining mixed vinaigrette.

321. Pesto Salmon

Preparation Time: 15 minutes
Cooking Time: 15 minutes
Servings: 2

Ingredients:
- 2 salmon fillets
- Salt and black pepper
- 1 tablespoon of melted butter
- 1 cup mayonnaise
- 1 teaspoon of pesto
- 6 tablespoons Greek yogurt
- Salt and black pepper, to taste

Directions:
1. Brush the salmon with butter and season the salmon with salt and pepper.

2. Combine mayonnaise, pesto, Greek yogurt, salt, and black pepper in a bowl and set aside.

3. Arrange the fish fillets inside the basket of the air fryer.

4. Cook the salmon for 10 minutes at 390 degrees Fahrenheit.

5. Flip the salmon and continue cooking.

6. Serve the salmon with the pesto sauce.

322. Bread Pizza

Preparation Time: 15 minutes
Cooking Time: 5 minutes
Servings: 2

Ingredients:
- 1 loaf French
- Any pizza sauce
- Shredded mozzarella cheese
- Crumbled cooked sausage or ground beef
- Diced bell peppers, red onion, mushrooms
- Pizza toppings of the choice
- Italian seasonings optional

Directions:
1. Cut the French bread into slices.

2. Keep the slices in the air fryer basket, and then spread with pizza sauce.

3. Add toppings to the pizza sauce with cheese, meat, and vegetables, along with the preferred pizza toppings.

4. Keep the pizzas in the air fryer for 4-5 minutes at 350 degrees Fahrenheit 170 degrees

323. Mozzarella Pizza

Preparation Time: 15 minutes
Cooking Time: 7 minutes
Servings: 2

Ingredients:
- 4 slices of Buffalo mozzarella
- 1 can of Pizza dough
- 2 teaspoons of Olive oil
- 4 tablespoons Tomato sauce
- others:
- Fresh basil, parmesan cheese, pepper flakes

Directions:
1. Preheat the air fryer to 400 degrees or 204 degrees C.

2. Grease the air fryer basket with oil.

3. Roll out pizza dough and arrange it in the air fryer basket.
Then spray with olive oil.

4. Spread the tomato sauce over the pizza and add toppings with buffalo mozzarella.

5. Bake for about 5-7 minutes until the cheese starts melting.

6. You can add pizza toppings with basil, grated parmesan, and pepper flakes.

7. Serve the crispy pizza and enjoy.

324. Indian Bread

Preparation Time: 15 minutes
Cooking Time: 6 minutes
Servings: 2

Ingredients:
- 1 1/2 cups warm water
- 1 tablespoon sugar
- 2 teaspoons active dry yeast
- pinch of salt
- 3 cups flour

Directions:
1. Take a bowl and add warm water, sugar, and yeast and mix it well until it gets foamy.
2. Then add salt and flour to the mixture.
3. Prepare the dough and knead well until it gets tight.
4. Cover the dough with a towel and let it sit for 45 minutes.
5. Make 8 balls from the dough.
6. Roll the dough, spray olive oil, and cook in the air fryer for 8 minutes at 204 degrees C or 400 degrees F.
7. Serve.

325. Air Fryer Bread Low Carb

Preparation Time: 15 minutes
Cooking Time: 12 minutes
Servings: 2

Ingredients:
- 1 1/2 cups warm water
- 1 tablespoon sugar
- 2 teaspoons active dry yeast
- pinch of salt
- 3 cups flour

Directions:
1. Combine the dry ingredients in a bowl.
2. And mix the wet ingredients in a separate bowl.
3. Next, combine the ingredients of both bowls.
4. Using the hands, make the mixture into a bun or bagel.
5. Bake the bun in the air fryer for 6 minutes at 350 degrees F or
170 degrees C
6. Then flip the bun and bake for another 6 to 8 minutes
7. Once the bun becomes golden brown, serve and enjoy.

326. Classic Bread

Preparation Time: 15 minutes
Cooking Time: 10 minutes
Servings: 2

Ingredients:
- 2 tablespoons melted unsalted butter
- 1.5 teaspoons sugar
- 1.5 teaspoons active dry yeast
- 1.5 teaspoons kosher salt
- cups all-purpose flour
- 1 tablespoon of butter, for greasing

Directions:
1. Grease the pan with the butter
2. Add the butter, yeast, sugar, salt, flour, and 1 cup of warm water to the dough maker.
3. Knead on slow to medium speed for 8-10 minutes.
4. Take the prepared dough and let it sit for 1 hour to double in size.
5. Place the pan with the dough in the air fryer and set it to 380 degrees F or 170 degrees

328. Pork Momos

Preparation Time: 12 minutes
Cooking Time: 15 minutes
Servings: 4

Ingredients:
- 2 tbsp. olive oil
- 1 lb. (454 g) ground pork
- 1 shredded carrot
- 1 onion, chopped
- 1 tsp. soy sauce
- 16 wonton wrappers
- Salt and ground black pepper, to taste
- Cooking spray

Directions:
1. Heat the olive oil in a nonstick skillet over medium heat until shimmering.
2. Add the ground pork, carrot, onion, soy sauce, salt, and ground black pepper and sauté for 10 minutes or until the pork is well browned and carrots are tender.
3. Unfold the wrappers on a clean work surface, then divide the
cooked pork and vegetables on the wrappers. Fold the edges
around the filling to form momos. Nip the top to seal the momos.
4. Arrange the momos in the air fryer basket and spritz with cooking spray.
5. Put the air fryer basket on the baking pan and slide into Rack Position 2, select Air Fry, set temperature to 320ºF (160ºC) and set time to 10 minutes.
6. When cooking is complete, the wrappers will be lightly browned.
7. Serve immediately.

329. Lobster Tails Casserole

Preparation Time: 9 minutes
Cooking Time: 8 minutes
Servings: 2

Ingredients:
- 2 6oz lobster tails
- 1 tsp. salt
- 1 tsp. chopped chives
- 2 tbsp. unsalted butter melted
- 1 tbsp. minced garlic
- 1 tsp. lemon juice

Directions:
1. Combine butter, garlic, salt, chives, and lemon juice to prepare butter mixture.
2. Butterfly lobster tails by cutting through shell followed by
removing the meat and resting it on top of the shell.
3. Place them on the tray in the Instant Pot duo Crisp Air Fryer basket and spread butter over the top of lobster meat. Close the Air Fryer lid, select the Air Fry option and cook on 380°F for 4 minutes.
4. Open the Air Fryer lid and spread more butter on top, cook for extra 2-4 minutes until done.

330. Okra and Green Beans Stew

Preparation Time: 5 minutes
Cooking Time: 12 minutes
Servings: 4

Ingredients:
- 1 lb. green beans; halved
- 4 garlic cloves; minced
- 1 C. okra
- 3 tbsp. tomato sauce
- 1 tbsp. thyme; chopped.
- Salt and black pepper to taste.

Directions:
1. In a pan that fits your air fryer, mix all the ingredients, toss, introduce the pan in the air fryer and cook at 370°F for 15
Mins.
2. divide the stew into bowls and serve.

331. Chicken Legs with dilled Brussels Sprouts

Preparation Time: 5 minutes
Cooking Time: 10 minutes
Servings: 2

Ingredients:
- 2 chicken legs
- 1/2 tsp. paprika

- 1/2 tsp. kosher salt
- 1/2 tsp. black pepper
- 1/2 lb. Brussels sprouts
- 1 tsp. dill, fresh or dried

Directions:
1. Start by preheating your Air Fryer to 370 degrees F.
2. Now, season your chicken with paprika, salt, and pepper. Transfer the chicken legs to the cooking basket. Cook for 10 minutes.
3. Flip the chicken legs and cook an additional 10 minutes.
Reserve.
4. Add the Brussels sprouts to the cooking basket; sprinkle with dill. Cook at 380 degrees F for 15 minutes, shaking the basket halfway through.
5. Serve with the reserved chicken legs.

332. Chili Chicken Sliders

Preparation Time: 5 minutes
Cooking Time: 10 minutes
Servings: 4

Ingredients:
- 1/3 tsp. paprika
- 1/3 C. scallions, peeled and chopped
- 3 cloves garlic, peeled and minced
- 1 tsp. ground black pepper, or to taste
- 1/2 tsp. fresh basil, minced
- 1 ½ C. chicken,minced
- 1 ½ tbsp. coconut aminos
- 1/2 tsp. grated fresh ginger
- 1/2 tbsp. chili sauce
- 1 tsp. salt

Directions:
1. Thoroughly combine all ingredients in a mixing dish. Then, form into 4 patties.
2. Cook in the preheated Air Fryer for 18 minutes at 355
degrees F.
3. Garnish with toppings of choice.

333. Roasted Grape and Goat Cheese Crostinis

Preparation Time: 5 minutes
Cooking Time: 10 minutes
Servings: 4

Ingredients:
- 1 lb. seedless red grapes
- 1 tsp. chopped rosemary
- 4 tbsp. olive oil
- 1 rustic French baguette
- 1 C. sliced shallots
- 2 tbsp. unsalted butter

99

- 8 oz. goat cheese
- 1 tbsp. honey

Directions:
1. Start by preheating toaster oven to 400°F.
2. Toss grapes, rosemary, and 1 tbsp. of olive oil in a large bowl.
3. Transfer to a roasting pan and roast for 20 minutes.
4. Remove the pan from the oven and set aside to cool.
5. Slice the baguette into 1/2-inch-thick pieces.
6. Brush each slice with olive oil and place on baking sheet.
7. Bake for 8 minutes, then remove from oven and set aside.
8. In a medium skillet add butter and one tbsp. of olive oil.
9. Add shallots and sauté for about 10 minutes.
10. Mix goat cheese and honey in a medium bowl, then add
contents of shallot pan and mix thoroughly.
11. Spread shallot mixture onto baguette, top with grapes, and
serve.

334. Glazed Lamb Chops

Preparation Time: 10 minutes
Cooking Time: 15 minutes
Servings: 4

Ingredients
- 1 tbsp. dijon mustard
- ½ tbsp. fresh lime juice
- 1 tsp. honey
- ½ tsp. olive oil
- Salt and ground black pepper, as required
- 4 (4-ounce) lamb loin chops

Directions:
1. In a black pepper large bowl, mix together the mustard, lemon juice, oil, honey, salt, and black pepper.
2. Add the chops and coat with the mixture generously.
3. Place the chops onto the greased "Sheet Pan".
4. Press "Power Button" of Ninja Foodi digital Air Fry Oven and turn the dial to select the "Air Bake" mode.
5. Press the Time button and again turn the dial to set the cooking time to 15 minutes.
6. Now push the Temp button and rotate the dial to set the temperature at 390 degrees F.
7. Press "Start/Pause" button to start.
8. When the unit beeps to show that it is preheated, open the lid.
9. Insert the "Sheet Pan" in oven.
10. Flip the chops once halfway through.
11. Serve hot.

335. Onion Omelet

Preparation Time: 7 minutes
Cooking Time: 15 minutes
Servings: 2

Ingredients
- 4 eggs
- ¼ tsp. low-sodium soy sauce
- Ground black pepper, as required
- 1 tsp. butter
- 1 medium yellow onion, sliced
- ¼ C. Cheddar cheese, grated

Directions:
1. In a skillet, melt the butter over medium heat and cook the onion and cook for about 8-10 minutes.
2. Remove from the heat and set aside to cool slightly.
3. Meanwhile, in a bowl, add the eggs, soy sauce and black pepper and beat well.
4. Add the cooked onion and gently, stir to combine.
5. Place the zucchini mixture into a small baking pan.
6. Press "Power Button" of Air Fry Oven and turn the dial to select the "Air Fry" mode.
7. Press the Time button and again turn the dial to set the cooking time to 5 minutes.
8. Now push the Temp button and rotate the dial to set the temperature at 355 degrees F.
9. Press "Start/Pause" button to start.
10. When the unit beeps to show that it is preheated, open the lid.
11. Arrange pan over the "Wire Rack" and insert in the oven.
12. Cut the omelet into 2 portions and serve hot.

336. Italian Meatballs

Preparation Time: 10 minutes
Cooking Time: 13 minutes
Servings: 4

Ingredients
- 2-lb. lean ground turkey
- ¼ C. onion, minced
- 2 cloves garlic, minced
- 2 tbsp. parsley, chopped
- 2 eggs
- 1½ C. parmesan cheese, grated
- ½ tsp. red pepper flakes
- ½ tsp. Italian seasoning Salt and black pepper to taste

Directions:

1. Toss all the meatball Ingredients: in a bowl and mix well.
2. Make small meatballs out this mixture and place them in the air fryer basket.
3. Press "Power Button" of Air Fry Oven and turn the dial to select the "Air Fry" mode.
4. Press the Time button and again turn the dial to set the cooking time to 13 minutes.
5. Now push the Temp button and rotate the dial to set the temperature at 350 degrees F.
6. Once preheated, place the air fryer basket inside and close its lid.
7. Flip the meatballs when cooked halfway through.
8. Serve warm.

337. Fried Paprika Tofu

Preparation Time: 5 minutes
Cooking Time: 12 minutes
Servings: 2

Ingredients
• 1 block extra firm tofu; pressed to remove excess water and cut into cubes
• 1/4 C. cornstarch
• 1 tbsp. smoked paprika
• salt and pepper to taste

Directions:
1. Line the Air Fryer basket with aluminum foil and brush with oil. Preheat the Air Fryer to 370 - degrees Fahrenheit.
2. Mix all ingredients in a bowl. Toss to combine. Place in the
Air Fryer basket and cook for 12 minutes.

338. Chicken Caprese Sandwich

Preparation Time: 5 minutes
Cooking Time: 3 minutes
Servings: 2

Ingredients:
• 2 leftover chicken breasts, or pre-cooked breaded chicken
• 1 large ripe tomato
• 4 oz. mozzarella cheese slices
• 4 slices of whole grain bread
• 1/4 C. olive oil
• 1/3 C. fresh basil leaves
• Salt and pepper to taste

Directions:
1. Start by slicing tomatoes into thin slices.
2. Layer tomatoes then cheese over two slices of bread and place on a greased baking sheet.

3. Toast in the toaster oven for about 2 minutes or until the cheese is melted.
4. Heat chicken while the cheese melts.
5. Remove from oven, sprinkle with basil, and add chicken.
6. drizzle with oil and add salt and pepper.
7. Top with other slice of bread and serve.

339. Saucy Chicken with Leeks

Preparation Time: 5 minutes
Cooking Time: 3 minutes
Servings: 2

Ingredients:
• 2 leeks, sliced
• 2 large-sized tomatoes, chopped
• 3 cloves garlic, minced
• ½ tsp. dried oregano
• 6 chicken legs, boneless and skinless
• ½ tsp. smoked cayenne pepper
• 2 tbsp. olive oil
• A freshly ground nutmeg

Directions:
1. In a mixing dish, thoroughly combine all ingredients, minus the leeks. Place in the refrigerator and let it marinate overnight.
2. Lay the leeks onto the bottom of an Air Fryer cooking basket.
Top with the chicken legs.
3. Roast chicken legs at 375 degrees F for 18 minutes, turning halfway through. Serve with hoisin sauce.

340. Air Fried Steak Sandwich

Preparation Time: 8 minutes
Cooking Time: 16 minutes
Servings: 4

Ingredients:
• Large hoagie bun, sliced in half
• 6 oz. of sirloin or flank steak, sliced into bite-sized pieces
• ½ tbsp. of mustard powder
• ½ tbsp. of soy sauce
• 1 tbsp. of fresh bleu cheese, crumbled
• 8 medium-sized cherry tomatoes, sliced in half
• 1 C. of fresh arugula, rinsed and patted dry

Directions:
1. Preparing the ingredients. in a small mixing bowl, combine the soy sauce and onion powder; stir with a fork until thoroughly combined.
2. Lay the raw steak strips in the soy-mustard mixture, and fully immerse each piece to marinate.
3. Set the instant crisp air fryer to 320 degrees for 10 minutes.

4. Arrange the soy-mustard marinated steak pieces on a piece of tin foil, flat and not overlapping, and set the tin foil on one side of the instant crisp air fryer basket. The foil should not take up more than half of the surface.

5. Lay the hoagie-bun halves, crusty-side up and soft-side down, on the other half of the air-fryer.

6. Air frying. Close air fryer lid.

7. After 10 minutes, the instant crisp air fryer will shut off; the hoagie buns should be starting to crisp and the steak will have begun to cook.

8. Carefully, flip the hoagie buns so they are now crusty-side down and soft-side up; crumble a layer of the bleu cheese on each hoagie half.

9. With a long spoon, gently stir the marinated steak in the foil to ensure even coverage.

10. Set the instant crisp air fryer to 360 degrees for 6 minutes.

11. After 6 minutes, when the fryer shuts off, the bleu cheese will be perfectly melted over the toasted bread, and the steak will be juicy on the inside and crispy on the outside.

12. Remove the cheesy hoagie halves first, using tongs, and set on a serving plate; then cover one side with the steak, and top with the cherry-tomato halves and the arugula. Close with the other cheesy hoagie-half, slice into two pieces, and enjoy.

341. Cheese-stuffed Meatballs

Preparation Time: 7 minutes
Cooking Time: 10 minutes
Servings: 4

Ingredients
- ⅓ C. soft bread crumbs
- 3 tbsp. milk
- 1 tbsp. ketchup
- 1 egg
- ½ tsp. dried marjoram
- Pinch salt
- Freshly ground black pepper
- 1-lb. 95 percent lean ground beef
- 20 ½-inch cubes of cheese
- Olive oil for misting

Directions:
1. Preparing the ingredients. in a large bowl, combine the bread

crumbs, milk, ketchup, egg, marjoram, salt, and pepper, and

mix well. Add the ground beef and mix gently but thoroughly with your hands. Form the mixture into 20 meatballs. Shape each meatball around a cheese cube. Mist the meatballs with olive oil and put into the instant crisp air fryer basket.

2. Air frying. Close air fryer lid. Bake for 10 to 13 minutes or until the meatballs register 165°f on a meat thermometer.

342. Bbq Chicken Breasts

Preparation Time: 7 minutes
Cooking Time: 10 minutes
Servings: 4

Ingredients:
- 4 boneless skinless chicken breast about 6 oz. each
- 1-2 tbsp. bbq seasoning

Directions:
1. Cover both sides of chicken breast with the BBq seasoning.

Cover and marinate the in the refrigerator for 45 minutes.

2. Choose the Air Fry option and set the temperature to 400°F.

Push start and let it preheat for 5 minutes.

3. Upon preheating, place the chicken breast in the Instant Pot duo Crisp Air Fryer basket, making sure they do not overlap. Spray with oil.

4. Cook for 13-14 Mins.

5. flipping halfway.

6. Remove chicken when the chicken reaches an internal temperature of 160°F. Place on a plate and allow to rest for 5 minutes before slicing.

343. Toast with Garlic and Cheese

Preparation Time: 7 minutes
Cooking Time: 8 minutes
Servings: 2

Ingredients:
- Enough French loaves cut in half
- 3 tbsp. olive oil
- 1 tbsp. butter
- 1 pinch of salt
- 1 pinch of black pepper
- Enough sliced cheese

Directions:
1. In a small cup, produce a paste of butter, olive oil, crushed garlic and season to taste with salt, pepper, and oregano.

2. Over the bread slices, pass this mixture over. Top with sliced cheese on top of each part.

3. Put in the 360-degree F air fryer for approximately 8 minutes or until golden, as required.

344. Fried Ravioli

Preparation Time: 7 minutes
Cooking Time: 5 minutes
Servings: 2

Ingredients:
- 1 (9-oz.) box cheese ravioli, store-bought or meat ravioli
- 1 cup buttermilk
- 2 cups Italian-style bread crumbs
- 1 tsp olive oil
- 1 (14-oz.) jar marinara sauce
- ¼ cup Parmesan cheese, shredded

Directions:
1. Dip the ravioli in buttermilk.
2. Combine breadcrumbs and olive oil, and press the ravioli into the breadcrumbs.
3. Move the breaded ravioli into a preheated air fryer or baking paper.
4. Allow cooking for 5 minutes at 200-degree F.
5. Serve while warm alongside marinara sauce for dipping and cheese topping.

345. Grilled Bruschetta

Preparation Time: 7 minutes
Cooking Time: 5 minutes
Servings: 6

Ingredients:
- 1 cup chopped celery
- 3 tablespoons Dijon mustard
- 1-lb. plum tomatoes, seeded and chopped 3 tablespoons balsamic vinegar
- 1/4 cup minced fresh basil 3 tablespoons olive oil
- 2 garlic cloves, minced 1/2 teaspoon salt

Spread:
- 1 tablespoon finely chopped green onion 1/4 cup Dijon mustard
- 1 garlic clove, minced
- 3/4 teaspoon dried oregano 1/2 cup mayonnaise
- loaf French bread, sliced

Direction:
1. Take the first eight ingredients in a bowl and mix them together. Cover this prepared topping and refrigerate for about 30 minutes. Now take mayonnaise, onion, garlic, oregano, and mustard in a bowl. Mix them well and prepare the mayonnaise spread.
2. Prepare and heat it up to the medium temperature configuration of the
Barbecue.
3. Once preheated, open the lid and place the bread slices on the grill in batches.
4. Cover the grill lid and let it grill for 2 minutes in the 'Grilling Mode.' Next, flip the bread slices and grill again for 2 minutes.
5. Top the grilled bread with mayonnaise spread and tomato relish. Serve fresh.

346. Hot Dogs

Preparation Time: 7 minutes
Cooking Time: 10 minutes
Servings: 6

Ingredients:
- 2 jumbo hot dogs
- 1 tsp taco seasoning mix
- 2 hot dog buns
- 1/3 cup guacamole
- 4 tbsp. salsa
- 6 pickled jalapeno slices

Directions:
1. Ensure that the air fryer is preheated for at least four minutes at 390- degree F.
2. On each hot dog, cut five slits and sprinkle 1/2 teaspoon of taco seasoning on each hot dog.
3. Allow the hot dogs to cook for about 5 minutes in the air fryer before placing them on the bus and back in the air fryer basket.
4. Cook until the buns are toasted and the hot dogs are crispy this time around. This takes 4 minutes or so or so.
5. Top the hot dogs, all in equal amounts, with guacamole, salsa and jalapenos.

347. XXL burger

Preparation Time: 10 minutes
Cooking Time: 5 minutes
Servings: 6

Ingredients:
- 2 burgers (beef)
- 2 burger buns
- Mayonnaise to taste
- Ketchup to taste
- Lollo rosso lettuce
- 1 tomato, sliced
- 1 red onion, chopped
- 2 slices cheddar cheese
- Garden cress

Directions:
1. Ensure that your air fryer is preheated before cooking the meat. Set the burgers in the air fryer and allow them to cook at 390-degree F for five minutes. Cut the bread buns along the center to produce the needed two bottom halves and a top half.
2. Add some mayonnaise on one bottom half and some ketchup on the other.
3. Combine the lettuce, the sliced tomatoes, and the chopped onions, and add the mixture to the bottoms. Open the air fryer, and add the cheddar cheese to the burgers. Allow cooking for 2 minutes at 390-degree F.

After putting the hamburger together, and strengthen it with a cocktail stick.

103

348. Chicken Avocado Burgers

Preparation Time: 10 minutes
Cooking Time: 12 minutes
Servings: 2

Ingredients:
- 14 oz. avocado, peeled
- 14 oz. chicken, minced
- 1 tbsp. Mexican seasoning

Directions:
1. Slice the peeled avocado and cut three slices into small cubes. Keep the rest aside as whole slices.
2. Transfer the minced chicken into a mixing bowl, and add the chunks of avocado alongside the Mexican seasoning.
3. After mixing the bowl contents above thoroughly, form the mixture into chicken burger patty shapes.
4. Transfer the burger into the air fryer and allow it to cook for 12 minutes at 360-degree F.
5. To get that ideal Mexican meal, serve the burger alongside potato wedges.

349. Basic Hot Dogs

Preparation Time: 10 minutes
Cooking Time: 12 minutes
Servings: 2

Ingredients:
- 4 hot dog buns
- 4 hot dogs

Directions:
1. Ensure that your air fryer is preheated to 390-degree F.
2. Move your burns into the air fryer basket and allow cooking for 2 minutes.
3. Remove the cooked buns to a plate.
4. Replace the buns with the hot dogs, and allow cooking for 3 minutes.
5. Remove and place on the same plate as the buns.
6. Serve.

350. Cheese and Onion Nuggets

Preparation Time: 10 minutes
Cooking Time: 12 minutes
Servings: 2

Ingredients:
- 2 spring onion
- 7 oz. Edam cheese
- 2 tbsp. Kyle's mayonnaise
- Salt and ground black pepper to taste
- 1 tbsp. thyme
- 1 tbsp. coconut oil

- ¼ shortcrust pastry
- 1 small egg, beaten

Directions:
1. Dice the cleaned spring onion into thin pieces.
2. Grate the cheese.
3. Combine the onion, mayonnaise, salt, pepper, dried thyme, and coconut oil in a medium mixing bowl. Mix thoroughly and make the mixture into eight small balls. Keep the balls in the fridge for an hour.
4. Make eight nugget shapes out of your shortcrust pastry. Ensure that there are no gaps by sealing them up.
5. With the aid of a pastry brush, brush the egg over the pastry. This gives them an Eggy glow when cooked.
6. Allow the egg to cook in the air fryer at 356 F for 12 minutes.
7. Serve warm with the cheese still melting.

351. Bacon Cashews

Preparation Time: 10 minutes
Cooking Time: 14 minutes
Servings: 2

Ingredients:
- 3 cups raw cashews
- 2 tbsp. blackstrap molasses
- 3 tbsp. liquid smoke
- 2 tsp salt

Directions:
1. Take a bowl, combine all the ingredients, and brush the cashews generously and evenly mix.
2. Transfer the coated cashews to the air-freezer basket and cook at 350- degree F for 8-10 minutes.
3. Shake the basket at intervals of 2 minutes when cooking. This means that the cashews cook evenly. For the last 2 minutes, be extra vigilant and shake/check consistently to avoid burning the cashews.
4. It takes about 15 minutes to cause the cooked cashews to cool to room temperature.
5. Then transfer and serve the cool cashews in an airtight storage container.

352. Potato Tots

Preparation Time: 10 minutes
Cooking Time: 15 minutes
Servings: 4

Ingredients:
- 12 potato tots
- 12 bacon strips

Directions:
1. Wrap the potato tots with bacon strips.
2. Add to the air fryer.
3. Set it to air dry.
4. Cook at 400 degrees F for 8 minutes, turning once or twice.

353. Coconut Shrimp

Preparation Time: 10 minutes
Cooking Time: 12 minutes
Servings: 3

Ingredients:
- 9 shrimp, peeled and deveined
- ½ cup flour
- 1 egg
- 1 cup breadcrumbs
- 1 cup coconut flakes

Directions:
1. Coat shrimp with flour.
2. Dip in egg.
3. Dredge with a mixture of breadcrumbs and coconut flakes.
4. Arrange shrimp in the air fryer.
5. Set it to air dry.
6. Cook at 320 degrees F for 6 minutes per side.

354. Chicken Breast

Preparation Time: 10 minutes
Cooking Time: 12 minutes
Servings: 3

Ingredients:
- 2 chicken breasts
- 2 tsp olive oil
- Salt and ground black pepper to taste

Directions:
1. Switch the air fryer basket in your air fryer with a grill pan.
2. Arrange the chicken breasts in the grill pan.
3. On each breast, apply a combination of a teaspoon of olive oil, salt, and pepper (as seasoning).
4. Set your Air Fryer to 350-degree F and let the chicken breasts cook for
12 minutes.
5. Slice the cooked chicken to your taste with your knife.
6. Serve.

355. Thai Mango Chicken

Preparation Time: 10 minutes
Cooking Time: 20 minutes
Servings: 2

Ingredients:
- Mixed herbs chicken seasoning
- ½ mango peeled and diced
- Salt and ground black pepper to taste
- Spicy chicken seasoning
- 1 tsp red Thai curry paste
- 2 tbsp. olive oil
- 1 lime rind and juice

- 2 chicken breasts

Directions:
1. Ensure that your Air Fryer is preheated to 355-degree F.
2. In a clean mixing cup, make a combination of your mixed spices, mango, salt, pepper, spicy chicken seasoning, Red Thai Curry Paste, olive oil, and lime. Ensure that you blend well to spread the spice in the mixture.
3. Cut slightly into your chicken with the help of your vegetable knife without the cut touching the bottom of the breasts.
4. spray the seasoning mixture to ensure sufficient seasoning gets into the cuts in the mixing bowl.
5. On the baking mat, move the sprinkled chicken onto your air fryer. Set the timer and allow it to cook for 15 minutes. Often check well to ensure that the chicken in the middle is well-cooked.
6. Serve with the cooked chicken and garnish with fresh tomatoes and extra lime.

356. Chicken Cutlets

Preparation Time: 10 minutes
Cooking Time: 20 minutes
Servings: 2

Ingredients:
- 3 medium chicken breasts
- 7 oz. gluten-free oats
- 2 medium eggs beaten
- Salt and ground black pepper
- 1 tbsp. mustard powder
- 1 tbsp. basil, dried
- 1 oz. parmesan cheese, grated
- 2 tbsp. garlic, dried

Directions:
1. The first step is to give your chicken a butterfly. Inevitably, if you use three chicken breasts, you would have six bits of butterfly chicken.
2. Divide the oats that are gluten-free into two; mix one half until the appearance of fine oats appears.
3. Get three clean bowls in each bowl: add your egg, blended oats, and unblended oats.
4. Combine the mixed oats and 1/4 of the undifferentiated oats and apply
the mixed pepper, salt and mustard to taste.
5. Add the pepper, salt, basil, parmesan cheese, and dried garlic and mix
the pure oats and 1/4 of the blended oats.
6. Place the chicken cutlets first, then the egg and the fake breadcrumbs in the fake flour.
7. Set an Air Fryer to 350-degree F and cook for 11 minutes. Cook two cutlets at a go, with the best results.
8. Just serve.

357. Brazilian Mini Turkey Pies

Preparation Time: 10 minutes
Cooking Time: 20 minutes
Servings: 2

Ingredients:
- 1 oz. turkey stock
- 2 oz. whole milk
- 2 oz. coconut milk
- 8 oz. homemade tomato sauce
- 1 tsp oregano
- 1 tbsp. coriander
- Salt and ground black pepper to taste
- 2 oz. turkey, cooked and shredded
- Flour
- 8 slices filo pastry
- 1 small egg beaten

Directions:
1. Get a clean mixing bowl and put all your wet ingredients, except the egg. Mix well.
2. The result should be a pale-looking sauce – the stock for your pie. Now add the seasoning and turkey before mixing again. Finally, set the mixture aside.
3. To each of your little pie cases, line them with a bit of flour before the filo pastry. This prevents them from sticking. Each pie should use up one sheet of filo, and it should be centrally positioned such that you can easily fold over the extra pastry for the top of the pie.
4. Add the mixture to every mini pie pot until they are ¾ full.
5. Cover the top with the remaining pastry before brushing the egg along the top.
6. Transfer the mini pie pot into the air fryer, set the temperature to 360- degree F and allow to cook for 10 minutes.
7. Serve

358. Arancini

Preparation Time: 15 minutes
Cooking Time: 15 minutes
Servings: 16

Ingredients:
- 2 cups cooked and cooled leftover rice or risotto
- Two beaten eggs
- 1 1/2 cup bread crumbs (split panko)
- 1/2 cups of Parmesan cheese, grated
- 2 tbsp of fresh basil, minced
- melted mozzarella cheese cubes measuring 16" x 3/4"
- 2 tablespoons olive oil

Directions:
1. Combine the rice, eggs, 1/2 cups of bread crumbs, Parmesan cheese, and basil in a medium mixing basin. Make 16 1 1/2- inch balls out of this mixture.
2. Make a hole with your finger in each of the balls and insert a mozzarella cube. Wrap the cheese in the rice mixture tightly.
3. In a small dish, mix the remaining 1 cup bread crumbs with the olive oil. Coat the rice balls with the bread crumbs.
4. Arancini should be cooked in batches for 8 to 11 minutes, or until golden brown.

359. Tortellini in a spicy sauce with fried Tortellini Sauce

Preparation Time: 10 minutes
Cooking Time: 10-15 minutes
Servings: 4

Ingredients:
- one-quarter cup mayonnaise
- 2 tablespoons mustard
- One egg
- 1/2 cups of all-purpose flour
- 1/2 tsp. dried oregano
- 1 ½ cup bread crumbs
- 2 tablespoons olive oil
- 2 cups of frozen tortellini with cheese

Directions:
1. In a small mixing dish, combine the mayonnaise and mustard.
2. Place aside.
3. Beat the egg in a small basin. Combine the flour and oregano in a separate basin. Mix up the bread crumbs and olive oil in a separate bowl.
4. To coat, dip a few tortellini at a time into the egg, then into the flour, then back into the egg, and lastly into the bread crumbs. Cooking in batches in the air fryer basket.
5. Cook for 10 minutes, shaking halfway through, or until the tortellini are crisp and golden brown on the exterior. Serve with mayonnaise.

360. Toast topped with shrimp

Preparation Time: 10 minutes Cooking Time: 6-12 minutes Servings: 12

Ingredients:
- 3 firm slices of white bread
- 2/3 cup raw shrimp, peeled and deveined, coarsely chopped
- 1 egg white, beaten
- 2 minced garlic cloves.
- 2 tablespoons cornstarch
- 1/4 teaspoon powdered ginger
- A pinch of salt
- Freshly ground black pepper.
- 2 tablespoons olive oil

Directions:
1. Using a sharp knife, remove the crusts off the bread; crush the crusts to form bread crumbs. Place aside.
2. Mix the shrimp, egg white, garlic, cornstarch, ginger, salt, and pepper in a small bowl.
3. Spread the shrimp mixture evenly on the bread, all the way to the edges. Cut each slice into four strips using a sharp knife.
4. Pat the bread crumbs and olive oil mixture onto the shrimp mixture. Place the shrimp toasts in a single layer in the air fryer basket; you may need to cook in batches.
5. Cook for 3–6 minutes, or until crispy and golden brown.

361. Tater Tots with bacon

Preparation Time: 5 minutes
Cooking Time: 5 minutes
Servings: 4

Ingredients:
- 24 tater tots (frozen)
- Six precooked bacon slices.
- 2 tablespoons maple syrup
- 1 cup shredded Cheddar cheese

Directions:
1. In the air fryer basket, place the tater tots. Shake the basket midway during the frying time and air-fry for 10 minutes.
2. Meanwhile, shred the cheese and chop the bacon into 1-inch pieces.
3. Remove the potato tots from the air fryer basket and place them in a 6-by-6-by2-inch baking dish. Drizzle with maple syrup and sprinkle with bacon. Minutes in the air fryer or until the tots and bacon are crisp.
4. Place the cheese on top and air-fry for 2 minutes, or until the cheese is melted.

362. Poutine, Waffle Fry

Preparation Time: 10 minutes
Cooking Time: 15 minutes
Servings: 4

Ingredients:
- 2 cups frozen waffle sliced fries
- 2 tbsp extra-virgin olive oil
- 1 red bell pepper, chopped
- Two sliced green onions.
- 1 cup shredded Swiss cheese
- 1/2 cup chicken gravy (canned)

Directions:
1. Place the waffle fries in the air fryer basket and toss with olive oil. Air fries the fries for 10 to 12 minutes, or until crisp and light brown.
2. Shake the basket halfway during the cooking time to brown.
3. Top the fries with the pepper, green onions, and cheese in a
6-by-6-by-2-inch pan. 3 minutes in the air fryer or until the veggies are crisp and tender.
4. Remove the air fryer pan from the oven and sprinkle the gravy over the fries.
5. 2 minutes in the air fryer or until the gravy is hot. Serve it right away.

363. Buffalo chicken bites

Preparation Time: 10 minutes
Cooking Time: 15 minutes
Servings: 4

Ingredients:
- 2/3 pound soured cream
- 1/4 cups of salad dressing (creamy blue cheese)
- 1/4 cups of blue cheese crumbles
- 1 celery stalk, finely sliced
- 1 pound chicken tenders, cut into thirds crosswise
- 3 tablespoons Buffalo chicken wing sauce
- 1 cup panko bread crumbs
- 2 tablespoons olive oil

Directions:
1. Set aside the sour cream, salad dressing, blue cheese, and celery in a small dish.
2. Combine the chicken pieces and Buffalo wing sauce in a medium mixing bowl and toss to coat. Allow it to sit while you prepare the bread crumbs.
3. In a dish, combine the bread crumbs and olive oil.
4. Coat the chicken in the bread crumb mixture, pressing each piece down to ensure the crumbs adhere.
5. Cook the chicken in batches for 7 to 9 minutes, shaking the basket once, until it reaches 165°F and is golden brown. Serve with a side of blue cheese sauce.

364. Mariscos Tacos

Preparation Time: 15 minutes
Cooking Time: 12 minutes
Servings: 4

Ingredients:
- 1 pound white fish fillets, such as snapper
- 1 tablespoon of olive oil
- 3 tbsp. lemon juice, divided
- 1 1/2 cups of red cabbage, chopped
- 1/2 cup of salsa
- 1/3-cup soured cream
- 6 soft flour tortillas
- Two peeled and sliced avocados

Directions:
1. Brush the fish with olive oil and season with 1 tablespoon of lemon juice. Place the fish in the air fryer basket and cook for

9 to 12 minutes, or until it flakes when checked with a fork.

2. Meanwhile, in a medium mixing bowl, combine the remaining

2 tablespoons of lemon juice, cabbage, salsa, and sour cream. When the fish is done, take it from

the air fryer basket and cut it into big chunks.

3. Allow each person to create their own taco by mixing the fish, tortillas, cabbage mixture, and avocados.

4. In this dish, you may use scallops, shrimp, lobster tails, or a variety of seafood. In the air fryer, cook until done, and then assemble the tacos with the other ingredients.

onion, and garlic in a 6-inch metal bowl.

2. Cook for 4 to 6 minutes, stirring once, until crisp and tender in the air fryer. Stir in the soy sauce, honey, and tuna.

3. Cook for 3 to 6 minutes more, stirring once, until the tuna is cooked to your liking. Tuna may be served rare, medium-rare, or cooked till done.

365. Asian Tuna Steamed

Preparation Time: 10 minutes
Cooking Time: 10 minutes
Servings: 4

Ingredients:
- 4 tuna steaks, tiny
- 2 tbsp. of low-sodium soy sauce
- 2 tbsp. sesame oil.
- 2 tablespoons rice wine vinegar
- 1 teaspoon grated fresh ginger
- 1/8 teaspoon ground black pepper
- 1 lemongrass stalk, halved
- 3 tbsp lemon juice
- On a dish, arrange the tuna steaks.

Direction:
1. In a small mixing bowl, add the soy sauce, sesame oil, rice wine vinegar, and ginger. Pour this mixture over the tuna and let it marinate for 10 minutes. Gently rub the soy sauce mixture into both sides of the tuna.

2. Season with salt to taste.

3. Place the lemongrass on top of the steaks in the air fryer basket. In the pan under the basket, combine the lemon juice and 1 tablespoon of water.

4. Steam the tuna for 8 to 10 minutes, or until it reaches a temperature of at least 145°F. Remove the lemongrass before serving the tuna.

367. Scallops with spring vegetables

Preparation Time: 10 minutes
Cooking Time: 10 minutes
Servings: 4

Ingredients:
- 1/2 pound asparagus, cut into 2-inch sections after removing the ends
- 1 pound sugar snap peas
- One pound of sea scallops
- 1 teaspoon fresh lemon juice
- 2 tbsp extra-virgin olive oil
- 1/2 tsp. dried thyme
- A pinch of salt
- Freshly ground black pepper.

Directions:
1. Fill the air fryer basket halfway with asparagus and sweet snap peas. Cook for 2 to 3 minutes, or until the veggies begin to soften.

2. Meanwhile, look for a little muscle linked to the side of the scallops and peel it off and discard it.

3. Toss the scallops with the lemon juice, olive oil, thyme, salt, and pepper in a medium bowl. Place it on top of the veggies in the air fryer basket.

4. Steam for 5 to 7 minutes, flipping the basket once during cooking, until the scallops are firm when touched with a finger and opaque in the middle, and the veggies are soft. Serve it right away.

366. Stir-Fry with Tuna

Preparation Time: 15 minutes
Cooking Time: 12 minutes
Servings: 4

Ingredients:
- 1 tablespoon of olive oil
- 1 red bell pepper, chopped
- 1 cup peeled and cut into 2-inch pieces green beans
- 1 onion, sliced
- Two garlic cloves, sliced
- 2 tbsp. of low-sodium soy sauce
- 1 tablespoon honey
- 1/2 pound fresh tuna, cubed

Directions:
1. Combine the olive oil, pepper, green beans,

368. Snapper Scampi

Preparation Time: 5 minutes
Cooking Time: 10 minutes
Servings: 4

Ingredients:
- 4 skinless snapper or arctic char fillets (6 oz.)
- 1 tablespoon of olive oil
- 3 tbsp. lemon juice, divided
- 1/2 tsp. dried basil
- A pinch of salt
- Freshly ground black pepper.
- 2 tbsp. melted butter
- 2 minced garlic cloves.

Directions:
1. Rub the fish fillets with 1 tablespoon each of

lemon juice and olive oil.

2. Place it in the air fryer basket and season with basil, salt, and pepper.

3. Grill the salmon for 7 to 8 minutes, or until it flakes easily with a fork. Place the fish on a serving platter after removing it from the basket.

4. Cover up to stay warm.

5. In a 6-by-6-by-2-inch pan, combine the butter, remaining 2 tablespoons lemon juice, and garlic. Cook for 1 to 2 minutes

in the air fryer, or until the garlic is sizzling. Pour this over the fish and serve.

369. Asian Turkey Meatballs

Preparation Time: 5 minutes
Cooking Time: 10 minutes
Servings: 4

Ingredients:
- split 2 tbsp. of peanut oil,
- 1 small onion, minced
- 1/4 cups of coarsely chopped water chestnuts
- 1/2 teaspoons of ginger powder
- 2 tbsp. of low-sodium soy sauce
- 1/4 cups of bread crumbs (panko)
- 1 egg, beaten
- 1 pound ground turkey

Direction:
1. Combine the peanut oil and onion in a 6-by-6-by-2-inch pan.
Cook for 1 to 2 minutes, or until the vegetables are crisp and tender. Place the onions in a medium mixing basin.

2. Mix in the water chestnuts, ground ginger, soy sauce, and bread crumbs with the onions. Stir in the egg well. Incorporate the ground turkey until well blended.

3. Make 1-inch meatballs out of the mixture. Drizzle the meatballs with the remaining 1 tablespoon of oil.

4. In batches, bake the meatballs in the 6-by-6-by-2-inch pan for

10 to 12 minutes, or until a meat thermometer reads 165°F.

370. Chicken with Pineapple Stir-Fry

Preparation Time: 10minutes
Cooking Time: 15 minutes
Servings: 4

Ingredients:
- 2 chicken breasts, skinless and boneless
- 2 tablespoons cornstarch
- 1 egg white, gently beaten
- 1 tablespoon olive or peanut oil
- 1 onion, sliced
- 1 red bell pepper, chopped
- 1 can (8 oz.) pineapple tidbits, drained, reserved juice
- 2 tbsp soy sauce (reduced sodium).

Directions:
1. Cut the chicken breasts into cubes and place them in a medium mixing dish. Mix in the cornstarch and the egg white completely. Place aside.

2. Combine the oil and onion in a 6-inch metal bowl. Cook for 2 to 3 minutes in the air fryer, or until the onion is crisp and tender.

3. Drain the chicken and combine it with the onions in a mixing dish; toss thoroughly. Cook for 7 to 9 minutes, or until the chicken reaches an internal temperature of 165°F.

4. Toss the chicken mixture, and then stir in the pepper, pineapple tidbits, 3 tablespoons of the conserved pineapple juice, and soy sauce. Cook for 2 to 3 minutes, or until the food is cooked through and the sauce has thickened somewhat.

371. Satay Chicken

Preparation Time: 10minutes
Cooking Time: 15 minutes
Servings: 4

Ingredients:
- 1/2 cups of peanut butter (crunchy)
- 1/3 cups of chicken broth
- Low-sodium soy sauce, 3 tbsp.
- 2 tablespoons lemon juice
- 2 minced garlic cloves.
- 2 tablespoons olive oil
- 1 teaspoon curry powder
- 1 pound of chicken tenders

Directions:
1. In a medium mixing bowl, whisk together the peanut butter, chicken broth, soy sauce, lemon juice, garlic, olive oil, and curry powder until smooth. Two tablespoons of this mixture should be placed in a small bowl. Set aside the leftover sauce in a serving dish.

2. Stir the chicken tenders into the dish with the 2 tablespoons

of sauce. Allow it to marinade for a few minutes before slicing using a bamboo slicing knife.

3. Insert a skewer lengthwise through each chicken tender.

4. Place the chicken in the air fryer basket and cook in batches for 6 to 9 minutes, or until a meat thermometer reads 165°F. Serve the chicken with the reserved sauce on the side.

372. Cheesecake with Marbles

Preparation Time: 15minutes
Cooking Time: 15 minutes
Servings: 8

Ingredients:
- 1 cup graham crackers, crushed
- 3 tbsp of softened butter.
- softened cream cheese, 1 1/2 (8-ounce) packets
- 1/3 pound of sugar
- Two beaten eggs
- 1 tablespoon flour
- 1 tsp vanilla extract
- 1/4-cup cocoa syrup

Directions:
1. In a small dish, combine the graham cracker crumbs and butter and stir thoroughly. Place it in the freezer to firm the bottom of a 6-by-6-by-2-inch baking pan.

2. In a medium mixing bowl, add the cream cheese and sugar

and stir thoroughly. One at a time, beat in the eggs. Mix in the flour and vanilla extract.

3. Transfer 23 cups of the filling to a small mixing dish and whisk in the chocolate syrup until well mixed.

4. Pour the vanilla filling into the crust-lined baking dish. Drop spoonful of the chocolate filling over the vanilla filling. To marbleize the fillings, mix them in a zigzag pattern with a clean butter knife.

5. Bake the cheesecake for 15 minutes, or until it is barely set.

6. Cool for 1 hour on a wire rack before cooling in the refrigerator until the cheesecake is hard.

373. Breakfast Calzone

Preparation Time: 15minutes
Cooking Time: 15 minutes
Servings: 4

Ingredients:
- 1 1/2 cups shredded mozzarella cheese
- 1/2 cup finely ground almond flour
- 1 ounce full-fat cream cheese
- 1 large whole egg
- 4 large eggs, scrambled
- 1/2 pound cooked breakfast sausage, crumbled
- 8 tbsp shredded mild Cheddar cheese

Directions:
1. Get a microwave-safe bowl and add mozzarella cheese, almond flour and cream cheese inside. Microwave for 1 minute. Mix until the mixture is even and forms a ball then add the egg and mix until the dough forms.

2. Set dough between two sheets of parchment and roll out to

1/4" thickness. Cut the dough into four rectangles.

3. Get a container and mix the scrambled egg with the sausage.

Place the mixture between each piece of dough, placing it on the bottom half of the rectangle.. Sprinkle each with 2 tbsp Cheddar.

4. Fold over the rectangle to cover the egg and meat mixture.

Pinch, roll, or use a wet fork to close the edges completely.

5. Divide a piece of parchment to fit your air fryer basket and place the calzones onto the parchment. Place parchment into the air fryer basket.

6. Set the temperature to 380F and set the timer for 15 min.

7. Flip the calzones halfway through the cooking time. When done, calzones should be golden in color. At that point you can serve.

374. Walnut Pancake

Preparation Time: 15minutes
Cooking Time: 15 minutes
Servings: 4

Ingredients:
- 3 tbsp melted butter, divided
- 1 cup flour
- 2 tbsp sugar
- 1½ tsp baking powder
- ¼ tsp salt
- 1 egg, beaten
- ¾ cup milk
- 1 tsp pure vanilla extract
- ½ cup roughly chopped walnuts
- Maple syrup or fresh sliced fruit, for serving

Directions:
1. Grease a baking pan with 1 tbsp of melted butter.

2. Mix together the flour, sugar, baking powder, and salt in a medium bowl. Add the beaten egg, the remaining 2 tbsp of melted butter, milk, and vanilla and stir until the batter is sticky but slightly lumpy.

3. Slowly pour the batter into the greased baking pan and scatter with the walnuts.

4. Place the pan on the bake position.

5. Select Bake, set temperature to 330°F (166°C) and set time to

15 min.

6. When cooked, the pancake should be golden brown and cooked through.

110

375. Buttermilk Biscuits

Preparation Time: 15 minutes
Cooking Time: 15 minutes
Servings: 8

Ingredients:
- 2 ½ cups all-purpose flour
- 1 tbsp baking powder
- 1 tsp kosher salt
- 1 tsp sugar
- ½ tsp baking soda
- 1 cup buttermilk, chilled
- 8 tbsp unsalted butter, at room temperature

Directions:
1. Stir together the flour, baking powder, salt, sugar and baking powder in a large bowl.
2. Add the butter and stir to mix well. Pour in the buttermilk and stir with a rubber spatula just until incorporated.
3. Place the dough onto a lightly floured surface and roll the dough out to a disk, ½ inch thick. Cut out the biscuits with a
2-inch round cutter and re-roll any scraps until you have 16 biscuits.
4. Arrange the biscuits in the air fryer basket in a single layer.
5. Place the basket on the bake position.
6. Select Bake, set temperature to 325 degs F (163 degs C), and set time to 15 min.
7. When cooked, the biscuits will be golden brown.
8. Remove from the air fryer grill to a plate and serve hot.

376. Golden Asparagus Frittata

Preparation Time: 15 minutes
Cooking Time: 15 minutes
Servings: 2-4

Ingredients:
- 1 cup asparagus spears, cut into 1-inch pieces
- 1 tsp vegetable oil
- 1 tbsp milk
- 6 eggs, beaten
- 2 ounces (57 g) goat cheese, crumbled
- 1 tbsp minced chives, optional
- Kosher salt and pepper, to taste

Directions:
1. Add the asparagus spears to a small bowl and drizzle with the vegetable oil. Toss until well coated and transfer to the air fry basket.
2. Place the basket on the air fry position.
3. Select Air Fry. Set temperature to 400 degs F (205 degs C)
and set time to 5 min. Flip the asparagus halfway through.

4. When cooking is complete, the asparagus should be tender and slightly wilted.
5. Remove the asparagus from the air fryer grill to a baking pan.
6. Stir together the milk and eggs in a medium bowl. Pour the mixture over the asparagus in the pan. Sprinkle with the goat
cheese and the chives (if using) over the eggs. Season with salt and pepper.
7. Place the pan on the bake position.
8. Select Bake, set temperature to 320 degs F (160 degs C) and set time to 15 min.
9. When cooking is complete, the top should be golden and the eggs should be set.
10. Transfer to a serving dish. Slice and serve.

377. Sausage Quiche

Preparation Time: 5 minutes
Cooking Time: 15 minutes
Servings: 4

Ingredients:
- 12 large eggs
- 1 cup heavy cream
- Salt and black pepper, to taste
- 2 cups shredded Cheddar cheese
- 12 ounces (340 g) sugar-free breakfast sausage
- Cooking Spray

Directions:
1. Coat a casserole dish with cooking spray.
2. Beat together the eggs, heavy cream, salt and pepper in a large bowl until creamy. Stir in the breakfast sausage and Cheddar cheese.
3. Pour the sausage mixture into the prepared casserole dish.
4. Place the dish on the bake position. Select Bake, set temperature to 375 degs F (190 degs C) and set time to 15 min.
5. When done, the top of the quiche should be golden brown and the eggs will be set.
6. Remove from the air fryer grill and let sit for 5 to 10 min before serving.

378. Tomato Breakfast Quiche

Preparation Time: 5 minutes
Cooking Time: 15 minutes
Servings: 4

Ingredients:
- 2 tbsp yellow onion, chopped
- 2 eggs
- 1/4 cup milk
- 1/2 cup gouda cheese, shredded
- 1/4 cup tomatoes, chopped
- Salt and black pepper to the taste

111

- Cooking Spray

Directions
1. Set a ramekin with cooking spray.
2. Crack eggs, add onion, milk, cheese, tomatoes, salt and pepper and stir.
3. Attach this in your air fryer's pan and cook at 340 degs F for
30 min.
4. Serve hot.
5. Enjoy!

379. Sausages Casserole

Preparation Time: 15minutes
Cooking Time: 15 minutes
Servings: 4

Ingredients:
- 3 spring onions, chopped
- 1 green bell pepper, sliced
- ¼ tsp salt
- ¼ tsp ground turmeric
- ¼ tsp ground paprika
- 10 oz Italian sausages
- 1 tsp olive oil
- 4 eggs

Directions:
1. Preheat the air fryer to 360F. Then pour olive oil in the air fryer basket. Add bell pepper and spring onions. Then sprinkle the vegetables with ground turmeric and salt. Cook them for 5 minutes.
2. When the time is finished, shake the air fryer basket gently.

Chop the sausages roughly and add in the air fryer basket. Cook the ingredients for 10 minutes. Then crack the eggs over the sausages and cook the casserole for 10 minutes more.

380. Banana Bread Pudding

Preparation Time: 15minutes
Cooking Time: 15 minutes
Servings: 8

Ingredients:
- 2 medium ripe bananas, mashed
- ½ cup low-fat milk
- 2 tbsp maple syrup
- 2 tbsp peanut butter
- 1 tsp vanilla extract
- 1 tsp ground cinnamon
- 2 slices whole-grain bread, torn into bite-sized pieces
- ¼ cup quick oats
- Cooking Spray

Directions:
1. Spritz the sheet pan with cooking spray.
2. In a large bowl, combine the bananas, maple syrup, peanut butter, milk, vanilla extract and cinnamon. You can use an immersion blender to mix until well combined.

3. Stir in the bread pieces to coat well. Add the oats and stir until everything is combined.
4. Transfer the mixture to the sheet pan. Cover with the aluminium foil.
5. Place the pan on the air fry position.
6. Select Air Fry, set temperature to 375ºF (190ºC) and set time to 15 min.
7. After 10 min, remove the foil and continue to cook for 8 min.
8. Serve immediately.

381. Artichokes and Parsley Frittata

Preparation Time: 5minutes
Cooking Time: 12 minutes
Servings: 4

Ingredients:
- 1 pound artichoke hearts, steamed and chopped
- Salt and black pepper to the taste
- 4 eggs, whisked
- green onion, chopped
- Tablespoon parsley, chopped
- Cooking Spray

Directions:
1. Grease a pan that fits your air fryer with cooking spray. In a bowl, mix all the other ingredients, whisk well and pour evenly into the pan.
2. Introduce the pan in the air fryer, cook at 390 degs F for 12 minutes, divide between plates and serve for breakfast.

382. Lush Vegetable Frittata

Preparation Time: 5minutes
Cooking Time: 12 minutes
Servings: 4

Ingredients:
- 4 eggs
- 1/3 cup milk
- 2 tsps olive oil
- 1 large zucchini, sliced
- 2 asparagus, sliced thinly
- 1/3 cup sliced mushrooms
- 1 cup baby spinach
- 1 small red onion, sliced
- 1/3 cup crumbled feta cheese
- 1/3 cup grated Cheddar cheese
- 1/4 cup chopped chives
- Salt and ground black pepper, to taste

Directions:
1. Line a baking pan with parchment paper.
2. Whisk together the eggs, salt, ground black pepper, and milk in a large bowl. Set aside.

3. Warm up the olive oil in a nonstick skillet over medium heat until shimmering.
4. Add the mushrooms, zucchini, spinach, asparagus, and onion to the skillet and sauté for 5 min or until tender.
5. Pour the sautéed vegetables into the prepared baking pan, then spread the egg mixture over and scatter with cheeses.
6. Place the pan on the bake position.
7. Select Bake, set temperature to 380 degs F (193 degs C) and set time to 15 min. Stir the mixture halfway through.
8. When cooking is complete, the egg should be set and the edges should be lightly browned.
9. Remove the frittata from the air fryer grill and sprinkle with chives before serving.

383. Spiced Crab Meatballs

Preparation Time: 10minutes
Cooking Time: 9 minutes
Servings: 2

Ingredients:
- 10 oz crab meat
- 1 garlic clove, minced
- 1 tbsp green onions, chopped
- 1 tsp ground nutmeg
- ½ tsp salt
- ½ tsp ground turmeric
- 2 tbsp coconut flour
- 1 tsp coconut oil, melted

Directions:
1. Put the crab meat in the bowl and churn it with the help of the fork. Then add minced garlic, green onion, ground nutmeg, salt, ground turmeric, and coconut flour.
2. Stir the mixture until homogenous and make 4 crab meatballs preheat the air fryer to 375F.
3. Put the meatballs in the air fryer and sprinkle them with coconut oil. Cook them for 5 minutes. Then flip them on another side and cook for 4 minutes more.

384. Cheesy Green Chiles Nachos

Preparation Time: 10minutes
Cooking Time: 10 minutes
Servings: 6

Ingredients:
- 8 ounces (227 g) tortilla chips
- 3 cups shredded Monterey Jack cheese, divided
- 2 (7-ounce / 198-g) cans chopped green chiles, drained
- 1 (8-ounce / 227-g) can tomato sauce
- 1/4 tsp dried oregano
- 1/4 tsp granulated garlic
- 1/4 tsp freshly ground black pepper
- Pinch cinnamon

- Pinch cayenne pepper

Directions:
1. Arrange the tortilla chips close together in a single layer on the sheet pan.
2. Sprinkle 1 - 1/2 cups of the cheese over the chips. Arrange the green chiles over the cheese as evenly as possible. Top with the remaining 11/2 cups of the cheese.
3. Place the pan on the toast position.
4. Select Toast, set temperature to 375 degs F (190 degs C) and set time to 10 min.
5. After 5 min, rotate the pan and continue cooking.
6. Meanwhile, stir together the remaining ingredients in a bowl.
7. When cooking is complete, the cheese will be melted and starting to crisp around the edges of the pan. Remove the pan from the air fryer grill. Drizzle the sauce over the nachos and serve warm.

385. Crispy Prosciutto-Wrapped Asparagus

Preparation Time: 10minutes
Cooking Time: 15 minutes
Servings: 4

Ingredients:
- 12 asparagus spears, woody ends trimmed
- 24 pieces thinly sliced prosciutto
- Cooking Spray

Directions:
1. Place the crisper tray on the air fry position. Select Air Fry, set the temperature to 360 degs F (182 degs C), and set the time to 4 min.
2. Wrap each asparagus spear with 2 slices of prosciutto, then repeat this process with the remaining asparagus and prosciutto.
3. Spray the crisper tray with cooking spray, then place 2 to 3 bundles in the crisper tray. Air fry for 4 min. Repeat this process with the remaining asparagus bundles.
4. Remove the bundles and allow to cool on a wire rack for 5 min before serving.

386. Lemon Tempeh

Preparation Time: 8 minutes
Cooking Time: 12 minutes
Servings: 4

Ingredients:
- 1 tsp lemon juice
- 1 tbsp sunflower oil
- 1/4 tsp ground coriander
- 6 oz tempeh, chopped

Directions:
1. Sprinkle the tempeh with lemon juice, sunflower oil, and ground coriander. Massage the tempeh gently with the help of the fingertips. After this, preheat the air fryer to 325F. Put the tempeh in the air fryer and cook it for 12 minutes.
2. Flip the tempeh every 2 minutes during cooking.

387. Bruschetta with Tomato and Basil

Preparation Time: 5 minutes
Cooking Time: 6 minutes
Servings: 6

Ingredients:
- 4 tomatoes, diced
- 1/3 cup shredded fresh basil
- 1/4 cup shredded Parmesan cheese
- 1 tbsp balsamic vinegar
- 1 tbsp minced garlic
- 1 tsp olive oil
- 1 tsp salt
- 1 tsp freshly ground black pepper
- 1 loaf French bread, cut into 1-inch-thick slices
- Cooking Spray

Directions:
1. Place the crisper tray on the bake position. Select Bake, set the temperature to 250 degs F (121 degs C), and set the time to 3 min.
2. Get a bowl and mix in the tomatoes, basil, cheese, vinegar, garlic, olive oil, salt and pepper until well incorporated. Set aside.
3. Spritz the crisper tray with cooking spray. Working in batches, lay the bread slices in the crisper tray in a single layer. Spray the slices with cooking spray.
4. Bake for 3 min until golden brown.
5. Remove from the crisper tray to a plate. Repeat with the remaining bread slices.
6. Top each slice with a generous spoonful of the tomato mixture and serve.

388. Spiced Almonds

Preparation time: 5 minutes
Cooking time: 10 minutes
Servings: 4

Ingredients:
- ½ tsp ground cinnamon
- ½ tsp smoked paprika
- 1 cup almonds
- 1 egg white
- Sea salt to taste

Directions:
1. Preheat air fryer to 310 F. Grease the air fryer basket with cooking spray. In a bowl, beat the egg white with cinnamon and paprika and stir in almonds.
2. Spread the almonds on the bottom of the frying basket and Air Fry for 12 minutes, shaking once or twice. Remove and sprinkle with sea salt to serve.

389. Roasted Coconut Carrots

Preparation time: 5 minutes
Cooking time: 10 minutes
Servings: 4

Ingredients:
- 1 tbsp coconut oil, melted
- 1 lb horse carrots, sliced
- Salt and black pepper to taste
- ½ tsp chili powder

Directions:
1. Preheat air fryer to 400 F.
2. In a bowl, mix the carrots with coconut oil, chili powder, salt, and pepper. Place in the air fryer and AirFry for 7 minutes. Shake the basket and cook for another 5 minutes until golden brown. Serve.

390. Walnut & Cheese Filled Mushrooms

Preparation time: 5 minutes
Cooking time: 10 minutes
Servings: 4

Ingredients:
- 4 large portobello mushroom caps
- ⅓ cup walnuts, minced
- 1 tbsp canola oil
- ½ cup mozzarella cheese, shredded
- 2 tbsp fresh parsley, chopped

Directions:
1. Preheat air fryer to 350 F. Grease the air fryer basket with cooking spray.
2. Rub the mushrooms with canola oil and fill them with mozzarella cheese. Top with minced walnuts and arrange on the bottom of the greased air fryer basket. Bake for 10 minutes or until golden on top. Remove, let cool for a few minutes and sprinkle with freshly chopped parsley to serve.

391. Crispy Dumplings

Preparation Time: 10 minutes
Cooking Time: 10 minutes
Servings: 8

Ingredients:
- .5 lb. Ground pork
- 1 tbsp. Olive oil
- .5 tsp each Black pepper and salt
- Half of 1 pkg. Dumpling wrappers

Directions:
1. Set the Air Fryer temperature setting at 390°

Fahrenheit.

2. Mix the fixings together.

3. Prepare each dumpling using two teaspoons of the pork mixture.

4. Seal the edges with a portion of water to make the triangle form.

5. Lightly spritz the Air Fryer basket using a cooking oil spray as needed. Add the dumplings to air-fry for eight minutes.

6. Serve when they're ready.

2. Beat the egg in a first bowl and sprinkle with salt and black pepper. Combine the Parmesan and bread crumbs in the second bowl.

3. Dredge the chicken in the first bowl to coat well, then in the second the bowl. Shake the excess off.

4. Cook the chicken in the preheated air fryer for 12 minutes or until the internal temperature reaches at least 165°F (74°C). Flip the chicken halfway through the cooking time.

5. Transfer the chicken to a plate and serve with rosemary on top.

392. Easy Ritzy Chicken Nuggets

Preparation Time: 20 minutes
Cooking Time: 8 minutes
Servings: 4

Ingredients:
• 1 ½ pounds chicken tenderloins, cut into small pieces
• 1/2 teaspoon garlic salt
• 1/2 teaspoon cayenne pepper
• 1/4 teaspoon black pepper, freshly cracked
• 4 tablespoons olive oil
• 1/3 cup saltines (e.g. Ritz crackers), crushed
• 4 tablespoons Parmesan cheese, freshly grated

Directions:
1. Start by preheating your Air Fryer to 390 degrees F.

2. Season each piece of the chicken with garlic salt, cayenne pepper, and black pepper.

3. In a mixing bowl, thoroughly combine the olive oil with crushed saltines. Dip each piece of chicken in the cracker mixture.

4. Finally, roll the chicken pieces over the Parmesan cheese.

Cook for 8 minutes, working in batches.

5. Later, if you want to warm the chicken nuggets, add them to the basket and cook for 1 minute more. Serve with French fries, if desired.

393. Parmigiana Chicken

Preparation Time: 3 minutes
Cooking Time: 12 minutes
Servings: 4

Ingredients:
• 2 eggs
• ½ cup Parmesan cheese, grated
• 1 cup seasoned bread crumbs
• 1-pound (454 g) chicken breast halves
• 2 sprigs rosemary, chopped
• From the cupboard:
• Salt and ground black pepper, to taste

Directions:
1. Preheat the air fryer to 380°F (193°C). Spritz the air fryer basket with cooking spray.

394. Easy Paprika Chicken

Preparation Time: 7 minutes
Cooking Time: 18 minutes
Servings: 4

Ingredients:
• 4 chicken breasts
• 1 tablespoon paprika
• ¼ teaspoon garlic powder
• 2 tablespoons fresh thyme, chopped
• From the cupboard:
• Salt and ground black pepper, to taste
• 2 tablespoons butter, melted

Directions:
1. Preheat the air fryer to 360°F (182°C). Spritz the air fryer basket with cooking spray.

2. On a clean work surface, rub the chicken breasts with paprika, garlic powder, salt, and black pepper, then brush with butter.

3. Cook the chicken in the preheated air fryer for 18 minutes or until the internal temperature reaches at least 165°F (74°C). Flip the chicken with tongs halfway through the cooking time.

4. Serve the cooked chicken on a plate immediately with thyme on top.

395. Chicken Wings with Sweet Chili Sauce

Preparation Time: 6 minutes
Cooking Time: 14 minutes
Servings: 4

Ingredients:
• 1-pound (454 g) chicken wings
• 1 teaspoon garlic powder
• 1 tablespoon tamarind powder
• ¼ cup sweet chili sauce
• From the Cupboard:
• Salt and ground black pepper, to taste

Directions:
1. Preheat the air fryer to 390°F (199°C). Spritz the air fryer with cooking spray.

2. On a clean work surface, rub the chicken wings with garlic powder, tamarind powder, salt, and black pepper.

3. Place the wings in the basket and cook for 6 minutes, then spread the chili sauce on top and cook for an additional 8 minutes or until the internal temperature of the wings reaches at least 165°F (74°C).

4. Remove the wings from the air fryer. Allow to cool for a few minutes and serve.

396. Cheesy Chicken Thighs With Marinara Sauce

Preparation Time: 10 minutes
Cooking Time: 10 minutes
Servings: 4

Ingredients:
- 2 tablespoons grated Parmesan cheese
- ½ cup Italian bread crumbs
- 4 chicken thighs
- ½ cup shredded Monterrey Jack cheese
- ½ cup marinara sauce
- From the Cupboard:
- 1 tablespoon butter, melted

Directions:
1. Preheat the air fryer to 380°F (193°C). Spritz the air fryer basket with cooking spray.

2. Combine the Parmesan and bread crumbs in a bowl.

3. On a clean work surface, brush the chicken thighs with butter, then dredge the thighs in the Parmesan mixture to coat.

4. Place the chicken thighs in the preheated air fryer and cook for 5 minutes, then spread the Monterrey Jack cheese over and pour the marinara sauce on the thighs, and then cook for 4 more minutes until the thighs are golden brown and the cheese melts.

5. Transfer the thighs onto a plate and serve warm.

397. Chicken In Bacon Wrap

Preparation Time: 5 minutes
Cooking Time: 15 minutes
Servings: 4

Ingredients:
- 2 chicken breasts
- 8 ounces (227 g) onion and chive cream cheese
- 6 slices turkey bacon
- 1 tablespoon fresh parsley, chopped
- Juice from ½ lemon
- From the Cupboard:
- 1 tablespoon butter
- Salt, to taste

- Special Equipment:
- 2 or 4 toothpicks, soaked for at least 30 minutes

Directions:
1. Preheat the air fryer to 390°F (199°C). Spritz the air fryer basket with cooking spray.

2. On a clean work surface, brush the chicken breasts with cream cheese and butter on both sides. Sprinkle with salt.

3. Wrap each chicken breast with 3 slices of bacon and secure with 1 or 2 toothpicks.

4. Arrange the bacon-wrapped chicken in the preheated air fryer and cook for 14 minutes or until the bacon is well browned and a meat thermometer inserted in the chicken reads at least 165°F (74°C). Flip them halfway through the cooking time.

5. Remove them from the air fryer basket and serve with parsley and lemon juice on top.

398. Shrimp, Spinach And Rice Frittata

Preparation Time: 15 minutes
Cooking Time: 15 minutes
Servings: 4

Ingredients:
- ½ cup chopped shrimp, cooked
- ½ cup baby spinach
- ½ cup of rice, cooked
- 4 eggs
- ½ cup grated Monterey Jack cheese
- ½ teaspoon dried basil
- Pinch salt
- Cooking spray

Direction:
1. Spritz a 6×6×2-inch baking pan with cooking spray. Place the cooked shrimp, rice, and spinach into the pan and stir to combine well. Put the pan into the air fryer basket.

2. Put the air fryer lid on and bake in the preheated air fryer at
325°F for 14 to 18 minutes, or until puffy and golden brown.

3. Remove from the pan and cool for 3 minutes before cutting into wedges to serve.

399. Cheese Rice Fish Balls

Preparation Time: 5 minutes
Cooking Time: 15 minutes
Servings: 6

Ingredients:
- 1 cup smoked fish, flaked
- 2 cups cooked rice
- 2 eggs, lightly beaten
- 1 cup grated Grana Padano cheese
- ¼ cup finely chopped thyme
- Salt and black pepper to taste

- 1 cup panko crumbs

Directions:
1. In a bowl, add fish, rice, eggs, Parmesan cheese, thyme, salt and pepper into a bowl; stir to combine. Shape the mixture into 12 even-sized balls. Roll the balls in the crumbs then spray with oil.
2. Arrange the balls into the fryer and cook for 15 minutes at
400 F, until crispy.

400. Raisins Cinnamon Peaches

Preparation Time: 10 minutes
Cooking Time: 15 minutes
Servings: 4

Ingredients:
- 4 peaches, cored and cut into chunks
- 1 tsp vanilla
- 1 tsp cinnamon
- 1/2 cup raisins
- 1 cup of water

Directions:
1. Put all of the ingredients in the inner pot of air fryer and stir well.
2. Seal pot and cook on high for 15 minutes.
3. As soon as the cooking is done, let it release pressure naturally for 10 minutes then release remaining using quick release. Remove lid.
4. Stir and serve.

401. Corn & Beans Fries

Preparation Time: 10 minutes
Cooking Time: 10 minutes
Servings: 2

Ingredients:
- ¼ cup corn flakes crumbs
- 1 egg
- 10 oz green beans
- 1 tablespoon canola oil
- ½ teaspoon salt
- 1 teaspoon garlic powder

Directions:
1. Preheat the air fryer to 400 F.
2. Put the green beans in the bowl.
3. Beat the egg in the green beans and stir carefully until homogenous.
4. Then sprinkle the green beans with the salt and garlic powder.
5. Shake gently.
6. Then coat the green beans in the corn flakes crumbs well.
7. Put the green beans in the air fryer basket in one layer.
8. Cook the green beans for 7 minutes
9. Shake the green beans twice during the cooking.
10. When the green beans are cooked – let them chill and serve.
11. Enjoy!

402. Chinese Long Beans Mix

Preparation Time: 10 minutes
Cooking Time: 10 minutes
Servings: 4

Ingredients:
- ½ teaspoon coconut aminos
- 1 tablespoon olive oil
- A pinch of salt and black pepper
- garlic cloves, minced
- long beans, trimmed and sliced

Directions:
1. In a pan that fits your air fryer, combine long beans with oil, aminos, salt, pepper and garlic, toss, introduce in your air fryer and cook at 350 degrees F for 10 minutes
1. Divide between plates and serve as a side dish.
2. Enjoy!

403. Our Daily Bean

Preparation Time: 5 minutes
Cooking Time: 10 minutes
Servings: 4

Ingredients:
- 1 (15-ounce) can pinto beans, Dry out
- ¼ cup tomato sauce
- tablespoons nutritional yeast
- large garlic cloves, pressed or minced
- ½ teaspoon dried oregano
- ½ teaspoon cumin
- ¼ teaspoon sea salt
- ⅛ Teaspoon freshly ground black pepper
- Cooking oil spray (sunflower, safflower, or refined coconut)

Directions:
1. In a medium bowl, stir together the beans, tomato sauce, nutritional yeast, garlic, oregano, cumin, salt, and pepper until well combined.
3. Spray the 6-inch round, 2-inch deep baking pan with oil and pour the bean mixture into it. Bake it for 4 minutes Remove, stir well, and Bake it for another 4 minutes, or until the mixture has thickened and is heated through. It will most likely form a little crust on top and be lightly browned in spots. Serve hot. This will keep, refrigerated in an airtight container, for up to a week.

404. Mexican Baked Zucchini

Preparation Time: 10 minutes
Cooking Time: 15 minutes
Servings: 4

Ingredients:
- 1 tablespoon olive oil
- 1 ½ pounds cubed zucchini
- ½ cup chopped onion
- ½ teaspoon garlic salt
- ½ teaspoon paprika
- ½ teaspoon dried oregano
- ½ teaspoon cayenne pepper
- ½ cup cooked long-grain rice
- ½ cup cooked pinto beans
- 1 ¼ cups salsa
- ¾ cup shredded cheddar cheese

Directions:
1. Grease the air fryer basket with olive oil.
4. Put onions and zucchini and cook for 10 minutes at 360 degrees F.
5. Halfway through cooking, give a stir.
6. Season with paprika, cayenne, oregano, garlic salt, and mix well.
7. Next, add in salsa, beans, and rice while stirring.
8. Cook for 5 minutes.
9. Next, stir in cheese and cover the pan with foil.
10. Serve hot and enjoy!

405. Chocolate Berry Cake

Preparation Time: 10 minutes
Cooking Time: 3 minutes
Servings: 6

Ingredients:
- 2 eggs
- ⅔ cup all-purpose flour
- 5 tablespoons sugar
- ⅔ cup unsalted butter
- Salt as needed
- 1 cup melted chocolate chips
- ⅓ cup raspberries

Directions:
1. Preheat the air fryer to 355 degrees for 5 minutes.
2. Grease 6 ramekins with cooking oil spray and dust with some sugar.
3. Thoroughly mix sugar and butter in a bowl.
4. Add eggs and whisk till fluffy.
5. Stir in flour and salt.
6. Add in chocolate chips while mixing.
7. Pour the batter into the ramekins about ¾ full.
8. Place the ramekins in the air fryer basket and cook for 3 minutes.
9. Remove from the basket and serve warm with raspberries on top.

406. Easy Baked Chocolate Mug Cake

Preparation Time: 5 minutes
Cooking Time: 15 minutes
Servings: 3

Ingredients:
- 1 cup coconut cream
- 1 package room temperature cream cheese
- ½ cup cocoa powder
- ½ cup stevia powder
- 1 tablespoon vanilla extract
- 1 tablespoon butter

Directions:
1. Set the air fryer to 350 degrees F.
2. Combine all the ingredients in a bowl.
3. Mix everything with an egg beater.
4. Grease mugs and pour the batter in them.
5. Add the mugs to the air fryer basket.
6. Bake for 15 minutes and place the mugs in the fridge to chill.
7. Serve once cooled.

407. Spicy Wax Bean Meal

Preparation Time: 10 minutes
Cooking Time: 8 minutes
Servings: 4

Ingredients:
- ½ teaspoon black pepper
- 1 teaspoon sea salt flakes
- ½ cup all-purpose flour
- 1 teaspoon smoky chipotle powder
- 2 beaten eggs
- 10 oz. wax beans
- ½ cup crushed saltines

Directions:
1. Combine flour, chipotle, pepper and salt in a bowl.
2. Coat the beans with the flour mixture and the beaten egg mixture
3. Then, coat with the crushed saltines
4. Spray cooking oil spray on the coated beans.
5. Preheat the air fryer to 360 degrees for 4 minutes, ensuring the basket is in there.
6. Add the beans to the air fryer basket and cook for 4 minutes.
7. Remove, shake and cook for 3 more minutes.
8. Serve immediately once done.

408. Cheesy Mushrooms

Preparation Time: 10 minutes
Cooking Time: 12 minutes
Servings: 5

Ingredients:
- 2 tablespoons chopped coriander
- ⅓ teaspoon kosher salt
- 20 stemless mushrooms
- ½ cup grated gorgonzola cheese
- ½ teaspoon crushed red pepper flakes
- ½ cup breadcrumbs
- 2 pressed cloves garlic
- 1 ½ tablespoons olive oil
- ¼ cup low-fat mayonnaise
- 1 teaspoon drained prepared horseradish
- 1 tablespoon finely chopped parsley

Directions:
1. Preheat the air fryer at 380 degrees F for 4 minutes.
11. Combine red pepper, bread crumbs, garlic, coriander, salt, and olive oil in a bowl, except for mushroom and cheese.
12. Fill the mushroom caps with the bread mixture and top with cheese.
13. Put the filled mushrooms on the air fryer basket and cook for 12 minutes.
14. Combine mayonnaise, horseradish and parsley in a bowl.
15. Serve with the cooked mushrooms.

409. Mayonnaise Tortellini Appetizer

Preparation Time: 10 minutes
Cooking Time: 10 minutes
Servings: 5

Ingredients:
- ½ cup flour
- ½ teaspoon dried oregano
- 1 ½ cups breadcrumbs
- ¾ cup mayonnaise
- 2 tablespoons mustard
- 1 egg
- 2 tablespoons olive oil
- 2 cups frozen cheese tortellini

Directions:
1. Preheat the air fryer to 355 degrees F for 4 minutes.
2. Combine mayonnaise and mustard in a bowl.
3. In a separate bowl, whisk the egg.
4. Mix flour and oregano in a separate bowl.
5. In a different bowl, combine breadcrumbs and olive oil.
6. Take the tortellini and coat with the egg, then flour and then egg once again.
7. Finish with a breadcrumb coating.
8. Repeat and add the tortellini to the air fryer basket.
9. Cook for 10 minutes or until golden.
10. Remove and serve immediately with the mayonnaise mixture.

410. Easy Bacon Avocado Fries

Preparation Time: 5 minutes
Cooking Time: 10 minutes
Servings: 4

Ingredients:
- 1 sliced into 8 pieces Avocado
- 6 thin strips of bacon
- ½ teaspoon ranch dressing

Directions:
1. Wrap every 8 slices of avocado with bacon strips.
2. Cut off excess bacon strips.
3. Cook in the air fryer at 400 degrees for 8 minutes.
4. Serve immediately with ranch dressing.

411. Quick Sweet Potato Fries

Preparation Time: 10 minutes
Cooking Time: 10 minutes
Servings: 4

Ingredients:
- 2 medium peeled sweet potatoes
- 2 teaspoons coconut oil
- ½ teaspoon kosher salt
- ½ teaspoon garlic powder
- ¼ teaspoon sweet paprika
- Black pepper as needed

Directions:
1. Preheat the air fryer to 400 degrees F for 6 minutes.
2. Use coconut oil to grease the basket.
3. Cut potatoes into ½ thick fries.
4. Combine with the seasonings.
5. Bake in the air fryer for 8 minutes.
6. Flip it once you cook evenly.
7. Serve once done!

412. Lovely Salmon & Sauce

Preparation Time: 5 minutes
Cooking Time: 10 minutes
Servings: 2

Ingredients:
- 1 cup water
- 6 oz. fresh salmon
- 2 teaspoon vegetable oil
- Salt as needed
- ½ cup plain Greek yogurt
- ½ cup sour cream

- 2 tablespoons finely chopped dill

Directions:
1. Add water to the air fryer tray and heat at 285 degrees F.
2. Drizzle oil over fish and add salt.
3. Put it in the tray and cook for 10 minutes.
4. Combine yogurt, cream, dill, and salt to make the sauce.
5. Serve the fish with the sauce once done.

413. Crispy Paprika Fish Fillets

Preparation Time: 5 minutes
Cooking Time: 15 minutes
Servings: 4

Ingredients:
- ½ cup seasoned breadcrumbs
- 1 tablespoon balsamic vinegar
- ½ teaspoon seasoned salt
- 1 teaspoon paprika
- ½ teaspoon ground black pepper
- 1 teaspoon celery seed
- 2 halved fish fillets
- 1 beaten egg

Directions:
1. Add all the ingredients to the food processor except fish and egg.
2. Process for 30 seconds.
3. Coat the fish with egg and then the breadcrumb mixture.
4. Put the fish on the rack and then into the middle of the air fryer.
5. Cook at 350 degrees F for 15 minutes.
6. Serve hot once done.

414. Crumbed Fish

Preparation Time: 15 minutes
Cooking Time: 12 minutes
Servings: 4

Ingredients:
- 1 sliced lemon
- 1 beaten egg
- 4 flounder fillets
- 1/4 cup of vegetable oil
- 1 cup of dry bread crumbs

Directions:
1. Heat up the Air fryer to 356 F.
2. In a bowl, mix together the oil with bread crumbs, stirring until crumbly.
3. Dip fillets in the beaten egg; let any excess drip off, you can also shake.
4. Dredge fillets in bread crumb to coat evenly.
5. Gently arrange the finely coated fillets in the Air fryer.
6. Cook about 12 minutes until fish easily flakes with a fork.
7. Garnish with slices of lemon.

415. Breaded Shrimp

Preparation Time: 15 minutes
Cooking Time: 12 minutes
Servings: 4

Ingredients:
- 2 eggs
- ½ cup of freshly peeled and diced onion
- 1 pound of peeled and deveined shrimps
- ½ cup of panko breadcrumbs
- 1 tsp of black pepper
- 1 tsp of garlic powder
- 1 tsp of ginger

Directions:
1. Preheat the air fryer. The temperature should be 350°F.
2. Take one bowl and beat the eggs. In another bowl, mix the panko breadcrumbs, spices, and onions
3. Dip the shrimps in the eggs and put them in the panko breadcrumbs bowl.
4. The shrimps should be well coated.
5. Fry the shrimp for 10 minutes. Flip the shrimps midway and cook for another 10 minutes.
6. Serve the shrimps with your favourite chutney, dip, or sauce.

416. Tasty Fryer Fillets

Preparation Time: 5 minutes
Cooking Time: 12 minutes
Servings: 4

Ingredients
- 1/2 lime juice
- 1/2 lime wedges
- 1 Tbs coconut oil
- 1 tsp powdered garlic
- 1 pound diced salmon fillets
- 2 tsps seafood seasoning
- 2 tsps lime pepper seasoning
- salt, to taste

Directions:
1. Ensure the salmon fillets are completely dry then combine the lime juice and coconut oil together.
2. Thoroughly coat the dry salmon with the oil mixture then sprinkle with the salt and remaining seasonings.
3. Prepare the fryer basket with parchment paper then place in the salmon fillets and air fry at 360°F for 12 minutes.
4. Allow the fillets to cool off for a bit then serve, garnished with the lime wedges and enjoy.

120

417. Provencal Pork

Preparation Time: 5 minutes
Cooking Time: 12 minutes
Servings: 4

Ingredients:
- 1 Red onion, sliced
- 1 Yellow bell pepper, cut into strips
- 1 Green bell pepper, cut into strips
- Salt and black pepper to taste
- 2 tsp. Provencal herbs
- ½ tsp. Mustard
- 1 tbsp. Olive oil
- 7 ounces Pork tenderloin

Directions:
1. In a dish, mix salt, pepper, onion, green bell pepper, yellow bell pepper, herbs and half the oil, and toss well.
2. Season pork with mustard, salt, pepper and rest of the oil.
3. Toss well and add to veggies.
4. Cook in the air fryer at 370F for 15 minutes.
5. Serve.

418. Pork Taquitos

Preparation Time: 10 minutes
Cooking Time: 10 minutes
Servings: 10

Ingredients:
- Cooking spray, as required
- 3 cups of shredded chicken or pork tenderloin
- 10 small flour tortillas
- 1 lime freshly juiced
- 1½ cups of fat-free shredded mozzarella cheese
- Nutrition Information:
- Fat 4 g
- Carbohydrates 4 g
- Protein 17 g

Directions:
1. Preheat the air fryer to 380°F.
2. Sprinkle some lime juice on the pork and mix it gently.
3. Take 5 tortillas and microwave them with a damp paper towel over them.
4. Within 10 seconds, the tortillas will be soft.
5. Add ¼ cup of cheese and 3 ounces of pork to a tortilla.
6. Roll up the tortillas gently so that the filler is contained within.
7. On a foil-lined pan which has already been greased, arrange the tortillas in a single line.
8. Spray some cooking spray over the tortillas.
9. Air fry the tortillas until they are golden brown and quite crisp. Flip the tortillas halfway through cooking.
10. Serve the taquitos with your favorite sauce or dip.

419. Jalapeno Poppers

Preparation Time: 10 minutes
Cooking Time: 7 minutes
Servings: 5

Ingredients
- 1 diced onion
- 1 minced garlic clove
- 4 ounces goat cheese
- 5 medium jalapenos
- salt, to taste
- powdered chili
- crushed red pepper
- a handful of cilantro

Instructions
1. Deseed the jalapenos then half each one of them.
2. Combine the onion, garlic, cilantro, red pepper, chili, salt and goat cheese together.
3. Spoon the cheese mixture into the halved jalapenos and arrange in the fryer basket.
4. Air fry for 7 minutes at 350°F.
5. Serve and enjoy as desired.

420. Marinara Eggplant

Preparation Time: 15 minutes
Cooking Time: 14 minutes
Servings: 4

Ingredients
- 1 large eggplant
- 1 cup of marinara sauce
- 2 Tbs of olive oil
- 1 cup of walnuts
- 1 Tbs of dried basil
- 1 Tbs of dried rosemary
- Salt and pepper to taste

Instructions
1. Slice the eggplant into ½ inch slices. Set aside.
2. In a food processor, blend the walnuts for about 10-15 seconds.
3. Thinly chop the basil and the rosemary.
4. Heat air fryer to 375 F.
5. Oil each eggplant slice with olive oil and place them into the fryer.
6. Top each slice with walnuts, marinara sauce, basil, and rosemary.
7. Cook for 12 minutes. Add salt and pepper.
8. Serve and enjoy!

421. Eggplant Fries & Salsa

Preparation Time: 15 minutes
Cooking Time: 15 minutes
Servings: 2

Ingredients:
- ¼ cup olive oil
- ¼ cup cornstarch
- ¼ cup water
- 1 eggplant, cut into long strips
- Salt to taste
- 2 tomatoes, chopped
- 2 Tbs sweet chili sauce

Directions:
1. Preheat your air fryer to 390 degrees F.
2. Mix olive oil, cornstarch and water.
3. Dip eggplant strips in the mixture.
4. Season with salt.
5. Cook eggplant in the air fryer for 15 minutes.
6. In a bowl, combine tomatoes and sweet chili sauce.
7. Serve eggplant fries with tomato salsa.

422. Cheesecake

Preparation Time: 7 minutes
Cooking Time: 2 minutes
Servings: 2

Ingredients:
- 1/2 cup erythritol
- 1/2 cup almond flour
- 1/2 tsp vanilla extract
- 2 Tbs erythritol
- 4 Tbs divided heavy cream
- 8 ounces cream cheese

Directions:
1. Allow the cream cheese to soften then incorporate with the 2 Tbs heavy cream, vanilla, and 1/2 cup erythritol until smooth and combined.
2. Transfer the mixture onto a baking sheet lined with parchment paper then place in the freezer until firm.
3. Using a medium sized bowl, add in the almond flour and 1 Tbs erythritol then mix together.
4. Dip the cheesecake bites into the remaining heavy cream then run through the flour mixture.
5. Arrange the bites into the fryer basket and air fry for 2 minutes at 300°F.
6. Serve and enjoy as desired.

423. Strawberry Egg Rolls

Preparation Time: 15 minutes
Cooking Time: 15 minutes
Servings: 4

Ingredients:
- 16 ounces cream cheese
- 4 Tbs granulated sugar
- 1 Tbs freshly squeezed lemon juice
- 15 strawberries, diced
- 8 egg roll wrappers
- 2 ounces butter, melted

Directions:
1. Beat cream cheese with sugar and lemon juice.
2. Fold in the strawberries.
3. Scoop the cheese mixture on top of each egg roll. Fold corners and roll.
16. Seal the edges.
17. Put the rolls in the air fryer basket.
18. Brush with butter.
19. Cook at 375 degrees F for 15 minutes.

424. Italian Chicken

Preparation Time: 10 minutes
Cooking Time: 15 minutes
Servings: 4

Ingredients
- 5 Chicken thighs
- 1 tbsp. Olive oil
- 2 cloves Garlic, minced
- 1 tbsp Thyme, chopped
- ½ cup Heavy cream
- ¾ cup Chicken stock
- 1 tsp Red pepper flakes, crushed
- ¼ cup Parmesan, grated
- ½ cup Sun-dried tomatoes
- 2 tbsp Basil, chopped
- Salt and black pepper to taste

Instructions
1. Season chicken with salt and pepper, and rub with half of the oil.
2. Place in the preheated air fryer at 350F and cook for 3 minutes.
3. Meanwhile, heat rest of the oil in a pan and add garlic, thyme, pepper flakes, tomatoes, stock, heavy cream, salt, parmesan and pepper.
4. Bring to a simmer and remove from the heat. Place the mixture in a dish.
5. Add chicken thighs on top and cook in the air fryer at 320F for 12 minutes.
6. Serve with basil sprinkled on top.

425. Paneer Cheese Balls

Preparation Time: 10 minutes
Cooking Time: 15 minutes
Serving: 6

Ingredients:
- 1 cup paneer, crumbled
- 1 cup cheese, grated
- 1 potato, boiled and mashed
- 1 onion, chopped finely
- 1 green chili, chopped finely
- 1 teaspoon red chili flakes
- Salt to taste
- 4 tablespoon coriander leaves, chopped finely
- ½ cup all-purpose flour
- ¾ cup of water
- Breadcrumbs as needed

Direction:
1. Mix flour with water in a bowl and spread the breadcrumbs in a tray.
2. Add the rest of the ingredients to make the paneer mixture.
3. Make golf ball-sized balls out of this mixture.
4. Dip each ball in the flour liquid then coat with the breadcrumbs.
5. Rotate the SELECT/CONFIRM dial until its indicator reaches the "Air Fry" mode.
6. Turn the TIME DIAL to change the cooking time to 15 minutes.
7. Rotate the TEMPERATURE DIAL to change the temperature to 360 degrees F.
8. Press the START/STOP button to begin preheating.
9. Place the cheese balls in the air fryer basket and spray it with cooking spray. Close the door and cook.
10. Serve.

426. Plantains Chips

Preparation Time: 10 minutes
Cooking Time: 10 minutes
Serves: 4

Ingredients:
- 2 ripe plantains, sliced
- 2 teaspoons avocado oil
- ⅛ teaspoon salt

Direction:
1. Gently toss the plantains with oil and salt in a bowl.
2. Rotate the SELECT/CONFIRM dial until its indicator reaches the "Air Fry" mode.
3. Turn the TIME DIAL to change the cooking time to 10 minutes.
4. Rotate the TEMPERATURE DIAL to change the temperature to 360 degrees F.
5. Press the START/STOP button to begin preheating.
6. Spread the plantains in the air fryer basket. Close the door and cook.
7. Serve fresh.

427. Pasta Chips

Preparation Time: 10 minutes
Cooking Time: 10 minutes
Serves: 2

Ingredients:
- ½ tablespoon olive oil
- ½ tablespoon nutritional yeast
- 1 cup bow tie pasta
- ⅔ teaspoon Italian seasoning blend
- ¼ teaspoon salt

Direction:
1. Cook and boil the pasta in salted water in half of the time as stated on the box then drain it.
2. Toss the boiled pasta with salt, Italian seasoning, nutritional yeast, and olive oil in a bowl.
3. Rotate the SELECT/CONFIRM dial until its indicator reaches the "Air Fry" mode.
4. Turn the TIME DIAL to change the cooking time to 5 minutes.
5. Rotate the TEMPERATURE DIAL to change the temperature to 390 degrees F.
6. Press the START/STOP button to begin preheating.
7. Spread this pasta in the air fryer basket. Close the door and cook.
8. Enjoy.

428. Bacon-Wrapped Jalapeno Poppers

Preparation Time: 10 minutes
Cook Time: 15 minutes
Serves: 5

Ingredients:
- 4 ounces of cream cheese
- ½ tablespoon garlic salt
- 5 jalapeno peppers, halved
- 10 sausages
- 10 slices of bacon

Preparation:
1. Mix cheese and garlic salt in a bowl.
2. Stuff each of the half pepper with cream cheese mixture.
3. Top the peppers with sausages then wrap them with bacon slices.
4. Rotate the SELECT/CONFIRM dial until its indicator reaches the "Air Fry" mode.
5. Turn the TIME DIAL to change the cooking time to 15 minutes.
6. Rotate the TEMPERATURE DIAL to change the temperature to 375 degrees F.

7. Press the START/STOP button to begin preheating.
8. Place the wrapped jalapeno peppers in the air fryer basket.
9. Close the door and cook. Serve.

429. Russet Potato Hay

Preparation Time: 10 minutes
Cooking Time: 15 minutes
Serves: 4

Ingredients:
- 2 Russet potatoes
- 1 tablespoon olive oil
- Salt and black pepper to taste

Direction:
1. Pass the potatoes through a spiralizer to get potato spirals.
2. Soak these potato spirals in a bowl filled with water for about 20 minutes.
3. Drain and rinse the soaked potatoes then pat them dry.
4. Toss the potato spirals with salt, black pepper, and oil in a bowl.
5. Rotate the SELECT/CONFIRM dial until its indicator reaches the "Air Fry" mode.
6. Turn the TIME DIAL to change the cooking time to 15 minutes.
7. Rotate the TEMPERATURE DIAL to change the temperature to 360 degrees F.
8. Press the START/STOP button to begin preheating.
9. Spread the seasoned potato spirals in the air fryer basket.
10. Close the door and cook.
11. Serve.

430. Breaded Sea Scallops

Preparation Time: 10 minutes
Cooking Time: 5 minutes
Serves: 4

Ingredients:
- ½ cup crushed buttery crackers
- ½ tablespoon garlic powder
- ½ tablespoon old bay seasoning
- 2 tablespoons melted butter
- 1 pound sea scallops, pat dried
- Cooking spray
- Lemon wedges

Direction:
1. In a bowl, mix the crackers, garlic powder and old bay until well combined.
2. Place the butter in a shallow bowl.

3. Dip the scallops in butter then coat them with the cracker mixture.
4. Rotate the SELECT/CONFIRM dial until its indicator reaches the "Air Fry" mode.
5. Turn the TIME DIAL to change the cooking time to 5 minutes.
6. Rotate the TEMPERATURE DIAL to change the temperature to 390 degrees F.
7. Press the START/STOP button to begin preheating.
8. Place the scallops in the air fryer basket leaving a space between each piece.
9. Mist the scallops with cooking spray.
10. Close the door and cook.
11. Garnish with lemon wedges and serve.

431. Loaded Potato Foil Packs

Preparation Time: 10 minutes
Cooking Time: 15 minutes
Serves: 4

Ingredients:
- 3 potatoes, cut into ¼ inch thick slices
- 3 tablespoons olive oil
- 2 tablespoons chopped parsley
- 1 tablespoon salt
- ½ tablespoon black pepper
- 4 double-walled aluminum foils

Direction:
1. In a bowl, add the potatoes, olive oil, parsley, salt and pepper and toss to mix.
2. Divide the potato slices among the aluminum foil. Fold them and seal.
3. Rotate the SELECT/CONFIRM dial until its indicator reaches the "BAKE" mode.
4. Turn the TIME DIAL to change the cooking time to 15 minutes.
5. Rotate the TEMPERATURE DIAL to change the temperature to 350 degrees F.
6. Press the START/STOP button to begin preheating.
7. Arrange the foil pack in the roasting pan. Close the door and cook.
8. Serve.

432. Buffalo Chicken Pizza

Preparation Time: 10 minutes
Cooking Time: 10 minutes
Serves: 4

Ingredients:
- Cooking spray
- 4 naan bread
- ½ cup pizza sauce

- 1 cup cooked chicken, diced
- 1 cup buffalo hot sauce
- 1 cup mozzarella cheese, shredded

Directions:
1. Grease the pizza pan of with cooking spray.
2. Rotate the SELECT/CONFIRM dial until its indicator reaches the "BAKE" mode.
3. Turn the TIME DIAL to change the cooking time to 7 minutes.
4. Rotate the TEMPERATURE DIAL to change the temperature to 350 degrees F.
5. Press the START/STOP button to begin preheating.
6. Place the pieces of naan bread on the pan and spread the pizza sauce over the bread.
7. In a bowl, add the chicken and hot sauce. Toss to mix.
8. Spread the chicken over the bread pieces then sprinkle them with cheese.
9. Close the door and cook.
10. Serve.

433. Lemon Air Fryer Broccolini

Preparation Time: 5 minutes
Cooking Time: 7 minutes
Serves: 4

Ingredients:
- 12 ounces broccolini
- 1 tablespoon olive oil
- 1 tablespoon lemon juice
- 1 clove garlic minced
- ½ teaspoon Kosher salt

Directions:
1. Preheat your Air Fryer Oven to 380° F
2. Rinse and shake dry the broccolini. Then trim the tips.
3. In a mixing bowl, mix lemon juice, salt, olive oil and garlic.
4. Toss and mix with broccolini. Lay a single layer in the Air Fryer Basket.
5. Roast for six to seven minutes on Air Fry mode.

434. Italian Vegetables

Preparation Time: 10 minutes
Cook Time: 15 minutes
Serves: 4

Ingredients:
- 2 medium bell peppers cored, chopped
- 2 medium carrots, peeled and sliced
- 1 small zucchini, ends trimmed, sliced
- 1 medium broccoli, florets
- ½ red onion, peeled and diced
- 2 tablespoons olive oil

- 1 ½ teaspoon Italian seasoning
- 2 garlic cloves, minced
- Salt and freshly ground black pepper
- 1 cup grape tomatoes
- 1 tablespoon fresh lemon juice

Directions:
1. Toss all the veggies with olive oil, Italian seasoning, salt, black pepper, and garlic in a large salad bowl.
2. Rotate the SELECT/CONFIRM dial until its indicator reaches the "BAKE" mode.
3. Turn the TIME DIAL to change the cooking time to 15 minutes.
4. Rotate the TEMPERATURE DIAL to change the temperature to 400 degrees F.
5. Press the START/STOP button to begin preheating.
6. Spread this broccoli-zucchini mixture on the roasting pan lined with parchment paper.
7. Close the door and cook.
8. Enjoy.

435. Rainbow Vegetables

Preparation Time: 10 minutes
Cooking Time: 20 minutes
Serves: 4

Ingredients:
- 1 red bell pepper, seeded and diced
- 1 yellow summer squash, diced
- 1 zucchini, cut into chunks
- 4 ounces fresh mushrooms, cleaned and halved
- ½ sweet onion, cut into wedges
- 1 tablespoon olive oil
- Salt and black pepper to taste

Directions:
1. Rotate the SELECT/CONFIRM dial until its indicator reaches the "Air Fry" mode.
2. Turn the TIME DIAL to change the cooking time to 20 minutes.
3. Rotate the TEMPERATURE DIAL to change the temperature to 350 degrees F.
4. Press the START/STOP button to begin preheating.
5. Toss the red bell pepper, zucchini, summer squash, mushrooms, and onion in a large bowl.
6. Stir in black pepper, salt, and olive oil to season the veggies.
7. Spread these vegetables in the air fryer basket lined with parchment paper.
8. Close the door and cook.
9. Serve warm.

436. Healthy Buffalo Cauliflower

Preparation Time: 10 minutes
Cook Time: 15 minutes
Serves: 2

Ingredients:
- 2 ¼ pound cauliflower head, trimmed and cut into florets
- ¼ cup cayenne pepper sauce
- 2 tablespoon butter, melted
- 2 tablespoon vinegar
- ⅛ tablespoon garlic powder
- Salt to taste
- For garnishing: chopped parsley

Directions:
1. In a bowl, mix the cauliflower, pepper sauce, butter, vinegar, garlic powder and salt.
2. Rotate the SELECT/CONFIRM dial until its indicator reaches the "Air Fry" mode.
3. Turn the TIME DIAL to change the cooking time to 12 minutes.
4. Rotate the TEMPERATURE DIAL to change the temperature to 400 degrees F.
5. Press the START/STOP button to begin preheating.
6. Transfer the cauliflower to the air fryer basket. Close the door and cook.
7. Garnish the cauliflower with parsley and serve.

437. Air Fryer Lobster Tails with Lemon-Garlic Butter

Preparation Time: 10 minutes
Cooking Time: 20 minutes
Serves: 2

Ingredients:
- 2 lobster tails
- Butter, 4 tablespoons
- Lemon zest, 1 teaspoon
- 1 clove garlic
- Salt and ground black pepper, to taste
- Chopped parsley, 1 teaspoon
- Lemon, 2 wedges

Direction:
1. Using kitchen shears, cut through the centers of the top shells and meat to butterfly the lobster tails. Cut to the bottom but not through the shells. Spread the tail halves apart and place them in the Air Fryer Oven Basket, meat facing up.
2. Take a small saucepan and melt butter over medium heat.
3. Then add garlic and lemon zest and heat for about 30 seconds.
4. Take two tablespoons of the butter mixture and transfer it to a small bowl. Brush it onto the

lobster tails and discard the unused.
5. Cook the lobsters for about 5 to seven minutes in the Air Fryer Oven at 380° F on Air Fry mode. Pour the remaining butter from the saucepan with a spoon over the lobster meat.

438. Air Fryer Fish Fingers

Preparation Time: 10 minutes
Cooking Time: 15 minutes
Serves: 2

Ingredients:
- 1 pound fish fillets
- All-purpose flour, ½ cup
- Salt divided, 1 teaspoon
- Ground black pepper divided, ½ teaspoon
- 2 eggs
- Dried breadcrumbs, 1 cup

Directions:
1. Thaw completely if using frozen fish. Season with salt and let it sit idle for 20 to 30 minutes.
2. Take the flour and season with salt and pepper.
3. Then, dredge the fillets in the flour. Dip in egg and thoroughly coat with breadcrumbs.
4. Air fry them in Air Fryer Oven for about 10 minutes at 400° F, flip, and cook for another 5 minutes.

439. Paprika Broiled Lobster Tail

Preparation Time: 10 Minutes
Cook Time: 10 Minutes
Serves: 4

Ingredients:
- 6 ounces of lobster tails, shell cut from the top
- ⅛ teaspoon salt
- ⅛ teaspoon black pepper
- ⅛ teaspoon paprika
- 1 tablespoon butter
- ½ lemon, cut into wedges
- Chopped parsley for garnish

Directions:
1. Place the lobster tails in the oven's baking tray.
2. Whisk the rest of the ingredients in a bowl and pour over the lobster tails
3. Select the Bake mode.
4. Set the temperature at 350 F and the cooking time to 10 minutes
5. Serve warm.

440. Juicy Steak Bites

Preparation Time: 10 minutes
Cooking Time: 9 minutes
Servings: 4

Ingredients:
- 1 lb. sirloin steak, cut into bite-size pieces
- 1 tbsp. steak seasoning
- 1 tbsp. olive oil
- Pepper
- Salt

Directions:
1. Warm air fryer to 390 F. Add steak pieces into the large mixing bowl. Add steak seasoning, oil, pepper, and salt over steak pieces and toss until well coated.
2. Transfer steak pieces on air fryer pan and air fry for 5 minutes.
3. Turn steak pieces to the other side and cook for 4 minutes more. Serve and enjoy.

441. Beef Patties

Preparation Time: 10 minutes
Cooking Time: 13 minutes
Servings: 4

Ingredients:
- 1 lb. ground beef
- 1/2 tsp. garlic powder
- 1/4 tsp. onion powder
- Pepper
- Salt

Directions:
1. Warm air fryer to 400 F. Add ground meat, garlic powder, onion powder, pepper, and salt into the mixing bowl and mix until well combined.
2. Make even shape patties from meat mixture and arrange an air fryer pan. Place pan in the air fryer. Air fry patties for 10 minutes Turn patties after 5 minutes. Serve and enjoy.

442. Vegetable Pita Sandwiches

Preparation Time: 15 minutes
Cooking Time: 12 minutes
Servings: 4

Ingredients:
- 1 baby eggplant, peeled and chopped
- 1 red bell pepper, sliced
- 1/2 cup diced red onion
- 1/2 cup shredded carrot
- 1 teaspoon olive oil
- 1/3 cup low-fat Greek yogurt
- 1/2 teaspoon dried tarragon
- low-sodium whole-wheat pita bread, halved crosswise

Directions:
1. In a 6-by-2-inch pan, stir together the eggplant, red bell pepper, red onion, carrot, and olive oil. Put the vegetable mixture into the air fryer basket and roast for 7 to 9 minutes, stirring once, until the vegetables are tender. Drain if necessary. In a small bowl, thoroughly mix the yogurt and tarragon until well combined.
2. Stir the yogurt mixture into the vegetables. Stuff one-fourth of this mixture into each pita pocket.
3. Place the sandwiches in the air fryer and air fry for 2 to 3 minutes, or until the bread is toasted. Serve immediately.

443. Ground beef

Preparation Time: 15 minutes
Cooking Time: 12 minutes
Servings: 6

Ingredients:
- 1-1/2 lb. ground beef
- 1 tbsp. salt
- 1/2 tbsp. pepper
- 1/2 tbsp. garlic powder

Directions:
1. Put the beef in a baking tray then season well with salt, pepper, and garlic powder.
2. Stir well using a wooden spoon.
3. Select the air fry setting on the Air Fryer.
4. Set the temperature at 400°F for 5 minutes.
5. Stir well when halfway cooked and continue cooking for the remaining minutes.
6. Crumble the meat well and leave the broth. Use the beef in your favorite recipe.

444. Zucchini Gratin

Preparation Time: 10 minutes
Cooking Time: 12 minutes
Servings: 4

Ingredients:
- Two Zucchini
- 1 Tablespoon Flour of Coconut
- 1 Parsley tablespoon
- 1 Butter Teaspoon
- 5 ounces of Cheese Parmesan, Shredded

Directions:
1. In a tub, blend the coconut flour, black pepper and cheese together.
2. Shake well then cut your zucchini into slices. Cut the squares of your zucchini, and then spread them out in the air-fryer. Heat your air fryer to 400, then mix it all together and cook for 13 minutes.

445. Kale Mash

Preparation Time: 10 minutes
Cooking Time: 10 minutes
Servings: 4

Ingredients:
- 1 lb. Kale of the Italian Dark Leaf
- 7 Parmesan Ounces, Shredded
- 1 Heavy Cream Cup
- 1 Butter Teaspoon
- 1 Onion, Diced

Directions:
1. Chop the kale and then add it to the basket of your air fryer. Sprinkle with the rest of the ingredients, and then heat up your air fryer to 250.
2. Cook for twelve minutes and then before serving, mix well.

446. Spaghetti Squash

Preparation Time: 10 minutes
Cooking Time: 2 minutes
Servings: 4

Ingredients:
- 1 lb. Squash Winter
- 1 Chicken Stock Cup
- Heavy Cream 4 Tablespoons
- 1 Sea Salt Teaspoon, Black Pepper
- 1 Butter Teaspoon

Directions:
1. Start by peeling and grating your winter squash, then heat your air fryer in your basket to 400, cover with chicken stock and season with salt and pepper. For ten minutes, cook.
2. Strain the liquid, and then apply the butter and heavy cream to the mixture. Serve it sweet.

447. Tuscan Cantucci

Preparation Time: 20 minutes
Cooking Time: 15 minutes
Servings: 2

Ingredients:
- 250 g of flour
- 150 g of coarsely chopped almonds
- 150 g of sugar
- 50 g of soft butter
- 2 eggs
- 8 g of baking powder
- 1/2 glass of white wine

Directions:
1. In the mixer or by hand, combine the butter and sugar. Add the yeast and almonds. In two or three times, add the flour, taking care to mix well. Combine the wine several times

to obtain a dough from which to obtain a roll of about 3 inches in diameter. Cut slices from the roll about 1/2 inch thick. Arrange on baking paper.
2. Preheat the air fryer to 180C/355F.
3. Place the paper in the basket and insert it into the fryer. Cook for 8-10 minutes. Turn the cookies over to the other side and bake another 5 minutes until golden brown.
4. Traditionally they are dipped in sweet wine.

448. Pumpkin Cookies

Preparation Time: 15 minutes
Cooking Time: 15 minutes
Servings: 4

Ingredients:
- 2 1/2 cups flour
- 1/2 teaspoon baking soda
- tablespoon flax seed, ground
- 1/2 cup dark chocolate chips
- 3 tablespoons water
- 1/2 cup pumpkin flesh, mashed
- 1/4 cup honey
- 1 tablespoons butter
- 2 teaspoon vanilla extract

Directions:
1. In a bowl, blend flax seed with water, mix and leave aside for a couple minutes.
2. In another bowl, blend flour in with salt and preparing pop.
3. In a third bowl, blend nectar in with pumpkin puree, spread, vanilla concentrate and flaxseed.
4. Consolidate flour with nectar blend and chocolate chips and mix.
5. Scoop 1 tablespoon of treat batter on a lined heating sheet that accommodates your air fryer, rehash with the remainder of the batter, present them in your air fryer and cook at 350 degrees F for 15 minutes.
6. Leave treats to chill off and serve.

449. Apple Dumplings

Preparation Time: 10 minutes
Cooking Time: 25 minutes
Servings: 4

Ingredients:
- 2 tbsp. melted coconut oil
- 2 puff pastry sheets
- 1 tbsp. brown sugar
- 2 tbsp. raisins
- 2 small apples of choice

Directions:
1. Ensure your air fryer oven is preheated to 356 degrees
2. Core and peel apples and mix with raisins

and sugar.

3. Place a bit of apple mixture into puff pastry sheets and brush sides with melted coconut oil.

4. Place into the air fryer. Cook 25 minutes, we were turning halfway through. It will be golden when done.

450. Cookie Custards

Preparation Time: 10
Cooking Time: x
Servings: 5

Ingredients:
- 2 tbsp. margarine
- A pinch of baking soda and baking powder
- 1 C. all-purpose flour
- ½ C. icing sugar
- ½ C. custard powder

Directions:
1. Cream the margarine and sugar together. Add the remaining ingredients and fold them together.

2. Prepare a baking tray by greasing it with butter. Make balls out of the dough, coat them with flour and place them in the tray.

3. Preheat the fryer to 300 Fahrenheit for five minutes. You will need to place the baking tray in the basket and cover it. Cook till you find that the balls have turned golden brown. Remove the tray and leave it to cool outside for half an hour. Store in an airtight container.

451. Mini Pecan Pies

Preparation Time: 8
Cooking Time: 10
Servings: 6

Ingredients:
- Nonstick cooking spray
- 1 sheet puff pastry, thawed
- 4 tbsp. brown sugar
- ½ stick butter, melted
- 2 tbsp. maple syrup
- ½ C. pecans, chopped fine

Directions:
1. Place baking pan in position 2. Lightly spray fryer basket with cooking spray.

2. In a plastic bowl, stir together butter, syrup and pecans.

3. Freeze 10 minutes.

4. Unfold pastry on a lightly floured surface. Gently roll it out.

5. Cut in 8 equal triangles.

6. Spoon 2 tsp. of pecan mixture onto the right side of rectangles, leaving a border. Fold left side over filling and seal edges with a fork. Pierce the tops of each pie.

7. Place half the pies in the fryer basket and put it on the baking pan. Set oven to air fryer on 375°F for 10 minutes. Cook pies

8. 7 minutes or until puffed and golden brown. Repeat with remaining pies. Serve warm.

452. Raspberry Muffins

Preparation Time: 6
Cooking Time: 15
Servings: 4

Ingredients:
- 2 C. almond flour
- ¾ C. Swerve
- 1¼ tsp. baking powder
- ⅓ tsp. ground allspice
- ⅓ tsp. ground anise star
- ½ tsp. grated lemon zest
- ¼ tsp. salt
- 2 eggs
- 1 C. sour cream
- ½ C. coconut oil
- ½ C. raspberries

Directions:
1. Line a muffin pan with 6 paper liners.

2. In a mixing bowl, mix the almond flour, Swerve, baking powder, allspice, anise, lemon zest, and salt.

3. In another mixing bowl, beat the eggs, sour cream, and coconut oil until well mixed. Add the egg mixture to the flour mixture and stir to combine. Mix in the raspberries.

4. Scrape the batter into the prepared muffin cups, filling each about three-quarters full.

5. Put the muffin pan into Rack Position 1, select Convection Bake, set temperature to 345°F (174ºC), and set time to 15 minutes.

6. When cooking is complete, the tops should be golden and a toothpick inserted in the middle should come out clean.

7. Allow the muffins to cool for 10 minutes in the muffin pan before removing and serving.

453. Nutella Brownies

Preparation Time: 10
Cooking Time: 15
Servings: 8

Ingredients:
- ½ stick unsalted butter
- ¼ C. half-and-half
- 4 oz chocolate chips
- ½ C. Nutella spread
- 1 C. sugar
- 3 large eggs
- 1 C. all-purpose flour
- ½ C. Dutch cocoa powder
- ½ tsp. salt
- ½ tsp. vanilla extract

Directions:
1. Preheat oven to 350°F.

2. Whisk together sugar and eggs in one bowl.

3. Whisk together flour, cocoa and salt in

another bowl.

4. In smart oven, simmer butter and half-and-half together over low heat.
5. Add chocolate chips and stir until melted, about 2 minutes.
6. Add in Nutella and continue stirring until incorporated.
7. Remove from heat.
8. Pour sugar mixture into chocolate mixture in smart oven.
9. Carefully add flour mixture and fold until just incorporated.
10. Bake for 15 minutes, but start checking at 10 minutes until you will have a brownie with a fudge-like consistency.

454. Healthy Sesame Bars

Preparation Time: 10
Cooking Time: 15
Servings: 8

Ingredients:
- 1 1/4 C. sesame seeds
- 1/4 C. applesauce
- 3/4 C. coconut butter
- 10 drops liquid stevia
- 1/2 tsp. vanilla
- Pinch of salt

Directions:
1. Fit the Cuisinart oven with the rack in position
2. In a large bowl, add applesauce, coconut butter, vanilla, liquid stevia, and sea salt and stir until well combined.
3. Add sesame seeds and stir to coat.
4. Pour mixture into a greased baking dish.
5. Set to bake at 350 F for 15 minutes. After 5 minutes place the baking dish in the preheated oven.
6. Cut into pieces and serve.

455. Caramelized Peaches

Preparation Time: 15
Cooking Time: 15
Servings: 4

Ingredients:
- 2 tbsp. sugar
- ¼ tsp. ground cinnamon
- 4 peaches, cut into wedges
- Cooking spray

Directions:
1. Toss the peaches with the sugar and cinnamon in a medium bowl until evenly coated.
2. Lightly spray the air fryer basket with cooking spray. Place the peaches in the basket in a single

layer. Lightly mist the peaches with cooking spray.
3. Put the air fryer basket on the baking pan and slide into Rack Position 2, select Air Fry, set temperature to 350°F (180°C), and set time to 10 minutes.
4. After 5 minutes, remove from the oven and flip the peaches.
5. Return to the oven and continue cooking for 5 minutes.
6. When cooking is complete, the peaches should be caramelized. If necessary, continue cooking for 3 minutes. Remove from the oven. Let the peaches cool for 5 minutes and serve warm.

456. Sago Payada

Preparation Time: 12
Cooking Time: 10
Servings: 4

Ingredients:
- 3 tbsp. powdered sugar
- 3 tbsp. unsalted butter
- 2 C. milk
- 2 cups-soaked sago
- 2 tbsp. custard powder

Directions:
1. Boil the milk and the sugar in a pan and add the custard powder followed by the sago and stir till you get a thick mixture.
2. Preheat the fryer to 300 Fahrenheit for five minutes. Place the dish in the basket and reduce the temperature to 250 Fahrenheit. Cook for ten minutes and set aside to cool.

457. Blueberry Pudding

Preparation Time: 10
Cooking Time: 10
Servings: 4

Ingredients:
- 2 tbsp. custard powder
- 3 tbsp. powdered sugar
- 3 tbsp. unsalted butter
- 1 C. blueberry juice
- 2 C. milk

Directions:
1. Boil the milk and the sugar in a pan and add the custard powder followed by the blueberry juice and stir till you get a thick mixture.
2. Preheat the fryer to 300 Fahrenheit for five minutes. Place the dish in the basket and reduce the temperature to 250 Fahrenheit. Cook for ten minutes and set aside to cool.

458. Gluten-free Fried Bananas

Preparation Time: 10
Cooking Time: 12
Servings: 8

Ingredients:
- 8 bananas
- 3 tbsp. vegetable oil
- 3 tbsp. cornflour
- 1 egg white
- ¾ C. breadcrumbs

Directions:
1. Preheat Cuisinart on Toast function to 350 F. Combine the oil and breadcrumbs in a small bowl.
2. Coat the bananas with the corn flour first, brush them with egg white, and dip them in the breadcrumb mixture. Arrange on a lined baking sheet and cook for 8-12 minutes. Serve.

459. Fried Pickles

Preparation Time: 6
Cooking Time: 3
Servings: 5

Ingredients:
- Cold dill pickle slices, 36.
- Chopped fresh dill, 2 tbsps.
- Salt, 1 tsp.
- Divided cornstarch, 1 cup
- Ranch dressing
- Cayenne, ¼ tsp.
- Black pepper, 2 tsps.
- Almond meal, ½ cup
- Large egg, 1.
- Almond milk, ¾ cup
- Paprika, 2 tsps.
- Canola oil

Directions:
1. Whisk together cayenne, milk, and egg.
2. Spread half-cup cornstarch in a shallow dish.
3. Mix the remaining ½-cup cornstarch with almond meal, salt, pepper, dill, and paprika.
4. Dredge the pickle slices first through the cornstarch then dip them in an egg wash.
5. Coat them with almond meal mixture and shake off the excess.
6. Place them in the fryer basket and spray them with oil.
7. Return the basket to the fryer and air fry the pickles for 3 minutes at 3700 F working in batches as to not crowd the basket.
8. Serve warm.

460. Marshmallow Pastries

Preparation Time: 4
Cooking Time: 5
Servings: 4

Ingredients:
- 4 phyllo pastry sheets, thawed
- 2 oz. butter, melted
- ¼ C. chunky peanut butter
- 4 tsp. marshmallow fluff
- Pinch of salt

Directions:
1. Brush 1 sheet of phyllo with butter.
2. Place a second sheet of phyllo on top of first one and brush it with butter.
3. Repeat until all 4 sheets are used.
4. Cut the phyllo layers in 4 (3x12-inch) strips.
5. Place 1 tbsp. of peanut butter and 1 tsp. of marshmallow fluff on the underside of a strip of phyllo.
6. Carefully, fold the tip of sheet over the filling to make a triangle.
7. Fold repeatedly in a zigzag manner until the filling is fully covered.
8. Press "Power Button" of Air Fry Oven and turn the dial to select the "Air Fry" mode.
9. Press the Time button and again turn the dial to set the cooking time to 5 minutes.
10. Now push the Temp button and rotate the dial to set the temperature at 360 degrees F.
11. Press "Start/Pause" button to start.
12. When the unit beeps to show that it is preheated, open the lid.
13. Arrange the pastries in greased "Air Fry Basket" and insert in the oven.
14. Sprinkle with a pinch of salt and serve warm.

461. Chocolate Paradise Cake

Preparation Time: 10
Cooking Time: 15
Servings: 6

Ingredients:
- 2 eggs, beaten
- 2/3 C. sour cream
- 1 C. almond flour
- 2/3 C. swerve
- 1/3 C. coconut oil, softened
- 1/4 C. cocoa powder
- 2 tbsp. chocolate chips, unsweetened
- 1 ½ tsp. baking powder
- 1 tsp. vanilla extract
- 1/2 tsp. pure rum extract
- Chocolate Frosting:
- 1/2 C. butter, softened
- 1/4 C. cocoa powder
- 1 C. powdered swerve

- 2 tbsp. milk

Directions:
1. Mix all ingredients for the chocolate cake with a hand mixer on low speed. Scrape the batter into a cake pan.
2. Bake at 330 degrees F for 15 to 20 minutes. Transfer the cake to a wire rack
3. Meanwhile, whip the butter and cocoa until smooth. Stir in the powdered swerve. Slowly and gradually, pour in the milk until your frosting reaches desired consistency.
4. Whip until smooth and fluffy; then, frost the cooled cake.
5. Place in your refrigerator for a couple of hours. Serve well chilled.

462. Chocolate Coffee Cake

Preparation Time: 10
Cooking Time: 15
Servings: 8

Ingredients:
- 1 ½ C. almond flour
- 1/2 C. coconut meal
- 2/3 C. swerve
- 1 tsp. baking powder
- 1/4 tsp. salt
- 1 stick butter, melted
- 1/2 C. hot strongly brewed coffee
- 1/2 tsp. vanilla
- 1 egg
- Topping:
- 1/4 C. coconut flour
- 1/2 C. confectioner's swerve
- 1/2 tsp. ground cardamom
- 1 tsp. ground cinnamon
- 3 tbsp. coconut oil

Directions:
1. Mix all dry ingredients for your cake; then, mix in the wet ingredients. Mix until everything is well incorporated.
2. Spritz a baking pan with cooking spray. Scrape the batter into the baking pan.
3. Then, make the topping by mixing all ingredients. Place on top of the cake. Smooth the top with a spatula.
4. Bake at 330 degrees F for 15 minutes or until the top of the cake springs back when gently pressed with your fingers. Serve with your favorite hot beverage.

463. Bebinca

Preparation Time: 15
Cooking Time: 10
Servings: 4

Ingredients:
- 2 tbsp. custard powder
- 3 tbsp. powdered sugar
- 3 tbsp. unsalted butter

- 1 C. coconut milk
- 1 C. almond flour
- 2 C. milk

Directions:
1. Boil the milk and the sugar in a pan and add the custard powder followed by the flour and coconut milk and stir till you get a thick mixture.
2. Preheat the fryer to 300 Fahrenheit for five minutes. Place the dish in the basket and reduce the temperature to 250 Fahrenheit. Cook for ten minutes and set aside to cool.

464. Margherita Pizza

Preparation Time: 14
Cooking Time: 15
Servings: 4

Ingredients:
- 1 whole-wheat pizza crust
- 1/2 C. mozzarella cheese, grated
- 1/2 C. can tomatoes
- 2 tbsp. olive oil
- 3 Roma tomatoes, sliced
- 10 basil leaves

Directions:
1. Fit the Cuisinart oven with the rack in position
2. Roll out whole wheat pizza crust using a rolling pin. Make sure the crust is ½-inch thick.
3. Sprinkle olive oil on top of pizza crust.
4. Spread can tomatoes over pizza crust.
5. Arrange sliced tomatoes and basil on pizza crust. Sprinkle grated cheese on top.
6. Place pizza on top of the oven rack and set to bake at 425 F for 15 minutes.
7. Slice and serve.

465. Steak with Bell Peppers

Preparation Time: 15 minutes
Cooking Time: 12 minutes
Servings: 4

Ingredients:
- 1 teaspoon dried oregano, crushed
- 1 teaspoon onion powder
- 1 teaspoon garlic powder
- 1 teaspoon red chili powder
- 1 teaspoon paprika
- Salt, as required
- 1¼ pounds flank steak, cut into thin strips
- 3 green bell peppers, seeded and cubed
- 1 red onion, sliced
- 2 tablespoons olive oil
- 3-4 tablespoons feta cheese, crumbled

Directions:
1. In a large bowl, mix together the oregano and spices.
2. Add the steak strips, bell peppers, onion, and oil and mix until well combined.
3. Arrange the steak mixture into the greased air fry basket.
4. Select "Air Fry" and adjust the temperature to 390 degrees F.
5. Set the timer for 12 minutes and press "Start/Stop" to begin preheating.
6. When the unit beeps to show that it is preheated, insert the air fry basket in the oven.
7. When the cooking time is completed, remove the air fry basket from the oven and place the steak mixture onto serving plates.
8. Serve immediately with the topping of feta.

466. Glazed Beef Short Ribs

Preparation Time: 15 minutes
Cooking Time: 8 minutes
Servings: 4

Ingredients:
- 2 pounds bone-in beef short ribs
- 3 tablespoons scallions, chopped
- ½ tablespoon fresh ginger, finely grated
- ½ cup low-sodium soy sauce
- ¼ cup balsamic vinegar
- ½ tablespoon Sriracha
- 1 tablespoon Erythritol
- ½ teaspoon ground black pepper

Directions:
1. In a resealable bag, place all the ingredients except for spinach.
2. Seal the bag and shake to coat well.
3. Refrigerate overnight.
4. Arrange the ribs into the greased air fry basket.
5. Adjust the temperature to 380 degrees F.
6. Set the timer for 8 minutes and press "Start/Stop" to begin preheating.
7. When the unit beeps to show that it is preheated, insert the air fry basket in the oven.
8. When the cooking time is completed, remove the air fry basket from the oven and serve hot alongside the spinach.

467. Smoky Beef Burgers

Preparation Time: 15 minutes
Cooking Time: 10 minutes
Servings: 4

Ingredients:
- 1-pound ground beef
- 1 tablespoon Worcestershire sauce
- 1 teaspoon Maggi seasoning sauce
- 3-4 drops liquid smoke
- 1 teaspoon dried parsley
- ½ teaspoon garlic powder

- ½ teaspoon onion powder
- Salt and ground black pepper, as required
- Olive oil cooking spray
- 6 cups fresh greens
- 1 large cucumber, chopped

Directions:
1. In a large bowl, mix together the beef, sauces, liquid smoke, parsley, and spices.
2. Make 4 equal-sized patties from the mixture.
3. Arrange the patties into the greased air fry basket.
4. Select "Air Fry" and adjust the temperature to 350 degrees F.
5. Set the timer for 10 minutes and press "Start/Stop" to begin preheating.
6. When the unit beeps to show that it is preheated, insert the air fry basket in the oven.
7. When the cooking time is completed, remove the air fry basket from the oven and serve hot alongside the greens and cucumber.

468. Pork with Green Beans

Preparation Time: 15 minutes
Cooking Time: 13 minutes
Servings: 3

Ingredients:
- 3 (6-ounces) pork tenderloins
- 2 tablespoons olive oil
- Salt and ground black pepper, as required
- ¾ pound frozen green beans

Directions:
1. Coat the pork tenderloins with oil and then rub with salt and black pepper.
2. Arrange the pork tenderloins into the greased air fry basket.
3. Adjust the temperature to 392 degrees F.
4. Set the timer for 12 minutes and press "Start/Stop" to begin preheating.
5. When the unit beeps to show that it is preheated, insert the air fry basket in the oven.
6. After 6 minutes of cooking, arrange the green beans around the tenderloins.
7. When the cooking time is completed, remove the air fry basket from the oven and place the pork tenderloins onto a platter.
8. Cut each tenderloin into desired sized slices and serve alongside the green beans.

133

469. Cajun Salmon

Preparation Time: 10 minutes
Cooking Time: 7 minutes
Servings: 2

Ingredients:
- 2 (7-ounce) (¾-inch thick) salmon fillets
- 1 tablespoon Cajun seasoning
- ½ teaspoon Erythritol
- 1 tablespoon fresh lemon juice
- 3 cups fresh salad greens

Directions:
1. Sprinkle the salmon fillets with Cajun seasoning and Erythritol evenly.
2. Arrange the salmon fillets into the greased air fry basket, skin- side up.
3. Adjust the temperature to 356 degrees F.
4. Set the timer for 7 minutes and press "Start/ Stop" to begin preheating.
5. When the unit beeps to show that it is preheated, insert the air fry basket in the oven.
6. When the cooking time is completed, remove the air fry basket from the oven and transfer the salmon fillets onto serving plates.
7. Drizzle with the lemon juice and serve hot alongside the salad greens.

470. Stuffed Pork Roll

Preparation Time: 15 minutes
Cooking Time: 15 minutes
Servings: 4

Ingredients:
- 1 scallion, chopped
- ¼ cup sun-dried tomatoes, chopped finely
- 2 tablespoons fresh parsley, chopped
- Salt and ground black pepper, as required
- 4 (6-ounce) pork cutlets, pounded slightly
- 2 teaspoons paprika
- ½ tablespoons olive oil
- 6 cups fresh spinach

Directions:
1. In a bowl, mix together the scallion, tomatoes, parsley, salt, and black pepper.
2. Spread the tomato mixture over each pork cutlet.
3. Roll each cutlet and secure with cocktail sticks.
4. Rub the outer part of rolls with paprika, salt and black pepper.
5. Coat the rolls with oil evenly.
6. Arrange pork rolls into the greased air fry basket in a single layer.
7. Adjust the temperature to 390 degrees F.
8. Set the timer for 15 minutes and press "Start/ Stop" to begin preheating.
9. When the unit beeps to show that it is preheated, insert the air fry basket in the oven.
10. When the cooking time is completed, remove the air fry basket from the oven and transfer the pork rolls onto serving plates.
11. Serve hot alongside the spinach.

471. Eggs with Turkey

Preparation Time: 10 minutes
Cooking Time: 13 minutes
Servings: 2

Ingredients:
- 2 teaspoons coconut oil, softened
- 2 ounces cooked turkey breast, sliced thinly
- 4 large eggs, divided
- 1 tablespoon coconut milk
- Salt and ground black pepper, as required
- 1/8 teaspoon smoked paprika
- 3 tablespoons low-fat Parmesan cheese, grated finely
- 2 teaspoons fresh chives, minced

Directions:
1. In the bottom of a baking dish, spread the coconut oil.
2. Arrange the turkey slices over the coconut oil.
3. In a bowl, add 1egg, coconut milk, salt and black pepper and beat until smooth.
4. Place the egg mixture over the turkey slices evenly.
5. Carefully crack the remaining eggs on top and sprinkle with paprika, salt, black pepper, cheese and chives evenly.
6. Adjust the temperature to 320 degrees F.
7. Set the timer for 13 minutes and press "Start/ Stop" to begin preheating.
8. When the unit beeps to show that it is preheated, arrange the baking dish over the wire rack.
9. When the cooking time is completed, remove the baking dish from the oven and set aside for about 5 minutes before serving.
10. Cut into equal-sized wedges and serve.

472. Spicy Chicken Legs

Preparation Time: 15 minutes
Cooking Time: 15 minutes
Servings: 6

Ingredients:
- 2½ pounds chicken legs
- 2 tablespoons olive oil
- 1 teaspoon smoked paprika
- 1 teaspoon garlic powder
- ½ teaspoon ground cumin
- Salt and ground black pepper, as required
- 8 cups fresh baby greens

Directions:
1. In a large bowl, add all the ingredients except for baby greens and mix well.
2. Arrange the chicken legs onto the greased enamel roasting pan.
3. Adjust the temperature to 400 degrees F.
4. Set the timer for 15 minutes and press "Start/Stop" to begin preheating.
5. When the unit beeps to show that it is

preheated, insert the roasting pan in the oven.

6. When the cooking time is completed, remove the roasting pan from the oven and transfer the chicken pieces onto a platter.

7. Serve hot alongside the baby greens.

473. Lemony Chicken Kabobs

Preparation Time: 15 minutes
Cooking Time: 9 minutes
Servings: 2

Ingredients:
- 1 (8-ounce) chicken breast, cut into medium-sized pieces
- 1 tablespoon fresh lemon juice
- 3 garlic cloves, grated
- 1 tablespoon fresh oregano, minced
- ½ teaspoon lemon zest, grated
- Salt and ground black pepper, as required
- 1 teaspoon plain low-fat Greek yogurt
- 1 teaspoon olive oil
- 1 carrot, peeled and chopped
- 3 cups fresh arugula

Directions:
1. In a large bowl, add the chicken, lemon juice, garlic, oregano, lemon zest, salt and black pepper and toss to coat well.
2. Cover the bowl and refrigerate overnight.
3. Remove the bowl from refrigerator and stir in the yogurt and oil.
4. Thread the chicken pieces onto the metal skewers.
5. Arrange the skewers into the greased air fry basket.
6. Adjust the temperature to 350 degrees F.
7. Set the timer for 9 minutes and press "Start/Stop" to begin preheating.
8. When the unit beeps to show that it is preheated, insert the air fry basket in the oven.
9. Flip the skewers once halfway through.
10. When the cooking time is completed, remove the air fry basket from the oven and transfer the kabobs onto a serving platter.
11. Serve hot alongside the carrot and arugula.

474. Beef & Veggie Frittata

Preparation Time: 15 minutes
Cooking Time: 14 minutes
Servings: 2

Ingredients:
- 1 tablespoon olive oil
- ¼ cup cooked ground beef
- 4 cherry tomatoes, halved
- 6 fresh mushrooms, sliced
- Salt and ground black pepper, as required
- 3 eggs
- 1 tablespoon fresh parsley, chopped
- ½ cup low-fat Parmesan cheese, grated

Directions:
1. In a baking dish, place the bacon, tomatoes, mushrooms, salt, and black pepper and mix well.
2. Place the baking dish in the air fry basket.
3. Adjust the temperature to 320 degrees F.
4. Set the timer for 14 minutes and press "Start/Stop" to begin preheating.
5. When the unit beeps to show that it is preheated, insert the air fry basket in the oven.
6. Meanwhile, in a bowl, add the eggs and beat well.
7. Add the parsley and cheese and mix well.
8. After 6 minutes of cooking, top the bacon mixture with egg mixture evenly.
9. When the cooking time is completed, remove the air fry basket from the oven and transfer the frittata onto a plate.
10. Cut into equal-sized wedges and serve hot.

475. Fruity Oats & Coconut Granola

Preparation Time: 15 minutes
Cooking Time: 15 minutes
Servings: 6

Ingredients:
- 1 medium banana, peeled and mashed
- ¼ cup creamy almond butter
- ¼ cup unsweetened applesauce
- 1½ cups rolled oats
- ¾ cup unsweetened coconut flakes
- ½ cup walnuts, chopped
- ¼ cup pecans, chopped
- 1 tablespoon pumpkin pie spice
- 1½ ounces dried apples

Directions:
1. In a bowl, add bananas, almond butter and applesauce and beat until well combined.
2. In a large bowl, add the oats, coconut, nuts and pumpkin pie spice and mix well.
3. Add the banana mixture and mix until well combined.
4. Line the Air Fryer Basket with parchment paper.
5. Set the temperature of Air Fryer to 350 degrees F to preheat for 5 minutes.
6. After preheating, place the oat mixture into the prepared Air
7. Fryer Basket.
8. Slide the basket into Air Fryer and set the time for 15 minutes.
9. While cooking, stir the granola after every 5 minutes.
10. When cooking time is completed, transfer the granola onto a baking sheet and set aside to cool completely.
11. Add the apple pieces and stir to combine.
12. Break the granola into chunks and serve with your favorite non-dairy milk.

476. Glazed Carrots

Preparation Time: 10 minutes
Cooking Time: 12 minutes
Servings: 4

Ingredients:
- 3 cups carrots, peeled and cut into large chunks
- 1 tablespoon olive oil
- 1 tablespoon maple syrup
- 1 tablespoon fresh thyme, finely chopped
- Salt and ground black pepper, as required

Directions:
1. In a bowl, add the carrot, oil, maple syrup, thyme, salt and black pepper and mix until well combined.
2. Set the temperature of Air Fryer to 390 degrees F to preheat for 5 minutes.
3. After preheating, arrange the carrot chunks into the greased
4. Air Fryer Basket in a single layer.
5. Slide the basket into Air Fryer and set the time for 12 minutes.
6. When cooking time is completed, open the lid and transfer the carrot chunks onto serving plates.
7. Serve hot.

477. Spicy Green Beans

Preparation Time: 10 minutes
Cooking Time: 15 minutes
Servings: 3

Ingredients:
- 1 garlic clove, minced
- 1 teaspoon soy sauce
- 1 tablespoon sesame oil
- 1 teaspoon rice wine vinegar
- ½ teaspoon red pepper flakes
- 12 ounces fresh green beans, trimmed

Directions:
1. In a bowl, add all ingredients except for green beans and beat until well combined.
2. Add the green beans and toss to coat well.
3. Set aside for about 5 minutes.
4. Set the temperature of Air Fryer to 400 degrees F to preheat for 5 minutes.
5. After preheating, arrange the green beans into the greased Air Fryer Basket in 2 batches.
6. Slide the basket into Air Fryer and set the time for 12 minutes.
7. When cooking time is completed, transfer the green beans onto a platter.
8. Serve hot.

478. Balsamic Brussels Sprout

Preparation Time: 10 minutes
Cooking Time: 10 minutes
Servings: 4

Ingredients:
- 1 pound Brussels sprouts, trimmed and halved
- 1 tablespoon balsamic vinegar
- 1 tablespoon extra-virgin olive oil
- Salt and ground black pepper, as required
- ¼ cup whole-wheat breadcrumbs
- 2-3 tablespoons nutritional yeast

Directions:
1. In a bowl, mix together the Brussels sprouts, vinegar, oil, salt, and black pepper.
2. Set the temperature of Air Fryer to 400 degrees F to preheat for 5 minutes.
3. After preheating, open the lid and arrange the Brussels sprouts into the greased Air Fryer Basket.
4. Slide the basket into Air Fryer and set the time for 10 minutes.
5. While cooking, flip the Brussels sprouts once after 5 minutes and sprinkle with breadcrumbs, followed by the nutritional yeast.
6. When cooking time is completed, transfer the Brussels sprouts onto serving plates.
7. Serve hot.

479. Soy Sauce Mushrooms

Preparation Time: 10 minutes
Cooking Time: 10 minutes
Servings: 2

Ingredients:
- 1 (8-ounce) package Cremini mushrooms, sliced
- 2 tablespoons avocado oil
- 1 teaspoon low-sodium soy sauce
- ½ teaspoon garlic granules
- Salt and ground black pepper, as required

Directions:
1. In a bowl, add all ingredients and toss to coat well.
2. Set the temperature of Air Fryer to 375 degrees F to preheat for 5 minutes.
3. After preheating, arrange the mushrooms into the greased Air
4. Fryer Basket.
5. Slide the basket into Air Fryer and set the time for 10 minutes.
6. While cooking, shake the Air Fryer Basket occasionally.
7. When cooking time is completed, transfer the mushrooms onto a platter.
8. Serve hot.

480. Lemony Spinach

Preparation Time: 10 minutes
Cooking Time: 6 minutes
Servings: 6

Ingredients:
- 2 pounds fresh spinach, chopped
- 1 garlic clove, minced
- 1 jalapeño pepper, minced
- 2 tablespoons olive oil
- Salt and ground black pepper, as required
- 1 tablespoon fresh lemon juice
- 1 teaspoon fresh lemon zest, grated

Directions:
1. In a bowl, add the spinach, garlic, jalapeño, oil, salt and black pepper and mix well.
2. Set the temperature of Air Fryer to 340 degrees F to preheat for 5 minutes.
3. After preheating, arrange the spinach mixture into the greased Air Fryer Basket.
4. Slide the basket into Air Fryer and set the time for 15 minutes.
5. When cooking time is completed, transfer the spinach mixture into a bowl.
6. Immediately stir in the lemon juice and zest and serve hot.

481. Kale with Pine Nuts

Preparation Time: 15 minutes
Cooking Time: 15 minutes
Servings: 3

Ingredients:
- 1 pound fresh kale, tough ribs removed and chopped
- 2 tablespoons olive oil
- ¼ teaspoon ground cumin
- ¼ teaspoon red pepper flakes, crushed
- Salt and ground black pepper, as required
- 2 tablespoons pine nuts
- ½ tablespoon fresh lime juice

Directions:
1. In a bowl, add the kale, oil, spices, salt and black pepper and mix well.
2. Set the temperature of Air fryer to 340 degrees F to preheat for 5 minutes.
3. After preheating, arrange the kale into the greased Air Fryer Basket.
4. Slide the basket into Air Fryer and set the time for 15 minutes.
5. When cooking time is completed, open the lid and immediately transfer the kale mixture into a bowl.
6. Stir in the pine nuts and lime juice and serve hot.

482. Broccoli with Cauliflower

Preparation Time: 15 minutes
Cooking Time: 15 minutes
Servings: 2

Ingredients:
- 1½ cups broccoli, cut into 1-inch pieces
- 1½ cups cauliflower, cut into 1-inch pieces
- 1 tablespoon olive oil
- Salt, as required

Directions:
1. In a bowl, add the vegetables, oil, and salt and toss to coat well.
2. Set the temperature of Air Fryer to 375 degrees F to preheat for 5 minutes.
3. After preheating, arrange the veggie mixture into the greased Air Fryer Basket.
4. Slide the basket into Air Fryer and set the time for 15 minutes.
5. Toss the veggie mixture once halfway through.
6. When cooking time is completed, transfer the veggie mixture into a bowl.
7. Serve hot.

483. Veggie Fried Rice

Preparation Time: 10 minutes
Cooking Time: 15 minutes
Servings: 4

Ingredients:
- 3 cups cooked cold white rice
- 1¼ cups frozen vegetables (carrot, corn and green peas)
- 1/3 cup soy sauce
- 1 tablespoon olive oil

Directions:
1. In a bowl, add all ingredients and stir to combine.
2. Place the mixture into a baking pan.
3. Set the temperature of Air Fryer to 360 degrees F to preheat for 5 minutes.
4. After preheating, arrange the baking pan into the Air Fryer Basket.
5. Slide the basket into Air Fryer and set the time for 15 minutes.
6. While cooking, stir the rice mixture after every 4 minutes.
7. When cooking time is completed, transfer the rice mixture onto a platter.
8. Serve hot.

137

484. Tofu in Orange Sauce

Preparation Time: 15 minutes
Cooking Time: 10 minutes
Servings: 4

Ingredients: For Tofu:
- 1 pound extra-firm tofu, pressed and cubed
- 1 tablespoon cornstarch
- 1 tablespoon low-sodium soy sauce

For Sauce:
- ½ cup water
- 1/3 cup fresh orange juice
- 1 tablespoon maple syrup
- 1 teaspoon orange zest, grated
- 1 teaspoon garlic, minced
- 1 teaspoon fresh ginger, minced
- 2 teaspoons cornstarch
- ¼ teaspoon red pepper flakes, crushed
- Ground black pepper, as required

Directions:
1. In a bowl, add the tofu, cornstarch, and soy sauce and toss to coat well.
2. Set the tofu aside to marinate for at least 15 minutes.
3. Set the temperature of Air Fryer to 390 degrees F to preheat for 5 minutes.
4. After preheating, arrange the tofu cubes into the greased Air Fryer Basket.
5. Slide the basket into Air Fryer and set the time for 10 minutes.
6. While cooking, flip the tofu cubes once halfway through.
7. Meanwhile, for the sauce: in a small pan, add all the ingredients over medium-high heat and bring to a boil, stirring continuously.
8. Remove from the heat and transfer the sauce into a large bowl.
9. When cooking time is complete, transfer the tofu cubes into the bowl with the sauce and gently stir to combine.
10. Serve immediately.

485. Eggplant Fries

Preparation Time: 15 minutes
Cooking Time: 15 minutes
Servings: 4

Ingredients:
- 1 medium eggplant
- 1-1½ tablespoons olive oil
- 2 teaspoons maple syrup
- 1 teaspoon smoked paprika
- Salt and ground black pepper, as required
- 1 cup almond flour

Directions:
1. Cut the eggplant into ½-inch rounds and then cut each round into ¼-inch sticks.
2. With paper towels, pat dry the eggplant sticks.
3. In a shallow bowl, mix together the oil, maple syrup, paprika, salt and black pepper.
4. In a second shallow bowl, place the flour.
5. Dip the eggplant sticks into the oil mixture and then coat with flour.
6. Arrange the coated eggplant sticks onto a platter and set aside for about 5 minutes.
7. Set the temperature of Air Fryer to 370 degrees F to preheat for 5 minutes.
8. After preheating, arrange the eggplant sticks into the greased Air Fryer Basket.
9. Slide the basket into Air Fryer and set the time for 14-16 minutes.
10. After 10 minutes of cooking, shake the basket once.
11. When cooking time is completed, transfer the eggplant fries onto a platter and serve immediately.

486. Fudge Brownies

Preparation Time: 10 minutes
Cooking Time: 15 minutes
Servings: 4

Ingredients:
- ½ cup all-purpose flour
- ¾ cup white sugar
- 6 tablespoons unsweetened cocoa powder
- ¼ teaspoon baking powder
- ¼ teaspoon salt
- ½ cup unsweetened applesauce
- ¼ cup coconut oil, melted
- 1 tablespoon vegetable oil
- ½ teaspoon vanilla extract

Directions:
1. In a large bowl, mix together the flour, sugar, cocoa powder, baking powder and salt.
2. Add the remaining ingredients and mix until well combined.
3. Place the mixture into a generously greased 7-inch baking pan evenly.
4. Set the temperature of Air Fryer to 330 degrees F to preheat for 5 minutes.
5. After preheating, arrange the baking pan into the Air Fryer Basket.
6. Slide the basket into Air Fryer and set the time for 15 minutes.
7. When cooking time is completed, remove the baking pan and place onto a wire rack to cool completely.
8. Cut into desired sized squares and serve.

487. Apple Crumble

Preparation Time: 15 minutes
Cooking Time: 15 minutes
Servings: 4

Ingredients:
- 3 cups Gala apples, cored and chopped
- 3 tablespoons almond flour, divided
- 1 tablespoon pure maple syrup
- 2 teaspoons fresh lemon juice
- ½ teaspoon ground cinnamon
- 1/3 cup quick oats
- ¼ cup brown sugar
- 2 tablespoons coconut oil, melted

Directions:
1. In a bowl, add the apple pieces, 1 tablespoon of the almond flour, maple syrup, lemon juice and cinnamon and mix until well combined.
2. In another bowl, add the remaining almond flour, oats and brown sugar and mix well.
3. Add the melted coconut oil and mix until a crumbly mixture forms.
4. Place the mixture into a lightly greased baking pan.
5. Set the temperature of Air Fryer to 350 degrees F to preheat for 5 minutes.
6. After preheating, arrange the baking pan into the Air Fryer Basket.
7. Slide the basket into Air Fryer and set the time for 15 minutes.
8. When cooking time is completed, remove the baking pan and set aside to cool slightly before serving.

488. Corn Pancakes

Preparation Time: 15 minutes
Cooking Time: 14 minutes
Servings: 4

Ingredients:
- 1 tablespoon flaxseed meal
- 3 tablespoons hot water
- 1 cup all-purpose flour
- ¼ cup yellow cornmeal
- 3 tablespoons white sugar
- 1 tablespoon baking powder
- ¼ teaspoon salt
- 1 tablespoon coconut oil, melted
- ¾ teaspoon soy milk
- 3 cups corn kernels, drained
- ¼ cup fresh chives, chopped
- Non-stick cooking spray

Directions:
1. In a large bowl, add flaxseed and water and mix well. Set aside for about 5 minutes.
2. In another bowl, add flour, cornmeal, sugar, baking powder and salt and mix well.
3. In the bowl of flaxseed mixture, add coconut oil, melted and soy milk and mix until well combined.
4. Add corn and chives and gently stir to combine.
5. Make 4 equal-sized patties from the mixture.

6. Set the temperature of Air Fryer to 380 degrees F to preheat for 5 minutes.
7. After preheating, arrange the patties into the greased Air Fryer Basket.
8. Spray the top of each patty with cooking spray.
9. Slide the basket into Air Fryer and set the time for 14 minutes.
10. After 7 minutes of cooking, flip the patties.
11. When cooking time is completed, remove the patties and serve alongside yogurt sauce.

489. Protein Oatmeal

Preparation Time: 10 minutes
Cooking Time: 10 minutes
Servings: 2

Ingredients:
- 1 cup quick oats
- 4 tablespoons unflavored vegan protein powder
- 3 tablespoons coconut sugar
- ½ teaspoon baking powder
- 1/8 teaspoon ground cinnamon
- ¾ cup plus 2 tablespoons unsweetened almond milk
- 1/3 cup almond milk yogurt
- ½ teaspoon vanilla extract

Directions:
1. Lightly grease a 2 (8-ounce) ramekins.
2. In a food processor, add oats, protein powder, coconut sugar, baking powder and cinnamon and pulse until blended finely.
3. In a bowl, add the almond milk, yogurt and vanilla extract and eat until well combined.
4. In the bowl of yogurt mixture, add the oat mixture and stir until a smooth mixture is formed.
5. Divide the mixture into prepared ramekins evenly.
6. Set the temperature of Air Fryer to 355 degrees F to preheat for 5 minutes.
7. After preheating, arrange the ramekins into the Air Fryer Basket.
8. Slide the basket into Air Fryer and set the time for 10 minutes.
9. When cooking time is completed, remove the ramekins from Air Fryer and set aside for about 5 minutes before serving.

490. Strawberry buttermilk pancakes

Preparation Time: 10 minutes
Cooking Time: 15 minutes
Servings: 2

Ingredients:
- Two cups of whole-grain pastry flour
- One teaspoon of baking powder
- A quarter teaspoon of baking soda
- A quarter teaspoon of salt (optional)
- Two cups of low-fat buttermilk
- Half cup of egg substitute
- One cup of sliced fresh strawberries

- Canola oil cooking spray
- Sliced strawberries or other fruit or low-sugar fruit jams as garnish (optional)
- Sugar-free syrup (optional)

Directions:
1. In a mixing bowl, whisk together flour, baking powder, baking soda, and salt, then make a well in the center of the mixture.
2. In a separate bowl, combine the buttermilk and egg and whisk to blend. Pour buttermilk mixture into the well and fold in the flour with a spatula until the mixture is smooth.
3. Gently fold in strawberries and allow the batter to stand for 5 minutes. In the meantime, spray a griddle with cooking oil and heat over medium heat.
4. Drop a few droplets of water onto the heated griddle. When water droplets bead, the griddle is hot enough. Pour Two tablespoons of batter onto the griddle for each pancake. Cook pancakes until the surface of the pancake begin to bubble, and the edges turn golden brown (about 3 minutes).
5. Flip the pancake over and cook until another side is golden brown. Repeat this process until all the batter is gone.
6. Keep cooked pancakes on a warm platter or in a low-heat oven (175 degrees) while preparing the other pancakes.
7. Serve warm, garnished with sliced strawberries, low-sugar fruit jam, or sugar-free syrup, if desired.

491. Tomato and garlic bruschetta

Preparation Time: 10 minutes
Cooking Time: 10 minutes
Servings: 2

Ingredients:
- Four slices (Half-inch thick) of a French baguette or a crusty whole-grain bread
- One teaspoon of extra-virgin olive oil
- One and a quarter cup of chopped plum tomatoes
- One and a half teaspoons of minced fresh garlic
- One teaspoon of balsamic vinegar
- Half teaspoon of dried basil
- A quarter teaspoon of non-caloric sweetener
- A quarter teaspoon of freshly ground pepper

Directions:
1. Place slices of bread on an ungreased baking sheet. Brush each slice with olive oil and bake at 500 degrees for 3–4 minutes until golden brown.
2. Combine tomatoes, garlic, vinegar, basil, sweetener, and pepper in a small bowl. Mix well and spoon mixture over bread slices.

492. Codfish in sundried tomato pesto sauce

Preparation Time: 10 minutes
Cooking Time: 15 minutes
Servings: 2-4

Ingredients:
- Four medium tomatoes, chopped
- Four cloves fresh garlic, chopped
- A quarter cup of market-fresh sundried tomato pesto
- One tablespoon of sambuca
- Two tablespoons of chopped sundried tomatoes, drained
- One teaspoon of capers, drained and well rinsed
- Ten Kalamata olives pitted and halved
- Four (6-ounce) fillets of cod
- 2/3 cup of dry vermouth
- One bay leaf
- A quarter teaspoon of peppercorns
- Salt and freshly ground pepper to taste
- Four lemon wedges for garnish
- Four fresh parsley sprigs for garnish

Directions:
1. In a large, heavy skillet, add tomatoes, garlic, pesto, Sambuca, sundried tomatoes, capers, and olives. Cook mixture over medium-low heat. Stir often to marry flavors.
2. Reduce heat to low to keep sauce warm. In a separate skillet, add cod, vermouth, bay leaf, peppercorns, and salt and pepper to taste.
3. Bring to a boil and reduce heat to simmer; cover and simmer for 10–12 minutes or until fish is opaque in color and flakes easily. Meanwhile, warm a platter in the oven at 175 degrees. When fish is ready, transfer to a warm platter and return the platter to the oven to keep the fish warm.

493. Linguine and mixed seafood

Preparation Time: 10 minutes
Cooking Time: 15 minutes
Servings: 2-4

Ingredients:
- Eight ounces of natural clam juice
- Two cups of good dry white wine (not cooking wine)
- A quarter-pound of baby octopus, cleaned
- A quarter-pound of shrimp, peeled and deveined
- A quarter-pound of calamari, cleaned, cut into 1/4-inch rings
- Twenty mussels, scrubbed and debearded (discard any open mussels)
- A quarter-pound of bay scallops
- Three tablespoons of extra-virgin olive oil
- Four cloves fresh garlic, minced
- A quarter teaspoon of freshly chopped hot pepper
- Eight small ripe plum tomatoes, chopped into

small chunks
- Pinch of low-calorie baking sweetener
- Half tablespoon chopped fresh parsley
- Half tablespoon chopped fresh oregano
- Salt and freshly ground pepper to taste
- Half pound linguine
- Ten arugula leaves, chopped for garnish
- Ten pitted Kalamata black olives, halved, for garnish

Directions:
1. In a large deep skillet, add clam juice, wine, octopus, shrimp, calamari, mussels, and scallops. Bring to boil, cover, and reduce heat to simmer, occasionally stirring, until calamari and squid are almost tender.
2. Remove mussels and shell all but 9–12; set these aside for garnish and return shelled mussels to seafood skillet to keep warm.
3. In a separate skillet, over medium heat, add olive oil and garlic and sauté until golden brown. Add hot pepper to garlic mixture, reduce heat to simmer, and cook for 1–2 additional minutes.
4. Add tomatoes, sweetener, parsley, oregano, and salt and pepper to taste, and simmer another 3–4 minutes. Cover to keep warm and set aside. Bring water to a boil, add pasta, and cook pasta until al dente.
5. Remove from heat, drain pasta, and return to pot, drizzling with the scant amount of olive oil to keep the pasta from sticking together. Set aside.
6. With a slotted spoon, remove seafood from the skillet and strain the remaining liquid through a sieve or cheesecloth.
7. Return seafood and one cup of strained liquid to skillet; add pasta and tomato mixture and toss all ingredients.
8. Spoon the entire pasta and seafood dish into a large pasta bowl, garnish with arugula, olives, and remaining unshelled mussels, and serve.

494. Tuna Pasta

Preparation Time: 10 minutes
Cooking Time: 10 minutes
Servings: 2-4

Ingredients
- Ten ounces can of tuna, drained
- Fifteen ounces of whole wheat rotini pasta
- Four ounces of mozzarella cheese, cubed
- Half cup of parmesan cheese, grated
- One teaspoon of dried basil
- Fourteen ounces can tomato, diced
- Four cups of vegetable broth
- One tablespoon of garlic, minced
- Eight ounces of mushrooms, sliced
- Two zucchinis, sliced
- One onion, chopped
- Two tablespoons of olive oil
- Pepper
- Salt

Directions:
1. Warm olive oil in a pot, then sauté the mushrooms, zucchini, and onion until onion is softened.
2. Add garlic and sauté for a minute. Add pasta,

basil, tuna, tomatoes, and broth and stir well.
3. Seal pot with lid and cook on high for 4 minutes. Add the remaining ingredients and stir well and serve.

495. Pork and Orzo in a Bowl

Preparation Time: 15 minutes
Cooking Time: 15 minutes
Servings: 2-4

Ingredients
- Twenty-four ounces of pork tenderloin
- One teaspoon of coarsely ground pepper
- Two tablespoons of olive oil
- Three quarts of water
- One and a quarter cups of orzo pasta, uncooked
- A quarter teaspoon of salt
- One 6 ounces package of fresh baby spinach
- One cup of halved grape tomatoes
- 3/4 cup of feta cheese, crumbled

Directions:
1. Rub pepper onto the pork; slice into an inch-size cube. Warm-up oil on medium heat in a large non-stick skillet and stir-cook pork for 8 to 10 minutes.
2. Meanwhile, boil water and cook the orzo. Add salt. Keep uncovered and cook for 5 minutes. Add in the spinach and cook until orzo turns tender (about 45 to 60 seconds). Drain.
3. Add tomatoes and heat through. Stir in the orzo and cheese.

496. Za'atar Chicken Tenders

Preparation Time: 10 minutes
Cooking Time: 15 minutes
Servings: 2-4

Ingredients
- Olive oil cooking spray
- One pound of chicken tenders
- One and a half tablespoons of za'atar
- Half teaspoon of kosher salt
- A quarter teaspoon of freshly ground black pepper

Directions:
1. Preheat the oven to 450°F. Lightly spray with olive oil cooking spray.
2. In a large bowl, combine the chicken, za'atar, salt, and black pepper. Mix well, covering the chicken tenders fully.
3. Arrange in a single sheet on the baking sheet and bake for 15 minutes, turning the chicken over once midway through cooking.

497. Crisped Coco-Shrimp with Mango Dip

Preparation Time: 10 minutes
Cooking Time: 15 minutes
Servings: 2-4

Ingredients
- One cup of shredded coconut
- One lb. Of raw shrimp, peeled and deveined
- Two egg whites
- Four tablespoons of tapioca starch
- Pepper and salt to taste

Mango Dip
- One cup of mango, chopped
- One jalapeño, thinly minced
- One teaspoon of lime juice
- 1/3 cup of coconut milk
- Three teaspoons of raw honey

Directions:
1. Preheat oven to 400°F.
2. Ready a pan with a wire rack on top.
3. In a medium bowl, add tapioca starch and season with pepper and salt.
4. In a second medium bowl, add egg whites and whisk.
5. In a third medium bowl, add coconut.
6. To ready shrimps, dip first in tapioca starch, then egg whites, and then coconut. Place dredged shrimp on a wire rack. Repeat until all shrimps are covered.
7. Pop shrimp in the oven and roast for 10 minutes per side
8. Meanwhile, make the dip by adding all ingredients to a blender. Puree until smooth and creamy. Transfer to a dipping bowl.
9. Once shrimps are golden brown, serve with mango dip.

498. Minty-Cucumber Yogurt Topped Grilled Fish

Preparation Time: 10 minutes
Cooking Time: 5 minutes
Servings: 2-4

Ingredients
- A quarter cup of 2% plain Greek yogurt
- A quarter teaspoon plus 1/8 teaspoon of salt
- A quarter teaspoon of black pepper
- Half green onion, finely chopped
- Half teaspoon of dried oregano
- One tablespoon of finely chopped fresh mint leaves
- Three tablespoons of finely chopped English cucumber
- Four 5-ounces cod fillets
- Cooking oil as needed

Directions:
1. Brush grill grate with oil and preheat grill to high.
2. Season cod fillets on both sides with pepper, A quarter teaspoon of salt, and oregano.

3. Grill cod for 3 minutes per side or until cooked to desired doneness.
4. Mix thoroughly 1/8 teaspoon of salt, onion, mint, cucumber, and yogurt in a small bowl. Serve cod with a dollop of the dressing. This dish can be paired with salad greens or brown rice.

499. Vegetable and tortellini soup

Preparation Time: 10 minutes
Cooking Time: 15 minutes
Servings: 2

Ingredients
- One large white onion, chopped
- Four cloves fresh garlic, chopped
- Three celery stalks, chopped
- Two tablespoons of olive oil
- Thirty-two ounces low-sodium, fat-free chicken broth
- One cup of frozen corn
- One cup of chopped carrot
- One cup of frozen cut green beans
- One cup of diced raw potato
- One teaspoon of dried sweet basil
- One teaspoon of dried thyme
- One teaspoon of minced chives
- Two (14.5-ounce) cans of diced tomatoes, undrained
- Three cups of fresh chicken-filled tortellini
- Shredded fat-free or low-fat cheddar cheese (optional)
- Crusty croutons for garnish (optional)

Directions:
1. In a large pot, sauté onion, garlic, celery, and olive oil until soft and fragrant. Add broth, corn, carrot, beans, potato, basil, thyme, and chives. Bring to a boil.
2. Reduce heat, cover, and let simmer for about 15 minutes or until vegetables are tender. Add tomatoes and tortellini and let simmer uncovered for another 5 minutes or until heated through.
3. Serve hot with a sprinkling cheddar cheese and a few crusty croutons, if desired.

500. Beef Back Ribs

Prep Time: 10 minutes
Cook Time: 15 minutes
Servings: 6-8

Ingredients:
- 1 cup of BBQ sauce
- 1 tablespoon of garlic powder
- 2 pounds beef back ribs
- 1 tablespoon of onion powder
- 1 tablespoon of kosher salt
- 1 tablespoon of black pepper

Directions:
1. The ribs should be placed bone-side up

on your work surface once removed from the container. Grasp the membrane with a paper towel and carefully pull it away from the bone with your fingers. The membrane may fall off in little chunks.

2. Check for proper fit. Test your air fryer's capacity by fitting the full slab of ribs in it. Chop the ribs down into small slabs that fit easily inside the air fryer's cooking chamber. If you have a small air fryer, you may need to cut them into pieces with just one or two bones if you have a smaller air fryer.

3. Season the ribs with salt and pepper. Combine the pepper, salt, onion powder, garlic powder, and onion powder in a small mixing bowl until well combined. Season the ribs on both sides with a generous coating of seasoning mix and thoroughly massage it in.

4. The ribs should be cooked in the oven. Preheat your air fryer to 375 degrees Fahrenheit. Grilled ribs should be cooked for about 20 minutes or until the temperature of the meat hits 195°F when placed in an air fryer basket with the bone side down.

5. Apply a generous amount of BBQ sauce. Apply a generous Kansas City-style BBQ sauce coating on the ribs before grilling. Make careful to cover both sides of the ribs with the sauce. Turn up the heat on your air fryer to 400 degrees Fahrenheit and cook for an additional 5 minutes. When the ribs are cooked, the internal temperature should be approximately 203°F.

6. Take a break and get to work! Take the ribs from the air fryer and wrap them in aluminum foil to keep them warm. Allow for around 10-20 minutes of resting time. Cut them up into separate ribs and get to eating!

501. Garlic Bread

Prep Time: 5 minutes

Cook Time: 8 minutes

Servings: 5 slices

Ingredients:
- Half cup of Parmesan cheese grated
- Parsley, for garnishing
- 1 baguette of sliced ¾" thick
- 2-3 teaspoons of Italian seasoning parsley or a combination of fresh chopped herbs such as oregano, thyme, and basil
- 5 tablespoons of sea salt butter room temperature
- 3 teaspoons of minced garlic or 5-6 fresh cloves chopped fine

Directions:
1. Slice baguette into 34" pieces and keep aside. You will only be liable for 5 pieces of pizza if you want to create more than 5 slices. Just then, double garlic butter components and cook them in two batches in the air fryer.

2. Preheat the air fryer at 360 degrees for 5 minutes before using.

3. A small bowl filled with soft butter, cheese, minced garlic, and herbs should create garlic butter.

4. Garlic butter should be spread on both sides of the bread.

5. Remove from the oven, insert 5 slices into the heated basket (or whatever will easily fit in your air fryer), and cook for 5 minutes on high heat. Cook for another 3 minutes on the opposite side of each slice.

6. Transfer the dish from the air fryer basket to a serving platter and decorate with parsley. Serve as soon as possible.

502. Korean Fried Chicken

Prep Time: 15 minutes

Cook Time: 15 minutes

Servings: 6

Ingredients:
- 2 cloves of garlic, minced
- 4 scallions, thinly sliced
- Toasted sesame seeds
- 1 tablespoon of soy sauce
- 2 teaspoons of fresh ginger, minced
- 1 and ½ pounds boneless, skinless chicken thighs, cut into bite-size pieces
- 2 tablespoons of rice vinegar
- ¾ teaspoon of kosher salt
- 3 tablespoons of gochujang
- 3 tablespoons of honey
- ½ teaspoon of black pepper, freshly ground
- 2 large eggs, beaten
- 1 cup of cornstarch
- 3 tablespoons of ketchup
- 2 tablespoons of soy sauce
- 1 tablespoon of sesame oil

Directions:
1. Prepare the air fryer basket by lining it with parchment paper.

2. In a medium-sized mixing bowl, mix the vinegar, chicken, ginger, soy sauce, salt, and pepper, tossing to evenly cover the chicken with the ingredients. Allow 10 to 20 minutes for the marinade to work its magic. In order to marinate the chicken for an extended period of time, cover it with plastic wrap and freeze it up overnight.

3. In a small bowl, whisk together the eggs.

4. Place the cornstarch in a small bowl and set it aside.

5. Toss the chicken pieces in the egg first, then cornstarch to cover them completely. Place the breaded chicken pieces on a sheet of parchment paper in the air fryer and cook for 15 minutes.

6. Spritz or spray the chicken with cooking oil once it has been coated and positioned in the air fryer (you will most likely need to do this in two batches).

7. Cook the chicken for 8 minutes at 400 degrees Fahrenheit in the air fryer. Continue to cook for yet another 5 minutes at 400 degrees Fahrenheit after turning the chicken over and spritzing or brushing with a little extra oil.

8. Make the sauce while the chicken is roasting in the oven. Mix all ingredients in a small bowl until everything is completely incorporated, including the ketchup and gochujang paste. Add the sesame oil, soy sauce, and garlic and mix well.

503. Lime Dipping Sauce with Avocado Fries

Prep Time: 5 minutes
Cook Time: 10 minutes
Servings: 4

Ingredients:
- 8 ounces small avocados, pitted, peeled, and cut in 16 wedges
- 1 egg, lightly beaten
- 3 tablespoons of light mayonnaise
- 2 teaspoons of fresh lime juice
- 3/4 cup of breadcrumbs
- 1/4 teaspoons of lime chili seasoning salt, such as Tajin

Classic
- 1/4 cup of Greek Yogurt
- 1/2 teaspoon of lime chili seasoning salt, such as Tajin Classic
- 1/8 teaspoon of kosher salt

Directions:
1. Preheat the air fryer to 390 degrees Fahrenheit.
2. Put the egg in a small bowl and set it aside. On a separate dish, mix the panko and 1 teaspoon Tajin together.
3. 1/4 teaspoon Tajin is used to season the avocado wedges.
4. Each piece should be dipped in egg first, then in panko.
5. After spraying both sides with oil, transport to an air fryer and cook for 7 to 8 minutes, rotating halfway through, serve while still hot, with dipping sauce on the side.

504. Cheese Curds

Prep Time: 10 minutes
Cook Time: 15 minutes
Servings: 8

Ingredients:
- Twelve ounces of cheese curds, cut into 1 and ½ inch pieces.
- ½ teaspoon Italian seasoning
- ½ teaspoon of salt
- 1 and ½ cups panko bread crumbs
- ¼ teaspoon of pepper
- ¼ cup of all-purpose flour
- ½ cup of grated Parmesan cheese
- 3 eggs, lightly beaten

Directions:
1. Put all of the ingredients (bread crumbs, Italian seasoning, parmesan, chopped parsley, and salt & pepper) in a small mixing bowl.
2. Whisk the eggs until well combined in a second bowl, then add the flour to the third bowl.
3. Each cheese curd should be dipped in the flour, then the egg, and finally the bread crumb mixture. Make certain that it is completely

covered each time.
4. Dip the cheese curd down into the egg and then back into the bread crumb combination to coat it once more.
5. Then, using an oil mister, spray the interior of the air fryer basket with olive oil (**DO NOT use aerosol cooking spraying, as it might harm the inside of the basket**).
6. In an air fryer basket, arrange cheese curds in a single layer, being cautious not to overcrowd them. Air fry at 400° for 5-8 minutes, turning once halfway through. Check often to make sure they don't get overcooked!
7. Repeat the process as required until all of the cheese curds are finished.

505. Shredded Brussels sprouts, Red Onion, and Baby Red Potato Hash

Prep Time: 15 minutes
Cook Time: 11 minutes
Servings: 4

Ingredients:
- 2 cups of brussels sprouts
- 2 cups of baby red potatoes
- 2 Tablespoons of avocado oil
- 1 small to medium red onion
- 1/2 teaspoons of black pepper
- 4 eggs, optional
- 1/2 teaspoons of salt
- 1 avocado, optional

Directions:
1. Pour water over the potatoes in a medium-sized stockpot and bring to a boil. Bring the water to a boil after adding a lot of salt. Reduce the heat to low and cook until the vegetables are fork soft, approximately 15 minutes. Drain the water from the potatoes and set them aside to cool before slicing them in half. Store in an airtight container in the refrigerator for up to five days until you're prepared to use it!
2. Shred or finely chop the brussels sprouts until thinly sliced using a mandolin or a sharp knife. Quarter-inch-thick pieces of onion should be used.
3. Preheat your air fryer to 375 degrees Fahrenheit (180 degrees Celsius). To prepare the air fryer basket, place a layer of parchment paper on top of it and poke a few holes in it with a knife or fork. Toss the potatoes into the basket in an equal layer to prevent them from sticking together. Half of the oil should be sprayed or drizzled over, followed by a mild seasoning of salt and pepper.
4. If you're using pre-boiled potatoes, heat them for 10 minutes, turning them once halfway through the cooking process. If you're using raw potatoes, simmer them for 20-25 minutes, turning them every 7-8 minutes until they're tender.
5. Once the potatoes begin to crisp, put the onions and brussels sprouts into the air

fryer, spray or pour the remaining oil over all of the veggies, and cook for another 6 minutes, tossing or shaking once midway through the cooking time.

6. Season with more pepper and salt to your liking. Distribute the hash amongst four plates. If you're providing a full meal, combine the avocado with the eggs or protein of your choice and serve immediately.

506. Easy Air Fryer Tacos

Prep Time: 15 minutes

Cook Time: 4 minutes

Servings: 12

Ingredients:
- 12 Corn Taco Shells (Hard, Crispy Shells)
- Taco Seasoning
- Lettuce, Shredded
- 1 lb. of Ground Turkey
- Onions
- Salsa
- Black Beans, Rinsed & Drained
- Mexican Cheese, Shredded
- Tomatoes

Directions:
1. Brown the turkey in a medium-sized pan over medium heat.
2. Drain if necessary, and then pour in the taco seasoning according to the package directions.
3. Tacos are constructed by layering cooked meat, lettuce, shell, beans, and cheese.
4. Place the tacos in the air fryer and cook until crispy. It's preferable to line the pan with aluminum foil and coat it with nonstick cooking spray. Note: Using foil to line the baskets of the air fryer is optional; however, if you do, make sure that the foil does not completely cover the basket to enable proper air circulation.
5. Cook at 355°F or 360°F for 4 minutes, or until the bacon is crispy. (The temperature of certain air fryers may be set to 355 degrees Fahrenheit, while others can only be set to 350 or 360 degrees).

507. Pasta Chips

Prep Time: 15 minutes

Cook Time: 10 minutes

Servings: 1

Ingredients:
- 1 pound of bowtie pasta
- 3 tablespoons of olive oil
- 1 teaspoon of garlic powder
- 1/4 cup of grated Parmesan cheese
- 1 teaspoon of Italian seasoning
- 1 teaspoon of crushed red pepper

Directions:
1. Prepare a big saucepan of salted water by bringing it to a boil.
2. Cook the pasta according to the package guidelines until it is al dente.
3. Drain the pasta and combine it with the other ingredients in a mixing bowl.
4. Toss the spaghetti with olive oil.
5. Combine the grated garlic powder, Parmesan cheese, Italian seasoning, and chopped red pepper in a mixing bowl until well combined.
6. Toss everything together.
7. Preheat the air fryer to 405 degrees Fahrenheit (180 degrees Celsius).
8. Add the pasta to the preheated air fryer basket, making sure it covers the base of the basket and does not overlap in the basket.
9. Preheat the oven to 400 degrees F and cook for 4 minutes.
10. Cook for another 3-5 minutes at 400 degrees F, tossing halfway through until the vegetables are crisp to your liking.
11. Continue until you have finished making all of the spaghetti chips.
12. Toss with marinara sauce and serve with bread.

508. Steak Bites and Mushrooms

Prep Time: 1 hour 5 minutes

Cook Time: 1 hour 15 minutes

Serving: 2

Ingredients:
- 1 teaspoon of kosher salt
- 2 Tablespoons of Worcestershire Sauce
- 2 Tablespoons of avocado oil
- 8 oz. of Mushrooms, sliced
- 1 pound of steak, cut into 1.5 inch cubes
- ½ teaspoon of garlic powder
- ¼ teaspoon of black pepper

Directions:
1. In a large mixing bowl, combine all the marinade ingredients and stir well.
2. Toss the sliced mushrooms and steak cubes in the marinade in a large mixing dish until everything is well coated.
3. Allow about 1 hour of marinating time between the steak and the mushrooms.
4. For 5 minutes, heat your Air Fryer to 400 degrees Fahrenheit.
5. Make sure you coat the interior of your air fryer with cooking spray before placing your mushrooms and steak in the air fryer basket. Cook for about 10 minutes.
6. Cook the mushrooms and steak for 4 minutes at 400 degrees Fahrenheit in an Air Fryer. Open the basket and stir the mushrooms

and steak to ensure that they are cooked equally throughout. Continue cooking for an additional 5 minutes.

7. Check the steak's internal temperature using an inner meat thermometer. Cook in 3-minute intervals until a thermometer inserted in the middle of 1 steak bite reaches the specified temperature. If the steak is not done to your liking, continue to cook in 3-minute intervals until it is. Serve

509. Fried Oreos

Prep Time: 5 minutes
Cook Time: 5 minutes
Serving: 8

Ingredients:
- 1 package of crescent dough sheet or Crescents Rolls
- Powdered sugar, for dusting only (optional)
- 8 Oreo cookies or other brand sandwich cookies

Directions:
1. Rectangles of crescent dough should be spread out on a counter or cutting board.
2. Press it down through each perforated line with your finger so that it becomes a single large sheet of paper.
3. Divide the dough into eighths to make it easier to work with.
4. Place one Oreo cookie in the middle of each square using a crescent roll square and roll each edge up.
5. Bunch up the remainder of the crescent roll to ensure that it completely covers the Oreo cookie surface. Stretching the crescent roll too thinly can result in the roll breaking.
6. Preheat the air fryer to 325 degrees for around 3-5 minutes, depending on how big it is.
7. Place the Air Fried Oreos in the air fryer in a single, even row, ensuring they do not touch one other. Cooking in batches is recommended if you have a small air fryer.
8. Using a 320-degree oven, bake the Oreos for 5-6 minutes, or until golden brown on the exterior.
9. Take the Air Fryer Oreos from the air fryer with care and immediately coat them with powdered sugar, if preferred.
10. Allow for two minutes of cooling time before serving.

510. Cake

Prep Time: 15 minutes
Cook Time: 25 minutes
Serving: 6

Ingredients:
- 1 cup of granulated sugar
- ¾ cup of plus 2 tablespoons all-purpose flour
- 1 teaspoon of vanilla extract
- Half teaspoon of baking soda
- ½ teaspoon of kosher salt

- 1 large egg, beaten
- Half cup of unsweetened cocoa powder
- 1 teaspoon of baking powder
- ¼ cup of vegetable oil
- ½ cup of buttermilk
- ½ cup of boiling water

Directions:
1. Preheat your air fryer to 350 degrees Fahrenheit (180 degrees Celsius).
2. Baking sprays the interior of a 7-inch air fryer-safe baking dish and line the pan with a 9-inch circular piece of parchment paper, allowing the paper to hang over the edges a little. Set aside after spraying with more cooking spray.
3. In a large mixing dish, combine the sugar, baking powder, cocoa powder, salt, baking soda, and flour. Combine the buttermilk, vegetable oil, and vanilla extract egg in a large mixing bowl. Mix for 1 minute or until everything is fully blended. Using a whisk, incorporate the hot water to form a thin batter.
4. Pour the batter into the pan that has been prepared and set it in the air fryer basket to cook for 15 minutes.
5. Cook for 25-30 minutes, just until the cake is completely made through and a toothpick inserted into the center comes out clean. Allow 10 minutes of cooling time in the pan before fully transferring to a cooling rack.
6. Optional decorations include frosting and sprinkles.

511. Lava Cakes

Prep Time: 10 minutes
Cook Time: 10 minutes
Serving: 2

Ingredients:
- Half cup of semi-sweet chocolate chips
- 4 tablespoons of butter
- 1/4 teaspoon of salt
- 1 tablespoon of butter, softened
- 1 tablespoon of powdered sugar
- 1 tablespoon of all-purpose flour
- 1 egg, beaten
- 1 teaspoon of vanilla extract
- Half cup of powdered sugar
- 2 tablespoons of Nutella

Directions:
1. Preheat your air fryer to 370 degrees Fahrenheit before you begin.
2. In a separate microwave-safe dish, combine the chocolate chips, butter, and heat in 30-second increments, stirring until thoroughly melted and smooth after each interval. In a large mixing bowl, whisk the flour, salt, eggs, vanilla, and powdered sugar until well combined.
3. In a second dish, combine the softened butter, Nutella, and powdered sugar until well combined. Set aside.
4. Spritz the ramekins with oil and cover each one-half filled with the chocolate chips mixture before placing them on a baking

sheet. About half of the Nutella filling should be placed in the middle of each ramekin, followed by the leftover chocolate chip mixture, ensuring that the Nutella is well covered.

5. Carefully insert the lava cakes into the air fryer and cook for 7 to 11 minutes, depending on the size of the cakes.

6. Carefully take the lava cakes from the air fryer and set them aside to cool for 5 minutes before reassembling them. Remove the cake from the oven and turn it onto a serving platter using a butter knife to run around the outer edges.

7. Add ice cream, chocolate syrup, and additional toppings to your liking, and enjoy!

512. Cinnamon Rolls

Prep Time: 10 minutes
Cook Time: 4 minutes
Servings: 8

Ingredients:

- 1 can of Pillsbury cinnamon rolls, 8 counts (not Grands)

Directions:
1. Preheat the air fryer to 350 degrees Fahrenheit.
2. Placing the cinnamon rolls on top of the parchment in the air fryer (advised) and allowing a tiny space between them is a good way to start.
3. Cook the cinnamon buns for approximately 4 minutes at a medium temperature.
4. Carefully take the rolls from the air fryer and set them aside to chill for several minutes before drizzling the icing on top of the rolls... Enjoy!

513. Breakfast Potatoes

Prep Time: 10 minutes
Cook Time: 15 minutes
Servings: 4

Ingredients:
- 1 teaspoon of salt
- 1/2 teaspoon of sweet paprika
- cooking spray
- 1 teaspoon of garlic powder
- 1/2 teaspoon of onion powder
- 3-4 russets of potatoes
- 2-3 tablespoons of olive oil

Directions:
1. Peel and chop the potatoes into 1-inch pieces once they have been peeled.
2. Coat the potatoes with olive oil and then toss them in the spice, ensuring they're all uniformly coated in the seasoned mixture.
3. Spray the air fryer basket with nonstick cooking spray before adding the potatoes.
4. Cook for 20 minutes at 400 degrees Fahrenheit in an air fryer, turning at least once halfway through.
5. When you're finished, serve right away.

514. Chicken Fajitas

Prep Time: 10 minutes
Cook Time: 10 minutes
Servings: 4

Ingredients:
- Half pound boneless and skinless chicken breasts, cut into 1/2-inch wide strips
- 1 large red or yellow bell pepper, cut into strips
- 1 tablespoon of Mazola Corn Oil
- 1 tablespoon of chili powder
- 1 medium red onion, cut into strips
- 2 teaspoons of lime juice
- A pinch of cayenne pepper
- tortillas, for Serving
- 1 teaspoon of cumin
- Salt, to taste
- Pepper, to taste

Directions:
1. Preheat your air fryer to 370 degrees Fahrenheit before you begin.
2. Toss the chicken strips with the bell pepper and onion in a large mixing bowl before adding the cumin, lime juice, Mazola Corn Oil, cayenne pepper, chili powder, pepper, and salt.
3. Bake in the air fryer for 10-15 minutes, moving the basket halfway through, or until the chicken is cooked to your liking. The fajitas are ready to serve when the chicken reaches 166 degrees F at its widest point.
4. Take the fajitas from the air fryer, reheat the tortillas if necessary, and serve immediately.

515. Cinnamon Apples

Preparation Time: 15 Minutes
Cooking Time: 15 Minutes
Servings: 4

Ingredients:
- (2 Servings)
- 2 apples, cored, bottom intact
- 2 tbsp butter, cold
- 3 tbsp Sugar
- 3 tbsp crushed walnuts
- 2 tbsp raisins
- 1 tsp cinnamon.

Direction:
1. Preheat the air fryer to 350 F.
2. In a bowl, add butter, Sugar , walnuts, raisins, and cinnamon
3. Mix well until you obtain a crumble. Stuff the apples with the filling mixture.
4. Bake in the air fryer for 15 minutes.

516. Hearty Banana Pastry

Preparation Time: 15 Minutes
Cooking Time: 12 Minutes
Servings: 4

Ingredients:
- (2 Servings)
- 3 bananas, sliced
- 3 tbsp honey
- 2 puff pastry sheets, cut into thin strips
- 1 cup fresh berries to serve

Direction:
1. Preheat the air fryer to 340 F.
2. Place banana slices into a greased baking dish.
3. Cover with pastry strips and drizzle with honey. Bake inside the air fryer for 12 minutes until golden.
4. Serve with berries.

517. Korean Chili Chicken Wings

Preparation Time: 10 Minutes
Cooking Time: 15 Minutes
Servings: 4
Ingredients:
- (4 Servings)
- 8 chicken wings
- Salt to taste
- 1 tsp sesame oil
- Juice from half lemon
- ¼ cup sriracha chili sauce
- 1-inch piece ginger, grated
- 1 tsp garlic powder
- 1 tsp sesame seeds

Direction:
1. Preheat the air fryer to 370 F.
2. Grease the air frying basket with cooking spray. In a bowl, mix salt, ginger, garlic, lemon juice, sesame oil, and chili sauce.
3. Coat the wings in the d Transfer the wings to the basket and AirFry for 15 minutes, flipping once.
4. Sprinkle with sesame seeds and serve.

518. Air-Fried Chicken Thighs

Preparation Time: 10 Minutes
Cooking Time: 12 Minutes
Servings: 4

Ingredients:
- (4 Servings)
- 1 ½ lb chicken thighs
- 2 eggs, lightly beaten
- 1 cup seasoned breadcrumbs
- ½ tsp oregano
- Salt and black pepper to taste

Direction:
1. Preheat the air fryer to 390 F.
2. Season the thighs with oregano, salt, and black pepper.

3. In a bowl, add the beaten eggs.
4. In a separate bowl, add the breadcrumbs Dip the thighs in the egg wash. Then roll them in the breadcrumbs and press firmly, so the breadcrumbs stick well.
5. Spray the thighs with cooking spray and arrange them in the frying basket in a single layer, skin-side up.
6. AirFry for 12 minutes, turn the thighs over, and cook for 6-8 more minutes until crispy.
7. Serve and enjoy!

519. Crunchy Chicken Egg Rolls

Preparation Time: 15 Minutes
Cooking Time: 15 Minutes
Servings: 4

Ingredients:
- (4 Servings)
- 2 tsp olive oil
- 2 garlic cloves, minced
- ¼ cup soy sauce
- 1 tsp grated fresh ginger
- 1 lb ground chicken
- 2 cups white cabbage, shredded
- 1 onion, chopped
- 1 egg, beaten
- 8 egg roll wrappers

Direction:
1. Heat olive oil in a pan over medium heat and add garlic, onion, ginger, and ground chicken.
2. Sauté for 5 minutes until the chicken is no longer pink.
3. Pour in the soy sauce and shredded cabbage and stir-fry for another 5-6 minutes until the cabbage is tender.
4. Remove from the heat and let cool slightly.
5. Fill each egg wrapper with the mixture, arranging it just below the center of the wrappers Fold in both sides and roll up tightly.
6. Use the beaten egg to seal the edges.
7. Brush the tops with the remaining beaten egg.
8. Place the rolls in the greased frying basket, spray them with cooking spray, and AirFry for 12-14 minutes at 370 F until golden, turning once halfway through.
9. Let cool slightly and serve.

520. Herby Meatballs

Preparation Time: 15 Minutes
Cooking Time: 15 Minutes
Servings: 4

Ingredients:
- (4 Servings)
- 1 lb ground beef
- 1 onion, finely chopped
- 2 garlic cloves, finely chopped
- 1 egg
- 1 cup breadcrumbs
- ½ cup Mediterranean herbs
- Salt and black pepper to taste
- 1 tbsp olive oil.

Direction:
1. In a bowl, add the ground beef, onion, garlic, egg, breadcrumbs, herbs, salt, and pepper and mix with your hands to combine.
2. Shape into balls and brush them with olive oil.
3. Arrange the meatballs in the frying basket and AirFry for 15 minutes at 380 F, turning once halfway through.
4. Serve immediately.

521. Quick Pickle Chips

Preparation Time: 5 Minutes
Cooking Time: 10 Minutes
Servings: 4

Ingredients:
- (4 Servings)
- 36 sweet pickle chips, drained 1 cup flour
- ¼ cup cornmeal

Direction:
1. Preheat the air fryer to 400 F.
2. In a bowl, mix flour, cayenne pepper, and cornmeal Dip the pickles in the flour mixture and spritz with cooking spray.
3. AirFry for 10 minutes until golden brown, turning once.

522. Mexican-Style Air Fryer Nachos

Preparation Time: 5 Minutes
Cooking Time: 8 Minutes
Servings: 4

Ingredients:
- (4 Servings)
- 8 corn tortillas, cut into wedges
- 1 tbsp olive oil
- ½ tsp ground cumin
- ½ tsp chili powder
- ½ tsp paprika
- ½ tsp cayenne pepper
- ½ tsp salt
- ½ tsp ground coriander

Direction:
1. Preheat the air fryer to 370 F.
2. Brush the tortilla wedges with olive oil and arrange them in the frying basket in an even layer.
3. Mix the spices thoroughly in a small bowl.
4. Sprinkle the tortilla wedges with the spice mixture. Air Fry for 2-3 minutes, shake the basket, and fry for another 2-3 minutes until crunchy and nicely browned.
5. Serve the nachos immediately.

523. Low-Carb Radish Chips

Preparation Time: 8 Minutes
Cooking Time: 8 Minutes
Servings: 4

Ingredients:
- (4 Servings)
- 10-15 radishes, thinly sliced
- Salt to season.

Direction:
1. Preheat the air fryer to 400 F
2. Grease the frying basket with cooking spray.
3. Add in the sliced radishes and AirFry for 8 minutes, flipping once halfway through.
4. Season with salt and consume immediately.

524. Smoked Fish Balls

Preparation Time: 8 Minutes
Cooking Time: 15 Minutes
Servings: 4

Ingredients:
- (4 Servings)
- 1 cup smoked mackerel, flaked
- 2 cups cooked rice
- 2 eggs, lightly beaten
- 1 cup Grana Padano cheese, grated
- ¼ cup fresh thyme, chopped
- Salt and black pepper to taste
- 1 cup panko breadcrumbs Cooking spray

Direction:
1. In a bowl, add fish, rice, eggs, Grana Padano cheese, thyme, salt, and black pepper; stir to combine.
2. Shape the mixture into 12 even-sized balls.
3. In a bowl, add fish, rice, eggs, Grana Padano cheese, thyme, salt, and black pepper; stir to combine.
4. Shape the mixture into 12 even-sized balls.

525. Salmon Mini Tarts

Preparation Time: 10 Minutes
Cooking Time: 10 Minutes
Servings: 4-6

Ingredients:
- (4-6 Servings)
- 15 mini tart shells
- 4 eggs, lightly beaten
- 2 tbsp fresh dill, chopped
- ½ cup heavy cream
- 3 oz smoked salmon
- 6 oz cream cheese, divided into 15 pieces

Direction:
1. Mix together the eggs and heavy cream in a bowl.
2. Arrange the tarts on a greased air fryer muffin tray.
3. Pour the mixture into the tarts, about halfway up the side, and top with a piece of salmon and cheese.
4. Bake in the fryer for 10 minutes at 340 F, regularly checking them to avoid overcooking.
5. When ready, remove them from the tray and let cool.
6. Sprinkle with freshly chopped dill and enjoy

526. Salmon Croquettes

Preparation Time: 30 Minutes
Cooking Time: 12 Minutes
Servings: 4

Ingredients:
- (4 Servings)
- 1 (15 oz) tinned salmon, flaked
- 1 cup onions, grated
- 1 cup carrots, grated
- 3 large eggs
- 1 ½ tbsp fresh chives, chopped
- 4 tbsp mayonnaise
- 4 tbsp breadcrumbs 2
- ½ tsp Italian seasoning
- Salt and black pepper to taste
- 2 ½ tsp lemon juice

Direction:
1. In a bowl, mix well the salmon, onions, carrots, eggs, chives, mayonnaise, crumbs, Italian seasoning, salt, black pepper, and lemon juice.
2. Form croquettes out of the mixture and refrigerate for 45 minutes.
3. Preheat the air fryer to 400 F.
4. Grease the basket with cooking spray.
5. Arrange the croquettes in a single layer and spray with cooking spray.
6. AirFry for 10-12 minutes until golden, flipping once.

527. Parsley & Lemon Fried Shrimp

Preparation Time: 20 Minutes
Cooking Time: 12 Minutes
Servings: 4
Ingredients:
- (4 Servings)
- 1 ½ lb shrimp, peeled and deveined
- ½ cup fresh parsley, chopped
- Juice of 1 lemon
- 1 egg, beaten
- ½ cup flour
- ¾ cup seasoned breadcrumbs
- 2 tbsp chili garlic sauce

Direction:
1. Add the shrimp, parsley, and lemon juice in a resealable bag and massage until well-coated.
2. Place in the fridge to marinate for 20 minutes.
3. Preheat the air fryer to 400 F.
4. Put beaten egg, flour, and breadcrumbs each in a bowl.
5. Dredge shrimp in the flour, then in the egg, and finally in the crumbs.
6. Add to the frying basket and spray with cooking spray.
7. AirFry for 10-12 minutes, shaking once.
8. Remove to a serving plate and drizzle with chili garlic sauce to serve.

528. Cheesy Balls

Preparation time: 10 minutes
Cooking time: 14 minutes
Servings: 8

Ingredients:
- 3 zucchinis, grated
- Salt and black pepper to the taste
- 1 tablespoon almond flour
- 2 tablespoons mozzarella, shredded
- 2 tablespoons cheddar cheese, shredded
- ½ tablespoon lemon juice
- 1 tablespoon dill, chopped

Directions:
1. In a bowl, mix the zucchinis with the flour and the other ingredients, toss, shape medium balls out of this mix, place them in your Air Fryer's basket and cook at 400 degrees F for 14 minutes.
2. Divide into bowls and serve.

529. Pepper Salsa

Preparation time: 4 minutes
Cooking time: 12 minutes
Servings: 2

Ingredients:
- 1 yellow bell pepper, cut into strips
- 1 orange bell pepper, cut into strips
- 1 red bell pepper, cut into strips
- 1 cup cherry tomatoes, cubed
- 1 cup black olives, pitted and sliced

- 2 tablespoons balsamic vinegar
- Salt and black pepper to the taste
- 1 green onion, chopped
- 1 tablespoon chives, chopped

Directions:
1. In the Air Fryer's pan, mix the peppers with the tomatoes and the other ingredients, put the pan in the machine and cook at 400 degrees F for 12 minutes.
2. Divide the salsa into bowls and serve.

530. Cream Cheese Dip

Preparation time: 4 minutes
Cooking time: 10 minutes
Servings: 6

Ingredients:
- 2 cups cream cheese, soft
- 1 cup heavy cream
- ½ teaspoon turmeric powder
- Salt and black pepper to the taste
- 1 tablespoon chives, chopped
- 1 tablespoon basil, chopped

Directions:
1. In the Air Fryer's pan, mix the cream cheese with the cream and the other ingredients, whisk, put the pan in the machine and cook at 360 degrees F for 10 minutes.
2. Serve as a snack.

531. Italian Shrimp Platter

Preparation time: 5 minutes
Cooking time: 12 minutes
Servings: 4

Ingredients:
- 1 pound shrimp, peeled and deveined
- 1 tablespoon Italian seasoning
- ½ teaspoon cumin, ground
- ½ teaspoon mustard seeds, crushed
- 2 tablespoons lemon juice
- Salt and black pepper to the taste
- A drizzle of olive oil

Directions:
1. In the Air Fryer's basket, combine the shrimp with the seasoning and the other ingredients, toss and cook at 390 degrees F for 12 minutes, flipping them halfway.
2. Arrange the shrimp on a platter and serve as an appetizer.

532. Kale Dip

Preparation time: 10 minutes
Cooking time: 15 minutes
Servings: 4

Ingredients:
- 2 cups baby kale
- 1 cup heavy cream
- 1 cup Greek Yogurt
- 4 garlic cloves, minced
- 1 avocado, peeled, pitted, and cubed

Directions:
1. In a blender, mix the kale with the cream and the other ingredients, pulse well, transfer this to the Air Fryer's pan, cook at 380 degrees F for 15 minutes and serve cold as a party dip.

533. Shrimp Dip

Preparation time: 5 minutes
Cooking time: 12 minutes
Servings: 4

Ingredients:
- 1 pound shrimp, peeled, deveined, and chopped
- 1 cup heavy cream
- 1 teaspoon garam masala
- 2 green onions, chopped
- 2 teaspoons olive oil
- Salt and black pepper to the taste

Directions:
1. In your Air Fryer's pan, mix the shrimp with the cream, masala and the other ingredients, toss, put the pan in the machine and cook at 350 degrees F for 12 minutes.
2. Divide into bowls and serve as a party dip.

534. Broccoli Dip

Preparation time: 4 minutes
Cooking time: 15 minutes
Servings: 4

Ingredients:
- 1 pound broccoli florets, chopped
- 1 cup heavy cream
- 1 teaspoon sweet paprika
- Salt and black pepper to the taste
- 1 teaspoon olive oil
- 2 teaspoons garlic powder
- 1 tablespoon chives, chopped

Directions:
1. In a blender, mix the broccoli with the cream and the other ingredients, pulse well, transfer to the Air Fryer's pan, put the pan in the machine and cook at 400 degrees F for 15 minutes.
2. Divide into bowls and serve as a party dip.

535. Chicken Sandwiches

Preparation time: 5 minutes
Cooking time: 10 Minutes
Servings: 4

Ingredients:
- 2 chicken breasts; skinless, boneless, and cubed
- 1/2 cup Italian seasoning
- 1/2 tsp. thyme; dried
- 1 red onion; chopped.
- 1 red bell pepper; sliced
- 2 cups butter lettuce; torn
- 4 pita pockets
- 1 cup cherry tomatoes; halved
- 1 tbsp. olive oil

Directions:
1. In your Air Fryer, mix chicken with onion, bell pepper, Italian seasoning, and oil; toss and cook at 380 °F for 10 minutes.
2. Transfer chicken mix to a bowl; add thyme, butter lettuce and cherry tomatoes, toss well; stuff pita pockets with this mix and serve for lunch.

536. Prosciutto Sandwich

Preparation time: 5 minutes
Cooking time: 5minutes
Servings: 1

Ingredients:
- 2 bread slices
- 2 prosciutto slices
- 2 basil leaves
- 1 tsp. olive oil
- 2 mozzarella slices
- 2 tomato slices
- A pinch of salt and black pepper

Directions:
1. Arrange mozzarella and prosciutto on a bread slice.
2. Season with salt and pepper; place in your Air Fryer and cook at 400 °F, for 5 minutes. Drizzle oil over prosciutto, add tomato and basil; cover with the other bread slice, cut the sandwich in half and serve.

539. Wrapped Pears

Preparation time: 5 minutes
Cooking time: 15 minutes
Servings: 4

Ingredients:
- 4 puff pastry sheets
- 14 ounces vanilla custard
- 2 pears, halved
- 1 egg, whisked
- ½ teaspoon cinnamon powder
- 2 tablespoons sugar

Directions:
1. Place puff pastry slices on a working surface, add a spoonful of vanilla custard in the center of each, top with pear halves and wrap.
2. Brush pears with egg, sprinkle sugar and cinnamon, place them in your Air Fryer's basket and cook at 320 degrees F for 15 minutes.
3. Divide parcels among plates and serve.
4. Enjoy!

540. Tuna Sandwiches

Preparation time: 5 minutes
Cooking time: 14 minutes
Servings: 4

Ingredients:
- 16 oz. canned tuna; drained
- 6 bread slices
- 6 provolone cheese slices
- 2 spring onions; chopped.
- 1/4 cup mayonnaise
- 2 tbsp. mustard
- 1 tbsp. lime juice
- 3 tbsp. butter; melted

Directions:
1. In a bowl, mix the tuna, mayo, lime juice, mustard, and spring onions; stir until combined.
2. Spread the bread slices with the butter, place them in the preheated Air Fryer and bake them at 350°F for 5 minutes
3. Spread tuna mix on half of the bread slices and top with the cheese and the other bread slices
4. Place the sandwiches in your Air Fryer's basket and cook for 4 minutes more. Divide between plates and serve.

541. Chicken Pie Recipe

Preparation time: 5 minutes
Cooking time: 15 minutes
Servings: 4

Ingredients:
- 2 chicken thighs; boneless, skinless, and cubed
- 1 carrot; chopped
- 1 tsp. Worcestershire sauce
- 1 tbsp. flour
- 1 tbsp. milk
- 2 puff pastry sheets
- 1 tbsp. butter; melted
- 1 yellow onion; chopped
- 2 potatoes; chopped
- 2 mushrooms; chopped
- 1 tsp. soy sauce
- Salt and black pepper to the taste
- 1 tsp. Italian seasoning
- 1/2 tsp. garlic powder

Directions:
1. Heat a pan over medium high heat, add

potatoes, carrots, and onion; stir and cook for 2 minutes.

2. Add chicken and mushrooms, salt, soy sauce, pepper, Italian seasoning, garlic powder, Worcestershire sauce, flour, and milk; stir well and take off the heat.

3. Place 1 puff pastry sheet on the bottom of your Air Fryer's pan and trim edge excess.

4. Add chicken mix, top with the other puff pastry sheet; trim excess, and brush pie with butter.

5. Place in your Air Fryer and cook at 360 °F for 6 minutes.

6. Leave the pie to cool down; slice and serve for breakfast.

542. Beef Meatballs

Preparation time: 5 minutes
Cooking time: 15 Minutes
Servings: 4

Ingredients:
- 1/2 lb. beef; ground
- 1/2 tsp. garlic powder
- 1/2 tsp. onion powder
- 1/2 lb. Italian sausage; chopped.
- 1/2 cup cheddar cheese; grated
- Mashed potatoes for serving
- Salt and black pepper to the taste

Directions:
1. In a bowl, mix beef with sausage, garlic powder, onion powder, salt, pepper, and cheese; stir well and shape 16 meatballs out of this mix.

2. Place meatballs in your Air Fryer and cook them at 370 °F for 15 minutes. Serve your meatballs with some mashed potatoes on the side.

543. Special Pancake

Preparation time: 5 minutes
Cooking time: 12 Minutes
Servings: 2

Ingredients:
- 1 cup small shrimp; peeled and deveined
- 1 tbsp. butter
- 3 eggs; whisked
- 1/2 cup flour
- 1/2 cup milk
- 1 cup salsa

Directions:
1. Preheat your Air Fryer at 400 degrees F; add fryer's pan, add 1 tbsp. butter, and melt it.

2. In a bowl, mix eggs with flour and milk, whisk well, and pour into Air Fryer's pan, spread, cook at 350 degrees for 12 minutes and transfer to a plate. In a bowl, mix shrimp with salsa; stir and serve your pancake with this on the side.

544. Prawn Burgers

Preparation time: 15 minutes
Cooking time: 6 minutes
Servings: 2

Ingredients:
- ½ cup prawns, peeled, deveined, and finely chopped
- ½ cup breadcrumbs
- 2-3 tablespoons onion, finely chopped
- 3 cups fresh baby greens
- ½ teaspoon ginger, minced
- ½ teaspoon garlic, minced
- ½ teaspoon red chili powder
- ½ teaspoon ground cumin
- ¼ teaspoon ground turmeric
- Salt and ground black pepper, as required

Directions:
1. Preheat the Air fryer to 390 degrees F and grease an Air fryer basket.

2. Mix the prawns, breadcrumbs, onion, ginger, garlic, and spices in a bowl.

3. Make small-sized patties from the mixture and transfer them to the Air fryer basket.

4. Cook for about 6 minutes and dish out on a platter.

5. Serve immediately warm alongside the baby greens.

545. Buttered Scallops

Preparation time: 15 minutes
Cooking time: 4 minutes
Servings: 2

Ingredients:
- ¾ pound sea scallops, cleaned and patted very dry
- 1 tablespoon butter, melted
- ½ tablespoon fresh thyme, minced
- Salt and black pepper, as required

Directions:
1. Preheat the Air fryer to 390 degrees F and grease an Air fryer basket.

2. Mix scallops, butter, thyme, salt, and black pepper in a bowl.

3. Arrange scallops in the Air fryer basket and cook for about 4 minutes.

4. Dish out the scallops in a platter and serve hot.

153

546. Spring Rolls

Preparation Time: 10 minutes
Cooking Time: 5 minutes
Servings: 2

Ingredients
- Two spring roll wraps
- 7 oz. Chicken breast, cooked
- One egg
- 2 oz. Carrot
- 2 oz. Mushroom
- 1 oz. Onion, diced
- 1 tsp. Chives

Directions
1. Shred the grilled chicken breast.
2. Cut the carrot into the strips.
3. Slice the mushrooms. Combine the shredded chicken breast, carrot strips, and sliced mushrooms in the bowl.
4. Add diced onion and chives. Stir the mixture carefully.
5. Then place the chicken filling into the roll wraps and roll them.
6. Beat the egg in the bowl and whisk it.
7. Seal the spring rolls with the help of the whisked egg.
8. Preheat the air fryer to 360 F.
9. Cook the spring rolls for 5 minutes.
10. When the meal is cooked – serve it immediately.

547. Running Eggs

Preparation Time: 5 minutes
Cooking Time: 6 minutes
Servings: 2

Ingredients:
- Four eggs
- One pinch salt
- 3 oz. Cheddar cheese, shredded
- 1 tbsp. Dill, chopped
- 1/4 tsp. Butter

Directions:
1. Preheat the air fryer to 360 f.
2. Toss the butter in the air fryer and melt it.
3. Beat the eggs in the melted butter.
4. Sprinkle the eggs with the salt and chopped dill.
5. Cook the eggs for 4 minutes.
6. After this, sprinkle the eggs with the shredded cheese and cook them for 2 minutes more.
7. Transfer the cooked eggs to the serving plates.

548. French Toast

Preparation Time: 5 Minutes
Cooking Time: 6 Minutes
Servings: 2

Ingredients:
- Four slices of bread
- Two eggs
- ⅔ cup of milk
- One teaspoon of vanilla
- One tablespoon of cinnamon

Directions:
1. Preheat your air fryer to 320F. Place all ingredients except for the bread in a medium bowl and use a fork to mix them.
2. Make sure everything is well combined, and toe egg is broken up.
3. Dip the bread in the liquid mixture and shake off any extra liquid.
4. Spray an air fryer safe pan with cooking spray and place the bread in the pan
5. Place the pan in the basket of your preheated air fryer and set the timer for 6 minutes. Flip the bread halfway through
6. Serve immediately.

549. Baked Oatmeal

Preparation Time: 8 Minutes
Cooking Time: 10 Minutes
Servings: 1

Ingredients:
- 1 cup of milk
- One egg
- 2 cup of mixed berries, divided
- 1 cup of rolled oats
- ½ teaspoon of baking powder
- ½ teaspoon of ground cinnamon
- ⅓ teaspoon of salt
- ¼ cup of brown sugar
- ⅛ cup of slivered almonds

Directions:
1. Preheat the air fryer to 320F. Coat an air fryer safe pan with cooking spray.
2. Put the milk and egg together in a bowl.
3. Mix the baking powder, oats, brown sugar, salt, and cinnamon in a medium bowl.
4. Put ¼ cup of fruit in the pan, then the oat and brown sugar mixture, and finally the milk mixture.
5. Allow the mixture to rest for 10 minutes, then top with more fruit. Season with nutmeg and add the almonds.
6. Place the pan in the basket of your preheated air fryer and set the timer for 10 minutes. Check the oats after 10 minutes and cook for a couple more minutes if necessary.
7. Allow the oats to cool for a couple of minutes before serving.

550. Breakfast Sandwich

Preparation Time: 5 Minutes
Cooking Time: 7 Minutes
Servings: 1

Ingredients:
- Online egg, beaten
- Two streaky bacon stripes
- 1 English muffin
- A pinch of salt and pepper

Directions:
1. Beat one egg into an ovenproof cups or bowl.
2. Preheat the Air fryer to 390°F
3. Place the egg in the cup, bacon stripes, and muffin to the fryer and cook for 6-7 minutes.
4. Get the sandwich together and enjoy it.

551. Morning Vegetables on Toast

Preparation Time: 7 Minutes
Cooking Time: 11 Minutes
Servings: 4

Ingredients:
- Four slices French or Italian bread
- One red bell pepper, cut into strips
- 1 cup sliced button or cremini mushrooms
- One small yellow squash, sliced
- Two green onions, sliced
- One tablespoon olive oil
- Two tablespoons softened butter;
- ½ cup soft goat cheese

Directions:
1. Sprinkle the air fryer with olive oil and preheat the appliance to 350 F. Add red pepper, mushrooms, squash, and green onions mix well and cook for 7 minutes or until the vegetables are tender, shaking. the basket once during cooking time.
2. Transfer vegetables to a plate and set aside.
3. Spread bread slices with butter and place in the air fryer, butter-side up. Toast for 2 to 4 minutes or until golden brown.
4. Spread the goat cheese on the toasted bread and top with the vegetables.
5. Serve warm.

552. Egg Cups

Preparation Time: 10 minutes
Cooking Time: 18 minutes
Serve: 12

Ingredients:
- 12 eggs
- 4 oz cream cheese
- 12 bacon strips, uncooked
- 1/4 cup buffalo sauce
- 2/3 cup cheddar cheese, shredded
- Pepper Salt

Directions:
1. In a bowl, whisk together eggs, pepper, and salt.
2. Line each silicone muffin mold with one bacon strip.
3. Pour egg mixture into each muffin mold and place in the air fryer basket. (In batches)
4. Cook at 350 F for 8 minutes.
5. In another bowl, mix together cheddar cheese and cream cheese and microwave for 30 seconds. Add buffalo sauce and stir well.
6. Remove muffin molds from air fryer and add 2 tsp cheese mixture in the center of each egg cup.
7. Return muffin molds to the air fryer and cook for 10 minutes more.
8. Serve and enjoy.

553. Mushroom Cheese Salad

Preparation Time: 10 minutes
Cooking Time: 15 minutes
Serve: 3

Ingredients:
- 10 mushrooms, halved
- 1 tbsp fresh parsley, chopped
- 1 tbsp olive oil
- 1 tbsp mozzarella cheese, grated
- 1 tbsp cheddar cheese, grated
- 1 tbsp dried mix herbs
- Pepper Salt

Directions:
1. Add all ingredients into the bowl and toss well.
2. Transfer bowl mixture into the air fryer baking dish.
3. Place in the air fryer and cook at 380 F for 15 minutes.
4. Serve and enjoy.

554. Chicken Meatballs

Preparation Time: 10 minutes
Cooking Time: 12 minutes
Serve: 4

Ingredients:
- 1 lb ground chicken
- 1/3 cup frozen spinach, drained and thawed
- 1/3 cup feta cheese, crumbled
- 1 tsp greek seasoning
- ½ oz pork rinds, crushed
- Pepper Salt

Directions:
1. Spray air fryer basket with cooking spray.
2. Add all ingredients into the large bowl and mix until well combined.
3. Make small balls from meat mixture and place into the air fryer basket and cook for 12 minutes.
4. Serve and enjoy.

555. Shrimp Stew

Preparation Time: 15 minutes
Cooking Time: 12 Minutes
Servings: 4

Ingredients:
- 1 ½ lb. shrimp; peeled and deveined 1 red bell pepper; chopped.
- 14 oz. chicken stock 2 tbsp. tomato sauce
- 1 tbsp. olive oil
- 3 spring onions; chopped.
- Salt and black pepper to taste.

Directions:
1. In your air fryer's pan greased with the oil, mix the shrimp and the other ingredients, toss, introduce the pan in the machine and cook at 360°F for 12 minutes, stirring halfway
2. Divide into bowls and serve for lunch.

556. Lime Cheesecake

Preparation time: 15
Cooking Time: 4 minutes
Servings: 10

Ingredients:
- 2 tablespoons butter, melted
- 2 teaspoons sugar
- 4 ounces flour
- ¼ cup coconut, shredded For the filling:
- 1 pound cream cheese
- Zest from 1 lime, grated
- Juice form 1 lime
- 2 cups hot water
- 2 sachets lime jelly

Cooking Instructions:
1. In a bowl, mix coconut with flour, butter and sugar, stir well and press this on the bottom of a pan that fits your air fryer.
2. Meanwhile, put the hot water in a bowl, add jelly sachets and stir until it dissolves.
3. Put cream cheese in a bowl, add jelly, lime juice and zest and whisk really well.
4. Add this over the crust, spread, introduce in the air fryer and cook at 300 °F for 4 minutes.
5. Keep in the fridge for 4 hours before serving.

557. Maple Salmon

Preparation Time: 15 minutes
Cooking Time: 10 Minutes
Servings: 2

Ingredients:
- 2 salmon fillets; boneless
- 1 tbsp. olive oil
- 2 tbsp. mustard
- 1 tbsp. maple syrup
- Salt and black pepper to taste

Directions:
1. In a bowl, mix the mustard with the oil and the maple syrup; whisk well and brush the salmon with this mix.
2. Place the salmon in your air fryer and cook it at 370°F for 5 minutes on each side. Serve immediately with a side salad

558. Tiger Shrimp

Preparation Time: 15 minutes
Cooking Time: 10 Minutes
Servings: 2

Ingredients:
- 20 tiger shrimp; peeled and deveined
- 1/4 tsp. smoked paprika
- 1/2 tsp. Italian seasoning
- 1 tbsp. extra virgin olive oil
- Salt and black pepper to taste

Directions:
1. Add all the ingredients to a bowl and toss
2. Put the shrimp in the air fryer's basket and cook at 380°F for 10 minutes. Divide into bowls and serve.

559. Coconut Shrimp

Preparation Time: 15 minutes
Cooking Time: 10 Minutes
Servings: 4

Ingredients:
- 12 large shrimp; deveined and peeled 1 tbsp. parsley; chopped.
- 1 tbsp. cornstarch
- 1 cup coconut cream
- Salt and black pepper to taste

Directions:
1. Add all ingredients to a pan that fits your air fryer and toss.
2. Place the pan in the fryer and cook at 360°F for 10 minutes.
3. Serve hot and enjoy!

560. Shrimp and Mushrooms

Preparation Time: 15 minutes
Cooking Time: 13 Minutes
Servings: 2

Ingredients:
- 1 lb. shrimp; peeled and deveined
- 8 oz. mushrooms; roughly sliced
- 1/2 cup beef stock
- 1/4 cup heavy cream
- 2 garlic cloves; minced
- 1 tbsp. butter; melted 1 tbsp. chives; chopped.
- 1 tbsp. parsley; chopped.
- A drizzle of olive oil
- A pinch of red pepper flakes
- Salt and black pepper to taste

Directions:
1. Season the shrimp with salt and pepper and grease with the oil.
2. Place the shrimp in your air fryer, cook at 360°F for 7 minutes and divide between plates
3. Heat up a pan with the butter over medium heat, add the mushrooms, stir and cook for 3-4 minutes.
4. Add all remaining ingredients; stir and then cook for a few minutes more
5. Drizzle the butter / garlic mixture over the shrimp and serve.

561. Churros

Preparation Time: 10 minutes
Cooking Time: 5 minutes
Servings: 3

Ingredients:
- 1/4 cup butter
- 1/2 cup milk
- One pinch salt
- 1/2 cup flour
- Two eggs
- 1/4 cup white sugar
- 1/2 tsp. ground cinnamon

Directions:
1. Melt butter over medium to high heat in a saucepan. Pour over rice, and then apply salt. Reduce heat to medium, and bring to a boil with a wooden spoon, always stirring. Instantly apply all the flour at once. Keep stirring until the dough joins in.
2. Remove from heat and allow cooling for five to seven minutes. Mix the eggs and the wooden spoon before the choux pastry comes together. Spoon dough fitted with a large star tip to a pastry bag. Pip dough directly into the air-fryer basket into bits.
3. Air fry the churros for 5 minutes at 340 degrees F (175 degrees C).
4. In a prepared small bowl, mix sugar and cinnamon, then pour over a shallow plate.
5. Eliminate fried air fryer churros and spread out the cinnamon-sugar blend.

562. Home Fries

Preparation Time: 10 minutes
Cooking Time: 20 minutes
Servings: 2

Ingredients
- 1 tsp. salt
- Three russet potatoes, cubed
- 1 tsp. chili powder
- 3 tbsp. of paprika seasoning
- Olive oil - 2 tbsp.
- Pepper - 1/2 tsp.
- Garlic powder - 3 tbsp.

Directions
1. To heat, set the temperature of the air fryer to 400°F. Prepare the potatoes by scrubbing and chopping them into cubes.
2. Using a glass dish, combine the cubed potatoes with paprika, olive oil, chili powder, and garlic powder until integrated.
3. In a single layer, assemble the potatoes in the air fryer basket. Fry for approximately 25 minutes.
4. Open the lid about every 10 minutes to toss the potatoes for it to be cooked fully.
5. Remove from the basket, distribute to a serving dish, then serve immediately.

563. Maple-Glazed Bacon

Preparation Time: 10 minutes
Cooking Time: 10 minutes
Servings: 2

Ingredients
- Brown sugar - 3 tbsp.
- Water - 2 tbsp.
- Eight slices bacon
- Maple syrup - 2 tbsp.

Directions
1. Adjust the air fryer to heat at 400°F. Remove the basket and cover the base with baking paper.
2. Empty the water into the base of the fryer while preheating.
3. In a glass dish, whisk the 2 tbsp. Of maple syrup and the 3 tbsp. of brown sugar together.
4. Place the wire rack into the basket and arrange the bacon into a single layer.
5. Spread the sugar glaze on the bacon until completely covered.
6. Put the basket into the air fryer and steam for 8 minutes.
7. Move the bacon from the basket and wait about 5 minutes before serving hot.

564. Roasted Carrots

Preparation Time: 5 minutes
Cooking Time: 10 minutes
Servings: 4

Ingredients
- 20 oz. carrots, julienned
- 1 tbsp. olive oil
- 1 tsp. cumin seeds
- 2 tbsp. fresh cilantro, chopped

Directions
1. In a bowl, mix olive oil, carrots, and cumin seeds; stir to coat. Place the carrots in a baking tray and cook in your Bake function at 300 F for 10 minutes.
2. Scatter fresh coriander over the carrots and serve.

565. Meat Lovers' Pizza

Preparation Time: 10 minutes
Cooking Time: 12 minutes
Servings: 2

Ingredients
- One pre-prepared 7-inch pizza crust, defrosted if necessary.
- 1/3 cup of marinara sauce.
- 2 ounces of grilled steak, sliced into bite-sized pieces
- 2 ounces of salami, sliced fine
- 2 ounces of pepperoni, sliced fine
- ¼ cup of American cheese
- ¼ cup of shredded mozzarella cheese

Directions:
1. Preheat the Air Fryer Oven to 350 degrees. Lay the pizza dough flat on a sheet of parchment paper or tin foil, cut large enough to hold the entire pie crust but small enough that it will leave the edges of the air frying basket uncovered to allow for air circulation.
2. Using a fork, stab the pizza dough several times across the surface – piercing the pie crust will allow air to circulate throughout the crust and ensure even cooking. With a deep soup spoon, scoop the marinara sauce onto the pizza dough, and spread evenly in expanding circles over the pie-crust surface. Be sure to leave at least ½ inch of bare dough around the edges to ensure that extra-crispy crunchy first bite of the crust!
3. Distribute the steak pieces and the slices of salami and pepperoni evenly over the sauce-covered dough, then sprinkle the cheese in an even layer on top.
4. Set the air fryer timer to 12 minutes, and place the pizza with foil or paper on the fryer's basket surface. Again, be sure to leave the edges of the basket uncovered to allow for proper air circulation, and don't let your bare fingers touch the hot surface. After 12 minutes, when the Air Fryer Oven shuts off, the cheese should be perfectly melted and lightly crisped, and the pie crust should be golden brown. If necessary, using a spatula – or two, remove the pizza from the air fryer basket and set it on a serving plate.
5. Wait a few minutes until the pie is cool enough to handle, then cut into slices and serve.

566. Country Fried Steak

Preparation Time: 5 minutes
Cooking Time: 12 minutes
Servings: 2

Ingredients
- 1 tsp. pepper
- 2 C. almond milk
- 2 tbsp. almond flour
- 6 ounces ground sausage meat
- 1 tsp. pepper
- 1 tsp. salt
- 1 tsp. garlic powder
- 1 tsp. onion powder
- 1 C. panko breadcrumbs
- 1 C. almond flour
- Three beaten eggs
- 6 ounces sirloin steak, pounded till thin

Directions:
1. Season panko breadcrumbs with spices.
2. Dredge steak in flour, then egg, and then seasoned panko mixture.
3. Place into air fryer basket.
4. Set temperature to 370°F, and set time to 12 minutes.
5. To make sausage gravy, cook sausage and drain off fat, but reserve 2 tbsps.
6. Add flour to sausage and mix until incorporated. Gradually mix in milk over medium to high heat till it becomes thick.
7. Season mixture with pepper and cook 3 minutes longer.
8. Serve steak topped with gravy and enjoy.

567. Warming Winter Beef with Celery

Preparation Time: 5 minutes
Cooking Time: 12 minutes
Servings: 4

Ingredients
- 9 ounces tender beef, chopped
- 1/2 cup leeks, chopped
- 1/2 cup celery stalks, chopped
- Two cloves of garlic smashed
- 2 tbsps. red cooking wine
- 3/4 cup cream of celery soup
- Two sprigs of rosemary, chopped
- 1/4 tsp. smoked paprika
- 3/4 tsp. salt
- 1/4 tsp. black pepper, or to taste

Directions:
1. Add the beef, leeks, celery, and garlic to the baking dish; cook for about 5 minutes at 390 degrees F.
2. Once the meat is starting to tender, pour in the wine and soup. Season with rosemary, smoked paprika, salt, and black pepper. Now, cook an additional 7 minutes.

568. Beef & Veggie Spring Rolls

Preparation Time: 5 minutes
Cooking Time: 12 minutes
Servings: 10

Ingredients
- 2-ounce Asian rice noodles
- 1 tbsp. sesame oil
- 7-ounce ground beef
- One small onion, chopped
- Three garlic cloves, crushed
- 1 cup fresh mixed vegetables
- 1 tsp. soy sauce
- One packet spring roll skins
- 2 tbsps. water
- Olive oil, as required

Directions:
1. Soak the noodles in warm water till soft.
2. Drain and cut into small lengths. In a pan, heat the oil and add the onion and garlic and sauté for about 4-5 minutes.
3. Add beef and cook for about 4-5 minutes.
4. Add vegetables and cook for about 5-7 minutes or till cooked through.
5. Stir in soy sauce and remove from the heat.
6. Immediately, stir in the noodles and keep aside till all the juices have been absorbed.
7. Preheat the Air Fryer Oven to 350 degrees F.
8. Place the spring rolls skin onto a smooth surface.
9. Add a line of the filling diagonally across.
10. Fold the top point over the filling and then fold in both sides.
11. On the final point, brush it with water before rolling to seal.
12. Brush the spring rolls with oil.
13. Arrange the rolls in batches in the air fryer and Cook for about 8 minutes.
14. Repeat with remaining rolls. Now, place spring rolls onto a baking sheet.
15. Bake for about 6 minutes per side.

569. Beef Korma

Preparation Time: 10 minutes
Cooking Time: 20 minutes
Servings: 6

Ingredients
- ½ cup yogurt
- 1 kg (2.2 lbs.) boneless beef steak, cut in chunks
- 1 tbsp. curry powder
- 1 tbsp. olive oil
- One onion, chopped
- 3 cloves garlic, minced
- One tomato, diced
- ½ cup frozen baby peas, thawed

Directions:
1. In a medium bowl, combine the steak, yogurt, and curry powder. Stir and set aside.
2. In a 6-inch metal bowl, combine the olive oil, onion, and garlic.
3. Cook for 3 to 4 minutes or until crisp and tender.
4. Add the steak along with the yogurt and the diced tomato. Cook for 12 to 13 minutes or until the steak is almost tender.
5. Stir in the peas and cook for 2 to 3 minutes or until hot.

570. Restaurant-Style Beef Burgers

Preparation Time: 5 minutes
Cooking Time: 15 minutes
Servings: 3

Ingredients
- 3/4 pound ground beef
- 2 cloves garlic, minced
- One small onion, chopped
- Kosher salt and ground black pepper to taste
- 3 hamburger buns

Directions
1. Mix the beef, garlic, onion, salt, and black pepper until everything is well combined. Form the mixture into three patties.
2. Cook the burgers at 380 degrees F for about 15 minutes or until cooked through; make sure to turn them over halfway through the cooking time.
3. Serve your burgers on the prepared buns and enjoy!

571. New York Strip Steak

Preparation Time: 10 minutes
Cooking Time: 10 minutes
Servings: 4

Ingredients
- 1½ pound New York strip steak
- 4 tbsps. butter, melted
- Sea salt and ground black pepper to taste
- 1 tsp. paprika
- 1 tsp. dried thyme
- 1 tsp. dried rosemary

Directions
1. Toss the beef with the remaining ingredients; place the beef in the Air Fryer cooking basket.
2. Cook the beef at 400 degrees F for 15 minutes, turning it over halfway through the cooking time.
3. Enjoy!

572. BBQ Pork Steaks

Preparation Time: 5 minutes
Cooking Time: 15 minutes
Servings: 4

Ingredients:
- Four pork steaks
- 1 tbsp. Cajun seasoning
- 2 tbsps. BBQ sauce
- 1 tbsp. vinegar
- 1 tsp. soy sauce

- ½ cup brown sugar
- ½ cup ketchup

Directions:
1. Sprinkle pork steaks with Cajun seasoning.
2. Combine remaining ingredients and brush onto steaks.
3. Add coated steaks to the air fryer oven. Select the AIR FRY function and cook at 290°F (143°C) for 15 minutes, or until just browned.
4. Serve immediately.

573. Fast Lamb Satay

Preparation Time: 5 minutes
Cooking Time: 8 minutes
Servings: 2

Ingredients:
- ¼ tsp. cumin
- 1 tsp. ginger
- ½ tsp. nutmeg
- Salt and ground black pepper to taste
- Two boneless lamb steaks
- Cooking spray

Directions:
1. Combine the cumin, ginger, nutmeg, salt, and pepper in a bowl.
2. Cube the lamb steaks and massage the spice mixture into each one.
3. Leave to marinate for 10 minutes, and then transfer onto metal skewers.
4. Spritz the skewers with the cooking spray and place them in the air fryer basket.
5. Select the AIR FRY function and cook at 400°F (204°C) for 8 minutes.
6. Take care when removing them from the air fryer oven and serve.

574. Lamb Ribs

Preparation Time: 5 minutes
Cooking Time: 18 minutes
Servings: 4

Ingredients:
- 2 tbsps. mustard
- 1 pound (454 g) lamb ribs
- 1 tsp. rosemary, chopped
- Salt and ground black pepper to taste
- ¼ cup mint leaves, chopped
- 1 cup Greek yogurt

Directions:
1. To add the mustard to the ribs of the lamb, use a brush and season with rosemary, salt, and pepper. Transfer to the air fryer basket.
2. Select the AIR FRY function and cook at 350°F (177°C) for 18 minutes.
3. Meanwhile, in a dish, combine the mint leaves and yogurt.
4. When baked, remove the lamb ribs from the air-fryer oven and serve with mint yogurt.

575. Simple Haddock

Preparation Time: 15 minutes
Cooking Time: 8 minutes
Servings: 2

Ingredients:
- 2 (6-oz.) haddock fillets
- 1 tbsp. olive oil
- Salt and ground black pepper, as required

Directions:
1. Coat the fish fillets with oil and then sprinkle with salt and black pepper.
2. Press the "Power Button" of the Air Fry Oven and turn the dial to select the "Air Fry" mode.
3. Press the Time button and again turn the dial to set the cooking time to 8 minutes.
4. Now push the Temp button and rotate the dial to set the temperature at 355 degrees F.
5. Press the "Start/Pause" button to start.
6. When the unit beeps to show that it is preheated, open the lid.
7. Arrange the haddock fillets in greased "Air Fry Basket" and insert them in the oven.
8. Serve hot.

576. Mango Jam Cookies

Preparation Time: 15 minutes
Cooking Time: 6 minutes
Servings: 2

Ingredients:
- 1 cup plain flour
- 2 tbsps. cornstarch
- 2 tbsps. icing sugar
- 3 tbsps. custard powder
- 1/8 tsp. salt
- ½ cup unsalted butter, chilled
- One egg yolk
- cold water, if needed
- 1 cup ready-made mango jam
- 1 tsp. lemon juice

Directions:
1. Sift together the plain flour, cornstarch, icing sugar, custard powder, and salt in a bowl.
2. Rub in the butter until the mixture resembles breadcrumbs.
3. Mix in the egg yolk and knead to form a dough. Add some cold water if the dough is too dry.
4. Divide the dough into two equal portions and wrap each portion with plastic wrap.
5. Chill in the refrigerator for at least 30 minutes.
6. While the dough is chilling, make the mango filling by mixing the mango jam with the lemon juice with a fork until it becomes smoother.

7. Preheat the Air Fryer to 300°F/150°C.
8. Roll out the dough onto a lightly floured work surface until ¼-inch thick.
9. Cut out cookies using cookie cutters.
10. Arrange the cookies in the Air Fryer Basket and use the Air Fryer
11. Double Layer Rack if needed.
12. Set the timer for 6 minutes or until the cookies are golden brown.
13. Remove the cookies from the Air Fryer and allow cooling.
14. Spread each cookie with the mango jam.
15. Serve and enjoy!

577. Pumpkin Cookies

Preparation Time: 10 minutes
Cooking Time: 15 minutes
Servings: 24

Ingredients:
- 2 and ½ cups flour
- ½ tsp. baking soda
- 1 tbsp. flax seed, ground
- 3 tbsps. water
- ½ cup pumpkin flesh, mashed
- ¼ cup honey
- 2 tbsps. butter
- 1 tsp. vanilla extract
- ½ cup dark chocolate chips

Directions:
1. In a bowl, mix flax seed with water, stir and leave aside for a few minutes.
2. In another bowl, mix flour with salt and baking soda.
3. In a third bowl, mix honey with pumpkin puree, butter, vanilla extract and flax seed.
4. Combine flour with honey mix and chocolate chips and stir.
5. Scoop 1 tbsp. of cookie dough on a lined baking sheet that fits your air fryer, repeat with the rest of the dough, introduce them in your air fryer and cook at 350 degrees F for 15 minutes.
6. Leave cookies to cool down and serve.
7. Enjoy!

578. Figs and Coconut Butter Mix

Preparation Time: 6 minutes
Cooking Time: 4 minutes
Servings: 3

Ingredients:
- 2 tbsps. coconut butter
- 12 figs, halved
- ¼ cup sugar
- 1 cup almonds, toasted and chopped

Directions:
1. Put butter in a pan that fits your air fryer and melt over medium-high heat.
2. Add figs, sugar, and almonds, toss, introduce in your air fryer and cook at 300 degrees F for 4 minutes.
3. Divide into bowls and serve cold.
4. Enjoy!

579. Plum Bars

Preparation Time: 10 minutes
Cooking Time: 16 minutes
Servings: 8

Ingredients:
- 2 cups dried plums
- 6 tbsps. water
- 2 cup rolled oats
- 1 cup brown sugar
- ½ tsp. baking soda
- 1 tsp. cinnamon powder
- 2 tbsps. butter, melted
- 1 egg, whisked
- Cooking spray

Directions:
1. In your food processor, mix plums with water and blend until you obtain a sticky spread.
2. In a bowl, mix oats with cinnamon, baking soda, sugar, egg, and butter and whisk really well.
3. Press half of the oats mix in a baking pan that fits your air fryer sprayed with cooking oil, spread plums mix, and top with the other half of the oats mix.
4. Introduce in your air fryer and cook at 350 degrees F for 16 minutes.
5. Leave mix aside to cool down, cut into medium bars, and serve.
6. Enjoy!

580. Air-Fried S'mores

Preparation Time: 10 minutes
Cooking Time: 10 minutes
Servings: 4

Ingredients:
- Whole graham crackers (4)
- Marshmallows (2)
- Chocolate - such as Hershey's (4 pieces)

Directions:
1. Break the graham crackers in half to make eight squares. Cut the marshmallows in half crosswise with a pair of scissors.
2. Place the marshmallows cut side down on four graham squares. Place marshmallow side up in the basket of the Air Fryer and cook at 390° Fahrenheit for four to five minutes, or until golden.
3. Remove them from the fryer and place a piece Break all graham crackers in half to create eight squares. Cut marshmallows in half crosswise.
4. Place the marshmallows, cut side down, on four graham squares of chocolate and graham square on top of each toasted marshmallow and serve.

581. Banana S'mores

Preparation Time: 10 minutes
Cooking Time: 5 minutes
Servings: 4

Ingredients:
- Bananas (4)
- Mini-peanut butter chips (3 tbsp.)
- Graham cracker cereal (3 tbsp.)
- Mini-chocolate chips - semi-sweet (3 tbsp.)

Directions:
1. Heat the Air Fryer in advance at 400° Fahrenheit.
2. Slice the un-peeled bananas lengthwise along the inside of the curve.
3. Don't slice through the bottom. Open slightly - forming a pocket.
4. Fill each pocket with chocolate chips, peanut butter chips, and marshmallows. Poke the cereal into the filling.
5. Arrange the stuffed bananas in the fryer basket, keeping them upright with the filling facing up.
6. Air-fry until the peel has blackened about 6 minutes.
7. Chill for 1-2 minutes. Spoon out the filling to serve.

582. Cherry Tomatoes Mix

Preparation time: 10 minutes
Cooking time: 15 minutes
Servings: 1

Ingredients:
- 1 tbsp. shallot, chopped
- 1 garlic clove, minced
- ¾ C. cashews, soaked for a couple of hours and drained
- 2 tbsps. nutritional yeast
- ½ C. veggie stock
- Salt and black pepper to the taste
- 2 tsps. lemon juice
- 1 C. cherry tomatoes, halved
- 5 tsps. olive oil
- ¼ tsp. garlic powder

Directions:
1. Place tomatoes in a pan that fits your air fryer, drizzle the oil over them, season with salt, black pepper, and garlic powder, toss to coat, and cook in your air fryer at 350°F for 15 minutes.
2. Meanwhile, in a food processor, mix garlic with shallots, cashews, veggie stock, nutritional yeast, lemon juice, a pinch of sea salt, and black pepper to the taste and blend well
3. Divide tomatoes between plates, drizzle the sauce over them, and serve as a side dish.

583. Potatoes With Green Beans

Preparation time: 10 minutes
Cooking time: 15 minutes
Servings: 1

Ingredients:
- 1 lb. red potatoes, cut into wedges
- 1 lb. green beans
- 2 garlic cloves, minced
- 2 tbsps. olive oil
- Salt and black pepper to the taste
- ½ tsp. oregano, dried

Directions:
1. Using a pan that fits your air fryer, combine potatoes with green beans, garlic, oil, salt, pepper, and oregano, toss, introduce in your air fryer, and cook at 380°F for 15 minutes.
2. Divide among dishes and serve as a side dish.

584. Oregano Bell Peppers

Preparation time: 10 minutes
Cooking time: 15 minutes
Servings: 1

Ingredients:
- 1 tbsp. olive oil
- 1 sweet onion, chopped
- 1 red bell pepper, chopped
- 1 orange bell pepper, chopped
- 1 green bell pepper, chopped
- Salt and black pepper to the taste
- ½ C. cashew cheese, shredded
- 1 tbsp. oregano, sliced

Directions:
1. In a pan that fits your air fryer, combine onion with red bell pepper, green bell pepper, orange bell pepper, salt, pepper, oregano, and oil, and toss.
2. Introduce in the fryer and cook at 320°F for 10 minutes.
3. Add cashew cheese, toss, introduce in the fryer for 4 minutes more, divide between plates, and serve as a side dish.

585 Colored Veggie Mix

Preparation time: 10 minutes
Cooking time: 12 minutes
Servings: 1

Ingredients:
- 1 zucchini, sliced in half, and roughly chopped
- 1 orange bell pepper, roughly chopped
- 1 green bell pepper, roughly chopped
- 1 red onion, roughly chopped
- 4 oz. brown mushrooms, halved
- Salt and black pepper to the taste
- 1 tsp. Italian seasoning
- 1 C. cherry tomatoes, halved
- ½ C. kalamata olives, pitted and halved
- ¼ C. olive oil

- 3 tbsps. balsamic vinegar
- 2 tbsps. basil, chopped

Directions:
1. In a bowl, mix zucchini with mushrooms, orange bell pepper, green bell pepper, red onion, salt, pepper, Italian seasoning, and oil, toss well, transfer to preheated air fryer at 380°F and cook them for 12 minutes.
2. In a large bowl, combine mixed veggies with tomatoes, olives, vinegar, and basil, toss, divide between plates and serve cold as a side dish.

586. Pork Rinds

Preparation time: 5 minutes
Cooking time: 10 minutes
Servings: 8

Ingredients:
- ½ tsp. black pepper
- 1 tsp. chili flakes
- ½ tsp. sea salt, fine
- 1 tsp. olive oil
- 1 lb. pork rinds

Directions:
1. Start by heating your air fryer to 365°F, and then spray it down with olive oil.
2. Place your pork rinds in your air fryer basket, and sprinkle with your seasoning. Mix well, and then cook for 7 minutes.
3. Shake gently, and then serve cooled.

587. Roasted Parsnips

Preparation time: 5 minutes
Cooking time: 40 minutes
Servings: 4

Ingredients:
- 2 lbs. parsnips, peeled & cut into chunks
- 2 tbsps. maple syrup
- 1 tbsp. olive oil
- 1 tbsp. parsley flakes

Directions:
1. Start by heating your air fryer to 360°F, and then add in your ingredients. Make sure that your parsnips are well coated.
2. Cook for 40 minutes, and then serve warm.

588. Parmesan Sticks

Preparation time: 5 minutes
Cooking time: 15 minutes
Servings: 4

Ingredients:
- ¼ tsp. black pepper
- 4 tbsps. almond flour
- 1 egg

- ½ C. heavy cream
- 8 oz. Parmesan cheese

Directions:
1. Crack your egg into a bowl, beating it. Add in your almond flour and cream, mixing well.
2. Sprinkle your cream mixture with black pepper, whisking well.
3. Cut your cheese into short, thick sticks, and then dip it in the cream mixture. Place these sticks in a plastic bag and place them in the freezer. Let them freeze.
4. Turn your air fryer to 400°F, and then place your frozen sticks on the air fryer rack, and then cook for 8 minutes.

589. Garlic Mozzarella Sticks

Preparation time: 15 Minutes
Cooking time: 10 minutes
Servings: 4

Ingredients:
- 1 tbsp. Italian seasoning
- 1 C. Parmesan cheese
- 8 string slices cheese, diced
- 2 eggs, beaten
- 1 clove garlic, minced

Directions:
1. Start by combining parmesan, garlic, and Italian seasoning in a bowl. Dip your cheese into the egg, and mix well.
2. Roll it into your cheese crumbles, and then press the crumbs into the cheese.
3. Place them in the fridge for 1 hour, and then preheat your air fryer to 375°F.
4. Spray your air fryer down with oil, and then arrange the cheese strings into the basket. Cook for 8–9 minutes at 365°F.
5. Allow them to cool for at least 5 minutes before serving.

590. Brownie Muffins

Preparation time: 10 minutes
Cooking time: 10 minutes
Servings: 12

Ingredients:
- 1 package of Betty Crocker fudge brownie mix
- ¼ C. walnuts, chopped
- 1 egg
- ⅓ C. vegetable oil
- 2 tsps. water

Directions:
1. Grease 12 muffin molds. Set aside.
2. In a bowl, put all ingredients together.
3. Place the mixture into the prepared muffin molds.
4. To select the "Air Fry" mode, press the "Power Button" on the air fry oven and spin the dial.

5. To adjust the cooking time to 10 minutes, press the "Time" button and then turn the dial again.
6. To set the temperature, press the "Temp" button and crank the dial to 300°F.
7. Press the "Start/Pause" button to start.
8. When the unit beeps to show that it is preheated, open the lid.
9. Arrange the muffin molds in the air fryer basket and insert them in the oven.
10. Place the muffin molds onto a wire rack to cool for about 10 minutes.
11. Carefully, invert the muffins onto the wire rack to completely cool before serving.

591. Honey Fruit Compote

Preparation time: 10 minutes
Cooking time: 3 minutes
Servings: 4

Ingredients:
* ⅓ C. honey
* 1 ½ C. blueberries
* 1 ½ C. raspberries

Directions:
1. Put all of the ingredients in the air fryer basket and stir well.
2. Seal pot with lid and cook on high for 3 minutes.
3. Once done, allow to release pressure naturally. Remove lid.
4. **Serve and enjoy.**

592. Potatoes Salad

Preparation time: 10 minutes
Cooking time: 20 minutes
Servings: 1

Ingredients:
* 1 ½ lb. baby potatoes, halved
* 2 garlic cloves, chopped
* 2 red onions, chopped
* 9 oz. cherry tomatoes
* 3 tbsps. olive oil
* 1 ½ tbsp. balsamic vinegar
* 2 thyme springs, chopped
* Salt and black pepper to the taste

Directions:
1. In your food processor, mix garlic with onions, oil, vinegar, thyme, salt, and pepper, and pulse really well.
2. In a bowl, mix potatoes with tomatoes and balsamic mix, toss, transfer to your air fryer and cook at 380°F for 20 minutes.
3. Divide between plates and serve cold as a side dish.

593. Rice With Veggies and Coconut Cream

Preparation time: 10 minutes
Cooking time: 10 minutes
Servings: 1

Ingredients:
* 2 C. rice, cooked
* 1 tbsp. olive oil
* Salt and black pepper to the taste
* 4 garlic cloves, minced
* 2 tbsps. carrot, chopped
* 3 tbsps. small broccoli florets
* 10 tbsp. coconut cream

Directions:
1. Heat your air fryer to 340°F, add oil, garlic, carrots, broccoli, salt, and pepper, and toss.
2. Add rice and coconut cream, toss, cover, and cook for 10 minutes.
3. Divide rice with veggies and coconut cream between plates and serve as a side dish.

594. Flavored Beets

Preparation time: 10 minutes
Cooking time: 10 minutes
Servings: 1

Ingredients:
* 1 ½ lb. beets, peeled and quartered
* A drizzle of olive oil
* 2 tsps. orange zest, grated
* 2 tbsps. cider vinegar
* ½ C. orange juice
* 2 tbsps. Stevia
* 2 scallions, chopped
* 2 tsps. mustard

Directions:
1. Rub beets with the oil and orange juice, place them in your air fryer's basket, and cook at 350°F for 10 minutes.
2. Transfer beets to a bowl, add scallions, orange zest, Stevia, mustard, and vinegar, toss, divide between plates and serve as a side dish.

595. Minty Leeks Medley

Preparation time: 10 minutes
Cooking time: 12 minutes
Servings: 1

Ingredients:
* 6 leeks, roughly chopped
* 1 tbsp. cumin, ground
* 1 tbsp. mint, chopped
* 1 tbsp. parsley, chopped
* 1 tsp. garlic, minced

- A drizzle of olive oil
- Salt and black pepper to the taste

Directions:
1. Using a pan that fits your air fryer, combine leeks with cumin, mint, parsley, garlic, salt, pepper, and the oil, toss, introduce in your air fryer, and cook at 350°F for 12 minutes.
2. Divide minty leeks medley between plates and serve as a side dish.

596. Tomatoes With Basil and Garlic

Preparation time: 10 minutes
Cooking time: 14 minutes
Servings: 1

Ingredients:
- 1 bunch basil, chopped
- 3 garlic cloves, minced
- A drizzle of olive oil
- Salt and black pepper to the taste
- 2 C. cherry tomatoes, halved

Directions:
1. Using a pan that fits well with your air fryer, combine tomatoes with garlic, salt, pepper, basil, and oil, toss, introduce in your air fryer, and cook at 320°F for 12 minutes.
2. Divide between plates and serve as a side dish.

597. Soft Tofu With Veggies

Cooking time: 14 minutes
Servings: 1

Ingredients:
- 1 broccoli head, florets separated, and steamed
- 1 tomato, chopped
- 3 carrots, chopped and steamed
- 2 oz. soft tofu, crumbled
- 1 tsp. parsley, chopped
- 1 tsp. thyme, chopped
- Salt and black pepper to the taste

Directions:
1. Using a pan that fits well with your air fryer, combine broccoli with tomato, carrots, thyme, parsley, salt, and pepper, toss, introduce the fryer and cook at 350°F for 10 minutes.
2. Add tofu, toss, introduce in the fryer for 4 minutes more, divide between plates, and serve as a side dish.

598. Squash Mix

Preparation time: 10 minutes
Cooking time: 10
Servings: 1

Ingredients:
- 3 oz. coconut cream
- ½ tsp. oregano, dried
- Salt and black pepper
- 1 big yellow summer squash, peeled and cubed

- ⅓ C. carrot, cubed
- 2 tbsps. olive oil

Directions:
1. In a pan that fits your air fryer, combine squash with carrot, oil, oregano, salt, pepper, and coconut cream, toss, transfer to your air fryer and cook at 400°F for 10 minutes.
2. Divide among dishes and serve as a side dish.

599. Corn With Tomatoes Salad

Preparation time: 10 minutes
Cooking time: 10 minutes
Servings: 1

Ingredients:
- 3 C. corn
- A drizzle of olive oil
- Salt and black pepper to the taste
- 1 tsp. sweet paprika
- 1 tbsp. Stevia
- ½ tsp. garlic powder
- ½ iceberg lettuce head, cut into medium strips
- ½ romaine lettuce head, cut into medium strips
- 1 C. canned black beans, drained
- 3 tbsps. cilantro, chopped
- 4 green onions, chopped
- 12 cherry tomatoes, sliced

Directions:
1. Put the corn in a pan that fits your air fryer, drizzle the oil, add salt, pepper, paprika, Stevia, and garlic powder, introduce in your air fryer and cook at 350°F for 10 minutes.
2. Transfer corn to a salad bowl, add lettuce, black beans, tomatoes, green onions, and cilantro, toss, divide between plates and serve as a side salad.

600. Corn and Tomatoes

Preparation time: 10 minutes
Cooking time: 13 minutes
Servings: 1

Ingredients:
- 2 C. corn
- 4 tomatoes, roughly chopped
- 1 tbsp. olive oil
- Salt and black pepper to the taste
- 1 tbsp. oregano, chopped
- 1 tbsp. parsley, chopped
- 2 tbsps. soft tofu, pressed and crumbled

Directions:
1. In a pan that fits your air fryer, combine corn with tomatoes, oil, salt, pepper, oregano, and parsley, toss, introduce the pan in your air fryer and cook at 320°F for 10 minutes.
2. Add tofu, toss, introduce in the fryer for 3 minutes more, divide between plates, and serve as a side dish.

165

601. Pork Chop Fries

Preparation time: 10 minutes
Cooking time: 15 minutes
Servings: 4

Ingredients:
- 1 lb. pork chops, cut into fries
- ½ C. parmesan cheese, grated
- 3.5 oz. pork rinds, crushed
- ½ C. ranch dressing
- Pepper
- Salt

Directions:
1. In a shallow dish, mix crushed pork rinds, parmesan cheese, pepper, and salt.
2. Add pork chop pieces and ranch dressing into the zip-lock bag, seal bag, and shake well.
3. Remove pork chop pieces from zip-lock bag and coat with crushed pork rind mixture.
4. Place the cooking tray in the air fryer basket. Line the air fryer basket with parchment paper.
5. Select "Bake" mode.
6. Set time to 15 minutes and temperature 400°F, then press "Start."
7. The air fryer display will prompt you to "Add Food" once the temperature is reached, then place breaded pork chop fries in the air fryer basket.
8. Serve and enjoy.

602. Tilapia

Preparation Time: 5 minutes
Cooking Time: 12 minutes
Servings: 2

Ingredients:
- 2 tilapia fillets, wild-caught, 1 ½ inch thick
- 1 tsp. old bay seasoning
- ¾ tsp. lemon-pepper seasoning
- ½ tsp. salt

Directions
1. Switch on the Air Fryer, insert fryer basket, grease it with olive oil, then shut with its lid, set the fryer to 400°F, and preheat for 5 minutes.
2. Meanwhile, spray tilapia fillets with oil and then season with salt, lemon, pepper, and old bay seasoning until evenly coated.
3. Open the fryer, add tilapia in it, close the lid and cook for 7 minutes until nicely golden and cooked, turning the fillets halfway through the frying.
4. When the Air Fryer beeps, open its lid, transfer tilapia fillets onto a serving plate and serve.

603. Shrimp Scampi

Preparation Time: 5 minutes
Cooking Time: 12 minutes
Servings: 4

Ingredients
- 1-lb. shrimp, peeled, deveined
- 1 tbsp. garlic, minced
- 1 tbsp. basil, minced
- 1 tbsp. lemon juice
- 1 tsp. chives, dried
- 1 tsp. basil, dried
- 2 tsp. red pepper flakes
- 4 tbsp. butter, unsalted
- 2 tbsp. chicken stock

Directions
1. Switch on the Air Fryer, insert fryer pan, grease it with olive oil, then shut with its lid, set the fryer to 330°F, and preheat for 5 minutes.
2. Add butter in it along with red pepper and garlic and cook for 2 minutes or until the butter has melted.
3. Then add remaining ingredients in the pan, stir until mixed and continue cooking for 5 minutes until shrimps have cooked, stirring halfway through.
4. When done, remove the pan from the Air Fryer, stir the shrimp scampi, let it rest for 1 minute and then stir again.
5. Garnish shrimps with basil leaves and serve.

604. Salmon Cakes

Preparation Time: 5 minutes
Cooking Time: 12 minutes
Servings: 2

Ingredients
- ½ C. almond flour
- 15 oz. pink salmon, cooked
- ¼ tsp. black pepper, ground
- 2 tsp. Dijon mustard
- 2 tbsp. fresh dill, chopped
- 2 tbsp. mayonnaise, reduced-fat
- 1 egg, pastured
- 2 wedges lemon

Directions
1. Switch on the Air Fryer, insert fryer basket, grease it with olive oil, then shut with its lid, set the fryer to 400°F, and preheat for 5 minutes.
2. Meanwhile, place all the ingredients in a bowl, except for lemon wedges, stir until combined, and then shape into four patties, each about 4-inches.
3. Open the fryer, add salmon patties in it, spray oil over them, close the lid and cook for 12 minutes until nicely golden and crispy, flipping the patties halfway through the frying.
4. When the Air Fryer beeps, open its lid, transfer salmon patties onto a serving plate and serve.

605. Scallops With Green Vegetables

Preparation Time: 15 Minutes
Cooking Time: 8–11 Minutes
Servings: 4

Ingredients
- 1 C. green beans
- 1 C. peas, frozen
- 1 C. broccoli, frozen and chopped
- 2 tsp. olive oil
- ½ tsp. basil, dried
- ½ tsp. oregano, dried
- 12 oz. sea scallops

Directions
1. In a big bowl, toss the green beans, peas, and broccoli with olive oil. Place in the Air Fryer basket. Air-fry for 4–6 minutes, or until the vegetables are crisp-tender.
2. Remove the vegetables from the Air Fryer basket and sprinkle them with the herbs. Set aside.
3. In the Air Fryer basket, put the scallops and air-fry for 4–5 minutes, or until the scallops are firm and reach an internal temperature of just 145°F on a meat thermometer.
4. Toss scallops with the vegetables and serve immediately.

606. Steak Burgers

Preparation Time: 10 minutes
Cooking Time: 12 minutes
Servings: 4

Ingredients
- 1 lb. beef, ground
- 1/8 tsp. cayenne pepper
- 2 tsp. paprika
- 2 tsp. mustard powder
- 1 tsp. Worcestershire sauce
- 1 tsp. tomato paste
- 3 garlic cloves, minced
- ½ small onion, minced
- Pepper
- Salt

Directions
1. Add all ingredients into the big bowl and mix until well combined.
2. Place the dehydrating tray in a multi-level Air Fryer basket and place the basket in the instant pot.
3. Make small patties from the meat mixture and place them on dehydrating tray.
4. Seal pot with the Air Fryer lid and select air fry mode then set the temperature to 320ºF and timer for 12 minutes. Turn patties halfway through.
5. Serve and enjoy.

605. Lamb Roast

Preparation Time: 10 minutes
Cooking Time: 15 minutes
Servings: 2

Ingredients
- 10 oz. lamb leg roast
- 1 tsp. thyme, dried
- 1 tsp. Rosemary, dried
- 1 tbsp. olive oil
- Pepper
- Salt

Directions
1. Coat lamb roast with olive oil and rub with thyme, rosemary, pepper, and salt.
2. Place the dehydrating tray in a multi-level Air Fryer basket and place the basket in the instant pot.
3. Place lamb roast on dehydrating tray.
4. Seal pot with the Air Fryer lid and select air fry mode then set the temperature to 360ºF and timer for 15 minutes.
5. Serve and enjoy.

607. Honey-Glazed Salmon

Preparation Time: 10 minutes
Cooking Time: 15 minutes
Servings: 2

Ingredients
- 6 tsp. gluten-free soy sauce
- 2 pcs salmon fillets
- 3 tsp. sweet rice wine
- 1 tsp. water
- 6 tbsp. honey

Directions
1. In a bowl, mix sweet rice wine, soy sauce, honey, and water.
2. Set half of it aside.
3. In the other half of it, marinate the fish and let it rest for 2 hours.
4. Let the air fryer preheat to 180ºC.
5. Cook the fish for 8 minutes, flip halfway through and cook for another 5 minutes.
6. Baste the salmon with marinade mixture after 3 or 4 minutes.
7. The half of marinade, pour in a saucepan, reduce to half, serve with a sauce.

167

608. Crispy Air Fryer Fish

Preparation Time: 10 minutes
Cooking Time: 17 minutes
Servings: 4

Ingredients
- 2 tsp. old bay
- 4–6 whiting fish fillets, cut in half
- ¾ C. fine cornmeal
- ¼ C. flour
- 1 tsp. paprika
- ½ tsp. garlic powder
- 1-½ tsp. salt
- ½ tsp. black pepper freshly ground

Directions
1. In a Ziploc bag, add all ingredients and coat the fish fillets with it.
2. Spray oil on the basket of the air fryer and put the fish in it.
3. Cook for 10 minutes at 400°F. Flip fish if necessary and coat with oil spray and cook for another 7-minute.
4. Serve with a green salad.

609. Air-Fried Fish Nuggets

Preparation Time: 15 minute
Cooking Time: 10 minutes
Servings: 4

Ingredients
- 2 C. fish fillets in cubes, skinless
- 1 egg, beaten
- 5 tbsp. flour
- 5 tbsp. water
- Kosher salt and pepper to taste
- Breadcrumbs mix
- 1 tbsp. paprika, smoked
- ¼ C. whole wheat breadcrumbs
- 1 tbsp. garlic powder

Directions
1. Season the fish cubes with kosher salt and pepper.
2. In a bowl, add flour and gradually add water, mixing as you add.
3. Then mix in the egg. And keep mixing but do not over mix.
4. Coat the cubes in batter, then in the breadcrumb mix. Coat well.
5. Place the cubes in a baking tray and spray with oil.
6. Let the air fryer preheat to 200°C.
7. Place cubes in the air fryer and cook for 12 minutes or until well cooked and golden brown.

610. Crumbed Fish

Preparation Time: 10 minutes
Cooking Time: 12 minutes
Servings: 2

Ingredients
- 4 fish fillets
- 4 tbsp. Olive oil
- 1 egg, beaten
- ¼ C. whole wheat breadcrumbs

Directions
1. Let the air fryer preheat to 180°C.
2. In a bowl, mix breadcrumbs with oil. Mix well.
3. First, coat the fish in the egg mix (egg mix with water), then in the breadcrumb mix. Coat well.
4. Place in the air fryer, let it cook for 10–12 minutes.
5. Serve hot with salad green and lemon.

611. Parmesan Shrimp

Preparation Time: 5 minutes
Cooking Time: 10 minutes
Servings: 4

Ingredients
- 2 tbsp. olive oil
- 8 C. jumbo shrimps, cooked, peeled, deveined
- ⅔ C. parmesan cheese, grated
- 1 tsp. onion powder
- 1 tsp. pepper
- 4 garlic cloves, minced
- ½ tsp. oregano
- 1 tsp. basil
- lemon wedges

Directions
1. Mix parmesan cheese, onion powder, oregano, olive oil, garlic, basil, and pepper in a bowl. Coat the shrimp in this mixture.
2. Spray oil on the air fryer basket put shrimp in it.
3. Cook for 10 minutes, at 350°F, or until browned.
4. Drizzle the lemon on shrimps before serving with a green salad.

612. Crispy Fish Sandwiches

Preparation Time: 10 minutes
Cooking Time: 10 minutes
Servings: 2

Ingredients
- 2 Cod fillets
- 2 tbsp. all-purpose flour
- ¼ tsp. pepper
- 1 tbsp. lemon juice
- ¼ tsp. salt
- ½ tsp. garlic powder

- 1 egg
- ½ tbsp. mayo
- ½ C. whole wheat bread crumbs

Directions
1. In a bowl, add salt, flour, pepper, and garlic powder.
2. In a separate bowl, add lemon juice, mayo, and egg.
3. In another bowl, add the breadcrumbs.
4. Coat the fish in flour, then in egg, then in breadcrumbs.
5. With cooking oil, spray the basket and put the fish in the basket. Also, spray the fish with cooking oil.
6. Cook at 400ºF for 10 minutes. This fish is soft, be careful if you flip.

613. Air Fryer Tuna Patties

Preparation Time: 15 minutes
Cooking Time: 10 minutes
Servings: 10

Ingredients
- ½ C. whole wheat breadcrumbs
- 4 C. fresh tuna, diced
- Lemon zest
- 1 tbsp. lemon juice
- 1 egg
- 3 tbsp. parmesan cheese, grated
- 1 stalk celery, chopped
- ½ tsp. garlic powder:
- ½ tsp. herbs, dried
- 3 tbsp. onion, minced
- Salt to taste
- Black pepper, freshly ground

Directions
1. In a bowl, add lemon zest, bread crumbs, salt, pepper, celery, eggs, dried herbs, lemon juice, garlic powder, parmesan cheese, and onion. Mix everything. Then add in tuna gently. Shape into patties. If the mixture is too loose, cool in the refrigerator.
2. Add air fryer baking paper to the air fryer basket. Spray the baking paper with cooking spray.
3. Spray the patties with oil.
4. Cook for 10 minutes at 360°F. Turn the patties halfway over.
5. Serve with lemon slices.

614. Sushi Roll

Preparation Time: 20 Minutes
Cooking Time: 10 minutes
Servings: 3

Ingredients

For the kale salad:
- ½ tsp. rice vinegar
- 1-½ C. kale, chopped
- 1/8 tsp. garlic powder
- 1 tbsp. sesame seeds
- ¾ tsp. sesame oil, toasted
- ¼ tsp. ginger, ground

- ¾ tsp. soy sauce

Sushi rolls:
- ½ avocado, sliced
- Sushi Rice, cooked and cooled
- ½ C. whole wheat breadcrumbs
- 3 Sushi sheets

Directions
Kale salad:
1. In a bowl, add vinegar, garlic powder, kale, soy sauce, sesame oil, and ground ginger.
2. With your hands, mix with sesame seeds and set them aside.

Sushi rolls:
1. Lay a sheet of sushi on a flat surface. With damp fingertips, add a tbsp. rice, and spread it on the sheet. Cover the sheet with rice, leaving a ½-inch space at one end.
2. Add kale salad with avocado slices. Roll up the sushi, use water if needed.
3. Add the breadcrumbs to a bowl. Coat the sushi roll with Sriracha Mayo, then in breadcrumbs.
4. Add the rolls to the air fryer. Cook for 10 minutes at 390ºF, shake the basket halfway through.
5. Take out from the fryer, and let them cool, then cut with a sharp knife.
6. Serve with light soy sauce.

615. Buttermilk Fried Chicken

Preparation Time: 20 minutes
Cooking Time: 10 minutes
Servings: 4

Ingredients
- 3 tbsp. cornmeal, ground
- 1-lb. chicken breasts, pastured
- 6 tbsp. cornflakes
- 1 tsp. garlic powder
- ¼ tsp. black pepper, ground
- 1 tsp. paprika
- ¼ tsp. salt
- ¼ tsp. hot sauce
- ⅓ C. buttermilk, low-fat

Directions
1. Pour milk in a bowl, add hot sauce and whisk until well mixed.
2. Cut the chicken in half lengthwise into four pieces, then add into buttermilk, toss well until well coated and let it sit for 15 minutes.
3. Place cornflakes in a blender or food processor, pulse until mixture resembles crumbs, then add remaining ingredients, pulse until well mixed, and then tip the mixture into a shallow dish.
4. After 15 minutes, remove chicken from the buttermilk, then coat with cornflakes mixture until evenly coated and place the chicken on a wire rack.
5. Switch on the air fryer, insert the fryer

basket, grease it with olive oil, then shut with its lid, set the fryer at 375°F, and preheat for 5 minutes.

6. Then open the fryer, add chicken in a single layer, spray with oil, close the lid and cook for 10 minutes until nicely golden and cooked, turning the chicken halfway through the frying.

7. When the air fryer beeps, open its lid, transfer the chicken onto a serving plate and serve.

616. Pork Satay

Preparation Time: 15 minutes
Cooking Time: 9 to 14 minutes
Servings: 4

Ingredients
- 1 (1-lb. / 454-g) pork tenderloin, cut into 1½-inch cubes
- ¼ C. onion, minced
- 2 garlic cloves, minced
- 1 jalapeño pepper, minced
- 2 tbsp. lime juice, freshly squeezed
- 2 tbsp. coconut milk
- 2 tbsp. peanut butter, unsalted
- 2 tsp. curry powder

Directions
1. In a medium bowl, mix the pork, onion, garlic, jalapeño, lime juice, coconut milk, peanut butter, and curry powder until well combined. Let stand for 10 minutes at room temperature.

2. With a slotted spoon, remove the pork from the marinade. Reserve the marinade.

3. Thread the pork onto about 8 bamboo or metal skewers. Air fry at 380°F (193°C) for 9 to 14 minutes, brushing once with the reserved marinade until the pork reaches at least 145°F (63°C) on a meat thermometer. Discard any remaining marinade. Serve immediately.

617. Pork Dumplings

Preparation Time: 30 minutes
Cooking Time: 20 minutes
Servings: 6

Ingredients
- 18 dumpling wrappers
- 1 tsp. olive oil
- 4 C. Bok choy, chopped
- 2 tbsp. rice vinegar
- 1 tbsp. ginger, diced
- ¼ tsp. red pepper, crushed
- 1 tbsp. garlic, diced
- ½ C. lean pork, ground
- Cooking spray
- 2 tsp. lite soy sauce
- ½ tsp. honey

- 1 tsp. sesame oil, toasted
- Scallions, finely chopped

Directions
1. In a large skillet, heat olive oil, add bok choy, cook for 6 minutes, and add garlic, ginger, and cook for 1 minute. Move this mixture on a paper towel, and pat dry the excess oil

2. In a bowl, add bok choy mixture, crushed red pepper, and lean ground pork and mix well.

3. Lay a dumpling wrapper on a plate and add 1 tbsp. filling in the wrapper's middle. With water, seal the edges and crimp them.

4. Air spray the air fryer basket, add dumplings in the air fryer basket and cook at 375°F for 12 minutes or until browned.

5. In the meantime, to make the sauce, add sesame oil, rice vinegar, scallions, soy sauce, and honey in a bowl mix together.

6. Serve the dumplings with sauce.

618. Tomato Dip

Preparation Time: 10 minutes
Cooking Time: 15 minutes
Servings: 4

Ingredients
- 1 lb. tomatoes
- Salt and black pepper to the taste
- 2 tbsp. avocado oil
- 2 tbsp. balsamic vinegar
- 1 tbsp. basil, chopped
- 1 C. heavy cream

Directions
1. In your air fryer's basket, combine the tomatoes with the oil and the other ingredients except for the cream, toss and cook at 220°F for 15 minutes.

2. Peel and transfer the tomatoes to a blender, add the cream, pulse, divide into bowls and serve.

619. Macaroons

Preparation Time: 10 minutes
Cooking Time: 8 minutes
Servings: 20

Ingredients
- 2 tbsp. sugar
- 4 egg whites
- 2 C. coconut
- 1 tbsp. vanilla extract

Directions
1. Mix in egg whites with stevia in a bowl and whisk using a mixer.

2. Put the coconut and vanilla extract, beat again, get small balls out of the mix, put in the air fryer, and cook at 340°F for 8 minutes.

3. Serve cold.

620. Crab Dip

Preparation Time: 8 minutes
Cooking Time: 18 minutes
Servings: 4

Ingredients:
- 1 oz. full-fat cream cheese; softened.
- (6-oz. can lump crabmeat
- ¼ cup chopped pickled jalapeños.
- ¼ cup full-fat sour cream.
- ¼ cup sliced green onion
- ½ cup shredded Cheddar cheese
- ¼ cup full-fat mayonnaise
- 1 tbsp. lemon juice
- ½ tsp. hot sauce

Directions:
1. Place all ingredients into a 4-cup round baking dish and stir until fully combined. Place dish into the air fryer basket. Adjust the temperature to 400°F and set the timer for 8 minutes. Dip will be bubbling and hot when done. Serve warm.

621. Sesame Shrimp

Preparation Time: 8 minutes
Cooking Time: 15 minutes
Servings: 4

Ingredients:
- 1 lb. shrimp; peeled and deveined
- 1 tbsp. olive oil
- 1 tbsp. sesame seeds, toasted
- ½ tsp. Italian seasoning
- A pinch salt and black pepper

Directions:
1. Take a bowl and mix the shrimp with the rest of the ingredients and toss well Put the shrimp in the air fryer's basket, cook at 370°F for 12 minutes, and divide into bowls and serve,

622. Cod and Endives

Preparation Time: 10 minutes
Cooking Time: 25 minutes
Servings: 4

Ingredients:
- salmon fillets; boneless
- endives; shredded
- tbsp. olive oil
- ½ tsp. sweet paprika
- Salt and black pepper to the taste

Directions:
1. In a pan that fits the air fryer, combine the fish with the rest of the ingredients, toss, introduce in the fryer and cook at 350°F for 20 minutes, flipping the fish halfway Divide between plates and serve right away

623. Salmon Burgers

Preparation Time: 10 minutes
Cooking Time: 10 minutes
Servings: 4

Ingredients:
- 14.75 oz. can salmon, drain & flake
- ¼ cup onion, chopped fine
- 1 egg
- ¼ cup multi-grain crackers, crushed
- tsp. fresh dill, chopped
- ¼ tsp. pepper
- Nonstick cooking spray

Directions:
1. In a medium bowl, combine all ingredients until combined. Form into 4 patties.
2. Lightly spray fryer basket with cooking spray. Place the baking pan in position 2 of the oven.
3. Set oven to air fryer on 350°F.
4. Place the patties in the basket and set them on the baking pan. Set Timer for 8 minutes. Cook until burgers are golden brown, turning over halfway through cooking time. Serve on toasted buns with a choice of toppings.

624. Crispy Coated Scallops

Preparation Time: 10 minutes
Cooking Time: 10 minutes
Servings: 4

Ingredients:
- Nonstick cooking spray
- 1 lb. sea scallops, patted dry
- 1 tsp. onion powder
- ½ tsp. pepper
- 1 egg
- 1 tbsp. water
- ¼ cup Italian breadcrumbs
- Paprika
- 1 tbsp. fresh lemon juice

Directions:
1. Lightly spray fryer basket with cooking spray. Place baking pan in position 2 of the oven.
2. Sprinkle scallops with onion powder and pepper.
3. In a shallow dish, whisk together egg and water.
4. Place bread crumbs in a separate shallow dish.
5. Dip scallops in egg then bread crumbs coating them lightly.
6. Place in fryer basket and lightly spray with cooking spray. Sprinkle with paprika.
7. Place the basket in the air fryer and set it to 400°F. Bake for 10–12 minutes until scallops are firm on the inside and golden brown on the outside. Drizzle with lemon juice and serve.

625. Mediterranean Sole

Preparation Time: 15 minutes
Cooking Time: 20 minutes
Servings: 6

Ingredients:
- Nonstick cooking spray
- tbsp. olive oil
- scallions, sliced thin
- cloves garlic, diced fine
- tomatoes, chopped
- ½ cup dry white wine
- tbsp. fresh parsley, chopped fine
- 1 tsp. oregano
- 1 tsp. pepper
- lb. sole, cut in 6 pieces
- oz. feta cheese, crumbled

Directions:
1. Place the rack in position 1 of the oven. Spray an 8x11-inch baking dish with cooking spray.
2. Heat the oil in a medium skillet over medium heat. Add scallions and garlic and cook until tender, stirring frequently.
3. Add the tomatoes, wine, parsley, oregano, and pepper. Stir to mix. Simmer for 5 minutes, or until sauce thickens. Remove from heat.
4. Pour half the sauce on the bottom of the prepared dish. Lay fish on top then pour remaining sauce over the top. Sprinkle with feta.
5. Set the oven to bake at 400°F for 25 minutes. After 5 minutes, place the baking dish on the rack and cook 15–18 minutes or until fish flakes easily with a fork. Serve immediately.

626. Friedamari

Preparation Time: 5 minutes
Cooking Time: 15 minutes
Servings: 6 - 8

Ingredients:
- ½ tsp. salt
- ½ tsp. Old Bay seasoning
- 1/3 cup plain cornmeal
- ½ cup semolina flour
- ½ cup almond flour
- 5–6 cups olive oil
- 1 ½ pounds baby squid

Directions:
1. Rinse squid in cold water and slice tentacles, keeping just ¼- inch of the hood in one piece.
2. Combine 1–2 pinches of pepper, salt, Old Bay seasoning, cornmeal, and both flours together. Dredge squid pieces into flour mixture and place into the air fryer. Spray liberally with olive oil.
3. Cook 15 minutes at 345°F till coating turns a golden brown.

627. Paprika Lobster Tail

Preparation Time: 10 minutes
Cooking Time: 10 minutes
Servings: 4

Ingredients:
- 2 (4 to 6 oz.) lobster tails, shell cut from the top
- 1/8 tsp. salt
- 1/8 tsp. black pepper
- 1/8 tsp. paprika
- 2 tbsp. butter
- 1/2 lemon, cut into wedges
- Chopped parsley for garnish

Directions:
1. Place the lobster tails in the oven's baking tray.
2. Whisk the rest of the ingredients in a bowl and pour over the lobster tails.
3. Press the "power button" of the air fryer and turn the dial to select the "broil" mode.
4. Press the Time button and again turn the dial to set the cooking time to 10 minutes.
5. Now push the temp button and rotate the dial to set the temperature at 350°F.
6. Once preheated, place the lobster's baking tray in the oven and close its lid.
7. Serve warm.

628. Sheet Pan Seafood Bake

Preparation Time: 10 minutes
Cooking Time: 14 minutes
Servings: 4

Ingredients:
- 2 corn ears, husked and diced
- 1 lb. Red potatoes, boiled, diced
- 2 lb. Clams, scrubbed
- 1 lb. Shrimp, peeled and de-veined
- 12 oz. Sausage, sliced
- 1/2 red onion, sliced
- 4 lobster tails, peeled
- Black pepper to taste
- 1 lemon, cut into wedges
- 1 cup butter
- 3 tsp. minced garlic
- 1 tbsp. old bay seasoning
- Fresh parsley for garnish

Directions:
1. Toss all the veggies, corn, seafood, oil, and seasoning in a baking tray.
2. Press the "power button" of the air fryer and turn the dial to select the "broil" mode.
3. Press the Time button and again turn the dial to set the cooking time to 14 minutes.
4. Now push the temp button and rotate the dial to set the temperature at 425°F.
5. Once preheated, place the seafood's baking tray in the oven and close its lid.
6. Serve warm.

629. Pineapple & Veggie Skewers

Preparation Time: 20 minutes
Cooking Time: 15 minutes
Servings: 6

Ingredients:
- 1/3 cup olive oil
- 1½ tsp. dried basil
- ¾ tsp. dried oregano
- Salt and ground black pepper, as required
- 2 zucchinis, cut into 1-inch slices
- 2 yellow squash, cut into 1-inch slices
- ½ pound whole fresh mushrooms
- 1 red bell pepper, cut into chunks
- 1 red onion, cut into chunks
- 12 cherry tomatoes
- 1 fresh pineapple, cut into chunks

Directions:
1. In a bowl, add oil, herbs, salt, and black pepper and mix well.
2. Thread the veggies and pineapple onto pre-soaked wooden skewers.
3. Brush the veggies and pineapple with the oil mixture evenly.
4. Place the water tray in the bottom of the Smokeless Electric Grill.
5. Place about 2 cups of lukewarm water into the water tray.
6. Place the drip pan over the water tray and then arrange the heating element.
7. Now, place the grilling pan over the heating element.
8. Plug in the Smokeless Electric Grill and press the 'Power' button to turn it on.
9. Then press the "Fan" button.
10. Set the temperature settings according to the manufacturer's directions.
11. Cover the grill with a lid and let it preheat.
12. After preheating, remove the lid and grease the grilling pan.
13. Place the skewers over the grilling pan.
14. Cover with the lid and cook for about 10–15 minutes, flipping occasionally.

630. Marinated Veggie Skewers

Preparation Time: 20 minutes
Cooking Time: 10 minutes
Servings: 4

Ingredients:

For Marinade:
- 2 garlic cloves, minced
- 2 tsp. fresh basil, minced
- 2 tsp. fresh oregano, minced
- ½ tsp. cayenne pepper
- Sea Salt and ground black pepper, as required
- 2 tbsp. fresh lemon juice
- 2 tbsp. olive oil

For Veggies:
- 2 large zucchinis, cut into thick slices
- 8 large button mushrooms, quartered
- 1 yellow bell pepper, seeded and cubed
- 1 red bell pepper, seeded and cubed

Directions:
1. For the marinade: in a large bowl, add all the ingredients and mix until well combined.
2. Add the vegetables and toss to coat well.
3. Cover and refrigerate to marinate for at least 6–8 hours.
4. Remove the vegetables from the bowl and thread onto pre-soaked wooden skewers.
5. Place the water tray in the bottom of the Smokeless Electric Grill.
6. Place about 2 cups of lukewarm water into the water tray.
7. Place the drip pan over the water tray and then arrange the heating element.
8. Now, place the grilling pan over the heating element.
9. Plug in the Smokeless Electric Grill and press the 'Power' button to turn it on.

631. Mediterranean Veggies

Preparation Time: 5 minutes
Cooking Time: 10 minutes
Servings: 4

Ingredients:
- 1 cup mixed bell peppers, chopped
- 1 cup eggplant, chopped
- 1 cup zucchini, chopped
- 1 cup mushrooms, chopped
- ½ cup onion, chopped
- ½ cup sun-dried tomato vinaigrette dressing

Directions:
1. In a large bowl, add all ingredients and toss to coat well.
2. Refrigerate to marinate for about 1 hour.
3. Place the water tray in the bottom of the Smokeless Electric Grill.
4. Place about 2 cups of lukewarm water into the water tray.
5. Place the drip pan over the water tray and then arrange the heating element.
6. Now, place the grilling pan over the heating element.
7. Plug in the Smokeless Electric Grill and press the 'Power' button to turn it on.
8. Then press the "Fan" button.
9. Set the temperature settings according to the manufacturer's directions.
10. Cover the grill with a lid and let it preheat.
11. After preheating, remove the lid and grease the grilling pan.
12. Place the vegetables over the grilling pan.
13. Cover with the lid and cook for about 8–10 minutes, flipping occasionally.

632. Buttered Corn

Preparation Time: 10 minutes
Cooking Time: 20 minutes
Servings: 6

Ingredients:
- 6 fresh whole corn on the cob
- ½ cup butter, melted
- Salt, as required

Directions:
1. Husk the corn and remove all the silk.
2. Brush each corn with melted butter and sprinkle with salt.
3. Place the water tray in the bottom of the Smokeless Electric Grill.
4. Place about 2 cups of lukewarm water into the water tray.
5. Place the drip pan over the water tray and then arrange the heating element.
6. Now, place the grilling pan over the heating element.
7. Plugin the Smokeless Electric Grill and press the 'Power' button to turn it on.
8. Then press the "Fan" button.
9. Set the temperature settings according to the manufacturer's directions.
10. Cover the grill with a lid and let it preheat.
11. After preheating, remove the lid and grease the grilling pan.
12. Place the corn over the grilling pan.
13. Cover with the lid and cook for about 20 minutes, rotating after every 5 minutes and brushing with butter once halfway through. Serve warm.

633. Cheesy Steak Fries

Preparation Time: 5 minutes
Cooking Time: 20 minutes
Servings: 5

Ingredients:
- 1 (28-ounce / 794-g) bag frozen steak fries
- Cooking spray
- ½ cup beef gravy
- 1 cup shredded Mozzarella cheese
- Two scallions, green parts only, chopped

Directions:
1. Preheat the air fryer oven to 400°F (204°C).
2. Place the frozen steak fries in the air fryer basket.
3. Place the air fryer basket onto the baking pan.
4. Slide into Rack Position 2, select Air Fry, and set time to 10 minutes.
5. Shake the basket and spritz the fries with cooking spray.
6. Sprinkle with salt and pepper. Air fry for an additional 8 minutes.
7. Pour the beef gravy into a medium, microwave-safe bowl—microwave for 30 seconds, or until the sauce is warm.
8. Sprinkle the fries with the cheese. Air fry for an additional 2 minutes until the cheese is melted.
9. Transfer the fries to a serving dish. Drizzle the fries with gravy and sprinkle the scallions on top for a green garnish. Serve warm.

634. Balsamic Salmon

Preparation Time: 10 minutes
Cooking Time: 3 minutes
Servings: 2

Ingredients:
- 2 salmon fillets
- 1 cup of water
- 2 tbsp balsamic vinegar
- 1 1/2 tbsp honey
- Pepper
- Salt

Directions:
1. Season salmon with pepper and salt.
2. Mix together vinegar and honey.
3. Brush fish fillets with vinegar honey mixture.
4. Pour water into the instant pot then place trivet into the pot.
5. Place fish fillets on top of the trivet.
6. Seal pot with lid and cook on manual high pressure for 3 minutes.
7. Once done then release pressure using the quick-release method than open the lid.
8. Garnish with parsley and serve.

635. Oiled Crab Sticks

Preparation time: 10 minutes
Cooking time: 12 minutes
Servings: 4

Ingredients:
- Cajun seasoning, 2 tsps.
- Sesame oil, 2 tsps.
- Halved crab-sticks, 10.

Directions:
1. Set up a bowl and add in crab sticks. Toss in Cajun seasoning and sesame oil.
2. Set the crab sticks into the air fryer's basket to cook for 12 minutes at 3500F.
3. Serve on plates as an appetizer and enjoy.

636. Sweet Buttered Banana

Preparation time: 10 minutes
Cooking time: 15 minutes
Servings: 8

Ingredients:
- Chocolate chips, ¾ c.
- Peanut butter, ¼ c.
- Vegetable oil, 1 tbsp.
- Peeled and sliced banana, 1.
- Crust, 16 baking cups

Directions:
1. Heat up a small pot with chocolate chips over low heat.
2. Stir until the chocolate chips melt and remove from heat.
3. Set a mixing bowl in place to combine coconut oil and peanut butter.
4. Set up a cup with 1 tbsp chocolate mix topped with 1 tsp butter mix and 1 banana slice.
5. Repeat the process to the remaining cups and set them to a dish that fits the air fryer.
6. Set the air fryer to cook for 5 minutes at 320ºF.
7. Refrigerate till serving them as a snack.

637. Yogurt Cake

Preparation time: 5 minutes
Cooking time: 30 minutes
Servings: 8

Ingredients:
- 1½ cups white flour
- 1 teaspoon baking soda
- ¾ cup sugar
- 1 banana, mashed
- ½ teaspoon baking powder
- 2 tablespoons vegetable oil
- 1 cup Greek yogurt
- 8 ounces canned pumpkin puree
- Cooking spray
- 1 egg
- ½ teaspoon vanilla extract

Directions:
1. In a bowl, combine all ingredients (except the cooking spray) and stir well.
2. Pour the mixture into a cake pan greased with cooking spray and put it in your air fryer's basket.
3. Cook at 330 degrees F for 30 minutes.

638. Strawberry Cream

Preparation time: 5 minutes
Cooking time: 15 minutes
Servings: 6

Ingredients:
- 1 teaspoon gelatin
- 8 ounces cream cheese
- 4 ounces strawberries
- 2 tablespoons water
- ½ tablespoon lemon juice
- ¼ teaspoon sugar
- ½ cup heavy cream

Directions:
1. Place all ingredients in your blender and pulse.
2. Divide the mixture into 6 ramekins and place them in your air fryer.
3. Cook at 330 degrees F for 15 minutes.
4. Refrigerate (or place briefly in freezer) and serve the cream really cold.

639. Fried Corn

Preparation Time: 5 minutes
Cooking Time: 10 minutes
Servings: 4

Ingredients:
- Tablespoons corn kernels
- 2½ tablespoons butter

Directions:
1. In a saucepan that fits your air fryer, mix the corn with the butter.
2. Place the pan inside the air fryer and cook at 400 degrees F for 10 minutes.
3. Serve as a snack and enjoy!

640. Chicken Rolls

Preparation time: 10 minutes
Cooking time: 10 minutes
Servings: 4

Ingredients:
- 4 oz. blue cheese; crumbled
- 2 celery stalks; finely chopped.
- 1/2 cup tomato sauce
- 12 egg roll wrappers
- 2 cups chicken; cooked and chopped.
- 2 green onions; chopped
- Salt and black pepper to the taste
- Cooking spray

Directions:
1. In a bowl; mix chicken meat with blue cheese, salt, pepper, green onions, celery and tomato sauce; stir well and keep in the fridge for 2 hours.
2. Place egg wrappers on a working surface, divide chicken mix on them, roll and seal edges.
3. Place rolls in your air fryer's basket, spray them with cooking oil and cook at 350 °F, for 10 minutes; flipping them halfway.

641. Cheesy Chicken Rolls

Preparation time: 10 minutes
Cooking time: 10 minutes
Servings: 4

Ingredients:
- 4 oz. blue cheese; crumbled
- 2 celery stalks; finely chopped.
- 1/2 cup tomato sauce
- 12 egg roll wrappers
- 2 cups chicken; cooked and chopped.
- 2 green onions; chopped
- Salt and black pepper to the taste
- Cooking spray

Directions:
1. In a bowl; mix chicken meat with blue cheese, salt, pepper, green onions, celery and tomato sauce; stir well and keep in the fridge for 2 hours.
2. Place egg wrappers on a working surface, divide chicken mix on them, roll and seal edges. Place rolls in your air fryer's basket, spray them with cooking oil and cook at 350 °F, for 10 minutes; flipping them halfway.

642. Cheesy Bombs in Bacon

Preparation Time: 10 minutes
Cooking Time: 10 minutes
Servings: 8

Ingredients
- Bacon Slices, cut in half
- 16 oz Mozzarella Cheese, cut into 8 pieces
- tbsp Butter, melted

Directions:
1. Wrap each cheese string with a slice of bacon and secure the ends with toothpicks. Set aside.
2. Grease the crisp basket with the melted butter and add in the bombs. Close the crisping lid, select Air Fry mode, and set the temperature to 370 F and set the time to 10 minutes.
3. At the 5-minute mark, turn the bombs. When ready, remove to a paper-lined plate to drain the excess oil. Serve on a platter with toothpicks.

643. Coffee Cream

Preparation time: 5 minutes
Cooking time: 10 minutes
Servings: 6

Ingredients:
- 2 tablespoons butter
- 8 ounces cream cheese
- 3 tablespoons coffee
- 3 eggs
- ⅓ cup sugar
- 1 tablespoon caramel syrup

Directions:
1. Place all ingredients in your blender and pulse.
2. Divide the mixture between 6 ramekins, and place in the fryer. Cook at 320 degrees F; bake for 10 minutes.
3. Let cool down and then place in the freezer before serving.

644. Mini cheesecakes

Preparation time: 15 minutes
Cooking time: 10 minutes
Servings: 2

Ingredients:
- ¾ cup erythritol
- 2 eggs
- 1 teaspoon vanilla extract
- ½ teaspoon fresh lemon juice
- 16 oz. Cream cheese, softened
- 2 tablespoon sour cream

Directions:
1. In a blender, add the erythritol, eggs, vanilla extract and lemon juice and pulse until smooth.
2. Add the cream cheese and sour cream and pulse until smooth.
3. Place the mixture into 2 (4-inch) springform pans evenly.
4. Press "power button" of air fry oven and turn the dial to select the "air fry" mode.
5. Press the time button and again turn the dial to set the cooking time to 10 minutes.
6. Now push the temp button and rotate the dial to set the temperature at 350 degrees f.
7. Press "start/pause" button to start.
8. When the unit beeps to show that it is preheated, open the lid.
9. Arrange the pans in "air fry basket" and insert in the oven.
10. Place the pans onto a wire rack to cool completely.
11. Refrigerate overnight before serving.

645. Ricotta cheesecake

Preparation time: 15 minutes
Cooking time: 25 minutes
Servings: 8

Ingredients:
- 17.6 oz. Ricotta cheese
- 3 eggs
- ¾ cup sugar
- 3 tablespoons corn starch
- 1 tablespoon fresh lemon juice
- 2 teaspoons vanilla extract
- 1 teaspoon fresh lemon zest, finely grated

Directions:
1. In a large bowl, place all ingredients and

mix until well combined.

2. Place the mixture into a baking pan.
3. Press "power button" of air fry oven and turn the dial to select the "air fry" mode.
4. Press the time button and again turn the dial to set the cooking time to 25 minutes.
5. Now push the temp button and rotate the dial to set the temperature at 320 degrees f.
6. Press "start/pause" button to start.
7. When the unit beeps to show that it is preheated, open the lid.
8. Arrange the pan in "air fry basket" and insert in the oven.
9. Place the cake pan onto a wire rack to cool completely.
10. Refrigerate overnight before serving.

646. Brown butter cookies

Preparation time: 20 minutes
Cooking time: 40 minutes
Servings: 6

Ingredients
• 1 ½ cups butter
• 2 cups brown sugar
• 2 eggs
• 3 cups flour
• 2/3 cup pecans
• 2 tbsp. Vanilla extract
• 1 tbsp. Baking soda
• ½ tbsp. Baking powder

Directions:
1. Warm pan with the butter over medium heat, turn till it melts, put brown sugar and mix till it melts.
2. Mix flour with vanilla extract, baking soda, pecan, baking powder and eggs and turn properly.
3. Put brown butter, turn properly and assemble spoonful of mix on a lined baking sheet.
4. Put it in fryer and cook at 340 ° f for 10 minutes.
5. Allow cookies to cool
6. Serve.

647. Yams chips

Preparation Time: 10 minutes
Cooking Time: 20 minutes
Servings: 4

Ingredients
• Yams
• 1 Teaspoon seasoned salt, or more to taste

Directions:
1. Preheat the Air fryer toaster oven to 175 ° C. Coating 2 baking trays with an oil. Prepare a longitudinal cut in the inside of each yams.
2. Cut the yams into pieces using a spiral slicer. Place the pieces in the Silpat. Coating with an oil. Spice collective with seasoned salt.
3. Bake in the preheated Air fryer toaster oven for 20 to 25 minutes up to the corners start to form into a curved. Season with more salt. Let cool for 10 minutes up to crispy.

648. Breakfast Pockets

Preparation Time: 10 minutes
Cooking Time: 10 minutes
Servings: 6

Ingredients
• 1 box puff pastry sheet
• 5 eggs
• ½ cup loose sausage, cooked
• ½ cup bacon, cooked
• ½ cup cheddar cheese, shredded

Directions:
1. Stir cook egg in a skillet for 1 minute then mix with sausages, cheddar cheese, and bacon. Spread the pastry sheet and cut it into four rectangles of equal size.
2. Divide the egg mixture over each rectangle. Fold the edges around the filling and seal them. Place the pockets in the Air Fryer basket.
3. Set the Air Fryer basket inside the Air Fryer toaster oven and close the lid. Select the Air Fry mode at 370 degrees F temperature for 10 minutes. Serve warm.

649. Sausage Burritos

Preparation Time: 10 minutes
Cooking Time: 10 minutes
Servings: 6

Ingredients
• 6 medium flour tortillas
• 6 scrambled eggs
• ½ lb. ground sausage, browned
• ½ bell pepper, minced
• 1/3 cup bacon bits
• ½ cup shredded cheese
• Oil, for spraying

Directions:
1. Mix eggs with cheese, bell pepper, bacon, and sausage in a bowl.
2. Spread each tortilla on the working surface and top it with ½ cup egg filling.
3. Roll the tortilla like a burrito then place 3 burritos in the Air Fryer basket. Spray them with cooking oil.
4. Set the Air Fryer basket inside the Air Fryer toaster oven and close the lid.
5. Select the Air Fry mode at 330 degrees F temperature for 5 minutes. Cook the remaining burritos in the same manner. Serve fresh.

649. Asian Cod Fillets

Prep Time: 10 Minutes.
Cook Time: 10 Minutes.
Serves: 2

Ingredients:
- 2 cod fillets
- 1 tablespoon butter, melted
- ⅛ teaspoon paprika
- ⅛ teaspoon garlic powder
- ¼ teaspoon curry powder
- ⅛ teaspoon sea salt

Directions:
1. In a small bowl, mix together curry powder, paprika, garlic powder, and salt and set aside.
2. Place cod fillets into the baking pan.
3. Brush fish fillets with butter then sprinkle with spice mixture.
4. Place the pan on the bottom rack at position 1 of the Air Fryer oven then close the door.
5. Use the function dial to select the "BAKE" mode for cooking.
6. Set the TEMP DIAL to 360 degrees F and turn the TIME DIAL to 10 Minutes.
7. Once the machine's timer goes off, open the air fryer oven's door and remove the food from the air fryer oven.

651. Simple & Spicy scallops

Prep Time: 10 Minutes.
Cook Time: 4 Minutes.
Serves: 2

Ingredients:
- 8 scallops
- 1 tablespoon olive oil
- ¼ teaspoon cayenne
- ¼ teaspoon paprika
- Pepper
- Salt

Directions:
1. Brush scallops with oil and season with cayenne, paprika, pepper, and salt.
2. Place scallops into the baking pan.
3. Place the pan on the bottom rack at position 1 of the Air Fryer oven then close the door.
4. Use the function dial to select the "BAKE" mode for cooking.
5. Set the TEMP DIAL to 390 degrees F and turn the TIME DIAL to 4 Minutes.
6. Once the machine's timer goes off, open the air fryer oven's door and remove the food from the air fryer oven.
7. Serve.

650. Old Bay Shrimp

Prep Time: 10 Minutes.
Cook Time: 6 Minutes.
Serves: 2

Ingredients:
- ½ lb. shrimp, peeled and deveined
- 1 tablespoon olive oil
- ¼ teaspoon paprika
- ½ teaspoon old bay seasoning
- ½ teaspoon cayenne pepper
- Pinch of salt

Directions:
1. Add shrimp and remaining ingredients into a suitable bowl and toss well to coat.
2. Add shrimp into the baking pan.
3. Place the pan on the bottom rack at position 1 of the Air Fryer oven then close the door.
4. Use the function dial to select the "BAKE" mode for cooking.
5. Set the TEMP DIAL to 390 degrees F and turn the TIME DIAL to 6 Minutes.
6. Once the machine's timer goes off, open the air fryer oven's door and remove the food from the air fryer oven.
7. Serve.

652. Bagel White Fish Fillets

Prep Time: 10 Minutes.
Cook Time: 10 Minutes.
Serves: 4

Ingredients:
- 4 white fish fillets
- 1 tablespoon mayonnaise
- 1 teaspoon lemon pepper seasoning
- 2 tablespoon almond flour
- ¼ cup bagel seasoning

Directions:
1. In a small bowl, mix together almond flour, bagel seasoning, and lemon pepper seasoning.
2. Brush mayonnaise over fish fillets. Sprinkle almond flour mixture over fish fillets.
3. Place fish fillets into the baking pan.
4. Place the pan on the bottom rack at position 1 of the Air Fryer oven then close the door.
5. Use the function dial to select the "AIR FRY" mode for cooking.
6. Set the TEMP DIAL to 400 degrees F and turn the TIME DIAL to 10 Minutes.
7. Once the machine's timer goes off, open the air fryer oven's door and remove the food from the air fryer oven.
8. Serve.

178

653. Southwestern Fish Fillets

Prep Time: 10 Minutes.
Cook Time: 16 Minutes.
Serves: 4

Ingredients:
- 1 lb. trout fillets
- 1 teaspoon garlic powder
- 3 tablespoon breadcrumbs
- 1 tablespoon olive oil
- 1 teaspoon chili powder
- 1 teaspoon onion powder

Directions:
1. In a small bowl, mix breadcrumbs, onion powder, garlic powder, and chili powder.
2. Brush fish fillets with oil and coat with breadcrumbs.
3. Place coated fish fillets into the baking pan.
4. Place the pan on the bottom rack at position 1 of the Air Fryer oven then close the door.
5. Use the function dial to select the "BAKE" mode for cooking.
6. Set the TEMP DIAL to 375 degrees F and turn the TIME DIAL to 16 Minutes.
7. Once the machine's timer goes off, open the air fryer oven's door and remove the food from the air fryer oven.
8. Serve.

654. Honey Sriracha Shrimp

Prep Time: 10 Minutes.
Cook Time: 6 Minutes.
Serves: 4

Ingredients:
- 12 oz shrimp, peeled & deveined
- 1 ½ tablespoon honey
- 1 ½ tablespoon butter, melted
- 2 tablespoon sriracha sauce
- ½ lime juice
- 1 ½ tablespoon soy sauce

Directions:
1. In a suitable bowl, add shrimp and the remaining ingredients into a zip-lock bag. Seal bag and place in refrigerator for 30 Minutes.
2. Add marinated shrimp into the baking pan.
3. Place the pan on the bottom rack at position 1 of the Air Fryer oven then close the door.
4. Use the function dial to select the "BAKE" mode for cooking.
5. Set the TEMP DIAL to 400 degrees F and turn the TIME DIAL to 6 Minutes.
6. Once the machine's timer goes off, open the air fryer oven's door and remove the food from the air fryer oven.
7. Serve.

655. Air Fryer Catfish

Prep Time: 10 Minutes.
Cook Time: 13 Minutes.
Serves: 4

Ingredients:
- 1 tablespoon chopped parsley
- 1 tablespoon olive oil
- ¼ cup fish seasoning
- 4 catfish fillets

Preparation:
1. Rinse off catfish fillets and pat dry.
2. Add fish fry seasoning to a Ziploc bag, then the catfish. Shake the bag and ensure the fish gets well coated.
3. Spray each fillet with olive oil.
4. Add fillets to the air fryer basket.
5. Place the basket in the position 2 of the Air Fryer oven then close the door.
6. Use the function dial to select the "AIR FRY" mode for cooking.
7. Set the TEMP DIAL to 350 degrees F and turn the TIME DIAL to 12 Minutes.
8. Once the machine's timer goes off, open the air fryer oven's door and remove the food from the air fryer oven.
9. Serve.

656. Simple Scallops

Prep Time: 10 Minutes.
Cook Time: 5 Minutes.
Serves: 2

Ingredients:
- 12 medium sea scallops
- 1 teaspoon fine sea salt
- ¾ teaspoon ground black pepper, plus more for garnish if desired
- Fresh thyme leaves, for garnish (optional)

Preparation:
1. Spray the Air Fryer basket with avocado oil.
2. Rinse the scallops and pat them completely dry.
3. Spray avocado oil on the scallops and season them with salt and pepper.
4. Place them in the air fryer basket, spacing them apart.
5. Place the basket in the position 2 of the Air Fryer oven then close the door.
6. Use the function dial to select the "AIR FRY" mode for cooking.
7. Set the TEMP DIAL to 390 degrees F and turn the TIME DIAL to 5 Minutes.
8. Once the machine's timer goes off, open the air fryer oven's door and remove the food from the air fryer oven.
9. Serve.

657. Lemon Chili Prawns

Prep Time: 10 Minutes.
Cook Time: 12 Minutes.
Serves: 3

Ingredients:
• 1 pound of prawns
• Pinch of salt
• ½ tablespoon of ginger garlic paste
• 2 tablespoons of lemon juice
• 1 teaspoon of chili garlic paste
• A dash of soya sauce
• 2 tablespoons of cooking oil

Preparation:
1. Remove the veins from the prawns. Wash and dry them and keep aside.
2. Mix the salt, ginger garlic paste, lemon juice, chili garlic paste, and the soya sauce in a suitable bowl.
3. Marinate the prawns in the sauce. Leave for one hour.
4. Coat the base of the Air Fryer basket with cooking oil.
5. Put the prawns into the basket and coat lightly with the oil.
6. Place the basket in the position 2 of the Air Fryer oven then close the door.
7. Use the function dial to select the "AIR FRY" mode for cooking.
8. Set the TEMP DIAL to 400 degrees F and turn the TIME DIAL to 12 Minutes.
9. Once the machine's timer goes off, open the air fryer oven's door and remove the food from the air fryer oven.

658. Blackened Mahi-Mahi

Prep Time: 10 Minutes.
Cook Time: 17 Minutes.
Serves: 4

Ingredients:
• 4 mahi-mahi fillets
• 1 teaspoon cumin
• 1 teaspoon paprika
• ½ teaspoon cayenne pepper
• 1 teaspoon oregano
• 1 teaspoon garlic powder
• 1 teaspoon onion powder
• ½ teaspoon pepper
• 3 tablespoon olive oil
• ½ teaspoon salt

Preparation:
1. Brush fish fillets with oil and place them into the baking pan.
2. Mix the remaining ingredients and sprinkle over fish fillets.
3. Place the pan on the bottom rack at position

1 of the Air Fryer oven then close the door.
4. Use the function dial to select the "BAKE" mode for cooking.
5. Set the TEMP DIAL to 50 degrees F and turn the TIME DIAL to 17 Minutes.
6. Once the machine's timer goes off, open the air fryer oven's door and remove the food from the air fryer oven.
7. Serve.

659. Greek Chicken

Prep Time: 10 Minutes.
Cook Time: 30 Minutes.
Serves: 4

Ingredients:
• 1 lb. chicken breasts, skinless & boneless
• For marinade:
• ¼ teaspoon oregano
• 2 garlic cloves, minced
• 1 tablespoon lemon juice
• 3 tablespoon olive oil
• ½ teaspoon dill
• 1 teaspoon onion powder
• ¼ teaspoon basil
• ¼ teaspoon pepper
• ½ teaspoon salt

Directions:
1. Add all the marinade ingredients into a suitable bowl and mix well.
2. Add chicken to the bowl and coat well. Cover and place in the refrigerator overnight.
3. Place the chicken in the baking pan.
4. Place the pan on the bottom rack at position 1 of the Air Fryer oven then close the door.
5. Use the function dial to select the "BAKE" mode for cooking.
6. Set the TEMP DIAL to 390 degrees F and turn the TIME DIAL to 35 Minutes.
7. Once the machine's timer goes off, open the air fryer oven's door and remove the food from the air fryer oven.

660. Crispy Chicken Cutlets

Prep Time: 10 Minutes.
Cook Time: 14 Minutes.
Serves: 4

Ingredients:
• 2 eggs
• 1 lb. chicken cutlets
• 1 cup potato chips, crushed
• 1 tablespoon Italian seasoning

Directions:
1. In a shallow bowl, whisk eggs.
2. In a different shallow dish, mix crushed potato chips and seasoning.

3. Dip each chicken in egg then coat with crushed potato chips.
4. Place coated chicken into the air fryer basket.
5. Place the basket in the position 2 of the Air Fryer oven then close the door.
6. Use the function dial to select the "AIR FRY" mode for cooking.
7. Set the TEMP DIAL to 380 degrees F and turn the TIME DIAL to 14 Minutes.
8. Once the machine's timer goes off, open the air fryer oven's door and remove the food from the air fryer oven.

661. Lemon Pepper Chicken

Prep Time: 10 Minutes.
Cook Time: 20 Minutes.
Serves: 4

Ingredients:
- 2 lbs. chicken wings
- 3 teaspoon lemon zest, grated
- 1 tablespoon olive oil
- 2 teaspoon black peppercorns, crushed
- 1 teaspoon garlic salt

Directions:
1. In a suitable bowl, toss chicken wings with remaining ingredients until well coated.
2. Add the chicken wings to the air fryer basket.
3. Place the basket in the position 2 of the Air Fryer oven then close the door.
4. Use the function dial to select the "AIR FRY" mode for cooking.
5. Set the TEMP DIAL to 360 degrees F and turn the TIME DIAL to 20 Minutes.
6. Once the machine's timer goes off, open the air fryer oven's door and remove the food from the air fryer oven.
7. Turn halfway through.
8. Serve.

662. BBQ Chicken Legs

Prep Time: 10 Minutes.
Cook Time: 20 Minutes.
Serves: 8

Ingredients:
- 8 chicken legs
- 2 tablespoon canola oil
- 2 teaspoons paprika
- ½ teaspoon garlic powder
- 2 teaspoon brown sugar
- Pepper
- Salt

Directions:
1. Add chicken legs and remaining ingredients to

a suitable bowl and toss well.
2. Add chicken legs to the air fryer basket and then place it in the baking pan.
3. Place the basket at position 2 of the Air Fryer oven then close the door.
4. Use the function dial to select the "AIR FRY" mode for cooking.
5. Set the TEMP DIAL to 400 degrees F and turn the TIME DIAL to 20 Minutes.
6. Once the machine's timer goes off, open the air fryer oven's door and remove the food from the air fryer oven.

663. Sweet and Sour Chicken

Prep Time: 10 Minutes.
Cook Time: 25 Minutes.
Serves: 6

Ingredients:
- 3 chicken breasts, cubed
- ½ cup flour
- ½ cup cornstarch
- 2 red peppers, sliced
- 1 onion, chopped
- 2 carrots, julienned
- ¾ cup sugar
- 2 tablespoon cornstarch
- ⅓ cup vinegar
- ⅔ cup water
- ¼ cup Soy sauce
- 1 tablespoon ketchup

Preparation:
1. Combine the flour, cornstarch, and chicken in an air-tight container and shake to combine.
2. Remove chicken from the container and shake off any excess flour.
3. Add chicken to the Air Fryer pan.
4. Place the pan on the bottom rack at position 1 of the Air Fryer oven then close the door.
5. Use the function dial to select the "BAKE" mode for cooking.
6. Set the TEMP DIAL to 375 degrees F and turn the TIME DIAL to 20 Minutes.
7. Once the machine's timer goes off, open the air fryer oven's door and remove the food from the air fryer oven.
8. In a saucepan, whisk together sugar, water, vinegar, soy sauce, and ketchup.
9. Bring to a boil over medium heat, reduce the heat, then simmer for 2 Minutes.
10. After cooking the chicken for 20 Minutes, add the vegetables and sauce mixture to the Air fryer and cook for 5 Minutes.

664. Turkey Wings

Prep Time: 10 Minutes.
Cook Time: 20 Minutes.
Serves: 4

Ingredients:
- 3 chicken breasts, cubed
- ½ cup flour
- ½ cup cornstarch
- 2 red peppers, sliced
- 1 onion, chopped
- 2 carrots, julienned
- ¾ cup sugar
- 2 tablespoon cornstarch
- ⅓ cup vinegar
- ⅔ cup water
- ¼ cup Soy sauce
- 1 tablespoon ketchup

Preparation:
1. Combine the flour, cornstarch, and chicken in an air-tight container and shake to combine.
2. Remove chicken from the container and shake off any excess flour.
3. Add chicken to the Air Fryer pan.
4. Place the pan on the bottom rack at position 1 of the Air Fryer oven then close the door.
5. Use the function dial to select the "BAKE" mode for cooking.
6. Set the TEMP DIAL to 375 degrees F and turn the TIME DIAL to 20 Minutes.
7. Once the machine's timer goes off, open the air fryer oven's door and remove the food from the air fryer oven.
8. In a saucepan, whisk together sugar, water, vinegar, soy sauce, and ketchup.
9. Bring to a boil over medium heat, reduce the heat, then simmer for 2 Minutes.
10. After cooking the chicken for 20 Minutes., add the vegetables and sauce mixture to the Air fryer and cook for 5 Minutes.

665. Herbed Duck Legs

Prep Time: 10 Minutes.
Cook Time: 30 Minutes.
Serves: 2

Ingredients:
- ½ tablespoon fresh thyme, chopped
- ½ tablespoon fresh parsley, chopped
- 2 duck legs
- 1 garlic clove, minced
- 1 teaspoon five-spice powder
- Salt and black pepper, to taste

Preparation:
1. Grease the Air Fryer basket.
2. Mix the garlic, herbs, five-spice powder, salt, and black pepper in a suitable bowl.

3. Rub the duck legs with garlic mixture generously and arrange them into the Air fryer basket.
4. Place the basket in the position 2 of the Air Fryer oven then close the door.
5. Use the function dial to select the "BAKE" mode for cooking.
6. Set the TEMP DIAL to 390 degrees F and turn the TIME DIAL to 25 Minutes.
7. Once the machine's timer goes off, open the air fryer oven's door and remove the food from the air fryer oven.
8. Serve warm.

666. Parmesan Chicken Tenders

Prep Time: 10 Minutes.
Cook Time: 8 Minutes.
Serves: 4

Ingredients:
- 1 pound chicken tenderloins
- 3 large egg whites
- ½ cup Italian-style bread crumbs
- ¼ cup grated Parmesan cheese

Preparation:
1. Spray the Air Fryer basket with olive oil.
2. Trim off any white fat from the chicken tenders.
3. In a small bowl, beat the egg whites until frothy.
4. In a separate small mixing bowl, combine the bread crumbs and Parmesan cheese. Mix well.
5. Dip the chicken tenders into the egg mixture, then into the Parmesan and bread crumbs. Shake off any excess breading.
6. Place the chicken tenders in the greased Air Fryer basket in a single layer.
7. Generously spray the chicken with olive oil to avoid powdery, uncooked breading.
8. Place the basket in the position 2 of the Air Fryer oven then close the door.
9. Use the function dial to select the "AIR FRY" mode for cooking.
10. Set the TEMP DIAL to 370 degrees F and turn the TIME DIAL to 8 Minutes.
11. Once the machine's timer goes off, open the air fryer oven's door and remove the food from the air fryer oven.

667. Chicken Cordon Bleu

Prep Time: 10 Minutes.
Cook Time: 12 Minutes.
Serves: 6

Ingredients:
- 6 slices (4.4 oz each) Sargento reduced fat Swiss cheese, cut into half
- Cooking spray
- 6 slices (5 oz each) lean deli ham, thinly sliced into half
- 12 (3 oz each) skinless, boneless chicken breasts, thinly sliced
- 4 tablespoons parmesan cheese, grated
- 2 large egg whites
- Salt and pepper, to taste
- ½ cup seasoned breadcrumbs
- 1 large egg
- 1 tablespoon water

Preparation:
1. Wash chicken cutlets and pat dry with a paper towel. Pound lightly to make chicken thinner and season chicken with pepper and salt.
2. Lay seasoned chicken on a flat surface followed by a slice of ham. Place cheese over ham slice and roll.
3. Add 2 large egg whites, 1 whole egg, and 1 tablespoon water to a suitable bowl and whisk well. Take another bowl and combine 4 tablespoons of Parmesan along with half a cup of seasoned breadcrumbs.
4. Dip chicken into the egg wash, then coat the chicken with bread crumbs.
5. Spray each side of the chicken with oil—place chicken in the Air Fry basket.
6. Place the pan on the bottom rack at position 1 of the Air Fryer oven then close the door.
7. Use the function dial to select the "AIR FRY" mode for cooking.
8. Set the TEMP DIAL to 400 degrees F and turn the TIME DIAL to 12 Minutes.
9. Once the machine's timer goes off, open the air fryer oven's door and remove the food from the air fryer oven.

668. Fried Chicken Livers

Prep Time: 10 Minutes.
Cook Time: 12 Minutes.
Serves: 6

Ingredients:
- 1 pound chicken livers
- 1 cup flour
- ½ cup cornmeal
- 2 teaspoons your favorite seasoning blend
- 3 eggs
- 2 tablespoons milk

Preparation:
1. Clean and rinse the livers, pat dry.
2. Beat eggs in a shallow bowl and mix in milk.
3. In another bowl, combine flour, cornmeal, and seasoning, mixing until even.
4. Dip the livers in the egg mix, and then toss them in the flour mix.
5. Spread the pieces in the air fryer basket.
6. Place the basket in the position 2 of the Air Fryer oven then close the door.
7. Use the function dial to select the "AIR FRY" mode for cooking.
8. Set the TEMP DIAL to 375 degrees F and turn the TIME DIAL to 10 Minutes.
9. Once the machine's timer goes off, open the air fryer oven's door and remove the food from the air fryer oven.

669. Steak Fajitas

Prep Time: 10 Minutes.
Cook Time: 12 Minutes.
Serves: 6

Ingredients:
- 2 lbs. beef skirt steak, cut into ½-inch strips
- ½ tablespoon garlic powder
- ¼ teaspoon paprika
- 1 tablespoon cumin
- 1 ½ tablespoon chili powder
- ½ tablespoon dried oregano
- 2 tablespoon brown sugar
- 2 tablespoon canola oil
- 1 ¼ tablespoon lime juice
- 8 oz mushrooms, quartered
- 4 bell peppers, sliced
- 1 onion, sliced
- Salt

Directions:
1. Add all ingredients except mushrooms, bell peppers, and onion into the large bowl and mix until well combined. Cover and place in refrigerator for 1 hour.
2. Add marinated steak pieces, mushrooms, bell peppers, and onion to a baking sheet.
3. Place the pan on the bottom rack at position 1 of the Air Fryer oven then close the door.
4. Use the function dial to select the "BAKE" mode for cooking.
5. Set the TEMP DIAL to 400 degrees F and turn the TIME DIAL to 25 Minutes.
6. Once the machine's timer goes off, open the air fryer oven's door and remove the food from the air fryer oven.

670. Tomahawk Ribeye Steak

Prep Time: 10 Minutes.
Cook Time: 25 Minutes.
Serves: 6

Ingredients:
- 2 tomahawk ribeye steaks
- 2 tablespoon canola oil
- 1 teaspoon garlic powder
- Pepper
- Salt

183

Directions:
1. Season steaks with garlic powder, pepper, and salt.
2. Set a pan greased with oil over medium heat. Add prepared steaks to the pan and sear for 3 Minutes on each side.
3. Place steaks on a baking sheet.
4. Place the pan on the bottom rack at position 1 of the Air Fryer oven then close the door.
5. Use the function dial to select the "BAKE" mode for cooking.
6. Set the TEMP DIAL to 375 degrees F and turn the TIME DIAL to 25 Minutes.
7. Once the machine's timer goes off, open the air fryer oven's door and remove the food from the air fryer oven.
8. Serve.

671. Lamb Patties

Prep Time: 10 Minutes.
Cook Time: 8 Minutes.
Serves: 4

Ingredients:
• 1 lb. ground lamb
• 1 cup feta cheese, crumbled
• 1 tablespoon garlic, minced
• 1 jalapeno pepper, minced
• 5 basil leaves, minced
• 10 mint leaves, minced
• ¼ cup fresh parsley, chopped
• 1 teaspoon dried oregano
• ¼ teaspoon pepper
• ½ teaspoon kosher salt

Directions:
1. Add all the ingredients into the bowl and mix until well combined.
2. Make four equal shape patties from the meat mixture and place on a baking sheet.
3. Place the pan on the bottom rack at position 1 of the Air Fryer oven then close the door.
4. Use the function dial to select the "BAKE" mode for cooking.
5. Set the TEMP DIAL to 390 degrees F and turn the TIME DIAL to 13 Minutes.
6. Once the machine's timer goes off, open the air fryer oven's door and remove the food from the air fryer oven.

672. Creole Pork Chops

Prep Time: 10 Minutes.
Cook Time: 10 Minutes.
Serves: 6

Ingredients:
• 6 pork chops, boneless
• 1 tablespoon Italian seasoning
• 2 tablespoon Creole mustard

• ½ cup zesty Italian dressing

Directions:
1. Add pork chops to a suitable bowl.
2. Pour remaining ingredients over pork chops and coat well and place them in the refrigerator for 30 Minutes.
3. Arrange marinated pork chops on the air fryer's baking pan.
4. Place the pan on the bottom rack at position 1 of the Air Fryer oven then close the door.
5. Use the function dial to select the "BAKE" mode for cooking.
6. Set the TEMP DIAL to 375 degrees F and turn the TIME DIAL to 15 Minutes.
7. Once the machine's timer goes off, open the air fryer oven's door and remove the food from the air fryer oven.

673. Pork Skewers

Prep Time: 10 Minutes.
Cook Time: 15 Minutes.
Serves: 6

Ingredients:
• 2 lbs. country-style pork ribs, cut into pieces
• ¼ cup soy sauce
• 0.7 oz Italian dressing
• ½ cup olive oil
• Skewers

Directions:
1. Add meat pieces and remaining ingredients into the zip-lock bag. Seal bag and place in the refrigerator for 2 hours.
2. Soak wooden skewers into the water.
3. Remove meat pieces from the marinade and thread onto the soaked skewers.
4. Place meat skewers into the baking pan.
5. Place the pan on the bottom rack at position 1 of the Air Fryer oven then close the door.
6. Use the function dial to select the "BAKE" mode for cooking.
7. Set the TEMP DIAL to 380 degrees F and turn the TIME DIAL to 15 Minutes.
8. Once the machine's timer goes off, open the air fryer oven's door and remove the food from the air fryer oven.
9. Serve.

674. Flax Mozzarella Wraps

Preparation time: 10 minutes
Cooking time: 2 minutes
Servings: 1

Ingredients:
• 1 cucumber
• 1 egg
• 3 oz. flax seeds
• 3 oz. mozzarella, grated
• 1 tablespoon water
• ½ tablespoon butter

184

- ¼ teaspoon baking soda
- ¼ teaspoon salt

Directions:
1. Crack the egg into a bowl and whisk it.
2. Sprinkle the whisked egg with the flax seeds, grated mozzarella, water, baking soda, and salt.
3. Whisk the mixture.
4. Preheat the air fryer to 360 F.
5. Toss the butter in the air fryer basket and melt it.
6. Separate the egg liquid into 2 servings.
7. Pour the first part of the serving in the air fryer basket.
8. Cook it for 1 minute on one side.
9. Turnover and cook for another minute.
10. Repeat the same steps with the remaining egg mixture.
11. Cut the cucumber into cubes.
12. Separate the cubed cucumber into 2 parts.
13. Place the cucumber cubes in the center of each egg pancake.
14. Wrap the eggs.

675. Keto Almond Buns

Preparation time: 15 minutes
Cooking time: 13 minutes
Servings: 1

Ingredients:
- 1 cup almond flour
- 5 tablespoon sesame seeds
- 1 tablespoon pumpkin seeds, crushed
- 1 teaspoon stevia extract
- ½ tablespoon baking powder
- 1 teaspoon apple cider vinegar
- ¼ teaspoon salt
- ½ cup water, hot
- 4 eggs

Directions:
1. Place the almond flour, sesame seeds, crushed pumpkin seeds, baking powder, and salt in a large mixing bowl.
2. Then crack the eggs in a separate bowl.
3. Whisk them and add stevia extract and apple cider vinegar.
4. Stir the egg mixture gently.
5. Pour the hot water into the almond flour mixture.
6. Stir and add the whisked egg mixture.
7. Knead the dough until well combined.
8. Preheat the air fryer to 350 F.
9. Cover the air fryer basket with some parchment paper.
10. Make 10 small buns from the dough and put them in the air fryer.
11. Cook the sesame cloud buns for 13 minutes.
12. Check if the buns are cooked. If they require a little more time – cook for 1 minute more.

676. Jalapeno Bacon Bites

Preparation time: 15 minutes
Cooking time: 11 minutes
Servings: 1

Ingredients:
- 6 oz. bacon, sliced
- 1 cup jalapeno pepper
- ½ teaspoon salt
- ½ teaspoon paprika
- 1 teaspoon olive oil

Directions:
1. Wash the jalapeno peppers carefully.
2. Combine the salt, paprika, and olive oil together.
3. Stir gently.
4. Brush the jalapeno peppers with the olive oil mixture generously.
5. Wrap each jalapeno pepper in the bacon slices.
6. Secure the jalapeno bites with toothpicks.
7. Preheat the air fryer to 360 F.
8. Put the jalapeno bites in the air fryer rack.
9. Cook for 11 minutes or until the bacon is crisp.
10. Transfer the cooked jalapeno pepper bites to a plate and cover them with paper towels to remove excess grease before serving.

677. Moroccan Lamb Balls

Preparation time: 15 minutes
Cooking time: 14 minutes
Servings: 1

Ingredients:
- 1 teaspoon cumin seeds
- 1 teaspoon coriander seeds
- 1 garlic clove, sliced
- 12 oz. ground lamb
- 2 tablespoon fresh lemon juice
- 1 egg
- 1 teaspoon dried mint
- 2 tablespoon heavy cream

Directions:
1. Combine the ground lamb and sliced garlic in a bowl.
2. Sprinkle the meat mixture with the coriander seeds and cumin seeds.
3. Coat the ground lamb with the fresh lemon juice and dried mint.
4. Stir the ground lamb mixture with a fork.
5. Crack the egg into the mixture.
6. Stir well.
7. Preheat the air fryer 360 F.
8. Make the meatballs from the lamb mixture and place them in the air fryer.
9. Cook for 8 minutes.
10. Drizzle the lamb balls with the heavy cream and cook for 6 minutes.
11. Place a cocktail stick in every lamb ball and serve them.

185

678. Chicken Coconut Poppers

Preparation time: 10 minutes
Cooking time: 10 minutes
Servings: 1

Ingredients:
- ½ cup coconut flour
- 1 teaspoon chili flakes
- 1 teaspoon ground black pepper
- 1 teaspoon garlic powder
- 11 oz. chicken breast, boneless, skinless
- 1 tablespoon olive oil

Directions:
1. Cut the chicken breast into medium cubes and put them in a large bowl.
2. Sprinkle the chicken cubes with the chili flakes, ground black pepper, garlic powder, and stir them well using your hands.
3. After this, sprinkle the chicken cubes with the almond flour.
4. Shake the bowl with the chicken cubes gently to coat the meat.
5. Preheat the air fryer to 365 F.
6. Grease the air fryer basket tray with the olive oil.
7. Place the chicken cubes inside.
8. Cook the chicken poppers for 10 minutes.
9. Turn the chicken poppers over after 5 minutes of cooking.
10. Allow the cooked chicken poppers to cool before serving.

679. Paprika Pulled Pork

Preparation time: 15 minutes
Cooking time: 20 minutes
Servings: 1

Ingredients:
- 1 tablespoon chili flakes
- 1 teaspoon ground black pepper
- ½ teaspoon paprika
- 1 teaspoon cayenne pepper
- 1/3 cup cream
- 1 teaspoon kosher salt
- 1-pound pork tenderloin
- 1 teaspoon ground thyme
- 4 cup chicken stock
- 1 teaspoon butter

Directions:
1. Pour the chicken stock into the air fryer basket tray.
2. Add the pork steak and sprinkle the mixture with the chili flakes, ground black pepper, paprika, cayenne pepper, and kosher salt.
3. Preheat the air fryer to 370 F and cook the meat for 20 minutes.
4. Strain the liquid and shred the meat with 2 forks.
5. Then add the butter and cream and mix it.
6. Cook the pulled pork for 4 minutes more at 360 F.
7. When the pulled pork is cooked allow to rest briefly.

680. Coriander Chicken

Preparation time: 20 minutes
Cooking time: 16 minutes
Servings: 1

Ingredients:
- 3 oz. fresh coriander root
- 1 teaspoon olive oil
- 3 tablespoon minced garlic
- ¼ lemon, sliced
- ½ teaspoon salt
- 1 teaspoon ground black pepper
- ½ teaspoon chili flakes
- 1 tablespoon dried parsley
- 1-pound chicken thighs

Directions:
1. Peel the fresh coriander and grate it.
2. Then combine the olive oil with the minced garlic, salt, ground black pepper, chili flakes, and dried parsley.
3. Combine the mixture and sprinkle over the chicken tights.
4. Add the sliced lemon and grated coriander root.
5. Mix the chicken thighs carefully and leave them to marinate for 10 minutes in the fridge.
6. Meanwhile, preheat the air fryer to 365 F.
7. Put the chicken in the air fryer basket tray.
8. Add all the remaining liquid from the chicken and cook for 15 minutes.
9. Turn the chicken over and cook it for 1 minute more.

681. Paprika Beef Tongue

Preparation time: 10 minutes
Cooking time: 20 minutes
Servings: 1

Ingredients:
- 1-pound beef tongue
- 1 teaspoon salt
- 1 teaspoon ground black pepper
- 1 teaspoon paprika
- 1 tablespoon butter
- 4 cup water

Directions:
1. Preheat the air fryer to 365 F.
2. Put the beef tongue in the air fryer basket tray and add water.
3. Sprinkle the mixture with salt, ground black pepper, and paprika.
4. Cook the beef tongue for 15 minutes.
5. Strain the water from the beef tongue.
6. Cut the beef tongue into strips.
7. Toss the butter in the air fryer basket tray and add the beef strips.
8. Cook the strips for 5 minutes at 360 F.
9. When the beef tongue is cooked transfer to a serving plate.

186

682. Pepper Beef Stew

Preparation time: 15 minutes
Cooking time: 23 minutes
Servings: 1

Ingredients:
- 10 oz. beef short ribs
- 1 cup chicken stock
- 1 garlic clove
- 3 oz chive stems
- 4 oz. green peas
- ¼ teaspoon salt
- 1 teaspoon turmeric
- 1 green pepper
- 2 teaspoon butter
- ½ teaspoon chili flakes
- 4 oz. kale

Directions:
1. Prehcat the air fryer to 360 F.
2. Place the butter in the air fryer basket tray.
3. Add the beef short ribs.
4. Sprinkle the beef short ribs with the salt, turmeric, and chili flakes.
5. Cook the beef short ribs for 15 minutes.
6. Meanwhile, remove the seeds from the green pepper and chop it.
7. Chop the kale and dice the chives.
8. When the time is over – pour the chicken stock in the beef short ribs.
9. Add the chopped green pepper and diced chives.
10. After this, sprinkle the mixture with the green peas.
11. Peel the garlic clove and add it to the mixture too.
12. Mix it up using the wooden spatula.
13. Then chop the kale and add it to the stew mixture.
14. Stir the stew mixture one more time and cook it at 360 F for 8 minutes more.
15. When the stew is cooked – let it rest little.
16. Then mix the stew up and transfer to the serving plates.

683. Beef Strips with Zucchini Zoodles

Preparation time: 15 minutes
Cooking time: 13 minutes
Servings: 1

Ingredients:
- 1-pound beef brisket
- 1 teaspoon ground black pepper
- 1 tomato
- 1 teaspoon salt
- 1 zucchini
- 1 teaspoon olive oil
- 1 teaspoon Italian spices
- 4 tablespoon water

Directions:
1. Cut the beef brisket into strips.
2. Sprinkle the beef strips with the ground black pepper and salt.
3. Chop the tomato roughly and transfer it to a blender.
4. Blend well until you get a smooth puree.
5. Grease the air fryer basket tray with the olive oil and put the beef strips inside.
6. Cook the beef strips for 9 minutes at 365 F.
7. Stir the beef strips carefully after 4 minutes of cooking.
8. Meanwhile, wash the zucchini carefully and make spirals using a spiralizer.
9. When meat is cooked – add the zucchini spirals over the meat.
10. Sprinkle with the tomato puree, water, and Italian spices.
11. Cook the dish for 4 minutes more at 360 F.
12. Stir with a wooden spatula before serving.

682. Beef with Broccoli

Preparation time: 10 minutes
Cooking time: 13 minutes
Servings: 1

Ingredients:
- 6 oz. broccoli
- 10 oz. beef brisket
- 4 oz chive stems
- 1 teaspoon paprika
- 1/3 cup water
- 1 teaspoon olive oil
- 1 teaspoon butter
- 1 tablespoon flax seeds
- ½ teaspoon chili flakes

Directions:
1. Cut the beef brisket into medium pieces.
2. Coat the beef pieces with the paprika and chili flakes.
3. Combine using your hands.
4. Preheat the air fryer to 360 F.
5. Grease the air fryer basket tray with the olive oil.
6. Put the beef pieces in the air fryer basket tray and cook the meat for 7 minutes.
7. Stir once during the cooking.
8. Meanwhile, separate the broccoli into the florets.
9. Add the broccoli florets in the air fryer basket tray.
10. Sprinkle the ingredients with the flax seeds and butter.
11. Add water.
12. Dice the chives and add them in the air fryer basket tray.
13. Stir gently using the wooden spatula.
14. Cook the dish at 265 F for 6 minutes more.
15. When the broccoli is tender the dish is cooked.

683. Garlic Beef Mash

Preparation time: 10 minutes
Cooking time: 15 minutes
Servings: 1

Ingredients:
- 1-pound ground beef
- 3 oz chive stems
- 1 teaspoon garlic, sliced
- 1 teaspoon ground white pepper
- ¼ cup cream
- 1 teaspoon olive oil
- 2 green peppers
- 1 teaspoon dried dill
- 1 teaspoon cayenne pepper
- 2 teaspoon chicken stock

Directions:
1. Dice the chive stems.
2. Combine the chives with the sliced garlic.
3. Combine the mixture carefully with a teaspoon.
4. Sprinkle the ground beef with the ground white pepper.
5. Add dried dill and cayenne pepper.
6. Grease the air fryer basket tray with the olive oil.
7. Preheat the air fryer to 365 F.
8. Put the spiced ground beef in the air fryer basket tray.
9. Cook the beef mixture for 3 minutes.
10. Stir it carefully.
11. Add the chives mixture and chicken stock.
12. Mix it gently and cook at the same temperature for 2 minutes more.
13. Meanwhile, chop the green peppers into the small pieces.
14. Add the chopped green peppers in the air fryer.
15. Add the cream and stir it until well combined.
16. Cook the ground beef mixture for 10 minutes more.
17. Mix the ground beef mixture with a hand blender.
18. Serve hot.

684. Pork Meatballs Stuffed with Cheddar Cheese

Preparation time: 15 minutes
Cooking time: 8 minutes
Servings: 1

Ingredients:
- 1-pound ground pork
- 5 oz. Cheddar cheese
- 1 tablespoon dried oregano
- 1 large egg
- ½ teaspoon salt
- 1 teaspoon paprika
- 1 tablespoon butter
- ½ teaspoon nutmeg
- 1 teaspoon minced garlic
- ½ teaspoon ground ginger

Directions:
1. Crack the egg into a bowl and whisk it.
2. Add salt, paprika, nutmeg, and ground ginger to the bowl.
3. Stir gently and add the ground pork.
4. Add dried oregano and minced garlic.
5. Mix well using a spoon until well combined and make 6 medium balls.
6. Cut the Cheddar cheese into 6 medium cubes.
7. Fill the pork meatballs with the cheese cubes.
8. Preheat the air fryer to 365 F.
9. Toss the butter in the air fryer basket tray and melt it.
10. Add the pork meatballs and cook them for 8 minutes, stirring halfway through.

685. Chicken Liver Burgers

Preparation time: 15 minutes
Cooking time: 10 minutes
Servings: 1

Ingredients:
- ½ teaspoon turmeric
- ½ teaspoon ground coriander
- 1 teaspoon ground thyme
- ½ teaspoon salt
- 2 teaspoon butter
- 1 tablespoon almond flour
- 1 tablespoon coconut flour
- 1 teaspoon chili flakes
- 1-pound chicken liver
- 1 egg

Directions:
1. Grind the chicken liver.
2. Put the ground chicken in a mixing bowl.
3. Crack the egg in a separate bowl and whisk it.
4. Add the turmeric, ground coriander, ground thyme, and salt in the whisked egg mixture.
5. Add the whisked egg mixture to the ground liver.
6. Add the coconut flour and almond flour.
7. Mix with a spoon. You should get a non-sticky liver mixture. Add more almond flour if desired.
8. Preheat the air fryer to 360 F.
9. Then melt the butter and grease the air fryer basket tray with the melted butter.
10. Make medium liver burgers and put them in the prepared air fryer basket tray.
11. Cook the burgers for 5 minutes on each side. The burger should be a little bit crunchy.
12. When the liver burgers are cooked – let them chill a little before serving.

188

686. Cheddar Chicken Pizza

Preparation time: 15 minutes
Cooking time: 12 minutes
Servings: 1

Ingredients:
- 10 oz. ground chicken
- 1 teaspoon minced garlic
- 1 teaspoon almond flour
- ½ teaspoon salt
- 1 teaspoon ground black pepper
- 1 large egg
- 6 oz. Cheddar cheese, shredded
- ½ teaspoon dried dill

Directions:
1. Put the ground chicken in a bowl.
2. Coat it with the minced garlic, almond flour, salt, ground black pepper, and dried dill.
3. Crack the egg into the ground chicken mixture and mix with a spoon.
4. Combine to get a smooth texture.
5. Preheat the air fryer to 380 F.
6. Cover the air fryer pizza tray with the parchment.
7. Place the ground chicken mixture in the air fryer pizza tray and make the shape of a pizza crust.
8. Cook the chicken pizza crust for 8 minutes.
9. Remove the chicken pizza crust from the air fryer and sprinkle it with the shredded cheese generously.
10. Cook the pizza for 4 minutes more at 365 F.

687. Keto Blueberry Muffins

Preparation time: 10 minutes
Cooking time: 14 minutes
Serving: 1

Ingredients:
- 1 cup almond flour
- 1 Tbsp powdered stevia
- 1/4 cup entire milk
- 1 egg
- 1/4 tsp salt
- 1/4 tsp ground cinnamon
- 1 1/2 tsp preparing powder
- 1/2 cup frozen or new blueberries

Direction:
1. Preheat your air fryer to 350 degrees F.
2. Splash 12 silicone biscuit cups gently with cooking shower.
3. In a huge bowl, mix together the almond flour, Stevie, salt, cinnamon, and heating powder.
4. Add the eggs and milk and mix well.
5. Overlap in the blueberries.
6. Gap the biscuit hitter between every biscuit cup, filling about 3/4 of the way full.
7. Spot the biscuit into the air fryer container and cook for 14 minutes or until a toothpick comes out neatly when embedded into the middle.
8. Eliminate from the air fryer and let cool.
9. Serve and appreciate!

688. Raspberry Muffins

Preparation time: 10 minutes
Cooking time: 15 minutes
Serving: 1

Ingredients:
- 1 cup almond flour
- 1 Tbsp powdered Stevie
- 1/4 cup entire milk
- 1 egg
- 1/4 tsp salt
- 1/4 tsp ground cinnamon
- 1 1/2 tsp heating powder
- 1/2 cup frozen or new raspberries

Directions:
1. Preheat your air fryer to 350 degrees F.
2. Splash 12 silicone biscuit cups delicately with cooking shower.
3. In a huge bowl, mix together the almond flour, stevia, salt, cinnamon, and preparing powder.
4. Add the eggs and milk and mix well.
5. Overlap in the raspberries.
6. Separation the biscuit hitter between every biscuit cup, filling about 3/4 of the way full.
7. Spot the biscuits into the air fryer bushel and cook for 14 minutes or until a toothpick come out neatly when embedded into the middle.
8. Eliminate from the air fryer and let cool.

689. Strawberry Muffins

Preparation time: 10 minutes,
Cooking time: 15 minutes,
Serving: 1

Ingredients:
- 1 cup almond flour
- 1 Tbsp powdered stevia
- 1/4 cup entire milk
- 1 egg
- 1/4 tsp salt
- 1/4 tsp ground cinnamon
- 1 1/2 tsp heating powder
- 1/2 cup hacked strawberries

Directions:
1. Preheat your air fryer to 350 degrees F.
2. Splash 12 silicone biscuit cups delicately with cooking shower.

189

3. In an enormous bowl, mix together the almond flour, stevia, salt, cinnamon, and preparing powder.
4. Add the eggs and milk and mix well.
5. Overlap in the strawberries.
6. Separation the biscuit player between every biscuit cup, filling about 3/4 of the way full.
7. Spot the biscuits into the air fryer bushel and cook for 14 minutes or until a toothpick come out neatly when embedded into the middle.
8. Eliminate from the air fryer and let cool.
9. Serve and appreciate!

690. Keto Chocolate Chip Muffins

Preparation time: 10 minutes
Cooking time: 14 minutes
Serving: 1

Ingredients:
- 1 cup almond flour
- 1 Tbsp powdered stevia
- 1/4 cup entire milk
- 1 egg
- 1/4 tsp salt
- 1 1/2 tsp heating powder
- 1/2 cup smaller than expected dim chocolate chips (sugar free)

Direction:
1. Preheat your air fryer to 350 degrees F.
2. Shower 12 silicone biscuit cups softly with cooking splash.
3. In an enormous bowl, mix together the almond flour, stevia, salt, cinnamon, and heating powder.
4. Add the eggs and milk and mix well.
5. Crease in the chocolate chips
6. Separation the biscuit hitter between every biscuit cup, filling about 3/4 of the way full.
7. Spot the biscuits into the air fryer bushel and cook for 14 minutes or until a toothpick come out neatly when embedded into the middle.
8. Eliminate from the air fryer and let cool.

691. Ham Hash

Preparation Time: 10 minutes
Cooking Time: 10 minutes
Serving: 1

Ingredients:
- 1 egg
- 1 cup ham, chopped
- ½ onion, chopped
- 1 tbsp. butter
- 1/3 cup parmesan, grated

Direction:
1. Pre-heat your fryer to 350°F.

2. Whisk the egg into a bowl well, before adding in the ham, onion, and butter. Combine well and add seasoning if desired.
3. Scoop equal portions into three ramekins, adding a sprinkle of parmesan on top.
4. Place into fryer and cook for ten minutes. Take care when removing the ramekins, and serve hot.

692. Spicy Grilled Steak

Preparation Time: 7 minutes
Cooking Time: 9 minutes
Serving: 1

Ingredients:
- 2 tablespoons low-sodium salsa
- 1 tablespoon chipotle pepper, apple cider vinegar
- 1 teaspoon ground cumin
- 1/8 tsp. red pepper flakes
- ¾ lb. sirloin tip steak, mildly pounded to about 1/3 inch thick

Directions:
1. Thoroughly mix the salsa, chipotle pepper, cider vinegar, cumin, black pepper, and red pepper flakes. Scrub this mixture into both sides of each steak piece. Let stand for 15 minutes at room temperature.
2. Grill the steaks in the air fryer, two at a time, for 6 to 9 minutes.
3. Position the steaks to a clean plate and cover with aluminum foil to keep warm. Repeat with the remaining steaks.
4. Chop the steaks thinly against the grain and serve.

693. Creamy Halibut Chowder

Preparation time: 5 minutes
Cooking time: 10 minutes
Servings: 1

Ingredients:
- One halibut fillet, cut into cubes
- Salt and pepper, to taste
- ½ tsp. olive oil
- ½ tsp. lemon juice
- 1 cup fish stock
- ¼ cup cream
- ¼ cup mushrooms, sliced
- 1 tbsp. ginger, minced
- 1 tbsp. onion, chopped
- 1 tbsp. dill, chopped

Directions
1. Preheat the air fryer up to 350 degrees Fahrenheit /180 degrees Celsius.
2. Place the halibut fillets in the air fryer baking pan and season with salt and pepper.
3. Drizzle with olive oil and lemon juice.
4. Place the air fryer baking pan in the air fryer basket and set the timer for 2 minutes.
5. Add the mushrooms, ginger, and onions

then pour the fish stock and cream and add them.
6. Stir well to combine.
7. Set the timer for 8 minutes.
8. Top with the fresh dill.
9. Serve and enjoy!

694. Kimchi Stuffed Squid

Preparation time: 5 minutes
Cooking time: 12 minutes
Servings: 1

Ingredients:
- 1 large squid, cleaned
- 1 cup kimchi

Directions
1. Preheat the air fryer up to 350 degrees Fahrenheit /180 degrees Celsius.
2. Stuff the squid with the kimchi and secure it with a toothpick.
3. Place the squid in the air fryer basket and spray it with some cooking spray.
4. Turn the timer for 12 minutes or until the squid is cooked.
5. Halfway through the cooking time, use kitchen tongs to rearrange the squid to be cooked evenly.
6. Serve and enjoy!

695. Chicken-Lettuce Wraps

Preparation time: 15 minutes
Cooking time: 12 to 16 minutes
Servings: 1

Ingredients:
- 1/2-pound boneless, skinless chicken thighs, trimmed
- 1 teaspoon vegetable oil
- tablespoons lime juice
- 1 shallot, minced
- 1 tablespoon fish sauce, plus extra for serving
- 1teaspoons packed brown sugar
- 1 garlic clove, minced
- 1/8 teaspoon red pepper flakes
- 1 mango, peeled, pitted, and cut into ¼-inch pieces
- 1/3 cup chopped fresh mint
- 1/3 cup chopped fresh cilantro
- 1/3 cup chopped fresh Thai basil
- 1 head Bibb lettuce, leaves separated (8 ounces / 227 g)
- ¼ cup chopped dry-roasted peanuts
- Thai chiles, stemmed and sliced thin

Directions
1. Pat the chicken dry with paper towels and rub with oil. Place the chicken in air fryer basket. Select the Air Fry function and cook at 400 degrees Fahrenheit (204 degrees Celsius) for 12 to 16 minutes, or until the chicken registers 175 degrees Fahrenheit (79 degrees Celsius),

flipping and rotating chicken halfway through cooking.
2. Meanwhile, whisk lime juice, shallot, fish sauce, sugar, garlic, and pepper flakes together in large bowl; set aside.
3. Transfer chicken to cutting board, let cool slightly, then shred into bite-size pieces using 2 forks. Add the shredded chicken, mango, mint, cilantro, and basil to bowl with dressing and toss to coat.
4. Serve the chicken in the lettuce leaves, passing peanuts, Thai chiles, and extra fish sauce separately.

696. Veggie Salsa Wraps

Preparation time: 5 minutes
Cooking time: 7 minutes
Servings: 1

Ingredients:
- 1 cup red onion, sliced
- 1 zucchini, chopped
- 1 poblano pepper, deseeded and finely chopped
- 1 head lettuce
- ½ cup salsa
- 8ounces (227 g) Mozzarella cheese

Directions
1. Place the red onion, zucchini, and poblano pepper in the air fryer basket. Select the Air Fry function and cook at 390 degrees Fahrenheit (199 degrees Celsius) for 7 minutes, or until they are tender and fragrant.
2. Divide the veggie mixture among the lettuce leaves and spoon the salsa over the top. Finish off with Mozzarella cheese. Wrap the lettuce leaves around the filling.
3. Serve immediately.

697. Cheesy Chicken Sandwich

Preparation time: 10 minutes
Cooking time: 5 to 7 minutes
Servings: 1

Ingredients:
- 1/3 cup chicken, cooked and shredded
- 2Mozzarella slices
- 1 hamburger bun
- ¼ cup shredded cabbage
- 1 teaspoon mayonnaise
- 2teaspoons butter, melted
- 1 teaspoon olive oil
- ½ teaspoon balsamic vinegar
- ¼ teaspoon smoked paprika
- ¼ teaspoon black pepper
- ¼ teaspoon garlic powder
- Pinch of salt

Directions
1. Select the Bake function and preheat Maxx to

370 degrees Fahrenheit (188 degrees Celsius).

2. Brush some butter onto the outside of the hamburger bun.
3. In a bowl, coat the chicken with the garlic powder, salt, pepper, and paprika.
4. In a separate bowl, stir together the mayonnaise, olive oil, cabbage, and balsamic vinegar to make coleslaw.
5. Slice the bun in two. Start building the sandwich, starting with the chicken, followed by the Mozzarella, the coleslaw, and finally the top bun.
6. Transfer the sandwich to the air fryer oven and bake for 5 to 7 minutes.
7. Serve immediately.

698. Beef Parmigiana Sliders

Preparation time: 5 minutes
Cooking time: 15 minutes
Servings: 1

Ingredients:
- 1/4-pound lean ground chuck
- 1 ounce bacon bits
- 2 tablespoons tomato paste
- 3 tablespoons shallots, chopped
- 1 garlic clove, minced
- 1/4 cup parmesan cheese, grated
- 1 teaspoon cayenne pepper
- Salt and black pepper, to taste
- 1 pretzel rolls

Preparation
1. Thoroughly combine the ground chuck, bacon bits, tomato paste, shallots, garlic, parmesan cheese, cayenne pepper, salt, black pepper.
2. Shape the mixture into 4 equal patties.
3. Spritz your patties with a nonstick cooking spray. Air fry your burgers at 380 degrees Fahrenheit for about 11 minutes or to your desired degree of doneness.
4. Place your burgers on pretzel rolls and serve with favorite toppings. Enjoy!

699. Shrimp Bacon Bites

Preparation time: 8 to 10 minutes.
Cooking time: 8 minutes.
Servings: 1

Ingredients:
- 1/2 teaspoon red pepper flakes, crushed
- 1 tablespoon salt
- 1 teaspoon chili powder
- 1 ¼ pounds shrimp, peeled and deveined
- 1 teaspoon paprika
- 1/2 teaspoon black pepper, ground
- 1 tablespoon shallot powder
- 1/4 teaspoon cumin powder

- ¼ pounds thin bacon slices

Directions:
1. Place your Air Fryer on a flat kitchen surface; plug it and turn it on. Set temperature to 360°F and let it preheat for 4–5 minutes.
2. Take out the Air-frying basket and gently coat it using cooking oil or spray.
3. In a bowl of medium size, thoroughly mix the shrimp and seasoning until they are coated well.
4. Now wrap a slice of bacon around the shrimps; secure them with a toothpick and refrigerate for 30 minutes.
5. Add the shrimps to the basket. Push the Air-frying basket in the Air Fryer. Cook for 8 minutes.
6. Slide-out the basket; serve with cocktail sticks or your choice of dip (optional).

700. Baked Cheese Crisps

Preparation time: 5 minutes.
Cooking time: 15 minutes.
Servings: 1

Ingredients:
- 1/2 cup Parmesan cheese, shredded
- 1 cup Cheddar cheese, shredded
- 1 teaspoon Italian seasoning
- 1/2 cup marinara sauce

Directions:
1. Begin by preheating your Air Fryer and set it to 350°F. Place a piece of parchment paper in the cooking basket.
2. Mix the cheese with the Italian seasoning.
3. Add around one tablespoon of the cheese mixture (per crisp to the basket, making sure they are not touching—Bake for 6 minutes or until browned to your liking.
4. Work in batches and place them on a large tray to cool slightly.
5. Serve with the marinara sauce. Bon appétit!

701. Taquitos

Preparation Time: 10 minutes
Cooking Time: 12 minutes
Serving: 1

Ingredients:
- 1 corn tortillas
- 1 large egg
- 1 tbsp. taco seasoning
- 1/4 lb. ground beef
- ½ cup bread crumbs
- Olive oil spray

Directions:
1. Preheat the Ninja Air Fryer to 350 degrees F.

2. Combine the eggs, breadcrumbs, taco seasoning and beef in a large bowl.
3. Equally divide the beef mixture and place into the center of each tortilla.
4. Roll the tortillas and secure with a toothpick.
5. Arrange the taquitos into a single layer in the air fryer basket.
6. Spray with olive oil and cook for 12 minutes. Turn halfway through the cooking process.
7. Serve with salsa or guacamole.

702. Spicy Fries

Preparation Time: 10 minutes
Cooking Time: 15 minutes
Serving: 4

Ingredients:
- 3 potatoes, sliced., rinsed
- 2-tsp. cayenne pepper
- 1-tsp. paprika
- 2-tsp. olive oil
- Salt and black pepper

Directions:
1. Place the fries into a bowl and sprinkle with oil, cayenne, paprika, salt and black pepper. Toss and place them in the fryer.
2. Cook for 7 minutes at 360 degrees F., until golden and crispy.
3. Give it a toss after 7-8 minutes and continue cooking for another 8 minutes. Serve.

703. Seafood Tostadas

Preparation Time: 10 minutes
Cooking Time: 20 minutes
Serving: 4

Ingredients:
- 18 shrimps, peeled and deveined.
- 1/4 cup sour cream
- 1/4 cup cheese sauce
- 1/2 cup tomatoes, diced.
- 12 ounces nacho chips
- 2-tbsp. olives, sliced.
- 1-tsp. garlic powder
- 1-tsp. paprika
- salt and pepper, to taste.

Directions:
1. Preheat the Air Fryer to 350 degrees F. Season the shrimps with the garlic powder, paprika, salt and pepper.
2. Place the shrimps in the Air Fryer Basket and cook for 3 to 5 minutes or until the shrimps are cooked through
3. Remove from the Air Fryer and set aside.
4. Place the nachos into the Air Fryer Basket and

cook for 3 to 5 minutes or until they are well toasted.
5. Remove the chips from the Air Fryer and arrange them on a serving plate. Top the nachos with the shrimps, tomatoes and olives. Dollop with the sour cream and cheese sauce. Serve and enjoy!

704. BBQ Chicken

Preparation Time: 10 minutes
Cooking Time: 20 minutes
Serving: 3

Ingredients:
- 1 whole small chicken, cut into pieces
- 1 cup BBQ sauce
- 1-tsp. garlic powder
- 1-tsp. smoked paprika
- 1-tsp. salt

Directions:
1. Mix salt, paprika and garlic powder and coat chicken pieces. Place in the air fryer.
2. Cook for 15 minutes at 400 degrees F. Remove to a plate and brush with barbecue sauce.
3. Wipe fryer out from the chicken fat. Return the chicken to the air fryer, skin-side up and cook for 5 minutes at 340 degrees F. Serve.

705. Squash Chips

Preparation Time: 10 minutes
Cooking Time: 15 minutes
Serving: 2

Ingredients:
- 1/2 cup parmesan cheese, finely grated.
- 1/2 cup all-purpose flour
- 1 medium squash, thinly sliced.
- 1-tsp. garlic powder
- olive oil spray
- 1-tsp. paprika
- salt and pepper, to taste.

Directions:
1. Preheat the Air Fryer to 350 degrees F. Mix the flour, garlic powder, parmesan cheese and paprika together in a bowl.
2. Coat the squash slices in the flour mixture.
3. Place the squash slices (chips in the Air Fryer Basket and spray lightly with cooking spray.)
4. Cook for 15 minutes or until the chips become golden brown.
5. Halfway through the cooking time, give the Air Fryer Basket a shake to allow even cooking. Season with salt and pepper to taste. Serve and enjoy!

193

706. Yummy Fish Bites

Preparation Time: 10 minutes
Cooking Time: 15 minutes
Serving: 4

Ingredients:
- 1/4 cup parsley, chopped
- 4 trout fillets; cut into 3-inch sticks
- 1/2 cup panko
- 2-tbsp. lime rinds, grated.
- 1-tsp. lime juice
- salt and pepper, to taste.

Directions:
1. Preheat the Air Fryer to 350 degrees F. Season the fish sticks with salt and pepper and spray with cooking spray.
2. Coat the fish sticks evenly with the panko and arrange them in the Air Fryer Basket. Use the Air Fryer Double Layer Rack if needed.
3. Drizzle over with the lime juice. Cook for 5 minutes or until just tender. Garnish with the parsley and lime rinds. Serve and enjoy!

707. Chicken with Rice

Preparation Time: 30 minutes
Cooking Time: 20 minutes
Serving: 4

Ingredients:
- 4 chicken legs
- 2 cups water
- 2 tomatoes, cubed
- 1 onion
- 3 minced cloves garlic
- 1 cup rice
- 3-tbsp. butter
- 1-tbsp. tomato paste
- Salt and black pepper

Directions:
1. Rub the chicken legs with butter. Sprinkle with salt and pepper and fry in a preheated air fryer for 30 minutes at 380 degrees F.
2. Then, add small onion and a little bit of oil; keep stirring. Add the tomatoes, the tomato paste and the garlic and cook for 5 more minutes.
3. Meanwhile, in a pan, boil the rice in 2 cups of water for around 20 minutes. In a baking tray, place the rice and top it with the air fried chicken and cook in the air fryer for 5 minutes. Serve and enjoy!

708. Kimchi-Spiced Salmon

Preparation Time: 10 minutes
Cooking Time: 15 minutes
Serving: 4

Ingredients:
- 2-tbsp. soy sauce
- 2-tbsp. sesame oil
- 2-tbsp. mirin
- 2-tbsp. ginger puree
- 1-tsp. kimchi spice
- 1-tsp. sriracha sauce
- 2-lb. salmon fillets
- 1 lime, cut into wedges

Directions:
1. Preheat your Air Fryer to 350 degrees F.
2. Grease the air fryer basket with cooking spray. Take a bowl and, mix together soy sauce, mirin, ginger puree, kimchi spice and sriracha sauce.
3. Add the salmon fillets and toss to coat. Place in the air fryer basket and drizzle with sesame oil.
4. Cook for 10 minutes, flipping once halfway through. Garnish with lime wedges and serve.

709. Peppery and Lemony Haddock

Preparation Time: 10 minutes
Cooking Time: 15 minutes
Serving: 4

Ingredients:
- 4 haddock fillets
- 1 cup breadcrumbs
- 2-tbsp. lemon juice
- 1/2-tsp. black pepper
- 1/4 cup dry air fryer to flakes
- 1 egg, beaten
- 1/4 cup Parmesan cheese
- 3-tbsp. flour
- 1/4-tsp. salt

Directions:
1. Combine flour, black pepper and salt, in a small bowl. In another bowl, combine lemon, breadcrumbs, Parmesan cheese and potato flakes.
2. Dip the fillets in the flour first, then in the egg and coat them with the lemony crumbs.
3. Arrange on a lined sheet and place in the air fryer. Cook for 10 minutes at 370 degrees F.

710. Sockeye Fish

Preparation Time: 10 minutes
Cooking Time: 20 minutes
Serving: 2

Ingredients:
- 2-3 fingerling potatoes, thinly sliced
- 1/2 bulb fennel, thinly sliced
- 4-tbsp. melted butter
- Salt and pepper to taste
- 1-2-tsp. fresh dill
- 2 sockeye salmon fillets
- 8 cherry tomatoes, halved
- 1/4 cup fish stock

Directions:
1. Preheat your Air Fryer to 400 degrees F. Bring to a boil salted water over medium heat. Add the potatoes and blanch for 2 minutes; drain. Cut 2 large-sized rectangles of parchment paper of 13x15 inch size.
2. In a large bowl, mix potatoes, fennel, pepper and salt. Divide the mixture between parchment paper pieces and sprinkle with dill. Top with fillets.
3. Add cherry tomatoes on top and drizzle with butter; pour fish stock on top. Fold the squares and seal them. Cook the packets in the air fryer for 10 minutes.

711. Herbed Garlic Lobster

Preparation Time: 10 minutes
Cooking Time: 15 minutes
Serving: 3

Ingredients:
- 4 oz. lobster tails, halved
- 1-tsp. garlic, minced.
- 1-tbsp. butter
- Salt and pepper to taste
- 1/2-tbsp. lemon Juice

Directions:
1. Add all the ingredients to a food processor, except shrimp and blend well. Clean the skin of the lobster and cover with the marinade.
2. Preheat the air fryer to 380 degrees F. Place the lobster in your air fryer's cooking basket and cook for 10 minutes. Serve with fresh herbs and enjoy!

712. Tuna Sushi

Preparation Time: 10 minutes
Cooking Time: 13 minutes
Serving: 1

Ingredients:
- 2 ounces sashimi grade tuna, cut into small cubes.
- 1 cup of cooked sushi rice
- 1 stalk green onion, thinly sliced.
- 1-tbsp. rice vinegar
- 1/2-tsp. sriracha sauce
- 1/2-tsp. of sugar

Directions:
1. Preheat Air Fryer to 400 degrees F. Combine the rice, vinegar and sugar and set aside.
2. Place rice on a flat surface. Mold and roll into a long strip. Cut into bite sizes.
3. Carefully place rice bites into the Air Fryer and cook for 13 minutes. Mix together the tuna and onions.
4. Top each rice bite with some tuna and sriracha sauce. Serve and enjoy!

713. Shrimp Balls

Preparation Time: 10 minutes
Cooking Time: 13 minutes
Serving: 1

Ingredients:
- 1-lb. shrimps, peeled and deveined.
- 1/2 knob of ginger; peeled and minced
- 2 eggs
- 2 garlic cloves, minced.
- 1 cup breadcrumbs
- 4 green onions, minced.
- 1-tsp. white sugar
- 1-tsp. sesame oil
- 1-tsp. paprika
- salt and pepper, to taste.

Directions:
1. Combine the shrimps, garlic, sugar, ginger, sesame oil and onions in a food processor. Add an egg and season with salt and pepper.
2. Blend until smooth. Transfer into a bowl and chill for 30 minutes.
3. Preheat the Air Fryer to 300 degrees F. Mix the breadcrumbs and paprika in a bowl and set aside.
4. Whisk the other egg in a bowl and set aside. Scoop out balls of the shrimp mix and dip into the whisked egg.
5. Evenly coat the balls with the breadcrumbs and leave to set for a few minutes. Arrange the shrimp balls in the Air Fryer Basket and use the Air Fryer Double Layer Rack if needed.
6. Spray the balls with cooking spray and cook for 10 minutes. Serve and enjoy!

714. Salmon Taquitos

Preparation Time: 10 minutes
Cooking Time: 13 minutes
Serving: 1

Ingredients:
- 2-tbsp. olive oil
- 1-lb. smoked salmon, chopped
- Salt to taste
- 2-tbsp. taco seasoning
- 1 cup cheddar cheese
- 1 lime, juiced
- 1/2 cup chopped cilantro
- 8 corn tortillas

Directions:
1. Preheat the Air Fryer to 390 degrees F. Take a bowl and, mix salmon, taco seasoning, lime juice, cheddar cheese, salt and cilantro.
2. Wrap the tortillas around the filling and place in the air fryer basket. Cook for 12 minutes, turning once halfway through. Serve with hot salsa.

715. Fisherman's Stew

Preparation Time: 10 minutes
Cooking Time: 13 minutes
Serving: 1

Ingredients:
- 1 trout fillet, cubed.
- 6 ounces mussels, cleaned.
- 4 lemon slices
- 1/2 cup shrimps, peeled and deveined.
- 2 cups fish stock
- 1-tbsp. olive oil
- 1-tbsp. ginger, sliced.
- 1-tbsp. fresh cilantro, chopped
- 1-tbsp. lemon juice
- 2-tbsp. tomato paste
- 1-tbsp. olives
- 1/2-tsp. paprika
- salt and pepper, to taste.

Directions
1. Preheat the Air Fryer to 350 degrees F. Place the trout cubes and shrimps in the Air Fryer Baking Pan and season them with the paprika, salt and pepper.
2. Add the mussels to the Air Fryer Baking Pan and drizzle over with the olive oil and lemon juice. Cook for 5 minutes.
3. Mix together the fish stock and tomato paste and add to the Air Fryer Baking Pan.
4. Mix in the olives, lemon slices and ginger slices and return the Air Fryer Baking Pan to the Air Fryer.
5. Cook for 8 minutes. Top with the fresh cilantro. Serve and enjoy!

716. Shrimp Spring Rolls

Preparation Time: 10 minutes
Cooking Time: 15 minutes
Serving: 4

Ingredients:
- 1 tablespoon peanut oil
- 1 teaspoon sesame oil
- 2 cloves garlic, crushed and minced
- 1 teaspoon fresh ginger, grated
- ¼ cup water chestnuts, cut into small strips
- ½ cup carrots, shredded
- ½ cup cabbage, shredded
- ¼ cup scallions, sliced
- 1 tablespoon soy sauce
- 1 teaspoon five spice powder
- 1 teaspoon salt
- 1 teaspoon pepper
- ¼ pound shrimp, cleaned, deveined and sliced
- ½ cup bean sprouts
- 12-14 spring roll wrappers
- 1 egg, lightly beaten

Directions:
1. Heat the peanut oil and sesame oil in a large skillet over medium heat.
2. Add the garlic, ginger, chestnuts, carrots, cabbage, scallions, and soy sauce.
3. Season the mixture with five spice powder,

salt, and pepper. Sauté the mixture for 3-5 minutes.
4. Add the shrimp and bean sprouts. Cook just until the shrimp is pink, and then remove the skillet from the heat.
5. Lay the spring roll wrappers out on the counter or other flat surface.
6. Brush the ends with the beaten egg mixture.
7. Place a generous spoonful of the mixture onto each spring roll wrapper.
8. Roll each one up, fold in the ends, and press the edge to seal.
9. Lightly brush the spring roll with the egg mixture again, if desired.
10. Set the air fryer to 390°F.
11. Place the spring rolls in the basket of the air fryer and cook for 5 minutes.
12. Serve with your favorite dipping sauce, if desired.

717. Flakey Fried Whitefish

Preparation Time: 10 minutes
Cooking Time: 15 minutes
Serving: 4

Ingredients:
- 1 pound whitefish fillets, cut into 3-4 inch pieces
- 2 teaspoons fresh lemon juice
- 1 teaspoon salt
- 1 teaspoon black pepper
- ½ cup flour
- 2 eggs, lightly beaten
- 1 cup panko bread crumbs
- 1 tablespoon fresh tarragon, chopped
- 1 tablespoon fresh parsley chopped
- 1 tablespoon olive oil

Directions:
1. Set the air fryer to 390°F.
2. Sprinkle the whitefish fillets with lemon juice and season them with salt and black pepper.
3. Place the flour in one bowl and the eggs in a second bowl.
4. In a third bowl, combine the panko bread crumbs, tarragon, parsley, and olive oil. Mix until the olive oil is worked through the crumbs.
5. Dust a piece of whitefish with the flour, and then dip it into the egg mixture.
6. Next, place it into the panko mixture and use your hands to pat the crumbs onto the fish. Repeat until all the pieces are coated.
7. Place the whitefish pieces in the basket of the air fryer.
8. Cook for 12-15 minutes, or until the fish is cooked through.

718. Cod with Simple Olive Caper Sauce

Preparation Time: 10 minutes
Cooking Time: 15 minutes
Serving: 4

Ingredients:
- 1 pound cod pieces
- 1 tablespoon plus 1 teaspoon olive oil
- 1 teaspoon lemon juice
- 1 teaspoon salt
- 1 teaspoon black pepper
- 1 cup cherry tomatoes, halved
- 2 cloves garlic, crushed and minced
- ¼ cup Kalamata olives, diced
- 1 tablespoon capers
- ¼ cup fresh basil, chopped

Directions:
1. Set the air fryer to 355°F.
2. Lightly brush the cod with 1 teaspoon of the olive oil.
3. Sprinkle the cod with lemon juice and season it with salt and black pepper.
4. Place the cod in the basket of the air fryer.
5. Cook for 12 minutes, or until the cod is flakey and tender.
6. While the cod is cooking, heat the remaining olive oil in a large skillet over medium.
7. Add the tomatoes and cook for 2-3 minutes, or until they begin to break down and release their juices.
8. Next, add the garlic, olives, capers, and basil to the skillet. Cook, stirring frequently, for 4-5 minutes.
9. Remove the cod from the air fryer and transfer it to serving plates Top the cod with the olive caper sauce before serving.

719. Sesame Soy Striped Bass

Preparation Time: 10 minutes
Cooking Time: 15 minutes
Serving: 4

Ingredients:
- 1 pound striped bass steaks
- 1 cup soy sauce
- ½ cup mirin
- 2 tablespoons sesame oil
- 2 tablespoons brown sugar
- 1 tablespoon lime juice
- 1 tablespoon garlic chili paste
- ¼ cup apple juice

Directions:
1. Place the bass steaks in a shallow baking dish.
2. In a bowl, combine the soy sauce, mirin, sesame oil, brown sugar, lime juice, garlic chili paste, and apple juice. Use a whisk to blend.
3. Cover the steaks with the sesame soy sauce, cover, and refrigerate for one hour.
4. Set the air fryer to 390°F.
5. Remove the bass from the marinade and blot up any extra.
6. Place the steaks in the air fryer and cook for approximately 10 minutes, or until the fish is cooked through and flakey.
7. Remove the bass from the air fryer and let it rest several minutes before serving.

720. Garlic Tarragon Buttered Salmon

Preparation Time: 10 minutes
Cooking Time: 15 minutes
Serving: 4

Ingredients:
- ¼ cup butter
- 1 tablespoon shallot, diced
- 1 tablespoon fresh tarragon, chopped
- 1 teaspoon fresh lemon zest
- 1 pound salmon fillets
- 1 teaspoon salt
- 1 teaspoon black pepper
- Fresh lemon slices for garnish

Directions:
1. Set the air fryer to 350°F.
2. Melt the butter in a saucepan over medium heat.
3. Once the butter has melted, add the shallot, tarragon, and lemon zest. Cook, stirring frequently, for 2-3 minutes. Remove it from the heat and set it aside.
4. Season the salmon fillets with salt and black pepper.
5. Liberally brush both sides of each piece of salmon with the garlic tarragon butter.
6. Place the salmon pieces in the air fryer and cook for 15 minutes, turning once halfway through.
7. Remove the salmon from the air fryer and garnish with any remaining butter sauce and fresh lemon slices.

721. Sweet Potato Croquettes

Preparation Time: 10 minutes
Cooking Time: 10 minutes
Serving: 4

Ingredients:
- 2 cups mashed sweet potatoes
- ½ cup freshly grated Asiago cheese
- 1 egg, plus 1 egg yolk
- 2 tablespoons flour, divided
- 1 tablespoon fresh thyme, chopped
- ½ teaspoon nutmeg
- 1 teaspoon salt
- 1 teaspoon black pepper
- ½ cup seasoned bread crumbs

Directions:
1. Set the air fryer to 390°F.
2. In a bowl, combine the mashed sweet potatoes, Asiago cheese, egg yolk, 1 tablespoon of the flour, thyme, nutmeg, salt, and black pepper.
3. Take heaping spoonfuls of the mixture and using your hands, form golf ball sized mounds.
4. Dust each one with the remaining flour.
5. Lightly beat the remaining egg and coat

each croquette with it before rolling it in the seasoned bread crumbs.
6. Place the croquettes in the air fryer and cook, working in batches if necessary, for 8-9 minutes.
7. Remove the croquettes from the air fryer and serve with your favorite dipping sauce, if desired.

722. Roasted Caprese Stacks

Preparation Time: 10 minutes
Cooking Time: 15 minutes
Serving: 4

Ingredients:
- 2 cups heirloom tomatoes, sliced thick
- 1 cup fresh mozzarella cheese, sliced thin
- ¼ cup fresh basil, chopped
- 1 teaspoon salt
- 1 teaspoon black pepper
- 2 tablespoons balsamic vinegar
- 1 tablespoon olive oil

Directions:
1. Set the air fryer to 390°F.
2. Begin by dividing the tomatoes into groups of three slices.
3. Place one tomato from each group onto a baking sheet.
4. Top each with a slice of mozzarella cheese, a drizzle of balsamic vinegar, and a sprinkling of salt and black pepper.
5. Top each with an additional piece of tomato.
6. Next, add on the remaining cheese, fresh basil, and any remaining balsamic vinegar, salt, and black pepper.
7. Top each with the last piece of tomato from each group.
8. Brush each stack lightly with olive oil.
9. Carefully place the stacks in the basket of the air fryer.
10. Cook for 12-15 minutes.

723. Portabella White Pizzas

Preparation Time: 10 minutes
Cooking Time: 5 minutes
Serving: 4

Ingredients:
- 4 large portabella mushroom caps
- 2 teaspoons olive oil
- 1 teaspoon salt
- 1 teaspoon black pepper, coarsely ground
- ½ teaspoon rubbed sage
- ¼ cup crème fraîche
- 1 tablespoon fresh chives, chopped
- ½ cup goat cheese, crumbled
- ½ cup fresh mozzarella cheese, shredded
- ¼ cup walnuts, chopped

Directions:
1. Set the air fryer to 325°F.
2. Brush the mushroom caps with olive oil and season them with salt, black pepper, and rubbed sage.
3. Combine the crème fraîche with the chives, and spread a layer on each mushroom cap.
4. Top each mushroom with goat cheese, mozzarella cheese, and walnuts.
5. Place the mushroom caps in the air fryer and cook for 5 minutes.

724. Jerk Party Wings

Preparation Time: 20 minutes
Cooking Time: 15 minutes
Serving: 6

Ingredients:
- 1 tablespoon olive oil
- 4 cloves garlic, crushed and minced
- 1 jalapeño pepper, diced
- ½ teaspoon cayenne powder
- 2 teaspoons allspice
- 1 teaspoon cinnamon
- ½ teaspoon ground ginger
- 1 teaspoon black pepper, coarsely ground
- ¼ cup soy sauce
- 1 tablespoon garlic chili paste
- 1 tablespoon brown sugar
- 2 tablespoons lime juice
- 2 pounds chicken wings

Directions:
1. Set the air fryer to 390°F.
2. In a bowl, combine the olive oil, garlic, jalapeño pepper, cayenne powder, allspice, cinnamon, ground ginger, and black pepper. Mix well.
3. To the seasoned olive oil add the soy sauce, garlic chili paste, brown sugar, and lime juice. Whisk together until blended.
4. Place the chicken wings in a shallow baking dish and pour the marinade over the wings.
5. Let the chicken marinate for at least 20 minutes, or up to 2 hours.
6. Remove the chicken from the marinade and place it in the basket of the air fryer.
7. Cook for approximately 15 minutes, or until the wings are cooked through.

725. Cranberry Ham and Cheese

Preparation Time: 10 minutes
Cooking Time: 5 minutes
Serving: 4

Ingredients:
- 8 slices sourdough bread (or preferred bread)
- 2 tablespoons butter, melted
- 1 tablespoon Dijon mustard
- ¼ cup cranberry sauce
- ½ pound smoked ham, shaved

- ¼ cup Brie cheese, sliced
- ½ cup Gruyere cheese, shredded
- 1 cup arugula leaves

Directions:
1. Set the air fryer to 355°F.
2. Lay the bread out on a counter or clean surface. Liberally brush the butter over one side of each piece, and then flip the bread over.
3. On four of the slices, apply the Dijon mustard and cranberry sauce.
4. Follow by placing the ham, Brie, Gruyere, and arugula on the bread.
5. Top each with an additional piece of bread.
6. Working in batches, place the sandwiches into the air fryer and cook for 5 minutes.

726. Pork Chops with Roasted Pepper Mango Salsa

Preparation Time: 10 minutes
Cooking Time: 15 minutes
Serving: 4

Ingredients:
- ¼ cup olive oil
- 2 tablespoons pineapple juice
- 2 cloves garlic, crushed and minced
- 1 tablespoon fresh mint, divided
- 2 tablespoons fresh cilantro, chopped and divided
- 1 tablespoon Dijon mustard
- 1 sprig fresh rosemary
- 1 pound pork chops, approximately 1 inch thick
- 1-2 jalapeño peppers, depending upon heat preference
- 1 red bell pepper, whole
- 1 cup mango, chopped
- ½ teaspoon salt
- ½ teaspoon pepper
- ½ teaspoon cumin
- ½ teaspoon coriander

Directions:
1. In a bowl, combine the olive oil, pineapple juice, garlic, mint, 1 tablespoon of the cilantro, Dijon mustard, and rosemary.
2. Place the pork chops in a shallow baking dish and cover them with the marinade.
3. Cover and refrigerate for 2 hours.
4. Remove the pork chops from the refrigerator and let them sit at room temperature for 15 minutes.
5. Set the air fryer to 390°F.
6. Place the jalapeño peppers and red pepper in the basket of the air fryer and cook for 3 minutes.
7. Remove the peppers from the air fryer and place them in a bowl. Cover the bowl with plastic wrap and let the peppers sweat for 5-10 minutes.
8. Remove the peppers from the bowl, peel away the skin, and dice.
9. Combine the diced peppers with the mango,

salt, pepper, cumin, coriander, and remaining cilantro. Mix well and set aside.
10. Set the air fryer to 390°F again.
11. Place the pork chops in the basket, working in batches if necessary.
12. Cook for approximately 10 minutes, or until cooked through.
13. Serve with the fresh mango salsa.

727. Italian Beef Rolls

Preparation Time: 10 minutes
Cooking Time: 15 minutes
Serving: 6

Ingredients:
- 1 cup fresh basil
- 1 cup fresh parsley
- ¼ cup pine nuts
- 2 cloves garlic
- 1 teaspoon lemon zest
- ½ teaspoon salt
- ½ teaspoon black pepper
- ¼ cup Parmesan cheese, freshly grated
- 3 tablespoons olive oil
- 1 ½ pounds flank steak, butterfly cut
- 1 cup fresh mozzarella cheese, sliced
- 1 cup fresh spinach, torn
- 1 cup roasted red peppers, sliced

Directions:
1. In a blender or food processor combine the basil, parsley, pine nuts, garlic, lemon zest, salt, black pepper, Parmesan, and olive oil. Pulse until well blended.
2. Lay the steak out on the counter and open up the butterfly cut.
3. Spread the herb sauce over the steak.
4. Next, layer on the mozzarella cheese, spinach, and roasted red peppers.
5. Roll the steak up and secure it with cooking twine or toothpicks throughout.
6. Set the air fryer to 400°F.
7. Place the steak roll in the air fryer and cook for 15 minutes, or until the desired doneness is reached.
8. Remove the steak roll from the air fryer and let it rest for 10 minutes before removing the twine or toothpicks and slicing.

728. Cajun Rubbed Ribeye Steaks

Preparation Time: 10 minutes
Cooking Time: 15 minutes
Serving: 4

Ingredients:
- 1 tablespoon Cajun seasoning
- 1 teaspoon black pepper, coarsely ground
- 1 teaspoon garlic powder
- 1 teaspoon powdered ground coffee
- 1 tablespoon olive oil
- 1 ½ pounds ribeye steaks

Directions:
1. Set the air fryer to 400°F.

2. Combine the Cajun seasoning, black pepper, garlic powder, and powdered ground coffee.
3. Add the olive oil to the spice mixture and combine until a paste forms.
4. Rub both sides of each steak with the Cajun spice paste.
5. Place the steaks in the basket of the air fryer and cook for 15 minutes, adjusting for desired doneness. Turn once halfway through cooking.
6. Remove the steaks from the air fryer and let them rest for 10 minutes before serving.

729. Lime Shrimp

Preparation Time: 10 minutes
Cooking Time: 15 minutes
Serving: 4

Ingredients:
- 1 pound shrimp, cleaned and deveined
- 1 cup unsweetened, shredded coconut
- 1 tablespoon lime zest, grated
- ½ teaspoon cayenne powder
- 1 cup flour
- 1 tablespoon cornstarch
- 1 teaspoon salt
- 1 teaspoon pepper
- 1 egg white

Directions:
1. Set the air fryer to 350°F.
2. In a bowl, combine the unsweetened shredded coconut, lime zest, and cayenne powder.
3. In a second bowl, combine the flour, cornstarch, salt, and pepper.
4. Place the egg white in a third bowl.
5. One at a time, dip each shrimp first in the flour mixture, then the egg white, and then in the coconut mixture, patting on the coconut with your fingers to make sure it sticks.
6. Place the shrimp in the basket of the air fryer.
7. Cook for 10 minutes, turning once halfway through.

730. Root Vegetable Snack Chips

Preparation Time: 10 minutes
Cooking Time: 20 minutes
Serving: 6

Ingredients:
- 1 ½ cups beet, thinly sliced
- 1 ½ cups sweet potato, thinly sliced
- 1 ½ cups parsnip, thinly sliced
- 1 cup purple carrots, thinly sliced
- 1 ½ tablespoons olive oil
- 1 teaspoon salt
- 1 teaspoon black pepper
- ½ teaspoon cayenne powder
- 1 teaspoon chili powder
- 1 teaspoon brown sugar

Directions:
1. Set the air fryer to 420°F.
2. Place the sliced root vegetables in a bowl and drizzle them with the olive oil. Toss the vegetables to coat evenly.

3. Working in batches if necessary, place the vegetable chips in the basket of the air fryer and cook for 18-20 minutes.
4. While the chips are cooking, combine the salt, black pepper, cayenne powder, chili powder, and brown sugar.
5. Remove the root vegetables from the air fryer and immediately toss them with the seasoning mixture.

731. Breakfast Empanadas

Preparation Time: 10 minutes
Cooking Time: 20 minutes
Serving: 4

Ingredients:
- 1 pound crumbled breakfast sausage
- ½ cup sweet yellow onion, diced
- ½ cup red bell pepper, diced
- 1 cup sweet potato, shredded
- ½ cup cheddar cheese, shredded
- ½ teaspoon ground sage
- ½ teaspoon thyme
- ½ teaspoon salt
- 1 teaspoon black pepper
- 1 package prepared empanada shells
- 1 egg yolk, whisked
- Crème fraîche for garnish (optional)

Directions:
1. Set the air fryer to 350°F.
2. Place the breakfast sausage in a skillet over medium heat and cook until thoroughly browned. Drain off the excess grease, leaving about one tablespoon remaining in the skillet.
3. Remove the sausage to a medium mixing bowl, and set it aside.
4. To the skillet add the onion, red bell pepper, and shredded sweet potatoes. Cook, stirring frequently, for 5 minutes or until the vegetables are firm tender.
5. Transfer the vegetables to the bowl with the cooked sausage.
6. Season the mixture with ground sage, fresh thyme, salt, and black pepper and mix.
7. Lay out the empanada shells on a counter or other flat surface.
8. Spoon the sausage mixture onto one half of each of the shells and top with a sprinkling of cheese.
9. Fold each shell in half and crimp it shut with your fingers.
10. Using a fork, press the edges together, ensuring that they are well sealed.
11. Brush each empanada with egg yolk to give it a nice, glossy look when cooked.
12. Place the empanadas in the frying basket and cook for 10-12 minutes.
13. Serve with crème fraîche, if desired.

732. Old Englishman's Breakfast

Preparation Time: 10 minutes
Cooking Time: 20 minutes
Serving: 4

Ingredients:
* 1 egg
* 1 tablespoon vegetable oil
* 1 cup lamb sausage, cooked and crumbled
* ¼ cup milk
* 1 cup flour
* 1 teaspoon baking powder
* 1 teaspoon ground sage (optional if using sage derby cheese)
* ½ teaspoon salt
* 1 teaspoon black pepper, coarsely ground
* ½ cup sage derby or white cheddar cheese, shredded
* 1 teaspoon Worcestershire sauce

Directions:
1. Set the air fryer to 375°F.
2. In a bowl, combine the egg and vegetable oil. Whisk together until blended.
3. Add the lamb sausage and stir.
4. Next, add the milk and blend.
5. Slowly add the flour and baking powder, and season with the ground sage, salt, and black pepper.
6. Finally, stir in the sage derby or white cheddar and Worcestershire sauce.
7. Transfer the mixture to four lightly oiled ramekins.
8. Place the ramekins in the air fryer, working in two batches if necessary.
9. Cook for 20 minutes, or until golden brown.

734. THAI MUSSELS

Prep Time: 5 minutes
Cook Time: 10 minutes
Servings: 4

Ingredients:
* 2 tablespoons coconut oil
* ¼ teaspoon sea salt fine grain 3 shallots diced
* 1 ½ tablespoons Thai red curry paste
* 1 ½ cups chicken bone broth
* 14 ounces coconut milk can
* 2 pounds mussels frozen, (on the half shell), thawed (see
* Note)
* ¼ cup fresh cilantro
* ¼ cup green onions sliced into ½ inch pieces
* 1 lime, juiced

Directions:
1. Heat the coconut oil in a large deep pot, such as a Dutch oven, over medium-high heat. Add the shallots and sauté until tender, about 2 minutes. Reduce heat to low. Whisk in the curry paste, broth and coconut milk. Simmer

on low, uncovered for 20-40 minutes or until broth reduces a bit. The longer you simmer, the thicker your sauce will be. Season with the salt.
2. Lower the heat under the pot to medium. Place the thawed mussels in the coconut milk and broth mixture to heat through, about 5 minutes.
3. Once the mussels are warmed through stir in chopped cilantro, green onions and squeeze in juice from 1 lime and stir. Immediately remove from heat and place in serving bowls. Garnish with additional sliced green onion, cilantro leaves.

735. Chicken Piccata

Prep Time: 5 minutes
Cook Time: 10 minutes
Servings: 4

Ingredients:
* 4 chicken thighs boneless, skinless
* 1 teaspoon fresh ground black pepper
* ½ teaspoon sea salt fine grain
* 2 tablespoons butter (or other Paleo fat if dairy sensitive)
* 1 clove garlic (or 1 teaspoon minced garlic)
* ¼ cup chicken bone broth (boxed will work, homemade preferred)
* 3 tablespoons lemon juice
* 2 tablespoons capers
* Fresh flat-leaf parsley for garnish

Directions:
1. Pat the chicken thighs with paper towel to get off excess moisture.
Using a heavy skillet, pound out chicken thighs to an even thickness of about ½ inch and season both sides well with pepper
2. And salt.
3. Place butter in a cast iron skillet. Heat to medium-high. Sear the chicken thighs on both sides for 5 minutes per side, or until cooked through and chicken is no longer pink inside. Remove chicken from pan and onto a serving platter.
4. Add the garlic to the pan. Add the stock to the pan to deglaze. Use a whisk to scrape bits off the bottom of the pan. Add lemon juice and simmer on medium-low for 2 minutes.
5. Serve chicken with drippings from the pan. Garnish with fresh chopped parsley and capers.

736. AMAZING COLESLAW

Prep Time: 5 minutes
Cook Time: 8 minutes
Servings: 6

Ingredients:
- 1 pound cabbage shredded (about 4 cups)
- 4 slices bacon diced small
- ¼ cup MCT oil or macadamia nut oil
- 3 teaspoons Confectioners Swerve (or equivalent)
- 3 tablespoons coconut vinegar (or apple
- Cider vinegar)
- Sea salt and pepper to taste

Directions:
1. Place the cabbage in a large bowl. Set aside In a large sauté pan, cook the bacon slowly over medium heat until it is crisp and golden brown, 8 to 10 minutes.
2. Leaving the bacon and the drippings in the pan. Add the natural sweetener, the oil, and the vinegar to the pan and bring to a boil. Pour the hot dressing over the cabbage, tossing to wilt the cabbage and coat it with the dressing.
3. Season with salt and pepper and serve

737. Grecian Chicken Pasta

Prep Time: 5 minutes
Cook Time: 15 minutes
Servings: 4

Ingredients:
- 1 pound chicken breasts boneless skinless,
- Cut into 1 inch chunks MARINADE if desired
- ¼ cup MCT oil
- 1 lemon juiced
- 2 tablespoons fresh oregano chopped

PASTA:
- 1 medium daikon swirled into "noodles" (about 4 cups)
- 2 tablespoons coconut oil
- 1 teaspoon sea salt fine grain
- ½ teaspoon fresh ground black pepper
- 3 clove garlic (or 3 teaspoons minced garlic)
- 1 tablespoon fresh oregano chopped
- 1 cup black olives
- 1 cup marinated red peppers chopped into 1 inch pieces
- ½ cup cherry tomatoes cut in ½
- ½ cup chicken bone broth boxed will work but homemade preferred
- 4 ounces feta cheese omit if dairy free

Directions:
1. Place the chicken in a glass pan and cover in the marinade ingredients. Cover and refrigerate for 2 hours.
1. Remove chicken from marinade and season

with salt and pepper.
2. Heat a cast iron skillet to medium heat. Add the coconut oil and sear the chicken on all sides until cooked through, about 6 minutes.
3. Remove chicken from the skillet and add in the daikon noodles, olives, tomatoes, red peppers, oregano and garlic. Sauté for 5 minutes or until daikon is softened. Add the chicken stock and cook another 4 minutes. Season with salt and pepper. Add chicken to the skillet and top with feta cheese if desired.

738. Cinnamon Syrup

Prep Time: 5 minutes
Cook Time: 5 minutes
Servings: 12

Ingredients:
- ½ cup butter browned
- ½ cup Confectioners Swerve
- 1 tablespoon cinnamon
- ½ cup unsweetened almond milk or hemp milk for dairy free

Directions:
1. Place the butter in a saucepan over high heat. Before you begin, make sure you have everything ready to go – the almond milk and the butter next to the pan, ready to put in. Work fast or the sweetener will burn.
2. Heat butter on high heat in a heavy-bottomed 2-quart (2 L) or 3-quart (3 L) saucepan. As soon as it comes to a boil, watch for specks of brown (this is brown butter....so good on veggies!).
3. Immediately add the Swerve, cinnamon and the almond milk to the pan. Whisk until sauce is smooth.

739. Dairy Free Ranch Dressing

Prep Time: 2 minutes
Cook Time: 0 minutes
Servings: 12

Ingredients:
- 1 cup organic mayo
- ¾ cup beef bone broth or chicken/veggie broth, boxed will work
- ½ teaspoon dried chives
- ¼ teaspoon dried parsley
- ½ teaspoon dried dill weed
- ¼ teaspoon garlic powder
- ¼ teaspoon onion powder
- 1/8 teaspoon sea salt
- 1/8 teaspoon fresh ground black pepper

Directions:
1. Lace all the ingredients a large jar and shake vigorously until well combined.
2. Cover and refrigerate for 2 hours before serving (it will thicken up as it rests).

740. Bacon Vinaigrette

Prep Time: 10 minutes
Cook Time: 0 minutes
Servings: 6

Ingredients:
- 4 slices bacon
- 2 tablespoons onion diced
- 3 tablespoons coconut vinegar or red wine vinegar
- 1 teaspoon Dijon mustard
- 2 drops stevia glycerite
- 3 tablespoons MCT oil or expeller pressed olive oil

Directions:
1. Place the diced bacon in a skillet and sauté until crisp, about 5 minutes.
2. Remove bacon from pan, leaving the drippings. Add the onion, 3 tablespoons coconut vinegar, 1 teaspoon Dijon, and stevia if using. Heat on medium until onions soften, about 2 minutes.
3. Using a whisk, slowly add the oil into the pan. Whisk well to combine.

741. Gochujang Chicken Wings

Prep Time: 10 minutes
Cook Time: 0 minutes
Servings: 6

Ingredients:
- 2 pounds chicken wings, thawed
- 1 tbsp olive oil
- ½ tsp salt
- ½ tsp black pepper
- 1 tbsp gochujang (Korean red chili paste)
- ½ tbsp rice vinegar
- ½ tbsp maple syrup or honey
- 1 tbsp light soy sauce
- 1 tbsp toasted sesame oil
- ½ garlic clove, minced
- ½ tbsp fresh ginger, minced
- ½ tbsp sesame seeds
- ¼ cup scallions, chopped

Directions:
1. Preheat the air fryer to 390°F (200°C).
2. Pat the wings dry with a paper towel.
3. Using a large bowl, toss the wings with the olive oil and season with salt and black pepper.
4. Place in the air fryer basket and cook for 20 minutes, turning the wings halfway through.
5. Meanwhile, using a small bowl, combine the gochujang, rice vinegar, maple syrup or honey, soy sauce, sesame oil, garlic, and ginger.
6. Using tongs, remove the wings to a large bowl.
7. Pour about half of the gochujang sauce on the wings and toss to coat well.
8. Return the wings to the air fryer basket and cook for 5 minutes more, until the sauce has glazed.
9. Transfer to a serving plate and sprinkle with the sesame seeds and scallions.
10. Serve with the remaining sauce.

742. Hawaiian Salmon

Prep Time: 10 minutes
Cook Time: 20 minutes
Servings: 2

Ingredients:
- 2 garlic cloves, minced
- 2 medium halibut fillets
- 2 tsp. olive oil
- 6 sun-dried tomatoes, chopped
- salt and black pepper to taste
- 2 small red onions, sliced
- ½ tsp. red pepper flakes, crushed
- 9 black olives, pitted and sliced
- 1 fennel bulb, sliced
- 4 rosemary sprigs, chopped

Directions:
1. Season the fish with salt, pepper, rub it with garlic and oil and place it in a pan suitable for your air fryer. Add the onion slices, sundried tomatoes, fennel, olives, rosemary and sprinkle with chili flakes; transfer to the air fryer and cook at 380°F for 10 minutes. Divide the fish and vegetables among plates and serve.

743. Honey Sea Bass

Prep Time: 10 minutes
Cook Time: 10 minutes
Servings: 2

Ingredients:
- zest from ½ orange, grated
- 2 sea bass fillets
- juice from ½ orange
- 2 tbsp. mustard
- 1 pinch of salt and black pepper
- 2 tsp. honey
- ½ pound canned lentils, drained
- 2 tbsp. olive oil
- 1 small bunch of dill, chopped
- 1 small bunch of parsley, chopped
- 2 ounces watercress

Directions
1. Spice the fish fillets with salt and pepper, add the zest and orange juice, rub with 1 tbsp. oil, honey, and mustard, rubbing, transfer into an air fryer to air and bake at 350°F for 10 minutes, turning on the medium. Meanwhile, put the lentils in a saucepan, heat them over medium heat, add the rest of the oil, watercress, dill, and parsley, mix well and divide into plates. Add the fish fillets and serve immediately.

203

744. Chicken with Garlic

Prep Time: 10 minutes
Cook Time: 15 minutes
Servings: 2

Ingredients:
- 1 lb. roasted chicken, sliced
- salt and pepper to taste
- 1 tbsp. lemon juice
- 2 tbsp. butter
- 1 onion, chopped
- 2 carrots, chopped
- 2 garlic cloves, minced

Directions:
1. Add roasted chicken into the air fryer pot. Combine the lemon juice, butter, onion, carrots, garlic with salt and pepper. Bake at 300°F for 15 minutes. Serve and enjoy.

745. Chicken with Apple

Prep Time: 10 minutes
Cook Time: 20 minutes
Servings: 2

Ingredients:
- 1 tbsp. fresh ginger, finely grated
- 1 shallot, thinly sliced
- 1 tsp. fresh thyme, minced
- 2 tbsp. maple syrup
- 1 large apple, cored and cubed
- ½ cup apple cider
- salt and ground black pepper to taste
- 2 (4 ounces) boneless, skinless chicken thighs, sliced into chunks

DIRECTIONS:
1. In a portable bowl, combine the shallot, ginger, thyme, apple cider, maple syrup, salt, and black pepper. Add the chicken pieces and toss generously with the marinade. Marinate in the refrigerator for 6-8hours.
2. Set the air-fryer temperature to 390°F. Grease a fryer basket. Place the chicken pieces and the diced apple in the air fryer basket. Air fry for about 20 minutes, flipping once halfway. Remove from the fryer and transfer the chicken mixture to a serving plate. Serve hot.

746. Shrimp and Beef with Lettuce

Prep Time: 10 minutes
Cook Time: 20 minutes
Servings: 2

Ingredients:
- 3 tbsp. lemon juice
- 2 tbsp. olive oil
- ½ cup cilantro, chopped
- 1 lb. beef
- salt and pepper to taste
- ½ cup cilantro dressing
- 1 lb. shrimp, pieces
- 2 avocados
- 4 cups lettuce

DIRECTIONS:
1. Add olive oil into the air fryer pot. Toss the shrimp with salt, pepper, and lemon juice. Add the meat. Bake at 300°F for 20 minutes. Meanwhile, combine avocado, lettuce, and cilantro in a bowl. When you are ready, serve the meat with the avocado and cilantro mixture.

747. Quick Beef

Prep Time: 10 minutes
Cook Time: 20 minutes
Servings: 2

Ingredients:
- 1 tbsp. canola oil
- ¼ cup ground beef
- 1 sliced green onion, separated green and white parts
- 3 cups short grain rice, cooked
- 1 tsp. sesame oil
- 1 tsp. butter
- 1 egg

DIRECTIONS:
1. Add canola oil into the air fryer pot. Combine the green onion, sesame oil, butter, and egg.
2. Add the ground beef and rice. Bake at 300°F for 20 minutes. When it's ready, serve.

748. Broccoli Quiche

Prep Time: 10 minutes
Cook Time: 14 minutes
Servings: 4

Ingredients:
- 1 cup broccoli florets
- ¾ cup chopped roasted red peppers
- 1¼ cups grated Fontina cheese
- 6 eggs
- ¾ cup heavy cream
- ½ teaspoon salt
- Freshly ground black pepper, to taste
- Cooking spray

Directions:
1. Spritz the baking pan with cooking spray.
2. Place the baking pan on the air fry position. Select Air Fry, set the temperature to 325°F (163°C), and set the time to 10 minutes.
3. Add the broccoli florets and roasted red peppers to the pan and scatter the grated Fontina cheese on top.
4. In a bowl, beat together the eggs and heavy cream. Sprinkle with salt and pepper. Pour the egg mixture over the top of the cheese. Wrap the pan in foil.
5. Air fry for 8 minutes. Remove the foil and continue to cook another 2 minutes until the quiche is golden brown.
6. Rest for 5 minutes before cutting into wedges and serve warm.

749. Western Omelet

Prep Time: 10 minutes
Cook Time: 14 minutes
Servings: 4

Ingredients:
- ¼ cup chopped bell pepper, green or red
- ¼ cup chopped onion
- ¼ cup diced ham
- 1 teaspoon butter
- 4 large eggs
- 2 tablespoons milk
- ⅛ teaspoon salt
- ¾ cup shredded sharp Cheddar cheese

Directions:
1. Place the baking pan on the air fry position. Select Air Fry, set the temperature to 390ºF (199ºC), and set the time to 6 minutes.
2. Put the bell pepper, onion, ham, and butter in the baking pan and mix well.
3. Air fry for 1 minute. Stir and continue to cook for an additional 4 to 5 minutes until the veggies are softened.
4. Meanwhile, whisk together the eggs, milk, and salt in a bowl.
5. Pour the egg mixture over the veggie mixture.
6. Reduce the grill temperature to 360ºF (182ºC) and bake for 13 to 15 minutes more, or until the top is lightly golden browned and the eggs are set.
7. Scatter the omelet with the shredded cheese. Bake for another 1 minute until the cheese has melted.
8. Let the omelet cool for 5 minutes before serving.

750. Sweet-and-Sour Chicken Breasts

Prep Time: 10 minutes
Cook Time: 14 minutes
Servings: 4

Ingredients:
- 1 cup cornstarch
- Chicken seasoning or rub, to taste
- Salt and ground black pepper, to taste
- 2 eggs
- 2 (4-ounce/ 113-g) boneless, skinless chicken breasts, cut into 1- inch pieces
- 1½ cups sweet-and-sour sauce
- Cooking spray

Directions:
1. Spritz the perforated pan with cooking spray.
2. Combine the cornstarch, chicken seasoning, salt, and pepper in a large bowl. Stir to mix well. Whisk the eggs in a separate bowl.
3. Dredge the chicken pieces in the bowl of cornstarch mixture first, then in the bowl of whisked eggs, and then in the cornstarch mixture again.
4. Arrange the well-coated chicken pieces in the perforated pan.
5. Spritz with cooking spray.
6. Select Air Fry. Set temperature to 360ºF (182ºC) and set time to 15 minutes. Press Start to begin preheating.
7. Once preheated, place the pan into the oven. Flip the chicken halfway through.
8. When cooking is complete, the chicken should be golden brown and crispy.
9. Transfer the chicken pieces on a large serving plate, then baste with sweet-and-sour sauce before serving.

751. Dill Chicken Strips

Prep Time: 15 minutes
Cook Time: 10 minutes
Servings: 4

Ingredients:
- 2 whole boneless, skinless chicken breasts, halved lengthwise
- 1 cup Italian dressing
- 3 cups finely crushed panato chips
- 1 tablespoon dried dill weed
- 1 tablespoon garlic powder
- 1 large egg, beaten
- Cooking spray

Directions:
1. In a large resealable bag, combine the chicken and Italian dressing. Seal the bag and refrigerate to marinate at least 1 hour.
2. In a shallow dish, stir together the panato chips, dill, and garlic powder. Place the beaten egg in a second shallow dish.
3. Remove the chicken from the marinade. Roll the chicken pieces in the egg and the panato chip mixture, coating thoroughly.
4. Place the baking pan on the bake position. Select Bake, set the temperature to 325ºF (163ºC), and set the time to 10 minutes.
5. Place the coated chicken in the baking pan and spritz with cooking spray.
6. Bake for 5 minutes. Flip the chicken, spritz it with cooking spray, and bake for 5 minutes more until the outsides are crispy and the insides are no longer pink. Serve immediately.

752. Rosemary Chicken

Prep Time: 15 minutes
Cook Time: 10 minutes
Servings: 4

Ingredients:
- ¼ cup balsamic vinegar
- ¼ cup honey
- 2 tablespoons olive oil
- 1 tablespoon dried rosemary leaves
- 1 teaspoon salt
- ½ teaspoon freshly ground black pepper
- 2 whole boneless, skinless chicken breasts (about 1 pound / 454 g each), halved
- Cooking spray

Directions:
1. In a large resealable bag, combine the vinegar, honey, olive oil, rosemary, salt, and pepper. Add the chicken pieces, seal the bag, and refrigerate to marinate for at least 2 hours.
2. Place the crisper tray on the bake position. Select Bake, set the temperature to 325°F (163°C), and set the time to 20 minutes.
3. Line the crisper tray with parchment paper.
4. Remove the chicken from the marinade and place it on the parchment. Spritz with cooking spray.
5. Bake for 10 minutes. Flip the chicken, spritz it with cooking spray, and bake for 10 minutes more until the internal temperature reaches 165°F (74°C) and the chicken is no longer pink inside. Let sit for 5 minutes before serving.

753. Mayonnaise-Mustard Chicken

Prep Time: 15 minutes
Cook Time: 10 minutes
Servings: 4

Ingredients:
- 6 tablespoons mayonnaise
- 2 tablespoons coarse-ground mustard
- 2 teaspoons honey (optional)
- 2 teaspoons curry powder
- 1 teaspoon kosher salt
- 1 teaspoon cayenne pepper
- 1 pound (454 g) chicken tenders

Directions:
1. Place the crisper tray on the bake position. Select Bake, set the temperature to 350°F (177°C), and set the time to 15 minutes.
2. In a large bowl, whisk together the mayonnaise, mustard, honey (if using), curry powder, salt, and cayenne. Transfer half of the mixture to a serving bowl to serve as a dipping sauce. Add the chicken tenders to the large bowl and toss until well coated.
3. Place the tenders in the crisper tray. Bake for 15 minutes. Use a meat thermometer to ensure the chicken has reached an internal temperature of 165°F (74°C).
4. Serve the chicken with the dipping sauce.

754. Ginger Chicken Thighs

Prep Time: 15 minutes
Cook Time: 10 minutes
Servings: 4

Ingredients:
- ¼ cup julienned peeled fresh ginger
- 2 tablespoons vegetable oil
- 1 tablespoon honey
- 1 tablespoon soy sauce
- 1 tablespoon ketchup
- 1 teaspoon garam masala
- 1 teaspoon ground turmeric
- ¼ teaspoon kosher salt
- ½ teaspoon cayenne pepper
- Vegetable oil spray
- 1 pound (454 g) boneless, skinless chicken thighs, cut crosswise into thirds
- ¼ cup chopped fresh cilantro, for garnish

Directions:
1. In a small bowl, combine the ginger, oil, honey, soy sauce, ketchup, garam masala, turmeric, salt, and cayenne. Whisk until well combined. Place the chicken in a resealable plastic bag and pour the marinade over. Seal the bag and massage to cover all of the chicken with the marinade. Marinate at room temperature for 30 minutes or in the refrigerator for up to 24 hours.
2. Place the crisper tray on the bake position. Select Bake, set the temperature to 350°F (177°C), and set the time to 10 minutes.
3. Spray the crisper tray with vegetable oil spray and add the chicken and as much of the marinade and julienned ginger as possible.
4. Bake for 10 minutes. Use a meat thermometer to ensure the chicken has reached an internal temperature of 165°F (74°C).
5. To serve, garnish with cilantro.

756. Turkey Hoisin Burgers

Prep Time: 15 minutes
Cook Time: 20 minutes
Servings: 4

Ingredients:
- 1 pound (454 g) lean ground turkey
- ¼ cup whole-wheat bread crumbs
- ¼ cup hoisin sauce
- 2 tablespoons soy sauce
- 4 whole-wheat buns
- Olive oil spray

Directions:
1. In a large bowl, mix together the turkey, bread crumbs, hoisin sauce, and soy sauce.
2. Form the mixture into 4 equal patties. Cover with plastic wrap and refrigerate the patties for 30 minutes.

3. Spray the crisper tray lightly with olive oil spray.
4. Place the crisper tray on the air fry position. Select Air Fry, set the temperature to 370°F (188°C), and set the time to 20 minutes.
5. Place the patties in the crisper tray in a single layer. Spray the patties lightly with olive oil spray.
6. Air fry for 10 minutes. Flip the patties over, lightly spray with olive oil spray, and air fry for an additional 5 to 10 minutes, until golden brown.
7. Place the patties on buns and top with your choice of low- calorie burger toppings like sliced tomatoes, onions, and cabbage slaw. Serve immediately.

757. Easy Asian Turkey Meatballs

Prep Time: 15 minutes
Cook Time: 15 minutes
Servings: 4

Ingredients:
• 2 tablespoons peanut oil, divided
• 1 small onion, minced
• ¼ cup water chestnuts, finely chopped
• ½ teaspoon ground ginger
• 2 tablespoons low-sodium soy sauce
• ¼ cup panko bread crumbs
• 1 egg, beaten
• 1 pound (454 g) ground turkey

Directions:
1. Place the baking pan on the air fry position. Select Air Fry, set the temperature to 400°F (204°C), and set the time to 2 minutes.
2. In the baking pan, combine 1 tablespoon of peanut oil and onion. Air fry for 1 to 2 minutes or until crisp and tender. Transfer the onion to a medium bowl.
3. Add the water chestnuts, ground ginger, soy sauce, and bread crumbs to the onion and mix well. Add egg and stir well. Mix in the ground turkey until combined.
4. Form the mixture into 1-inch meatballs. Drizzle the remaining 1 tablespoon of oil over the meatballs. Arrange the meatballs in the pan.
5. Bake for 10 to 12 minutes, or until they are 165°F (74°C) on a meat thermometer. Rest for 5 minutes before serving.

758. Chicken Kebabs with Corn Salad

Prep Time: 15 minutes
Cook Time: 15 minutes
Servings: 4

Ingredients:
• 1 pound (454 g) boneless, skinless chicken breast, cut into 1½- inch chunks
• 1 green bell pepper, deseeded and cut into 1-inch pieces
• 1 red bell pepper, deseeded and cut into 1-inch pieces
• 1 large onion, cut into large chunks
• 2 tablespoons fajita seasoning
• 3 tablespoons vegetable oil, divided
• 2 teaspoons kosher salt, divided
• 2 cups corn, drained
• ¼ teaspoon granulated garlic
• 1 teaspoon freshly squeezed lime juice
• 1 tablespoon mayonnaise
• 3 tablespoons grated Parmesan cheese

Directions:
1. Place the chicken, bell peppers, and onion in a large bowl. Add the fajita seasoning, 2 tablespoons of vegetable oil, and 1½ teaspoons of kosher salt. Toss to coat evenly.
2. Alternate the chicken and vegetables on the skewers, making about 12 skewers.
3. Place the corn in a medium bowl and add the remaining vegetable oil. Add the remaining kosher salt and the garlic, and toss to coat. Place the corn in an even layer on a baking pan and place the skewers on top.
4. Select Roast. Set temperature to 375°F (190°C) and set time to 10 minutes. Press Start to begin preheating.
5. Once preheated, place the pan into the oven.
6. After about 5 minutes, remove the pan from the oven and turn the skewers. Return the pan to the oven and continue cooking.
7. When cooking is complete, remove the pan from the oven.
8. Place the skewers on a platter. Put the corn back to the bowl and combine with the lime juice, mayonnaise, and Parmesan cheese. Stir to mix well. Serve the skewers with the corn.

759. Chicken Livers

Prep Time: 15 minutes
Cook Time: 15 minutes
Servings: 4

Ingredients:
• 2 eggs
• 2 tablespoons water
• ¾ cup flour
• 2 cups panko bread crumbs
• 1 teaspoon salt
• ½ teaspoon ground black pepper
• 20 ounces (567 g) chicken livers
• Cooking spray

Directions:
1. Spritz the perforated pan with cooking spray.
2. Whisk the eggs with water in a large bowl. Pour the flour in a separate bowl. Pour the panko on a shallow dish and sprinkle with salt and pepper.
3. Dredge the chicken livers in the flour. Shake the excess off, then dunk the livers in the whisked eggs, and then roll the livers over the panko to coat well.
4. Arrange the livers in the perforated pan and spritz with cooking spray.

5. Select Nuwave Air Fryer Oven. Set temperature to 390ºF (199ºC) and set time to 10 minutes. Press Start to begin preheating.
6. Once preheated, place the pan into the oven. Flip the livers halfway through.
7. When cooking is complete, the livers should be golden and crispy.
8. Serve immediately.

759. Spaghetti Squash Tots

Prep Time: 5 minutes
Cook Time: 15 minutes
Servings: 10

Ingredients:
- ¼ tsp. pepper
- ½ tsp. salt
- 1 thinly sliced scallion
- 1 spaghetti squash

Directions:
1. Wash and cut the squash in half lengthwise. Scrape out the seeds.
2. With a fork, remove spaghetti meat by strands and throw out skins.
3. In a clean towel, toss in squash and wring out as much moisture as possible. Place in a bowl and with a knife slice through meat a few times to cut up smaller.
4. Add pepper, salt, and scallions to squash and mix well.
5. Create "tot" shapes with your hands and place in air fryer.
6. Spray with olive oil.
7. Cook 15 minutes at 350 degrees until golden and crispy!

760. Cinnamon Butternut Squash Fries

Prep Time: 5 minutes
Cook Time: 10 minutes
Servings: 2

Ingredients:
- 1 pinch of salt
- 1 tbsp. powdered unprocessed sugar
- ½ tsp. nutmeg
- 2 tsp. cinnamon
- 1 tbsp. coconut oil
- 10 ounces pre-cut butternut squash fries

Directions:
1. In a plastic bag, pour in all ingredients. Coat fries with other components till coated and sugar is dissolved.
2. Spread coated fries into a single layer in the air fryer. Cook 10 minutes at 390 degrees until crispy.

761. Chicken Fajita Rollups

Prep Time: 5 minutes
Cook Time: 10 minutes
Servings: 2

Ingredients:
- ½ tsp. oregano
- ½ tsp. cayenne pepper
- 1 tsp. cumin
- 1 tsp. garlic powder
- 2 tsp. paprika
- ½ sliced red onion
- ½ yellow bell pepper, sliced into strips
- ½ green bell pepper, sliced into strips
- ½ red bell pepper, sliced into strips
- 3 chicken breasts

Directions:
1. Mix oregano, cayenne pepper, garlic powder, cumin and paprika along with a pinch or two of pepper and salt. Set to the side.
2. Slice chicken breasts lengthwise into 2 slices.
3. Between two pieces of parchment paper, add breast slices and pound till they are ¼-inch thick. With seasoning, liberally season both sides of chicken slices.
4. Put 2 strips of each color of bell pepper and a few onion slices onto chicken pieces.
5. Roll up tightly and secure with toothpicks.
6. Repeat with remaining ingredients and sprinkle and rub mixture that is left over the chicken rolls.
7. Lightly grease your air fryer basket and place 3 rollups into the fryer. Cook 12 minutes at 400 degrees.
8. Repeat with remaining rollups.
9. Serve with salad!

762. Mexican Chicken Burgers

Prep Time: 5 minutes
Cook Time: 20 minutes \
Servings: 2

Ingredients:
- 1 jalapeno pepper
- 1 tsp. cayenne pepper
- 1 tbsp. mustard powder
- 1 tbsp. oregano
- 1 tbsp. thyme
- 3 tbsp. smoked paprika
- 1 beaten egg
- 1 small head of cauliflower
- 4 chicken breasts

Directions:
1. Ensure your air fryer is preheated to 350 degrees.
2. Add seasonings to a blender. Slice cauliflower into florets and add to blender.
3. Pulse till mixture resembles that of

breadcrumbs.

4. Take out ¾ of cauliflower mixture and add to a bowl. Set to the side. In another bowl, beat your egg and set to the side.
5. Remove skin and bones from chicken breasts and add to blender with remaining cauliflower mixture. Season with pepper and salt.
6. Take out mixture and form into burger shapes. Roll each patty in cauliflower crumbs, then the egg, and back into crumbs again.
7. Place coated patties into the air fryer, cooking 20 minutes.
8. Flip over at 10-minute mark. They are done when crispy!

763. Crispy Southern Fried Chicken

Prep Time: 5 minutes
Cook Time: 20 minutes
Servings: 4

Ingredients:
- 1 tsp. cayenne pepper
- 2 tbsp. mustard powder
- 2 tbsp. oregano
- 2 tbsp. thyme
- 3 tbsp. coconut milk
- 1 beaten egg
- ¼ C. cauliflower
- ¼ C. gluten-free oats
- 8 chicken drumsticks

Directions:
1. Ensure air fryer is preheated to 350 degrees.
2. Lay out chicken and season with pepper and salt on all sides.
3. Add all other ingredients to a blender, blending till a smooth- like breadcrumb mixture is created. Place in a bowl and add a beaten egg to another bowl.
4. Dip chicken into breadcrumbs, then into egg, and breadcrumbs once more.
5. Place coated drumsticks into air fryer and cook 20 minutes.
6. Bump up the temperature to 390 degrees and cook another 5 minutes till crispy.

764. Air Fryer Turkey Breast

Prep Time: 10 minutes
Cook Time: 15 minutes
Servings: 4

Ingredients:
- Pepper and salt
- 1 oven-ready turkey breast
- Turkey seasonings of choice

Directions:
1. Preheat air fryer to 350 degrees.
2. Season turkey with pepper, salt, and other desired seasonings.
3. Place turkey in air fryer basket.
4. Cook 60 minutes. The meat should be at 165 degrees when done.
5. Allow to rest 10-15 minutes before slicing. Enjoy!

765. Cheesy Chicken Fritters

Prep Time: 10 minutes
Cook Time: 15 minutes
Servings: 4

Ingredients:
Chicken Fritters:
- ½ tsp. salt
- 1/8 tsp. pepper
- 1 ½ tbsp. fresh dill
- 1 1/3 C. shredded mozzarella cheese
- 1/3 C. coconut flour
- 1/3 C. vegan mayo
- 2 eggs
- 1 ½ pounds chicken breasts
Garlic Dip:
- 1/8 tsp. pepper
- ¼ tsp. salt
- ½ tbsp. lemon juice
- 1 pressed garlic cloves
- 1/3 C. vegan mayo

Directions:
1. Slice chicken breasts into 1/3" pieces and place in a bowl.
2. Add all remaining fritter ingredients to the bowl and stir well. Cover and chill 2 hours or overnight.
3. Ensure your air fryer is preheated to 350 degrees. Spray basket with a bit of olive oil.
4. Add marinated chicken to air fryer and cook 20 minutes, making sure to turn halfway through cooking process.
5. To make the dipping sauce, combine all the dip ingredients until smooth.

766. Bacon Wrapped Pork Tenderloin

Prep Time: 10 minutes
Cook Time: 15 minutes
Servings: 4

Ingredients:
Pork:
- 1-2 tbsp. Dijon mustard
- 3-4 strips of bacon
- 1 pork tenderloin

Apple Gravy:
- ½ - 1 tsp. Dijon mustard
- 1 tbsp. almond flour
- 2 tbsp. ghee
- 1 chopped onion
- 2-3 Granny Smith apples
- 1 C. vegetable broth

Directions:
1. Spread Dijon mustard all over tenderloin and wrap meat with strips of bacon.
2. Place into air fryer and cook 10-15 minutes at 360 degrees. Use a meat thermometer to check for doneness.
3. To make sauce, heat ghee in a pan and add shallots. Cook 1-2 minutes.
4. Then add apples, cooking 3-5 minutes until softened.

5. Add flour and ghee to make a roux. Add broth and mustard, stirring well to combine.
6. When sauce starts to bubble, add 1 cup of sautéed apples, cooking till sauce thickens.
7. Once pork tenderloin I cook, allow to sit 5-10 minutes to rest before slicing.
8. Serve topped with apple gravy. Devour!

767. Cajun Pork Steaks

Prep Time: 15 minutes
Cook Time: 15 minutes
Servings: 4

Ingredients:
• 4-6 pork steaks
BBQ sauce:
• Cajun seasoning
• 1 tbsp. vinegar
• 1 tsp. low-sodium soy sauce
• ½ C. brown sugar
• ½ C. vegan ketchup

Directions:
1. Ensure your air fryer is preheated to 290 degrees.
2. Sprinkle pork steaks with Cajun seasoning.
3. Combine remaining ingredients and brush onto steaks.
4. Add coated steaks to air fryer. Cook 15minutes till just browned.

768. Louisiana Shrimp Po Boy

Prep Time: 5 minutes
Cook Time: 10 minutes
Servings: 1-2

Ingredients:
• 1 tsp. creole seasoning
• 8 slices of tomato
• Lettuce leaves
• ¼ C. buttermilk
• ½ C. Louisiana Fish Fry
• 1 pound deveined shrimp

Remoulade sauce:
• 1 chopped green onion
• 1 tsp. hot sauce
• 1 tsp. Dijon mustard
• ½ tsp. creole seasoning
• 1 tsp. Worcestershire sauce
• Juice of ½ a lemon
• ½ C. vegan mayo

Directions:
1. To make the sauce, combine all sauce ingredients until well incorporated. Chill while you cook shrimp.
2. Mix seasonings together and liberally season shrimp.

3. Add buttermilk to a bowl. Dip each shrimp into milk and place in a Ziploc bag. Chill half an hour to marinate.
4. Add fish fry to a bowl. Take shrimp from marinating bag and dip into fish fry, then add to air fryer.
5. Ensure your air fryer is preheated to 400 degrees.
6. Spray shrimp with olive oil. Cook 5 minutes, flip and then cook another 5 minutes.
7. Assemble "Keto" Po Boy by adding sauce to lettuce leaves, along with shrimp and tomato.

769. Panko-Crusted Tilapia

Prep Time: 15 minutes
Cook Time: 11 minutes
Servings: 1

Ingredients:
• 2 tsp. Italian seasoning
• 2 tsp. lemon pepper
• 1/3 C. panko breadcrumbs
• 1/3 C. egg whites
• 1/3 C. almond flour
• 3 tilapia fillets
• Olive oil

Directions:
1. Place panko, egg whites, and flour into separate bowls. Mix lemon pepper and Italian seasoning in with breadcrumbs.
2. Pat tilapia fillets dry. Dredge in flour, then egg, then breadcrumb mixture. Add to air fryer basket and spray lightly with olive oil.
3. Cook 10-11 minutes at 400 degrees, making sure to flip halfway through cooking.

770. Bacon Wrapped Scallops

Prep Time: 15 minutes
Cook Time: 6 minutes
Servings: 1

Ingredients:
• 1 tsp. paprika
• 1 tsp. lemon pepper
• 5 slices of center-cut bacon
• 20 raw sea scallops

Directions:
1. Rinse and drain scallops, placing on paper towels to soak up excess moisture.
2. Cut slices of bacon into 4 pieces.
3. Wrap each scallop with a piece of bacon, using toothpicks to secure. Sprinkle wrapped scallops with paprika and lemon pepper.
4. Spray air fryer basket with olive oil and add scallops.
5. Cook 5-6 minutes at 400 degrees, making sure to flip halfway through.

771. Fried Sushi Roll

Prep Time: 15 minutes
Cook Time: 10 minutes
Servings: 3

Ingredients:
Kale Salad:
* 1 tbsp. sesame seeds
* ¾ tsp. soy sauce
* ¼ tsp. ginger
* 1/8 tsp. garlic powder
* ¾ tsp. toasted sesame oil
* ½ tsp. rice vinegar
* 1 ½ C. chopped kale

Sushi Rolls:
* ½ of a sliced avocado
* 3 sheets of sushi nori
* 1 batch cauliflower rice

Sriracha Mayo:
* Sriracha sauce
* ¼ C. vegan mayo

Coating:
* ½ C. panko breadcrumbs

Directions:
1. Combine all of kale salad ingredients together, tossing well. Set to the side.
2. Lay out a sheet of nori and spread a handful of rice on. Then place 2-3 tbsp. of kale salad over rice, followed by avocado. Roll up sushi.
3. To make mayo, whisk mayo ingredients together until smooth.
4. Add breadcrumbs to a bowl. Coat sushi rolls in crumbs till coated and add to air fryer.
5. Cook rolls 10 minutes at 390 degrees, shaking gently at 5 minutes.
6. Slice each roll into 6-8 pieces and enjoy!

772. Apple Dumplings

Prep Time: 15 minutes
Cook Time: 25 minutes
Servings: 2

Ingredients:
* 2 tbsp. melted coconut oil
* 2 puff pastry sheets
* 1 tbsp. brown sugar
* 2 tbsp. raisins
* 2 small apples of choice

Directions:
1. Ensure your air fryer is preheated to 356 degrees.
2. Core and peel apples and mix with raisins and sugar.
3. Place a bit of apple mixture into puff pastry sheets and brush sides with melted coconut oil.
4. Place into air fryer. Cook 25 minutes, turning halfway through. Will be golden when done.

773. Breaded Prawns

Prep Time: 15 minutes
Cook Time: 15 minutes
Servings: 3

Ingredients:
* 12 large prawns
* 3 tablespoons butter, melted
* 6 eggs
* Wheat flour to the point
* Salt to taste
* 1 tbsp. of virgin olive oil

Directions:
1. Cook the prawns in the air fryer at 320-degree F, and be careful not to cook them for about 10 minutes.
2. Then, peel the prawns and place them in the melted butter, resting.
3. Separate the 6 egg whites from yolks, beat the whites in the snow, then add the wheat flour until it sighs, season with salt and the spoon of oil.
4. Then, place the prawns in this pasta, and with a spoon, remove each shrimp, accompanied by a little pasta.
5. Put back in the air fryer for 5 minutes.

774. Thai Fish Cakes with Mango Salsa

Ingredients:
* 1 ripe mango, peeled
* 3 tbsp. fresh coriander or flat-leaf parsley
* 1½ tsp red chili paste
* Juice and zest of 1 lime
* 1 lb. white fish fillet (pollack, cod, pangasius, tilapia)
* 1 egg, beaten
* 1 green onion, finely chopped
* 2 oz. ground coconut

Directions:
1. Make sure that your air fryer is preheated to 375-degree F.
2. Cut the peeled mangoes into small cubes and blend them with a tablespoon of coriander, 1/2 teaspoon of red chili paste, juice, and half a lime zest in a cup.
3. Purée the fish and apply one shell, one teaspoon of salt, and the remaining lime zest, red chili paste, and lime juice to the food processor. Mix these with the remaining coriander, 2 tablespoons of coconut, and the green onion.
4. Get a clean plate of soup and move the rest of the coconut into this one. Out of the fish mixture, make 12 portions, with each part made into round cakes. Finally, coat the coconut with each cake.
5. In your air fryer basket, arrange six fish cakes and fry the fish cakes for about 7 minutes, or until the golden-brown color is visible. For the other fish cakes, do the same.
6. Take the fried cakes from the fish and serve with the mango salsa. Pandan rice and stir-fried pak choi can also be mixed with it.

211

775. Vegetable Supreme Pan Pizza

Prep Time: 15 minutes
Cook Time: 15 minutes
Servings: 3

Ingredients:
- 8 slice White Onion
- 12 slice Tomato
- 2 tablespoon olive oil
- 3/2 cup shredded mozzarella
- 8 Cremini mushrooms
- 1/2 green pepper
- 4 tablespoon Pesto
- 1 Pizza Dough
- 1 cup spinach

Directions:
1. Roll the pizza dough halves until they each meet the size of the Air Flow racks.
2. Grease all sides of each dough lightly with olive oil.
3. Put each pizza on a rack, and place the racks on the electric fryer's upper and lower shelves.
4. Press the power button and the cooking time to 13 minutes by pressing the French Fries button (400-degree F).
5. Flip the dough onto the top shelf after 5 minutes and switch the racks.
6. Switch the dough onto the top shelf after 4 minutes.
7. Take both racks out and drizzle the toppings with the pizzas.
8. Place the racks on the electric fryer's upper and lower shelves.
9. Then, push the power button and the cooking time to 7 minutes by pressing the French Fries button (400-degree F).
10. Rotate the pizzas after 4 minutes.
11. If the pizzas are done, let them rest for 4 minutes before cutting them.

776. Sticky BBQ Pork Strips

Prep Time: 15 minutes
Cook Time: 15 minutes
Servings: 2

Ingredients:
- 6 pcs pork loin chops
- Freshly ground pepper
- 2 tbsp. honey
- 2 tbsp. soy sauce
- 1 tsp balsamic vinegar
- ¼ tsp ground ginger (or ½ tsp freshly grated ginger)
- 1 garlic clove, chopped

Directions:
1. Ensure that the air fryer is preheated to 400-degree F.
2. Spray the air-fryer basket with cooking spray.
3. Mix the eggs and milk in a shallow cup.
4. Get another shallow bowl and put the pecans alongside the breadcrumbs.
5. Coat the pork chops with flour and shake to remove the excess flour.
6. Dip the coated pork chops in the egg and crumb mixture. Pat will occasionally ensure that the blends do not slip off. Also, you should work in batches if you have lots of pork chops.
7. Place the chops into a single sheet in the air fryer basket and lightly spray with the cooking spray.
8. Allow the pork chops to cook inside the air fryer for 12 to 15 minutes or until they become golden brown. After 6-7 minutes, turn the chops and spray gently again.
9. After cooking, depart and keep warm. Then cook the other chops.
10. While boiling, place the unused ingredients in a small saucepan and boil until the mixture is slightly thickened while stirring. This should, at maximum, take 6 to 8 minutes.
11. Serve the chops with butter.

777. Fried Chicken Drumettes

Prep Time: 15 minutes
Cook Time: 15 minutes
Servings: 2

Ingredients:
- 1½ lbs. chicken wing Drumettes
- Olive oil cooking spray
- 1 tbsp. lower-sodium soy sauce
- ½ tsp cornstarch
- 1 tsp finely chopped garlic
- ½ tsp finely chopped fresh ginger
- 1 tsp Sambal Oelek (ground fresh chili paste)
- 1/8 tsp kosher salt
- 1 tsp fresh lime juice
- 2 tsp honey
- 2 tbsp. chopped scallions

Directions:
1. Using paper towels, pat the rinsed chicken Drumettes dry and then brush with olive oil
2. Make sure the air fryer is preheated to 400-degree F.
3. Transfer the chicken Drumettes, keeping a single coat, to the air fryer.
4. Allow the air fryer to cook for 22 minutes, shaking two or three times.
5. When crispy, withdraw the Drumettes.
6. Take a clean saucepan and mix the soy sauce and cornstarch with the Drumettes in your air fryer.
7. Place the garlic, ginger, Sambal, salt, lime juice, and honey together.
8. Thoroughly swirl the blend and move to medium-high pressure.
9. Cook until the mixture has thickened and bubbles start to form.
10. Remove the Drumettes from the chicken and put them in a big bowl.
11. Over the Drumettes, pour the sauce mixture and stir mildly.
12. Before eating, add chopped scallions and toppings.

778. Pizza Dogs

Prep Time: 15 minutes
Cook Time: 7 minutes
Servings: 2

Ingredients:
- 2 hot dogs
- 4 slices pepperoni, halved
- ½ cup pizza sauce
- 2 hot dog buns
- ¼ cup shredded mozzarella cheese
- 2 tsp. sliced olives

Directions:
1. Ensure that your air fryer is heated to 200-degree F.
2. Cut four slits into each hot dog and position them in the air-fryer basket.
3. Allow cooking for 3 minutes before using tongs to pull on a cutting board.
4. In each of the slits in the hot dogs, put half the pepperoni. Divide the buns into the pizza sauce and fill them with the olives, hot dogs, and mozzarella cheese.
5. Place the hot dogs in the air-fryer basket and allow them to cook again.
6. When the cheese is melted, remove it, and the buns appear crisp, which takes about 2 minutes.

779. Fried Pizza Sticks

Prep Time: 15 minutes
Cook Time: 7 minutes
Servings: 2

Ingredients:
- 12 egg roll wrappers
- 36 slices pepperoni
- 12 pieces string cheese
- Oil for frying
- Marinara sauce for dipping

Directions:
1. The first step is to lay an egg roll wrapper out flat.
2. On the wrapper, lay three pieces of pepperoni towards the center on the diagonal.
3. Now, lay a mozzarella stick on top of the pepperoni.
4. Fold the corners of the egg wrapper down over the cheese, and then fold one or both larger corners down over the cheese. Once folded, start rolling the folded cheese until you have used up the entire wrapper.
5. Add drops of water to hold the edges shut. Do the same for the other 11 mozzarella sticks.
6. Transfer the wrapped mozzarella sticks into a deep-frying pan containing an already heated oil.
7. Now, fry the wrapped cheese for about a minute or until a golden-brown colour is on both sides.
8. Serve while hot, alongside marinara sauce for dipping.

780. Chicken Quesadillas

Prep Time: 10 minutes
Cook Time: 5 minutes
Servings: 2

Ingredients:
- Cooking spray
- Soft taco shells
- Mexican cheese, shredded
- Chicken fajita strips
- ½ cup onions, sliced
- ½ cup green peppers, sliced
- Sour cream, optional
- Salsa, optional

Directions:
1. Ensure that your air fryer is preheated to 370 F for 3 minutes, and spray the pan with some vegetable oil.
2. Get a pan and place one soft taco shell in it; add the shredded cheese to the shell.
3. Arrange the fajita chicken strips to form a single layer and add the onions and green peppers to the strips.
4. Add extra shredded cheese.
5. Now, place another soft taco shell on the top and spray with some vegetable oil. To hold the shell in place, put the rack that came with the air fryer on the top.
6. Set the air fryer timer for 4 minutes, and then change to the other side using a large spatula.
7. Spray again with vegetable oil and place the rack on the top of the shell to hold it in place.
8. Set the timer for four minutes.
9. If you want it to be crispier, let it stay a couple of additional minutes in the air fryer.
10. Remove when you are satisfied with the crispiness.
11. Now, cut into four or six slices.
12. Serve alongside sour cream and Salsa (not compulsory).

781. Healthy Chicken Tenders

Prep Time: 10 minutes
Cook Time: 10 minutes
Servings: 2

Ingredients:
- 12 oz. of chicken breasts
- Salt and ground black pepper to taste
- 1/8 cup flour
- 1 egg white
- 1¼ oz. panko bread crumbs

Directions:
1. Before you cut the chicken breast into tenders, remove excess fat by trimming. Use the combination of salt and pepper to season each side.
2. Get your flour, egg, and panko breadcrumbs

into different clean bowls.

3. Then dip the chicken tenders into flour, eggs, and panko breadcrumbs, respectively.

4. Arrange the coated chicken into the basket of your air fryer, and spray with olive spray.

5. Set your air fryer to 350-degree F and cook.

6. Let the chicken cook through – for about 10 minutes.

782. Thai Mango Chicken

Prep Time: 10 minutes
Cook Time: 15 minutes
Servings: 2

Ingredients:
- Mixed herbs chicken seasoning
- ½ mango, peeled and diced
- Salt and ground black pepper to taste
- Spicy chicken seasoning
- 1 tsp red Thai curry paste
- 2 tbsp. olive oil
- 1 lime rind and juice
- 2 chicken breasts

Directions:
1. Ensure that your air fryer is preheated to 355-degree F.

2. In a clean mixing cup, make a combination of your mixed spices, mango, salt, pepper, spicy chicken seasoning, Red Thai Curry Paste, olive oil, and lime. Ensure that you blend well so that the spice is spread equally in the mixture.

3. Cut slightly into your chicken with the help of your vegetable knife without the cut touching the bottom of the breasts.

4. In the mixing bowl, spray the seasoning mixture to ensure sufficient seasoning gets into the cuts.

5. On the baking mat, move the sprinkled chicken onto your air fryer. Then set the timer and allow it to cook for 15 minutes. Often check well to ensure that the chicken in the middle is well-cooked.

6. Serve with the cooked chicken and garnish with fresh tomatoes and extra lime.

783. Crusty Bread

Prep Time: 10 minutes
Cook Time: 6 minutes
Servings: 2

Ingredients:
- Stale or baked and frozen loaves of bread (various types)
- Sufficient water

Directions:
1. At the bottom of the container, scatter the loaves of bread and sprinkle a little water.

2. Select 400-degree F, close the lid, and set the time to 6 minutes.

3. Then serve the newly flavored crispy bread.

784. Empanadas Mini Sausages

Prep Time: 10 minutes
Cook Time: 11 minutes
Servings: 2

Ingredients:
- ½ lb. mini sausages
- 3 ½ oz. already prepared puff pastry (refrigerated or frozen, thawed)
- 1 tbsp. of mustard powder

Directions:
1. Preheat to 400-degree F with the fryer. Completely drain the sausages and gently pat dry on a sheet of paper towels.

2. Break the puff pastry into strips of 5 x 1½ cm and put a thin layer of powdered mustard over the strips. Wrap a spiral strip of dough for each sausage.

3. In the basket, put half the sausages covered in batter and slip them into the fryer.

4. Set the timer to 10-11 minutes, then bake until golden brown with the breaded sausages. In the same way, cook the leftover sausages. Serve the sausages, followed by a cup of mustard on a plate.

785. Halloween Cookie

Prep Time: 15 minutes
Cook Time: 10 minutes
Servings: 8

Ingredients:
- 1 cup butter at room temperature
- 1 cup granulated sugar
- 2 eggs
- 3 tsp vanilla
- 2 ¼ cups all-purpose flour
- 2 tsp baking powder
- ½ tsp salt

Directions:
1. To 350-degree F, preheat the air fryer.

2. Beat the butter and sugar using a hand mixer for about two minutes or before soft. Then scrape down the sides of the bowl.[S2]

3. Apply the vanilla and eggs and stir until well mixed.

4. Combine flour, baking powder, and salt. Mix until it is fully implemented; the dough will be messy.

5. Through a mug, spill the candy. Remove the cookie dough and put it on a granulated part of the cup. Then roll in the drizzled section of the dough until 1 cup of black and orange granules is filled. Next, reshape the dough into a ball before putting it on a baking sheet lined with parchment paper.

6. The cookies can scatter widely while cooking.

7. Bake for 10 minutes at 350-degree F.

214

786. Sweet Potato Hash

Prep Time: 15 minutes
Cook Time: 10 minutes
Servings: 8

Ingredients:
- 2 sweet potatoes, cubed
- 2 slices bacon, diced
- 2 tablespoons olive oil
- 1 tablespoon smoked paprika
- Salt and pepper to taste
- 1 teaspoon dried dill weed

Directions:
1. Pick the Air Fry configuration.
2. Preheat to 400 degrees F.
3. Combine all the ingredients in a bowl.
4. Pour it into a saucepan.
5. Set the air fryer in place.
6. Cook, stirring every 3 minutes, for 15 minutes.

787. KFC Chicken in the Air Fryer

Prep Time: 15 minutes
Cook Time: 18 minutes
Servings: 8

Ingredients:
- 1 whole chicken
- 1 oz. KFC spice blend
- 10 oz. bread crumbs
- 4 oz. plain flour
- 3 small eggs, beaten

Directions:
1. After chopping your chicken into pieces of desired sizes, set them aside.
2. You may separate the wings, things, drumsticks, breasts, or have the wings and the breast together.
3. Get a clean bowl, and make a mixture of the KFC spice and breadcrumbs.
4. Get another clean bowl and place your flour.
5. In a third clean bowl, place your beaten eggs.
6. After rolling the chicken pieces in the flour, roll it in the egg, and finally, in the spicy breadcrumbs.
7. Set your air fryer to 360-degree F and cook the rolled chicken for 18 minutes. Do not withdraw until it is well cooked in the middle. Then serve.

788. Barbeque Chicken Wings

Prep Time: 15 minutes
Cook Time: 18 minutes
Servings: 8

Ingredients:
- 2 tbsp. honey
- Salt and ground black pepper to taste
- BBQ chicken seasoning
- 1 tbsp. olive oil
- 1 lb. chicken wings

Directions:
1. Get a clean bowl, and in it, mix the honey, salt,

pepper, BBQ chicken seasoning, and olive oil.
2. Using the BBQ mixture, brush the chicken wings generously.
3. Ensure that your air fryer is preheated to 400-degree F.
4. Transfer the chicken wings into the air fryer while maintaining a single layer.
5. Allow frying for 18 minutes while turning the wings after 9 minutes.
6. Remove when both sides are fried.
7. Serve.

789. Panko Cheese Chicken

Prep Time: 10 minutes
Cook Time: 12 minutes
Servings: 4

Ingredients:
- 1 egg, whisked
- ½ cup all-purpose flour
- 1 teaspoon garlic powder
- 1 teaspoon cayenne pepper
- Sea salt and ground black pepper, to taste
- ¼ cup bread crumbs
- ¼ cup grated Parmesan cheese
- 1½ pounds (680 g) chicken breast, boneless, skinless, cut into strips

Directions:
1. Start by preheating the air fryer to 380°F (193°C).
2. Mix the egg and flour in a shallow bowl. In a separate bowl, whisk the garlic powder, cayenne pepper, salt, black pepper, bread crumbs, and Parmesan cheese.
3. Dip the chicken breasts into the egg mixture. Then, roll the chicken breasts over the bread crumb mixture.
4. Arrange the chicken in the crisper tray.
5. Place the crisper tray in the corresponding position in the air fryer. Select Air Fry and cook the chicken for 12 minutes, turning them over halfway through the cooking time.
6. Bon appétit!

790. Chicken Patties with Chili Sauce

Prep Time: 10 minutes
Cook Time: 17 minutes
Servings: 4

Ingredients:
- 1 pound (454 g) ground chicken
- 1 tablespoon olive oil
- 1 small onion, chopped
- 1 teaspoon minced garlic
- 1 tablespoon chili sauce
- Kosher salt and ground black pepper, to taste

Directions:
1. Start by preheating the air fryer to 380°F (193°C).
2. Mix all ingredients until everything is well combined. Form the mixture into four

patties.

3. Arrange the patties in the crisper tray.
4. Place the crisper tray in the corresponding position in the air fryer. Select Air Fry and cook the patties for about 17 minutes or until cooked through; make sure to turn them over halfway through the cooking time.
5. Bon appétit!

791. Chicken Salad with Cucumber

Prep Time: 10 minutes
Cook Time: 12 minutes
Servings: 4

Ingredients:
- 1 pound (454 g) chicken breasts, boneless, skinless
- 1 red onion, thinly sliced
- 1 bell pepper, sliced
- 4 Kalamata olives, pitted and minced
- 1 small Greek cucumber, grated and squeezed
- 4 tablespoons Greek yogurt
- 4 tablespoons mayonnaise
- 1 tablespoon fresh lemon juice
- Coarse sea salt and red pepper flakes, to taste

Direction:
1. Start by preheating the air fryer to 380°F (193°C).
2. Pat the chicken dry with paper towels. Place the chicken breasts in a lightly oiled crisper tray.
3. Place the crisper tray in the corresponding position in the air fryer. Select Roast and cook the chicken for 12 minutes, turning them over halfway through the cooking time.
4. Chop the chicken breasts and transfer it to a salad bowl; add in the remaining ingredients and toss to combine well.
5. Serve chilled.

792. Chicken Cheese Muffins

Prep Time: 5 minutes
Cook Time: 12 minutes
Servings: 4

Ingredients:
- 1 pound (454 g) chicken breasts
- 1 tablespoon olive oil
- Sea salt and black pepper, to taste
- 4 slices Cheddar cheese
- 4 teaspoons yellow mustard
- 4 English muffins, lightly toasted

Direction:
1. Start by preheating the air fryer to 380°F (193°C).
2. Pat the chicken dry with kitchen towels. Toss the chicken breasts with the olive oil, salt, and pepper. Place the chicken in the crisper tray.
3. Place the crisper tray in the corresponding position in the air fryer. Select Roast and cook the chicken for 12 minutes, turning them over halfway through the cooking time.
4. Shred the chicken using two forks and serve with cheese, mustard, and English muffins. Bon appétit!

793. Panko Chicken with Olives

Prep Time: 5 minutes
Cook Time: 12 minutes
Servings: 4

Ingredients:
- 1 pound (454 g) chicken fillets, boneless, skinless
- 2 eggs, whisked
- 1 teaspoon dried basil
- ½ teaspoon dried rosemary
- ½ teaspoon dried oregano
- ½ teaspoon crushed red pepper flakes
- ½ cup seasoned bread crumbs
- 2 ounces (57 g) Kalamata olives, pitted and sliced

Direction:
1. Start by preheating the air fryer to 380°F (193°C).
2. Pat the chicken dry with paper towels.
3. In a shallow bowl, thoroughly combine the eggs and spices.
4. Place the bread crumbs in a separate shallow bowl.
5. Dip the chicken fillets into the egg mixture. Then, roll the chicken fillets over the bread crumbs. Arrange the chicken fillets in the crisper tray.
6. Place the crisper tray in the corresponding position in the air fryer. Select Air Fry and cook the chicken fillets for 12 minutes, turning them over halfway through the cooking time.
7. Serve with Kalamata olives and enjoy!

794. Duck with Miso Paste

Prep Time: 5 minutes
Cook Time: 30 minutes
Servings: 5

Ingredients:
- 2 pounds (907 g) duck breasts
- 1 tablespoon butter, melted
- 2 tablespoons pomegranate molasses
- 2 tablespoons miso paste
- 1 teaspoon minced garlic
- 1 teaspoon peeled and minced ginger
- 1 teaspoon five-spice powder

Direction:
1. Start by preheating the air fryer to 330°F (166°C).
2. Pat the duck breasts dry with paper towels. Toss the duck breasts with the remaining ingredients. Place the duck breasts in the baking pan.
3. Place the baking pan in the corresponding position in the air fryer. Select Bake and cook the duck breasts for 15 minutes, turning them over halfway through the cooking time.
4. Increase the temperature to 350°F (180°C) and continue to cook for about 15 minutes or until cooked through.
5. Let it rest for 10 minutes before carving and serving. Bon appétit!

795. Chicken Fillets with Cheese

Prep Time: 5 minutes
Cook Time: 12 minutes
Servings: 5

Ingredients:
- 1½ pounds (680 g) chicken fillets
- 2 tablespoons olive oil
- 1 teaspoon smoked paprika
- 1 teaspoon Italian seasoning mix
- Sea salt and ground black pepper, to taste
- ½ cup grated Pecorino Romano cheese

Direction:
1. Start by preheating the air fryer to 380°F (193°C).
2. Pat the chicken fillets dry with paper towels. Toss the chicken fillets with the olive oil and spices. Place the chicken fillets in the crisper tray.
3. Place the crisper tray in the corresponding position in the air fryer. Select Air Fry and cook the chicken fillets for 12 minutes, turning them over halfway through the cooking time.
4. Top the chicken fillets with grated cheese and serve warm.
5. Bon appétit!

796. Chicken Cheese Tortilla

Prep Time: 5 minutes
Cook Time: 12 minutes
Servings: 5

Ingredients:
- 1 egg, whisked
- ½ cup grated Parmesan cheese
- ½ cup crushed tortilla chips
- ½ teaspoon onion powder
- ½ teaspoon garlic powder
- 1 teaspoon red chili powder
- 1½ pounds (680 g) chicken breasts, boneless, skinless, cut into strips

Direction:
1. Start by preheating the air fryer to 380°F (193°C).
2. Whisk the egg in a shallow bowl. In a separate bowl, whisk the Parmesan cheese, tortilla chips, onion powder, garlic powder, and red chili powder.
3. Dip the chicken pieces into the egg mixture. Then, roll the chicken pieces over the bread crumb mixture. Place the chicken in the crisper tray.
4. Place the crisper tray in the corresponding position in the air fryer. Select Air Fry and cook the chicken for 12 minutes, turning them over halfway through the cooking time.
5. Bon appétit!

797. Hot Chicken with Mustard

Prep Time: 5 minutes
Cook Time: 12 minutes
Servings: 5

Ingredients:
- ¾ pound (340 g) chicken breasts, boneless, skinless
- 1 teaspoon minced garlic
- ½ cup red wine
- ¼ cup hot sauce
- 1 tablespoon Dijon mustard
- Sea salt and cayenne pepper, to taste

Direction:
1. Place the chicken, garlic, red wine, hot sauce, and mustard in a ceramic bowl. Cover the bowl and let the chicken marinate for about 3 hours in the refrigerator.
2. Preheat the air fryer to 380°F (193°C).
3. Discard the marinade and place the chicken breasts in the crisper tray.
4. Place the crisper tray in the corresponding position in the air fryer. Select Roast and cook the chicken breasts for 12 minutes, turning them over halfway through the cooking time.
5. Season the chicken with the salt and cayenne pepper to taste.
6. Bon appétit!

798. Chicken Wings with Mustard

Prep Time: 5 minutes
Cook Time: 12 minutes
Servings: 5

Ingredients:
- ¾ pound (340 g) chicken wings, boneless
- 1 tablespoon butter, room temperature
- ½ teaspoon garlic powder
- ½ teaspoon shallot powder
- ½ teaspoon mustard powder

Direction:
1. Start by preheating the air fryer to 380°F (193°C).
2. Toss the chicken wings with the remaining ingredients.
3. Arrange the chicken wings in the crisper tray.
4. Place the crisper tray in the corresponding position in the air fryer. Select Air Fry and cook the chicken wings for 18 minutes, turning them over halfway through the cooking time.
5. Bon appétit!

799. Butter Chicken Fillets

Prep Time: 5 minutes
Cook Time: 12 minutes
Servings: 5

Ingredients:
- 1 pound (454 g) chicken fillets
- 2 tablespoons butter
- 2 bell peppers, seeded and sliced
- 1 teaspoon minced garlic
- Sea salt and ground black pepper, to taste
- 1 teaspoon red pepper flakes

Direction:
1. Start by preheating the air fryer to 380ºF (193ºC).
2. Toss the chicken fillets with the butter and place them in the crisper tray. Top the chicken with bell peppers, garlic, salt, black pepper, and red pepper flakes.
3. Place the crisper tray in the corresponding position in the air fryer. Select Air Fry and cook the chicken and peppers for 15 minutes, tossing crisper tray halfway through the cooking time.
4. Serve warm and enjoy!

800. Vanilla Pancake Cups

Prep Time: 5 minutes
Cook Time: 12 minutes
Servings: 5

Ingredients:
- ½ cup flour
- 2 eggs
- ⅓ cup coconut milk
- 1 tablespoon coconut oil, melted
- 1 teaspoon vanilla paste
- ¼ teaspoon ground cinnamon
- A pinch of ground cardamom

Direction:
1. Start by preheating the air fryer to 330ºF (166ºC).
2. Mix all the ingredients until well combined.
3. Let the batter stand for 20 minutes. Spoon the batter into a greased muffin tin. Transfer to the baking pan.
4. Place the baking pan in the corresponding position in the air fryer. Select Bake and cook for 4 to 5 minutes or until golden brown. Serve with toppings of choice.
5. Bon appétit!

801. Gulgulas with Yogurt

Prep Time: 5 minutes
Cook Time: 10 minutes
Servings: 4

Ingredients:
- ½ cup all-purpose flour
- ½ teaspoon baking powder
- ½ cup sugar
- ¼ teaspoon ground cardamom
- ¼ teaspoon sea salt
- 1 tablespoon ghee
- 2 eggs, whisked
- 2 tablespoons Indian yogurt

Direction:
1. Start by preheating the air fryer to 360ºF (182ºC).
2. In a mixing bowl, thoroughly combine all the ingredients.
3. Drop a spoonful of batter onto the greased baking pan.
4. Place the baking pan in the corresponding position in the air fryer. Select Bake and cook for 10 minutes, flipping them halfway through the cooking time.
5. Repeat with the remaining batter and serve warm. Enjoy!
6. Start by preheating the air fryer to 360ºF (182ºC).
7. In a mixing bowl, thoroughly combine all the ingredients.
8. Drop a spoonful of batter onto the greased baking pan.
9. Place the baking pan in the corresponding position in the air fryer. Select Bake and cook for 10 minutes, flipping them halfway through the cooking time.
10. Repeat with the remaining batter and serve warm. Enjoy!

802. Butter Toast

Prep Time: 5 minutes
Cook Time: 8 minutes
Servings: 3

Ingredients:
- ½ cup all-purpose flour
- ½ teaspoon baking powder
- ½ cup sugar
- ¼ teaspoon ground cardamom
- ¼ teaspoon sea salt
- 1 tablespoon ghee
- 2 eggs, whisked
- 2 tablespoons Indian yogurt

Direction:
1. Start by preheating the air fryer to 360ºF (182ºC).

2. In a mixing bowl, thoroughly combine all the ingredients.
3. Drop a spoonful of batter onto the greased baking pan.
4. Place the baking pan in the corresponding position in the air fryer. Select Bake and cook for 10 minutes, flipping them halfway through the cooking time.
5. Repeat with the remaining batter and serve warm. Enjoy!

809. Churros with Butter

Prep Time: 5 minutes
Cook Time: 20 minutes
Servings: 4

Ingredients:
* ¾ cup all-purpose flour
* ½ teaspoon baking powder
* ¾ cup water
* 4 tablespoons butter
* 1 tablespoon granulated sugar
* ½ teaspoon vanilla extract
* ½ teaspoon sea salt
* 1 large egg

Directions:
1. Start by preheating the air fryer to 360°F (182°C).
2. In a mixing bowl, thoroughly combine all ingredients. Place the batter in a piping bag fitted with a large open star tip.
3. Pipe the churros into 6-inch long ropes and lower them onto the greased baking pan.
4. Place the baking pan in the corresponding position in the air fryer. Select Bake and cook the churros for 10 minutes, flipping them halfway through the cooking time.
5. Repeat with the remaining batter and serve warm. Enjoy!

804. Shrimp, Chorizo Sausage, and Potatoes

Prep Time: 10 minutes
Cook Time: 15 minutes
Servings: 4

Ingredients:
* ½ red onion, chopped into 1-inch chunks
* 8 fingerling potatoes, sliced into 1-inch slices or halved lengthwise
* 1 teaspoon olive oil
* Salt and freshly ground black pepper
* 8 ounces (227 g) raw chorizo sausage, sliced into 1-inch chunks
* 16 raw large shrimp, peeled, deveined and tails removed
* 1 lime
* ¼ cup chopped fresh cilantro

* Chopped orange zest (optional)

Direction:
1. Combine the red onion and potato chunks in a bowl and toss with the olive oil, salt and freshly ground black pepper.
2. Transfer the vegetables to the air fryer basket. Select the AIR FRY function and cook at 380°F (193°C) for 6 minutes, shaking the basket a few times during the cooking process.
3. Add the chorizo chunks and continue to air fry for another 5 minutes.
4. Add the shrimp, season with salt and continue to air fry, shaking the basket every once in a while, for another 5 minutes.
5. Transfer the tossed shrimp, chorizo and potato to a bowl and squeeze some lime juice over the top to taste. Toss in the fresh cilantro, orange zest and a drizzle of olive oil, and season again to taste.
6. Serve with a fresh green salad.

805. Shrimp Spring Rolls

Prep Time: 10 minutes
Cook Time: 17 minutes
Servings: 4

Ingredients:
* 2 teaspoons minced garlic
* 2 cups finely sliced cabbage
* 1 cup matchstick cut carrots
* 2 (4-ounce / 113-g) cans tiny shrimp, drained
* 4 teaspoons soy sauce
* Salt and freshly ground black pepper, to taste
* 16 square spring roll wrappers
* Cooking spray

Direction:
1. Spray the air fryer basket lightly with cooking spray. Spray a medium sauté pan with cooking spray.
2. Add the garlic to the sauté pan and cook over medium heat until fragrant, 30 to 45 seconds. Add the cabbage and carrots and sauté until the vegetables are slightly tender, about 5 minutes.
3. Add the shrimp and soy sauce and season with salt and pepper, then stir to combine. Sauté until the moisture has evaporated, 2 more minutes. Set aside to cool.
4. Place a spring roll wrapper on a work surface so it looks like a diamond. Place 1 tablespoon of the shrimp mixture on the lower end of the wrapper.
5. Roll the wrapper away from you halfway, then fold in the right and left sides, like an envelope. Continue to roll to the very end, using a little water to seal the edge. Repeat with the remaining wrappers and filling.
6. Place the spring rolls in the air fryer basket in a single layer, leaving room between each roll. Lightly spray with cooking spray. You may need to cook them in batches.
7. Select the AIR FRY function and cook at 370°F (188°C) for 5 minutes. Turn the rolls over, lightly spray with cooking spray, and air fry until heated through and the rolls start to brown, 5 to 10 more minutes. Cool for 5 minutes before serving.

219

806. Baja Tilapia Tacos

Prep Time: 15 minutes
Cook Time: 10 minutes
Servings: 4

Ingredients:
Fried Fish:
- 1 pound (454 g) tilapia fillets (or other mild white fish)
- ½ cup all-purpose flour
- 1 teaspoon garlic powder
- 1 teaspoon kosher salt
- ¼ teaspoon cayenne pepper
- ½ cup mayonnaise
- 3 tablespoons milk
- 1¾ cups panko bread crumbs
- Vegetable oil, for spraying

Tacos:
- 8 corn tortillas
- ¼ head red or green cabbage, shredded
- 1 ripe avocado, halved and each half cut into 4 slices
- 12 ounces (340 g) pico de gallo or other fresh salsa
- Dollop of Mexican crema
- 1 lime, cut into wedges

Direction:
1. To make the fish, cut the fish fillets into strips 3 to 4 inches long and 1 inch wide. Combine the flour, garlic powder, salt, and cayenne pepper on a plate and whisk to combine. In a shallow bowl, whisk the mayonnaise and milk together. Place the panko on a separate plate. Dredge the fish strips in the seasoned flour, shaking off any excess. Dip the strips in the mayonnaise mixture, coating them completely, then dredge in the panko, shaking off any excess. Place the fish strips on a plate or rack.
2. Working in batches, spray half the fish strips with oil and arrange them in the air fryer basket, taking care not to crowd them. Select the AIR FRY function and cook at 400°F (204°C) for 4 minutes, then flip and air fry for another 3 to 4 minutes until the outside is brown and crisp and the inside is opaque and flakes easily with a fork. Repeat with the remaining strips.
3. Heat the tortillas in the microwave or on the stovetop. To assemble the tacos, place 2 fish strips inside each tortilla. Top with shredded cabbage, a slice of avocado, pico de gallo, and a dollop of crema. Serve with a lime wedge on the side.

807. Mayo Salmon Burgers

Prep Time: 10 minutes
Cook Time: 15 minutes
Servings: 4

Ingredients:
- 4 (5-ounce / 142-g) cans pink salmon in water, any skin and bones removed, drained
- 2 eggs, beaten
- 1 cup whole-wheat bread crumbs
- 4 tablespoons light mayonnaise
- 2 teaspoons Cajun seasoning
- 2 teaspoons dry mustard
- 4 whole-wheat buns
- Cooking spray

Direction:
1. In a medium bowl, mix the salmon, egg, bread crumbs, mayonnaise, Cajun seasoning, and dry mustard. Cover with plastic wrap and refrigerate for 30 minutes.
2. Spray the air fryer basket lightly with cooking spray.
3. Shape the mixture into four ½-inch-thick patties about the same size as the buns.
4. Place the salmon patties in the air fryer basket in a single layer and lightly spray the tops with cooking spray. You may need to cook them in batches.
5. Select the AIR FRY function and cook at 360°F (182°C) for 6 to 8 minutes. Turn the patties over and lightly spray with cooking spray. Air fry until crispy on the outside, 4 to 7 more minutes.
6. Serve on whole-wheat buns.

808. Crispy Shrimp Empanadas

Prep Time: 10 minutes
Cook Time: 15 minutes
Servings: 4

Ingredients:
- ½ pound (227g) raw shrimp, peeled, deveined and chopped
- ¼ cup chopped red onion
- 1 scallion, chopped
- 2 garlic cloves, minced
- 2 tablespoons minced red bell pepper
- 2 tablespoons chopped fresh cilantro
- ½ tablespoon fresh lime juice
- ¼ teaspoon sweet paprika
- ⅛ teaspoon kosher salt
- ⅛ teaspoon crushed red pepper flakes (optional)
- 1 large egg, beaten
- 10 frozen Goya Empanada Discos, thawed
- Cooking spray

Directions:
1. In a medium bowl, combine the shrimp, red onion, scallion, garlic, bell pepper, cilantro, lime juice, paprika, salt, and pepper flakes (if using).
2. In a small bowl, beat the egg with 1 teaspoon water until smooth.
3. Place an empanada disc on a work surface and put 2 tablespoons of the shrimp mixture in the center. Brush the outer edges of the disc with the egg wash. Fold the disc over and gently press the edges to seal. Use a fork and press around the edges to crimp and seal completely. Brush the tops of the empanadas with the egg wash.
4. Spray the bottom of the air fryer basket with cooking spray to prevent sticking. Working in batches, arrange a single layer of the empanadas in the air fryer basket. Select the AIR FRY function and cook at 380°F (193°C) for 8 minutes, flipping halfway, until golden brown and crispy.
5. Serve hot.

809. Golden Trout Fingers

Prep Time: 15 minutes
Cook Time: 6 minutes
Servings: 4

Ingredients:
- ½ cup yellow cornmeal, medium or finely ground (not coarse)
- ⅓ cup all-purpose flour
- 1½ teaspoons baking powder
- 1 teaspoon kosher salt, plus more as needed
- ½ teaspoon freshly ground black pepper, plus more as needed
- ⅛ teaspoon cayenne pepper
- ¾ pound (340 g) skinless trout fillets, cut into strips 1 inch wide and 3 inches long
- 3 large eggs, lightly beaten
- Cooking spray
- ½ cup mayonnaise
- 2 tablespoons capers, rinsed and finely chopped
- 1 tablespoon fresh tarragon
- 1 teaspoon fresh lemon juice, plus lemon wedges, for serving

Direction:
1. In a large bowl, whisk together the cornmeal, flour, baking powder, salt, black pepper, and cayenne. Dip the trout strips in the egg, then toss them in the cornmeal mixture until fully coated. Transfer the trout to a rack set over a baking sheet and liberally spray all over with cooking spray.
2. Transfer half the fish to the air fryer oven. Select the AIR FRY function and cook at 400ºF (204ºC) for 6 minutes, or until the fish is cooked through and golden brown. Transfer the fish sticks to a plate and repeat with the remaining fish.
3. Meanwhile, in a bowl, whisk together the mayonnaise, capers, tarragon, and lemon juice. Season the tartar sauce with salt and black pepper.
4. Serve the trout fingers hot along with the tartar sauce and lemon wedges.

810. Crab Cakes with Lush Salad

Prep Time: 10 minutes
Cook Time: 13 minutes
Servings: 2

Ingredients:
- 8 ounces (227 g) lump crab meat, picked over for shells
- 2 tablespoons panko bread crumbs
- 1 scallion, minced
- 1 large egg
- 1 tablespoon mayonnaise
- 1½ teaspoons Dijon mustard
- Pinch of cayenne pepper
- 2 shallots, sliced thin
- 1 tablespoon extra-virgin olive oil, divided
- 1 teaspoon lemon juice, plus lemon wedges for serving
- ⅛ teaspoon salt
- Pinch of pepper
- ½ (3-ounce / 85-g) small head Bibb lettuce, torn into bite-size pieces
- ½ apple, cored and sliced thin

Directions:
1. Line large plate with triple layer of paper towels. Transfer crab meat to prepared plate and pat dry with additional paper towels. Combine panko, scallion, egg, mayonnaise, mustard, and cayenne in a bowl. Using a rubber spatula, gently fold in crab meat until combined; discard paper towels. Divide crab mixture into 4 tightly packed balls, then flatten each into 1- inch-thick cake (cakes will be delicate). Transfer cakes to plate and refrigerate until firm, about 10 minutes.
2. Toss shallots with ½ teaspoon oil in separate bowl; transfer to air fryer basket. Select the AIR FRY function and cook at
3. 400ºF (204ºC) for 5 to 7 minutes, or until shallots are browned, tossing once halfway through cooking. Return shallots to now-empty bowl and set aside.
4. Arrange crab cakes in air fryer basket, spaced evenly apart.
5. Return basket to air fryer oven and air fry until crab cakes are light golden brown on both sides, 8 to 10 minutes, flipping and rotating cakes halfway through cooking.
6. Meanwhile, whisk remaining 2½ teaspoons oil, lemon juice, salt, and pepper together in large bowl. Add lettuce, apple, and shallots and toss to coat. Serve crab cakes with salad, passing lemon wedges separately.

811. Old Bay Crawfish

Prep Time: 15 minutes
Cook Time: 18 minutes
Servings: 4

Ingredients:
- ½ cup flour, plus 2 tablespoons
- ½ teaspoon garlic powder
- 1½ teaspoons Old Bay Seasoning
- ½ teaspoon onion powder
- ½ cup beer, plus 2 tablespoons
- 1 (12-ounce / 340-g) package frozen crawfish tail meat, thawed and drained
- Oil for misting or cooking spray

Coating:
- 1½ cups panko crumbs
- 1 teaspoon Old Bay Seasoning
- ½ teaspoon ground black pepper

Direction:
1. In a large bowl, mix together the flour, garlic powder, Old Bay Seasoning, and onion powder. Stir in beer to blend.
2. Add crawfish meat to batter and stir to coat.
3. Combine the coating ingredients in food processor and pulse to finely crush the

221

crumbs. Transfer crumbs to shallow dish.

4. Pour the crawfish and batter into a colander to drain. Stir with a spoon to drain excess batter.
5. Working with a handful of crawfish at a time, roll in crumbs and place on a cookie sheet. It's okay if some of the smaller pieces of crawfish meat stick together.
6. Spray breaded crawfish with oil or cooking spray and place all at once into air fryer basket.
7. Select the AIR FRY function and cook at 390°F (199°C) for 5 minutes. Shake basket or stir and mist again with olive oil or spray. Air fry for 5 more minutes, shake basket again, and mist lightly again. Continue cooking for 3 to 5 more minutes, until browned and crispy.

812. Fish Sticks

Prep Time: 15 minutes
Cook Time: 15 minutes
Servings: 4

Ingredients:
- 4 fish fillets
- ½ cup whole-wheat flour
- 1 teaspoon seasoned salt
- 2 eggs
- 1½ cups whole-wheat panko bread crumbs
- ½ tablespoon dried parsley flakes
- Cooking spray

Diections:
1. Spray the air fryer basket lightly with cooking spray.
2. Cut the fish fillets lengthwise into "sticks."
3. In a shallow bowl, mix the whole-wheat flour and seasoned salt.
4. In a small bowl, whisk the eggs with 1 teaspoon of water.
5. In another shallow bowl, mix the panko bread crumbs and parsley flakes.
6. Coat each fish stick in the seasoned flour, then in the egg mixture, and dredge them in the panko bread crumbs.
7. Place the fish sticks in the air fryer basket in a single layer and lightly spray the fish sticks with cooking spray. You may need to cook them in batches.
8. Select the AIR FRY function and cook at 400°F (204°C) for 5 to 8 minutes. Flip the fish sticks over and lightly spray with the cooking spray. Air fry until golden brown and crispy, 5 to 7 more minutes.
9. Serve warm.

813. Carne Asada Tacos

Prep Time: 5 minutes
Cook Time: 14 minutes
Servings: 4

Ingredients:
- ⅓ cup olive oil
- 1½ pounds (680 g) flank steak
- Salt and freshly ground black pepper, to taste
- ⅓ cup freshly squeezed lime juice
- ½ cup chopped fresh cilantro
- 4 teaspoons minced garlic
- 1 teaspoon ground cumin
- 1 teaspoon chili powder

Directions:
1. Brush the air fryer basket with olive oil.
2. Put the flank steak in a large mixing bowl. Season with salt and pepper.
3. Add the lime juice, cilantro, garlic, cumin, and chili powder and toss to coat the steak.
4. For the best flavor, let the steak marinate in the refrigerator for about 1 hour.
5. Put the steak in the air fryer basket. Select the AIR FRY function and cook at 400°F (204°C) for 7 minutes. Flip the steak. Air fry for 7 minutes more or until an internal temperature reaches at least 145°F (63°C).
6. Let the steak rest for about 5 minutes, then cut into strips to serve.

814. Cantonese Char Siew

Prep Time: 10 minutes
Cook Time: 20 minutes
Servings: 4

Ingredients:
- 1 strip of pork shoulder butt with a good amount of fat marbling
- Olive oil, for brushing the pan

Marinade:
- 1 teaspoon sesame oil
- 4 tablespoons raw honey
- 1 teaspoon low-sodium dark soy sauce
- 1 teaspoon light soy sauce
- 1 tablespoon rose wine
- 2 tablespoons Hoisin sauce

Directions:
1. Combine all the marinade ingredients together in a Ziploc bag. Put pork in bag, making sure all sections of pork strip are engulfed in the marinade. Chill for 3 to 24 hours.
2. Take out the strip 30 minutes before planning to roast.
3. Select the ROAST function and preheat MAXX to 350°F (177°C).
4. Put foil on small pan and brush with olive oil. Put marinated pork strip onto prepared pan.
5. Roast in the preheated air fryer oven for 20 minutes.
6. Glaze with marinade every 5 to 10 minutes.
7. Remove strip and leave to cool a few minutes before slicing.
8. Serve immediately.

815. American Beef Cheeseburgers

Prep Time: 10 minutes
Cook Time: 19 minutes
Servings: 2

Ingredients:
- ½ slice hearty white sandwich bread, crust removed, torn into ¼- inch pieces
- 1 tablespoon milk
- ½ teaspoon garlic powder
- ½ teaspoon onion powder
- 12 ounces (340 g) 85% lean ground beef
- Salt and pepper
- 2 slices American cheese (2 ounces / 57 g)
- 2 hamburger buns, toasted if desired

Directions:
1. Mash bread, milk, garlic powder, and onion powder into paste in medium bowl using fork. Break up ground beef into small pieces over bread mixture in bowl and lightly knead with hands until well combined. Divide mixture into 2 lightly packed balls, then gently flatten each into 1-inch-thick patty. Press center of each patty with fingertips to create ¼-inch-deep depression. Season with salt and pepper.
2. Arrange patties in air fryer basket, spaced evenly apart. Place basket in air fryer oven. Select the AIR FRY function and cook at 350°F (180°C) for 18 to 21 minutes, or until burgers are lightly browned and register 140°F (60°C) to 145°F (63°C) (for medium-well) or 150°F (66°C) to 155°F (68°C) (for well- done), flipping and rotating burgers halfway through cooking.
3. Top each burger with 1 slice cheese. Return basket to air fryer oven and cook until cheese is melted, about 30 seconds. Serve burgers on buns.

816. Maple Brussels Sprouts

Prep Time: 5 minutes
Cook Time: 13 minutes
Servings: 2

Ingredients:
- 2 cups Brussels sprouts, halved
- 1 tablespoon olive oil
- 1 tablespoon balsamic vinegar
- 1 tablespoon maple syrup
- ¼ teaspoon sea salt

Directions:
1. Evenly coat the Brussels sprouts with the olive oil, balsamic vinegar, maple syrup, and salt.
2. Transfer to the air fryer basket. Select the AIR FRY function and cook at 375°F (191°C) for 5 minutes.
3. Give the basket a good shake, turn the heat to 400°F (204°C) and continue to air fry for another 8 minutes.
4. Serve hot.

817. Eggplant and Rice Bowl

Prep Time: 15 minutes
Cook Time: 10 minutes
Servings: 4

Ingredients:
- ¼ cup sliced cucumber
- 1 teaspoon salt
- 1 tablespoon sugar
- 7 tablespoons Japanese rice vinegar
- 3 medium eggplants, sliced
- 3 tablespoons sweet white miso paste
- 1 tablespoon mirin rice wine
- 4 cups cooked sushi rice
- 4 spring onions
- 1 tablespoon toasted sesame seeds

Directions:
1. Coat the cucumber slices with the rice wine vinegar, salt, and sugar.
2. Put a dish on top of the bowl to weight it down completely.
3. In a bowl, mix the eggplants, mirin rice wine, and miso paste.
4. Allow to marinate for half an hour.
5. Put the eggplant slices in the air fryer oven. Select the AIR FRY function and cook at 400°F (204°C) for 10 minutes.
6. Fill the bottom of a serving bowl with rice and top with the eggplants and pickled cucumbers.
7. Add the spring onions and sesame seeds for garnish. Serve immediately.

818. Cream sausage

Preparation time: 8-10 min.
Cooking time: 20 min.
Servings: 2-3

Ingredients
- 2 cooked sausages, sliced
- 1 bread slice, make sticks
- ¼ cup cream
- 3 eggs
- ¼ cup mozzarella cheese, grated

Directions
1. Place your air fryer on a flat kitchen surface; plug it and turn it on. Set temperature to 355 degrees f and let it preheat for 4-5 minutes.
2. Take 2 ramekins and gently grease them.
3. In a bowl of medium size, thoroughly whisk the cream and eggs. Add the egg mixture into ramekins.
4. Arrange the sausage slices and bread sticks around the edges; add them in the egg mixture.
5. Top with the cheese evenly. Add the ramekins in the basket.
6. Push the air-frying basket in the air fryer. Let your air fryer cook the added mixture for the next 20 minutes.
7. Slide out the basket; serve warm!

819. Cloud eggs

Preparation time: 7 minutes
Cooking time: 7 minutes
Servings: 2

INGREDIENTS
- 2 eggs, whites, and yolks separated
- Pinch of salt
- Pinch of freshly ground black pepper
- 2 bread slices, toasted

DIRECTIONS
1. In a bowl, add the egg white, salt, and black pepper and beat until stiff peaks form.
2. Line a baking pan with parchment paper.
3. Carefully, make a pocket in the center of each egg white circle.
4. Place the oven rack at the top position of the air fryer and press preheat.
5. Select start/cancel to begin preheating.
6. When ready, place the baking pan on top of the rack.
7. Bake for 7 minutes at 350 °f
8. Place 1 egg yolk into each egg white pocket after 5 minutes of Cooking.
9. Serve alongside toasted bread slices.

820. Homemade giant pancake

Preparation time: 15 minutes
Cooking time: 15 minutes
Servings: 6

INGREDIENTS
- 3 cups all-purpose flour
- ¾ cup Sugar
- 5 eggs
- ⅓ cup olive oil
- ⅓ cup sparkling water
- ⅓ tsp salt
- 1 ½ tsp baking soda
- 2 tbsp maple syrup
- A dollop of whipped cream to serve

DIRECTIONS
1. Start by pouring the flour, Sugar, eggs, olive oil, sparkling water, salt, and baking soda into a food processor and blend until smooth.
2. Pour the batter into the cooker and let it sit in there for 15 minutes. Close the lid and secure the pressure valve.
3. Select the pressure mode on low pressure for 10 minutes.
4. Press start.
5. Once the timer goes off, press cancel, quick release the pressure valve to let out any steam and open the lid.
6. Gently run a spatula around the pancake to let lose any sticking.
7. Once ready, slide the pancake onto a serving plate and drizzle with maple syrup. Top with the whipped cream to serve.

821. Oregano squash

Preparation time: 5-10 minutes
Cooking time: 16 minutes
Servings: 4

INGREDIENTS
- 1 medium squash peeled, seeded butternut, cut into 1/2-inch slices
- 1 tablespoon olive oil
- 1 and 1/2 teaspoons oregano, dried
- 1 teaspoon thyme, dried
- 1/2 teaspoon salt
- 1/4 teaspoon black pepper

DIRECTIONS
1. Take a mixing bowl and add all Ingredients, combine well
2. Arrange the grill grate and close the lid
3. Pre-heat ninja foodi by pressing the "grill" option and setting it to "med" and timer to 16 minutes
4. Let it pre-heat until you hear a beep
5. Arrange the squash slices over the grill grate, lock lid and cook for 8 minutes
6. Flip them and close the lid, cook for 8 minutes more
7. Serve warm and enjoy!

822. Bacon and tomato omelet

Preparation time: 10 minutes
Cooking time: 10 minutes
Servings: 4

INGREDIENTS
- 4 whole eggs, whisked
- 1 tablespoon cheddar, grated
- 1/4-pound bacon, cooked and chopped
- 4 tomatoes, cubed
- 1 tablespoon parsley, chopped
- 1 tablespoon olive oil
- Salt and pepper to taste

DIRECTIONS
1. Take a small pan and place it over medium heat, add bacon and sauté for 2 minutes until crisp
2. Take a bowl and add bacon, add remaining Ingredients and gently stir. Sprinkle cheese on top
3. Pre-heat ninja foodi by pressing the "bake" option and setting it to "400 degrees f" and timer to 10 minutes
4. Let it pre-heat until you hear a beep
5. Pour mixture into a baking dish and transfer baking dish inside ninja foodi grill, let it bake for 8 minutes
6. Serve and enjoy!

823. French pineapple toast

Preparation time: 10 minutes
Cooking time: 15 minutes
Servings: 4

INGREDIENTS
- 10 bread slices
- 1/4 cup of Sugar
- 1/4 cup milk
- 3 large whole eggs
- 1 cup of coconut milk
- 10 slices pineapple, peeled
- 1/2 cup coconut flakes
- Cooking spray as needed

DIRECTIONS
1. Take a mixing bowl and whisk in coconut milk, Sugar, eggs, milk and stir well
2. Dup breads in the mixture and keep the mon the side for 2 minutes
3. Pre-heat ninja foodi by pressing the "grill" option and setting it to "med" and timer to 15 minutes
4. Let it pre-heat until you hear a beep
5. Arrange bread slices over grill grate, lock lid and cook for 2 minutes. Flip and cook for 2 minutes more, let them cook until the timer reads 0
6. Repeat with remaining slices, serve and enjoy!

824. Fresh chicken mix

Preparation time: 10 minutes
Cooking time: 22 minutes
Servings: 4

INGREDIENTS
- 2 chicken breasts, skinless, boneless and cubed
- 8 button mushrooms, sliced
- 1 red bell pepper, chopped
- 1 tablespoon olive oil
- ½ teaspoon thyme, dried
- 10 ounces alfredo sauce
- 6 bread slices
- 2 tablespoons butter, soft

DIRECTIONS
1. In your air fryer, mix chicken with mushrooms, bell pepper and oil, toss to coat well and cook at 350 degrees f for 15 minutes.
2. Transfer chicken mix to a bowl, add thyme and alfredo sauce, toss, return to air fryer and cook at 350 degrees F for 4 minutes more.
3. Spread butter on bread slices, add it to the fryer, butter side up and cook for 4 minutes more.
4. Arrange toasted bread slices on a platter, top each with chicken mix.

825. Tasty okra

Preparation time: 10 minutes
Cooking time: 12 minutes
Servings: 2

INGREDIENTS
- 1/2 lb. Okra, ends trimmed and sliced
- 1 tsp olive oil
- 1/2 tsp mango powder
- 1/2 tsp chili powder
- 1/2 tsp ground coriander
- 1/2 tsp ground cumin
- 1/8 tsp pepper
- 1/4 tsp salt

DIRECTIONS
1. Preheat the air fryer to 350 f.
2. Add all Ingredients into the large bowl and toss well.
3. Spray air fryer basket with cooking spray.
4. Transfer okra mixture into the air fryer basket and cook for 10 minutes. Shake basket halfway through.
5. Toss okra well and cook for 2 minutes more.
6. Serve and enjoy.

826. Cabbage wedges

Preparation time: 10 minutes
Cooking time: 14 minutes
Servings: 2

INGREDIENTS
- 1 small cabbage head, cut into wedges
- 3 tbsp olive oil
- 1/4 tsp red chili flakes
- 1/2 tsp fennel seeds
- 1 tsp garlic powder
- 1 tsp onion powder
- Pepper
- Salt

DIRECTIONS
1. Spray air fryer basket with cooking spray.
2. In a small bowl, mix together garlic powder, red chili flakes, fennel seeds, onion powder, pepper, and salt.
3. Coat cabbage wedges with oil and rub with garlic powder mixture.
4. Place cabbage wedges into the air fryer basket and cook at 400 F for 8 minutes.
5. Turn cabbage wedges to another side and cook for 6 minutes more.
6. Serve and enjoy.

225

827. Beef curry

Preparation time: 5 minutes
Cooking time: 35 minutes
Servings: 2

INGREDIENTS
- 2 pounds cubed beef
- 2 tablespoons olive oil
- 3 potatoes, diced
- 1 tomato, cubed
- 2½ tablespoons curry powder
- 2 yellow onions, chopped
- 2 garlic cloves, minced
- 10 ounces coconut milk
- Salt and black pepper to taste

DIRECTIONS
1. In a pan that fits your air fryer, heat up the oil over medium heat.
2. Add the meat and brown it for 2-3 minutes.
3. Then add the potatoes, tomato, curry powder, onions, garlic, salt, and pepper; toss, and cook for 2 more minutes.
4. Transfer the pan to your air fryer and cook at 380 degrees f for 25 minutes.
5. Add the coconut milk, toss, and cook for 5 minutes more.
6. Divide everything into bowls, serve, and enjoy.

828. Beef short ribs

Preparation time: 10 minutes
Cooking time: 35 minutes
Servings: 2

INGREDIENTS
- 1 2/3 lbs. Short ribs
- Salt and black pepper, to taste
- 1 teaspoon grated garlic
- 1/2 teaspoon salt
- 1 teaspoon cumin seeds
- ¼ cup panko crumbs
- 1 teaspoon ground cumin
- 1 teaspoon avocado oil
- ½ teaspoon orange zest
- 1 egg, beaten

DIRECTIONS
1. Place the beef ribs in a baking tray and pour the whisked egg on top.
2. Whisk rest of the crusting Ingredients in a bowl and spread over the beef.
3. Press "power button" of air fry oven and turn the dial to select the "air fry" mode.
4. Press the time button and again turn the dial to set the Cooking time to 35 minutes.
5. Now push the temp button and rotate the dial to set the temperature at 350 degrees F.
6. Once preheated, place the beef baking tray in the oven and close its lid.
7. Serve warm.

829. Tomato kebabs

Preparation time: 10 minutes
Cooking time: 6 minutes
Servings: 12

INGREDIENTS
- 3 tablespoon balsamic vinegar
- 24 cherry tomatoes
- 2 tablespoon olive oil
- 3 garlic cloves; minced
- 1 tablespoon thyme; chopped
- Salt and black pepper to the taste
- For the dressing:
- 2 tablespoon balsamic vinegar
- 4 tablespoon olive oil
- Salt and black pepper to the taste

DIRECTIONS
1. Take a medium bowl and add 2 tablespoon oil, 3 garlic cloves, thyme, salt, 2 tablespoon vinegar, and black pepper in it. Mix well, then toss in tomatoes and coat them liberally. Thread 6 tomatoes on each skewer.
2. Place these skewers in the air fryer basket inside the instant pot. Put on the instant air fryer lid and cook on air fry mode for 6 minutes at 360 degrees f. Once done, remove the lid and serve warm. Meanwhile, whisk 2 tablespoon vinegar with pepper, salt, and 4 tablespoon oil. Place the cooked skewers in the serving plates. Pour the vinegar dressing over them. Enjoy.

830. Saucy artichokes

Preparation time: 10 minutes
Cooking time: 6 minutes
Servings: 4

INGREDIENTS
- 2 artichokes; trimmed
- 1 tablespoon lemon juice
- 2 garlic cloves; minced
- A drizzle olive oil
For the sauce:
- 3 anchovy fillets
- 1/4 cup extra virgin olive oil
- 1/4 cup coconut oil
- 3 garlic cloves

DIRECTIONS
1. Toss artichokes with lemon juice, oil and 2 garlic cloves in a large bowl. Place the seasoned artichokes in the air fryer basket inside the instant pot. Put on the instant air fryer lid and cook on air fry mode for 6 minutes at 350 degrees f. Blend coconut oil with olive oil, anchovy and 3 garlic cloves in a food processor.
2. Place the artichokes in the serving plates. Pour the anchovy mixture over the artichokes. Enjoy fresh.

831. Mushroom cream pie

Preparation time: 10 minutes
Cooking time: 50 minutes
Servings: 6

INGREDIENTS
- 4 eggs
- 2 tablespoon parmesan cheese, grated
- 2 oz fresh spinach
- 2 teaspoon olive oil
- 1 teaspoon garlic, minced
- 4 oz mushrooms, sliced
- 1/2 cup mozzarella cheese, shredded
- 1/4 teaspoon nutmeg
- 1/2 teaspoon pepper
- 1/2 cup heavy cream
- 16 oz cottage cheese
- 1 teaspoon salt

DIRECTIONS
1. Heat oil in a suitable pan over moderate heat. Toss in garlic and mushrooms and sauté until soft. Stir in salt, black pepper, nutmeg, and spinach. Drain this mushrooms spinach mixture then adds spread it into a suitable pie dish. Whisk eggs with cream and cottage cheese in a bowl. Pour this egg mixture over the mushrooms and top it with cheese.
2. Place the mushroom pie in the instant pot. Put on the instant air fryer lid and cook on bake mode for 50 minutes at 350 degrees f. Once done, remove the lid and serve warm.

832. Spinach lentil

Preparation time: 10 mins
Cooking time: 12 mins
Servings: 3

INGREDIENTS
- ½ cup of water
- ½ tablespoon of oil
- ½ inch ginger, finely chopped
- 1 tomato, chopped
- 1 cup of spinach, chopped
- ¼ teaspoon of cumin seeds
- 2 garlic cloves, finely chopped
- ½ teaspoon of salt
- ½ cup of split pigeon pea, washed

DIRECTIONS
1. Set the instant vortex on air fryer to 375 degrees f for 8 minutes. Sauté garlic, ginger, and cumin seeds in the olive oil in a pan for about 1 minute. Stir in the tomato paste, water, lentils, and salt. Sauté for about 3 minutes and add spinach. Transfer this mixture into the Cooking dish and place on the Cooking tray.
2. Insert the Cooking tray in the vortex when it displays "add food". Remove from the vortex when cooking time is complete. Serve warm.

833. Kale rice

Preparation time: 10 mins
Cooking time: 20 mins.
Servings: 4

INGREDIENTS
- ¼ cup of white wine
- 3 tablespoons of vegetable stock
- 2 tablespoons of basil, chopped
- ½ cup of parmesan, grated
- 1½ cups of rice, boiled
- 1 bunch kale leaves, chopped and stems removed
- 1 cup of onions, finely chopped
- 2 garlic cloves, minced
- ½ teaspoon of salt
- ½ teaspoon of black pepper
- ½ teaspoon of red pepper flakes
- 2 tablespoons of apple cider vinegar
- 2 tablespoons of olive oil

DIRECTIONS
1. Set the instant vortex on air fryer to 375 degrees f for 12 minutes. Sauté onions and garlic in the olive oil in a pan for about 3 minutes. Stir in the rice, wine and vegetable broth. Transfer this mixture into the Cooking dish and place on the Cooking tray. Insert the Cooking tray in the vortex when it displays "add food". Remove from the vortex when cooking time is complete.
2. Stir in the kale leaves, chopped herbs, apple cider vinegar, salt, black pepper, cheese, and red pepper flakes. Cook again in the vortex for about 5 minutes and dish out to serve warm.

834. Parmesan pasta

Preparation time: 10 minutes
Cooking time: 20 minutes
Servings: 6

INGREDIENTS
- 3 tbsp pine nuts
- ¾ cup fresh basil leaves
- 2 garlic cloves
- 1 tbsp lemon juice
- 8 oz uncooked pasta
- 1 ½ cups water
- 1 cup skim milk
- 1 tsp salt
- 2 cups fresh broccoli florets
- 1 cup chopped zucchini
- ½ cup frozen peas
- 4 oz parmesan cheese

DIRECTION
1. Combine 2 tbsp of the roasted pine nuts with the basil, garlic and lemon juice in the bowl and grind it and set aside.
2. Add water and milk in the dry pasta; add the salt and the broccoli, zucchini and peas.
3. Cook the mixture in air fryer 13-16 minutes until the liquid is mostly absorbed (pasta and veggies will be cooked).
4. Remove from heat and stir in almost all the shredded parmesan and nuts mixture.

5. Cover the pan with a lid for 2-3 minutes until the cheese is melted and then stir until well combined and cheesy.

835. Chicken muffins

Preparation time: 20 minutes
Cooking time: 25 minutes
Servings: 16
INGREDIENTS
- 1 ½ lbs. Chicken breast
- 1 egg
- 1 egg whites
- 6 tbsp dried breadcrumbs
- ¾ tsp dried basil
- ¾ tsp dried thyme
- ¾ tsp oregano
- 2 garlic cloves, minced
- ½ a small onion
- ¾ tsp salt
- 1/3 tsp black pepper
- ¾ cup parmesan cheese
- ¾ cup pasta sauce
- ¾ cup mozzarella cheese
- Oregano or basil for garnish

DIRECTION
1. Preheat the fryer to 350. Lightly mist a muffin tin with Cooking spray and set aside.
2. In a large bowl, combine the ground chicken, egg, egg whites, breadcrumbs, basil, thyme, oregano, garlic, onion, salt, pepper and parmesan cheese and lightly mix together.
3. Form the meat mixture evenly into the 12 cups of your prepared muffin tin. Spread the pasta sauce evenly over the tops of each muffin. Bake for 20 minutes and remove from the fryer.
4. Top each muffin with about a tbsp of shredded cheese and then return to the fryer for 2-3 minutes until the cheese is melted. Garnish.

836. Roasted pumpkin

Preparation time: 10 minutes
Cooking time: 12 minutes
Servings: 4
INGREDIENTS
- 1 and ½ pound pumpkin, deseeded, sliced and roughly chopped
- 3 garlic cloves, minced
- 1 tablespoon olive oil
- A pinch of sea salt
- A pinch of brown Sugar
- A pinch of nutmeg, ground
- A pinch of cinnamon powder

DIRECTIONS
1. In your air fryer's basket, mix pumpkin with garlic, oil, salt, brown Sugar, cinnamon and nutmeg, stir and cover and for 12 minutes boil at 370 degrees f
2. Serve after dividing

837. Corn nuts

Preparation time: 10 minutes
Cooking time: 20 minutes
Servings: 6

INGREDIENTS
- 14 oz. Giant white corn
- 3 tablespoons vegetable oil
- 1 1/2 teaspoons salt

DIRECTIONS
1. Soak white corn in a bowl filled with water and leave it for 8 hours.
2. Drain the soaked corns and spread them in the air fryer basket.
3. Leave to dry for 20 minutes after patting them dry with a paper towel.
4. Add oil and salt on top of the corns and toss them well.
5. Set the air fryer basket in the instant pot.
6. Put on the air fryer lid and seal it.
7. Hit the "air fry button" and select 20 minutes of Cooking time, then press "start."
8. Shake the corns after every 5 minutes of Cooking, then resume the function.
9. Once the instant pot duo beeps, remove its lid.
10. Serve.

838. Air Fryer Honey French toast Sticks

Prep Time: 10 minutes
Cook Time: 8 minutes
Servings: 4

INGREDIENTS:
- 2 large eggs
- 1/3 c. heavy cream
- 1/3 c. whole milk
- 3 tbsp. granulated sugar
- 1/4 tsp. ground cinnamon
- 1/2 tsp. pure vanilla extract
- Kosher salt
- 6 thick slices Pullman or other white loaf or brioche, each slice cut into thirds
- Maple syrup, for serving

DIRECTIONS:
1. Beat eggs, cream, milk, sugar, cinnamon, vanilla, and a spot of salt in an enormous shallow baking dish. Add bread, go to cover a couple of times.
2. Organize French toast in bin of air fryer, working in clusters as important to not pack container. Set air fryer to 375° and cook until brilliant, around 8 minutes, throwing partially through.
3. Serve toast warm, sprinkled with maple syrup.

839. Air Fryer Spicy Pickles

Prep Time: 10 minutes
Cook Time: 10 minutes
Servings: 4

INGREDIENTS:
- 2 c. dill pickle slices
- 1 egg, whisked with 1 tbsp. water
- 1/2 c. bread crumbs
- 1/4 c. freshly grated Parmesan
- 1 tsp. dried oregano
- 1 tsp. garlic powder
- Ranch, for dipping

DIRECTIONS:
1. Utilizing paper towels, pat pickle chips dry. Mix bread scraps, Parmesan, oregano, and garlic powder in a medium bowl.
2. Dig pickle chips first in egg and afterward in the bread morsel combination. Working in clumps, place in a solitary layer in air fryer bushel. Cook at 400° for 10 minutes.
3. Serve warm with farm.

840. Mustard Garlic-Rosemary Brussels Sprouts

Cook Time: 13 minutes
Servings: 4

INGREDIENTS:
- 3 tablespoons olive oil
- 2 garlic cloves, minced
- 1/2 teaspoon salt
- 1/4 teaspoon pepper
- 1 pound Brussels sprouts, trimmed and halved
- 1/2 cup panko bread crumbs
- 1-1/2 teaspoons minced fresh rosemary

DIRECTIONS:
1. Preheat air fryer to 350°. Place initial 4 fixings in a little microwave-safe bowl; microwave on high 30 seconds.
2. Throw Brussels sprouts with 2 tablespoons oil blend. Place Brussels sprouts on plate in air-fryer crate; cook 4-5 minutes. Mix sprouts. Cook until sprouts are daintily sautéed and close to wanted delicacy, around 8 minutes longer, mixing partially through cooking time.
3. Throw bread scraps with rosemary and remaining oil combination; sprinkle over sprouts. Keep cooking until pieces are sautéed and fledglings are delicate, 3-5 minutes. Serve right away.

841. Garlic Red Potatoes

Prep Time: 10 minutes
Cook Time: 12 minutes
Servings: 4

INGREDIENTS:
- 2 pounds small unpeeled red potatoes, cut into wedges
- 2 tablespoons olive oil
- 1 tablespoon minced fresh rosemary or 1 teaspoon dried rosemary, crushed
- 2 garlic cloves, minced
- 1/2 teaspoon salt
- 1/4 teaspoon pepper

DIRECTIONS:
1. Preheat air fryer to 400°. Sprinkle potatoes with oil. Sprinkle with rosemary, garlic, salt and pepper; throw delicately to cover.
2. Place on ungreased plate in air-fryer bin. Cook until potatoes are brilliant brown and delicate, 10-12 minutes, blending once.

842. Nashville Hot Chicken

Prep Time: 10 minutes
Cook Time: 12 minutes
Servings: 4

INGREDIENTS:
- 2 tablespoons dill pickle juice, divided
- 2 tablespoons hot pepper sauce, divided
- 1 teaspoon salt, divided
- 2 pounds chicken tenderloins
- 1 cup all-purpose flour
- 1/2 teaspoon pepper
- 1 large egg
- 1/2 cup buttermilk
- Cooking spray
- 1/2 cup olive oil
- 2 tablespoons cayenne pepper
- 2 tablespoons dark brown sugar
- 1 teaspoon paprika
- 1 teaspoon chili powder
- 1/2 teaspoon garlic powder
- Dill pickle slices

DIRECTIONS:
1. In a bowl or shallow dish, consolidate 1 tablespoon pickle juice, 1 tablespoon hot sauce and 1/2 teaspoon salt. Add chicken and go to cover. Refrigerate, covered, somewhere around 60 minutes. Channel chicken, disposing of any marinade.
2. Preheat air fryer to 375°. In a shallow bowl, blend flour, staying 1/2 teaspoon salt and the pepper. In another shallow bowl, whisk egg, buttermilk, and the leftover 1 tablespoon pickle juice and 1 tablespoon hot sauce. Dunk chicken in flour to cover the two sides; shake off abundance. Plunge in egg blend, of course in flour combination.
3. In bunches, orchestrate chicken in a solitary layer on all around lubed plate in air-fryer

229

crate; spritz with cooking splash. Cook until brilliant brown, 5-6 minutes. Turn; spritz with cooking shower. Cook until brilliant brown, 5-6 minutes longer.

4. Whisk together oil, cayenne pepper, earthy colored sugar and flavors; pour over hot chicken and throw to cover. Present with pickles.

843. Wasabi Crab Cakes

Prep Time: 10 minutes
Cook Time: 12 minutes
Servings: 4

INGREDIENTS:
- 1 medium sweet red pepper, finely chopped
- 1 celery rib, finely chopped
- 3 green onions, finely chopped
- 2 large egg whites
- 3 tablespoons reduced-fat mayonnaise
- 1/4 teaspoon prepared wasabi
- 1/4 teaspoon salt
- 1/3 cup plus 1/2 cup dry bread crumbs, divided
- 1-1/2 cups lump crabmeat, drained
- Cooking spray

Sauce:
- 1 celery rib, chopped
- 1/3 cup reduced-fat mayonnaise
- 1 green onion, chopped
- 1 tablespoon sweet pickle relish
- 1/2 teaspoon prepared wasabi
- 1/4 teaspoon celery salt

DIRECTIONS:
1. Preheat air fryer to 375°. Consolidate initial 7 fixings; add 1/3 cup bread morsels. Tenderly overlap in crab.
2. Place remaining bread pieces in a shallow bowl. Drop piling tablespoons crab combination into pieces. Tenderly coat and shape into 3/4-in.- thick patties. In bunches, place patties in a solitary layer on lubed plate in air-fryer container. Spritz crab cakes with cooking splash. Cook until brilliant brown, 8-12 minutes, cautiously turning part of the way through cooking and spritzing with extra cooking shower.
3. In the interim, place sauce fixings in food processor; beat 2 or multiple times to mix or until wanted consistency is reached. Serve crab cakes quickly with plunging sauce

844. French toast Sticks

Prep Time: 10 minutes
Cook Time: 12 minutes
Servings: 4

INGREDIENTS:
- 6 slices day-old Texas toast
- 4 large eggs
- 1 cup 2% milk
- 2 tablespoons sugar
- 1 teaspoon vanilla extract
- 1/4 to 1/2 teaspoon ground cinnamon
- 1 cup crushed cornflakes, optional
- Confectioners' sugar, optional
- Maple syrup

DIRECTIONS:
1. Cut each slice of bread into thirds; place in an ungreased 13x9-in. dish. Whisk eggs, milk, sugar, vanilla, and cinnamon in an enormous bowl. Pour over bread; douse for 2 minutes, turning once. Whenever wanted, cover bread with cornflake morsels on all sides.
2. Place in a lubed 15x10x1-in. baking skillet. Freeze until firm, around 45 minutes. Move to a water/air proof cooler compartment and store in the cooler.
3. To utilize frozen French toast sticks: Preheat air fryer to 350°.
4. Place wanted number on lubed plate in air-fryer container. Cook for 3 minutes. Turn; cook until brilliant brown, 2-3 minutes longer. Sprinkle with confectioners' sugar whenever wanted. Present with syrup

845. Quinoa Arancini

Prep Time: 12 minutes
Cook Time: 8 minutes
Servings: 4

INGREDIENTS:
- 1 package (9 ounces) ready-to-serve quinoa or 1-3/4 cups cooked quinoa
- 2 large eggs, lightly beaten, divided use
- 1 cup seasoned bread crumbs, divided
- 1/4 cup shredded Parmesan cheese
- 1 tablespoon olive oil
- 2 tablespoons minced fresh basil or 2 teaspoons dried basil
- 1/2 teaspoon garlic powder
- 1/2 teaspoon salt
- 1/8 teaspoon pepper
- 6 cubes part-skim mozzarella cheese (3/4 inch each)
- Cooking spray
- Warmed pasta sauce, optional

DIRECTIONS:
1. Preheat air fryer to 375°. Plan quinoa as indicated by bundle bearings. Mix 1 egg, 1/2 cup bread morsels, Parmesan cheddar, oil, basil and flavors
2. Partition into 6 bits. Shape each piece

around a cheddar block to cover totally, framing a ball.

3. Place remaining egg and 1/2 cup bread morsels in discrete shallow dishes. Plunge quinoa balls in egg, then, at that point, roll in bread morsels. Place on lubed plate in air-fryer bin; spritz with cooking shower. Cook until brilliant brown, 6-8 minutes. Whenever wanted, present with pasta sauce.

846. Sriracha Spring Rolls

Prep Time: 12 minutes
Cook Time: 15 minutes
Servings: 4

INGREDIENTS:
- 3 cups coleslaw mix (about 7 ounces)
- 3 green onions, chopped
- 1 tablespoon soy sauce
- 1 pound boneless skinless chicken breasts
- 1 teaspoon sesame oil
- 1 teaspoon seasoned salt
- 2 packages (8 ounces each) cream cheese, softened
- 2 tablespoons Sriracha chili sauce
- 24 spring roll wrappers
- Cooking spray
- Optional: Sweet chili sauce and additional green onions

DIRECTIONS:
1. Preheat air fryer to 360°. Throw coleslaw blend, green onions, soy sauce and sesame oil; let stand while cooking chicken. Place chicken in a solitary layer on lubed plate in air-fryer bin. Cook until a thermometer embedded in chicken peruses 165°, 18-20 minutes. Eliminate chicken; cool marginally. Finely slash chicken; throw with prepared salt.

2. Increment air-fryer temperature to 400°. Mix cream cheddar and Sriracha stew sauce; mix chicken and coleslaw combination. With 1 corner of a spring roll covering confronting you, place around 2 tablespoons filling just beneath focus of covering. (Cover remaining coverings with a clammy paper towel until prepared to utilize.) Fold base corner over filling; saturate remaining edges with water. Crease side corners toward focus over filling; roll up firmly, squeezing tip to seal. Rehash.

3. In clumps, orchestrate spring rolls in a solitary layer on lubed plate in air-fryer bushel; spritz with cooking shower. Cook until gently seared, 5-6 minutes. Turn; spritz with cooking shower. Cook until brilliant brown and fresh, 5-6 minutes longer. Present with sweet bean stew sauce and sprinkle with green onions whenever wanted.

847. Pork Schnitzel

Prep Time: 12 minutes
Cook Time: 10 minutes
Servings: 4

INGREDIENTS:
- 1/4 cup all-purpose flour
- 1 teaspoon seasoned salt
- 1/4 teaspoon pepper
- 1 large egg
- 2 tablespoons 2% milk
- 3/4 cup dry bread crumbs
- 1 teaspoon paprika
- 4 pork sirloin cutlets (4 ounces each)
- Cooking spray
- 1 teaspoon sesame oil

DIRECTIONS:
1. Preheat air fryer to 375°. In a shallow bowl, blend flour, prepared salt and pepper. In a subsequent shallow bowl, whisk egg and milk until mixed. In a third bowl, blend bread morsels and paprika.

2. Pound pork cutlets with a meat hammer to 1/4-in. thickness.

3. Plunge cutlets in flour combination to cover the two sides; shake off abundance. Plunge in egg blend, then, at that point, in piece combination, tapping to assist covering with following.

4. Place pork in a solitary layer on lubed plate in air-fryer bin; spritz with cooking shower. Cook until brilliant brown, 4-5 minutes. Turn; spritz with cooking shower. Cook until brilliant brown, 4-5 minutes longer. Eliminate to a serving plate; keep warm.

5. In the meantime, in a little pan, whisk flour and stock until smooth. Heat to the point of boiling, blending continually; cook and mix 2 minutes or until thickened. Lessen hotness to low. Mix in harsh cream and dill; heat through (don't bubble). Present with pork.

848. Bacon Wrapped Honey and Lemon Avocado

Prep Time: 12 minutes
Cook Time: 8 minutes
Servings: 4

INGREDIENTS:
- 3 avocados
- 24 thin strips of bacon
- 1/4 c. ranch dressing, for serving

DIRECTIONS:
1. Cut every avocado into 8 similarly estimated wedges. Wrap each wedge with a portion of bacon, cutting bacon if necessary.

2. Working in groups, organize in air fryer crate in a solitary layer.

3. Cook at 400° for 8 minutes until bacon is cooked through and firm.

4. Serve warm with farm.

849. Herbs Mayo Salmon

Prep Time: 12 minutes
Cook Time: 10 minutes
Servings: 4

INGREDIENTS:
- 2 (6-oz.) salmon fillets
- Kosher salt
- Freshly ground black pepper
- 2 tsp. extra-virgin olive oil
- 2 tbsp. whole grain mustard
- 1 tbsp. packed brown sugar
- 1 clove garlic, minced
- 1/2 tsp. thyme leaves

DIRECTIONS:
1. Season salmon done with salt and pepper. Whisk together oil, mustard, sugar, garlic, and thyme in a little bowl. Spread on top of salmon.
2. Orchestrate salmon in air fryer container. Set air fryer to 400° and cook for 10 minutes.

850. Herb Turkey Breast

Prep Time: 12 minutes
Cook Time: 10 minutes
Servings: 4

INGREDIENTS:
- 2 lb. turkey breast, skin on
- Kosher salt
- Freshly ground black pepper
- 4 tbsp. butter, melted
- 3 cloves garlic, minced
- 1 tsp. freshly chopped thyme
- 1 tsp. freshly chopped rosemary

DIRECTIONS:
1. Pat turkey bosom dry and season on the two sides with salt and pepper.
2. Consolidate a little bowl of softened margarine, garlic, thyme, and rosemary. Brush margarine all over turkey bosom.
3. Place in bushel of air fryer, skin side up and cook at 375° for 40 minutes or until inner temperature comes to 160°, flipping partially through.
4. Let rest for 5 minutes before cutting.

851. Mustard Pork Chops

Prep Time: 12 minutes
Cook Time: 9 minutes
Servings: 4

INGREDIENTS:
- 4 boneless pork chops
- 2 tbsp. extra-virgin olive oil
- 1/2 c. freshly grated Parmesan
- 1 tsp. kosher salt
- 1 tsp. paprika
- 1 tsp. garlic powder
- 1 tsp. onion powder
- 1/2 tsp. freshly ground black pepper

DIRECTIONS:
1. Pat pork slashes dry with paper towels, then, at that point, cover the two sides with oil. In a medium bowl, consolidate Parmesan and flavors. Cover the two sides of pork cleaves with Parmesan blend.
2. Place pork slashes in crate of air fryer and cook at 375° for 9 minutes, flipping part of the way through.

852. Garlic Cinnamon Rolls

Prep Time: 12 minutes
Cook Time: 10 minutes
Servings: 4

INGREDIENTS:
- 2 tbsp. melted butter, plus more for brushing
- 1/3 c. packed brown sugar
- 1/2 tsp. ground cinnamon
- Kosher salt
- All-purpose flour, for surface
- 1 (8-oz.) tube refrigerated Crescent rolls

DIRECTIONS:
1. Make rolls: Line lower part of air fryer with material paper and brush with margarine. In a medium bowl, join spread, earthy colored sugar, cinnamon, and a huge touch of salt until smooth and fleecy.
2. On a gently floured surface, carry out bow rolls in a single piece.
3. Squeeze creases together and overlap down the middle. Roll into a 9"- x-7" square shape. Spread margarine blend over mixture, leaving 1/4-inch line. Beginning at a long edge, roll up batter like a jam roll, then, at that point, cut transversely into 6 pieces.
4. Organize pieces in pre-arranged air fryer, cut-side up, separated uniformly.

853. Keto Granola

Preparation time: 10 minutes
Cooking time: 12 minutes
Servings: 4

Ingredients:
- 1 teaspoon monk fruit
- 2 teaspoons coconut oil
- 3 pecans, chopped
- 1 teaspoon pumpkin pie spices
- 1 tablespoon coconut shred
- 3 oz. almonds, chopped
- 1 tablespoon flax seeds

Directions:
1. In the mixing bowl, mix all ingredients from

the list above.
2. Make the small balls from the mixture and put them in the air fryer.
3. Cook the granola for 6 minutes per side at 365F.
4. Cool the cooked granola.

1. Mix the ground chicken with Italian seasonings, egg, and coconut flour.
2. Make the small balls from the chicken mixture (popcorn) and put in the air fryer in one layer.
3. Sprinkle the popcorn balls with avocado oil and cook at 365F for 6 minutes per side.

854. Chicken Skin

Preparation time: 10 minutes
Cooking time: 10 minutes
Servings: 3

Ingredients:
- 6 oz. chicken skin
- 1 teaspoon avocado oil
- 1/2 teaspoon ground black pepper

Directions:
1. Chop the chicken skin roughly and mix it with avocado oil and ground black pepper.
2. Put the chicken skin in the air fryer basket and cook at 375F for 10 minutes. Shake the chicken skin every 3 minutes to avoid burning.

855. Seafood Balls

Preparation time: 15 minutes
Cooking time: 15 minutes
Servings: 4

Ingredients:
- 1-pound salmon fillet, minced
- 1 egg, beaten
- 3 tablespoons coconut, shredded
- 1/2 cup almond flour
- 1 tablespoon avocado oil
- 1 teaspoon dried basil

Directions:
1. In the mixing bowl, mix minced salmon fillet, egg, coconut, almond flour, and dried basil.
2. Make the balls from the fish mixture and put them in the air fryer basket.
3. Sprinkle the balls with avocado oil and cook at 365F for 15 minutes.

856. Popcorn Balls

Preparation time: 10 minutes
Cooking time: 12 minutes
Servings: 6

Ingredients:
- 2 cups ground chicken
- 1 teaspoon Italian seasonings
- 1 egg, beaten
- 1/4 cup coconut flour
- 1 tablespoon avocado oil

Directions:

857. Parsley Balls

Preparation time: 10 minutes
Cooking time: 8 minutes
Servings: 6

Ingredients:
- 4 pecans, grinded
- 3 tablespoons dried parsley
- 1 teaspoon onion powder
- 1 egg, beaten
- 2 oz. Parmesan, grated

Directions:
1. In the mixing bowl, mix pecans with dried basil, onion powder, egg, and Parmesan.
2. Make the balls and put them in the air fryer in one layer.
3. Cook them at 375F for 8 minutes (4 minutes per side).

858. Cheese Sticks

Preparation time: 15 minutes
Cooking time: 17 minutes
Servings: 8

Ingredients:
- 8 regular cheese sticks
- 1 large free-range egg
- 1/4 cup almond flour
- 1/2 cup grated parmesan cheese
- 1 teaspoon Italian seasoning
- 1/4 teaspoon ground rosemary
- 1 teaspoon garlic powder

Directions:
1. Whisk the egg properly in a bowl.
2. Add the almond flour, parmesan, Italian seasoning, and rosemary and garlic powder in another bowl. Mix well to combine properly.
3. Coat the cheese sticks with the egg by dipping it in the egg, drip off any excess and dip in the almond flour.
4. Line a baking pan with a baking sheet. Place the cheese sticks in the pan and place in the freezer for 10 minutes.
5. Heat the air fryer to 370F.
6. Set out the cheese sticks from the freezer then place in the air fryer.
7. Cook for 10 minutes, then serve and enjoy.

859. Sweets and Treats

Preparation time: 10 minutes
Cooking time: 12 minutes
Servings: 6-8

Ingredients:
- 2 free-range eggs
- 1 1/2 cups milk
- 1/4 cup butter
- 1 1/2 teaspoon vanilla extract
- 1 cup shredded coconut
- 1/2 cup Monk Fruit sweetener
- 1/2 cup coconut flour

Directions:
1. Heat the air fryer to 350F and oil a 6 inches pie plate with any oil of your choice. Set aside.
2. Attach all the ingredients to a large bowl. Mix properly to combine.
3. Pour the mixture into the pie plate and place in your air fryer.
4. Let it cook properly for 10-12 minutes.
5. Serve and enjoy!

860. Chicken Poppers

Preparation time: 5 minutes
Cooking time: 20 minutes
Servings: 5

Ingredients:
- 1 Teaspoon Garlic Powder
- 1 Teaspoon Black Pepper
- 1 Teaspoon Chili Flakes
- 1/2 Cup Coconut Flour
- 11 Ounces Chicken Breast, Boneless and Skinless
- 1 Tablespoon Canola Oil

Direction:
1. Start by cubing your chicken, and then place it in a bowl.
2. Sprinkle your chicken cubes with black pepper, garlic, and chili flakes. Stir well, and then sprinkle your almond flour over it.
3. Sake the bowl so that the meat is coated properly, and preheat your air fryer to 365.
4. Sprinkle your air fryer down with your canola oil, and then cook your chicken for ten minutes.
5. Turn them over, cooking for another five minutes. Serve warm.

861. Quick Paella

Preparation time: 7 minutes
Cooking time: 17 minutes
Servings: 4

Ingredients:
- 1 (10-ounce) package frozen cooked rice, thawed
- 1 (6-ounce) jar artichoke hearts, drained and chopped
- 1/4 cup vegetable broth
- 1/2 teaspoon turmeric
- 1/2 teaspoon dried thyme
- 1 cup frozen cooked small shrimp
- 1/2 cup frozen baby peas
- 1 tomato, diced

Directions:
1. In a 6-by-6-by-2-inch pan, combine the rice, artichoke hearts, vegetable broth, turmeric, and thyme, and stir gently.
2. Set in the air fryer and bake for 8 to 9 minutes or until the rice is hot.
3. Remove from the air fryer and gently stir in the shrimp, peas, and tomato. Cook for 5 to 8 minutes or until the shrimp and peas are hot and the paella is bubbling.
4. Substitution tip: If you like intensely flavored food, try using marinated artichoke hearts in this recipe. Be sure you taste the marinade first! For even more flavor, use the liquid in the jar of artichokes in place of the vegetable broth.

862. Hot Crab Dip

Preparation time: 10 minutes
Cooking time: 8 minutes
Servings: 4

Ingredients:
- 8 ounces full-fat cream cheese, softened
- 1/4 cup full-fat mayonnaise
- 1/4 cup full-fat sour cream
- 1 tablespoon lemon juice
- 1/2 teaspoon hot sauce
- 1/4 cup chopped pickled jalapeños
- 1/4 cup sliced green onion
- 2 (6-ounce) cans lump crabmeat
- 1/2 cup shredded Cheddar cheese

Directions:
1. Place all ingredients into a 4-cup round baking dish and stir until fully combined. Place dish into the air fryer basket.
2. Adjust the temperature to 400F and set the timer for 8 minutes.
3. Dip will be bubbling and hot when done. Serve warm.

863. Chicken Cutlets with Broccoli

Preparation Time: 5 minutes
Cooking Time: 15 minutes
Servings: 4

Ingredients:
- 1 pound chicken cutlets
- 1 pound broccoli florets
- 1 tablespoon olive oil
- Sea salt and ground black pepper, to taste

Directions
1. Pat the chicken dry with kitchen towels. Place the chicken cutlets in a lightly greased Air Fryer basket.
2. Cook the chicken cutlets at 380 degrees F for 6 minutes, turning them over halfway through the cooking time.
3. Turn the heat to 400 degrees F and add in the remaining ingredients. Continue to cook for 6 minutes more.
4. Bon appétit!

864. Chicken Couscous Bowl

Preparation Time: 10 minutes
Cooking Time: 25 minutes
Servings: 2

Ingredients:
- Water 120ml
- Tomato purees 2 tbsp.
- Vegetable stock cube 1/2
- Couscous 120g
- Sriracha sauce 1 tbsp.
- Chicken breasts, sliced 2
- Oil 1 tbsp.
- Tomatoes 2, diced
- Paprika 1 tsp.
- Garlic powder 1 tsp.
- Onion 1, peeled and diced
- Salt and pepper
- Bell pepper 1, deseeded and diced
- For garnishing parsley feta and cheese

Directions
1. Boil 120 ml of water and transfer some of the vegetable stock. Stir until the stock dissolves. In a bowl put the couscous and pour over it with vegetable stock. Cover and set the bowl on the side.
2. Ensure that a pot is placed, but remove the grill plate. Choose ROAST, set the temp to 200° C, and set the timer for 15 minutes. To commence preheating, click START/STOP.
3. Mix the chicken, paprika, oil, garlic powder, pepper, and salt together in a dish.
4. Once the device beeps to signal that it has preheated, insert the seasoned chicken and close the lid to start cooking.
5. Open the cover and put bell pepper, tomatoes and onion when 10 minutes are remaining on the timer. To keep cooking, close the lid.
6. Insert Sriracha, tomato puree and already cooked couscous and mix well when there are 3 minutes left on the timer.
7. Stir in the parsley and garnish with the feta cheese until the cooking phase has been finished. Serve it hot.

865. Beef Steak

Preparation time: 25 minutes
Cooking time: 25 minutes
Servings: 2 - 4

Ingredients:
- 1lb. of beef steak
- 1 tsp. of salt
- 1 tbsp. of freshly squeezed lemon juice
- 1 tsp. of paprika
- 3tbsp. of fresh rosemary
- 3tbsp. of balsamic vinegar
- 1 tbsp. of olive oil
- 1 tsp. of ground black pepper
- 1 cup of red wine
- 1 tbsp. of minced garlic
- 1 onion

Directions:
1. Mix salt, paprika, fresh rosemary, ground black pepper and minced garlic in a mixing bowl.
2. Peel the onion and chop it and place the chopped onion and spice mixture in a blender.
3. Add freshly squeezed lemon juice, balsamic vinegar, organic extra virgin olive oil, and burgundy or merlot wine.
4. Blend the amalgamation until it smoothens. Mix beef steak with all the spice mixture and then leave it in a refrigerator for a quarter-hour to marinate.
5. Switch to Sauté mode and transfer the marinated steak into pressure cooker and sauté the meat for ten minutes while stirring frequently.
6. Close the pressure cooker lid and cook the dish on Pressure mode for quarter-hour. Release pressure on the cooker and open the lid.
7. Serve the beef while hot.

865. Air-Fried Green Beans

Preparation Time: 10 minutes
Cooking Time: 10 minutes
Serving: 4

Ingredients
- 11/2 pounds (680 g) French green beans, stems removed and blanched
- 1/2tablespoon salt
- 1/2 pound (227 g) shallots, peeled and cut into quarters
- 1/2 teaspoon ground white pepper
- 1/2tablespoons olive oil

Directions
1. Coat the vegetables with the rest of the ingredients in a bowl.
2. Transfer to the air fryer basket and air fry at 400F (204C) for 10 minutes, making sure the green beans achieve a light brown color.
3. Serve hot.

886. Breakfast Enchilada

Preparation Time: 5 minutes
Cooking Time: 3 minutes
Servings: 1

Ingredients:
- 1 egg white, beaten
- 1 egg, beaten
- Cooking spray
- Salt and pepper to taste
- 1 oz. tofu, sliced into cubes and cooked
- 2 tbsps. salsa
- 1 tbsp. low-fat Mexican cheese, shredded

Direction:
1. Mix egg white and egg in a bowl.
2. Spray a pan with oil.
3. Place the pan over medium heat.
4. Add the eggs and cook for 1 to 2 minutes without stirring.
5. Season with salt and pepper.
6. Flip and cook for another 1 minute.
7. Transfer to a plate.
8. Cook eggs on the other side for about 2 minutes or until completely cooked and transfer to a plate.
9. Top the egg with tofu and cheese.
10. Roll it up.
11. Store in a food container.
12. Refrigerate for up to 1 day.
13. Reheat when ready to serve.
14. Serve with salsa.

867. Shrimp Sandwiches

Preparation Time: 10 minutes
Cooking Time: 5 minutes
Servings: 2

Ingredients:
- 1 and ¼ cups cheddar, shredded
- 6 oz. tiny shrimp, canned and drained
- 3 tbsps. mayonnaise
- 2 tbsps. green onions, chopped
- 4 whole wheat bread slices
- 2 tbsps. butter, soft

Directions:
1. In a bowl, mix shrimp with cheese, green onion, and mayo and stir well. Spread this on half of the bread slices, top with the other bread slices, cut into halves diagonally, and spread butter on top.
2. Place sandwiches in your air fryer and cook at 350°F for 5 minutes. Divide shrimp sandwiches on plates and serve them for breakfast. Enjoy!

868. Breakfast Pea Tortilla

Preparation Time: 10 minutes
Cooking Time: 7 minutes
Servings: 2

Ingredients:
- ½ lb. baby peas
- 4 tbsps. butter
- 1 and ½ cup yogurt
- 8 eggs
- ½ cup mint, chopped
- Salt and black pepper to the taste

Directions:
1. Heat up a pan that fits your air fryer with the butter over medium heat, add peas. Stir and cook for a couple of minutes.
2. Meanwhile, in a bowl, mix half of the yogurt with salt, pepper, eggs, and mint and whisk well.
3. Pour this over the peas, toss, introduce in your air fryer and cook at 350°F for 7 minutes.
4. Spread the rest of the yogurt over your tortilla, slice, and serve. Enjoy!

869. Easy Beef Roast

Preparation Time: 10 minutes
Cooking Time: 45 minutes
Servings: 6

Ingredients:
- 2 ½ lbs. beef roast
- 2 tbsps. Italian seasoning

Directions:
1. Arrange roast on the rotisserie spite.
2. Rub roast with Italian seasoning, then insert into the instant vortex air fryer oven.
3. Air fry at 350°F for 45 minutes or until the internal temperature of the beef roast (as read by a meat thermometer) reaches to 145°F.
4. Slice and serve.

870. Beef Sirloin Roast

Preparation Time: 10 minutes
Cooking Time: 50 minutes
Servings: 8

Ingredients:
- 2½ lbs. sirloin roast
- Salt and ground black pepper, as required

Directions:
1. Rub the roast with salt and black pepper generously.
2. Insert the rotisserie rod through the roast.
3. Insert the rotisserie forks, one on each side of the rod to secure the rod to the chicken.
4. Arrange the drip pan in the bottom of the

Instant Vortex Plus Air Fryer Oven cooking chamber.

5. Select "Roast" and then adjust the temperature to 350°F.
6. Set the timer for 50 minutes and press the "Start."
7. When the display shows "Add Food" press the red lever down and load the left side of the rod into the Vortex.
8. Now, slide the rod's left side into the groove along the metal bar, so it doesn't move. Then, close the door and touch "Rotate." Press the red lever to release the rod when cooking time is complete.
9. Remove from the Vortex and place the roast onto a platter for about 10 minutes before slicing. With a sharp knife, cut the roast into desired-sized slices and serve.

871. Garlicky Pork Tenderloin

Preparation Time: 15 minutes
Cooking Time: 20 minutes
Servings: 5

Ingredients:
- 1½ lbs. pork tenderloin
- Nonstick cooking spray
- 2 small heads roasted garlic
- Salt and ground black pepper, as required

Directions:
1. Lightly spray all the sides of pork with cooking spray and then, season with salt and black pepper.
2. Now, rub the pork with roasted garlic. Arrange the roast onto the lightly greased cooking tray.
3. Arrange the drip pan in the bottom of the Instant Vortex plus Air Fryer Oven cooking chamber.
4. Select "Air Fry" and then adjust the temperature to 400°F. Set the timer for 20 minutes and press the "Start."
5. When the display shows "Add Food," insert the cooking tray in the center position.
6. When the display shows "Turn Food," turn the pork.
7. When cooking time is complete, remove the tray from Vortex and place the roast onto a platter for about 10 minutes before slicing. With a sharp knife, cut the roast into desired-sized slices and serve.

872. Chimichanga

Preparation Time: 2 minutes
Cooking Time: 8 minutes
Servings: 1

Ingredients:
- 1 whole-grain tortilla
- ½ cup vegan beans, refried
- ¼ cup vegan cheese, grated (optional)
- Cooking oil spray (sunflower, safflower)
- ½ cup fresh salsa, or Green Chili Sauce
- 2 cups romaine lettuce, chopped (about ½ head)
- Guacamole (optional)
- Cilantro, chopped (optional)
- Cheesy Sauce (optional)

Directions:
1. Lay the tortilla on a flat surface and place the beans in the center. Top with the cheese, if using.
2. Wrap the bottom up over the filling, and then fold in the sides. Then roll it all up so as to enclose the beans inside the tortilla (you're making an enclosed burrito here).
3. Spray the air fryer basket with oil, place the tortilla wrap inside the basket, seam-side down, and spray the top of the chimichanga with oil.
4. Fry for 5 minutes. Spray the top (and sides) again with oil, flip over, and spray the other side with oil. Fry for an additional 2 or 3 minutes, until nicely browned and crisp.
5. Transfer to a plate. Top with the salsa, lettuce, guacamole, cilantro, and/or Cheesy Sauce, if using. Serve immediately.

873. Creamy Chicken

Preparation Time: 10 minutes
Cooking Time: 20 minutes
Servings: 4

Ingredients:
- Pepper and salt
- 1 tsp. Olive oil
- 0.5 tsp. Sweet paprika
- 0.25 cup cream cheese
- 4 Chicken breasts, cubed

Directions:
1. Turn on the air fryer to 370°F.
2. Prepare a pan that fits into the machine with some oil before adding the ingredients inside.
3. Add this to the air fryer and let it bake. After 17 minutes, you can divide between the few plates and serve!

874. Basil Chicken

Preparation Time: 15 minutes
Cooking Time: 25 minutes
Servings: 4

Ingredients:
- Pepper and salt
- 2 tsps.paprika, smoked
- 0.5 tsp. basil, dried
- 0.5 cup chicken stock
- 0.5 lb. chicken breasts, cubed

Directions:
1. Turn on the air fryer to 390°F.
2. Bring out a pan and toss the ingredients inside before putting it into the air fryer.
3. After 25 minutes of baking, divide this between a few plates and serve with a side salad.

875. Eggplant Bake

Preparation Time: 20 minutes
Cooking Time: 15 minutes
Servings: 4

Ingredients:
- 2 tsps. olive oil
- pepper and salt
- 4 spring onions, chopped
- 1 hot chili pepper, chopped
- 2 eggplants, cubed
- 4 garlic cloves, minced
- 0.5 cup cilantro, chopped
- 0.5 lb. cherry tomatoes, cubed

Directions:
1. Turn on the air fryer and let it heat up to 380°F.
2. Prepare a baking pan that will go into the air fryer and mix all of the ingredients onto it.
3. Place into the air fryer to cook. After 15 minutes, divide between four bowls and serve.

876. Salsa Chicken

Preparation Time: 40 minutes
Cooking Time: 15 minutes
Servings: 2

Ingredients:
- 1 lb. chicken breast fillet
- 1 oz. taco seasoning mix
- ½ cup salsa
- ½ cup chicken broth,reduced-sodium

Directions:
1. Season the chicken breast fillet with taco seasoning mix.
2. Add the chicken to your Instant Pot. Spread the salsa on top.
3. Pour in the chicken broth.
4. Lock the lid in place.
5. Choose the poultry setting. Set it to 15 minutes. Release pressure naturally.
6. Shred the chicken with a fork.

877. Chicken Curry

Preparation Time: 15 minutes
Cooking Time: 25 minutes
Servings: 4

Ingredients:
- 1 tbsp. coconut oil
- 1 onion, minced
- 2 cloves garlic, crushed and minced
- 3 tbsps. curry powder
- 2 tbsps. white sugar
- 8 oz. tomato sauce,canned
- 14 oz. tomatoes,canned and diced
- ½ cup chicken broth
- 2 lbs. chicken breast fillet
- Salt and pepper to taste
- 14 oz. milk,skimmed

Directions:
1. Choose the sauté function in your Instant Pot.
2. Pour in the coconut oil.
3. Cook the onion and garlic for 2 minutes.
4. Sprinkle with the curry powder and stir.
5. Press the "Cancel" button.
6. Add the sugar, tomato sauce, tomatoes, and chicken broth. Stir.
7. Season both sides of the chicken with salt and pepper.
8. Place the chicken in the pot.
9. Secure the pot.
10. Cook on high for 10 minutes.
11. Release pressure naturally.
12. Shred the chicken and return to the pot.
13. Press sauté setting.
14. Cook for 3 minutes.
15. Pour in the skimmed milk. Cook for 10 more minutes.

878. Mexican Rice

Preparation Time: 40 minutes
Cooking Time: 20 minutes
Servings: 4

Ingredients:
- 1 tbsp. avocado oil
- ½ onion, chopped
- 2 cloves garlic, crushed and minced
- 1 cup rice
- 1 ½cups chicken broth,reduced-sodium
- ½ cup tomato sauce,reduced-sodium
- Pinch cayenne pepper
- ¼ tsp. ground cumin
- Salt to taste

Directions:
1. Select the sauté function in your Instant Pot.
2. Pour the avocado oil into the pot.
3. Cook the onion and garlic for 5 minutes, stirring frequently.
4. Stir in the rice.

5. Coat with the oil.
6. Add the chicken stock.
7. Stir in the cayenne pepper, cumin, and salt.
8. Seal the pot.
9. Cook on high for 15 minutes.
10. Release pressure quickly.
11. Stir the rice and serve.

879. Crunchy Cauliflower

Preparation Time: 20 minutes
Cooking Time: 15 minutes
Servings: 5

Ingredients:
- 2 oz. cauliflower
- 1 tbsp. potato starch
- 1 tsp. olive oil
- Salt & pepper to taste

Directions:
1. Set the air fryer toaster oven to 400°F and preheat it for 3 minutes. Slice cauliflower into equal pieces and if you are using potato starch, then toss with the florets into the bowl.
2. Add some olive oil and mix to coat.
3. Use olive oil cooking spray for spraying the inside of the air fryer toaster oven basket, next add cauliflower.
4. Cook for 8 minutes, after that shake the basket and cook for another 5 minutes depending on your desired level of crispiness. Sprinkle roasted cauliflower with fresh parsley, kosher salt, and seasonings or sauce of your choice.

880. Crispy Broccoli

Preparation Time: 10 minutes
Cooking Time: 10 minutes
Servings: 4

Ingredients:
- 1 large head fresh broccoli
- 2 tsps. olive oil
- 1 tbsp. lemon juice

Directions:
1. Rinse the broccoli and pat dry. Cut off the florets and separate them. You can also use the broccoli stems too; cut them into 1 chunk and peel them.
2. Toss the broccoli, olive oil, and lemon juice in a large bowl until coated.
3. Roast the broccoli in the air fryer, in batches, for 10 to 14 minutes or until the broccoli is crisp-tender and slightly brown around the edges. Repeat with the remaining broccoli. Serve immediately.

881. Dill Mashed Potato

Preparation Time: 10 minutes
Cooking Time: 15 minutes
Servings: 2

Ingredients:
- 2 potatoes
- 2 tbsps. fresh dill, chopped
- 1 tsp. butter
- ½ tsp. salt
- ¼ cup half and half

Directions:
1. Preheat the air fryer to 390°F.
2. Rinse the potatoes thoroughly and place them in the air fryer.
3. Cook the potatoes for 15 minutes.
4. After this, remove the potatoes from the air fryer.
5. Peel the potatoes.
6. Mash the potatoes with the help of the fork well.
7. Then add chopped fresh dill and salt.
8. Stir it gently and add butter and half and half.
9. Take the hand blender and blend the mixture well. When the mashed potato is cooked, serve it immediately. Enjoy

882. Chard with Cheddar

Preparation Time: 10 minutes
Cooking Time: 11 minutes
Servings: 2

Ingredients:
- 3 oz. Cheddar cheese, grated
- 10 oz. Swiss chard
- 3 tbsps. cream
- 1 tbsp. sesame oil
- salt and pepper to taste

Directions:
1. Wash Swiss chard carefully and chop it roughly.
2. After this, sprinkle chopped Swiss chard with the salt and ground white pepper.
3. Stir it carefully.
4. Sprinkle Swiss chard with the sesame oil and stir it carefully with the help of 2 spatulas.
5. Preheat the air fryer to 260°F.
6. Put chopped Swiss chard in the air fryer basket and cook for 6 minutes.
7. Shake it after 3 minutes of cooking.
8. Then pour the cream into the air fryer basket and mix it up.
9. Cook the meal for 3 minutes more.
10. Then increase the temperature to 400°F.
11. Sprinkle the meal with the grated cheese and cook for 2 minutes more.
12. After this, transfer the meal in the serving plates. Enjoy!

883. Packet Lobster Tail

Preparation Time: 15 minutes
Cooking Time: 12 minutes
Servings: 2

Ingredients:
- 2 (6-oz.) lobster tails, halved
- 2 tbsps. butter, salted and melted
- 1 tsp. parsley, dried
- ½ tsp. Old Bay seasoning
- Juice of ½ medium lemon

Directions:
1. Place the 2 halved tails on a sheet of aluminum foil. Drizzle with butter, Old Bay seasoning, and lemon juice.
2. Seal the foil packets, completely covering tails. Place into the air fryer basket.
3. Adjust the temperature to 375°F and set the timer for 12 minutes. Once done, sprinkle with dried parsley and serve immediately.

884. Delicious Catfish

Preparation Time: 10 minutes
Cooking Time: 20 minutes
Servings: 4

Ingredients:
- 4 catfish fillets
- Black pepper and Salt
- A pinch sweet paprika
- 1 tbsp. parsley
- 1 tbsp. lemon juice
- 1 tbsp. olive oil

Directions:
1. Season catfish fillets with salt, paprika, pepper, drizzle oil, rub well. Then put in air fryer basket and cook at 400°F for 20 minutes. Flip the fish after 10 minutes of time.
2. Share fish on plates. Sprinkle parsley and drizzle some lemon juice over it, serve.

885. Triple Cheese Dip

Preparation Time: 5 minutes
Cooking Time: 12 minutes
Servings: 8

Ingredients:
- 8 ounces (227 g) cream cheese, softened
- ½ cup mayonnaise
- ¼ cup sour cream
- ½ cup shredded sharp Cheddar cheese
- ¼ cup shredded Monterey jack cheese

Directions:
1. In a large bowl, combine all ingredients. Scoop mixture into an ungreased 4-cup nonstick baking dish and place into air fryer basket.
2. Adjust the temperature to 375°F (190ºC) and set the timer for 12 minutes. Dip will be browned on top and bubbling when done. Serve warm.

886. Dilled Eggplant

Preparation Time: 15 minutes
Cooking Time: 13 minutes
Servings: 4

Ingredients:
- 1 eggplant, peeled and thinly sliced
- Salt, to taste
- ½ cup almond meal
- ¼ cup olive oil
- ½ cup water
- 1 teaspoon garlic powder
- ½ teaspoon dried dill weed
- ½ teaspoon ground black pepper, to taste

Directions:
1. Salt the eggplant slices and let them stay for about 30 minutes. Squeeze the eggplant slices and rinse them under cold running water.
2. Toss the eggplant slices with the other ingredients. Cook at 390°F (199ºC) for 13 minutes, working in batches.
3. Serve with a sauce for dipping. Bon appétit!

887. Prosciutto-Wrapped Rings with Guacamole

Preparation Time: 10 minutes
Cooking Time: 6 minutes
Servings: 8

Ingredients:
- 2 avocados, halved, pitted, and peeled
- 3 tablespoons lime juice, plus more to taste
- 2 small plum tomatoes, diced
- ½ cup finely diced onions
- 2 small cloves garlic, smashed to a paste
- 3 tablespoons chopped fresh cilantro leaves
- ½ scant teaspoon fine sea salt
- ½ scant teaspoon ground cumin
- 2 small onions (about 1½-inches in diameter), cut into ½-inch-thick slices
- 8 slices prosciutto

Directions:
1. Make the guacamole: Place the avocados and lime juice in a large bowl and mash with a fork until it reaches your desired consistency. Add the tomatoes, onions, garlic, cilantro, salt, and cumin and stir until well combined. Taste and add more lime juice if desired. Set aside half of the guacamole for serving. (Note: If you're making the guacamole ahead of time, place it in a large resealable plastic bag, squeeze out all the air, and seal it shut. It will keep in the refrigerator for up to 3 days when stored this way.)
2. Place a piece of parchment paper on a tray that fits in your freezer and place the onion slices on it, breaking the slices apart into 8 rings. Fill each ring with about 2 tablespoons of guacamole. Place the tray in the freezer for 2 hours.
3. Spray the air fryer basket with avocado oil. Preheat the air fryer to 400°F (205ºC).
4. Remove the rings from the freezer and wrap

each in a slice of prosciutto. Place them in the air fryer basket, leaving space between them (if you're using a smaller air fryer, work in batches if necessary), and cook for 6 minutes, flipping halfway through. Use a spatula to remove the rings from the air fryer. Serve with the reserved half of the guacamole.

5. Store leftovers in an airtight container in the refrigerator for up to 4 days. Reheat in a preheated 400°F (205°C) air fryer for about 3 minutes, until heated through.

888. Pepperoni Chips

Preparation Time: 10 minutes
Cooking Time: 8 minutes
Servings: 8

Ingredients:
- 14 slices pepperoni

Directions:
1. Place pepperoni slices into ungreased air fryer basket. Adjust the temperature to 350°F (180°C) and set the timer for 8 minutes. Pepperoni will be browned and crispy when done.

2. Let cool 5 minutes before serving. Store in airtight container at room temperature up to 3 days.

889. Salami Roll-Ups

Preparation Time: 10 minutes
Cooking Time: 6 minutes
Servings: 8

Ingredients:
- 4 ounces (113 g) cream cheese, broken into 16 equal pieces
- 16 (0.5-ounce / 14-g) deli slices Genoa salami

Directions:
1. Place a piece of cream cheese at the edge of a slice of salami and roll to close. Secure with a toothpick. Repeat with remaining cream cheese pieces and salami.

2. Place roll-ups in an ungreased 6-inch round nonstick baking dish and place into air fryer basket. Adjust the temperature to 350°F (180°C) and set the timer for 4 minutes. Salami will be crispy and cream cheese will be warm when done. Let cool 5 minutes before serving.

890. Mozzarella Pizza Crust

Preparation Time: 10 minutes
Cooking Time: 10 minutes
Servings: 8

Ingredients:
- ½ cup shredded whole-milk Mozzarella cheese

- 2 tablespoons blanched finely ground almond flour
- 1 tablespoon full-fat cream cheese
- 1 large egg white

Directions:
1. Place Mozzarella, almond flour, and cream cheese in a medium microwave-safe bowl. Microwave for 30 seconds.

2. Stir until smooth ball of dough forms. Add egg white and stir until soft round dough forms.

3. Press into a 6-inch round pizza crust.

4. Cut a piece of parchment to fit your air fryer basket and place crust on parchment. Place into the air fryer basket.

5. Adjust the temperature to 350°F (180°C) and set the timer for 10 minutes.

6. Flip after 5 minutes and at this time place any desired toppings on the crust. Continue cooking until golden. Serve immediately.

891. Cauliflower Buns

Preparation Time: 10 minutes
Cooking Time: 12 minutes
Servings: 8

Ingredients:
- 1 (12-ounce 340-g) steamer bag cauliflower, cooked according to package instructions
- ½ cup shredded Mozzarella cheese
- ¼ cup shredded mild Cheddar cheese
- ¼ cup blanched finely ground almond flour
- 1 large egg
- ½ teaspoon salt

Directions:
1. Let cooked cauliflower cool about 10 minutes. Use a kitchen towel to wring out excess moisture, then place cauliflower in a food processor.

2. Add Mozzarella, Cheddar, flour, egg, and salt to the food processor and pulse twenty times until mixture is combined. It will resemble a soft, wet dough.

3. Divide mixture into eight piles. Wet your hands with water to prevent sticking, then press each pile into a flat bun shape, about ½-inch thick.

4. Cut a sheet of parchment to fit air fryer basket. Working in batches if needed, place the formed dough onto ungreased parchment in air fryer basket. Adjust the temperature to 350°F (180°C) and set the timer for 12 minutes, turning buns halfway through cooking.

5. Let buns cool 10 minutes before serving. Serve warm.

892. Oregano Parmesan Calamari Rings

Preparation Time: 10 minutes
Cooking Time: 15 minutes
Servings: 8

Ingredients:
- 2 large egg yolks
- 1 cup powdered Parmesan cheese (or pork dust for dairy-free; see here)
- ¼ cup coconut flour
- 3 teaspoons dried oregano leaves
- ½ teaspoon garlic powder
- ½ teaspoon onion powder
- 1 pound (454 g) calamari, sliced into rings
- Fresh oregano leaves, for garnish (optional)
- 1 cup no-sugar-added marinara sauce, for serving (optional)
- Lemon slices, for serving (optional)

Directions:
1. Spray the air fryer basket with avocado oil. Preheat the air fryer to 400°F (205°C).
2. In a shallow dish, whisk the egg yolks. In a separate bowl, mix together the Parmesan, coconut flour, and spices.
3. Dip the calamari rings in the egg yolks, tap off any excess egg, then dip them into the cheese mixture and coat well. Use your hands to press the coating onto the calamari if necessary. Spray the coated rings with avocado oil.
4. Place the calamari rings in the air fryer, leaving space between them, and cook for 15 minutes, or until golden brown. Garnish with fresh oregano, if desired, and serve with marinara sauce for dipping and lemon slices, if desired.
5. Best served fresh. Store leftovers in an airtight container in the fridge for up to 5 days. Reheat in a preheated 400°F (205°C) air fryer for 3 minutes, or until heated through.

893. Cheesy Bacon Stuffed Sweet Pepper

Preparation Time: 10 minutes
Cooking Time: 8 minutes
Servings: 8

Ingredients:
- 8 mini sweet peppers
- 4 ounces (113 g) full-fat cream cheese, softened
- 4 slices sugar-free bacon, cooked and crumbled
- ¼ cup shredded pepper jack cheese

Directions:
1. Remove the tops from the peppers and slice each one in half lengthwise. Use a small knife to remove seeds and membranes.
2. In a small bowl, mix cream cheese, bacon, and pepper jack.
3. Place 3 teaspoons of the mixture into each sweet pepper and press down smooth. Place into the fryer basket.
4. Adjust the temperature to 400°F (205°C) and set the timer for 8 minutes.
5. Serve warm.

894. Lemon Chicken

Preparation Time: 10 minutes
Cooking Time: 25 minutes
Servings: 8

Ingredients:
- 8 bone-in chicken thighs, skin on
- 1 tablespoon olive oil
- 1½ teaspoons lemon-pepper seasoning
- ½ teaspoon paprika
- ½ teaspoon garlic powder
- ¼ teaspoon freshly ground black pepper
- Juice of ½ lemon

Directions:
1. Preheat the air fryer to 360°F (182°C).
2. Place the chicken in a large bowl and drizzle with the olive oil. Top with the lemon-pepper seasoning, paprika, garlic powder, and freshly ground black pepper. Toss until thoroughly coated.
3. Working in batches if necessary, arrange the chicken in a single layer in the basket of the air fryer. Pausing halfway through the cooking time to turn the chicken, air fry for 20 to 25 minutes, until a thermometer inserted into the thickest piece registers 165°F (74°C).
4. Transfer the chicken to a serving platter and squeeze the lemon juice over the top.

895. Aromatic Chicken

Preparation Time: 10 minutes
Cooking Time: 25 minutes
Servings: 8

Ingredients:
- 1 (4-pound / 1.8 kg) chicken, giblets removed
- ½ onion, quartered
- 1 tablespoon olive oil

Secret Spice Rub
- 2 teaspoons salt
- 1 teaspoon paprika
- ½ teaspoon onion powder
- ½ teaspoon garlic powder
- ½ teaspoon dried thyme
- ½ teaspoon freshly ground black pepper
- ¼ teaspoon cayenne

Directions:
1. Preheat the air fryer to 350°F (180°C).
2. Use paper towels to blot the chicken dry. Stuff the chicken with the onion. Rub the chicken with the oil.
3. To make the spice rub: In a small bowl, combine the salt, paprika, onion powder, garlic powder, thyme, black pepper, and cayenne; stir until thoroughly combined. Sprinkle the chicken with the spice rub until thoroughly coated.

4. Place the chicken breast side down in the air fryer basket. Air fry the chicken for 30 minutes. Use tongs to carefully flip the chicken over and air fry for an additional 30 minutes, or until the temperature of a thermometer inserted into the thickest part of the chicken registers 165°F (74°C).

5. Let the chicken rest for 10 minutes. Discard the onion and serve.

896. Broccoli Cheese Chicken

Preparation Time: 10 minutes
Cooking Time: 19 minutes
Servings: 4

Ingredients:
- 1 tablespoon avocado oil
- ¼ cup chopped onion
- ½ cup finely chopped broccoli
- 4 ounces (113 g) cream cheese, at room temperature
- 2 ounces (57 g) Cheddar cheese, shredded
- 1 teaspoon garlic powder
- ½ teaspoon sea salt, plus additional for seasoning, divided
- ¼ freshly ground black pepper, plus additional for seasoning, divided
- 2 pounds (907 g) boneless, skinless chicken breasts
- 1 teaspoon smoked paprika

Directions:
1. Heat a medium skillet over medium-high heat and pour in the avocado oil. Add the onion and broccoli and cook, stirring occasionally, for 5 to 8 minutes, until the onion is tender.

2. Transfer to a large bowl and stir in the cream cheese, Cheddar cheese, and garlic powder, and season to taste with salt and pepper.

3. Hold a sharp knife parallel to the chicken breast and cut a long pocket into one side. Stuff the chicken pockets with the broccoli mixture, using toothpicks to secure the pockets around the filling.

4. In a small dish, combine the paprika, ½ teaspoon salt, and ¼ teaspoon pepper. Sprinkle this over the outside of the chicken.

5. Set the air fryer to 400°F (205°C). Place the chicken in a single layer in the air fryer basket, cooking in batches if necessary, and cook for 14 to 16 minutes, until an instant-read thermometer reads 160°F (71°C). Place the chicken on a plate and tent a piece of aluminum foil over the chicken. Allow to rest for 5 to 10 minutes before serving.

897. Ham Chicken with Cheese

Preparation Time: 15 minutes
Cooking Time: 20 minutes
Servings: 4

Ingredients:
- ¼ cup unsalted butter, softened
- 4 ounces (113 g) cream cheese, softened
- 1½ teaspoons Dijon mustard
- 2 tablespoons white wine vinegar
- ¼ cup water
- 2 cups shredded cooked chicken
- ¼ pound (113 g) ham, chopped
- 4 ounces (113 g) sliced Swiss or Provolone cheese

Directions:
1. Preheat the air fryer to 380°F (193°C). Lightly coat a 6-cup casserole dish that will fit in the air fryer, such as an 8-inch round pan, with olive oil and set aside.

2. In a large bowl and using an electric mixer, combine the butter, cream cheese, Dijon mustard, and vinegar. With the motor running on low speed, slowly add the water and beat until smooth. Set aside.

3. Arrange an even layer of chicken in the bottom of the prepared pan, followed by the ham. Spread the butter and cream cheese mixture on top of the ham, followed by the cheese slices on the top layer. Air fry for 20 to 25 minutes until warmed through and the cheese has browned.

898. Buttery Strip Steak

Preparation Time: 7 minutes
Cooking Time: 12 minutes
Servings: 2

Ingredients:
- ½ cup (1 stick) unsalted butter, at room temperature
- 1 cup finely grated Parmesan cheese
- ¼ cup finely ground blanched almond flour
- 1½ pounds (680g) New York strip steak
- Sea salt, freshly ground black pepper, to taste

Directions:
1. Place the butter, Parmesan cheese, and almond flour in a food processor. Process until smooth. Transfer to a sheet of parchment paper and form into a log. Wrap tightly in plastic wrap. Freeze for 45 minutes or refrigerate for at least 4 hours.

2. While the butter is chilling, season the steak liberally with salt and pepper. Let the steak rest at room temperature for about 45 minutes.

3. Place the grill pan or basket in your air fryer, set it to 400°F (205°C), and let it preheat for 5 minutes.

4. Working in batches, if necessary, place the steak on the grill pan and cook for 4 minutes. Flip and cook for 3 minutes more, until the steak is brown on both sides.

5. Remove the steak from the air fryer and arrange an equal amount of the Parmesan butter on top of each steak. Return the steak to the air fryer and continue cooking for another 5 minutes, until an instant-read thermometer reads 120°F (49°C) for medium-rare and the crust is golden brown (or to your desired doneness).

6. Transfer the cooked steak to a plate; let rest for 10 minutes before serving.

899. Steak with Bell Pepper

Preparation Time: 15 minutes
Cooking Time: 20 minutes
Servings: 2

Ingredients:
- ¼ cup avocado oil
- ¼ cup freshly squeezed lime juice
- 2 teaspoons minced garlic
- 1 tablespoon chili powder
- ½ teaspoon ground cumin
- Sea salt, Freshly ground black pepper, to taste
- 1 pound (454 g) top sirloin steak or flank steak, thinly sliced against the grain
- 1 red bell pepper, cored, seeded, and cut into ½-inch slices
- 1 green bell pepper, cored, seeded, and cut into ½-inch slices
- 1 large onion, sliced

Directions:
1. In a small bowl or blender, combine the avocado oil, lime juice, garlic, chili powder, cumin, and salt and pepper to taste.
2. Place the sliced steak in a zip-top bag or shallow dish. Place the bell peppers and onion in a separate zip-top bag or dish. Pour half the marinade over the steak and the other half over the vegetables. Seal both bags and let the steak and vegetables marinate in the refrigerator for at least 1 hour or up to 4 hours.
3. Line the air fryer basket with an air fryer liner or aluminum foil. Remove the vegetables from their bag or dish and shake off any excess marinade. Set the air fryer to 400°F (205°C). Place the vegetables in the air fryer basket and cook for 13 minutes.
4. Remove the steak from its bag or dish and shake off any excess marinade. Place the steak on top of the vegetables in the air fryer, and cook for 7 to 10 minutes or until an instant-read thermometer reads 120°F (49°C) for medium-rare (or cook to your desired doneness).
5. Serve with desired fixings, such as keto tortillas, lettuce, sour cream, avocado slices, shredded Cheddar cheese, and cilantro.

900. Red Wine Rib

Preparation Time: 15 minutes
Cooking Time: 10 minutes
Servings: 2

Ingredients:
- 1½ pounds (680g) short ribs
- 1 cup red wine
- 1 lemon, juiced
- 1 teaspoon fresh ginger, grated
- 1 teaspoon salt
- 1 teaspoon black pepper
- 1 teaspoon paprika
- 1 teaspoon chipotle chili powder
- 1 cup keto tomato paste

- 1 teaspoon garlic powder
- 1 teaspoon cumin

Directions:
1. In a ceramic bowl, place the beef ribs, wine, lemon juice, ginger, salt, black pepper, paprika, and chipotle chili powder. Cover and let it marinate for 3 hours in the refrigerator.
2. Discard the marinade and add the short ribs to the Air Fryer basket. Cook in the preheated Air fry at 380°F (193°C) for 10 minutes, turning them over halfway through the cooking time.
3. In the meantime, heat the saucepan over medium heat; add the reserved marinade and stir in the tomato paste, garlic powder, and cumin. Cook until the sauce has thickened slightly.
4. Pour the sauce over the warm ribs and serve immediately. Bon appétit!

901. Mozzarella Bagels

Preparation Time: 15 minutes
Cooking Time: 14 minutes
Servings: 6

Ingredients:
- 1¾ cups shredded Mozzarella cheese or goat cheese
- 2 tablespoons unsalted butter or coconut oil
- 1 large egg, beaten
- 1 tablespoon apple cider vinegar
- 1 cup blanched almond flour
- 1 tablespoon baking powder
- ⅛ teaspoon fine sea salt
- 1½ teaspoons everything bagel seasoning

Directions:
1. Make the dough: Put the Mozzarella and butter in a large microwave-safe bowl and microwave for 1 to 2 minutes, until the cheese is entirely melted. Stir well. Add the egg and vinegar. Using a hand mixer on medium, combine well. Add the almond flour, baking powder, and salt and, using the mixer, combine well.
2. Lay a piece of parchment paper on the countertop and place the dough on it. Knead it for about 3 minutes. The dough should be a little sticky but pliable. (If the dough is too sticky, chill it in the refrigerator for an hour or overnight.)
3. Preheat the air fryer to 350°F (180°C). Spray a baking sheet or pie pan that will fit into your air fryer with avocado oil.
4. Divide the dough into 6 equal portions. Roll 1 portion into a log that is 6 -inches long and about ½ -inch thick. Form the log into a circle and seal the edges together, making a bagel shape. Repeat with the remaining portions of dough, making 6 bagels.
5. Place the bagels on the greased baking sheet. Spray the bagels with avocado oil and top with everything bagel seasoning, pressing the seasoning into the dough with your hands.
6. Place the bagels in the air fryer and cook for 14 minutes, or until cooked through and

golden brown, flipping after 6 minutes.

7. Remove the bagels from the air fryer and allow them to cool slightly before slicing them in half and serving. Store leftovers in an airtight container in the fridge for up to 4 days or in the freezer for up to a month.

902. Cheesy Roll

Preparation Time: 15 minutes
Cooking Time: 10 minutes
Servings: 4

Ingredients:
* 2½ cups shredded Mozzarella cheese
* 2 ounces (57 g) cream cheese, softened
* 1 cup blanched finely ground almond flour
* ½ teaspoon vanilla extract
* ½ cup erythritol
* 1 tablespoon ground cinnamon

Directions:
1. In a large microwave-safe bowl, combine Mozzarella cheese, cream cheese, and flour. Microwave the mixture on high 90 seconds until cheese is melted.
2. Add vanilla extract and erythritol, and mix 2 minutes until a dough forms.
3. Once the dough is cool enough to work with your hands, about 2 minutes, spread it out into a 12-inch × 4-inch rectangle on ungreased parchment paper. Evenly sprinkle dough with cinnamon.
4. Starting at the long side of the dough, roll lengthwise to form a log. Slice the log into twelve even pieces.
5. Divide rolls between two ungreased 6-inch round nonstick baking dishes. Place one dish into air fryer basket. Adjust the temperature to 375°F (190ºC) and set the timer for 10 minutes.
6. Cinnamon rolls will be done when golden around the edges and mostly firm. Repeat with second dish. Allow rolls to cool in dishes 10 minutes before serving.

903. Cheddar Omelet

Preparation Time: 5 minutes
Cooking Time: 12 minutes
Servings: 2

Ingredients:
* 4 large eggs
* 1½ cups chopped fresh spinach leaves
* 2 tablespoons peeled and chopped yellow onion
* 2 tablespoons salted butter, melted
* ½ cup shredded mild Cheddar cheese
* ¼ teaspoon salt

Directions:
1. In an ungreased 6-inch round nonstick baking dish, whisk eggs. Stir in spinach, onion, butter,

Cheddar, and salt.

2. Place dish into air fryer basket. Adjust the temperature to 320°F (160ºC) and set the timer for 12 minutes. Omelet will be done when browned on the top and firm in the middle.

3. Slice in half and serve warm on two medium plates.

904. Golden Bacon Calzones

Preparation Time: 15 minutes
Cooking Time: 12 minutes
Servings: 4

Ingredients:
* 2 large eggs
* 1 cup blanched finely ground almond flour
* 2 cups shredded Mozzarella cheese
* 2 ounces (57 g) cream cheese, softened and broken into small pieces
* 4 slices cooked sugar-free bacon, crumbled

Directions:
1. Beat eggs in a small bowl. Pour into a medium nonstick skillet over medium heat and scramble. Set aside.
2. In a large microwave-safe bowl, mix flour and Mozzarella.
3. Add cream cheese to bowl.
4. Place bowl in microwave and cook 45 seconds on high to melt cheese, then stir with a fork until a soft dough ball forms.
5. Cut a piece of parchment to fit air fryer basket. Separate dough into two sections and press each out into an 8-inch round.
6. On half of each dough round, place half of the scrambled eggs and crumbled bacon. Fold the other side of the dough over and press to seal the edges.
7. Place calzones on ungreased parchment and into air fryer basket. Adjust the temperature to 350°F (180ºC) and set the timer for 12 minutes, turning calzones halfway through cooking. Crust will be golden and firm when done.
8. Let calzones cool on a cooking rack 5 minutes before serving.

905. Parmesan Ramekin

Preparation Time: 5 minutes
Cooking Time: 8 minutes
Servings: 2

Ingredients:
* 2 teaspoons unsalted butter (or coconut oil for dairy-free), for greasing the ramekins
* 4 large eggs
* 2 teaspoons chopped fresh thyme
* ½ teaspoon fine sea salt
* ¼ teaspoon ground black pepper
* 2 tablespoons heavy cream (or unsweetened, unflavored almond milk

for dairy-free)

- 3 tablespoons finely grated Parmesan cheese (or Kite Hill brand chive cream cheese style spread, softened, for dairy-free)
- Fresh thyme leaves, for garnish (optional)

Directions:
1. Preheat the air fryer to 400°F (205°C). Grease two 4-ounce (113-g) ramekins with the butter.
2. Crack 2 eggs into each ramekin and divide the thyme, salt, and pepper between the ramekins. Pour 1 tablespoon of the heavy cream into each ramekin. Sprinkle each ramekin with 1½ tablespoons of the Parmesan cheese.
3. Place the ramekins in the air fryer and cook for 8 minutes for soft-cooked yolks (longer if you desire a harder yolk).
4. Garnish with a sprinkle of ground black pepper and thyme leaves, if desired. Best served fresh.

906. Warm Soufflés

Preparation Time: 15 minutes
Cooking Time: 12 minutes
Servings: 4

Ingredients:
- 3 large eggs, whites and yolks separated
- ¼ teaspoon cream of tartar
- ½ cup shredded sharp Cheddar cheese
- 3 ounces (85 g) cream cheese, softened

Direction:
1. In a large bowl, beat egg whites together with cream of tartar until soft peaks form, about 2 minutes.
2. In a separate medium bowl, beat egg yolks, Cheddar, and cream cheese together until frothy, about 1 minute. Add egg yolk mixture to whites, gently folding until combined.
3. Pour mixture evenly into four 4-inch ramekins greased with cooking spray. Place ramekins into air fryer basket. Adjust the temperature to 350°F (180°C) and set the timer for 12 minutes. Eggs will be browned on the top and firm in the center when done. Serve warm.

907. Pork Sausage and Cheese Balls

Preparation Time: 15 minutes
Cooking Time: 12 minutes
Servings: 16 balls

Ingredients:
- 1 pound (454 g) pork breakfast sausage
- ½ cup shredded Cheddar cheese
- 1 ounce (28 g) full-fat cream cheese, softened
- 1 large egg

Direction:
1. Mix all ingredients in a large bowl. Form into sixteen (1-inch) balls. Place the balls into the air fryer basket.
2. Adjust the temperature to 400°F (204°C) and air fry for 12 minutes.
3. Shake the basket two or three times during cooking. Sausage balls will be browned on the outside and have an internal temperature of at least 145°F (63°C) when completely cooked.
4. Serve warm.

908. Mexican-Style Shakshuka

Preparation Time: 5 minutes
Cooking Time: 6 minutes
Servings: 1

Ingredients:
- ½ cup salsa
- 2 large eggs, room temperature
- ½ teaspoon fine sea salt
- ¼ teaspoon smoked paprika
- ⅛ teaspoon ground cumin

For Garnish:
- 2 tablespoons cilantro leaves

Directions:
1. Preheat the air fryer to 400°F (204°C).
2. Place the salsa in a pie pan or a casserole dish that will fit into your air fryer. Crack the eggs into the salsa and sprinkle them with the salt, paprika, and cumin.
3. Place the pan in the air fryer and bake for 6 minutes, or until the egg whites are set and the yolks are cooked to your liking.
4. Remove from the air fryer and garnish with the cilantro before serving.
5. Best served fresh.

909. Simple Vinegary Pork Belly

Preparation Time: 5 minutes
Cooking Time: 12 minutes
Servings: 4

Ingredients:
- 1 pound (454 g) slab pork belly
- ½ cup apple cider vinegar
- Fine sea salt
- For Serving (Optional):
- Guacamole
- Pico de gallo

Directions:
1. Slice the pork belly into ⅛-inch-thick strips and place them in a shallow dish. Pour in the vinegar and stir to coat the pork belly. Place in the fridge to marinate for 30 minutes.
2. Spray the air fryer basket with avocado oil.

Preheat the air fryer to 400°F (205°C).

3. Remove the pork belly from the vinegar and place the strips in the air fryer basket in a single layer, leaving space between them. Cook in the air fryer for 10 to 12 minutes, until crispy, flipping after 5 minutes. Remove from the air fryer and sprinkle with salt. Serve with guacamole and pico de gallo, if desired.

4. Best served fresh. Store leftovers in an airtight container in the fridge for up to 5 days. Reheat in a preheated 400°F (205°C) air fryer for 5 minutes, or until heated through, flipping halfway through.

910. Turkey Kabobs

Preparation Time: 15 minutes
Cooking Time: 12 minutes
Servings: 8

Ingredients:
- 1 cup Parmesan cheese, grated
- 1½ cups of water
- 14 ounces (397 g) ground turkey
- 2 small eggs, beaten
- 1 teaspoon ground ginger
- 2½ tablespoons olive oil
- 1 cup chopped fresh parsley
- 2 tablespoons almond meal
- ¾ teaspoon salt
- 1 heaping teaspoon fresh rosemary, finely chopped
- ½ teaspoon ground allspice

Directions:
1. Mix all of the above ingredients in a bowl. Knead the mixture with your hands.
2. Then, take small portions and gently roll them into balls.
3. Now, preheat your Air Fryer to 380°F (193°C). Air fry for 8 to 10 minutes in the Air Fryer basket. Serve on a serving platter with skewers and eat with your favorite dipping sauce.

911. Dilled Chicken Breasts

Preparation Time: 10 minutes
Cooking Time: 14 minutes
Servings: 4

Ingredients:
- 1 cup Parmesan cheese, grated
- 1½ cups of water
- 14 ounces (397 g) ground turkey
- 2 small eggs, beaten
- 1 teaspoon ground ginger
- 2½ tablespoons olive oil
- 1 cup chopped fresh parsley
- 2 tablespoons almond meal
- ¾ teaspoon salt
- 1 heaping teaspoon fresh rosemary, finely chopped

- ½ teaspoon ground allspice

Directions:
1. Mix all of the above ingredients in a bowl. Knead the mixture with your hands.
2. Then, take small portions and gently roll them into balls.
3. Now, preheat your Air Fryer to 380°F (193°C). Air fry for 8 to 10 minutes in the Air Fryer basket. Serve on a serving platter with skewers and eat with your favorite dipping sauce.

912. Mackerel with Spinach

Preparation Time: 10 minutes
Cooking Time: 20 minutes
Servings: 4

Ingredients:
- 1-pound (454 g) mackerel, trimmed
- 1 bell pepper, chopped
- ½ cup spinach, chopped
- 1 tablespoon avocado oil
- 1 teaspoon ground black pepper
- 1 teaspoon keto tomato paste

Directions:
1. In the mixing bowl, mix bell pepper with spinach, ground black pepper, and tomato paste.
2. Fill the mackerel with spinach mixture.
3. Then brush the fish with avocado oil and put it in the air fryer.
4. Cook the fish at 365F (185°C) for 20 minutes.

913. Mackerel Fillet

Preparation Time: 10 minutes
Cooking Time: 20 minutes
Servings: 4

Ingredients:
- 12 oz mackerel fillet
- 2 oz Parmesan, grated
- 1 teaspoon ground coriander
- 1 tablespoon olive oil

Directions:
1. Sprinkle the mackerel fillet with olive oil and put it in the air fryer basket.
2. Top the fish with ground coriander and Parmesan.
3. Cook the fish at 390F (199°C) for 7 minutes.

247

914. Easy Sardines

Preparation Time: 15 minutes
Cooking Time: 10 minutes
Servings: 5

Ingredients:
- 12 oz sardines, trimmed, cleaned
- 1 cup coconut flour
- 1 tablespoon coconut oil
- 1 teaspoon salt

Directions:
1. Sprinkle the sardines with salt and coat in the coconut flour.
2. hen grease the air fryer basket with coconut oil and put the sardines inside.
3. Cook them at 385F (196°C) for 10 minutes.

915. Bacon Halibut Steak

Preparation Time: 15 minutes
Cooking Time: 10 minutes
Servings: 5

Ingredients:
- 24 oz halibut steaks (6 oz each fillet)
- 1 teaspoon avocado oil
- 1 teaspoon ground black pepper
- 4 oz bacon, sliced

Direction:
1. Sprinkle the halibut steaks with avocado oil and ground black pepper.
2. Then wrap the fish in the bacon slices and put in the air fryer.
3. Cook the fish at 390F (199°C) for 5 minutes per side.

916. Marshmallow Chocolate Pie

Preparation Time: 15 minutes
Cooking Time: 5 minutes
Servings: 4

Ingredients:
- 4 graham cracker sheets, snapped in half
- 8 large marshmallows
- 8 squares each of dark, milk, and white chocolate

Directions:
1. Arrange the crackers on a cutting board. Put 2 marshmallows onto half of the graham cracker halves.
2. Place 2 squares of chocolate on top of the crackers with marshmallows. Put the remaining crackers on top to create 4 sandwiches.
3. Wrap each one in baking paper, so it resembles a parcel. Bake in the preheated air fryer for 5 minutes at 340°F (171°C).
4. Serve at room temperature or chilled. Enjoy!

917. Fruit Skewers with Caramel Sauce

Preparation Time: 15 minutes
Cooking Time: 8 minutes
Servings: 4

Ingredients:
- 1 cup blueberries
- 1 banana, sliced
- 1 mango, peeled and cut into cubes
- 1 peach, cut into wedges
- 2 kiwi fruit, peeled and quartered
- 2 tablespoon caramel sauce

Directions:
1. Preheat air fryer to 340°F (171°C). Thread the fruit through your skewers.
2. Transfer to the greased frying basket and Air Fry for 6 to 8 minutes, turning once until the fruit caramelize slightly.
3. Drizzle with the caramel sauce and serve. Enjoy!

918. Almond-Drizzled Banana Fritters with Honey

Preparation Time: 10 minutes
Cooking Time: 10 minutes
Servings: 3

Ingredients:
- 3 ripe bananas, peeled
- 1 egg, whisked
- ¼ cup almond flour
- ¼ cup plain flour
- ½ teaspoon baking powder
- 1 teaspoon canola oil
- 1 tablespoon honey

Directions:
1. Mash your bananas in a bowl. Now, stir in the egg, almond flour, plain flour, and baking powder.
2. Drop spoonful of the batter into the preheated Air Fryer cooking basket. Brush the fritters with canola oil.
3. Cook the banana fritters at 360°F (182°C) for 10 minutes, flipping them halfway through the cooking time.
4. Drizzle with some honey just before serving. Enjoy!

919. Griddle Cakes

Preparation Time: 10 minutes
Cooking Time: 5 minutes
Servings: 2

Ingredients:
- ¾ cup self-rising flour
- ¼ teaspoon fine sea salt
- 2 tablespoons sugar
- ½ cup milk
- 2 eggs, lightly beaten
- 1 tablespoon butter
- Topping:
- 1 cup Greek-style yogurt
- 1 banana, mashed
- 2 tablespoons honey

Directions:
1. Mix the flour, salt, and sugar in a bowl. Then, stir in the milk, eggs, and butter.
2. Mix until smooth and uniform. Drop tablespoons of the batter into the Air Fryer pan. Cook at 300ºF (150ºC) for 4 to 5 minutes or until bubbles form on top of the griddle cakes.
3. Repeat with the remaining batter. Meanwhile, mix all ingredients for the topping. Place in your refrigerator until ready to serve.
4. Serve the griddle cakes with the chilled topping. Enjoy!

920. Cinnamon-Pecans Coffeecake

Preparation Time: 15 minutes
Cooking Time: 15 minutes
Servings: 4

Ingredients:
Cake:
- ½ cup unbleached white flour
- ¼ cup yellow cornmeal
- 1 teaspoon baking powder
- 3 tablespoons white sugar
- 1 tablespoon unsweetened cocoa powder
- A pinch of kosher salt
- 3 tablespoons coconut oil
- ¼ cup milk 1 egg
Topping:
- 2 tablespoons polenta
- ¼ cup brown sugar
- 1 teaspoon ground cinnamon
- ¼ cup pecans, chopped
- 2 tablespoons coconut oil

Directions:
1. In a large bowl, combine together the cake ingredients. Spoon the mixture into a lightly greased baking pan.
2. Then, in another bowl, combine the topping ingredients.
3. Spread the topping ingredients over your cake.
4. Bake the cake at 330ºF (166ºC) for 12 to 15 minutes until a tester comes out dry and clean.
5. Allow your cake to cool for about 15 minutes before cutting and serving. Enjoy!

921. Banana Crepes

Preparation Time: 5 minutes
Cooking Time: 5 minutes
Servings: 2

Ingredients:
- 1 small ripe banana
- ⅛ teaspoon baking powder
- ¼ cup chocolate chips
- 1 egg, whisked

Directions:
1. Mix all ingredients until creamy and fluffy. Let it stand for about 20 minutes.
2. Spritz the Air Fryer baking pan with cooking spray. Pour ½ of the batter into the pan using a measuring cup.
3. Cook at 230ºF (110ºC) for 4 to 5 minutes or until golden brown. Repeat with another crepe. Enjoy!

922. Bruschetta with Chopped Tomato

Preparation Time: 5 minutes
Cooking Time: 6 minutes
Servings: 3

Ingredients:
- ½ Italian bread, sliced
- 2 garlic cloves, peeled
- 2 tablespoons extra-virgin olive oil
- 2 ripe tomatoes, chopped
- 1 teaspoon dried oregano Salt, to taste
- 8 fresh basil leaves, roughly chopped

Directions:
1. Place the bread slices on the lightly greased Air Fryer grill pan. Bake at 370ºF (188ºC) for 3 minutes.
2. Cut a clove of garlic in half and rub over one side of the toast; brush with olive oil. Add the chopped tomatoes. Sprinkle with oregano and salt. Increase the temperature to 380ºF (193ºC).
3. Cook in the preheated Air Fryer for 3 minutes more. Garnish with fresh basil and serve. Serve and enjoy!

923. Hot Roasted Cauliflower Florets

Preparation Time: 10 minutes
Cooking Time: 12 minutes
Servings: 3

Ingredients:
- ½ cup plain flour
- ½ teaspoon shallot powder
- 1 teaspoon garlic powder
- ¼ teaspoon dried dill weed
- ½ teaspoon chipotle powder
- Sea salt and ground black pepper, to taste
- ½ cup rice milk
- 2 tablespoons coconut oil, softened
- 1 pound (454 g) cauliflower florets

Directions:
1. In a mixing bowl, thoroughly combine the flour, spices, rice milk and coconut oil. Mix to combine well.
2. Coat the cauliflower florets with the batter and allow the excess batter to drip back into the bowl.
3. Cook the cauliflower florets at 400°F (205°C) for 12 minutes, shaking the basket once or twice to ensure even browning.
4. Serve with some extra hot sauce, if desired. Enjoy!

924. Trout with Yogurt

Preparation Time: 10 minutes
Cooking Time: 12 minutes
Servings: 3

Ingredients:
- 4 trout pieces
- 2 tablespoon olive oil
- Salt to taste
- ½ cup greek yogurt
- 2 garlic cloves, minced
- 2 tablespoon fresh dill, finely chopped

Directions:
1. Preheat air fryer to 380°F (193°C). Drizzle the trout with olive oil and season with salt. Place the seasoned trout into the frying basket and Air Fry for 12 to 14 minutes, flipping once.
2. In a bowl, mix Greek yogurt, garlic, chopped dill, and salt. Top the trout with the dill sauce and serve.

945. Herbed Crab Croquettes

Preparation Time: 10 minutes
Cooking Time: 15 minutes
Servings: 4

Ingredients:
- 1½ pounds (680 g) lump crab meat
- ⅓ cup sour cream
- ⅓ cup mayonnaise
- 1 red pepper, finely chopped
- ⅓ cup red onion, chopped
- ½ celery stalk, chopped
- 1 teaspoon fresh tarragon, chopped
- 1 teaspoon fresh chives, chopped
- 1 teaspoon fresh parsley, chopped
- 1 teaspoon cayenne pepper
- 1 ½ cups breadcrumbs
- 2 teaspoon olive oil
- 1 cup flour
- 3 eggs, beaten
- Salt to taste
- Lemon wedges to serve

Directions:
1. Heat olive oil in a skillet over medium heat and sauté red pepper, onion, and celery for 5 minutes or until sweaty and translucent. Turn off the heat. Pour the breadcrumbs and salt on a plate.

2. In 2 separate bowls, add the flour and beaten eggs, respectively, set aside. In a separate bowl, add
3. crabmeat, mayo, sour cream, tarragon, chives, parsley, cayenne pepper, and vegetable sauteed mix.
4. Form bite-sized oval balls from the mixture and place them onto a plate. Preheat air fryer to 390°F (199°C). Dip each crab meatball in the beaten eggs and press them in the breadcrumb mixture.
5. Place the croquettes in the greased fryer basket without overcrowding. Cook for 10 minutes until golden brown, shaking once halfway through. Serve hot with lemon wedges.

926. Tiger Prawns with Firecracker Sauce

Preparation Time: 10 minutes
Cooking Time: 10 minutes
Servings: 4

Ingredients:
- 1 pound (454 g) tiger prawns, peeled
- Salt and black pepper to taste
- 2 eggs
- ½ cup flour
- ¼ cup sesame seeds
- ¾ cup seasoned breadcrumbs
Firecracker sauce:
- ⅓ cup sour cream
- 2 tablespoon buffalo sauce
- ¼ cup spicy ketchup
- 1 green onion, chopped

Directions:
1. Preheat air fryer to 390°F (199°C). Beat the eggs in a bowl with salt. In another bowl, mix breadcrumbs with sesame seeds.
2. In a third bowl, mix flour with salt and pepper. Dip prawns in the flour and then in the eggs, and finally in the crumbs.
3. Spray with cooking spray and Air Fry for 10 minutes, flipping once. Meanwhile, mix well all thee sauce ingredients, except for green onion in a bowl.
4. Serve the prawns with firecracker sauce and scatter with freshly chopped green onions.

927. Creamy Wild Salmon

Preparation Time: 5 minutes
Cooking Time: 15 minutes
Servings: 2

Ingredients:
- 4 Alaskan wild salmon fillets
- 2 teaspoon olive oil Salt to taste
- ½ cup heavy cream
- ½ cup milk

- 2 tablespoon fresh parsley, chopped

Directions:
1. Preheat air fryer to 380ºF (193ºC). Drizzle the fillets with olive oil, and season with salt and black pepper.
2. Place salmon in the frying basket and Bake for 15 minutes, turning once until tender and crispy. In a bowl, mix milk, parsley, salt, and whipped cream. Serve the salmon with the sauce.

928. Chicken with Peppers

Preparation Time: 10 minutes
Cooking Time: 10 minutes
Servings: 4

Ingredients:
- 1 cup breadcrumbs
- ½ cup yogurt
- 1 pound (454 g) chicken breasts, cut into strips
- ½ teaspoon red chili pepper
- 1 tablespoon hot sauce
- 2 eggs, beaten
- 1 teaspoon sweet paprika
- 1 teaspoon garlic powder

Directions:
1. Preheat air fryer to 390ºF (199ºC). Whisk eggs with the hot sauce and yogurt. In a shallow bowl, combine the breadcrumbs, paprika, cayenne pepper, and garlic powder. Line a baking dish with parchment paper.
2. Dip the chicken in the egg/yogurt mixture first, and then coat with breadcrumbs. Arrange on the sheet and Bake in the air fryer for 8 to 10 minutes. Flip the chicken over and bake for 6-8 more minutes. Serve.

929. Roasted Boston Butt

Preparation Time: 10 minutes
Cooking Time: 32 minutes
Servings: 4

Ingredients:
- 1 pound (454 g) Boston butt, thinly sliced across the grain into
- 2-inch-long strips
- ½ teaspoon red pepper flakes, crushed Sea
- salt and ground black pepper, to taste
- ½ pound (226 g) tomatillos, chopped
- 1 small-sized onion, chopped
- 2 chili peppers, chopped
- 2 cloves garlic
- 2 tablespoons fresh cilantro, chopped
- 1 tablespoon olive oil
- 1 teaspoon sea salt

Directions:

1. Rub the Boston butt with red pepper, salt, and black pepper. Spritz the bottom of the cooking basket with a nonstick cooking spray.
2. Roast the Boston butt in the preheated Air Fryer at 390ºF (199ºC) for 10 minutes. Shake the basket and cook another 10 minutes.
3. While the pork is roasting, make the salsa. Blend the remaining ingredients until smooth and uniform. Transfer the mixture to a saucepan and add 1 cup of water.
4. Bring to a boil; reduce the heat and simmer for 8 to 12 minutes. Serve the roasted pork with the salsa verde on the side. Enjoy!

930. Pork Cutlets with Plum Sauce

Preparation Time: 10 minutes
Cooking Time: 13 minutes
Servings: 4

Ingredients:
- 4 pork cutlets
- 2 teaspoon sesame oil
- ½ teaspoon ground
- black pepper Salt, to taste
- 1 tablespoon Creole seasoning
- 2 tablespoons aged balsamic vinegar
- 2 tablespoons soy sauce
- 6 ripe plums, pitted and diced

Directions:
1. Preheat your Air Fryer to 390ºF (199ºC). Toss the pork cutlets with the sesame oil, black pepper, salt, Creole seasoning, vinegar, and soy sauce.
2. Transfer them to a lightly greased baking pan; lower the pan onto the cooking basket.
3. Cook for 13 minutes in the preheated Air Fryer, flipping them halfway through the cooking time. Serve warm.

931. Pork Loin with Creamy Mushroom

Preparation Time: 10 minutes
Cooking Time: 20 minutes
Servings: 4

Ingredients:
- 2 pounds (907 g) top loin, boneless
- 1 tablespoon olive oil
- 1 teaspoon Celtic salt
- ¼ teaspoon ground black pepper, or more to taste
- 2 shallots, sliced
- 2 garlic cloves, minced
- 1 cup mushrooms, chopped
- 2 tablespoons all-purpose flour
- ¾ cup cream of mushroom soup
- 1 teaspoon chili powder
- Salt, to taste

Directions:
1. Pat dry the pork and drizzle with olive oil. Season with Celtic salt and pepper. Cook in the preheated Air Fryer at 370ºF (188ºC) for

10 minutes. Top with shallot slices and cook another 10 minutes.

2. Test the temperature of the meat; it should be around 150 °F (66 °C). Reserve the pork and onion, keeping warm.

3. Add the cooking juices to a saucepan and preheat over medium-high heat. Cook the garlic and mushrooms until aromatic about 2 minutes. Combine the flour with the mushroom soup.

4. Add the flour mixture to the pan along with the chili powder and salt. Gradually stir into the pan. Bring to a boil; immediately turn the heat to medium and cook for 2 to 3 minutes stirring frequently. Spoon the sauce over the reserved pork and onion. Enjoy!

932. Cinnamon Banana Muffins

Preparation Time: 7 minutes
Cooking Time: 20 minutes
Servings: 4

Ingredients:
- 1 large egg, whisked
- 1 ripe banana, peeled and mashed
- 1/4 cup butter, melted
- 1/4 cup agave nectar
- 1/2 cup all-purpose flour
- 1/4 almond flour
- 1 teaspoon baking powder
- 1/4 cup brown sugar
- 1/2 teaspoon vanilla essence
- 1 teaspoon cinnamon powder
- 1/4 teaspoon ground cloves

Directions:
1. Start by preheating your Air Fryer to 320 degrees F.
2. Mix all ingredients in a bowl.
3. Scrape the batter into silicone baking molds; place them in the Air Fryer basket.
4. Bake your muffins for about 20 minutes or until a tester comes out dry and clean.
5. Allow the muffins to cool before unmolding and serving.

933. Bourbon Ciabatta Bread Pudding

Preparation Time: 7 minutes
Cooking Time: 31 minutes
Servings: 5

Ingredients:
- 1 ½ cups ciabatta bread, cubed
- 2 eggs, whisked
- 1/2 cup double cream
- 1/2 cup milk
- 1/2 teaspoon vanilla extract
- 1 tablespoon bourbon
- 1/4 cup honey
- 1/2 cup golden raisins

Directions:
1. Place the ciabatta bread in a lightly greased baking pan.
2. In a mixing bowl, thoroughly combine the eggs, double cream, milk, vanilla, bourbon, and honey.
3. Put the egg/cream mixture over the bread cubes.
4. Fold in the raisins and set aside for 15 minutes to soak.
5. Bake your bread pudding at 360 degrees F for about 20 minutes or until the custard is set but still a little wobbly.
6. Serve at room temperature. Bon appétit!

934. Quinoa Patties

Preparation Time: 8 minutes
Cooking Time: 20 minutes
Servings: 4

Ingredients:
- 1 ½ cups quinoa, cooked
- 1/2 cup bread crumbs
- 1/2 cup Pecorino cheese, grated
- 2 eggs, beaten
- 2 garlic cloves, minced
- 1/2 small onion, chopped
- 1 small bell pepper, seeded and chopped
- 1 tablespoon olive oil
- 2 tablespoons fresh Mediterranean herbs, finely chopped
- ¼ tsp Sea salt and ground black pepper

Directions:
1. First by preheating your Air Fryer to 370 degrees F.
2. Mix all fixings until everything is all around consolidated.
3. Structure the combination into patties.
4. Air fry the patties for around 20 minutes or until cooked through.
5. Turn them throughout part of the way through the cooking time.
6. Bon appétit!

935. Easy Cornbread Bites

Preparation Time: 9 minutes
Cooking Time: 26 minutes
Servings: 6

Ingredients:
- 1/2 cup all-purpose flour
- 1/2 cup yellow cornmeal
- 1 ½ teaspoons baking powder
- 4 tablespoons honey
- A pinch of sea salt
- A pinch of grated nutmeg
- 4 tablespoons coconut oil, room temperature
- 2 eggs, whisked
- 1/2 cup milk

Directions:
1. Preheating your Air Fryer to 350 degrees F.
2. Mix all ingredients until everything is well incorporated.
3. Scrape the batter into baking molds and place them in the Air Fryer basket.
4. Bake your mini cornbread for about 22 minutes or until a tester comes out dry and clean.
5. Allow your mini cornbread to cool before unmolding and serving.
6. Bon appétit!

936. Cheesy Cauliflower Risotto

Preparation Time: 8 minutes
Cooking Time: 16 minutes
Servings: 4

Ingredients:
- 2 cups rice, cooked
- 2 tablespoons olive oil
- 1/2 cup cauliflower, chopped
- 1/2 cup vegetable broth
- 4 tablespoons mozzarella cheese, shredded

Directions:
1. Start by preheating your Air Fryer to 350 degrees F.
2. Thoroughly combine all ingredients in a lightly greased baking pan.
3. Lower the pan into the Air Fryer cooking basket.
4. Cook for about 10 minutes or until cooked through.
5. Bon appétit!

937. Glazed Carrots

Preparation Time: 10 minutes
Cooking Time: 15 minutes
Servings: 8

Ingredients
- ¼ cup of butter
- ¼ teaspoon of salt
- 2 pounds of carrots, should be peeled and cut into steaks
- ¼ cup of packed brown sugar
- 1 /8 teaspoon of ground white pepper

Directions:
1. Place the carrots into a large saucepan, pour water to reach 1- inch depth, and bring to a boil.
2. Reduce the heat to low, cover, and simmer the carrots until they become tender in about 8-10 minutes.
3. Drain and transfer to a neat bowl.
4. Melt butter in the same saucepan, stir salt, brown sugar, and white pepper into the butter until the salt and sugar have dissolved.
5. Transfer the carrots into brown sugar sauce; cook and keep stirring until the carrots are glazed with the sauce in about 5 minutes.

938. Peanut Butter Banana Melties

Preparation Time: 10 minutes
Cooking Time: 15 minutes
Servings: 4

Ingredients
- ½ cup of peanut butter
- 4 large bananas
- ½ cup of chocolate chips

Directions:
1. Without peeling the bananas, slice each of them vertically.
2. Smear the inside of each of them with peanut butter and sprinkle with chocolate chips.
3. Place the 2 halves back together and wrap each banana individually in aluminum foil.
4. Now cook in the hot coal of a campfire until the banana becomes hot, and the chocolate has melted in about 10-15 minutes (this depends on the level of heat from the coals).

939. Blueberry Mint Smoothie

Preparation Time: 10 minutes
Servings: 2

Ingredients
- 1 cup of water
- 1 avocado, to be peeled and pitted
- 2 teaspoons of lemon juice
- 2 cups of frozen blueberries
- 1 cup of fresh mint leaves
- ½ cup of orange juice

Directions:
1. Blend blueberries, mint leaves, water, avocado, lemon juice, and orange juice in a blender until they become smooth.

940. New York Cheesecake

Preparation Time: 30 minutes
Cooking Time: 1 hour
Servings: 12

Ingredients
- 2 tablespoons of butter, to be melted
- 1 ½ cups of white sugar
- 4 large eggs
- 15 large rectangular piece or either 2 squares or 4 small rectangular pieces of graham crackers, to be crushed
- 4 (8 ounce) packages cream cheese
- ¾ cup of milk
- 1 cup of sour cream
- ¼ cup of all-purpose flour
- 4 large eggs
- 1 tablespoon of vanilla extract

Directions:

1. Preheat the oven to 3500F (1750C).
2. Then grease a 9-inch spring form pan.
3. Get a medium bowl and mix melted butter with graham cracker crumbs.
4. Then, press on the bottom of the spring form pan.
5. Get a large bowl and mix sugar with cream cheese until they become smooth.
6. Blend in milk, and after that, mix the eggs one after the other and let it incorporate.
7. Then mix in vanilla, sour cream, and flour until they become smooth.
8. Then pour filling into the prepared crust.
9. Bake in the already preheated oven for like 1 hour.
10. Turn off the oven and leave the cake to cool in it while the oven door is closed for about 5-6 hours; this is necessary to prevent cracking.
11. Then chill in the refrigerator until you are ready to serve.

Directions:
1. Preheat air fryer to 220°F (104°C).
2. Add sugar and butter to a medium-size ramekin and beat evenly.
3. Slowly whisk in egg and egg yolk until fresh yellow color is obtained.
4. Mix in the lemon juice.
5. Place the ramekin in the preheated air fryer when your air fryer displays "READY" (select the cooking preset, and make minor adjustments according to your desired doneness.) and choose a shake reminder.
6. Bake at 220°F (104°C) for 6 minutes.
7. Increase the temperature to 320°F (160°C) and cook for 13 to 15 minutes.
8. Remove the ramekin and use a spoon to check for any lumps.
9. Serve chilled. Enjoy!

941. Molten Chocolate Cake

Preparation Time: 4 minutes
Cooking Time: 18 minutes
Servings: 4

Ingredients:
- 2 tablespoons butter, melted
- 3 ½ tablespoon sugar
- 1 ½ tablespoon self-rising flour
- 3 ½ ounces (99 g) dark chocolate, melted
- 2 eggs

Directions:
1. Preheat air fryer to 360°F (182°C). In a bowl, beat the eggs and sugar until frothy.
2. Stir in butter and chocolate and gently fold in the flour.
3. Divide the mixture between 4 greased ramekins.
4. When your air fryer displays "READY" (select the cooking preset, and make minor adjustments according to your desired doneness.) and choose a shake reminder.
5. Bake in the air fryer for 18 minutes.
6. Let cool for a few minutes before inverting the lava cakes onto serving plates.
7. Enjoy!

942. Lemon Curd

Preparation Time: 6 minutes
Cooking Time: 13 minutes
Servings: 2

Ingredients:
- 3 tablespoons butter
- 3 tablespoons sugar
- 1 egg
- 1 egg yolk
- ¾ lemon, juiced

943. Chocolate Glazed Banana Chips

Preparation Time: 6 minutes
Cooking Time: 14 minutes
Servings: 2

Ingredients:
- 2 bananas, cut into slices
- ¼ teaspoon lemon zest
- 1 tablespoon agave syrup
- 1 tablespoon cocoa powder
- 1 tablespoon coconut oil, melted

Directions:
1. Preheat air fryer to 370°F (188°C).
2. Toss the bananas with the lemon zest and agave syrup.
3. Transfer your bananas to the parchment-lined cooking basket.
4. When your air fryer displays "READY" (select the cooking preset, and make minor adjustments according to your desired doneness.) and choose a shake reminder.
5. Bake in the preheated Air Fryer at 370°F (188°C) for 12 minutes, turning them over halfway through the cooking time.
6. In the meantime, melt the coconut oil in your microwave; add the cocoa powder and whisk to combine well.
7. Serve the baked banana chips with a few drizzles of the chocolate glaze.
8. Enjoy!

944. American Moon Pie

Preparation Time: 6 minutes
Cooking Time: 11 minutes
Servings: 4

Ingredients:
- 4 graham cracker sheets, snapped in half
- 8 large marshmallows
- 8 squares each of dark, milk, and white chocolate

Directions:
1. Preheat air fryer to 340ºF (171ºC).
2. Arrange the crackers on a cutting board.
3. Put 2 marshmallows onto half of the graham cracker halves.
4. Place 2 squares of chocolate on top of the crackers with marshmallows.
5. Put the remaining crackers on top to create 4 sandwiches.
6. Wrap each one in baking paper, so it resembles a parcel.
7. When your air fryer displays "READY" (select the cooking preset, and make minor adjustments according to your desired doneness.) and choose a shake reminder.
8. Bake in the preheated air fryer for 5 minutes at 340ºF (171ºC).
9. Serve at room temperature or chilled.

945. Coconut Pancake

Preparation Time: 9 minutes
Cooking Time: 4 minutes
Servings: 4

Ingredients:
- ½ cup flour
- 1/3 cup coconut milk
- 2 eggs
- 1 tablespoon coconut oil, melted
- 1 teaspoon vanilla
- A pinch of ground cardamom
- ½ cup coconut chips

Directions:
1. Preheat air fryer to 230ºF (110ºC).
2. Mix the flour, coconut milk, eggs, coconut oil, vanilla, and cardamom in a large bowl.
3. Let it stand for 20 minutes.
4. Spoon the batter into a greased muffin tin.
5. When your air fryer displays "READY" (select the cooking preset, and make minor adjustments according to your desired doneness.) and choose a shake reminder.
6. Cook at 230ºF (110ºC) for 4 to 5 minutes or until golden brown.
7. Repeat with the remaining batter.
8. Decorate your pancakes with coconut chips.
9. Enjoy!

946. Sweet Dough

Preparation Time: 6 minutes
Cooking Time: 8 minutes
Servings: 4

Ingredients:
- 8 ounces (227 g) bread dough
- 2 tablespoons butter, melted
- 2 ounces (57 g) powdered sugar

Directions:
1. Preheat air fryer to 350ºF (177ºC).
2. Cut the dough into strips and twist them together 3 to 4 times.
3. Then, brush the dough twists with melted butter and sprinkle sugar over them.
4. When your air fryer displays "READY" (select the cooking preset, and make minor adjustments according to your desired doneness.) and choose a shake reminder.
5. Cook the dough twists at 350ºF (177ºC) for 8 minutes, tossing the basket halfway through the cooking time.
6. Serve with your favorite dip. Enjoy!

947. Dill Pickle Fries

Preparation Time: 5 minutes
Cooking Time: 15 minutes
Servings: 12

Ingredients:
- 1½ (16-oz.) jars spicy dill pickle spears, drained and pat dried
- 1 cup all-purpose flour
- ½ tsp. paprika
- 1 egg, beaten
- ¼ cup milk
- 1 cup panko breadcrumbs
- Nonstick cooking spray

Directions:
1. In a bowl, mix well the flour and paprika.
2. In a second bowl, mix well milk and egg. In a third dish, put the breadcrumbs.
3. Coat the pickle spears with flour mixture, then dip into the egg mixture, and finally, coat evenly with the breadcrumbs.
4. Now, spray the pickle spears evenly with cooking spray.
5. Set the temperature of your Chefman air fryer oven to 440 ºF and time to 15 minutes.
6. Arrange the pickle spears in a Chefman air fryer oven basket in a single layer in 2 batches.
7. Flip once halfway through.
8. Serve.

948. Cherry-Choco Bars

Preparation Time: 8 minutes
Cooking Time: 15 minutes
Servings: 8

Ingredients:
- ¼ tsp. salt
- ½ cup almonds, sliced
- ½ cup chia seeds
- ½ cup dark chocolate, chopped
- ½ cup dried cherries, chopped
- ½ cup prunes, pureed
- ½ cup quinoa, cooked
- ¾ cup almond butter
- 1/3 cup honey
- 2 cups old-fashioned oats
- 2 tbsp. coconut oil

Directions:
1. Preheat the Chefman air fryer oven to 375°F for 5 minutes.
2. In a bowl, combine the oats, quinoa, chia seeds, almond, cherries, and chocolate.
3. In a saucepan, heat the almond butter, honey, and coconut oil.
4. Pour the butter mixture over the oat mix. Add salt and prunes.
5. Mix until well combined.
6. Pour over a baking dish that can fit inside the Chefman air fryer oven.
7. Cook for 15 minutes.
8. Let it cool before slicing into bars.

949. Crispy Peaches

Preparation Time: 8 minutes
Cooking Time: 15 minutes
Servings: 8

Ingredients:
- ¼ tsp. salt
- ½ cup almonds, sliced
- ½ cup chia seeds
- ½ cup dark chocolate, chopped
- ½ cup dried cherries, chopped
- ½ cup prunes, pureed
- ½ cup quinoa, cooked
- ¾ cup almond butter
- 1/3 cup honey
- 2 cups old-fashioned oats
- 2 tbsp. coconut oil

Directions:
1. Preheat the Chefman air fryer oven to 375°F for 5 minutes.
2. In a bowl, combine the oats, quinoa, chia seeds, almond, cherries, and chocolate.
3. In a saucepan, heat the almond butter, honey, and coconut oil

4. Pour the butter mixture over the oat mix. Add salt and prunes.
5. Mix until well combined.
6. Pour over a baking dish that can fit inside the Chefman air fryer oven.
7. Cook for 15 minutes.
8. Let it cool before slicing into bars.

950. Blueberry Apple Crumble

Preparation Time: 8 minutes
Cooking Time: 15 minutes
Servings: 2

Ingredients:
- 2 ramekins
- 1 red apple
- 1/2 cup frozen blueberries
- 1/4 cup plus
- 1 tbsp. brown rice flour
- 2 tbsp. sugar
- 1/2 tsp. ground cinnamon
- 2 tbsp. butter

Directions:
1. Finely dice the red apples.
1. Mix the fruit in one bowl and all other ingredients in another.
2. Preheat the Chefman air fryer oven to 350°F for 5 minutes
3. Put the fruit in ramekins and sprinkle the flour mixture over it.
4. Bake in the fryer for 15 minutes

951. Fried Banana Split

Preparation Time: 8 minutes
Cooking Time: 10 minutes
Servings: 8

Ingredients:
- 8 ripe bananas cut into 2
- 1 cup of dry breadcrumbs
- ½ cup of cornflour
- 2 eggs, lightly beaten
- 3 tbsp. of coconut oil
- 3 tbsp. of granulated sugar

Directions:
1. Preheat the Chefman air fryer oven at 280 F for 5 minutes.
2. Melt the coconut oil and stir into it the breadcrumbs until they become golden brown then transfer them to a bowl.
3. Roll each banana half in the cornflour, dip them in the beaten eggs and coat them with the breadcrumbs.
4. Place the banana halves in the Chefman air fryer oven and sprinkle the sugar on them, then set time to 10 minutes.
5. Once the time is up, allow the bananas to cool down completely, then serve them with your favorite ice cream and enjoy it.

952. Bread Pudding

Preparation Time: 8 minutes
Cooking Time: 12 minutes
Servings: 8

Ingredients:
- 2 slices of bread cut into 16 dices
- 1 cup of milk
- 1 egg
- 2 tbsp. of raisins, soaked for 15 min
- 1 tbsp. of brown sugar
- 1 tbsp. of chocolate chips
- ½ tsp. of cinnamon powder

Directions:
1. Preheat the Chefman air fryer oven at 356 °F for 5 minutes.
2. Beat the milk with egg, cinnamon, and sugar then fold in the raisins.
3. Place the bread dices in a small baking tray and pour on it the batter then let it chill for about 30 minutes in the fridge.
4. Sprinkle some sugar with chocolate chips on the bread mix then air fry it for 12 minutes.
5. Serve your bread pudding warm and enjoy.

953. Marble Cake

Preparation Time: 8 minutes
Cooking Time: 17 minutes
Servings: 6

Ingredients:
- 5 ¼ oz. of butter, melted
- oz. of self-raising flour
- oz. of castor sugar
- 1 ½ tbsp. of cocoa powder
- 3 eggs
- 1 pinch of Salt

Directions:
1. Preheat the Chefman air fryer oven at 356 °F for 5 minutes.
2. Combine 3 1/3 tbsp. Of the melted butter with cocoa powder and mix them until they become smooth, then set it aside.
3. Beat the rest of the butter with sugar until they become pale then add in the rest of the ingredients while beating them gradually until no lumps appear.
4. Pour the batter into a greased pan alternating between the white and cocoa batter, then Chefman air fryer oven it for 17 minutes.
5. Allow the cake to cool before serving.

954. Grilled Curried Fruit

Preparation Time: 6 minutes
Cooking Time: 8 minutes
Servings: 6

Ingredients:
- 2 peaches, pitted
- 2 firm pears
- 2 plums
- 2 tbsp. melted butter
- 1 tbsp. honey
- 2 tsp. curry powder

Directions:
1. Cut the peaches in half, and cut each half in half again. Cut the pears in half, core them, and remove the stem. Cut each half in half again. Do the same with the plums.
2. Arrange the fruit on a foil and drizzle with the butter and honey. Sprinkle with the curry powder.
3. Wrap the fruit in the foil, making sure to leave some air space in the packet.
4. Put the foil package in the basket and Set the temperature to 350°F, and set time to 8 minutes. Shake the basket once during the cooking time, until the fruit is soft and tender.

956. Sweet & Sour Chicken

Preparation Time: 8 minutes
Cooking Time: 40 minutes
Servings: 5

Ingredients:
- 2 lbs. boneless chicken breasts
- ¼ cup lime juice, freshly squeezed
- ½ cup honey
- 2 tbsp. soy sauce
- 1 tbsp. olive oil
- 2 cloves of garlic, minced
- ½ cup cilantro, chopped finely
- Salt and pepper to taste

Directions:
1. Place all ingredients in a sealable bag and give a good shake.
2. Allow marinating for two hours in the refrigerator.
3. Preheat the Chefman air fryer oven at 390°F for 5 minutes
4. Place the grill pan accessory in the Chefman air fryer oven.
5. Set the time to 40 minutes, flipping the chicken every 10 minutes to grill evenly on all sides.

957. Asian Pork Chops

Preparation Time: 8 minutes
Cooking Time: 40 minutes
Servings: 5

Ingredients:
- 1/2 cup hoisin sauce
- 3 tbsp. cider vinegar
- 1 tbsp. sweet chili sauce
- 1/4 tsp. garlic powder
- 4 (1/2-inch-thick) boneless pork chops
- 1 tsp. salt
- 1/2 tsp. pepper

Directions:
1. Stir together hoisin, chili sauce, garlic powder, and vinegar in a large mixing bowl.
2. Separate 1/4 cup of this mixture, then add pork chops to the bowl and marinate in the fridge for 2 hours.
3. Place the chops on a plate and sprinkle each side of the pork chop evenly with salt and pepper.
4. Cook at 360 °For 14 minutes, flipping halfway through.
5. Brush with reserved marinade and serve.

958. Lamb Chops

Preparation Time: 8 minutes
Cooking Time: 15 minutes
Servings: 2

Ingredients:
- 2 lamb chops
- 3 cloves of garlic, crushed
- Salt and black pepper to taste
- ½ bunch of rosemary

Directions:
1. Preheat the Chefman air fryer oven on 400°F for 5 minutes.
2. eason the chops with some salt and pepper, then rub the chops with garlic and rosemary, then set them aside to marinate for 3 hours.
3. Fry the chops for 18 minutes, then serve them warm and enjoy.

959. Herbed Lamb Chops

Preparation Time: 7 minutes
Cooking Time: 8 minutes
Servings: 2

Ingredients:
- 1 tbsp. fresh lemon juice
- 1 tbsp. olive oil
- 1 tsp. dried rosemary
- 1 tsp. dried thyme
- 1 tsp. Dried oregano
- ½ tsp. Ground cumin
- ½ tsp. ground coriander
- Salt and ground black pepper, as required
- 4 (4-oz.) lamb chops

Directions:
1. In a bowl, mix well the lemon juice, oil, herbs, and spices. Add the chops and coat evenly with the herb mixture.
2. Refrigerate to marinate for about 1 hour.
3. Set the temperature of the Chefman air fryer oven to 390 °F and time to 7 minutes.
4. Grease a Chefman air fryer oven basket. Arrange chops into the prepared Chefman air fryer oven basket in a single layer.
5. Flip once halfway through
6. Remove from the Chefman air fryer oven and transfer the chops onto plates.
7. Serve hot.

960. Garlic and Sesame Carrots

Preparation Time: 7 minutes
Cooking Time: 8 minutes
Servings: 2

Ingredients:
- 1 lb. baby carrots
- 1 tbsp. Sesame oil
- ½ tsp. dried dill Pinch
- Salt and black pepper to taste
- 6 cloves garlic, peeled
- 3 tbsp. sesame seeds

Directions:
1. Place the baby carrots in a medium bowl. Drizzle with sesame oil, add the dill, salt, and pepper, and toss to coat thoroughly.
2. Put the carrots in the basket of the Chefman air fryer oven.
3. Set temperature to 360°F and the time to 8 minutes shake the basket once during cooking time.
4. Add the garlic to the Chefman air fryer oven and set time to 8 minutes, shake the basket once during cooking time, or until the garlic and carrots become lightly brown.
5. Serve and sprinkle with the sesame seeds before serving.

961. Creamy Corn Casserole

Preparation Time: 9 minutes
Cooking Time: 15 minutes
Servings: 4

Ingredients:
- Nonstick baking spray with flour
- 2 cups frozen yellow corn
- 3 tbsp. flour
- 1 egg, beaten

258

- ¼ cup milk
- ½ cup light cream
- ½ cup grated Havarti cheese
- A Pinch of salt
- Freshly ground black pepper
- 2 tbsp. butter cut in cubes

Directions:
1. Spray a 6-by-6-by-2-inch baking pan with nonstick spray.
2. In a medium bowl, combine the corn, flour, egg, milk, and light cream, and mix until combined.
3. Stir in the cheese, salt, and pepper.
4. Pour the mix into a baking pan — dot with the butter.
5. Bake at 390°F for 15 minutes in your Chefman air fryer oven

962. Roasted Cashews

Preparation Time: 9 minutes
Cooking Time: 15 minutes
Servings: 4

Ingredients:
- 2 cups raw cashew nuts
- 1 tsp. butter, melted
- Salt and black pepper to taste

Directions:
1. Preheat your Chefman air fryer oven to 355°F for 4 minutes.
2. In a bowl, mix all the ingredients.
3. Place the cashews nuts in a Chefman air fryer oven basket in a single layer.
4. Set time to 4 minutes, shaking once halfway through.
5. Once done, transfer the hot nuts in a glass bowl and serve.

963. Primavera Chicken

Preparation Time: 10 minutes
Cooking Time: 25 minutes
Servings: 4

Ingredients:
- 4 chicken breasts, boneless
- 1 zucchini, sliced
- 3 medium tomatoes, sliced
- 2 yellow bell peppers, sliced
- ½ red onion, sliced
- 2 tablespoons olive oil
- 1 teaspoon Italian seasoning
- Kosher salt, to taste
- Freshly ground black pepper, to taste

- 1 cup shredded mozzarella
- Freshly chopped parsley for garnish

Direction:
1. Carve one side slit in the chicken breasts and stuff them with all the veggies.
1. Place these stuffed chicken breasts in a casserole dish, then drizzle oil, Italian seasoning, black pepper, salt, and Mozzarella over the chicken.
2. Transfer the dish to the 2nd rack position of Ninja Foodi XL Pro Air Oven and close the door.
3. Select the "Bake" Mode using the Function Keys and select Rack Level 2.
4. Set its cooking time to 25 minutes and temperature to 370degrees F, then press "START/STOP" to initiate cooking.
5. Garnish with parsley and serve warm.

964. Brine-Soaked Turkey

Preparation Time: 10 minutes
Cooking Time: 58 minutes
Servings: 4

Ingredients:
Brine
- ½ cup salt
- 1 lemon
- ½ onion
- 3 cloves garlic, smashed
- 5 sprigs of fresh thyme
- 3 bay leaves
- black pepper
Turkey Breast
- 4 tablespoons butter, softened
- ½ teaspoons black pepper
- ½ teaspoons garlic powder
- ¼ teaspoons dried thyme
- ¼ teaspoons dried oregano

Directions:
1. Mix the turkey brine ingredients in a pot and soak the turkey in the brine overnight.
2. The next day, remove the soaked turkey from the brine.
3. Whisk the butter, black pepper, garlic powder, oregano, and thyme.
4. Brush the butter mixture over the turkey, then place it in a roast tray.
5. Transfer the tray to the 2nd rack position of Ninja Foodi XL Pro Air Oven and close the door.
6. Select the "Air Roast" Mode using the Function Keys and select Rack Level 2.
7. Set its cooking time to 60 minutes and temperature to 375 degrees F, then press "START/STOP" to initiate cooking.
8. Slice and serve warm.

965. Parmesan Chicken Meatballs

Preparation Time: 10 minutes
Cooking Time: 12 minutes
Servings: 4

Ingredients:
- 1 pound ground chicken
- 1 large egg, beaten
- ½ cup Parmesan cheese, grated
- ½ cup pork rinds, ground
- 1 teaspoon garlic powder
- 1 teaspoon paprika
- 1 teaspoon kosher salt
- ½ teaspoon pepper

Crust:
- ½ cup pork rinds, ground

Directions:
1. Toss all the meatball ingredients in a bowl and mix well.
2. Make small meatballs out of this mixture and roll them in the pork rinds.
3. Place the coated meatballs in the air fryer basket.
4. Transfer the basket to the 2nd rack position of Ninja Foodi XL Pro Air Oven and close the door.
5. Select the "Bake" Mode using the Function Keys and select Rack Level 2.
6. Set its cooking time to 12 minutes and temperature to 400 degrees F, then press "START/STOP" to initiate cooking.
7. Serve warm.

966. Chicken and Rice Casserole

Preparation Time: 10 minutes
Cooking Time: 25 minutes
Servings: 4

Ingredients:
- 2 pounds bone-in chicken thighs
- Salt and black pepper
- 1 teaspoon olive oil
- 5 cloves garlic, chopped
- 2 large onions, chopped
- 2 large red bell peppers, chopped
- 1 tablespoon sweet Hungarian paprika
- 1 teaspoon hot Hungarian paprika
- 2 tablespoons tomato paste
- 2 cups chicken broth
- 3 cups brown rice, thawed
- 2 tablespoons parsley, chopped
- 6 tablespoons sour cream

Directions:
1. Season and rub the chicken with black pepper, salt, and olive oil.

2. Sear the chicken in a skillet for 5 minutes per side, then transfer to a casserole dish.
3. Sauté onion in the same skillet until soft.
4. Toss in garlic, peppers, and paprika, then sauté for 3 minutes.
5. Stir in tomato paste, chicken broth, and rice.
6. Mix well and cook until rice is soft, then add sour cream and parsley.
7. Spread the mixture over the chicken in the casserole dish.
8. Transfer the dish to the 2nd rack position of Ninja Foodi XL Pro Air Oven and close the door.
9. Transfer the sandwich to the 2nd rack position of Ninja Foodi XL Pro Air Oven and close the door.
10. Select the "Bake" Mode using the Function Keys and select Rack Level 2.
11. Set its cooking time to 10 minutes and temperature to 375 degrees F, then press "START/STOP" to initiate cooking.
12. Serve warm.

967. Chicken Potato Bake

Preparation Time: 10 minutes
Cooking Time: 25 minutes
Servings: 4

Ingredients:
- 4 potatoes, diced
- 1 tablespoon garlic, minced
- 1.5 tablespoons olive oil
- ⅛ teaspoon salt
- ⅛ teaspoon pepper
- 1.5 pounds boneless skinless chicken
- ¾ cup mozzarella cheese, shredded
- parsley chopped

Directions:
1. Toss chicken and potatoes with all the spices and oil in a sheet pan.
2. Drizzle the cheese on top of the chicken and potato.
3. Transfer the pan to the 2nd rack position of Ninja Foodi XL Pro Air Oven and close the door.
4. Select the "Bake" Mode using the Function Keys and select Rack Level 2.
5. Set its cooking time to 25 minutes and temperature to 375 degrees F, then press "START/STOP" to initiate cooking.
6. Serve warm.

968. Steak with Bell Peppers

Preparation Time: 15 minutes
Cooking Time: 11 minutes
Servings: 4

Ingredients:
- 1 teaspoon dried oregano, crushed
- 1 teaspoon onion powder
- 1 teaspoon garlic powder
- 1 teaspoon red chili powder
- 1 teaspoon paprika
- Salt, as required
- 1¼ pounds flank steak, cut into thin strips
- 3 green bell peppers, seeded and cubed
- 1 red onion, sliced
- 2 tablespoons olive oil
- 3-4 tablespoons feta cheese, crumbled

Directions:
1. In a large bowl, mix the oregano and spices together.
2. Add the steak strips, bell peppers, onion, and oil and mix until well combined.
3. Press "Power Button" of Ninja Foodi XL Pro Air Oven and select "Air Fry" function.
4. Press "Temp Button" to set the temperature at 390 degrees F.
5. Now press "Time Button" to set the cooking time to 11 minutes.
6. Press "START/STOP" button to start.
7. When the unit beeps to show that it is preheated, open the lid and grease the air fry basket.
8. Place the steak mixture into the prepared air fry basket and insert in the oven.
9. When cooking time is completed, open the lid and transfer the steak mixture onto serving plates.
10. Serve immediately with the topping of feta.

969. Lamb Burgers

Preparation Time: 10 minutes
Cooking Time: 10 minutes
Servings: 6

Ingredients:
- 2 pounds ground lamb
- ½ tablespoon onion powder
- ½ tablespoon garlic powder
- ¼ teaspoon ground cumin
- Salt and ground black pepper, as required

Directions:
1. In a bowl, add all the ingredients and mix well.
2. Make 6 equal-sized patties from the mixture.
3. Arrange the patties onto the greased sheet pan

in a single layer.
4. Press "Power Button" of Ninja Foodi XL Pro Air Oven and select "Air Fry" function.
5. Press "Temp Button" to set the temperature at 360 degrees F.
6. Now press "Time Button" to set the cooking time to 8 minutes.
7. Press "START/STOP" button to start.
8. When the unit beeps to show that it is preheated, open the lid.
9. Insert the sheet pan in oven.
10. Flip the burgers once halfway through.
11. When cooking time is completed, open the lid and serve hot.

970. Cloud Eggs

Preparation Time: 10 minutes
Cooking Time: 7 minutes
Servings: 1

Ingredients:
- 2 eggs, whites and yolks separated
- Pinch of salt
- Pinch of freshly ground black pepper

Directions:
1. In a bowl, add the egg white, salt and black pepper and beat until stiff peaks form.
2. Line a baking pan with parchment paper.
3. Carefully, make a pocket in the center of each egg white circle.
4. Now press "Time Button" to set the cooking time to 7 minutes.
5. Press "Power Button" of Ninja Foodi XL Pro Air Oven and select "Broil" function.
6. Press "START/STOP" button to start.
7. When the unit beeps to show that it is preheated, open the lid and insert the baking pan in the oven.
8. Place 1 egg yolk into each egg white pocket after 5 minutes of cooking.
9. When cooking time is completed, open the lid and serve.

971. Pasta Chips

Preparation Time: 10 minutes
Cooking Time: 7 minutes
Servings: 1

Ingredients:
- ½ tablespoons olive oil
- ½ tablespoons nutritional yeast
- 1 cup bow tie pasta
- ⅔ teaspoons Italian Seasoning Blend
- ¼ teaspoons salt

Directions:
1. Cook and boil the pasta in salted water half of the time as stated on the box, then drain it.
2. Toss the boiled pasta with salt, Italian seasoning, nutritional yeast, and olive oil in a bowl.
3. Spread this pasta in the air fryer basket.
4. Transfer the basket to the 3rd rack position of Ninja Foodi XL Pro Air Oven and close the door.
5. Select the "Air Fry" Mode using the Function Keys and select Rack Level 3.
6. Set its cooking time to 5 minutes and temperature to 390 degrees F, then press "START/STOP" to initiate cooking.
7. Toss the pasta and continue air frying for another 5 minutes.
8. Enjoy.

972. Glazed Chicken Wings

Preparation Time: 10 minutes
Cooking Time: 25 minutes
Servings: 4

Ingredients:
• 1½ pounds chicken wingettes and drumettes
• ⅓ cup tomato sauce
• 2 tablespoons balsamic vinegar
• 2 tablespoons maple syrup
• ½ teaspoon liquid smoke
• ¼ teaspoon red pepper flakes, crushed
• Salt, as required

Directions:
1. Arrange the wings onto the greased sheet pan.
2. Press "Power Button" of Ninja Foodi XL Pro Air Oven and select "Air Fry" function.
3. Press "Temp Button" to set the temperature at 380 degrees F.
4. Now press "Time Button" to set the cooking time to 25 minutes.
5. Press "START/STOP" button to start.
6. When the unit beeps to show that it is preheated, open the lid and insert the sheet pan in oven.
7. Meanwhile, in a small pan, add the remaining ingredients over medium heat and cook for about 10 minutes, stirring occasionally.
8. When cooking time is completed, open the lid and place the chicken wings into a bowl.
9. Add the sauce and toss to coat well.
10. Serve immediately.

973. Spicy Spinach Chips

Preparation Time: 10 minutes
Cooking Time: 10 minutes
Servings: 4

Ingredients:
• 2 cups fresh spinach leaves, torn into bite-sized pieces
• ½ tablespoon coconut oil, melted
• ⅛ teaspoon garlic powder
• Salt, as required

Directions:
1. In a large bowl, mix all the ingredients together.
2. Arrange the spinach pieces onto the greased sheet pan.
3. Press "Power Button" of Ninja Foodi XL Pro Air Oven and select "Air Fry" function.
4. Press "Temp Button" to set the temperature at 300 degrees F.
5. Now press "Time Button" to set the cooking time to 10 minutes.
6. Press "START/STOP" button to start.
7. When the unit beeps to show that it is preheated, open the lid.
8. Insert the sheet pan in oven.
9. Toss the spinach chips once halfway through.
10. When cooking time is completed, open the lid and transfer the spinach chips onto a platter.
11. Serve warm.

974. Beef Taquitos

Preparation Time: 15 minutes
Cooking Time: 8 minutes
Servings: 4

Ingredients:
• 6 corn tortillas
• 2 cups cooked beef, shredded
• ½ cup onion, chopped
• 1 cup pepper jack cheese, shredded
• Olive oil cooking spray

Directions:
1. Arrange the tortillas onto a smooth surface.
2. Place the shredded meat over one corner of each tortilla, followed by onion and cheese.
3. Roll each tortilla to secure the filling and secure with toothpicks.
4. Spray each taquito with cooking spray evenly.
5. Arrange the taquitos onto the greased sheet pan.
6. Place the tofu mixture in the greased sheet pan.
7. Press "Power Button" of Ninja Foodi XL Pro Air Oven and select "Air Fry" function.
8. Press "Temp Button" to set the temperature

at 400 degrees F.

9. Now press "Time Button" to set the cooking time to 8 minutes.
10. Press "START/STOP" button to start.
11. When the unit beeps to show that it is preheated, open the lid and insert the sheet pan in oven.
12. When cooking time is completed, open the lid and transfer the taquitos onto a platter.
13. Serve warm.

975. Persimmon Chips

Preparation Time: 15 minutes
Cooking Time: 8 minutes
Servings: 4

Ingredients:
• 2 ripe persimmons, cut into slices horizontally
• Salt and ground black pepper, as required

Directions:
1. Arrange the persimmons slices onto the greased sheet pan.
2. Press "Power Button" of Ninja Foodi XL Pro Air Oven and select "Air Fry" function.
3. Press "Temp Button" to set the temperature at 400 degrees F.
4. Now press "Time Button" to set the cooking time to 10 minutes.
5. Press "START/STOP" button to start.
6. When the unit beeps to show that it is preheated, open the lid.
7. Insert the sheet pan in oven.
8. Flip the chips once halfway through.
9. When cooking time is completed, open the lid and transfer the chips onto a platter.
10. Serve warm.

976. Pecan Brownies

Preparation Time: 15minutes
Cooking Time: 20 minutes
Servings: 6
Ingredients:
• Almond flour – 64 g
• Powdered erythritol – 64 g
• Unsweetened cocoa powder – 2 tbsps.
• Baking powder – ½ tsp.
• Unsalted butter – ¼ cup, softened
• Egg – 1
• Chopped pecans – 32 g
• Chocolate chips – 32 g
Directions:
1. Mix almond flour, baking powder, cocoa powder, and erythritol in a bowl. Stir in egg and butter. Fold in chocolate chips and pecans. Scoop mixture into a baking pan and place the pan into the air fryer basket. Cook at 300F for 20 minutes. Cool, sliced and serve.

977. Cherry Pie

Preparation Time: 30 minutes
Cooking Time: 30 minutes
Servings: 6

Ingredients:
• 2 rolls of refrigerated pie crust
• 400g All-purpose flour for dusting
• 1 can of cherry pie filling 120g
• 1 egg beaten
• 1 tablespoon of water
• 1 tablespoon of raw sugar

Directions:
1. Defrost the crust of the refrigerated pie and place it on a flat, floured surface of work.
2. Roll out the thawed pie crust, and reverse the dough with a shallow air fryer baking pan.
3. Cut the pan around, making your cut a half-inch wider than the pan itself.
4. Repeat with the crust of the second pie, only make the cut the same size or slightly smaller than the pan.
5. Layout the larger crust at the bottom of the baking pan, gently pressing into the dough to conform to the shape of the pan.
6. Spoon in the filling of a cherry pie. Place the smaller piece of crust over the filling, and pinch each crust edge together.
7. OR-cut the second piece into 1 "strips and weave in a lattice pattern before placing over the top of the pie. Make a few cuts at the top of the dough. In a small bowl, whisk the egg and water together. Sprinkle the egg gently over the top of the pie. Sprinkle with the raw sugar and place the pan in the air fryer basket. Bake at 320 degrees for 30 minutes, until golden brown and flaky.

978. Apple Cider Donuts

Preparation Time: 15 minutes
Cooking Time: 10 minutes
Servings: 5

Ingredients:
For the Muffins
• 4 large eggs
• 4 tbsp of coconut oil melted
• 3 tbsp of honey
• 168 gapple cider vinegar
• 128 g of coconut flour
• 1 tsp of cinnamon
• 1 tsp of baking soda
• pinch salt

Directions:
1. Oven preheats to 350 F. Prepare a donut baking pan by spraying liberally with cooking spray or using coconut oil to grease

well.

2. Wish the eggs, salt, honey, apple cider vinegar, and melted coconut oil together in a small bowl.
3. Sift cinnamon, baking soda, and coconut flour together in a separate bowl, to disperse the dry ingredients well.
4. Attach the dry ingredients to the wet ingredients until mixed thoroughly. The batter is going to be a bit humid. Transfer the batter to the baking pan for the donut and scoop the batter into the cavities. Use your fingers to evenly spread the batter inside the cavity.
5. Bake for 10 minutes at 350 F, until golden around the edges.
6. Remove from the oven and cool in baking for 5-10 minutes before flipping onto a removable wire rack. It's very important that these are cool before you remove them otherwise, they're going to fall apart. They need to be a little tough!

979. Pink Champagne Cupcakes

Preparation Time: 20 minutes
Cooking Time: 25 minutes
Servings: 12

Ingredients:
Cake:
- 1 box white cake mix
- 128 g pink champagne
- 64 g vegetable oil
- Three eggs
- Frosting:
- 2 (8-ounce) packages cream cheese
- 1 stick butter
- 512 g powdered sugar
- 32 g pink champagne

Directions:
1. Separate eggs and discard the yolks. Mix cake mix, oil, champagne, and egg whites.
2. Fill cupcake liners and place them on the wire rack in the fryer six at a time.
3. Bake it using your air fryer at 320 degrees for 25 minutes.
4. While waiting for the cupcakes to be baked, mix cream cheese and butter.
5. Slowly mix in powdered sugar and champagne alternating each one.
6. For additional effect, you can mix in a few drops of red food coloring to turn the frosting pink.
7. Allow the cupcakes to cool before adding frosting.

980. Pumpkin Muffins

Preparation Time: 20 minutes
Cooking Time: 15 minutes
Servings: 8

Ingredients:
- Pumpkin puree – 300g
- Oats – 200g
- Honey – 100g
- Egg – 2
- Coconut butter – 1 teaspoon
- Cocoa nibs – 1 tablespoon
- Nutmeg – 1 teaspoon
- Vanilla essence – 1 tablespoon

Directions:
1. Using a blender, combine all the ingredients making it a smooth paste.
2. Now fill the muffin mix in 12 muffin cases.
3. Place it in the air fryer basket.
4. Set the temperature to 180 degrees Celsius and cook for 15 minutes.
5. Serve when it becomes cool.

981 Apple Fries with Caramel

Preparation Time: 10 minutes
Cooking Time: 7 minutes
Servings: 4

Ingredients:
- Pink lady apples – 3
- Egg – 3 - Sugar - ¼ kg
- Flour - ½ kg
- Breadcrumbs – 200g
- Whipped cream cheese – 200g
- Caramel sauce – 100ml
- Cooking spray – as required

Directions:
1. Wash apples in running water, peel skin, cut into 8 wedges, remove the core and keep aside in a large bowl.
2. Put flour over it and toss to get a proper coating on the apple wedges. Beat the eggs in a medium bowl.
3. Put the crumbs in a flat plate.
4. Keep the apple wedges, beaten egg bowl and crumb plate in order. Dip the tossed apple wedges in the beaten egg and then dredge on the crumbs. Start frying by preheating the air fryer. Set the temperature at 190 degree Celsius.
5. Coat the air fryer basket with cooking spray.
6. Place the dipped wedges in the air fryer basket by not over layering. Set the timer for 5 minutes and start cooking.
7. Flip the apple wedges intermittently every 2 minutes.
8. When the cooking continues, let us make the caramel cream dip. In a bowl combine half of the caramel sauce and whipping cream. Mix it thoroughly.
9. Transfer the caramel cream dip into a serving bowl.
10. When the apple wedges cooking over, remove it into a serving bowl. Before serving, top it with the remaining caramel sauce.

982. Vanilla Almond Cookies

Preparation Time: 40minutes
Cooking Time: 40 minutes
Servings: 12

Ingredients:
- 8 egg whites
- ½ tsp almond extract
- 1 ⅓ cups sugar
- ¼ tsp salt
- 2 tsp lemon juice
- 1 ½ tsp vanilla extract
- Melted dark chocolate to drizzle

Directions:
1. In a mixing bowl, add egg whites, salt, and lemon juice. Beat using an electric mixer until foamy. Slowly add the sugar and continue beating until completely combined; add the almond and vanilla extracts. Beat until stiff peaks form and glossy.
2. Line a round baking sheet with parchment paper. Fill a piping bag with the meringue mixture and pipe as many mounds on the baking sheet as you can leaving 2-inch spaces between each mound.
3. Place the baking sheet in the fryer basket and bake at 250 F for 5 minutes. Reduce the temperature to 220 F and bake for 15 more minutes. Then, reduce the temperature once more to 190 F and cook for 15 minutes. Remove the baking sheet and let the meringues cool for 2 hours. Drizzle with the dark chocolate before serving.

983. Greek Kafta Kabobs

Preparation Time: 15 minutes
Cooking Time: 10 minutes
Servings: 14

Ingredients:
- One tablespoon coriander seed
- 1 tablespoon cumin seeds
- 1 teaspoon peppercorns
- 1 teaspoon allspice
- 1/2 teaspoon cardamom seeds
- 1/2 teaspoon turmeric powder
- 1 tablespoon oil
- 453 g 85% ground beef
- 32 g parsley
- One tablespoon minced garlic

Directions:
1. Grind the seeds and peppercorns into powder and combine with the turmeric and allspice.
2. Put altogether of the ingredients together in a blender and blend until well mixed.
3. Divide the meat into four equal parts and form a sausage around the skewers.
4. Cook in the air fryer at 370 degrees for 10 minutes.

984. Sesame Tuna Steak

Preparation Time: 15 minutes
Cooking Time: 8–10 minutes
Servings: 2

Ingredients:
- 1 tbsp. coconut oil, melted
- 2 x 300g. tuna steaks
- ½ tsp. garlic powder
- 2 tsp. black sesame seeds
- 2 tsp. white sesame seeds

Directions:
1. Apply the coconut oil to the tuna steaks with a brunch, then season with garlic powder.
13. Combine the black and white sesame seeds. Embed them in the tuna steaks, covering the fish all over. Place the tuna into your air fryer.
14. Cook for eight minutes at 400°F, turning the fish halfway through.
15. The tuna steaks are ready when they have reached a temperature of 145°F. Serve straightaway.

985. Chicken Alfredo

Preparation Time: 15 minutes
Cooking Time: 15-20 minutes
Servings: 4

Ingredients:
- 453 g chicken breasts, skinless and boneless
- ½kg button mushrooms, sliced
- 1 medium-sized onion, chopped
- 1 tablespoon olive oil
- 256 g cooked rice
- 1 jar (100g) Alfredo sauce
- 1 tablespoon Salt and pepper to taste
- ½ teaspoon thyme, dried

Directions:
1. Cut the chicken breasts into 1-inch cubes. Mix chicken, onion, and mushrooms in a large bowl. Season with salt and dried thyme and mix well.
16. Preheat your air fryer to 370°Fahrenheit and sprinkle basket with olive oil. Transfer chicken and vegetables to fryer and cook for 12-minutes and stir occasionally.
17. Stir in the Alfredo sauce. Cook for another 4-minutes. Serve with cooked rice

986. Bell Pepper and Sausage

Preparation Time: 10 Minutes
Cooking Time: 20 Minutes
Servings: 4

Ingredients:
- 1 lb. sausages; sliced
- 1 red bell pepper; cut into strips
- 1/2 cup yellow onion; chopped.
- 1/2 cup chicken stock
- 1/3 cup ketchup
- 3 tbsp. brown sugar
- 2 tbsp. mustard
- 2 tbsp. apple cider vinegar

Directions:
1. In a bowl; mix sugar with ketchup, mustard, stock and vinegar and whisk well.
2. In your air fryer's pan; mix sausage slices with bell pepper, onion and sweet and sour mix; toss and cook at 350 °F, for 10 minutes. Divide into bowls and serve for lunch.

987. Fried Thai Salad

Preparation Time: 5 Minutes
Cooking Time: 15 Minutes
Servings: 4

Ingredients:
- 12 big shrimp; cooked, peeled and deveined
- 1 cup carrots; grated
- 1 cup red cabbage; shredded
- A handful cilantro; chopped.
- 1 small cucumber; chopped.
- Juice from 1 lime
- 2 tsp. red curry paste
- A pinch of salt and black pepper

Directions:
1. In a pan, mix cabbage with carrots, cucumber and shrimp; toss, introduce in your air fryer and cook at 360 °F, for 5 minutes. Add salt, pepper, cilantro, lime juice and red curry paste; toss again, divide among plates and serve right away.

988. Seafood Stew

Preparation Time: 5 Minutes
Cooking Time: 15 Minutes
Servings: 4

Ingredients:
- 5 oz. white rice
- 3 oz. sea bass fillet; skinless, boneless and chopped.

- 2 oz. peas
- 1 red bell pepper; chopped.
- 14 oz. white wine
- 3 oz. water
- 2 oz. squid pieces
- 7 oz. mussels
- 6 scallops
- 5 oz. clams
- 4 shrimp
- 4 crayfish
- 1 tbsp. olive oil
- Salt and black pepper to the taste

Directions:
- In your air fryer's pan; mix sea bass with shrimp, mussels, scallops, crayfish, clams and squid.
- Add the oil, salt and pepper and toss to coat.
- In a bowl; mix peas salt, pepper, bell pepper and rice and stir.
- Add this over seafood, also add wine and water, place pan in your air fryer and cook at 400 °F, for 15 minutes; stirring halfway. Divide into bowls and serve for lunch.

989. Duck Breasts Recipe

Preparation Time: 10 Minutes
Cooking Time: 15 Minutes
Servings: 4

Ingredients:
- 4 duck breasts; skinless and boneless
- 4 garlic heads; peeled, tops cut off and quartered
- 2 tbsp. lemon juice
- 1/2 tsp. lemon pepper
- 1 ½ tbsp. olive oil
- Salt and black pepper to the taste

Directions:
1. In a bowl, mix duck breasts with garlic, lemon juice, salt, pepper, lemon pepper and olive oil and toss everything.
2. Transfer duck and garlic to your air fryer and cook at 350 °F, for 15 minutes. Divide duck breasts and garlic on plates and serve.

990. Chicken and Spinach Salad Recipe

Preparation Time: 10 Minutes
Cooking Time: 12 Minutes
Servings: 2

Ingredients:
- 2 chicken breasts; skinless and boneless
- 2 tsp. parsley; dried
- 1/2 tsp. onion powder

- 1 avocado; pitted, peeled and chopped
- 1/4 cup olive oil
- 1 tbsp. tarragon; chopped.
- 2 tsp. sweet paprika
- 1/2 cup lemon juice
- 5 cups baby spinach
- 8 strawberries; sliced
- 1 small red onion; sliced
- 2 tbsp. balsamic vinegar
- Salt and black pepper to the taste

Directions:
1. Put chicken in a bowl, add lemon juice, parsley, onion powder and paprika and toss.
2. Transfer chicken to your air fryer and cook at 360 °F, for 12 minutes.
3. In a bowl, mix spinach, onion, strawberries and avocado and toss.
4. In another bowl, mix oil with vinegar, salt, pepper and tarragon, whisk well, add to the salad and toss. Divide chicken on plates, add spinach salad on the side and serve.

991. Chicken and Capers Recipe

Preparation Time: 10 Minutes
Cooking Time: 20 Minutes
Servings: 2

Ingredients:
- 4 chicken thighs
- 3 tbsp. capers
- 4 garlic cloves; minced
- 1/2 cup chicken stock
- 1 lemon; sliced
- 4 green onions; chopped
- 3 tbsp. butter; melted
- Salt and black pepper to the taste

Directions:
1. Brush chicken with butter, sprinkle salt and pepper to the taste, place them in a baking dish that fits your air fryer.
2. Also add capers, garlic, chicken stock and lemon slices, toss to coat, introduce in your air fryer and cook at 370 °F, for 20 minutes; shaking halfway. Sprinkle green onions, divide among plates and serve.

992. Pork in Peanut Sauce

Preparation Time: 10 Minutes
Cooking Time: 15 Minutes
Servings: 4

Ingredients:
- Chilli paste – 2 tsps.

- Cubed pork chops – 14 ounces
- Salt and pepper
- Chopped peanuts – 3 ounces
- Ground coriander – 1 tsp
- Minced garlic cloves – 2
- Olive oil - 2 tbsps.
- Chopped shallot - 1
- Coconut milk – 7 ounces

Directions:
1. Put all the ingredients in a pan that suits your air fryer and stir well
2. Place the pan in the fryer and cook for 15 minutes at 400°F
3. Share into bowls and serve

993. Spice-Rubbed Steaks

Preparation Time: 10 Minutes
Cooking Time: 15 Minutes
Servings: 2

Ingredients:
- Sweet Paprika – 2 tbsps.
- Flank steak – 4
- An co chilli powder – ¼ cup
- Grated ginger – 2 tbsps.
- Cooking spray
- Dry mustard – 1 tbsps.
- Flank steaks – 4
- Dried Oregano – 1 tbsps.
- Salt and black pepper

Directions:
1. Mix all the spices in a bowl
2. Rub the steaks well with the mixture
3. Put the steaks in your air fryer basket and grease with cooking spray
4. Serve the sticks with a side salad and enjoy

994. Chickpeas and Lentils Mix

Preparation Time: 10 Minutes
Cooking Time: 15 Minutes
Servings: 6

Ingredients:
- 1 yellow onion, chopped
- 1 tablespoon olive oil
- 1 tablespoon garlic, minced
- 1 teaspoons sweet paprika
- 1 teaspoon smoked paprika
- Salt and black pepper to the taste
- 1 cup red lentils, boiled

- 15 ounces canned chickpeas, drained
- 29 ounces canned tomatoes and juice

Directions:
1. In your air fryer, mix onion with oil, garlic, sweet and smoked paprika, salt, pepper, lentils, chickpeas and tomatoes, stir, cover and cook at 360 degrees F for 15 minutes.
2. Ladle into bowls and serve hot.

995. Creamy Corn

Preparation Time: 10 Minutes
Cooking Time: 15 Minutes
Servings: 6

Ingredients:
- 1 yellow onion, chopped
- A drizzle of olive oil
- 1 red bell pepper, chopped
- 3 cups gold potatoes, chopped
- 4 cups corn
- 2 tablespoons tomato paste
- ½ teaspoon smoked paprika
- 1 teaspoon cumin, ground
- Salt and black pepper to the taste
- ½ cup almond milk
- 2 scallions, chopped

Directions:
1. In your air fryer, mix onion with the oil, bell pepper, potatoes, corn, tomato paste, paprika, cumin, salt, pepper, scallions and almond milk, stir, cover and cook at 365 degrees F for 15 minutes.
2. Divide between plates and serve

996. Cajun Mushrooms and Beans

Preparation Time: 10 Minutes
Cooking Time: 15 Minutes
Servings: 6

Ingredients:
- 2 tablespoons olive oil
- 1 green bell pepper, chopped
- 1 yellow onion, chopped
- 2 celery stalks, chopped
- 3 garlic cloves, minced
- 15 ounces canned tomatoes, chopped
- 8 ounces white mushrooms, sliced
- 15 ounces canned kidney beans, drained
- 1 zucchini, chopped
- 1 tablespoon Cajun seasoning
- Salt and black pepper to the taste

Directions:
1. In your air fryer's pan, mix oil with bell pepper, onion, celery, garlic, tomatoes, mushrooms, beans, zucchini, Cajun seasoning, salt and pepper, stir, cover and cook on at 370 degrees F for 15 minutes.
2. Divide veggie mix between plates and serve.

997. Eggplant Stew

Preparation Time: 10 Minutes
Cooking Time: 15 Minutes
Servings: 4

Ingredients:
- 24 ounces canned tomatoes, chopped
- 1 red onion, chopped
- 2 red bell peppers, chopped
- 2 big eggplants, roughly chopped
- 1 tablespoon smoked paprika
- 2 teaspoons cumin, ground
- Salt and black pepper to the taste
- Juice of 1 lemon
- 1 tablespoons parsley, chopped

Directions:
1. In your air fryer's pan, mix tomatoes with onion, bell peppers, eggplant, smoked paprika, cumin, salt, pepper and lemon juice, stir, cover and cook at 365 degrees F for 15 minutes
2. Add parsley, stir, divide between plates and serve cold.

998. Corn and Cabbage Salad

Preparation Time: 10 Minutes
Cooking Time: 15 Minutes
Servings: 4

Ingredients:
- 1 small yellow onion, chopped
- 1 tablespoon olive oil
- 2 garlic cloves, minced
- 1 and ½ cups mushrooms, sliced
- 3 teaspoons ginger, grated
- A pinch of salt and black pepper
- 2 cups corn
- 4 cups red cabbage, chopped
- 1 tablespoon nutritional yeast
- 2 teaspoons tomato paste
- 1 teaspoon coconut aminos
- 1 teaspoon sriracha sauce

Directions:
1. In your air fryer's pan, mix the oil with onion, garlic, mushrooms, ginger, salt,

pepper, corn, cabbage, yeast and tomato paste, stir, cover and cook at 365 degrees F for 15 minutes
2. Add sriracha sauce and aminos, stir, divide between plates and serve.

999. Okra and Corn Mix

Preparation time: 10 minutes
Cooking Time: 15 minutes
Servings: 6

Ingredients:
- 1 green bell pepper, chopped
- 1 small yellow onion, chopped
- 3 garlic cloves, minced
- 16 ounces okra, sliced
- 2 cup corn
- 12 ounces canned tomatoes, crushed
- 1 and ½ teaspoon smoked paprika
- 1 teaspoon marjoram, dried
- 1 teaspoon thyme, dried
- 1 teaspoon oregano, dried
- Salt and black pepper to the taste

Directions:
1. In your air fryer, mix bell pepper with onion, garlic, okra, corn, tomatoes, smoked paprika, marjoram, thyme, oregano, salt and pepper, stir, cover and cook at 360 degrees F for 15 minutes.
2. Stir, divide between plates and serve.

1000. Winter Green Beans

Preparation time: 10 minutes
Cooking Time: 16 minutes
Servings: 4

Ingredients:
- 1 and ½ cups yellow onion, chopped
- 1 pound green beans, halved
- 4 ounces canned tomatoes, chopped
- 4 garlic cloves, chopped
- 2 teaspoons oregano, dried
- 1 jalapeno, chopped
- Salt and black pepper to the taste
- 1 and ½ teaspoons cumin, ground
- 1 tablespoons olive oil

Directions:
1. Preheat your air fryer to 365 degrees F, add oil to the pan, also add onion, green beans, tomatoes, garlic, oregano, jalapeno, salt, pepper and cumin, cover and cook for 16 minutes.
2. Divide between plates and serve.

Made in the USA
Monee, IL
07 May 2022